S0-AYF-678

- showing countries settled
by emigrant families
featured in this book

POLAND

ETHERLANDS

YPT

INDIA

AUSTRALIA

SOUTH
AFRICA

NEW
ZEALAND

SCOTTISH EXODUS

Scottish Exodus

Travels Among a Worldwide Clan

JAMES HUNTER

MAINSTREAM
PUBLISHING

EDINBURGH AND LONDON

First published in Great Britain in 2005 by
MAINSTREAM PUBLISHING COMPANY
(EDINBURGH) LTD
7 Albany Street
Edinburgh EH1 3UG

ISBN 1 84018 469 8
ISBN 1 84596 153 6 (US Edition)

A catalogue record for this book is available
from the British Library

Typeset in Garamond

Printed in Great Britain by
Clays Ltd, St Ives plc

For
Clan MacLeod

And the Lord said, I have surely seen the affliction of my people which are in Egypt, and have heard their cry by reason of their taskmasters; for I know their sorrows. And I am come down to deliver them out of the hand of the Egyptians, and to bring them up out of that land unto a good land and a large, unto a land flowing with milk and honey.

Exodus 3: 6–8

Is there any wonder if, under the present discouraging circumstances, and considering the dark and gloomy prospects they have before them at home, the Highlanders should seek for refuge in some happier land, on some more hospitable shore, where freedom reigns and where, unmolested by Egyptian taskmasters, they may reap the produce of their own labour and industry?

*Informations Concerning
the Province of North Carolina*, 1773

This has been to me a truly wonderful day . . . Quite early I was awake and soon I heard a soldier's voice call out, 'Come on boys, here's land!' . . . And what was more, this first foreign land I ever laid eyes on was none other than Bonny Scotland. I was almost overcome by my emotions and wondered long if it were not, after all, a dream. But there it was; great old hills . . . planted here and there with farms. In fancy I saw, more than a century ago, the old sailboat with prow headed in the opposite direction from the way we were going – towards the west. And on board, leaning far over the sides with tears streaming down weather-beaten cheeks, my own forefathers, straining to see as long as they could a bit of their homeland. After a century or more, a son of theirs greets these same old hills . . . It was a sight I shall never forget, but shall retain the recollection of as a treasure above all price. *I have seen Scotland!*

William A. McLeod, whose ancestors left Skye for
North Carolina in 1802, writing to his wife in Texas
from an American troopship bound for Europe, 1918

'You are from here,' said the woman. 'No,' said my sister, 'I'm from Canada.' 'That may be,' said the woman. 'But you are really from here. You have just been away for a while.'

Alistair MacLeod, *No Great Mischief,* 1999

CONTENTS

MAPS

CHAPTER ONE

YOU ARE FROM HERE

Tennessee and Mississippi: Nashville and Greene County

Harry McLeod's surname is Scottish. His accent could only have come out of America's Deep South. We have met in Nashville, Tennessee, but though Harry has lived hereabouts for more than forty years, he is no Tennessean. 'I was raised,' he tells me, 'in Greene County, Mississippi.' His father, Harry says, belonged to that same district, not far from the Mississippi–Alabama border, where the Leaf and Chickasawhay rivers merge to form the Pascagoula. 'My dad's given name was Benjamin,' Harry goes on. 'When he was just ten or eleven he was set to work in *his* dad's lumber business.'

Because Harry McLeod, a former college professor, is well into his eighties, and because Benjamin McLeod was in his forties when Harry was born, we are talking of the 1880s. 'Back then,' Harry goes on, 'there were plenty of real big trees – mostly yellow pines, I guess – to be got in the vicinity of the Chickasawhay and the Leaf.' Thousands of those trees were felled by Greene County entrepreneurs like Benjamin McLeod's father, Sweyne. The resulting timber was floated down the Pascagoula to the Gulf of Mexico.

This was less straightforward than it sounds. First, a consignment of logs – each of them forty to sixty feet in length and three to five feet in diameter – had to be dragged and levered into the water. Next, the logs had to be pinned or lashed together to form a raft. Finally, the raft had to be decked to provide living quarters for the crew who had the job of getting it safely to the ocean. It was one of those rafting crews that Benjamin McLeod, Harry's father, joined when no more than a boy.

Steering log rafts downstream called for skills of a high order – the clumsy craft being at constant risk of snagging on reefs and other obstructions. Still more demanding was the job of putting rafts together in the first place. Known as 'running the logs', this involved venturing out on to the slippery, shifting surfaces of the floating timber from which rafts were constructed. One false move out there meant instant injury, even death. Log runners, therefore, needed perfect balance and great courage. These Benjamin McLeod possessed. 'I might have been just a kid when I started into river rafting,' he told Harry years later. 'But even then I could run logs a whole lot better than my old man.'

In 1841, a traveller set down his impressions of Greene County and its occupants. 'They were an industrious, enterprising and economical people,' he commented of 'the old Scotch families' who had settled the district twenty or thirty years before. 'There are yet living [among Greene County's inhabitants] some of the original immigrants who speak nothing but . . . Gallic [meaning Scots Gaelic] and whose years no one can compute.' Sometimes, it seems, Greene County's Gaelic speakers and their younger kin partied on home-distilled rye whiskey. But for the most part, they worked hard, lived soberly and, in consequence, did pretty well. Doing better than most was a man 'universally known as Long Johnny McLeod' who served in Mississippi's state legislature and owned as many as 2,000 cattle.[1]

Nearly two centuries later, there are still McLeods in Greene County. With his wife, Ruby Jean, Harry McLeod drives south from Nashville to attend the reunions which those McLeods organise each September. 'I've seen as many as 500 people at our Greene County gatherings,' Harry comments. Many of those people are descendants, as Harry is himself, of Peter and Sarah McLeod who moved into Greene County towards the close of the nineteenth century's second decade. All that is known of Peter McLeod and his wife, whose name before her marriage was McCaskill, is set out on two pages of faded typescript which Ruby Jean shows me. This document was compiled by a McLeod family historian. Peter, it states, was born in 1772 and emigrated 'from Glenly, Inverness-shire, Scotland [to] . . . Wilmington, North Carolina'. When this happened is uncertain; so is the date of Peter and Sarah's marriage. But after spending some years together in North Carolina, the couple are said to have struck out by way of South Carolina, Georgia and Alabama for the then undeveloped territory of Mississippi. On getting there in or about 1817, Peter McLeod took possession of a tract of farmland which remained in his possession until his death in

1850. This land was adjacent to the Chickasawhay River. On it Peter and Sarah established the home where they raised their thirteen children. 'Peter and Sarah had ten sons,' Harry remarks, 'and nearly all those sons went on to have big families of their own. That made for a lot of McLeods.'

Where is Glenly, Harry and Ruby Jean ask. There is no such place, I reply, but there is an Inverness-shire parish called Glenelg, and there are two good reasons for thinking this may be where Peter McLeod came from. First, the compiler of Ruby Jean's typescript history would have been unfamiliar with Scottish geography and, when trying to decipher the handwritten documentation on which the history is based, could easily have mistaken Glenelg for 'Glenly'. Second, Glenelg was home to a lot of MacLeods, and many of them are known to have left for North America in the decades prior to 1800. I cannot be certain that one of those emigrants was Harry McLeod's Greene County ancestor, I admit, but the circumstantial evidence is strong enough to allow Harry to be reasonably sure that Glenelg was the Scottish starting point of the 200-year-long journey which brought him here to Nashville.

Ontario: Windsor

I went to Nashville at the invitation of another of the city's residents, Dr Alexander C. McLeod, a retired physician. Alex is president of the Associated Clan MacLeod Societies, an international confederation with several thousand members, and it was in this capacity he got in touch with me. He had read some of my published thoughts about the causes and consequences of emigration from Scotland, Alex wrote, and he wondered if I might be interested in adding to those by compiling an account of how Clan MacLeod, once confined to the Scottish Highlands and Islands, had spread around the globe.

To begin with, I was sceptical. Like many Scots, I regard clan societies with suspicion – not least because they purvey, or so it seems to me, a soft-focus and villain-less version of an often brutal and miserable past. If I accepted a history-writing commission from the Associated Clan MacLeod Societies, I feared I would come under pressure to play down hardship and wrongdoing – especially if any of this could be laid at the doors of clan chiefs whose conduct, in some clan society circles, is deemed beyond reproach. But when I voiced those doubts, Alex McLeod was reassuring. What he wanted, he said, was an honest, warts-and-all explanation of why so many MacLeods had felt obliged, or had been forced, to quit Scotland.

What he also wanted, Alex went on, was a book which would not confine itself to the generalities in which histories of emigration usually deal. Lots of

ACMS members, Alex said, could tell me exactly how their families got to be where they now are. Their stories, the ACMS president argued, would enable me to put a human face on processes which are frequently analysed only in the abstract. From the MacLeods who would accommodate me during my travels, Alex continued, I might gain in addition some understanding of why Americans and others of Scottish descent feel strongly about what they call their heritage.

This last was the clincher. Modern Scotland's population is barely five million. Out there in the wider world, however, are many times that number of people who, for right reason or wrong, believe they have an emotional stake in our country. In principle, the existence of those people ought to be of huge advantage from a Scottish standpoint. But it is not – Scotland's relationship with its overseas diaspora being anything but easy. Of course, when our distant cousins come as individuals to our homes, we make them welcome. It is their collective behaviour, as can be seen from the Scottish media's treatment of New York's annual Tartan Day parade, we find mystifying or, worse, embarrassing. Hence Scotland's failure to mobilise its diaspora – as Ireland, in contrast, has done brilliantly – in support of national causes that could do with international backing. And hence, the more I thought about it, the attraction of getting first-hand insights into diaspora thinking, diaspora enthusiasms, diaspora obsessions. Why, I wished to know, do twenty-first-century Americans kit themselves out in kilts in order to signal their attachment to an essentially tribal grouping – Clan MacLeod – which had its beginnings in the medieval Hebrides and which, other than in a sentimental sense, ceased to exist more than 200 years ago? And why, I wanted to discover, does a Canadian teacher of literature turn out fiction imbued with its author's sense of his still being rooted in the clan-based community his family sailed away from in the eighteenth century? It was with a view to getting the beginnings of an answer to the first of those questions that I travelled to Tennessee. It is in the hope of making progress with the second that, driving out of Toronto, I take Highway 3 for Windsor, Ontario, home of Professor Alistair MacLeod whose 1999 novel, *No Great Mischief*, is reckoned one of the more important achievements of contemporary Canadian writing.

The Ontario landscape traversed by Highway 3, like other landscapes I encounter while researching this book, is spattered with placenames which are duplicates of Highlands and Islands originals – Aberfoyle, Appin, Glencoe, West Lorne, Mull, Iona Station. But that is not why I have chosen to take Highway 3 to Windsor. I have selected this route because Alexander MacDonald, the narrator of *No Great Mischief*, is driving it when the novel opens: 'As I begin to tell this, it is the golden month of September in southwestern Ontario. In the splendid autumn sunshine the bounty of the land is almost overwhelming . . . The roadside stands are burdened down by baskets of produce and arrangements of plants and flowers. Signs invite you to "pick your own" and whole families can be seen doing exactly that: stooping and straightening or staggering with overflowing bushel baskets, or standing on ladders that reach into the trees of apple and of pear.'[2]

Alexander is not headed for an orchard. His destination is Toronto – specifically a run-down, seedy, slightly frightening city district where the sidewalks are obstructed by 'chained-down garbage cans' and where the streets are strewn with broken glass. Here, crookedly hung, brown-painted doors give access to blocks of one-roomed apartments occupied largely by single ageing men: 'Behind the closed doors one can hear vague sounds. The most dominant one is, perhaps, that of men coughing and spitting. Almost all of the men smoke quite heavily, some of them rolling their own cigarettes, sitting in their underwear on the edge of their beds . . . Few of the people eat very much. Many of the rooms do not contain stoves, or ones with workable ovens. Tomato soup is heated on top of hot plates and filled with crackers. The smell of burned toast is often present, and sometimes jars of instant coffee or boxes of teabags sit on windowsills or on archaic radiators beside packages of purchased cookies so laced with preservatives that they may sit there for months without any signs of change.'

Alexander is a successful orthodontist but, drawn by blood ties of a kind central to the world of *No Great Mischief*, he has come to visit with his older brother, Calum, an ex-miner who is dying of drink. Entering Calum's room, Alexander gives his brother a bottle of brandy – 'brandy always works the fastest' – and then the two men talk. They speak, as you sense they have done often before, of their emigrant great-great-great-grandfather, *Calum Ruadh*, Red-Headed Calum or Malcolm. Calum Ruadh's colouring, Calum says, has been inherited by Alexander; his name, Alexander responds, has come down to Calum. Those facts restated for perhaps the thousandth time, Calum Ruadh's departure from Scotland, despite this departure having occurred in 1779, is discussed at length and in detail.

Elsewhere Alistair MacLeod has commented: 'It has often been said that the Celtic people are given to living a certain portion of their lives in the past.' This is certainly true of the Scottish-Canadian Celts who populate the pages of *No Great Mischief*. It is true of Alexander and of Calum; it is true, too, of Catriona, Alexander's twin sister and a woman who seems closer to him than the wife we barely glimpse. These are people who are incapable of getting out from under their history.[3]

The more recent segments of this history have unfolded in Cape Breton Island, Nova Scotia, where – following their founder's emigration – *Clann*

Chalum Ruaidh, Calum Ruadh's clan, lived until twentieth-century circumstance dispersed the clan's members across Canada. But if Cape Breton looms large in Clann Chalum Ruaidh's past, so do the more distant outlines of Scotland and of that other, broken apart, clan to which Calum Ruadh's own ancestors belonged. 'I see them sometimes,' his Cape Breton grandfather says in the little Alexander's hearing at a point when an adult conversation has turned to the clansmen who were Clann Chalum Ruaidh's remote forerunners. 'I see them . . . coming home across the wildness of Rannoch Moor in the splendour of the autumn sun. I imagine them coming with their horses and their banners and their plaids tossed arrogantly over their shoulders. Coming with their broadswords and their claymores . . . Singing the choruses of their rousing songs, while the sun gleams off the shining of their weapons and the black and redness of their hair.'

After this golden age of Scottish clanship, *No Great Mischief* implies, came a protracted and tragic fall which has ended in a direct descendant of those shouting, chanting warriors sitting blearily before a newly opened brandy bottle in his Toronto slum. But what if, instead of surrendering to booze's consolations or getting on determinedly with orthodontics, Calum Ruadh's twenty-first-century heirs were to return whence he came? In Scotland as it now is, they would discover few remnants of a clanship which, when it disintegrated, left thousands of folk with little option but to seek refuge across the Atlantic. But might they be able to find over there in Scotland – in the place where their family used to live – someone or something with the capacity to bridge the gap between the people they have become and the people they, or their great-great-great-grandparents, once were? *No Great Mischief* explores that possibility in a passage which takes Catriona MacDonald, its narrator's sister, to the West Highland locality which, prior to his 1779 leavetaking, was home to Calum Ruadh.

Approaching this locality from the east, as she afterwards tells her brother, Catriona drives along 'narrow winding tracks'. Reaching the coast, she leaves her car and walks on a rocky shore, 'looking at the seaweed and a pair of splashing seals'. Next she sees 'the form of an older woman' approach, carrying in her hand a bag of freshly gathered winkles: 'And then, she said, she met the woman face to face, and they looked into each other's eyes. "You are from here," said the woman. "No," said my sister, "I'm from Canada." "That may be," said the woman. "But you are really from here. You have just been away for a while."'

Catriona is next taken to a nearby house: '"This woman is from Canada," said my sister's guide to an old man who sat on a wooden chair inside the house. "Oh," said the old man and my sister could not judge his degree of comprehension. He had on a soiled tartan shirt covered with a black sweater and wore a cloth cap. His eyes seemed rheumy and she thought he might be hard of hearing and that, perhaps, his mind wandered . . . "Did you come far?" he said. "From Canada," she said, again uncertain of his degree of comprehension. "Ha," he said, "the land of trees. A lot of the people went there on the ships. And some to America. And some to Australia, the country back of the sun. Almost all gone now," he said.'

This is fiction, and it has fiction's semi-magical properties. But that is not to say that the paragraphs I have quoted – paragraphs which are the source, incidentally, of my chapter headings – deal in wholly imaginative constructs. I put this point to their author when we meet in Windsor, a town which would be a suburb of Detroit, Michigan, were it not for the fact that the river separating the two also separates Canada from the United States. 'I didn't want *No Great Mischief* to be seen as autobiographical,' Alistair MacLeod says. 'That's partly why I made its leading characters MacDonalds, not MacLeods.' This is fair enough; but it is difficult to believe, all the same, that there is nothing of its creator in a novel which features a narrator called Alexander, the English equivalent of the Gaelic *Alasdair* or Alistair, and which concerns a family whose founder left eighteenth-century Scotland, as Alistair MacLeod's emigrant forebear also did, for Nova Scotia's Cape Breton Island. When Catriona, visiting Scotland from Canada, is told she is 'really from here', might there be in this exchange something of Alistair MacLeod's own experiences?

Alistair MacLeod was born in 1936 in Saskatchewan. But both his mother and father were Cape Bretoners, and when he was still small they returned with him to Cape Breton – to the Gaelic-speaking community where Alistair's parents grew up and where he too was raised. Alistair's wife, Anita, a MacLellan before her marriage, also belongs to this same Cape Breton locality – settled 200 years ago by emigrants from the Hebridean island of Eigg and from the adjacent mainland district of Moidart. 'I'm a sixth-generation Canadian,' Alistair comments. But he is also, he goes on, a product of a Cape Breton community where people of Highlands and Islands origin customarily found husbands and wives among neighbouring families of identical background. When Alistair and Anita travelled to Moidart and Eigg, then, the first thing said about them was that they looked like people from those places. The second thing said was that they sounded like Eigg or Moidart folk as well.

Scots Gaelic is highly dialectal. The Gaelic of Eigg and Moidart is not the same as the Gaelic of Skye, which differs, in turn, from the Gaelic of Sutherland or Lewis. But when Alistair or Anita MacLeod risked a little Gaelic with new-made friends in Moidart or on Eigg, this Canadian couple's pronunciation and vocabulary were such as to identify them at once as belonging, in effect, to Eigg or Moidart families. 'People in Scotland were amazed that our Gaelic accents are the same as theirs,' Alistair remarks. 'It's a tremendous thing, a powerful thing, to have been away from a place for so long, to have been away for hundreds of years, and still to fit right in when you go back.'

Note that phrase: when you go back. Over and over again in the course of the travels I made among Clan MacLeod, those words or others like them were used of places in the Highlands and Islands by people who cannot, as a matter of literal fact, go back to Scotland – because they have never been there. What those people mean is that their ancestral connection with this or that Scottish locality entitles them to say, despite their being separated from the locality in question by several generations, that they come from there. So when Alistair MacLeod reached Moidart and went on to Eigg, which his great-great-great-grandfather left in 1791, he – just like Catriona in *No Great Mischief* – was not arriving. He was returning.

North Carolina: Asheville

Alistair MacLeod has always known his MacLeod ancestors came from Eigg. Catriona MacDonald was well informed about the origins of Clann Chalum Ruaidh. But what if, despite your being completely ignorant about your family history, you found yourself by chance in your equivalent of the spot where Catriona met with the woman who had been gathering winkles? Would you feel anything? For all my awareness of the extent to which Celtic cultures, including that of the Highlands and Islands, make a fetish of the ties which supposedly bind families to places they have long inhabited, my answer to that question would be a definite no. John MacLeod Tutterow would beg to differ.

I got to know John and his wife Lisa at *Fèis Shiàtail*. This is a week-long gathering organised every two years by Seattle-based admirers of everything having to do with the Highlands and Islands, our language, our songs, our stories, our heritage in all its forms. I was there to teach classes in Highlands and Islands history. John and Lisa, though they had come to Fèis Shiàtail mainly to expand their knowledge of Gaelic, were among my students.

So far, so alternative sounding. But John MacLeod Tutterow is no refugee from America's mainstream. He and Lisa are a professional couple who live regular lives in Asheville, North Carolina, an attractive town made all the more attractive by its being surrounded by the Blue Ridge Mountains. John is one of Asheville's attorneys, and when I visited the Tutterow home a year or so after our Fèis Shiàtail encounter, his weekends were given over to the military training he was undergoing in furtherance of his ambition to become a US army lawyer.

What causes such a man to have so intense an interest in Scotland? 'It all began ten years ago when I was in my early twenties,' John MacLeod Tutterow says. 'I was doing a lot of travelling, and I'd flown to London to meet with friends who'd rented a cottage in England – in Dorset to be exact. When I reached London, it occurred to me that it might be good to see more of Britain than Dorset. So, I took a train to Edinburgh on no better basis than that I'd heard it was a pretty kind of city.'

On the train to Scotland, John got talking to another American who turned out to be the father of one of his college friends. This man, who had been in Scotland before, advised John to head north from Edinburgh. 'So that's what I did,' John says. 'I took a train to Inverness, then another train from Inverness to Kyle of Lochalsh. Those trains travel through some real nice country, and I was impressed – who wouldn't be? – by Scotland's scenery. All the same, what I'd been doing up to this point was simply taking a vacation trip – an enjoyable trip, sure, but a trip no different from any other.

'That now changed completely. We'd just left Strathcarron Station and were coming out of one of the bends the railroad makes around Loch Carron when, all of a sudden, I saw a set of peaks away beyond us to the west. It was late in the day and the sun was setting on the far side of these same mountains, making them stand out against the sky. I've never seen anything so beautiful. I was – and this will sound a little mad – left breathless. My sighting of these peaks, I knew then and I know now, was the most profound experience I'd ever had or ever would have.

'On the train, I'd no idea what the mountains that I'd seen were called. I didn't even know exactly where they were. It wasn't until I got to Kyle that I discovered I'd been looking at the Cuillin and that the Cuillin are on the Isle of Skye. So now I had to go there and see the Cuillin from close quarters. At first, I meant to be on the island for no more than a day. I'll zip around quickly, I thought, then I'll head back south on one of the buses you can get from Skye, by way of Fort William, to Glasgow.

'But I couldn't leave. Again, I know, this'll strike most folk as crazy. But I just couldn't get away from Skye. I missed one bus, then another. All the time, I was calling my friends in Dorset to make excuses for my non-appearance. I was truly set on getting down there, but I kept manufacturing reasons for not going.

'Eventually I got myself on to a Glasgow bus. At Fort William, however, I grabbed my rucksack, got off the bus and headed back to Skye. By evening, I was in a little village called Elgol where, that night, some sort of local festival was taking place. People were singing in Gaelic, a local band was playing, everyone was welcoming and I felt totally at home.'

Three weeks later, having at last completed his long-postponed journey from Skye to the south of England, John Tutterow was back in North Carolina, visiting with his mother and telling her about his trip to Scotland. When he was growing up, John says, his parents never expressed any interest – not that he can remember anyway – in family history. But now John's mother took some papers from a drawer and handed them to him. 'What I was looking at was information about my mom's kinsfolk from way back,' John explains, 'and what leaped out at me were their names – McLeods, McCaskills, more McLeods.' Those people were John Tutterow's ancestors and, as he now realised, their forebears had emigrated to eighteenth-century North Carolina from the very island, Skye, to which he had been so irresistibly attracted.

Hence John Tutterow's adoption of his middle name, MacLeod. Hence his decision that he and Lisa – whose MacRae forebears emigrated to America from the Highland mainland district of Kintail – should marry in Skye. Hence John's membership of America's Clan MacLeod Society in which this North Carolina attorney is both active and prominent. Hence his being willing to make a transcontinental journey from Asheville to Seattle for the sole purpose of obtaining tuition in Gaelic. 'One way or another,' John MacLeod Tutterow says, 'I'm still reacting to whatever it was that grabbed me on the train beside Loch Carron.'

Scotland: Glenelg, Skye, Raasay, Harris, Lewis and Sutherland

This book deals in hard facts, so I offer no explanation of John MacLeod Tutterow's story. However, I have included it here, just as I have included Alistair MacLeod's fictional account of an analogous experience, because it seems to me essential, by way of prelude to my treatment of emigration from the lands once occupied by Clan MacLeod, to highlight the manner in which those lands continue to fascinate the scattered progeny of people long gone from them.

Where to begin an introductory tour of Clan MacLeod's territories? Perhaps at the point, just past the foot of Glen Shiel, where the main road from Glasgow and Fort William to Skye meets the sea in the shape of one of the fiord-like inlets which are common hereabouts. This particular inlet is Loch Duich. The main road continues along its northern shore in the direction of Kyle of Lochalsh and the Skye Bridge. But if you make instead for Loch Duich's southern side, you find yourself on a quite different kind of road: one of the narrow tracks which Catriona MacDonald, Alistair MacLeod's invention, encounters during her Highland explorations: the kind of road where drivers need, like Catriona, to be 'watchful for the

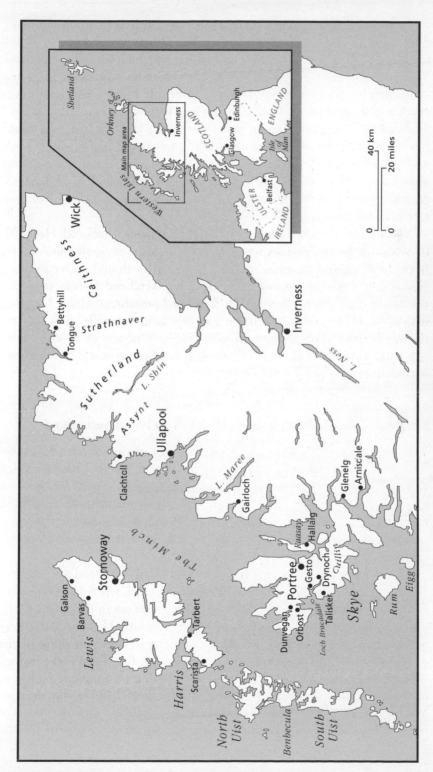

Map 1: The North-west Highlands and Islands of Scotland

sheep and mindful to pull over to one side at the sight of rare approaching vehicles'.

After a few minutes, this road climbs over Bealach Ràtagain, a high pass which gives access to Glenelg. It was in Glenelg, or so I conjectured when speaking with one of his descendants in Nashville, that Peter McLeod, the pioneer settler of Mississippi's Greene County, was born in 1772. Then, as it had been for ages and as it would be for another forty years, Glenelg – its high and rocky hills interspersed by fertile valleys – was one of the landholdings under Clan MacLeod's control.

More southerly parts of Skye, which can be reached on a ferry from Glenelg, were dominated by other clans. But heading north, through Broadford and on towards Sconser, you are soon in sight of Raasay – not part of Skye but a separate, and smaller, island a couple of miles off Skye's east coast. Like Glenelg, Raasay was one of Clan MacLeod's domains until the early nineteenth century.

Beyond Sconser and bearing west at Sligachan, you have the Cuillin on your left. Most of this mountain range's jagged and dark-looking peaks, the peaks which so captivated John Tutterow, belong to John MacLeod, who is his clan's current chief and who lives, as MacLeod chiefs have done since the thirteenth century, in nearby Dunvegan Castle – which, by the way, is where Lisa and John Tutterow, with John MacLeod's blessing, organised their wedding. Not just the Cuillin but all of this north-western corner of Skye – *Dùthaich MhicLèoid*, MacLeod's Country, as it is known in Gaelic – was owned by John MacLeod's predecessors in their capacity as the area's lairds or landlords. In the course of the last 250 years, much of the district has been acquired by other proprietors, but as of this writing John MacLeod remains in sole charge of the Cuillin as well as of the castle which is his home. Partly because of its role as John MacLeod's residence, Dunvegan Castle is treated as a potent symbol of their links with Scotland by members of the Associated Clan MacLeod Societies – to whom Chief John, as they call their clan's head, is a figure of significance. People make pilgrimages – the word is not too strong – to Dunvegan Castle, and every four years ACMS organises in the adjacent village a 'clan parliament' which attracts several hundred delegates from all over the world.

In August 2002, while compiling this book, I attended one of those events. The clan parliament's business sessions were held in a local church, and the proceedings were not uniformly riveting. But as my attention wandered to what could be seen through the church's windows – on one of those Skye days when sunshine and showers chased each other across the flat-topped hills called MacLeod's Tables – something kept drawing me back to what was going on around me. This something was the sheer range of voices to be heard – American voices, Canadian voices, Australian voices, French voices, English voices, South African voices, New Zealand voices. Listening to them, I remembered Alex McLeod saying to me in Nashville, 'If ACMS has any justification other than enabling folk to have a good time, then that justification's bound up with the way our Associated Clan MacLeod Societies have the capacity to bring people together in a manner that transcends nationality, class, religion and colour. Sure, all sorts of petty disputes and disagreements keep obscuring the ideal – tribal warfare's in our blood, after all. But if we can keep the ideal in sight, if we can get around at least some of the antagonisms that bedevil our planet, then Clan MacLeod in its present-day form will have something positive to say to the rest of humanity.'

People attending Clan MacLeod's parliament are clearly pleased to be in Dunvegan. But talking with delegates from overseas, I discover that attendance at parliament is widely seen as a prelude – a pleasurable prelude but a prelude nevertheless – to more vital business in the shape of ancestor-hunting expeditions that will take many delegates to the places where they know, or think, their families originated. From Dunvegan, some of those journeys are easy – occupying just the few minutes needed to drive north to Waternish, west to Glendale or south to Orbost, Roag, Ullinish, Struan, Gesto and the other communities constituting Dùthaich MhicLèoid, Skye's MacLeod Country. But because Clan MacLeod, as already indicated, was by no means confined to Skye in times past, other post-parliament trips are necessarily more complicated.

In this category are excursions made to Harris and Lewis. Those islands are accessed from Skye by seagoing ferries which crisscross the Minch – a stormy stretch of ocean separating the Highland mainland and the Inner Hebrides, the island group that includes Skye, from the Outer Hebrides, the group to which Lewis and Harris belong. Although they occupy a single landmass, being divided by mountains rather than by water, Harris and Lewis have always been considered separate entities. This makes sense in that their physical characters – Harris consists mostly of high hills and Lewis is largely moorland – are very different. But both, and together they are more extensive than Skye, were once in the possession of Clan MacLeod – Lewis from the Middle Ages until the early seventeenth century, Harris for a couple of hundred years longer.

Also under Clan MacLeod's jurisdiction during the clan's heyday were the peaks you see when looking eastwards across the Minch from Lewis. Those peaks rise above Assynt, part of the Highland mainland county of Sutherland. To get there from Lewis, you take yet another ferry – this one connecting Stornoway, Lewis's capital and the only town of consequence in the Hebrides, with Ullapool.

The road north from Ullapool to Assynt goes on to Durness before turning east along Sutherland's north coast. Because Assynt's MacLeods, over the centuries, spread across much of this area, any comprehensive overview of MacLeod lands should arguably take it in. This involves driving through several little settlements like Laid and Tongue before heading south through Strathnaver and the Strath of Kildonan to Helmsdale. From here it is possible to return to Ullapool via Strath Oykel. And from Ullapool it is equally possible, by making now for Gairloch, another of Clan MacLeod's former dominions, to get back to Glen Shiel – and thus to this MacLeod tour's starting point.

Some MacLeods inhabited other localities – one of them being Eigg, due south of Skye, where Alistair MacLeod's great-great-great-grandfather began his 1791 journey to Canada. But the route I have just delineated – this route starting in Glenelg and going on from Dunvegan to the Outer Hebrides and Sutherland – takes in most of the places which were home to the MacLeod emigrants mentioned in this book.

Since I lived in Skye for twelve years, and since my work has taken me repeatedly to practically every corner of the Highlands and Islands, I know those places well. I have seen them in every conceivable kind of weather – in shimmering heat, in gale-driven rain, in snow, in mist and, perhaps most memorably, on still and cloudless winter days when low-angled sunlight flushes out our Scottish landscape's many colours and turns every piece of water into a set of near-perfect reflections. On days like that, it is easy to understand why all the different MacLeod countries – Glenelg, Gairloch, Assynt, Raasay, Lewis and Harris as well as the district around Dunvegan – have inspired so much affection. But despite the bonds thus engendered between Clan MacLeod's territories and the people who resided on them, there were occasions when hundreds, even thousands, of MacLeods were eager to leave those territories and to emigrate to other lands far, far away. To explain why this was so is one of this book's aims. Another of its objectives is to stress that, having once quit Harris, Lewis, Assynt, Gairloch, Glenelg, Raasay or Skye, few MacLeod emigrants, and equally few of the more recent descendants of such emigrants, were or are interested in resuming or taking up residence in Scotland. This might appear at odds with what I have had to say about my conversations with John Tutterow and about the messages to be drawn from Alistair MacLeod's *No Great Mischief.* But neither John Tutterow nor his fictional counterpart, Catriona MacDonald, it needs remembering in this context, responded to their Scottish experiences – life changing though those may have been – by staying permanently in Scotland. Catriona went back to her Canadian home and her Canadian husband. John Tutterow returned to North Carolina. Why not?

After all, John MacLeod Tutterow, as he emphasises, is first and foremost an American. History has made him so, and he has no quarrel with it. 'I love this country,' he says. 'I love the United States, I love the South, I love North Carolina. At the same time, however, I'm conscious that all of us here – Native Americans excepted – are interlopers on this continent. We have been in America for two or three hundred years at best, and oftentimes much less. That's why so many of us are looking to connect with wherever our folks came from. In Skye, I have deeper roots than it's possible for me to have in North Carolina. That doesn't make me any less of an American. But it does add something precious to my sense of who I am.'

These are crucial points. Many of Scotland's difficulties with its diaspora stem from our expectation that Scottish-Americans, Scottish-Canadians, Scottish-Australians and all the rest should conform with, and defer to, our present-day conceptions of what it means to be Scottish. If we do not participate in Tartan Day parades, if we do not rush to join clan societies and if we do not treat clan chiefs like minor royalty, we are inclined to think, then neither should they. But this is to overlook the extent to which our diaspora possesses its own agenda – an agenda stemming from a past that, sometimes for many generations, has been different from Scotland's. When John Tutterow talks about his links with Skye, or when Alistair MacLeod writes about the Highlands and Islands in the way he does in *No Great Mischief*, it is tempting to leap to the conclusion that both want to acquire whatever it is today's Scots think constitutes Scottishness. But this is to misinterpret the motives that drive foreigners – which is how people like Alistair MacLeod or John Tutterow are regarded legally – of Scottish extraction to interest themselves in Scotland. Neither John Tutterow nor Alistair MacLeod, it seems to me, are trying to be or to become Scottish. They simply want to get a handle on the Scottish component of backgrounds which are essentially Canadian in Alistair MacLeod's case, American and Southern in John Tutterow's.

All of which is by way of saying that the Scottish diaspora is entitled to have, and to celebrate, identities that are the diaspora's own, not ours. If, in Scotland, we want to understand those identities a little better – and I believe we should – then we are going to have to go to the countries where Scots emigrants settled and, having done so, spend time with the sort of people who constitute the membership of the Associated Clan MacLeod Societies. That is what this book does.

Victoria: Tragowel

To grasp the full force of Roger McLeod's description of the landscape around Tragowel, Victoria, you need to know how Australian cities handled sanitation before the adoption of flushing lavatories and sewer systems. Until well into the twentieth century, the business of getting rid of what was euphemistically called 'night soil' was the responsibility of men who took it away daily and who, when negotiating tricky stairs and narrow alleys, had to balance heavy, foul-smelling containers of filth on their heads. Hence the phrase which Roger now applies to the terrain in Tragowel's vicinity. 'It's as flat as a shit-carrier's cap,' he says.

Roger and I are standing at the top of a re-erected poppet head in Bendigo's Rosalind Park. Poppet heads are the steel-built winding towers placed over mineshafts, and there was a time when Bendigo, then one of the world's premier goldmining centres, contained dozens of them. Today, no gold is dug in Bendigo, and the Rosalind Park poppet head serves mainly as a viewing platform. From this platform, which we have reached by way of 124 steep steps, Roger and I have an unrestricted outlook to the north. It is May, Australia's autumn, and a chilly breeze blowing off the Southern Ocean has swept the atmosphere clear of haze and dust. Out there, about sixty miles distant, is Tragowel, and the ruler-straight horizon in that direction is what has occasioned Roger's comment. Around Tragowel, it is obvious even from as far away as Bendigo, the land is as table-top level and featureless as it is possible for land to be.

Roger McLeod is a former Australian Air Force pilot who, since leaving the military, has been an aviation administrator. This morning I have driven in his company to Bendigo, where Roger spent part of his childhood, from Melbourne where he now lives. Along the way, we have talked a good deal about Tragowel – a locality which figures prominently in Roger's family history.

The McLeod connection with Tragowel, Roger explains, began with John McLeod, his great-grandfather, who emigrated from Scotland to Australia in 1856 and who afterwards became one of Tragowel's earliest settlers – getting there in 1876 at the end of a 200-mile journey from Inverleigh, to the south-west of Melbourne, where he had previously worked as a shepherd.

What attracted John McLeod to Tragowel was the prospect of obtaining his own farm and thus becoming his own boss. Victoria's colonial government was then looking to populate the colony's extensive rural hinterland, and whole districts had been thrown open to settlers. In those districts, of which Tragowel was one, farms could be got at a nominal price by anyone prepared to fence, plough, cultivate and crop them. The holding chosen by John McLeod extended to 320 acres, a big area by Scottish standards.

John McLeod was accompanied to Tragowel by his wife, Grace. Her surname before her marriage was Ross and, like her husband, she had emigrated from Scotland – with her parents in Grace's case – during the 1850s. Although married for just ten years, the couple had nine children, all daughters, who came north with them from Inverleigh by wagon. Within two years of their getting to Tragowel, three of the McLeod girls – Lily Ann, nine, Anne Williamina, four, and Dolina, one – died of diphtheria. Catastrophes of this kind were regular occurrences in the nineteenth century, but that would not have made John and Grace's loss any easier to bear. Worse was to come, however. In 1883, Grace too died, and the raising of John McLeod's children – his five surviving girls and the three little boys born since the family's arrival in Tragowel – now devolved to Hughina, John's eldest daughter who was just fifteen.

'Her life seemed to be a happy one,' Hughina's son Frederick recalled of what his mother told him about her youth. This was despite the 'many hardships' Hughina endured. There were meals to cook, a house to keep, small children and straying animals to round up and look after. During periods of drought, which were frequent, Hughina had to walk for several miles to find a river with enough water to enable her to wash a few clothes. And when John McLeod succeeded in getting some dairy cows, it was Hughina who milked them, made butter and got the butter to market. 'In the cold months of the year in the earlier times,' Frederick wrote of his mother, 'she travelled with her family [meaning her younger siblings] to Bendigo on more than one occasion to take butter to sell. The trip was per horse and dray, and they would bring back supplies.'[4]

At Tragowel, the McLeods lived initially in tents and in the canvas-covered wagon which had brought them from Inverleigh. In due course, the family moved into a one-roomed house built of mud-and-straw bricks which had been baked in the summer sun. In time, this basic home acquired an additional four rooms. But virtually all such progress, Roger McLeod tells me, was offset by further setbacks and disasters. In 1884, diphtheria returned and two of John McLeod's sons, Donald, six, and John William, two, died from its effects, leaving just one boy, William John, Roger's grandfather, to help John manage a farm which – quite apart from all the other troubles associated with it – was proving to be a bad investment agriculturally.

The plains around Tragowel looked like fertile grasslands that, with a modicum of cultivation, would yield good crops. In fact, the place was desperately dry and when, in an attempt to combat this, irrigation was introduced, Tragowel's soils proved so saline as to be almost unworkable. When he took over the McLeod farm from his father, William John, or Wally as he was called, could make no worthwhile living from it. A racing cyclist who won several prestige events in Melbourne and elsewhere, Wally invested his prize money in an alternative business, McLeod's Tragowel Cash Store. The store doubled as Tragowel's post office and, according to local historians, 'carried hardware, drapery and millinery . . . as well as groceries'. But given the problems Tragowel's farming population faced in a district that should arguably never have been settled, McLeod's Cash Store was no money spinner. In time, both the store and the farm which John McLeod established back in 1876 were sold as a result of Wally's decision to make a final break with an area where John and everyone connected with him had encountered nothing but difficulty.[5]

'My great-grandfather seems to have been dogged by trouble all his life,' Roger McLeod says. This is borne out by Roger's enquiries into the circumstances surrounding John McLeod's departure from Tongue, the place where this Tragowel pioneer was born and brought up.

The countryside around Tongue, a little village on Sutherland's rocky north coast, is as mountainous and rainy as the Tragowel district is flat and arid. But for all that the outlook from Tongue – an outlook dominated by the steep slopes of Ben Loyal and Ben Hope – would have been as appealing in the nineteenth century as it is in the twenty-first, Tongue in the 1850s, when John McLeod quit the place for ever, was a community in crisis. The causes of this crisis, which had its origins in the wholesale dispossessions known as the Highland Clearances, will be examined later. For the moment, it is enough to make the point that from mid-nineteenth-century Tongue, as from the rest of Sutherland, lots of people were leaving for Australia, often in conditions of extreme poverty. However, John McLeod, or so his great-grandson is convinced, was fleeing something other than destitution.

John's father, Donald McLeod, a retailer or merchant who also served as his locality's postmaster, was a man of some substance in Tongue. Because of this, John had a more secure start in life than most of his Sutherland contemporaries. But in 1855, when twenty-two years old, John fathered an illegitimate son. In Tongue, then firmly in the grip of the very demanding form of Presbyterianism associated with the Free Church of Scotland, this would have caused a scandal – all the more so in that the baby's father was a member of one of the village's leading families. Might his great-grandfather have been banished from Tongue in disgrace, Roger McLeod wonders. There is no proof of this, he concedes, but there is the indisputable fact that John took himself off, or was sent, to the far side of the world within months of his son's birth.

All that is known of the baby's mother is her name, Georgina MacKay. The boy himself was christened John, after his father presumably, and brought up in the Tongue household of one of his McLeod uncles, William, the emigrant John's older brother and the heir, in partnership with a further brother, Donald, of the trading business which had belonged to their father, now dead. Those details, Roger McLeod explains, come from 1861 and 1871 census returns – which show William McLeod, 'general merchant', sharing a Tongue home with his wife, Anne, and with the unmarried Donald McLeod, 'postmaster and merchant'. Also mentioned in the same returns are William and Anne's several children, two or three servants and a 'boarder' whose name is given as John McLeod. This John's age tallies with his having been the son of that other John McLeod who, by the 1860s, was shepherding in Inverleigh, Victoria.

Was the younger John well or badly treated by his uncles and his aunt? Nobody now knows. All that is certain is that in 1876, when twenty one, he emigrated from Sutherland to Australia, where he joined his father at Tragowel. In organising his son's emigration, as he must have done, was the elder John McLeod looking to help the young man? Or was he simply using him as a source of cheap farm labour and as a means of gaining access to the additional acres to which John McLeod junior, as a welcome addition to Victoria's rural population, was legally entitled? Again, nobody now knows. But it may be suggestive that the new arrival was never formally acknowledged as his father's son – being introduced to family members, friends and neighbours as the elder John McLeod's nephew. It may be equally suggestive that in 1882, six years after getting to Australia and with his father's other children still not knowing he was their half-brother, the younger John McLeod headed for Melbourne and was never heard from again.

While listening to Roger McLeod's account of those long ago events, it occurs to me that they could easily form the basis of a novel or, better still, a film. This production would open with the birth of John McLeod in 1830s Sutherland. His early circumstances are comparatively comfortable, but he grows up in a place where hunger, homelessness and despair are commonplace and where, partly in reaction to their misery, people have embraced a peculiarly stern religion. In defiance of one of this faith's tenets, John fornicates – the word Presbyterian preachers of his day would have used – with a young woman. An illegitimate son is born, taken from his mother and categorised as a 'boarder' in the home of one of the son's uncles. The child's father, meanwhile, has fled to Victoria, where twenty years later, having done well enough to obtain his own farm, he arranges for his now grown-up son to come and help him cultivate it – without acknowledging to the wife and children he has acquired in Victoria who the new arrival really is. By way of a judgement on this conduct, or so a fictionalised version of those events would imply, John McLeod's life is blighted. Three of his children die. His wife dies. Two more children die. John's farm turns out to be laced fatally with salt. And then – in the novel's concluding chapter or the movie's final scene – the unacknowledged son, in a grand act of belated protest, walks through the father's door, walks off the father's farm and vanishes into the vastness that is Australia. What becomes of him there, we are left to wonder. But at last, we hope, he will be able – in a way not permitted him previously – to shape his own life, follow his own desires, make his own destiny.

Of course, it may not have been quite like that. It may not have been like that at all. But emigration stories of the sort Roger McLeod tells are undeniably rich in dramatic potential. This may be why such stories have often been at the centre of the narratives which different branches of humanity have devised to account for their beginnings.

In the Bible, for example, population movement is central to the emergence of the Jews as a distinct, indeed a chosen, group. 'Get thee out of thy country,' God commands Abraham, 'and from thy kindred, and from thy father's house, unto a land that I will shew thee.' Doing as he has been told, Abraham leaves Mesopotamia and treks westward, becoming as a result the founding father not just of Judaism but of Christianity and Islam as well.[6]

Departures, journeys and fresh starts of this kind recur throughout the Old Testament. The most crucial, and perhaps the most familiar, of these migrations takes place when the Jews, Abraham's descendants, have fallen into captivity and slavery in Egypt. Just when it appears that the Jewish people's sufferings are going to last indefinitely, God gives Moses the instructions which, as the *Book of Exodus* records, will simultaneously set his nation free and send this nation on a long and difficult journey: 'And the Lord said, I have surely seen the affliction of my people which are in Egypt, and have heard their cry by reason of their taskmasters; for I know their sorrows. And I am come down to deliver them out of the hand of the Egyptians, and to bring them up out of that land unto a good land and a large, unto a land flowing with milk and honey.'[7]

Thousands of years later, when families from the Highlands and Islands began to quit Scotland for Britain's American colonies, they took comfort and inspiration from the *Exodus* story. Like the Jews of Moses's time, those people considered themselves victims of oppression. Also like the Jews, they believed they would find salvation in a land of promise far away. This is why, in the pro-emigration literature which circulated widely in the eighteenth-century Highlands and Islands, the landlords from whom emigrants were trying to escape are described as 'Egyptian taskmasters', while North Carolina, then the favoured emigrant destination, is presented as a happy land 'where freedom reigns' and where, because lairds of the Scottish type are unknown in North America, people 'may reap the produce of their own labour and industry.'[8]

Nor was this the first time that Scottish migrants turned to the *Book of Exodus* when trying to give their wanderings a higher meaning and purpose. Some thirteen or fourteen centuries in advance of the earliest departures to America *from* the Highlands and Islands, people were moving *into* the Hebrides and nearby mainland areas from Ireland. The Romans, whose Europe-wide empire was then starting to collapse, knew those incomers as *Scoti*, or Scots, and it was this Latin version of their name that came to be applied to the country they took over, *Scotia* or Scotland. The Scoti, however, called themselves Gaels, and in their Gaelic language they told a powerful tale as to who they were and whence ultimately they had come.

Gaels were Celtic in culture, and their origin myth embodies an awareness that Celtic influences – indeed Celtic migrants – had reached the British Isles from continental Europe hundreds of years before any Irish Gaels emigrated to Scotland. Hence this myth's insistence that the Gaels had come from the east; that they had come, in fact, from much the same area as the Jews; that their equivalent of Abraham was Nel, a warrior king who had married an Egyptian ruler's daughter and who, because of his sympathy with Moses, had been forced to flee Egypt with his family. According to the variant of this story incorporated into a letter which medieval Scotland's magnates sent to Pope John XXII from Arbroath Abbey on 6 April 1320, there followed much to-ing and fro-ing around the Mediterranean. But eventually, by way of Spain and Ireland, Nel's descendants, now one of Europe's more 'distinguished nations', found their way to Scotland, a country which Scots were pledged to defend, as the cleverly crafted document of 1320 puts it, 'for as long as a hundred of us remain alive'.[9]

This document, the Declaration of Arbroath, was despatched to Pope John in his capacity as the head of fourteenth-century Europe's only supranational institution. It was composed by men trying to get the pope's backing for their contention that the Scottish kingdom was ethically and legally entitled to wage war as a means of preventing its conquest by England. In the event, the declaration's contemporary impact was slight. Today, however, it has taken on a good deal of retrospective significance. For instance, when the United States Senate resolved in 1998 to designate 6 April as America's 'National Tartan Day', it did so with those words: 'April 6 has a special significance for all Americans, and especially those Americans of Scottish descent, because the Declaration of Arbroath, the Scottish Declaration of Independence, was signed on April 6, 1320, and the American Declaration of Independence was modelled on that inspirational document.' Whether such was truly the case is, to put it mildly, debatable. But that matters less in the present context than the way in which the sentiments expressed in the Arbroath letter of 1320 – sentiments which Tartan Day celebrates – link Scottish-Americans not just with transatlantic emigrants of relatively recent times but with the much earlier emigrants who first made Scotland Scottish. Medieval Scots may not literally have been the remote offspring of a Middle Eastern princeling and his Egyptian princess. However, a good deal of what made their kingdom distinctive would not have existed had Scotland's Gaelic-speaking settlers not brought with them their own ideas as to how society should be organised. Not the least of those ideas, and one that is central to this book, was the institution of clanship.

But if Clan MacLeod was primarily a product of thinking introduced to the Scottish Highlands and Islands by emigrants from Ireland, the clan's origins were also bound up with another, quite different, culture. Like that of the Gaels, this culture was introduced to the Highlands and Islands by folk who got there from another country. Those folk, however, were not Gaelic speaking. They were not Celts of any kind. They came from Norway. Scots and other Europeans, having borrowed the word – it means pirate or freebooter – from this new emigrant people's Norse language, called them Vikings.

CHAPTER TWO

THE SHINING OF THEIR WEAPONS

Iceland: Hvammur

It is characteristic of people of Scots descent that, wherever on earth they settle, they try to see something of Scotland in their surroundings. Sometimes, as around Tragowel, this proves impossible. But in places as far apart as Canada's Cape Breton and New Zealand's South Island, I have been shown landscapes said to look exactly like those of the Highlands and Islands. Although too polite to say so, I have mostly found those landscapes to be, from a Scottish standpoint, unmistakably alien. New Zealand is greener, grassier and more mountainous than any part of the Highlands and Islands, while Cape Breton is more heavily forested. It is a little paradoxical, therefore, that when in Iceland, which everyone tells me is like nowhere else on earth, I feel – perhaps because the two islands are volcanic in origin – that I am in a larger-scale Skye.

This is especially true of Hvammur, a farming community which I reach at the end of a three-hour drive from Reykjavik, Iceland's capital. It is early July and in Scotland the summer has been wet. But here, less than a hundred miles below the Arctic Circle, the sky is blue, the weather warm and, judging by the dust my rented car kicks up from Iceland's dirtroads, it has not rained for weeks. Nor does it get dark. The evening is well advanced by the time I get to Hvammur, but the sun is still shining and the outlook, to reiterate my earlier point, is one that strikes me as essentially Hebridean. Looking west and south from Hvammur, I might be in the vicinity of Dunvegan, at Orbost maybe, with the breeze-ruffled waters of Hvammsfjördur taking the place of Loch Bracadale and the high peaks of the Snæfellsnes Peninsula looking, for all the world, like a replica of the Cuillin. Might this spot's resemblance to the Dunvegan area have drawn its Viking settlers here? On this sunlit summer's evening, I am tempted to think so. Hvammur's first occupants, after all, were familiar with places like Skye.

The most prominent of them was a woman called *Audur Djúpúdga*, Audur the Deep-Minded. Audur lived more than a thousand years ago and, since neither she nor her Icelandic contemporaries were literate, no document survives from the Iceland of that era. Some two or three centuries after Audur's death, however, the medieval compilers of Iceland's sagas set down what they had heard of her. Because Audur and her family were important contributors to Iceland's early history, this amounted to a good deal. From Icelandic sources, therefore, it is possible to piece together an account of Audur's life. This account touches more than once on the Hebrides where there was established during Audur's lifetime – by her close kin among others – the social order which gave rise eventually to Clan MacLeod. This social order, Iceland's sagas indicate, took shape as a result of population movements to Scotland from Norway. The same social order, again according to the sagas, quickly produced its own outflows of people – outflows of the sort which brought Audur Djúpúdga to Hvammur. Hence Hvammur's appearance in this book. When writing about the Highlands and Islands exodus which began in the eighteenth century and continued into the twentieth, it is easy to give the impression that, before clanship's disintegration, people from the area felt no need, or had no opportunity, to venture far from their birthplaces. Nothing could be further from the truth. At almost every stage of clanship's development, starting in the period when Clan MacLeod's emergence had barely begun, residents of the Highlands and Islands travelled regularly overseas. Audur Djúpúdga's story proves as much.

Like many Viking stories, this one opens during the first half of the ninth century AD among the mountains of west-central Norway. Audur was born and brought up there in the household of her father – described by one of Iceland's sagamen as 'a great chieftain'. This chieftain, the same sagaman went on, was called Ketil, and possibly as a result of his having received a facial wound in battle, he was nicknamed Flatnose.[1]

At this time, Vikings from Norway and the rest of Scandinavia were starting to make their presence felt far from their homelands. From the 790s onwards, men like Ketil Flatnose, travelling in swift craft called longships, made voyages to other parts of Europe. Initially those voyages were in the nature of hit-and-run raids on coastal communities. Gradually, however, raiding gave way to trading and settlement. As a result, Viking colonies emerged in several widely separated localities. From eastern Scandinavia or Sweden, colonising effort was directed towards Russia – accessed by that country's great rivers. From southern Scandinavia or Denmark, the principal goal of settlement was England – reached by way of the North Sea. From western Scandinavia or Norway, aspiring colonisers made for Shetland and Orkney, island groups off Scotland's north coast, before turning south for the Hebrides and Ireland.

Ketil Flatnose, who had already 'raided there extensively', was one of the Norwegian Vikings who settled permanently in the Hebrides. When 'he made ready for his voyage from Norway west across the sea', an Icelandic sagaman wrote of Ketil's departure from Scandinavia, 'his daughter, Audur the Deep-Minded, and many . . . of his kinsmen went with him'. 'Ketil conquered the entire Hebrides and became chieftain over them,' a further sagaman added.[2]

Behind that last sentence there must lie a lot of fighting, politicking and intrigue. Nothing of this is now retrievable. Nor is it possible even to be sure of the dimensions of Ketil's Hebridean realm. Perhaps, as Iceland's sagamen suggested, Ketil ruled the entire island chain from Lewis, Harris and Skye southwards. Perhaps his territories were more limited. Either way, and this fact adds credence to the Icelandic contention that he was a man of substance, Ketil Flatnose's possessions were extensive enough to enable him to arrange a good marriage for Audur Djúpúdga, his daughter.

And so, at some point in the middle years of the ninth century, Audur the Deep-Minded became the wife of Olaf the White, another Norwegian warrior who had carved out his own Ketil-style kingdom in Ireland. This kingdom was centred on the Norse-dominated community which later evolved into Dublin. Audur now moved there and had a son who features in the sagas under the name of Thorstein the Red.

In time, Olaf the White, Thorstein's father and Audur's husband, fell victim to the warfare in which he engaged endlessly. This resulted in Audur, accompanied by her now grown-up son Thorstein, returning to the Hebrides. In the Hebrides, Thorstein the Red, as a saga puts it, married and 'had many children'. Also in the Hebrides, Thorstein appears to have inherited the dominant position once occupied by Ketil Flatnose, his grandfather, who by this stage had joined Olaf the White in the appropriately boisterous afterworld which Vikings expected to enter when dead. But where Ketil had looked south to Ireland for allies, Thorstein looked north to Orkney – entering into partnership with one of the first of that island group's many Norse *jarls* or earls, Sigurd the Powerful. 'Thorstein the Red became a warrior king,' an Icelandic saga notes of this arrangement, 'and joined forces with Earl Sigurd the Powerful; together they conquered Caithness, Sutherland, Ross, Moray and more than half Argyll. Thorstein ruled over those territories [comprising most of the Highlands and Islands] . . . until he was . . . killed in battle.'[3]

In the ninth century, Viking-controlled Scotland was both male-dominated and prone to violence. In consequence, her son's death placed the already fatherless and husbandless Audur Djúpúdga in a vulnerable position. Audur duly decided to leave Scotland. Her destination was Iceland – which Vikings had first reached not long before and which had begun to be settled by people from Norway. Among those people were Audur's brothers, Bjorn and Helgi Bjolan, whom Audur now aimed to join.

An Icelandic saga states: 'Audur the Deep-Minded was . . . in Caithness [today a Scottish county to the east of Sutherland] when Thorstein [her son] lost his life. When she learned that her son had been killed she realised that she had no further prospects there, now that her father too was dead. So she had a ship built secretly in a forest, and when it was completed she loaded it with valuables and prepared it for a voyage. She took with her all her surviving kinsfolk; and . . . it would be hard to find another example of a woman escaping from such hazards with so much wealth and such a large retinue.'[4]

From Caithness, Audur voyaged by way of Orkney and the Faroe Islands to Iceland – sailing into Breidafjördur, a broad, bight-like inlet in the north-western part of the island, before pressing on into one of Breidafjördur's many narrower offshoots, Hvammsfjördur. Hvammur, where Audur settled, is on Hvammsfjördur's northern shore. Audur's former landholding occupies a wide and flat-floored valley. This valley is south facing and, despite being at a high latitude, is clearly fertile. When I get back to Hvammur on the morning of my second day in the district, a local farmer, one of Audur the Deep-Minded's present-day successors, is taking a hay crop from his fields. From the summit of the high hill which I climb on the valley's western rim, I can hear the sound of the farmer's machinery. I can hear too, exactly as I would if this hill were in Skye, the occasional bleating of sheep. The sun is still shining and is warm on my back. Sitting on a rock, I look towards the spot where Audur the Deep-Minded lived out the last years of her life. From my pocket, I take a book containing a description, set down here in Iceland centuries ago, of how this life ended: 'Audur was a woman of great dignity. When she was growing weary with old age, she invited her kinsmen and relatives-by-marriage to a magnificent feast, and when the feast had been celebrated for three days . . . she declared that the feast would go on for another three days and that it would be her funeral feast. That very night she died.'[5]

Scotland: The Highlands and Islands

Traces of the Viking influence on the Hebrides are still apparent to anyone exploring Clan MacLeod's former heartlands. In Lewis, you pass through villages called Shulishader, Garrabost, Swordale, Sandwick, Leurbost and Laxay. Those names are Norse. So are many of their counterparts in Harris, and much the same is true of Skye, not least the area around Dunvegan. This area's parish or district names, Minginish, Bracadale, Duirinish and Waternish, are wholly Scandinavian – as are more localised designations like Waterstein, Holmisdale, Colbost, Skinidin and Orbost. All such placenames date from the time when Ketil Flatnose, and the other warlords who succeeded him, were in charge hereabouts. For a period, their control of Skye, Harris and Lewis was absolute. As is underlined by the persistence of Norse names on Hebridean maps and signposts, this period extended over several generations.

However, in the eleventh century a new political entity appeared. This was the Kingdom of Man. Its Norse rulers, whose principal base was the Isle of Man in the Irish Sea, owed allegiance to the Norwegian monarchy. But Norway was far away and, for the most part, its rulers were content to leave the Kingdom of Man to its own devices. The Kings of Man, therefore, were free to extend their jurisdiction northward. Soon all the Hebrides – Lewis, Harris and Skye included – had fallen under their sway.

But though the Kings of Man were Norwegian in name, ancestry and affiliation, their Hebridean territories ceased gradually to be Norse in speech. This happened because of a resurgence in the Highlands and Islands of the Celtic culture associated with those earlier arrivals in the region, the Scoti or Gaels, who – despite their having been overrun militarily by men like Ketil Flatnose – had by no means vanished from the Hebridean scene.

In addition to their Gaelic language, the Gaels brought with them to Scotland a new religion, Christianity. Appropriately, then, much the most renowned individual among the many Irish-born Gaels who moved from Ireland to the Hebrides was a churchman, *Colum Cille* or Columba, whose missionary journeys took him to many parts of the Highlands and Islands, including Skye. Skye, when Columba came there towards the close of the sixth century, was inhabited by pagan tribes who spoke a now long-extinct language, Pictish. The same was true at that time of the rest of the Highlands and Islands – outside the area, roughly coterminous with the modern county of Argyll, already occupied by Columba's fellow Gaels. In the course of the ensuing 200 years, however, most of the mainland Highlands and practically all the Hebrides were christianised and to some extent gaelicised. This revolution had complex causes, but its principal promoters can readily be identified. They were the many Gaelic-speaking monks who, in the manner of Columba, devoted themselves to spreading their faith.

Although they had little else in common with Vikings, those monks were daring sailors. In skin-covered craft of frightening fragility, they made voyage after voyage through the Hebrides – next pushing on, by way of Orkney, Shetland and Faroe, to Iceland. Had circumstances permitted, other Gaels might have followed where those fearless churchmen led – turning Iceland, which was uninhabited when its monastic discoverers got there, into a Gaelic-speaking country. But history, as already indicated, took a different course. The arrival of Gaels in Iceland coincided with the first outpourings of Vikings from Norway, and soon almost every part of the North Atlantic world – Iceland, Faroe, Shetland, Orkney, the Hebrides, most of the Highland mainland and much of Ireland – had become a Norse preserve.

It is hard to overestimate the terror generated among the Christian and Gaelic-speaking inhabitants of the Hebrides and Ireland by the sudden appearance off their shores of gangs of seaborne, and aggressively pagan, raiders from Norway. In 794, when Viking incursions had just started, a Gaelic-speaking monk wrote in anguish of the 'devastation' brought to the Hebrides 'by the heathen'. In 795, another monk noted that 'Skye [had been] overwhelmed and laid waste'. A further monk, freed temporarily from fear of Norse raiders by the winter gales howling round his monastery, composed a revealing Gaelic verse in praise of wild weather. 'The bitter wind is high tonight,' this monk wrote. 'It lifts the white locks of the sea.' By so doing, the same monk noted gratefully, January storms accomplished something no human agency could achieve. They kept Viking warriors at home.[6]

The nature of that churchman's fears can be deduced from an Icelandic poem composed by a Scandinavian participant in the warfare which flared intermittently in the Hebrides throughout the ninth and tenth centuries. This poem features ravens 'rinsed in dead men's blood'; it glories in the spectacle of 'fire over Lewis play[ing] high in the heavens'; it tells how one Viking leader 'sated the eagle's hunger' with human corpses as he 'harried far about Skye'.[7]

But horrors of this sort did not preclude Nordic–Gaelic contact of a more peaceful kind. Within a generation or two of their reaching the Hebrides, Vikings were marrying Celts. They were also beginning to adopt Christianity. One early convert was Audur the Deep-Minded. Another was one of Audur's relatives, Helgi the Lean, son of a Norse father and a Gaelic-speaking mother. Helgi's Christianity, to be sure, was somewhat tentative. 'He believed in Christ,' a sagaman recorded, 'but invoked Thor [a Viking god] when it came to voyages and difficult times.' Eventually, however, Christianity won out over paganism, and in time the Celtic and Nordic elements in the Hebridean population merged totally. This process, admittedly, took several generations. But it was underway by the second half of the ninth century, when Audur the Deep-Minded left for Iceland. Several of Audur's companions had Celtic names. So did many other early emigrants to Iceland from the Norse colonies in the British Isles – with this Celtic contribution to the settlement of Iceland being evident even today in the occurrence among Icelanders of personal names like Njal, a variant of the Gaelic Neil or Niall.[8]

In Iceland, those Gaelic influences notwithstanding, a part-Viking, part-Celtic society became wholly Norse speaking. In the Hebrides, as already indicated, the opposite happened. Here, although Norse was dominant for long enough to leave an indelible mark in the form of thousands of Norse-derived placenames, Gaelic took its place. The exact timing of this linguistic shift is impossible to determine. But it was well on its way to completion, and may even have been completed, by the early thirteenth century – a period when the Hebrides, like the rest of the semi-autonomous Kingdom of Man, still belonged formally to Norway, not Scotland.

Nor was the gradual celticising, or re-celticising, of islands like Skye a matter merely of people who had formerly spoken Norse starting to speak Gaelic. Other Celtic traits and characteristics were adopted also. As a result, the population of the Hebrides began to be organised into clans. These groupings had long been universal in Gaelic-speaking Ireland, and by the thirteenth century, if not before, they were becoming standard in the Gaelic-speaking Hebrides as well. At the centre of one such grouping was a man called Ljot or Leod, Clan MacLeod's founding chief. Not much is known about Leod personally. But the milieu in which he operated was such as to make it certain that his values had nothing in common with those prevailing in the present-day countries where Leod and his successors continue to be celebrated by members of the Associated Clan MacLeod Societies.

All the nations represented at ACMS's clan parliaments in Dunvegan are democracies governed in accordance with beliefs of the type enunciated in the opening sentence of America's Declaration of Independence: 'We hold these truths to be self-evident, that all men are created equal, that they are endowed by their Creator with certain inalienable rights, that among these are Life, Liberty and the pursuit of Happiness.' Irrespective of family or other circumstance, this implies, human beings ought to be given every opportunity to maximise their potential. Anyone, in other words, should be able to progress from a log cabin to the White House or from an inner-city slum to the presidency of a multinational corporation. Of course, few societies are actually organised in ways which ensure that each career path is open to everyone with the capacity to follow it. Since the Declaration of Independence was drawn up – with or without reference to its Arbroath precursor – in Philadelphia in 1776, however, thinking of the kind which gave rise to it has spread widely enough to ensure the removal of many once-insurmountable barriers to advancement. Among present-day millionaires are some who started as slum kids. Among present-day politicians are plenty who have overcome real disadvantage.

Most such social mobility is regarded nowadays as positive. This demonstrates the breadth of the gulf separating the modern world from the world of people like Leod. The men in charge of Clan MacLeod in the Middle Ages and later could never have been persuaded that people were created equal. Those men's mental universe – a determinedly hierarchical universe where a clan's leaders counted for a great deal and where nobody else mattered much – was one in which a person's position and status was fixed at the moment of their birth. By unalterable custom and practice, chiefs of Clan MacLeod, together with the clan's other foremost figures, were drawn from a tight-knit group of Leod's direct descendants. Wherever society was organised in accordance with clanship's dictates, this was simply how things had to be. Clans, to be sure, could disintegrate, go down to military defeat or fall prey, as some branches of Clan MacLeod did, to more successful competitors. A particular chief might be, and sometimes was, displaced by a rival from within his own ruling elite. But there could, by definition, be no route into this ruling elite from a clan's lower ranks. Hence the importance attached by upper-echelon clansfolk to their genealogies. And hence, incidentally, the ease with which many modern MacLeods are able to equip themselves with impressively long pedigrees. If you can establish a connection with a past MacLeod who was near the top of his clan's pecking order, there is little to stop you mapping out a family tree which starts with Leod himself.

In the twenty-first century, possession of such a family tree conveys – outside the Associated Clan MacLeod Societies – no practical advantage. But once it did. From the thirteenth century down to the first half of the century which witnessed the proclamation of America's Declaration of Independence, a man's chances of obtaining large landholdings, together with the power and prestige they brought with them, were enhanced immeasurably by his being of Leod's line.

In a purely Clan MacLeod context, such a man felt his status secured by his links with Leod. But those links were not, of themselves, sufficient to guarantee that he would be treated as an equal by senior representatives of other clans. In this wider setting, given the ancestry-obsessed climate in which inter-clan relationships developed, it was necessary for the principal men of each clan to insist that their clan's progenitor had himself been of high standing. Thus the chiefs of the MacDonalds – with whom Clan MacLeod had both friendly and unfriendly dealings over several centuries – claimed that their thirteenth-century founder was descended from Irish kings. MacLeod chiefs, not to be outdone, insisted on Leod's similarly royal antecedents. But those antecedents, in Leod's case, were not said to be Irish. They were said instead to be Norse.

This was what Iain Macleod, then a leading British politician, had in mind in 1957, when, in the course of a Whitehall reception, he proposed a toast to Norway's ambassador to the United Kingdom. 'The clan to which I have the honour to belong,' Macleod told Oslo's man in London, 'were a Norwegian clan and came a thousand years ago from your shores to the Highlands and Islands of Scotland, from where my forebears come.'[9]

Iain Macleod's father was a medical doctor in the English town of Skipton where the future politician was born. But his Macleod grandfather was a fish curer and merchant in Stornoway and, much further back, an ancestor was principal tenant or tacksman (a term explained later) of Pabbay, a small island to the south of Harris. It is by no means improbable, therefore, that Iain Macleod was related in some way to a seventeenth-century poet whose father had Pabbay connections and who, in a poem praising a prominent MacLeod of the poet's time, made the same point as Iain Macleod did in his London speech. '*Lochlannaich threun*,' this poem informed the man who was its subject, '*Toiseach bhur sgéil*': 'Mighty men of Norway came first in your history'.[10]

Historians of Clan MacLeod have tried hard to substantiate assertions of this sort. Such historians used to claim that Leod, Clan MacLeod's thirteenth-century creator, was a son of Olaf the Black, a King of Man who died in 1237. Later investigators have questioned this contention. The same investigators, however, tend to accept a more longstanding, though less precise, MacLeod tradition to the effect that MacLeod chiefs, by way of Leod's remoter precursors, were descended from high-born Vikings. Despite it now being thought improbable that Leod was Olaf the Black's son, then, it remains likely that there was some sort of overlap between Leod's line and that of the Kings of Man. Those Kings, to reiterate, were of Norwegian extraction. They may have been related to Norway's monarchs. They may also have been related to the ninth-century, and highly influential, kin-group centred on Ketil Flatnose, Audur the Deep-Minded's father.[11]

Clarifying those matters by means of historical research is virtually impossible – the requisite sources of information being almost non-existent. But when the Associated Clan MacLeod Societies persuaded several hundred of their members to participate in an experiment organised by a geneticist, the results went some way to confirming Clan MacLeod's time-honoured account of its own beginnings. Of the ACMS volunteers, more than a tenth were thought to have had Viking forebears, and about a third showed evidence of having a common ancestor who lived about a thousand years ago – not Leod necessarily but perhaps one of his family predecessors.[12]

Future advances in genetics may add new details. But for the moment, not a lot more can be said about the circumstances giving rise to Clan MacLeod's formation. Nor is it possible to be a great deal clearer about ensuing events. What is definite – and it does not amount to much – is that after Leod's death, which occurred in the second half of the thirteenth century, his clan split into two distinct, though connected, branches. The founders of those branches were Tormod, a gaelicised Norse name afterwards anglicised as Norman, and Torcuil, another Norse name eventually anglicised as Torquil. Tormod was one of Leod's sons. Torcuil, long assumed to have been Tormod's brother, is now thought to have been his nephew. Either way, both Tormod and Torcuil established – within the wider clan which Leod had launched – chieftainly lineages of their own. In Gaelic, the first was *Sìol Thormoid*, meaning Tormod's seed, the second *Sìol Thorcuil*.

Leod had made himself master of Lewis, Harris and a part of Skye, which – and this may be a further confirmation of his Norse roots – were the Hebridean islands most densely settled by the Vikings. When those territories were divided between Leod's Sìol Thormoid and Sìol Thorcuil successors, the former took charge of Harris and the Skye districts of Duirinish, Bracadale and Minginish – to which Sìol Thormoid's chiefs afterwards added Glenelg. The Sìol Thorcuil, for their part, acquired Lewis and the Skye district of Waternish – to which they later added Raasay and the mainland localities of Assynt and Gairloch. As indicated earlier, making a circuit of those MacLeod lands nowadays takes time and effort. Six or seven centuries back, however, all the areas under MacLeod control were in comparatively direct communication with each other. This was because Clan MacLeod's territories then constituted a seaborne empire – the clan's strength resting, from the outset, on its warships.

One such ship – a *birlinn* in Gaelic, a galley in English – is portrayed on the Harris tombstone of a sixteenth-century MacLeod chief, *Alasdair Crotach* of the Sìol Thormoid. As is evident from this carving and others like it, birlinns were – in design, construction and appearance – the lineal descendants of Viking longships. Indeed the principal builders of Clan MacLeod's galleys – reputedly a family resident for many generations in Colbost near Dunvegan – may well have been the inheritors of skills handed down directly from the Norsemen who first brought those skills to Skye.[13]

A Gaelic poem, dating from the period of Clan MacLeod's emergence, evokes the nature of Hebridean seapower in a series of verbal snapshots. A fleet of birlinns is bearing down on a hostile strongpoint. Because the fleet is powered by oars, as well as sails, it 'stays its course' irrespective of the vagaries of wind and weather. Each of the fleet's component ships has rows of highly polished shields slung over its 'long flanks'. The sun glints on those shields, on the 'red silk banner' which flies at each masthead, and on the 'fine helmets' worn by 'fierce, fearless warriors' who eagerly ready themselves for action: 'there's no hand lacks a sleek war-spear'.[14]

This was how war had been waged in the Hebrides since the time of Ketil Flatnose. This was how war continued to be waged when, during Leod's lifetime, the islands ceased to be possessions of Norwegian kings and became subject instead to Scotland's Edinburgh-based monarchy. The consequent snapping of their 500-year old ties with Norway had the effect of removing islands like Skye and Lewis from the Norse world to which they had formerly belonged. But chiefs of Clan MacLeod – this 'clan of galleys' in the words of an ancient Gaelic ballad – lost none of their significance as a result.[15]

For much of the fourteenth and fifteenth centuries, admittedly, the Sìol Thormoid and the Sìol Thorcuil were lacking in freedom of action – both branches of Clan MacLeod then being subordinate to the overarching authority of the Lordship of the Isles. By the 1490s, however, the lordship, a quasi-independent successor to the earlier Kingdom of Man, had fallen apart. Although its collapse had been engineered by Scotland's kings, who were anxious to be done with the threat posed by Lords of the Isles to their own position, those kings – for the next hundred or so years – lacked the means to impose their own rule on the Hebrides. During the sixteenth century, in consequence, Clan MacLeod chiefs – no longer subject to the lordship and, for most practical purposes, outside the jurisdiction of the Scottish monarchy – were able greatly to enlarge their sphere of operations.

From a Clan MacLeod perspective, the sixteenth century is bracketed by the careers of two of the most formidable chiefs the clan produced, Alasdair Crotach and *Ruaraidh Mòr*. Both headed the Sìol Thormoid – Alasdair assuming command of this branch of the clan in the years immediately prior to 1500, Ruaraidh taking on the Sìol Thormoid chieftainship nearly a century later. In Highlands and Islands tradition, the era in which Alasdair and Ruaraidh lived is remembered as *Linn nan Creach*, an age of forays, raids and plundering. This, however, is to give a retrospectively heroic gloss to ugly events – the Hebridean sixteenth century being one of frequent slaughter. Most fighting stemmed from the fact that, in the anarchic circumstances produced by the demise of the Lordship of the Isles, several Hebridean clans found themselves caught up in bitter wrangles over territory. The numerous conflicts into which MacLeod chiefs were drawn at this time generally involved one or other of two MacDonald clans, the MacDonalds of Sleat, whose land bordered that of the Clan MacLeod in Skye, and the MacDonalds of Clanranald, whose lands included islands to the south of Clan MacLeod's possessions in Harris. Alasdair Crotach, or so MacLeod lore has it, owed his name, which translates as Hump-Backed Alexander, to a disabling wound he received when battling with MacDonalds. Ruaraidh Mòr was often at war with them too. His Gaelic designation – Ruaraidh Mòr meaning Big Roderick in the sense of Roderick the Great – reflects a well-founded conviction on the part of MacLeod tradition bearers that, but for the military prowess of this most celebrated of its chieftains, Clan MacLeod might easily have been overwhelmed by its MacDonald, or other, enemies.

Like Alasdair Crotach before him, Ruaraidh Mòr held court in Dunvegan Castle. In the sixteenth century, the castle was described – in a document written in the Broad Scots of the Scottish Lowlands – as 'ane stark strenth biggit on ane craig'. There can be no argument with those words. Dunvegan's looming walls, still planted firmly on top of the steep-sided *craig* or rock which Leod himself may have selected as the perfect site for a fortress, have always conveyed – as they were meant to convey – an impression of unassailability. But if Dunvegan Castle's primary purpose was to intimidate, its secondary function was to provide Clan MacLeod chieftains with a setting appropriate to their station. Here in the years around 1600, MacLeod clansfolk were wined, dined and otherwise entertained by Ruaraidh Mòr in the grand style captured in the Gaelic verse of *Màiri Nighean Alasdair Ruaidh* or Mary MacLeod, the Pabbay-connected poet whose insistence on Clan MacLeod's Norse antecedents was cited earlier.[16]

''S ann 'na thigh mòr a fhuair mi am macnas,' Mary wrote of Ruaraidh Mòr, whose Dunvegan stronghold she first visited when still a girl. '*Dann's le sunnd air urlar farsaing, An fhìdhleireachd 'gam chur a chadal, A' phìobaireachd mo dhùsgadh maidne*': 'In his great house I have been joyful, dancing merrily on a wide floor, the fiddle playing to put me to sleep, the pipe playing to wake me in the morning'.[17]

Ireland: Ulster

When I am shown around Dunvegan Castle by John MacLeod, Clan MacLeod's present chief, we stand for a moment – along with some of the tourists who flock here each summer – in front of a glass cabinet containing Ruaraidh Mòr's intricately decorated drinking cup. The cup, of Irish design, was reputedly gifted to Ruaraidh by Hugh O'Neill, Earl of

Tyrone, in gratitude for the assistance which Clan MacLeod gave the earl in the course of the armed uprising he mounted during the 1590s with the aim of liberating Ireland from English rule. Like many such tales, the story of how Ruaraidh Mòr's drinking cup reached Dunvegan is impossible to verify. However, there is no doubt as to the involvement of Ruaraidh and his clan in Ireland's late-sixteenth-century wars – this involvement serving, incidentally, to make the point that, though Hebridean contact with Iceland had ceased long before, Hebrideans of Ruaraidh Mòr's time continued to be in touch with localities beyond their shores.

Links between the Hebrides and Ireland were not new, of course. As already stressed, the language spoken by sixteenth-century MacLeod clansfolk, those clansfolk's wider culture and, for that matter, the concept of clanship itself had all originated in Ireland. Partly for this reason, medieval Ireland and the medieval Hebrides constituted a single geographical entity – with people of all sorts wandering freely across Gaelic-speaking territories which stretched from Assynt and Lewis in the north to Cork and Kerry in the south. Among such itinerants were the Irish bards – accompanied, no doubt, by harpists and other musicians – who are known to have made stopovers at Dunvegan Castle. Hebridean poets probably made similar journeys in the reverse direction. Soldiers certainly did.

The practice of men from the Hebrides seeking military careers in Ireland was one that stretched back to the Viking period. It continued into the era of the Lordship of the Isles when so-called *gallvglaich* of Hebridean extraction provided Ireland's perpetually warring nobility with a ready supply of dependable troops. Galloglaich, a Gaelic term that passed into Shakespearian English as *galloglasses*, were mercenaries. Today, when people are expected to serve only in armies raised by their own countries, the notion of soldiers hiring themselves out to all-comers in return for cash is one that carries negative connotations. This was not so in the pre-modern world, however. Until at least the eighteenth century, soldiering tended to be treated as a trade like any other – with nobody seeing anything wrong in a man's military skills being on offer to the highest bidder.

Nor were galloglaich penniless unfortunates who went to war for lack of any alternative. On the contrary, most Hebridean galloglasses were drawn from clanship's higher ranks. This is reflected in galloglasses having been accompanied, as they trekked from one part of Ireland to another, by personal servants. It is reflected too in the nature of a galloglass's equipment. His weapons consisted primarily of a battleaxe or a huge two-handed sword known as a claymore. For protection, he wore a chainmail coat and an iron helmet. All those items were affordable only to individuals of above-average affluence.

But if a galloglass was typically a man of standing, there was nothing of the aristocratic amateur about him. On the contrary, he tended to be a deeply committed, highly capable and, above all, courageous professional. This was recognised by English commentators who encountered Hebridean galloglasses in the course of the wars caused by England's repeated attempts to annexe Ireland. Irish infantry were liable to scatter when a battle began to go against them, one Englishman wrote. In his experience, however, Hebrideans did 'not lightly abandon the field, but [bore] the brunt to the death'.[18]

One of Leod's younger sons, a man reputed to have made his home in Ireland, may have been an early galloglass. The expeditionary force which Ruaraidh Mòr led to Ireland in the mid-1590s was definitely in this tradition, although its several hundred participants – the invention of firearms having meanwhile rendered body armour useless – were more mobile and less heavily equipped than their galloglaich predecessors had been.

Ulster, where Ruaraidh Mòr and his men disembarked from their galleys in 1594, is the most northerly of Ireland's four provinces. In the sixteenth century, it was also the part of Ireland most committed to sustaining the country's Gaelic character and most hostile, therefore, to invaders and colonisers from England. Despite his English-sounding title, the Earl of Tyrone, Hugh O'Neill, shared this Ulster antagonism to England's expansionist ambitions. The earl, the most prominent of the province's native leaders, had concluded that, if he and Ulster folk more generally were to preserve their autonomy, the armies of England's Queen Elizabeth would have to be driven out of Ireland. This, from Ruaraidh Mòr's standpoint, was an ambition which made good sense. By the 1590s, Ruaraidh was uncomfortably aware that Scotland's monarch, James VI, was in agreement with Elizabeth of England on the desirability of curtailing the freedoms of Gaelic-speaking chieftains – not just in Ulster but in the Hebrides too. In going to the aid of Hugh O'Neill, therefore, Clan MacLeod was arguably endeavouring merely to preserve its own independence. In the event, neither this long-run objective nor Hugh O'Neill's more immediate goals were attained. But that, as far as one can judge from the sketchy record of Ruaraidh Mòr's Irish adventure, was not for want of trying on Clan MacLeod's part.

When you drive through modern Ulster, as I did with a view to tracing Ruaraidh Mòr's route of 400 years ago, there is no mistaking the failure of Earl Hugh O'Neill's efforts to keep the area Irish. Following the earl's defeat, which occurred in 1603, thousands of English-speaking families were installed hereabouts. Some of those families came from England, more came from the south of Scotland. But irrespective of their places of origin, all such incomers differed from the Irish people they displaced not only in speech but also in religion – England and the Scottish Lowlands having embraced the Protestant Reformation during the sixteenth century, Ireland having remained fervently Catholic. Thus there were engendered the intercommunal hatreds – Gaelic-speaking Catholics on one side, English-speaking Protestants on the other – which have been a feature of life in Ulster ever since.

Reminders of those enduring tensions – in the shape of rival banners, flags and slogans – are all around as I head westwards through Coleraine and Limavady. Minutes out of Limavady on the Derry road, I reach the shores of Lough Foyle – wider than most of its Scottish equivalents but with the Highland-looking hills of Donegal rising steeply on its far side. 'Around Loch Foyle he left none unharried,' a Gaelic poet wrote in celebration of Ruaraidh Mòr's Ulster 'triumphs'. However, no trace of those triumphs, if that is what they were, is detectable in present-day Northern Ireland. Nor are there any memorials to Clan MacLeod across the border in the Irish Republic – for all that Ruaraidh Mòr was engaged in anti-English activity of the kind to which Irish nationalists erected numberless public monuments when, in the 1920s, they finally gained independence for the greater part of Ireland. According to his bards, Ruaraidh Mòr 'set Ballymote aflame' and marched into nearby Sligo with 'herds of horses taken from the people of Connaught follow[ing] in his rear'. But so much further fighting has washed through Irish towns and villages in the interim that Clan MacLeod's impact on places like Sligo and Ballymote has long been forgotten. If you want to discover an enduring legacy of MacLeod entanglements in the foreign wars of Ruaraidh Mòr's time, then, you have to go somewhere other than Ireland. You have to go to continental Europe.[19]

France: Versailles

England's victory over Hugh O'Neill completed the English conquest of Gaelic Ireland and deprived MacLeod mercenaries of what had been the main market for their talents. Other markets soon appeared, however. When early-seventeenth-century Europe became embroiled in the Germany-centred conflict known as the Thirty Years War, demand for military manpower grew exponentially. Much of this manpower was supplied by the continent's least developed regions – the Balkans, Switzerland and Scotland. By the 1620s, in consequence, thousands of Scots had found their way into the armies of one or other of a dozen European monarchs. Among such Scots was Murdo MacLeod who came from Assynt and who is known to have been in action with the forces of the Danish king at the Battle of

Stralsund in 1628. Among them too was a further MacLeod, also in Danish pay, who that same year was killed in fierce fighting at Kiel.[20]

Once established, this pattern persisted for the remainder of the seventeenth century and well into the eighteenth. It persisted especially strongly in the case of the Netherlands, where set after set of MacLeods – fathers, sons, brothers and cousins – followed each other into that country's armed services. Beyond their names – Neil MacLeod, John MacLeod, Angus MacLeod and so on – little can now be discovered about most of those men. In one or two instances, however, details of their weddings survive – as in the case of a Corporal Donald MacLeod who, in 1725, married Agnes Harlestanee, a Dutch woman. Since plenty more such marriages must have occurred, it is not surprising that the name MacLeod became indigenous to Holland. Thus it came about that one of the most senior officers in the Royal Navy of the Netherlands at the start of the twentieth century was Admiral Norman MacLeod, whose Skye-born great-great-grandfather had joined the Dutch military in 1706.[21]

Holland's MacLeods did not confine themselves to Europe. During the nineteenth century, several were active in the Dutch East Indies, now Indonesia. Among this group was an army captain, Rudolph MacLeod, a nephew of the Dutch navy's Admiral Norman. In the mid-1890s, when Rudolph was on extended leave in Holland, he met and married Margarethe Zelle, who afterwards accompanied the captain back east and helped him set up home in Java. One of his contemporaries described Rudolph as 'a handsome man of dandified appearance'. But perhaps because of a big discrepancy in their ages – he was thirty-nine when they married, she was still a teenager – Rudolph and Margarethe did not get on well. The captain, rumour had it, maltreated his wife, and so bad had things got by 1902, when the MacLeods returned to Holland from Java, that Margarethe left her husband and moved to Paris. There, this young Dutchwoman commenced a spectacularly successful, and well-publicised, career as – in the terminology of the period – an exotic dancer. From the standpoint of Rudolph and his relatives, this was an outrageous development made all the more shocking by Margarethe's initial choice of stagename, Lady MacLeod. But such ill repute as attached itself to Paris's self-styled Lady MacLeod was as nothing to the notoriety forever to be associated with the designation Margarethe next adopted. By way of advertising the eastern origins of her dance routine, which was partly inspired by what she had seen of traditional dancing in Java, the former Lady MacLeod gave herself the oriental-sounding name of Mata Hari. Some ten years later, at the height of the First World War, it was as Mata Hari that Margarethe, still known formally as Madame Rudolph MacLeod, was arrested by the French authorities, accused of spying for

Kaiser Wilhelm's Germany, tried, found guilty and condemned to death.[22]

In his home in Versailles, on Paris's western outskirts, I discuss the Mata Hari case with Alain MacLeod of the *Association Française du Clan MacLeod*, France's Clan MacLeod Society. Alain, a retired military engineer, mentions that when Mata Hari was executed, his paternal grandfather, Colonel Alfred MacLeod, was one of millions of Frenchmen then engaged in what Alfred's generation called the Great War. Would this French-speaking artillery officer have been aware, I ask, that he shared his Hebridean-derived surname with the Dutch-born seductress who, from the moment her death was decreed, has been synonymous with an enticingly glamorous kind of treachery?

Alfred MacLeod died in the Great War's aftermath, before Alain was born, and Alain cannot answer my question. But he can supply other facts about his grandfather's career, he comments. So saying, Alain fetches some handwritten letters and spreads them across a table. They are more than a hundred years old and were sent by Alfred MacLeod, then sailing up the Senegal River in West Africa, to relatives in France. Picking up one of Alfred's letters, I discover that it is dated 1 November 1893 and that it contains an account of what Alfred MacLeod, then a young subaltern in France's colonial forces, saw from the deck of his river steamer: a flat, forested, tropical countryside, dotted with hutted settlements which are described in detail.

Nothing is more indicative of the extent of Clan MacLeod's dispersal around the world than the fact that, at the same time as a Dutchman called Rudolph MacLeod was helping to consolidate his country's grip on Indonesia, a Frenchman called Alfred MacLeod was contributing to the expansion of France's empire in Africa. But how did Alfred MacLeod, his several siblings and their many descendants – including Alfred's grandson Alain – get to be French in the first place? Alain is happy to explain. But his explanation, he warns, may take time – Alain's MacLeod forebears having reached France from Scotland by way of the Netherlands, England, Ireland and the West Indies.

'The earliest of our MacLeod ancestors we have been able to trace,' Alain MacLeod says of his family's genealogical researches, 'was called Robert MacLeod. Where he came from exactly in Scotland, we haven't been able to find out. We know him only as a mercenary officer in the army the Dutch king, William of Orange, led from Holland to England in 1688. Afterwards, Robert went with King William to Ireland. In time, he got land there, in or near Cork, and made his home on this land.'

The ground Alain has covered is historically complex. It includes the enforced ejection from England of the country's last Catholic monarch, James II, and his replacement by Robert MacLeod's aggressively Protestant commander, William of Orange; it includes the expelled James's raising of a Catholic and native Irish army in English-ruled Ireland; it includes, finally, the crushing of this army by King William at the Battle of the Boyne in July 1690. Since William of Orange was accompanied to Ireland by Alain MacLeod's ancestor, Robert, and since the events of 1690 were regarded by Protestant settlers as confirming their supremacy over Ulster's Catholic and Gaelic-speaking inhabitants, Robert MacLeod, in his role as one of William's soldiers, can be seen as having helped to deliver in Ireland exactly the opposite of what Ruaraidh Mòr was trying to accomplish when fighting there a century before.

But that is by the way. More important, in the context of Alain MacLeod's family history, was the gradual integration of Robert MacLeod's descendants into the nation Robert assisted William of Orange to conquer. During the eighteenth century, those Cork-based MacLeods, despite their having arrived in Ireland as Protestants, converted – and this was an unusual transition to make in eighteenth-century Ireland – to Catholicism. At the start of the nineteenth century, one member of the family, Charles John MacLeod, whose bust can still be seen in Cork Cathedral, was a prominent priest in the city. Another, Denis Francis MacLeod, held a senior position in Ireland's order of Capuchin Friars.

Not all of Cork's MacLeods pursued ecclesiastical careers. About twenty years into the nineteenth century, two further members of the family, brothers called Robert Francis and John, left Cork for the West Indies. There they set up as traders specialising in the import of wine from France. Perhaps as a result of this French connection or perhaps, family tradition hints, because they resented the way Catholics were then discriminated against in British-ruled Ireland, Robert Francis and John MacLeod, rather than return to Cork from the West Indies, moved instead to France, where they established themselves eventually in Vendôme, near Orléans. There, Robert Francis MacLeod's home, complete with a MacLeod coat of arms above its doorway, remains in the ownership of one of Alain MacLeod's relatives – Alain himself being a great-grandson of Robert Francis's brother, John.

France: Lorraine

On a warm autumn evening in a restaurant called La Chamade, at 17 Rue du Colonel Bange, Versailles, the Association Française du Clan MacLeod holds one of its regular dinners. There are between twenty and thirty people present. Alain MacLeod and his wife Catherine are here. So is Alain's cousin, Yves Gobilliard, who possesses all sorts of documentation concerning the ancestry of the Vendôme MacLeods. Also in attendance at this La Chamade gathering is another clan society member I get to know well in the day or two ahead. His name is Alex de Knoop and, on the following morning, he takes me to Lorraine to meet the Association Française du Clan MacLeod's president – who belongs, as Alex de Knoop does too, to a MacLeod family whose members quit Scotland more than half a millennium ago.

This family derives from men who served, either as archers or axe-carrying men-at-arms, in the royal guard established by France's late-medieval monarchs. Because the Scottish and French kingdoms were in the habit of backing each other in their quarrels with England, the French king's guards included a number of Scots. Those men were not always popular with their hosts. '*Sacs à vin et mangeurs de mouton*,' one Frenchman called them contemptuously. 'Wine bags and mutton eaters'. But if – by French standards – they were lacking in refinement, Scots, as even their critics conceded, were not short of fighting spirit. More and more of them, as a result, were brought to France – usually from the Scottish Lowlands but in some instances from the Highlands and Islands as well. Among the Highlands and Islands group were individuals named MacLeod.[23]

Most such MacLeods belonged to a single family – Alexander MacLeod, who was serving in France's royal guard by the 1430s, being followed into the French monarchy's service by his son, Robert, and by his grandson, Archibald. By way of Alexander's father, George, who appears to have been a younger son of William MacLeod, chief of the Sìol Thormoid branch of Clan MacLeod in the years around 1400, those Paris-based MacLeods were direct descendants of their clan's founder. In the course of the fifteenth century, however, their identification with France became total. This was recognised formally in 1495 when France's King Charles VIII granted all the rights and privileges of French nationality to Archibald MacLeod, whose links with his adopted country had been three generations in the making. Archibald's wife was Anne Fraser, the daughter of another royal guardsman of Scottish extraction, and after 1495 the children of this marriage, now French nationals, were entitled to acquire land in France. This they soon did – Archibald and Anne's son, David, becoming the owner of extensive estates in Lorraine.

There, near France's much-disputed borders with Germany, David's family – locally prestigious members of the Lorraine nobility – survived into the later nineteenth century. In Lorraine, their surname was rendered, from the sixteenth century if not before, as Maclot or Macklot, not MacLeod. But both David and his Maclot successors remained aware, indeed proud, of their Scottish origins. In 1754, one Lorraine Maclot, seeking information about his roots, supplied details of his MacLeod background to a prospective informant in Scotland. '*Je descends d'Archibal Macklot et d'Anne Fraser,*' this man wrote confidently. Equal certainty as to their antecedents was displayed by the later Maclots who, in Victorian times, got directly in touch with prominent Scottish MacLeods of their day.[24]

All this I go over at length with Alex de Knoop when, on the morning following the Association Française du Clan MacLeod's Versailles dinner, we drive into Lorraine. Alex, who worked for many years with IBM in Paris, is Belgian. He grew up in Liège, and his involvement with France's Clan MacLeod Society, Alex tells me, stems from his deciding – after the deaths of his mother and father in the early 1980s – to explore his parents' background. 'I began by researching the de Knoops, my father's people,' Alex says. 'Then I moved on to my mother's family. Before her marriage, she was a Maclot, and I had heard it said that the name Maclot could be Scottish. Mention was made, for instance, of the possibility that the Liège Maclots were descended from one of the Scots soldiers who came to Belgium around 1700 – when lots of troops were sent there by the British.'

The troops Alex mentions were commanded by the Duke of Marlborough – then engaged in a protracted war with Louis XIV's France. But the theory that his mother's surname had been introduced to Belgium by one of Marlborough's soldiers was readily disproved, Alex comments. 'I discovered that my Maclot ancestors had been in Liège since the 1550s,' he goes on. 'That was long before Marlborough's time.'

Suspecting now that his Maclot forebears reached Liège from France, Alex de Knoop – anxious to confirm this new hunch – next wrote in search of further genealogical data to every Maclot listed in France's telephone directories. 'And that,' he concludes, 'is how I got in touch with the man I'm taking you to meet.' This man is Michel Maclot – president, as already mentioned, of the Association Française du Clan MacLeod. Before his retirement, Michel was a master baker in Paris. Today he and his wife, Marie Madeleine, live in the Lorraine village of Vandières. Nearby is Prény – the still smaller settlement where, as Alex de Knoop explains, Michel Maclot's family are known to have resided since the seventeenth century. 'Michel will take us to Prény tomorrow,' Alex predicts. So it turns out.

Next day dawns foggy and damp. Michel, who has attended several Clan MacLeod parliaments where he formed a low opinion of Hebridean weather, is scathing. 'You have brought your Scottish climate to Lorraine,' he tells me. But soon the sun is shining and Michel, Alex and I are starting on what turns into a day-long, breakneck tour of practically every spot in Lorraine known to have been inhabited by Maclots. With him, Alex has brought the results of one of the most extensive genealogical exercises I have encountered. Hundreds, indeed thousands, of Maclot names are involved. The earliest of those date from the sixteenth century. The most recent belong to people, Alex and Michel included, still very much alive. Alex de Knoop's own ancestors – who came, Alex is now convinced, from Lorraine – are listed. So are the numerous Maclots who resided, century after century, in places like Verdun – which, Michel announces, will be our initial destination.

Verdun's Maclots, Alex remarks as we pause briefly in a city which I had previously associated with a First World War battle rather than with Clan MacLeod, were mostly jewellers, leather workers, wigmakers, lawyers, magistrates, priests and the like. Although linked with the family founded by Archibald MacLeod and Anne Fraser in the fifteenth century, those Maclots were not, as was the case with Archibald's more direct descendants, landowning aristocrats. They were professionals, craftsmen, artisans. It is among those people, Michel interjects, that his own origins are to be found – the Prény branch of the Maclots, to which Michel belongs, stemming from Gérard Maclot who, though Prény became his home eventually, was born in Verdun in 1651. 'Nine generations separate Michel from Gérard of Prény,' Alex adds. 'There are ten generations between Michel and Gérard's father, Jacques of Verdun; eleven generations between Michel and Jacques's father, Gilles of Verdun.'

From Verdun, we head for Varennes-en-Argonne where we stop at a café in this little town's main street. Inside, while I drink the blackest of black coffee and struggle to catch one word in twenty, Michel and Alex interrogate the woman behind the café's metal counter as to the whereabouts of any local archives. 'There are none,' she declares. How so? I ask, momentarily forgetting Lorraine's twentieth-century history. 'The Germans,' I am told, 'destroyed them all.'

This proves an exaggeration. In the Varennes-en-Argonne *mairie* or mayor's office, we are directed to a nineteenth-century register of births, marriages and deaths. The register contains several mentions of Maclots. The details go into one of Alex de Knoop's notebooks. They represent, he remarks, a tiny but nevertheless welcome addition to his Maclot database.

Back in Michel's car, we push on, by way of Clermont-en-Argonne, to Prény, Michel's ancestral village, which – with its hilltop castle and its sinuous streets – encapsulates the wider character of this much fought-over frontier region that has for so long been home to families whose roots are traceable to the Hebrides. It is now evening. In the restaurant where we draw proceedings to a close, I question Alex and Michel – at whose insistence I am eating a Lorraine delicacy consisting of the fatty flesh stripped from a calf's head – about matters arising from our joint exploration of what it meant, and means, to be a Maclot. Do they, I ask, feel themselves to be in any sense Scottish? 'No,' Michel replies. 'After all,' he continues, 'my ancestors have been French for more than 500 years.' There is no argument with this. In fact, had Michel Maclot been so inclined, he might have pointed out that, since the Hebrides were Norwegian until the 1260s, his family's residency in France has already lasted three or four times longer than their residency in Scotland. But one thing puzzles me, I tell Michel. While I am prepared to accept that he is in no way Scottish, this seems at odds with his prominent role in the affairs of Clan MacLeod. What is said next is said rapidly and in French. Its import, however, is clear. Although Clan MacLeod originated in Scotland, I am given to understand, it has ceased to belong exclusively to Scots.

Poland: Warsaw

More than 500 miles east of Lorraine and well over a thousand miles from the Hebrides, I sit at a pavement table in Rynek Starego Miasta, the pedestrian-only square at the heart of Warsaw's old town, and think about what happened here in the summer of 1944. Then Warsaw – on the orders of the German dictator, Adolf Hitler, whose Nazi troops had been occupying the city for five years – was given over to unremitting slaughter. The killing began at the start of August when, with Soviet forces closing in on Poland's capital from the east, units of the Polish Home Army launched an armed rebellion. The Home Army consisted of resistance fighters loyal to Poland's exiled government in London – where, in the aftermath of Nazi Germany's original attack on their country, a number of Polish politicians found refuge. Neither those politicians nor their Home Army followers had much reason to trust the Soviet Union, whose Communist supremo, Josef Stalin, had helped Adolf Hitler engineer Poland's destruction in 1939. In the interim, the Soviet Union had itself become a victim of Nazi aggression and was, in consequence, the nominal ally of Poland's London-based government. This meant, in theory anyway, that the Soviet troops who entered Nazi-controlled Poland in the summer of 1944 – and who had been pushing the Germans westward since the Nazi advance into Soviet territory stalled at Stalingrad – were Poland's liberators. But suspecting, correctly, that Stalin would not permit Poles to make their own political choices, the Home Army leadership concluded that Poland's interests would be best served by their men, as opposed to Soviet soldiers, ending Nazi rule in Warsaw. Hence the Warsaw Rising.

Had this rising been accompanied, as its organisers assumed it would be, by a continued Soviet advance, then the Home Army's Warsaw insurgents, who freed much of the Polish capital in the early days of August, would have achieved a great success. With characteristic opportunism, however,

Josef Stalin responded to events in Warsaw by ordering his divisions to halt just beyond the city's eastern outskirts. There they remained as Warsaw's Home Army fighters, whose leaders Stalin called 'power-seeking criminals', were gradually overwhelmed by their Nazi opponents. In effect, then, Josef Stalin's Red Army stood by while Adolf Hitler's troops turned Warsaw into a graveyard – a graveyard which, conveniently from the Soviet dictator's point of view, contained many of the Polish patriots who might otherwise have opposed the Communist regime the Soviet Union was about to impose on their country.[25]

Day after day, through August and into September, Warsaw was subject to ceaseless air and artillery bombardment. And day after day, the city's Home Army defenders – whose handguns and obsolete rifles were no match for the tanks and other heavy weapons at the disposal of their attackers – gradually gave ground. As each locality was surrendered, its buildings were dynamited by German demolition squads carrying out Hitler's instructions that Warsaw should cease to exist. And by the closing weeks of September, with the capital's death toll approaching 200,000, the few depleted Home Army detachments holding out in the blazing city centre were being kept in touch with one another only by girl runners – called *laczniczki* in Polish – who, though dying in dozens, continued to sprint heroically from one beleaguered command post to the next.

'It was a hell on earth,' one of those messengers wrote of this period. 'Houses collapsed in ruins, whole streets ceased to exist . . . and became a cemetery for hundreds of unknown members of our Home Army. Whenever I went out I saw corpses, while continually over the city the huge pall of smoke grew larger, and one heard the crashing roar of exploding bombs . . . [From our quarter] it became increasingly difficult to maintain liaison with those [other] parts [of Warsaw] which remained in [Home Army] possession. Hitherto we had managed by using the streets . . . But when this became impossible we had to use the underground sewers. These contained water in which floated bodies, while rats and other creatures scurried about. Sometimes the sewers were so narrow that we had to crawl, and the passage through the longest – two or three miles in length – took from ten to fifteen hours. Many people perished there.'[26]

In 1944, Wanda Machlejd, the author of those words, was seventeen years old. She survived the Warsaw Rising because she was fit, brave and very lucky. She survived what came next, in part at least, because she belonged to a family whose founder, Wanda's great-great-great-great-great-great-great-great-great-grandfather, was a mercenary soldier called MacLeod. This MacLeod's first name is uncertain. But he came, or so Polish sources contend, from the Isle of Skye, which he is believed to have left in the 1620s with a view to making a military career in Germany, then at the centre, as noted previously, of the bloody struggles known collectively as the Thirty Years War.[27]

Their Skye forefather, or so this seventeenth-century soldier's descendants maintain, was a younger son of one of the MacLeods of Gesto – a prominent family whose standing depended both on their extensive landholdings, some ten miles south of Dunvegan, and on their descent from one of Clan MacLeod's medieval chiefs. In Germany, this Gesto-born mercenary served in the army of the Swedish king, Gustav Adolf. Financially at any rate, he appears to have done well, becoming – as the Thirty Years War wound down – the owner of several properties, including a number of vineyards, which eventually came into the possession of the Gesto soldier's son, Jan or Johannes.

Despite their Skye ancestry, Johannes, his seven sons, seven daughters and innumerable grandchildren were, to all intents, German. At some point, however, members of this family moved into Poland. In so doing, they were following the 'great multitude' of Scots – as many as thirty or forty thousand according to one seventeenth-century calculation – who made much the same journey. As happened afterwards in the United States, Canada and elsewhere, Poland's Scottish immigrants left enduring imprints on maps of their adopted country – modern Polish placenames like Nowa Szkocja, Skotna Góra and Wzgórza being the exact counterparts of Nova Scotia, New Caledonia and the like. In the ethnic melting pot that was Central Europe in the aftermath of the Thirty Years War, however, the communities commemorated by such placenames merged into surrounding populations. In the process, surnames were polonised – MacAulay becoming Makalinski, MacLeod or its already germanised equivalent becoming Machlejd.[28]

Given the extent of the acculturation signalled by such developments, Poles of Scottish descent might be expected to have lost all recollection of their Scottishness. But this was not the Machlejd experience – as is underlined by the fact that, in the summer of 1937, Jerzy Machlejd, Wanda's uncle and a member of Poland's parliament, turned up at Dunvegan in the company of his wife, a Machlejd cousin and a family friend. The four Poles had travelled by car from Warsaw to Skye – no small feat in those days – with a view to reasserting their Clan MacLeod connection. Accounts of this 1937 expedition stress its carefree, almost nonchalant, character. Retrospectively, therefore, those accounts constitute a poignant prelude to the catastrophe shortly afterwards visited on the Machlejds and on the nation of which they had become part. By the summer of 1939, just twenty-four months after his Dunvegan trip, Jerzy Machlejd, together with his brother Jozef, Wanda's father, were prisoners of Poland's invaders. By the following summer, the two Machlejd brothers were dead – as a result of their falling victim to a Stalin-inspired massacre of captured Poles at Katyn in the Ukraine. Months later, Wanda Machlejd, aged ten when her uncle drove from Warsaw to Dunvegan, became a member of the Polish Home Army. At this point, she was just fourteen.

'I . . . was attached to a secret scouting unit,' Wanda recalled of her first months in Poland's resistance movement. 'Our task was propaganda . . . We chalked on the walls, or wrote in pitch on the pavements, inscriptions against the Germans, such as "Poland Fights!", "Poland Lives!"' In essence, the Warsaw Rising of 1944 was a desperate attempt to make a reality of these slogans. The rising ended, two months after it began, when the Home Army's surviving remnants, Wanda Machlejd among them, surrendered to the Germans. 'It was on 5 October that I saw my Warsaw for the last time,' Wanda remembered. 'My mother, whom I also saw, blessed me as I went . . . into captivity . . . We were very hungry and very tired and ragged; we had no uniforms, only red and white bands [red and white being Poland's national colours] on our right arms.'[29]

To begin with, Wanda was held in a hastily wired enclosure not far from Warsaw. 'I well remember the first dreadful night we spent behind the wires of the camp,' she wrote, 'confined in an incredibly small space and having to sleep on the swampy ground . . . Later we were separated, and then came sad farewells to companions-in-arms and friends. We women were loaded onto dirty cattle trucks, without bunks and with only one small, wired hole as a window. Fifty women were put in each of those trucks, and in this fashion we travelled for three days, the cars being opened only once a day for a few minutes. We had no maps, but I had a small compass which showed that we were travelling west all the time.'[30]

For a time, Wanda was imprisoned near Belsen. Subsequently, she was transferred to a labour camp on Germany's border with the Netherlands: 'We were compelled to work . . . We had no names and no privileges, we were just numbers. I loaded and unloaded goods trains. It was very tiring . . . The German guards often drove us far beyond our strength . . . We were always hungry; our [principal] food consisted of . . . soup and frozen turnips which we received once daily. Despite my hunger, I could not touch it. Our other rations consisted of black, and often musty, bread and minute quantities of margarine and sugar.'[31]

In the spring of 1945, with a resumed Soviet advance threatening Berlin and with American and British forces surging across the Rhine, Nazi Germany collapsed. Wanda Machlejd's prison camp, as luck would have it, was liberated by a Polish armoured division attached to the British army – its troops greeted, to their astonishment, by the Polish national anthem and by the unfurling of a Polish flag which Wanda and her fellow prisoners had made in secret. But the 'tears of happiness' which Wanda cried that day were not to last. Now she was merely one of the millions of 'displaced persons' the war had left scattered across Europe. As such, Wanda was moved to yet another camp – this one near Brussels – where, though well treated, she was as unable as before to determine her own future. Providentially, however, there was among the British officials dealing with those matters a man by the name of J.R. Stuart MacLeod who, before the war, had helped found an English branch of the Clan MacLeod Society and who had read, in the society's magazine, of the Dunvegan trip made by Wanda's relatives. Because it was one of Stuart MacLeod's wartime duties to keep in close touch with Polish exiles in London, he was aware that Wanda Machlejd had taken part in the Warsaw Rising and that she had afterwards been taken into Nazi custody. In the summer of 1945, by mobilising his diplomatic and other contacts, Stuart MacLeod discovered Wanda's whereabouts, established contact with her and arranged for Wanda to be provided with the documentation needed to get her into Britain. Thus it came about that, before 1945 ended, Wanda Machlejd – still a teenager and still out of touch with her mother in Poland – was installed in Dunvegan Castle as a guest of the castle's owner and Clan MacLeod's chief, Flora MacLeod. Wanda's seventeenth-century emigrant forebear, whose father was a man of influence in MacLeod circles and who had himself grown up at nearby Gesto during the time of that earlier, and famously hospitable, MacLeod chief, Ruaraidh Mòr, is bound to have been a regular visitor to Great Ruaraidh's castle. With Wanda's arrival here more than 300 years later, then, a wheel had come full circle.[32]

England, Scotland and Poland: Whitley Bay, Dunvegan, Warsaw

Sixty years after the Warsaw Rising, I meet with Moira MacLeod, the daughter of Wanda Machlejd's rescuer, to talk about her father. Stuart MacLeod, Moira tells me in her home at Whitley Bay in the north of England, was not British by birth but Australian. Like Wanda Machlejd, however, Stuart MacLeod possessed Skye ancestors who were part of Clan MacLeod's ruling group. His forebears, who were related to Wanda's because of their shared descent from their clan's chiefs, held land first in Glendale, west of Dunvegan, and later in Glen Brittle, on the northern edge of the Cuillin. 'Our people left Skye in the early nineteenth century,' Moira goes on, 'moving first to Ayrshire, then emigrating to Australia where my great-great-grandfather, James MacLeod, arrived in the 1850s.' Although James – a livestock rearer at one point, a storekeeper in the goldmining town of

Ballarat at another – appears to have had a chequered career, his Australian descendants prospered. This is evident from a photograph in Moira's possession of the substantial home in the Melbourne suburb of Kew, where her father grew up. 'It was called Glendale,' Moira says of this house.[33]

In 1914, when Britain went to war with Kaiser Wilhelm's Germany, Stuart MacLeod, like thousands of other Australians, joined the military force his country sent to Britain's aid. While fighting in France, Stuart was badly wounded. 'Both his knees were practically blown away,' Moira comments. At the war's end, Moira continues, her father, still recovering from his injuries, decided to set up home in England. He took a law degree at Cambridge University, joined the British civil service, married and raised a family.

While still a young man in Melbourne, Stuart MacLeod helped set up a Clan MacLeod Society. He also developed a life-long interest in MacLeod history. Among the material Moira shows me is a pamphlet written by her father in 1912 and examining in meticulous detail Clan MacLeod's Norse origins. Among the same material is an outline sketch of a book which Stuart MacLeod was intent at one time on compiling – a book, I am intrigued to see, which would have dealt with topics similar to those explored here. As often happens, his other commitments got in the way of Stuart MacLeod's researches, and the projected book never got beyond the planning stage. But Stuart MacLeod's Clan MacLeod involvements had far-reaching consequences for Moira, his daughter. Had her father's clan society interests not made him aware of Wanda Machlejd's existence, Wanda, with whom Moira became close friends, would not have found her way to Britain. Nor would Moira have met the man she married.

This was Stefan Machlejd, Wanda's second cousin and, like Wanda, a participant in the Warsaw fighting of 1944. In the wake of this fighting, Stefan, again like Wanda, was imprisoned by his country's German occupiers – in Holland initially in Stefan's case, then in Austria. Managing somehow to escape from the Austrian camp to which he and other Poles had been transferred with the aim of keeping them out of reach of the British and American armies then advancing into Holland and Germany, Stefan Machlejd hiked in winter through the mountains into Yugoslavia. There, until Germany's capitulation in May 1945, he continued his struggle with Poland's Nazi conquerors by linking up – a little ironically in view of the Red Army's failure to aid the Polish Home Army – with Josip Broz Tito's communist and anti-German guerrillas.

'Stefan came to Britain in 1947 with other Poles who'd found themselves outside Poland at the war's end,' Moira MacLeod says. 'My father befriended him, just as he'd befriended Wanda, and so I met Stefan in my parents'

London home. He was a stocky young man, wearing Polish uniform and speaking only the most limited English. But soon we were seeing a lot of each other, and in 1948 we were married.'

This marriage lasted until Stefan's death in 1989. It marked, in effect, the reunification of two sets of MacLeods who had long before been neighbours and kinsfolk in Skye but who were, for a lengthy period, so separated geographically as to make it little short of extraordinary that contact between them was resumed. 'Stefan became a civil engineer,' Moira goes on, 'I became a social worker. We had three children, Gustav, Julian and Mary. Now I have grandchildren as well.' How do she and her family spell their surname? I ask. 'MacLeod,' Moira replies. 'When Stefan got his British naturalisation papers from the authorities in 1956,' she adds, 'his name had been altered from Machlejd to MacLeod. I think that was because the official dealing with the case was Scottish. Or maybe there was some other explanation. Anyway, ever since 1956, we've all been MacLeods which, when you think about it, is what we all were – even the Machlejds – to start with.'

At Clan MacLeod's 2002 parliament in Dunvegan, I am introduced to Mary MacLeod, Moira's daughter, who has come north with her mother. Nearly 200 years after this Englishwoman's maternal ancestor left the island for Australia and nearly 400 years after her paternal MacLeod forebear left for Central Europe, Mary McLeod thinks it is meaningful to be in Dunvegan. Her Polish relatives, Mary tells me, feel much the same way. One of them, her cousin Michal Machlejd, a Warsaw banker, has travelled to Skye twice.

This is confirmed when I visit Warsaw and meet with Michal, with his father, Jerzy, and with Michal's daughter, Malgorzata. Before we get together, I wander through Warsaw's old town, painstakingly rebuilt in the Second World War's aftermath, and inspect its memorials to the dead of the 1944 rising. Jerzy, whose brother Stefan, Mary MacLeod's father, fought throughout the rising, remembers it well. 'We lived a little way outside the city,' Jerzy says in Polish, which his son and granddaughter, both of them fluent in English, translate for my benefit. 'My mother and father allowed Stefan to join the fighting, but they wouldn't let me go with him. They didn't want to lose one son. They certainly weren't going to lose two. So when Stefan went off to become part of the Home Army, I stayed at home, hearing the noise from the bombs and the heavy guns, seeing the smoke from all the burning buildings.'

By permitting Stefan to participate in the Warsaw Rising and by stopping Jerzy from doing the same, the brothers' parents, Henryk and Otylia Machlejd, were instrumental in determining – though nobody could have foreseen this in August 1944 – that, while two of their grandchildren, Michal and his brother Piotr, would be Poles like them, their three other grandchildren, Mary MacLeod and her brothers, would spend their lives in England.

Treading carefully through the many sensitivities surrounding such matters, I probe the issue of national identity as it has affected this family who were once Scottish, then German, then Polish and who are now, in some instances, English or British. 'Although we have been in Poland for a long time,' Michal says, 'we came here as Germans.' His family's German heritage survives, Michal goes on, in their religion. 'We Machlejds are and always have been Lutheran Protestants, and that makes us a bit of an oddity in what has always been a Catholic country.'

And yet, I say to Michal, Stefan Machlejd, his uncle, and Wanda Machlejd, his more distant relative, were prepared in 1944 to die fighting for Poland against Germany. Michal agrees. But not every member of his family, he adds, felt like that. 'When Hitler invaded in 1939, some of our relatives, my father's grandmother for example, signed papers saying they were German, not Polish. After that, we never spoke with those people – the people who said they were German – ever again.'

There are times, then, when your identity becomes desperately important. By putting their names to papers of the sort Michal mentions, Poles of German ancestry staked a claim to be treated as *Volksdeutsch* – the term Poland's Nazi occupiers applied to non-Germans of German ethnicity. This entitled such people to all sorts of privileges – including far more generous food rations than those made available to the generality of Poles whom the Nazis categorised as *untermenschen* or subhuman. But if it was advantageous to be Volksdeutsch in 1939, the opposite was the case six years later. Then, with the German occupation of Poland at an end, Poles who had opted for Volksdeutsch status risked losing everything, even their lives, as punishment for having collaborated with the Nazi enemy. Their fate is a reminder that, though genealogy is seen in peaceful times as no more than an obsessive hobby, there have been – and in some parts of the world there still are – occasions when you might almost literally be hanged from the branches of your family tree.

But in Warsaw, with my Machlejd hosts, I explore those difficult topics no further. Instead I talk with Michal about his visits to Skye, where he met in Dunvegan with someone who remembered Wanda convalescing there in 1945. Malgorzata, who works in the Warsaw office of a British legal firm, interjects. 'I, too, will be going to Scotland,' she says. And what of her grandfather, I ask – conscious that Jerzy's comparative lack of English, and my ignorance of Polish, have excluded him from our conversation. What, if anything, does he feel about his MacLeod background? My question is translated. Jerzy Machlejd replies forcefully. Malgorzata smiles. 'My grandfather wants you to know,' she says, 'that it matters to him to be part of Clan MacLeod. It matters a great deal.'

CHAPTER THREE

SOME TO AMERICA

New Jersey: Montville

The millions of Europeans who emigrated to the United States just before the First World War included Artur Juliusz Machlejd. While still a teenager, Artur, born in Poland in 1884, was drawn into insurrectionary activity of the sort which appears to have been a Machlejd speciality. Poland, at this time, was not an independent state – the country having been partitioned between the Russian, German and Austrian empires. Artur Juliusz Machlejd, like other patriotically minded Poles, thought this an intolerable situation, and when, in 1905, a nationalist uprising began in Russian-ruled Warsaw, Artur Juliusz joined it. Although Poland eventually regained its statehood, this did not happen in 1905 – a failure which led to Artur Juliusz's emigration. 'He received a gunshot wound in the chest during the Warsaw fighting and was forced to flee abroad,' I am told by Michele Winter, Artur Juliusz's granddaughter. 'He went first to Germany, then in 1906 he came to New York City where he found work as a baker.'

Today Artur Juliusz's descendants are scattered across the United States. Michele Winter's home is in Montville, New Jersey. But she is in touch with relatives in Florida, Ohio, Washington DC and New Hampshire. Some of her kinsfolk, Michele says, have changed their names from Machleid, the surname Artur Juliusz used in America, to MacLeid. Some MacLeids and Machleids, including Michele, are members of the USA's Clan MacLeod Society – which, Michele comments, has brought the American branch of Poland's Machlejd family into contact with people whose Hebridean ancestors may have known the family's founder before he left Skye to join King Gustav Adolf's army.

When this departure took place, emigration from Clan MacLeod's Scottish territories was exclusively in an easterly or southerly direction. Soon, however, MacLeods began to reach America. Among the first was a man entered as 'John Maclude' on a list of prisoners who left Gravesend, near London, for New England on 8 December 1651. This man, one of numerous soldiers from the Highlands and Islands captured three months before at the Battle of Worcester, probably spent the rest of his life in one or other of the then tiny Massachusetts settlements to which he and his fellow prisoners were sent – Boston, Cambridge, Ipswich, Reading and Salem. In those places, as in the rest of North America, people of Highlands and Islands background were rarities in the mid-seventeenth century and for several decades afterwards. But in due course John MacLeod was followed across the Atlantic by thousands of men, women and children who shared his surname. The motivations of those emigrants varied greatly, but all of them embarked on their Atlantic voyages as a result of profound changes which began to affect the Highlands and Islands in John MacLeod's time and which were to transform the area over the course of the next hundred years.[1]

Scotland: The Highlands and Islands

Before the seventeenth century, the world outside the Highlands and Islands took little interest in Clan MacLeod. Nor did Clan MacLeod have much to do with this wider world. By the 1650s, however, the clan's isolation had ended. This is shown by the presence of a MacLeod contingent at the Battle of Worcester – an episode in a struggle for power between an army answering to England's parliament and forces loyal to the Stuart monarchy which parliament had deposed. In itself, admittedly, the MacLeod presence on the royalist side at Worcester, where many MacLeods died, was neither here nor there. In Ruaraidh Mòr's late-sixteenth-century heyday, his clansmen had seen action in equally faraway theatres of war. But there was a difference between Ruaraidh Mòr's military adventures and those of his seventeenth-century successors. Ruaraidh's Irish campaign can be interpreted as an attempt to maintain the autonomy of those parts of the British Isles where clanship, or something like it, had long prevailed. During the seventeenth century, in contrast, Clan MacLeod's chiefs, while preserving some semblance of independence, became so enmeshed in the affairs of Lowland

Scotland and England that they found themselves hopelessly caught up, as Worcester proves, in southern politics.

Those involvements ended in MacLeod chiefs becoming enthusiastic participants in the public life of the United Kingdom. This new state started to take shape in 1603 when Scotland's King James VI became England's king also. The United Kingdom came fully into existence in 1707 when Scotland's governing class agreed to merge their Edinburgh parliament with its London equivalent. Because its rulers were committed to the eradication of local particularisms, the emerging United Kingdom was intolerant of people whose lifestyles differed from what was considered, whether in London or Edinburgh, the national norm. Hence the policy dilemma confronting clan chiefs from 1600 onwards. Naturally, they wanted to maintain their previous power and position. Equally naturally, they were anxious to remain on reasonable terms with their clansfolk. Increasingly, however, those two objectives were mutually incompatible. A chief who did what external authority demanded, and who duly adopted southern ways of doing things, might retain his territories. But such a chief was also likely, because of his abandonment of long-cherished custom and practice, to offend and alienate the people around him. This was an unattractive prospect. To most clan chiefs, however, it was marginally more enticing than the only alternative – a principled refusal to bend the knee to any outside agency. Because central government, thanks to its growing military strength, was increasingly capable of getting its way in the Highlands and Islands, chiefs who pursued an anti-government line usually came to grief – none more spectacularly so than the MacLeods of Lewis, the Sìol Thorcuil.

'The Clan Torkil in Lewis,' according to one seventeenth-century commentator, 'were the stoutest [meaning bravest] and prettiest men, but a wicked, bloody crew whom neither law nor reason could guide or model . . . till in the end they were expelled [from] that country, and the MacKenzies now possess it.' This is a less than objective account of the Sìol Thorcuil's downfall, but it contains some truth. Ruaraidh, the last of Lewis's MacLeod chiefs, conducted himself so piratically as to provide King James VI with plenty of justification for measures the king was set on anyway – measures designed to demonstrate that he and his Edinburgh-based government, not the region's clan chiefs, were in charge of the Highlands and Islands. Because they had proved themselves savages and law breakers, King James announced, the MacLeods of Lewis were to have their lands taken over by Lowland colonists sent north from Fife. The unfortunate Fife people were promptly killed or ejected by the clansfolk they aimed to displace. But if King James lacked the means at this stage to secure his Highlands and Islands objectives, he was not about to back down in the face of MacLeod defiance.

The MacKenzies of Kintail, sufficiently compliant to have won royal favour, were told by the king that Lewis was theirs for the taking. This proved to be not quite the case – because Neil MacLeod, one of the dead Chief Ruaraidh's five illegitimate sons and a more engaging man than his father, held out against the MacKenzies and their royal backer for several years. Eventually, however, Neil was pinned down with a handful of followers on a tiny island in Loch Roag, on Lewis's Atlantic coast. Attempting to escape, he was captured, taken to Edinburgh and, in April 1613, executed at the city's market cross. Lewis, though many of its MacLeod families survived the MacKenzie supremacy which now ensued, would never again be under MacLeod control.[2]

Clan MacLeod's lands in Assynt and Wester Ross also went to others. Raasay, however, remained in the ownership of its own MacLeod chiefs. So did the properties belonging to the MacLeods of Dunvegan, as the Sìol Thormoid had come to be known. Around 1700, those properties comprised: first, a 205,000-acre Skye estate centred on Dunvegan itself; second, a further 139,000-acre estate made up of Harris and of adjacent islands like Bernera, Pabbay and Scalpay; third, a 50,000-acre block of mainland territory around Glenelg. The proprietor of this enormous domain from 1706 until 1772 was Norman MacLeod. The MacLeods of Lewis having lost their possessions and the MacLeods of Raasay being relatively minor players on the Hebridean stage, Norman was Clan MacLeod's foremost chief. However, his chieftainship and his hundreds of thousands of acres had come his way only because his seventeenth-century forebears, unlike their Lewis kin, had made the adjustments required of them by King James VI and by King James's successors. As a result, Norman MacLeod's behaviour was not that of his warrior ancestors.[3]

In the wake of King James's failure to install a Lowland colony in Lewis, frontal attacks on clans and clansfolk, though not abandoned, had given way to a more insidious undermining of the belief system with which clanship was associated. At the heart of this subtle, but ultimately devastating, strategy were measures whose cumulative effect was to encourage clan chiefs to turn their backs on their heritage. Men such as the MacLeods of Dunvegan, it was decreed, were to have their sons educated in the south. They were themselves to put in regular appearances in Edinburgh. They were to give up their age-old practice of filling their castles with bards, musicians and other retainers. In short, they were to become less like tribal leaders and more like the Lowland and English gentry with whom they mixed increasingly and whose tastes, as was the southern establishment's intention, most clan chiefs came to share.

The last Dunvegan chief to live as chiefs lived formerly was *Iain Breac*, Pockmarked John, who died in 1693 and whose death was followed by

Dunvegan Castle ceasing to be, as it had been for centuries, a centre of Gaelic culture. '*Chaidh a' chuible mun cuairt*,' lamented one of the late chief's bards, Roderick Morrison: '*Ghrad thionndaidh gu fuachd am blàths*.' Time's wheel has gone round, Morrison complains, and warmth has given way to cold. Buildings once 'filled with song' are empty. Instead of keeping house in Dunvegan, Clan MacLeod's chieftains have taken up residence in the south. Instead of offering hospitality to poets and musicians, the same chieftains are squandering their resources on 'doublets', 'fine velvet trews' and other fripperies.[4]

Roderick Morrison lost out personally as a result of the developments he described, and his complaints need not be taken as gospel. However, the tale Roderick had to tell is substantiated by seventeenth-century documentation preserved in Dunvegan Castle – though this documentation, it should be acknowledged, shows that expenditure of the type the bard criticised began earlier than he implied. During the 1650s, for example, Iain Breac's predecessor laid out large sums annually on 'gold buttons', 'red satin', 'French serge', 'gold and silver lace', 'calico', 'black silk stockings' and further items of that sort. As this same chief's finances became more complicated, he also engaged the services of lawyers and other professionals. The predictable outcome was an accumulation of debts which were never cleared. Thus there originated a crisis which came to a head during the lifetime of Norman MacLeod, Iain Breac's grandson and the 1706 inheritor of Sìol Thormoid's territories. In principle, Norman could have economised. But that was not his style – his spending pattern being even more reckless than that of preceding chiefs. Eventually, bankruptcy loomed and desperate expedients had to be adopted. Their impact on Norman MacLeod's clansfolk was such as to come close to destroying the emotional and other linkages which had bound Clan MacLeod to its chief.[5]

Ireland: Donaghadee

On 10 November 1739, Thomas Montgomery and John Bailie, magistrates in Donaghadee, a small town and seaport near Belfast, sent an urgent dispatch to the Duke of Devonshire, the British politician who, from his base at Dublin Castle, was responsible for the governance of Ireland. Their dispatch, Bailie and Montgomery informed the duke, dealt with disturbances which had occurred in and around Donaghadee some nights previously. At the centre of those disturbances, the magistrates wrote, were a hundred or so men, women and children who 'had been forced with the most inhuman violence out of the islands of Skye and Harris and put on board the ship *William*'. The *William*, Montgomery and Bailie went on, was owned and skippered by a Donaghadee merchant, William Davison, and his vessel's ultimate destination, it appeared, was one of Britain's American colonies. There, if Davison's venture had gone to plan, the people constituting his human cargo would have been advertised for sale as 'indentured labourers'. Such labourers, just one step up from black slaves in the colonial pecking order, were obliged to work without wages for several years. At the end of this period, indentured labourers were set free, and aspiring emigrants who could not afford Atlantic passages consequently chose in some instances to sell themselves into servitude – the sums thus raised being used to pay the dues of the emigrants concerned. The Skye and Harris folk taken to Donaghadee by William Davison were not in this volunteer category, however. 'We examined them severally by an interpreter,' Thomas Montgomery and John Bailie reported of the Gaelic-speaking Hebrideans brought before them at the start of November 1739. All, 'from the youngest to the oldest', were agreed on the brutalities surrounding their departure from their native islands: 'Husbands were in the dead and darkest time of the night torn by ruffians . . . from their wives, wives from their husbands, mothers from their young children and children from their mothers.'[6]

According to John Bailie and Thomas Montgomery, the perpetrators of those crimes included William Davison. They also included individuals drawn from the upper ranks of Clan MacLeod. Of those, the most senior were a father and son, Donald and Norman MacLeod, known – because they tenanted the Harris and Skye landholdings in question – as MacLeod of Bernera and MacLeod of Unish.

Among the documents sent to Dublin Castle by the Donaghadee magistrates in November 1739 was a letter which Norman MacLeod of Unish had written the previous June. Norman's father, Donald of Bernera, is mentioned in this letter as party to a 'project' which is to be 'carried on with great privacy' and which, Norman assures his Donaghadee contact, will provide him with 'as many [people] as [his] brig [meaning ship] can carry'. Suspecting 'roguery' on Norman MacLeod's part, the Donaghadee skipper to whom Norman's June letter was addressed, one John McGown, refused to take matters further. Hence the eventual involvement of the less scrupulous William Davison and his ship, the *William*, which sailed from Donaghadee, ostensibly for Norway but actually for the Hebrides, on 13 August. Within the week, the *William* was at anchor in Loch Bracadale, four or five miles south of Dunvegan, and the business of filling her holds with human beings had been put in hand.[7]

Although some of the people crammed into the *William* came from estates belonging to Sir Alexander MacDonald of Sleat, most of them were taken from Norman MacLeod of Dunvegan's properties – many of those people, as the Donaghadee magistrates heard, having been 'brought to the shore . . . by force and violence'. One woman was 'dragged' across rocks. Boys and girls, between the ages of five and twelve, were 'brought down . . . in all appearance against their will'. Adults were 'tied' and 'carried' towards the waiting ship, and when, on one occasion, a youth came aboard the *William* with a letter for Norman MacLeod of Unish, then closeted with William Davison, the lad found himself 'seized', 'confined . . . under deck' and 'brought away'.[8]

From Loch Bracadale, the *William* sailed to Harris, where further unfortunates were made captive, before returning south. En route, the ship made brief halts to disembark small children, an elderly man and two expectant mothers – people, in other words, thought unlikely to survive an Atlantic crossing. As it was, a young woman 'of about twenty years of age' died prior to the *William* putting into Donaghadee, the ship's home port, where Captain Davison, still accompanied by MacLeod of Unish, intended to refit his vessel before sailing for America.[9]

At Donaghadee, which they reached on 20 October 1739, the Skye and Harris folk were brought ashore and locked up in barns belonging to Davison or his neighbours. On the night of 4 November, however, several of the captives broke out and made their way to the nearby settlement of Bangor. Pursued there by MacLeod of Unish and William Davison, the escapees, according to Donaghadee's magistrates, were recaptured, tied up and beaten 'with a cudgel and even with a piece of iron'.[10]

'When we called upon MacLeod and Davison to show by what law or right they imprisoned and held those poor, injured people in confinement here,' the Donaghadee authorities reported, 'they both fled and could not be apprehended.' The two men's disappearance, however, served only to heighten speculation back in Scotland about the part played in the *William* episode by Skye's leading chiefs, Norman MacLeod of Dunvegan and Sir Alexander MacDonald of Sleat. Since nothing of consequence could be accomplished in Skye without their sanction, the two clan chieftains, or so it was said in Edinburgh, must have had a hand in the business – must, in fact, have been among its intended beneficiaries. A surviving, and panicky, letter sent to a Scottish politician in January 1740 by Lady Margaret MacDonald, Sir Alexander's wife, rejects any such notion. 'I am positive of the falsehood of this,' Lady Margaret wrote in response to a rumour that her husband might be charged with complicity in kidnapping. 'One Norman MacLeod [of Unish], with a number of fellows that he had picked up to execute his intentions, were the real actors [in the] affair.' But even if MacLeod of Unish was the principal organiser of what had occurred, his activities – Lady Margaret's protestations notwithstanding – clearly had, at a minimum, the tacit backing of Sir Alexander and his MacLeod counterpart, Norman of Dunvegan. One of the men bundled aboard the *William* in Loch Bracadale was told that 'orders for seizing him' came from 'the Laird of MacLeod'. Comments to the same effect were made by MacLeod of Unish. He 'had the consent of . . . the Laird of MacLeod [and] several other proprietors,' Norman of Unish told his Donaghadee collaborators, 'to take away as many men, women and children as he could provide shipping for'. Hence the Dunvegan chief's decision to throw himself on the mercy of Duncan Forbes of Culloden, the British government's foremost representative in the north of Scotland and, as such, a man with the capacity to bury awkward legal proceedings. Insisting on his innocence but acknowledging the damaging nature of 'information come from Ireland', Norman of Dunvegan begged Forbes for help. 'A prosecution,' he wrote, 'would be attended with a multitude of inconveniences.'[11]

So with Duncan Forbes's connivance, the MacLeod chief's part in the happenings of 1739 was hushed up. As matters turned out, this gave Forbes useful leverage when, in July 1745, Prince Charles Edward Stuart arrived in the Hebrides from France to launch an armed uprising. The prince was the latest Stuart claimant to a throne from which his family had been ejected in the 1640s and again in the 1680s. As demonstrated by their presence at the Battle of Worcester, the MacLeods had long been Stuart supporters. On getting to Scotland, therefore, Prince Charles Edward lost no time in soliciting the backing of Norman MacLeod of Dunvegan. However, this was not forthcoming – partly, it is reasonable to guess, because Norman was well aware of his vulnerability to pressure from the staunchly pro-government Duncan Forbes. He had given 'no sort of countenance' to the rebel prince's emissaries, the MacLeod chief assured Duncan Forbes on 3 August 1745. Nor was this position to alter in the months ahead – months which saw Charles Edward Stuart conquer Scotland and advance deep into England. By the close of 1745, in fact, Norman MacLeod of Dunvegan was providing a beleaguered British government with badly needed troops in the shape of several companies raised from among his Harris, Skye and Glenelg clansmen. Had those companies been serving Prince Charles Edward instead of George II, the monarch Charles had come to overthrow, the rebel prince might conceivably have triumphed. As it was, he and his followers, known as Jacobites, were defeated at the Battle of Culloden in April 1746.[12]

The possible role of the *William* episode in the events of 1745 gives this episode wider significance. In the context of a book about emigration and its causes, however, what matters about the 1739 kidnappings – a 'grim foretaste of the clearances', the twentieth-century Gaelic poet Sorley MacLean called them – is what they have to say about Norman MacLeod's abandonment of the traditional obligations of chieftainship. Skye's eighteenth-century inhabitants still spoke of Norman's great-great-grandfather as Ruaraidh Mòr, Great Roderick. Their opinion of Norman can be gauged from his much less flattering designation. *An Droch Dhuine*, Norman was called: the evil, or wicked, man. Since it stemmed from Norman MacLeod's participation in a series of murky dealings, his nickname cannot be attributed solely to his involvement in the affair of the *William*. This affair nevertheless explains why, from the perspective of families who had formerly looked to clan chiefs for protection, those chiefs ceased, in the course of the eighteenth century, to be father figures and became people who were feared, even hated. Earlier chieftains, of course, were no angels – Ruaraidh Mòr, for example, having won favour with King James VI by helping to consign Neil MacLeod, the Lewis rebel, to his doom in Edinburgh. But no one would have suspected Ruaraidh, even at his most Machiavellian, of having a hand in a scheme which turned on a hundred or more of his clansfolk being sold, in effect, into slavery. The Wicked Man, however, was thought capable of almost anything. So when, towards the close of his long reign over them, Skye folk were presented with a chance to escape Chief Norman's sphere of influence, it is not surprising that many of them chose to take it.[13]

Scotland: Skye, Glenelg and Harris

Flora MacLeod, the clan chief who welcomed Wanda Machlejd to Dunvegan, was a woman who found it hard to think ill of her ancestors. She consequently tried to have the Wicked Man posthumously renamed the Red Man, because of the scarlet tartan he wears in his Dunvegan Castle portrait, and it is as the Red Man, therefore, that he features in some clan histories. Earlier members of Chief Norman's family were less forgiving. One of the chief's Skye relatives thought Norman had 'brought an ancient and honourable family from a flourishing condition to the brink of ruin'. This judgement is in accordance with the facts. Anxious to cut a dash socially and to make himself a figure of national standing politically, the so-called Wicked Man spent so far beyond his means that, at the end of the 1760s, his total liabilities were in the order of £50,000. This was an astonishing sum – equivalent to many millions of pounds today – and Norman MacLeod, if he was to stave off bankruptcy, had no alternative but to reduce the debts threatening to overwhelm him. Hence his adoption of a course of action which, though it added on paper at least to his income, so antagonised his clansfolk as to persuade many of them to leave their homes and make a fresh start in America.[14]

In 1769, Clan MacLeod's chief increased the rents he got from his

Glenelg, Skye and Harris properties by more than 75 per cent. Hardest hit by this imposition were Chief Norman's tacksmen. Tacksmen were so called because they held their land under lease – a lease being known in Scotland as a tack. This might suggest that tacksmen were simply tenant farmers. In fact, they constituted a managerial class whose members were central to the workings of clanship – tacksmen supervising a clan's day-to-day affairs in time of peace and directing its military operations in time of war. Given their importance in the overall scheme of things, and given the extent to which a clan was in practice as well as in principle an extended family, it comes as no surprise to discover that a clan's tacksmen were commonly related to the man at its head. This was certainly so in the case of Clan MacLeod. A majority of the clan's tacksmen descended from earlier chiefs, and by way of underlining their status, those tacksmen customarily added, as lesser mortals could not do, the names of their tacks to their own. Hence MacLeod of Bernera, MacLeod of Unish, MacLeod of Gesto, MacLeod of Talisker, MacLeod of Drynoch and the like. Together with their wives, sons and daughters, individuals of this type comprised, as eighteenth-century observers recognised, 'a kind of . . . gentry, a superior order of people'. Tacksmen, it followed, were usually 'men of education and of considerable endowments'. Travelling through Skye in 1773, Samuel Johnson, then one of England's leading writers, found 'nothing but civility, elegance and plenty' in the homes of the MacLeod tacksmen he encountered. Thomas Pennant, another pioneer tourist, was equally impressed by the tacksmen he met. 'I shall never forget the hospitality of the house,' Pennant wrote of his arrival – on a typically 'wet and boisterous' West Highland day – at the home of Donald MacLeod of Arnisdale, a tacksman on MacLeod of Dunvegan's Glenelg estate. 'Before I could utter a denial, three glasses of rum, cordialised with jelly of bilberries, were poured into me by the irresistible hand of good Madam MacLeod.'[15]

Until the middle decades of the eighteenth century, a tacksman like MacLeod of Arnisdale paid only a nominal rent to his chief. Although greatly to the financial disadvantage of the MacLeods of Dunvegan, this state of affairs had been tolerated by them because, but for the freely given support of his tacksmen, a clan chief – especially in the disorderly conditions often prevailing in the Highlands and Islands – would not have lasted long. One of a tacksman's key functions was to turn out the menfolk of his district when his, and their, chief went to war. A clan chief of the traditional type, therefore, had to make sure that he kept his tacksmen on side.

But Norman MacLeod of Dunvegan, the man responsible for the massive rent increase imposed on MacLeod tacksmen in 1769, was not, as the affair of the *William* demonstrated, a chief of the old sort. Especially after

1746, when – following the defeat of Charles Edward Stuart at Culloden – the British government set about disarming the Highlands and Islands, Norman's status and position in no way depended on his clan's military capacities. As was true of clan chiefs more generally, Chief Norman now needed a cash income more than he needed his tacksmen's backing. 'The number and bravery of their followers no longer support their grandeur,' it was remarked of men like Norman. 'The number and weight of their guineas only are put in the scale.' In those new circumstances, and with his supply of guineas not what it might have been, Norman MacLeod of Dunvegan, as he saw it, was acting reasonably when, in 1769, he sought to boost his revenues from estates which, or so Norman's Edinburgh-based advisers were happy to assure him, had long been under rented.[16]

The MacLeod chief's tacksmen, on the other hand, were outraged by this hike in their rents. From a tacksman's perspective, Thomas Pennant observed, chiefs who did what Norman MacLeod had done were behaving unforgivably: 'Many of the greater tacksmen were of the same blood with their [chief]. They were attached to [him] by ties of consanguinity as well as affection. They felt . . . [this] act of oppression as Caesar did the wound from his beloved Brutus.' In itself, such ill-feeling was of little consequence to the Wicked Man. It became a danger to him only because his leading tenants were in a position by 1769 to do something other than accede to their chief's demands. They could emigrate to America, and this, as Pennant commented, was exactly what happened: 'Resentment drove many to seek a retreat beyond the Atlantic . . . They found . . . a happy change of situation. They wrote . . . an account of [this] situation. Their friends caught the contagion, and numbers followed.'[17]

Scotland and North Carolina

The overseas banishment imposed on clansmen captured at Worcester in 1651 was also imposed, a century later, on clansmen taken prisoner during Charles Edward Stuart's failed uprising. Although Norman MacLeod of Dunvegan refused to back the Jacobite prince, other MacLeods rallied to Charles's side. Some of them were men who, despite their being Norman MacLeod's tenants, were so pro-Jacobite in their politics as to be willing to defy their chief. However, most MacLeods in Charles Edward's army came from MacLeod-inhabited districts, such as Raasay or Gairloch, not in Norman of Dunvegan's jurisdiction. Some men from those places were taken prisoner by government forces during the 1745–6 rebellion and afterwards exiled to Britain's American and Caribbean colonies. One such captive was John MacLeod, whose home was in Wester Ross and who found himself consigned, in the spring of 1747, to a vessel bound for the Leeward Islands. Had this ship, the *Veteran*, reached its destination unmolested, John MacLeod would have become a forced labourer on a sugar plantation. But this did not happen. While en route for the West Indies, the *Veteran* was scized by a French privateer whose crew – France then being at war with Britain – first restored John MacLeod to freedom and next landed him on the French-ruled island of Martinique.[18]

Other MacLeods were deported to Jamaica, Barbados, Maryland and Pennsylvania – some of the Pennsylvania and Maryland prisoners surviving long enough to be liberated, years later, in America. Might MacLeods in this category have written to family members back in Scotland and might their descriptions of their new homeland have helped fuel the 'epidemical fury of emigration' Samuel Johnson encountered in the course of his 1773 travels through the Hebrides? Perhaps. But of more immediate importance in this connection was the fact that, during the 1750s, men from the Highlands and Islands began to be recruited by the British army. The regiments thus raised were posted in the first instance to North America where they helped win the battles – on Cape Breton Island, in Quebec and elsewhere – which made Canada British rather than French. As is apparent from a 1772 account of Harris, few such men came home: 'From this parish there went to the army, during the late war, 118 men who were all sent to America. Only 14 of these . . . returned.' In part, this was because of deaths resulting from military action or disease. But it was also a consequence of the British army's practice, at the Canadian campaign's conclusion in 1763, of discharging its now surplus troops in North America – demobilised soldiers being settled on land made available to them by the colonial authorities. Some such settlers, it was noted in 1771, 'correspond with their relations and acquaintances in the Highlands and, by the accounts they give of their own happy situation, persuade them to forsake the Highlands, where they are so miserably enslaved, and to cross the Atlantic in order to live in freedom'.[19]

In the 1770s, the concept of America as a land of liberty was already an old one – its origins traceable to pronouncements made by the Pilgrim Fathers and by other seventeenth-century emigrants from England to Massachusetts. From a Highlands and Islands standpoint, however, Massachusetts was of less significance than North Carolina – a colony which, throughout the Highlands and Islands of the 1750s and 1760s, took on something of the aura of an earthly paradise. This development stemmed from North Carolina's role as a destination for people wanting to make their escape from Argyll, the first Highlands and Islands locality to experience rent rises of the sort afterwards enforced by Norman MacLeod of Dunvegan.

Argyll is the part of the Highlands and Islands closest to the Irish province of Ulster. People in Argyll were consequently well aware that, during the eighteenth century's opening decades, Ulster farmers of Lowland Scots descent responded to rent increases, as was said at the time, by 'quitting their lands . . . and transporting themselves to America'. Anyone able to get across the Atlantic, those Ulster emigrants informed relatives back in Ireland, would find in America 'a good poor man's country' where land was to be had for the taking and 'where there [were] no oppressions of any kind whatsoever'. Soon stories to the same effect were circulating in Argyll, and soon tacksmen from Argyll, rather than pay higher rents, were following the example set by their Ulster neighbours. Perhaps because its colonial governor, Gabriel Johnston, was a Scot with a soft spot for his compatriots, emigrants from Argyll tended to settle in North Carolina. There they were directed by Johnston to previously unclaimed territory in the Cape Fear River country, a district which thus began to acquire a settler population of Highlands and Islands extraction.[20]

By the time Norman MacLeod's 1769 rent increase took effect, therefore, his tenants were well aware of what North Carolina had to offer. It was during this period, for example, that there appeared in Scotland a pamphlet entitled *Informations Concerning the Province of North Carolina Addressed to Emigrants from the Highlands and Western Isles of Scotland*. Almost certainly written by a tacksman from Argyll, this publication, though it proclaimed itself 'impartial', was a classic early instance of what Americans later called 'boosterism' – the practice of enticing settlers to some newly opened-up region by exaggerating its attractions. North Carolina, readers of the *Informations* were assured, was 'the most temperate part of the earth on the north side of the equator . . . The sky in winter is commonly clear and serene . . . The climate in summer is said to resemble that of Italy.' Nor were emigrants to North Carolina at risk of being deposited in untamed wilderness. Thanks to the efforts of the Argyll folk who had preceded them, the author of the *Informations* explained, new arrivals would find the banks of the Cape Fear River 'agreeably adorned with fine . . . villas and pleasant farmhouses'. Practically anywhere in this easily navigable river's catchment area, a tacksman of even modest means might install himself and his family on an established plantation from which forest cover had begun to be removed: 'One of those plantations, consisting of 640 acres, and 70 or 80 acres of it clear, with a good mansion house . . . upon it, may be purchased for £160.'[21]

Not all prospective emigrants to North Carolina from the Highlands and Islands were men of means, the *Informations* acknowledged. In North Carolina, however, there were no limits on what the generality of people could accomplish: 'Here we see that a man of small substance, if upon a precarious footing at home, can . . . secure to himself a handsome, independent living . . . The poorest man, if he can but work, procures at once plenty of subsistence which grows yearly upon his hands until, by gentle and agreeable labour, he arrives at last in a state of affluence and ease.'[22]

In the unsettled conditions created by the announcement that their rents were to be racked up dramatically, material of this sort is bound to have struck a chord with Norman MacLeod's tenants. Equally appealing to them, it seems likely, were those passages in the *Informations* which dealt with the causes of their difficulties. 'The natives of the Highlands and Isles have always been remarkable for the strongest attachment to the place of their nativity and for the highest respect towards their masters and superiors,' the compiler of the *Informations* wrote. But there had been a 'very cogent and powerful' change in this regard, he continued, in consequence of Highlands and Islands landlords having ceased to live on their properties: 'Formerly the proprietors resided mostly among [their tenants] . . . and were familiar with them, were tender of them, cherished and patronised them.' But this was no longer so: 'The modern lairds, unlike their forefathers, live at a great distance from their estates. Whatever misfortunes may befall the tenants, whatever grievances they have to complain of, whatever oppression they may groan under, they have no access to their master; they scarce know where he lives or where to find him.'[23]

This might have been written with Norman MacLeod of Dunvegan in mind. As he grew older, Norman spent more and more time in the Lowlands and in England – putting in only occasional appearances at Dunvegan and never so much as visiting his Glenelg or Harris properties. Clan chiefs who had thus become absentees, according to the author of the *Informations Concerning the Province of North Carolina*, merited nothing but disdain. Interested only in extracting higher rents from their tenants, they had enslaved those tenants in much the same way as Egypt's pharaohs had enslaved the Children of Israel. This, the *Informations* concluded, was why the people of the Highlands and Islands were right to undertake their equivalent of the biblical exodus: 'Is there any wonder if, under the present discouraging circumstances . . . they have before them at home, the Highlanders should seek for refuge in some happier land, on some more hospitable shore, where freedom reigns, and where, unmolested by Egyptian taskmasters, they may reap the produce of their own labour and industry? For this purpose, where can they better betake themselves than to the large continent of America [and] to that part of it especially [North Carolina] to which some of their countrymen went some time ago [and] . . . send . . . to their friends and acquaintances in the Highlands . . . the most pressing invitations . . . to follow after them across the Atlantic.'[24]

Identical sentiments surface in Gaelic songs and poems dating from the 1760s and 1770s. In those, as in the *Informations*, America is identified with the promised land to which Moses led the Jews. Over there on the Atlantic's other shore, intending emigrants are told by one Hebridean bard whose imagery depended heavily on the *Book of Exodus*, they will discover a 'country of milk', a 'country of honey', 'a country without want', 'a country where you may buy land to your will'.[25]

'*Falbhamaid 's bitheadh beannachd Dhè leinn*,' runs a further song which, since it was composed in nearby Kintail, must have been known to MacLeod of Dunvegan's Glenelg tenants: 'Let us go and may God's blessing be with us. Let us go and charter a vessel. Better that than to remain under landlords who will not tolerate tenantry . . . We shall all go together . . . to where we shall find every kind of the most beautiful game to be seen. We shall get deer, buck and doe, and the right to take as many as we wish. We shall get woodcock and woodhen, teal, ducks and wild geese . . . Imagine how prosperous they are over yonder; even every herdsman has a horse!'[26]

North Carolina: The Cape Fear River Country

Emigrants from the Highlands and Islands to the Cape Fear River country included the Skye-born forebears of Alexander McLeod, president of the Associated Clan MacLeod Societies and the person who asked me to write this book. On a damp morning in April, I set out in Alex's company to see what is left of the homesteads occupied by successive generations of his family in the course of their first century in America. Our starting point is Sandy Grove Presbyterian Church on North Carolina's Fort Bragg Military Reservation. This area is set aside, as it has been since 1918, for the use of the US army. Much of the countryside in Sandy Grove's vicinity has been permitted, as a result, to revert to forest. But in the nineteenth century, when Sandy Grove's timber-built and white-painted church took shape, the same countryside consisted of farms created by settler families from the Highlands and Islands. This is evident from a hundred-year-old map in the possession of Daniel MacLeod. Daniel's great-great-great-grandparents reached America on the ship which also carried Alex's ancestors and he is one of several folk – word of our excursion having got around Clan MacLeod circles in North Carolina – waiting for Alex and me at Sandy Grove. Sheltering from the rain in Alex's car, we examine Daniel's map. It shows who owned land in this locality before the military took over, and it is covered with Highlands and Islands surnames: McNeill, Monroe, Bethune or Beaton, Gillis, McColl, McFadyen, Cameron, Campbell, McLean and, of course, McLeod.

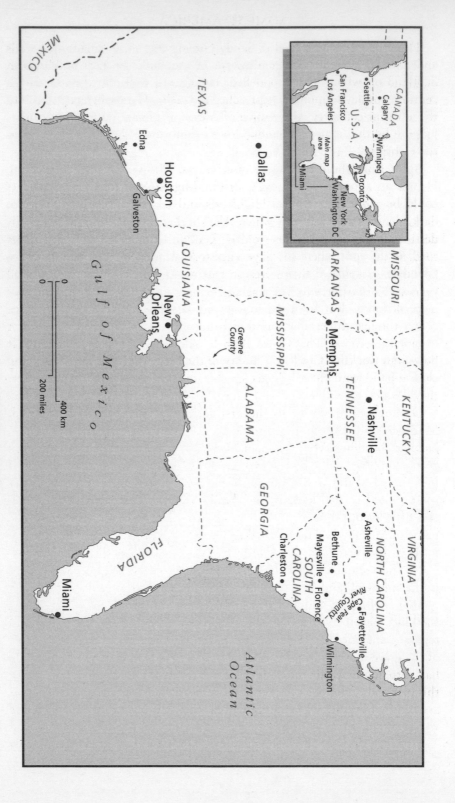

Map 2: South-eastern USA

Those people worshipped in Sandy Grove's church, its unadorned walls and narrow, upright pews reminiscent of the similarly stark buildings in Scotland on which it was modelled. Here, until well into the nineteenth century, Sunday sermons were preached in Gaelic. Here, when you step into the adjacent cemetery where some of Alex's people are buried, you might, judging by the names on Sandy Grove's tombstones, be in a graveyard in the Hebrides.

Apart from those tombstone inscriptions, admittedly, there is nothing Hebridean about Sandy Grove's surroundings. Indeed, few environments could be more alien from a Highlands and Islands standpoint than the dark, dense woodland into which Alex McLeod soon turns his car. His destination, Alex explains as we drive cautiously along a badly rutted dirt road, is the spot where his Skye ancestors, whose previous home was in Glendale, established themselves on getting to North Carolina some 200 years ago. This spot, when we reach it, seems at first glance to be just another piece of forest. But from the foot of the slope below our stopping place comes the just-discernible sound of running water – always an attraction to pioneer settlers. 'That's Field Branch,' Alex says of this little stream. 'It flows into Rockfish Creek, a tributary of the Cape Fear River, and its being close at hand would have helped convince my great-great-great-grandparents they'd hit on a good location for a farm.'

Occupying this farm, in the first instance, were Murdoch McLeod, Murdoch's wife Effie and their son John, Alex's great-great-grandfather, who had been born in Skye and who, on his arrival in America, was not quite two years old. 'I first came here forty years ago,' Alex tells me. 'I'd been drafted into the navy and, trying to find something constructive to do with my spare time, I started looking into family history. Where exactly Murdoch and Effie lived, I'd no idea. But I was put in touch with an old man by the name of McFadyen. His folk had neighboured with mine, and he was able to show me where Effie and Murdoch made their home.'

No trace remains of that home, a log cabin constructed from trees felled in the course of land clearance. But close to the McLeod cabin's site are the remnants of a post-and-wire fence which once surrounded a burial plot of the kind that, in North Carolina settlements, preceded the appearance of regular cemeteries like the one adjacent to the church at Sandy Grove. Most of the grave markers in this burial plot are of timber and, because they are half rotted, any words they might have carried have long gone. But it is in this plot and under one or other of those weathered markers, or so Alex was assured by his guide of forty years back, that Murdoch and Effie McLeod were interred.

Murdoch died in 1843. 'In the name of God amen,' reads Alex's copy of his great-great-great-grandfather's will, 'I, Murdoch McLeod, of the County of Cumberland and State of North Carolina, being afflicted in body but of sound mind and memory, have thought proper to make my last . . . testament.' Murdoch's 'home place' beside Field Branch was left to Effie 'during her lifetime' – this same 'home place', as Murdoch directed, eventually becoming the property of Archibald, the second of Murdoch's sons and a man whose name appears on the map which Daniel McLeod showed Alex and me when we met with him at Sandy Grove. Archibald's sisters, Nancy and Mary, were bequeathed a 'bay mare'; Archibald's younger brother, Donald, got some cash. Also dealt with in Murdoch McLeod's will was unfinished business involving Alex's great-great-grandfather. 'To . . . John,' Murdoch's will concludes, 'I give and bequeath forty dollars which he now owes me for the horse I sold him.'

This may seem a trifle peremptory. But if John McLeod gained nothing other than the cancellation of a $40 debt on his father's death, that was because John was already doing well financially. Just how well is evident from the home that John built in 1831, the year of his marriage to Flora Johnson who, since her brother was Cumberland County's sheriff, would have been seen as quite a catch on John's part.

John McLeod's 1831 house, unoccupied today but still in good condition, is located in North Carolina's Moore County. Visiting this house in the company of John's great-great-grandson Alex, I am impressed by its spaciousness. In the early 1830s, when John and Flora McLeod were starting married life here and beginning to raise a family that would number seven boys and six girls, John's cousins back in Skye – and such cousins definitely existed – would have been inhabiting single-roomed hovels of the kind then standard in the Highlands and Islands. John McLeod, in contrast, owned a one-and-a-half-storey, timber-framed home which ran to six sizeable rooms. And at a time when his Hebridean relatives would have been tenants – wholly insecure tenants at that – of no more than four or five acres of inferior soil, John, as his great-great-grandson's researches have revealed, was the outright possessor of 2,000 acres of North Carolina farmland. On this farmland, John McLeod pastured a large herd of cattle. On it, too, he grew maize, cotton and tobacco.

Flora Anne, one of John's children, lived on in her father's home until the 1930s. 'She died just three years before I was born,' Alex McLeod remarks of Flora Anne, 'and I heard a lot about her when I was growing up. She was a small woman, but real fiery, and one of the things she insisted on was the importance of our Scottish heritage. "Whatever you do," she'd say to younger members of the family, "always remember that we came from the Isle of Skye."'

The clouds are breaking now and, though we are barely into North Carolina's spring, it is warmer than it gets in Scotland most summers. A pair of wild turkeys, scattered by us on our arrival, have emerged cautiously from a nearby cluster of trees. A mile or so away, on what was once one of John McLeod's fields, a tractor is at work. Otherwise, the silence of this Moore County morning is broken only by Alex's account of one of the more dramatic episodes from his family history – an episode that reached its climax exactly where we are standing.

The tale in question dates from the early part of 1865, towards the close of America's Civil War. John McLeod had died a year or so before, and practically all the male members of his family, including Alex's great-grandfather, another Alexander McLeod, were serving, as were more than a thousand of their Moore County neighbours, with the forces of the Confederacy, the breakaway grouping of Southern states to which the McLeods, like most of North Carolina's white residents, were intensely loyal. There remained at home to look after the McLeod farm, and the farm's womenfolk, only one of John's sons, Sam, then in his early twenties.

The war, by this point, was going badly for the South. Some months before, a Northern or Union army under the command of General William T. Sherman had famously fought its way through Georgia – 'from Atlanta to the sea', as a marching song of the time puts it. This same army had then swung north and, having broken Confederate resistance in South Carolina, entered North Carolina – in the vicinity, as it happened, of the homestead occupied by Sam McLeod, his mother and his sisters. No conquering troops are ever received warmly by the people they conquer. But General Sherman's men, being under orders to destroy the Confederacy's infrastructure, were regarded with particular hostility. Often this hostility turned into loathing because of rumours about the Union, or Yankee, soldiery's propensity to rape as well as loot. Such rumours were rife in Moore County when, on a cold, wet afternoon about a week into March 1865, a detachment of Northern horsemen headed by Sherman's cavalry commander, Major-General Judson Kilpatrick, crossed the county boundary and, minutes later, approached the McLeod place.

'Sam had seen the Yankee cavalrymen coming,' Alex says, pointing. 'He'd mounted a horse, rounded up the cattle and was driving them down there into a swamp where the stock could more readily be kept out of the Northern army's clutches. Seeing what Sam was about, one of Kilpatrick's troopers gave chase. But Sam was carrying a gun and, turning in his saddle, he shot the Yankee trooper dead.'

Meanwhile, just as the elusive Sam disappeared deep into swampland where he could not be tracked, Judson Kilpatrick was personally confronting

Flora McLeod, Sam's mother. 'The Major-General wanted overnight quarters for himself and his officers in Flora's home,' Alex says. 'But there was no way she was going to agree to that until she'd established exactly who was boss. She came out on to the porch here, she folded her arms and she stared Kilpatrick down – telling him neither he nor his men would set foot in this house unless he guaranteed that her daughters would come to no harm. Well, the guarantee was given. In the Yankees came, and their behaviour – despite Flora's son having just killed one of Kilpatrick's soldiers – turned out to be impeccable.'

Sam McLeod, having survived his March 1865 encounter with the Union army, became a Baptist minister. As for the land on which the encounter took place, it passed into the possession of Sam's brother, Alexander, the great-grandfather, as well as the namesake, of the other Alex McLeod who is my source of this information. In the early 1880s, Alexander, every bit as accomplished a farmer as his father, built a new and larger home a mile or so from the house where he had grown up and where his mother had received Major-General Judson Kilpatrick. In this latest McLeod residence, which has been restored and extended by its present-day owners, Alexander and his wife raised a family including the present-day Alex McLeod's grandfather – who was named, as were many other Southerners then and later, after that most renowned of Confederate commanders, Robert E. Lee.

Robert Lee McLeod had a successful career in the lumber business – dealing in timber throughout North and South Carolina, Georgia and Texas. He was, then, a wealthy man, and his wealth is reflected in the home constructed for him, around 1910, in the little town of Maxton, not far from his father's farm. This home has all the porticoed splendour which a thousand Hollywood movies have taught the world to associate with a well-to-do Southern lifestyle. But what I take away from Robert L. McLeod's fine house is not so much an impression of its lavishness as a sense of having come across, in the course of the day Alex McLeod and I have spent together, a striking insight into the long-run outcome of emigration from places like Skye.

Think about the four-generation sequence of McLeod homes which starts with Murdoch's Field Branch cabin and ends with Robert's Maxton residence. Collectively, those homes testify to very marked upward mobility. In fact, they can be seen as constituting nothing less than the realisation, in timber, brick and stone, of what in the nineteenth century began to be called the American Dream. To believe in the American Dream was to be convinced that to get to the United States from Europe was to liberate oneself from the Old World's hardships and injustices. By crossing the ocean, it was thought, working men and women – who would otherwise have been condemned to lifelong poverty and exploitation – could gain the ability to shape their own lives, fulfil their potential, secure a good income.

In reality, matters were seldom so simple. Many people who left the Highlands and Islands for America did not even get there – dying, as a later chapter stresses, on overcrowded emigrant ships. And of those who made it over the Atlantic, by no means all did as well as Murdoch and Effie McLeod, their sons, their grandsons and their great-grandsons. As is indicated by this family's progression from pioneer farming to urban affluence, however, there were plenty of emigrants who managed to make the American Dream come true. This was not because people like Effie and Murdoch acquired new capacities in the United States. It was down to this country's more open, more democratic society enabling Murdoch, Effie and their numerous counterparts to do things in North Carolina they never could have done in Skye. That is why, from the late eighteenth century onwards, it made sense for America to feature in Gaelic songs and poems as a place of almost fabled opportunity; a country without landlords; a country where, as was then impossible in Scotland, ordinary families could acquire homes, farms and, ultimately, capital of their own.

Scotland: Skye and Glenelg

Between them, Norman MacLeod of Dunvegan and Sir Alexander MacDonald of Sleat owned the greater part of Skye. On Sir Alexander making known in 1770 that he intended to increase his tacksmen's rents to levels commensurate with those announced a year earlier by Norman of Dunvegan, discontents of the sort previously confined to Norman's tacksmen duly erupted across the island. Sir Alexander in particular, it was observed, had become an object of 'universal hatred' among his clansfolk – whose detestation of their laird and chief took practical form at a meeting held in Portree, Skye's only substantial village, in March 1771. During this meeting, about thirty of Sir Alexander MacDonald's tacksmen agreed to form a company with a view to buying a tract of territory in North Carolina. To this territory, they proposed to decamp as soon as possible and with as many other Skye residents as cared to join them. Hence the sensational nature of a report which soon reached Edinburgh from the Hebrides: 'Two thousand emigrants are preparing for their departure from the Isle of Skye to some part of our foreign settlements . . . That they may go as a formed colony, a parochial preacher and a thoroughbred surgeon are to go along with them . . . All this is owing to the exorbitant rents for land.'[27]

'Your people have been civiller than mine,' Sir Alexander complained in a letter he sent Norman MacLeod during this critical period. But if the MacLeod chief's tacksmen were more muted than their MacDonald counterparts in their immediate response to the prospect of higher rents, this was quickly to change. 'People going to America is become a very serious matter,' Norman MacLeod was told in February 1771 by the man responsible for the administration of his Skye estate. The following month, much the same point was made by Donald MacLeod of Arnisdale, the Glenelg tacksman whose hospitality Thomas Pennant enjoyed. 'The most material news here,' Donald wrote on 18 March, 'is those people going to North America from Sir Alexander's estate.' In the light of such comments, it is scarcely surprising that 'a spirit of emigration' was soon said to be spreading from the MacDonald estates to neighbouring properties. 'I grew out of this ground and have as strong an attachment to my native soil as any man,' Norman MacLeod was informed by one of his Skye tacksmen, 'but . . . it [is] out of my power [and the power of] . . . my neighbours, to pay our rents.' Those words were written by Alexander Morrison of Skinidin, whose lands were situated just a mile or two from Dunvegan Castle. Alexander's forebears, though not MacLeods by name, had adhered to Clan MacLeod for generations. He was also his laird's cousin. But this, if anything, seems to have intensified his hostility to Norman of Dunvegan's policies. If the MacLeod chief refused to 'come . . . to see [his] people [and] to give ease in their rents', Morrison warned in March 1771, his ancestral lands would rapidly be 'stripped' of their inhabitants. Within weeks, the Skinidin tacksman, whose call for rent reductions had been ignored, was doing all he could to make a reality of his own depopulating prophecies. That summer there were posted up notices in Skye advertising the fact that Alexander Morrison was shortly to leave for North Carolina aboard a chartered ship on which passages would be available to all-comers at a cost of just over £3 a head. In the event, some 300 people took up Morrison's offer and, by the North Carolina fall of 1772, the former tacksman had succeeded in exchanging his Skinidin landholdings for a 500-acre plantation in the Cape Fear River country. On this plantation, Alexander Morrison reported, 'he established himself and [his] family in circumstances very happy and independent'.[28]

From a Highlands and Islands perspective, the wholesale departure of tacksmen like Alexander Morrison was a serious blow from which, in some respects, the region did not recover until modern times. By taking themselves overseas or by moving to other parts of the United Kingdom, tacksmen deprived their home localities of capital, enterprise and leadership. Something of this was apparent to contemporaries. Emigrants from the Highlands and Islands to America, it was observed during the 1770s, were often 'people of property', 'gentlemen of wealth and merit', 'people in good circumstances'. In the preceding ten or so years, it was estimated in 1772, such folk had 'carried with them', from the Hebrides alone, gold coinage to the value of 'at least ten thousand pounds' – as well as huge quantities of furniture, agricultural implements and other possessions. This draining away of wealth was bad enough. Even more alarming, as far as lairds like Norman MacLeod were concerned, was the tendency of emigrating tacksmen to do what Alexander Morrison of Skinidin did in 1771 – charter a vessel which was immediately filled with scores of the departing tacksman's more modestly placed neighbours.[29]

Some of the tacksmen who took hundreds of people with them to America were motivated partly by a desire to make things as difficult as possible for the chiefs-cum-landowners whose policies such tacksmen had come to detest. But there were more straightforward reasons why Alexander Morrison and other emigrating tacksmen, instead of simply taking cabins on America-bound ships, hired such ships in their entirety. Tacksmen were nothing if not entrepreneurs, and in the emigration business they scented opportunity. By selling surplus berths on his chartered vessel, an emigrating tacksman could cover his costs – even make a profit. All he needed was a plentiful supply of prospective passengers. By the 1770s, such a supply, as shown by the ease with which Alexander Morrison sold passages to North Carolina, was readily available.

Underlying this eagerness to be off to America was the profound unrest engendered everywhere in the Highlands and Islands by clanship's disintegration. Two or three generations earlier, in 1695, one of the first Hebrideans to write about the Hebrides in English commented: 'The islanders have a great respect for their chiefs and heads of tribes, and they conclude grace after every meal with a petition to God for their [chief's] welfare and prosperity.' Seventy years later, such practices were in abeyance. On all sides, the old order was crumbling as chiefs like Norman MacLeod of Dunvegan placed a new, and unavoidably disruptive, stress on maximising the cash yields of their properties. Touring the Highlands and Islands in 1773, Samuel Johnson discerned everywhere 'a general discontent'. 'That adherence which was lately professed by every man to the chief of his name has now little prevalence,' he wrote. In such circumstances, Samuel Johnson went on, the notion of emigrating overseas was becoming daily more attractive: 'He that cannot live as he desires at home listens to the tale of fortunate islands, and happy regions, where every man may have land of his own, and eat the product of his labour, without a superior.'[30]

Samuel Johnson's remarks did not stem solely from what he saw of developments on MacLeod of Dunvegan's estates. But two individuals concerned directly with the management of those estates echoed Johnson's conclusions about emigration's origins. The first was John MacKenzie of Delvine, a Perthshire landowner and lawyer who became closely involved in Clan MacLeod affairs during the 1770s. The second was Norman MacLeod of Dunvegan's grandson and heir – who shared his grandfather's name and who, by way of minimising confusion, is here called Young Norman.* To MacKenzie, emigration seemed nothing less than 'a punishment for the imprudences, shall I say the sins, of chieftains who from avarice, or . . . [so] that they might plunge at large in the fashionable luxuries and vices of the age, must needs squeeze their tenants without discretion'. Young Norman MacLeod agreed. 'Sucked into the vortex of the nation,' he wrote of men like his grandfather, 'they degenerated from patriarchs and chieftains to landlords . . . In the Hebrides especially, this change was not gradual but sudden – and baleful were its effects. The people, freed . . . by the chieftains themselves from the bonds of affection, turned their eyes and hearts to new scenes. America seemed to open its arms . . . To those possessed of [even] small sums of money, it offered large possessions of uncultivated but excellent land in a preferable climate. To the poor, it held out large wages for labour. To all, it promised property and independence.'[31]

On Norman MacLeod of Dunvegan's possessions, as elsewhere in the Highlands and Islands, the group most attracted by the prospect of a more self-reliant existence in North Carolina consisted of folk standing below tacksmen in clanship's pecking order. 'There are a very great number of [people] on MacLeod's estates,' it was noted in 1769, 'who are cottars to such as have larger tacks and who, though they possess but small [pieces] of the worst of the lands, are burdened with the whole of the rents that are payed to the superior [meaning the laird], besides services.' Cottars were subtenants. Instead of renting their plots of land directly from MacLeod of Dunvegan, in other words, they rented those plots from a tacksman – to whom they were also liable, as indicated in the passage just quoted, for 'services' in the form of unpaid labour. Because tacksmen could pass on to their subtenants any uplift in their own rents, the prevalence of subtenancy – and there were hundreds of subtenants on the MacLeod estates – should, in principle, have provided Norman MacLeod's tacksmen with a way of spreading their rent burden. Unfortunately for such tacksmen and their chief, however, the levying of the new rents coincided with a severe agricultural downturn. Any such downturn would, of itself, have made it more difficult for subtenants and tacksmen alike to pay their rents – those rents being dependent, in the last analysis, on the prices fetched by the cattle which, for much of the eighteenth century, were central to the farming economy

* Afterwards he became General Norman MacLeod and features as such in later chapters.

of the Highlands and Islands. But making matters worse was the way the effects of the price slump were aggravated by a series of exceptionally bad winters. With thousands of cattle dying from lack of fodder, rents began, of necessity, to go unpaid. And with food as scarce as money, because crops too fell victim to the weather, subtenants and their families were frequently left hungry.[32]

The winter of 1771–2, according to Alexander MacLeod of Ullinish, Sheriff of Skye and one of Norman MacLeod's tacksmen, brought incessant frost and 'frequent snow'. Alexander, who occupied 'a very good farmhouse of two storeys' on the eastern shore of Loch Bracadale, was personally well provided for, and neither he nor his immediate kin suffered unduly. But the sheriff was greatly distressed, as his correspondence reveals, by the 'deplorable' plight of his less favoured neighbours: 'Never was a calamity so universal . . . It's moving to see the poor people carrying off dead cows' carcases to support life.'[33]

Other Skye residents were equally gloomy. Norman MacLeod of Fernilea, whose home was located a mile or so beyond the present-day Talisker Distillery on the south side of Loch Harport, reported: 'We have such a general loss of cattle . . . that I believe few [animals] will remain alive . . . Upon the whole, this country has a very ruinous aspect just now.'[34]

Writing at this time to a friend in the south, Flora MacDonald – who had famously come to the aid of Charles Edward Stuart when he fled to the Hebrides following Culloden – described Skye as a 'poor miserable island'. Flora's husband, Allan MacDonald, tacksman of Kingsburgh on Sir Alexander MacDonald's estate, was equally affected by the 'melancholy' he discerned all around him. By insisting on their 'great rents', he wrote, both Sir Alexander and Norman of Dunvegan had placed themselves on a collision course with their tenants. The result, in Allan MacDonald's opinion, was that island society had begun to fall apart: 'No respect of persons . . . stealing of sheep . . . thieving of corn, garden stuffs and potatoes . . . lying, backbiting and slandering . . . honesty entirely fled . . . villainy and deceit, supported by downright poverty, in its place.'[35]

In those circumstances, Allan MacDonald commented, further emigration was inevitable. 'I believe the whole will go for America,' he wrote. This was certainly to be Allan's own way out of Skye's developing crisis. In 1774, he and Flora sailed for North Carolina. With them, the MacDonalds took their daughter, Ann, and Ann's husband, Alexander MacLeod of Glendale. Alexander was Norman of Dunvegan's factor or land manager. As such, he had the thankless task of trying to prevent the MacLeod chief's tenants from simply throwing in their leases, as many of them were threatening to do by the disastrous spring of 1772, and leaving Skye for ever. 'A few of you some little time ago told me of your intention of your being quit of your lands . . . as you [were] not in condition . . . to pay your rents,' Alexander observed in the course of a circular sent that April to his father's tacksmen. He had hoped, Alexander MacLeod went on, that their chief might himself have journeyed to Skye to meet with his clansfolk. Sadly, Old Norman was too ill to make the trip. He had decided, however, to send Young Norman in his place. 'Everyone,' Alexander urged, 'ought . . . patiently to await this event.'[36]

Scotland: Skye, Assynt and Lewis

Just beyond Drynoch, in the mountainous heartland of Skye, a narrow road runs west through Gleann Oraid. To begin with, this road is hemmed in by moorland, but then, without warning, a wholly different landscape comes in sight. A mile or so short of the sea, Gleann Oraid's floor drops away steeply and the surrounding hills draw back to make space for green, grassy fields which an eighteenth-century visitor to those parts thought as 'flat as any in Holland'. To the west of this tract of farmland, the same visitor wrote, lay the ocean. On the 'other three sides' were 'high precipices enlivened by cataracts'. Below one of those precipices, in the eighteenth century, there stood a substantial, stone-built house. This house, altered somewhat in the interim, but still standing and still occupied, was home in the 1770s to Colonel John MacLeod of Talisker, a man who deserves to be remembered for the efforts he made to sustain the social cohesion which was one of clanship's more admirable characteristics.[37]

The first MacLeod of Talisker, who headed the MacLeod detachment which came to grief at Worcester in 1651, was a son of his clan's most acclaimed chief, Ruaraidh Mòr. Colonel John MacLeod, the Worcester veteran's great-grandson, studied medicine at St Andrew's University and was said, as a result, to have always retained a 'tincture of scholarship'. While still in his twenties, however, John MacLeod was given command of one of the units his chief raised to help the British government defeat Charles Edward Stuart. In the event, this unit saw little action against the Jacobites. But having got a taste for the military life, John MacLeod left in 1747 for the continent where, like many other MacLeods, he joined the Dutch army. For the next twenty years, then, John MacLeod was overseas, rising eventually to the rank of lieutenant-colonel and not getting back to Skye until 1767. What he found on his return appalled him. Particularly shocking, in Colonel John's opinion, was the gulf which had opened up between chiefs like his own kinsman, Norman MacLeod of Dunvegan, and the clansfolk to whom such chiefs, or so Colonel John considered, ought to have been offering leadership of the traditional kind. The Dunvegan laird's financial and other problems, John MacLeod of Talisker insisted, were of his own making. Practically all of those problems, the Talisker tacksman maintained, arose from the MacLeod chief's vainglorious desire to be regarded as an equal by southern aristocrats whose spending power he could match only by incurring ever greater debts. 'What is it,' John MacLeod asked, 'has brought our Highland chieftains to their present despicable state but their . . . vying in luxury and extravagance with people of much larger fortunes? Then the tenants must be squeezed to support a [chief] in . . . vice and dissipation whose face [his clanspeople] hardly know and who never thinks of them in any other way than as slaves whose labour affords him the means of indulging his follies.'[38]

Although disenchanted with Old Norman MacLeod of Dunvegan, John MacLeod of Talisker had high hopes of the chief's grandson, Young Norman. When his grandfather sent Young Norman to Skye in the spring of 1772, in fulfilment of Alexander MacLeod of Glendale's April promise to Old Norman's disaffected tacksmen, Colonel John consequently put himself at Young Norman's disposal. He would be happy, MacLeod of Talisker assured Young Norman, to 'cooperate' with him in 'everything'. The bond which thus developed between the two men – Young Norman in his teens, Colonel John in his fifties – became all the stronger when, in the summer of 1772, Old Norman died and Young Norman assumed the MacLeod chieftainship.[39]

'Your burden of debts is immense,' John MacLeod of Talisker told his new chief. If this burden was to be reduced, he went on, it was essential that Young Norman, together with his widowed mother and his sisters, leave the Lowlands, where they had lived previously, and set up home in Dunvegan Castle. Such a move, Colonel John acknowledged in a letter to Young Norman's mother, would be 'difficult' and 'disagreeable'. But it offered her and her son their only hope of 'salvation'. 'Augmented rents', 'dreadful seasons' and the 'entire neglect' shown them by their former chief had left Young Norman's clansfolk 'discontented', Colonel John warned. That was why 'flattering accounts received from America' had so readily fostered 'a spirit of emigration' which, 'if not soon suppressed', was likely to have 'dreadful consequences'. 'All these . . . circumstances,' Colonel John stressed, 'it is in the [chief's] power, and his only, to remove by residing among [his people], treating them with kindness and convincing them he has their real interest at heart.'[40]

Those arguments carried the day. Soon Norman MacLeod was in residence at Dunvegan – the first chief to live there since Iain Breac, Norman's great-great-grandfather, a century before. Perhaps predictably, this reversion to past practice was to end after just three or four years. But for the moment it seemed to John MacLeod of Talisker that Clan MacLeod might after all have a future. Hence the upbeat tenor of the remarks he made when trying, on Young Norman's behalf, to dissuade his fellow tacksmen from emigrating. 'I told them,' Colonel John informed Norman, 'that you were now resolved to take up your residence among them [and] . . . that your greatest ambition was to deserve the appellation of a real Highland chieftain who loved and cherished his people and who, in return, [was] loved and cherished by them.'[41]

Those appeals, though heartfelt, evoked no very positive response. This is evident from a comment made at the time by a visitor to Skye: 'Colonel MacLeod, instead of being all life and gaiety as I have seen him, was . . . grave and somewhat depressed by his anxious concern about [Young Norman] MacLeod's affairs, and by finding some gentlemen of the clan [meaning Norman's tacksmen] by no means disposed to act a generous or affectionate part to their chief in his distress, but bargaining with him as with a stranger.'[42]

However, a number of the hearts and minds which remained impervious to Colonel John's entreaties were won over by Young Norman himself. 'I was young,' he wrote later, 'and had the warmth of the liberal passions natural to that age. I called the people of the different districts of our estate together. I laid before them the situation of our family – its debts, its burthens, its distresses. I acknowledged the hardships under which they laboured. I described, and reminded them of, the manner in which . . . their ancestors lived with mine. I combated their passion for America with a real account of the dangers and hardships they might encounter there. I besought them to love their young chieftain and renew with him their ancient manners. I promised to live among them. I threw myself upon them . . . I desired every district to point out some of their oldest and most respected men to settle with me every claim, and I promised to do everything for their relief which in reason I could.'[43]

Young Norman's rhetoric was accompanied by more down-to-earth tokens of his goodwill. Dunvegan Castle accounts dating from 1772–3 contain details of cash laid out on providing for '565 men at meat'. The same accounts show that no fewer than thirty bottles of whisky were lavished on a separate set of estate residents. But if pleased enough to eat and drink at his expense, Young Norman's tenants were interested ultimately in one thing only. If they were to remain on his properties, they told him, they must be granted 'considerable abatements' in rent. In the end, just such abatements were agreed – senior tacksmen getting 'very high reductions', 'the lower and middling classes' settling for more 'reasonable' concessions.[44]

This helped reduce the rate of emigration from Norman MacLeod's estates in Harris, Skye and Glenelg. It did nothing to halt emigration from areas which had once been MacLeod territory but which had passed into the ownership of non-MacLeod lairds. One such area was the Sutherland district of Assynt. Although it had ceased to be a MacLeod possession in the seventeenth century, many of its inhabitants were still MacLeods. Their links with America dated back to 1735 when some fifteen individuals named MacLeod were among several dozen Sutherland men recruited for military service in Georgia – where Highland troops were used to garrison the fortified settlement of Darien on what was then the frontier between British North America and Spanish Florida. After the 1730s, however, this Sutherland–Darien connection appears to have lapsed. By the 1770s, most of the folk quitting Sutherland, like emigrants from the Highlands and Islands more generally, were making for North Carolina.[45]

'There is a migration going on in this country in imitation of the Isle of Skye people,' it was reported from Assynt in February 1772. Among the hundreds of men, women and children involved was a sixty-year-old farming tenant, Angus MacLeod. Rather than pay the inflated rent demanded by his landlord, Angus sailed for the Cape Fear River country where he intended, he said, 'to live by day labour'. Also bound for North Carolina were William MacLeod, then twenty-six, William's wife and their one-year-old son. He had decided to abandon Sutherland for America, William MacLeod told a customs officer at the family's port of embarkation, because 'he [had] a brother settled there who wrote to him to come out, assuring him that he would find [in North Carolina] a better farm than he possessed at home . . . for one-fourth of the money'.[46]

In the former MacLeod heartland of Lewis, meanwhile, whole communities were reportedly falling prey to an 'epidemical frenzy . . . for migrating to America'. On a single day in June 1773, between 700 and 800 Lewis folk, out of an island population then put at about 9,000, sailed from Stornoway, the island's only town and its principal seaport. In conformity with the now standard pattern, 'extravagant rents' were 'the sole cause given' by those emigrants when they were asked why they were leaving.[47]

Rent levels in Lewis were set by the Earl of Seaforth, a descendant of the MacKenzies who had displaced the island's MacLeod chiefs more than 150 years before. Described by one of his contemporaries as 'a lively, pretty young man', the earl, then in his early thirties, spent most of his time in London or in continental Europe. There, very much in the manner of Old Norman MacLeod of Dunvegan, he amassed enormous debts which caused him, also in the Old Norman manner, to impose massive rent increases on his island tenants. From the Earl of Seaforth's standpoint, it followed, the outflow of people from Lewis was a potentially devastating blow – for if the island continued to empty at the 1773 rate, his income was bound to fall sharply.[48]

That is why, when emigration from Lewis began again in the spring of 1774, the Earl of Seaforth was driven to desperate measures. He asked the authorities in Edinburgh to dispatch to Lewis 'a small command of troops' whose task would be to halt an exodus resulting, or so Lewis's proprietor alleged, from kidnappings akin to those which had occurred in Skye in 1739. 'There are now in the harbour of Stornoway,' the Earl of Seaforth's Lewis-based representatives explained, 'vessels from several parts of America, particularly from Philadelphia, the crews of which are . . . employed in ensnaring . . . the inhabitants to emigrate . . . and [who] not only carry off persons who are lessees and under engagements [to the Earl of Seaforth] . . . but also apprentices and infants . . . without the consent of their masters or parents.'[49]

The 'atrocious villains' conducting such operations, it was asserted, were plunging 'the whole [of Lewis] into anarchy and confusion'. Nobody would be safe until the military were deployed: 'The civil power in the island of Lewis is not sufficient to prevent these illegal practices and, if they are not contained, the island will soon become desolated.'[50]

Government ministers were unconvinced. When customs officers in Stornoway questioned passengers on the Philadelphia-registered *Friendship*, they found that her cargo of prospective emigrants consisted overwhelmingly of people who wanted 'to leave . . . in order to procure bread elsewhere'. The Earl of Seaforth's allegations notwithstanding, none of the men, women or children on the *Friendship* had been forced to quit Lewis – except, perhaps, by their own poverty. 'Necessity obliged them to emigrate,' it was reported of the *Friendship*'s passengers.[51]

Among those passengers, when the *Friendship* finally cleared Stornoway in May 1774, were Lewis boys like Angus MacLeod from Brenish and John MacLeod from Galson; both of them just fifteen; both of them sailing unaccompanied; both of them sent to make careers for themselves in America by parents who knew they would never see their sons again. Also aboard the *Friendship* were many entire families. John and Catherine MacLeod from Carloway sailed with their two daughters and two sons. Neil and Margaret MacLeod from Melbost left with their three children, Christina, twelve, Norman, nine, and Margaret, two.[52]

North Carolina: Glendale

By the early 1770s, families everywhere in the Highlands and Islands were well informed as to what they would find if they crossed the Atlantic. 'You would wonder to hear how exactly they know the geography of North America,' one eighteenth-century commentator remarked of people he had met in the north of Scotland. '[You would wonder] how distinctly they can speak of [America's] lakes, its rivers and the extent and richness of the soil in the respective territories where British colonies are settled. For my part, did I not know the contrary, I would be tempted to think they had lived for some time in that country.'[53]

Because of a paucity of reliable data, aggregate emigration from the Highlands and Islands in the 1770s cannot be calculated precisely. Neither can the number leaving particular properties, such as the estates belonging to Young Norman MacLeod. But this number was certainly large. Glenelg's minister recorded that 160 people left his parish for America between 1770 and 1774. Other ministers reported that Duirinish and Bracadale, Skye parishes wholly in the MacLeod chief's ownership, lost 539 folk during the same period. Since some such estimates appear to have excluded children, they may well understate the true position – all the more so if account is taken of the many references to emigration which can be found in the contemporary Lowland media. One of these, dating from July 1773, reports total emigration of around 800 from Skye that year. This is substantiated by a letter sent to Scotland from North Carolina in the course of the following winter: 'We have had come this year [1773] upwards of seven hundred souls from Skye and the neighbouring isles.' A 'great many' more people from Skye were expected in 1774, the same letter goes on. When those people put in their anticipated appearance, they were found to include Old Norman MacLeod's illegitimate son, Alexander MacLeod of Glendale, who, as mentioned earlier, was also his father's land manager or factor.[54]

Alexander, whose mother was an Edinburgh woman, had been born about 1730. Educated at his father's expense, he afterwards joined the Royal Navy which he left in 1766 to take up his factorship and, in addition, become the tenant of a couple of tacks, including the highly desirable farm of Hamara in Glendale. But if Alexander of Glendale, as he was designated on acquiring his Hamara tack, prospered in Old Norman's time, the latter's death left him out in the cold. Soon there was talk to the effect that, when in charge of his late father's affairs, MacLeod of Glendale was not as scrupulous as he should have been in handling money. Those allegations were dismissed by Alexander's father-in-law, Allan MacDonald of Kingsburgh, as 'jigripockry' got up by Alexander's 'antagonists'. But Dunvegan's new laird, Young Norman, who was also Alexander's nephew, took the matter seriously enough to have it looked into by one of Edinburgh's heavyweight lawyers. Understandably, then, the Glendale tacksman and his wife, Ann, were delighted to have the chance to leave Skye and to accompany Ann's parents, Allan and Flora MacDonald of Kingsburgh, to North Carolina.[55]

Alexander and Ann MacLeod, together with their two young children, reached the Cape Fear River country in December 1774. Judging by the reaction of Janet Schaw, an Edinburgh woman who got there a month or two after the MacLeods, their first glimpse of North Carolina is unlikely to have been inspiring. For hundreds of miles on either side of the Cape Fear River's estuary there stretched, as there still does, a low-lying, featureless coastline consisting, Schaw observed, of 'barren sand and melancholy, nodding pines'. Nor was Brunswick, the first population centre reached by ships entering the Cape Fear River, much more reassuring. 'The town is very poor,' Janet Schaw remarked of Brunswick, 'a few scattered houses on the edge of the woods, without street or regularity.' Some ten or fifteen miles upriver, however, was the larger and more attractive settlement of Wilmington. Here Ann and Alexander MacLeod, like the thousands of people from the Highlands and Islands who reached North Carolina before them, came ashore. But their journey, though approaching its end, was not yet over. From Wilmington, new arrivals such as the Glendale MacLeods were transported into the North Carolina interior on one of the numerous longboats and canoes then plying up and down the Cape Fear River. 'Nothing can be finer than the banks of this river,' Janet Schaw commented of her upstream voyage. 'A thousand beauties both of the flowery and sylvan tribe hang over it and are reflected from it with additional lustre.'[56]

Four or five days out of Wilmington, Ann and Alexander MacLeod got to Cross Creek, a trading centre serving the extensive district which had become home to as many as 15,000 people from the Highlands and Islands. Today it has evolved into the sprawling city of Fayetteville, but in 1774 Cross Creek was a comparatively tiny place, only a few years old. Even then, however, the town was bigger and busier than Portree, Skye's nearest approach to an equivalent community. Cross Creek's riverfront wharfs and jetties handled the goods that Cape Fear River country settlers produced for export. The town's stores were the source of everything the same settlers could not manufacture for themselves. In Cross Creek on Sundays, spiritual needs were catered for by Rev. John MacLeod, a Presbyterian preacher. During the rest of the week, bodily aches and ailments were treated by Murdo MacLeod, surgeon and apothecary. Both the Reverend John and Surgeon Murdo were emigrants from Scotland. The first, one of Alexander of Glendale's relatives, belonged originally to Skye. The second came from Raasay, where his father, also Murdo or Murdoch, was one of the island's tacksmen.[57]

During 1775, Ann and Alexander MacLeod leased a 300-acre plantation in a locality some forty miles west of Cross Creek. They named this plantation Glendale and on it they installed the twelve servants – six men and six women – who had accompanied them from Skye. With those folk's help, the MacLeods set about establishing a home of the sort they thought appropriate to people of their status. This home was no roughly built log cabin of the kind thrown up in eighteenth-century North Carolina by the generality of the colony's settlers. Nor were its furnishings in any way sparse or spartan. From Scotland, Ann and Alexander had brought, among other items, 324 books, 27 pairs of blankets, 20 pairs of sheets, 41 tablecloths, an array of high-grade china and a still larger quantity of silver cutlery. In the new Glendale they had conjured into existence so far from the old one, Alexander and Ann MacLeod intended to live in some style.[58]

The MacLeod plantation was located on a stream known as Wad's Creek or McDeed's Creek. This creek flows under today's US Highway 15/501 about three miles south of the modern town of Carthage. A day or two after our joint exploration of his own family's nineteenth-century homesteads, I accompany Alex McLeod of the Associated Clan MacLeod Societies to this spot – where, in Alex's recollection, there once stood one of those roadside markers which, in North Carolina, are commonly erected at sites of historical significance.

The marker has disappeared, we discover, because the surrounding area has recently been turned into a housing complex. This complex, as signs at its entrance inform passing traffic, is called Glendale – an indication that the place's past has not been entirely forgotten. Next, Alex and I drive into Glendale, its newly constructed homes hidden carefully from each other by woodland which, though cleared in colonial times, has re-advanced across Alexander MacLeod's former fields. Seeing a man and woman walking their dogs, we stop, explain that we are looking for the site of the MacLeod house of 1775, and ask where it might be found. The dog-walking couple do not know, but they direct us to a nearby farm whose occupants, we are told, have been in those parts a lot longer than most Glendale residents.

At the farm, Alex and I are received by more dogs and by a young woman carrying a baby. She can't help us either, she tells us regretfully. The man we really need to speak with, she adds, is Jody Hall, who farms here. Jody's not around right now, but she'll tell him we stopped by and, if he can be of any help, he'll surely call Alex and me at our hotel. A little pessimistically, we expect to hear nothing more. A day or so later, however, Jody Hall is in touch. He mentions some ruined buildings in the vicinity of his farm. Might those be what we're looking for? Anyway, we'd be welcome if we want to come and look.

That afternoon, Alex and I are back at Jody Hall's farm. In Jody's company, we quarter the surrounding woodland. The ruins Jody shows us turn out to be the remnants of nineteenth-century tobacco barns, not the foundations of an eighteenth-century house. By this point, having got – if nothing else – some sense of the Wad's Creek landscape, I am prepared to call a halt. But neither Alex nor Jody, both of them now determined to run the MacLeod plantation to ground, are minded to quit. When he gets home to Nashville, they agree, Alex will get in touch with the North Carolina agency responsible for erecting the now-vanished historical marker. This agency is bound to have some records dealing with the site. Those Alex will pass on to Jody who will be more than happy, he assures us, to do any further fieldwork that might be needed.

Two weeks later, when I am back in Scotland, I get from Alex a photocopy of a letter dated 9 November 1949 and written by a Mr R.E. Wicker. This was the document which convinced the North Carolina authorities to erect a marker beside Highway 15/501. It contains a map showing the precise location of Alexander MacLeod's 1775 home, and it explains how Mr Wicker had learned of this home's whereabouts from 'the late John R. Black' whose forebears, back in the 1770s, had been neighbours of Alexander, Ann and their family. 'Mr Black's aunt,' the Wicker letter continues, 'told the writer that "old Glendale" [meaning Alexander MacLeod] lost a silver shoe buckle on the place, which was found by some of the Black family, but was later again lost. This was related to the writer about 1914, at which time Miss Black [John R. Black's aunt] was a very old woman.' In the same Miss Black's possession in 1914 was 'a little gold brooch made in the shape of a key', which had been gifted to her ancestors by Flora MacDonald, Alexander MacLeod's mother-in-law and, according to Miss Black, a frequent visitor to Alexander's Glendale plantation.

All of this information, Alex tells me by email, he has passed to Jody Hall. There duly follows, in another week or two, a further photocopied letter. This one is from Jody to Alex. Enclosed with it are some photographs. One shows what Jody calls 'the approximate location' of the MacLeod house at Glendale – its site now occupied by Victory Baptist Church. Another shows the brooch mentioned by R.E. Wicker in 1949. It is now in the possession of Robert Moore, a descendant of the Black family and, it turns out, one of Jody Hall's neighbours.

North Carolina: Moore's Creek Bridge and Horse's Creek

Just as Alexander and Ann MacLeod were installing themselves in their home beside Wad's Creek, North Carolina became embroiled in the revolution which was shortly to result in the colony joining with a dozen others to form a new nation, the United States of America. This revolution's origins were bound up with a protracted series of disputes between Britain's American colonists and the London politicians in charge of colonial affairs. With one quarrel leading to another, the radical concept of turning the colonies into an independent republic began to attract support among Americans. The outcome was that argument and debate gradually gave way to open war between the British army and colonial militias. This fighting started in the summer of 1775. During the fall of that year, therefore, in North Carolina as elsewhere in North America, people were forced to decide who to back in what was turning into a continent-wide conflict: the rebel colonists or the British state. Without hesitation, Alexander MacLeod declared himself loyal to Britain and its monarch, George III. By so doing, he ensured that his family's connection with North Carolina would be brief.

By upbringing and conviction, men like Alexander MacLeod of Glendale and his kinsman-by-marriage, Allan MacDonald of Kingsburgh, were profoundly conservative. Although Alexander and Allan had recently put an ocean between themselves and the Highlands and Islands, they remained deeply attached to clanship's traditional values which, because of the stress those values placed on inherited position, were hopelessly at odds with the ideals motivating the makers of the United States. Republicanism and democracy, the twin principles on which the USA rested from its inception, were seen as alien, subversive and dangerous by Alexander MacLeod, by Allan MacDonald and by other recently arrived North Carolinians of similar background. Towards the close of 1775, therefore, Alexander and Allan sought out North Carolina's British governor, Josiah Martin, and offered to raise, from among colonists of Highlands and Islands extraction, a force whose objective would be to crush the colony's growing number of rebels.

This force went into action against American patriot opposition at a place called Moore's Creek Bridge on 27 February 1776. Among the loyalist troops present there that day were Allan MacDonald of Kingsburgh and Alexander MacLeod of Glendale. Commanding those troops was Captain Donald MacLeod, a professional military man ordered to North Carolina to help organise resistance to the colony's revolutionaries. Captain Donald was a son of John MacLeod of Pabbay, one of Young Norman MacLeod's Harris tacksmen. And at the Harris-born commander's side, as he led a brave but poorly conducted charge on well-armed rebel formations dug in behind a hastily constructed breastwork or embankment, was Captain John Campbell, the son, despite his not being a MacLeod by name, of another of Young Norman's Harris tacksmen, Donald Campbell of Scalpay.[59]

During the weeks preceding the Battle of Moore's Creek Bridge, John

Campbell and Donald MacLeod, with Alexander of Glendale's assistance, had managed to get a substantial proportion of the Cape Fear River country's male population to rally to the loyalist cause. As they hurtled towards their American enemies in the foggy half-light of a winter's dawn, therefore, John Campbell and Donald MacLeod were accompanied by lots of men – among them William MacLeod, Torcuil MacLeod, Norman MacLeod, John MacLeod and Daniel MacLeod – whose lives, like the lives of their commanders, had begun in the Hebrides. Many of those men died at Moore's Creek Bridge that cold and misty February morning in 1776. So did the loyalist force's two leaders. Their fate, and what followed from it, is described in a dispatch compiled by one of the Americans whose revolution the loyalist fighters had been trying in vain to snuff out: 'Captain MacLeod and Captain Campbell fell within twenty paces of the breastwork, the former of whom received upwards of twenty balls through his body. And in a very few minutes their whole army was put to flight.'[60]

Events in North Carolina notwithstanding, by no means all of America's Scottish settlers were on the side of Britain. In June 1775, the provincial congress of New York, the body at the centre of revolutionary activity in that colony, was petitioned by a MacLeod who, though he had 'nothing to recommend him but the vanity of calling himself a Highlander', offered to put at the New York congress's disposal a detachment of a hundred Gaelic-speaking soldiers. There were, then, MacLeod rebels as well as MacLeod loyalists, and even among the latter, as is suggested by the subsequent behaviour of men lucky enough to have survived the Moore's Creek Bridge debacle, there were some whose commitment to King George was less than total.[61]

Alexander MacLeod of Glendale, one of those who lived to tell the tale of Moore's Creek Bridge, returned to Skye with his wife and children rather than take up residence in an American republic. Several other families of the same status also left the Cape Fear River country in the later 1770s – either for Scotland or for the few North American colonies, in what is now Canada, which declined to become part of the USA. Significantly, however, no worthwhile number of the Cape Fear River country's rank-and-file MacLeods chose to do likewise. Mostly they simply hunkered down on their North Carolina homesteads and waited for America's Revolutionary War to pass them by. Unfortunately, this tactic did not always work, as I learned when visiting Martha MacLeod, a present-day descendant of eighteenth-century loyalists.

Martha lives where her loyalist ancestors also lived – on a farm near Horse's Creek in the neighbourhood of Aberdeen, North Carolina. Neil MacLeod, her great-great-grandfather, came to the Cape Fear River country from Skye in 1774. 'Neil was in his fifties when he emigrated, and had been married twice,' Martha says. 'Both his wives were dead but, between them, they had produced four sons, two grown up and two much younger. Neil brought his sons with him to America. One of the younger lads, Alex by name, was killed in the course of the troubles that followed the Battle of Moore's Creek Bridge. His brother John, my great-grandfather, was lucky not to be killed as well.'

Alex MacLeod's death resulted from his falling into the hands of patriot militiamen searching for the perpetrators of a massacre of pro-independence settlers at a place called Piney Bottom. The militia unit in question, commanded by a Captain Bogan, had descended on a farm belonging to Kenneth Clark, one of Neil MacLeod's neighbours and, as Martha MacLeod acknowledges, a known loyalist. In an attempt to get Clark, who had Argyll antecedents, to reveal the whereabouts of the men they were looking for, Bogan's troops, according to contemporary testimony, tortured the farmer 'by beating him or slapping him with their swords and [by] screwing his thumb [into] a gun lock [meaning a musket's firing mechanism] until the blood gushed out on each side'. When Kenneth Clark refused, even under duress, to provide the information Captain Bogan wanted, the captain lost his temper and decided to execute all the menfolk to be found on Clark's farm. Among those menfolk was Alex MacLeod, whose father, Neil, as Martha puts it, 'had sent him on an errand to the Clark place just before the patriot troops got there'.[62]

When setting out for Kenneth Clark's farm, Alex MacLeod, then in his teens, had invited his younger brother John, no more than eleven years old, to accompany him. 'He was just an itsy-bitsy boy at the time,' Martha MacLeod says of her great-grandfather. This, as things turned out, was to be his salvation. Seeing Captain Bogan and his militiamen approach their home, and fearing for the MacLeod lads' safety, the Clark womenfolk hid John MacLeod by shoving him up their cabin's brick-built chimney. They next tried to hide Alex, but because he was more full grown than his brother, he could not fit into the chimney alongside John. Alex was duly taken prisoner and, an hour or two later, was put to death on Captain Bogan's orders.

Accounts vary as to how exactly Alex MacLeod died. Martha believes he was shot. Some nineteenth-century sources, however, insist that Alex had his head split practically in two by a militiaman's sword – this having been the way in which victims of the Piney Bottom massacre, which Captain Bogan and his troops were out to avenge, had been dispatched by their loyalist killers.

'When he grew up,' Martha says, 'John MacLeod, my great-grandfather, married Christian Clark, a daughter of Kenneth Clark in whose chimney he was hiding the day his brother was killed.' This Clark–MacLeod marriage provides Martha's story with a happy ending of sorts and, on reaching it, she pauses. Outside, night is falling. Somewhere a dog barks. Otherwise there is silence – a silence reinforced by the nature of the room in which Martha and I are sitting. This room is raftered and panelled in dark wood. It looks, especially by American standards, extremely old. And so it is, for it was constructed, like much of the rest of Martha MacLeod's home, by Martha's great-grandfather in either 1797 or 1798 – at about the time, in other words, John MacLeod was looking to provide for his new wife.

Has she ever been to Skye, I ask Martha MacLeod. 'Yes,' she replies, 'several times.' And what did she think of it? 'I thought Skye was beautiful,' Martha says, 'really beautiful. It meant so much to me to have the chance to see it, to meet Skye folk, to hear Gaelic spoken. But what surprised me was how small Skye crofts are when compared with North Carolina farms. Most Skye crofters have to make do with just a few acres. In America, by comparison, we have so much land – land that's ours, not anybody else's. The fact that they'd managed to get hold of a piece of this land must have mattered a lot to my great-great-grandfather and his sons. I'm sure that's why, despite Alex's death, they were so intent on staying here.'

Martha, I am convinced, is right. The gentry of the clans – MacDonald of Kingsburgh, MacLeod of Glendale and the like – may have had ideologically rooted objections to becoming citizens of the United States. But such considerations did not count for much with less elevated clansfolk who, having hugely improved their prospects by emigrating to the Cape Fear River country, showed not the slightest interest in resuming their previous and all-too-precarious existences in Skye, Glenelg, Sutherland, Lewis or Harris.

'You would do well,' one of North Carolina's Gaelic-speaking settlers informed family members back in Scotland, 'to . . . take courage and come to this country.' Otherwise, the same man warned his stay-at-home kin, they would be condemned to remain for ever in the Highlands and Islands, where 'the landlord will sure be master . . . [and where] the face of the poor is kept to the grinding stone'. People holding such views, and there was no scarcity of them in the Cape Fear River country of the 1770s, were not about to accompany Alexander MacLeod of Glendale back to Scotland. To begin with, they might have been loyalists. In the end, it is safe to guess, they mostly shared the political convictions of a Skye-born emigrant whose tombstone stands outside North Carolina's Old Bethesda Presbyterian Church. 'Colin Bethune,' this Bethesda tombstone reads, 'Died 1820, aged 64. An honest man. A native of Scotland by accident, but a citizen of the US by choice.'[63]

North Carolina: Old Bethesda

Martha MacLeod's family have been associated with the Bethesda congregation since the congregation's eighteenth-century beginnings. John MacLeod, Martha's Skye-born great-grandfather, was session clerk here. Much of Martha's own life has revolved around this same church. So when Martha offers to help with my researches by organising a get-together of people of Highlands and Islands descent, the resulting gathering takes place in one of the church's meeting rooms. Twenty or so folk are in attendance. Not all of them are MacLeods by name, but all possess MacLeod ancestors and most, as a result, are members, as Martha is too, of the USA's Clan MacLeod Society.

To start with, our conversation is light hearted. Cary McLeod, a farmer, tells a story about a McLeod funeral in early-twentieth-century North Carolina. At such funerals, as had been the case long before in the Highlands and Islands, it was customary, despite the clergy's efforts to eradicate the practice, to have plenty of whiskey to hand. And on this particular occasion, it appears, the leading mourners were so 'liquored up', in Cary's phrase, they did not notice, when fording a flooded creek near the graveyard where the interment was to take place, that 'the casket containing the deceased,' as Cary puts it, 'had floated clean off the back of their wagon and was last seen headed for the Cape Fear River'. Several other such tales follow. But then, by way of getting clear exactly who is present, I ask everyone to introduce themselves – and the atmosphere is instantly serious.

I had expected that folk, on giving their names, would add little beyond their occupations. But this is not what happens. Entirely unprompted, and without even mentioning how he earns his living, Cary McLeod, to whom I have turned first, outlines his genealogy – a genealogy that extends, in Cary's case, all the way back to a pioneer forebear of more than 200 years ago. You asked me who I am, Cary is saying. Well, I'm telling you in the way that makes most sense in the context of what we're trying to accomplish this evening. I'm providing you with my name, my father's name, his father's name – with all the names that, taken together, connect me to the place my folk started out from when they left Scotland for America.

In the Gaelic-speaking Highlands and Islands from which Cary McLeod's family have been separated for seven or eight generations, a man would habitually identify himself by means of what was called his *sloinneadh* or lineage. I'm James, he'd say, son of Donald, son of James – this list extending, in some instances, through several centuries. With the possible exception of Martha MacLeod, who has been learning Gaelic, none of our Bethesda gathering's attendees is likely to be acquainted with the word sloinneadh. But instinctively, everyone makes himself or herself known in precisely the way their Highlands and Islands forebears would have done. In minutes, as a result, my note-taking gives out amid a hopelessly confusing welter of Murdochs, Williams, Kenneths, Johns and Alexanders.

Why, I ask a little despairingly, do your ancestors matter so much? Katharine McLeod, a lawyer, volunteers an answer. When she was growing up, it emerges, Katharine's name was Edna Bryan. On her marriage, it became Edna Bryan Chappell. Now Katharine is divorced, bringing up a son by herself and attempting to carve out a career in what she describes as a 'male-controlled' line of work. 'I've always been impressed by the way my McLeod ancestors handled themselves in the face of hardship and adversity,' Katharine says. 'That's why, though I don't have to confront what she confronted, I've taken my McLeod great-grandmother's name. By doing this, I guess, I'm making a statement about who I am, who I'd like to be, how I aim to live my life.'

The hardships Katharine mentions, I assume initially, were those her settler forebears encountered on their arrival here. But no. What Katharine has in mind, I discover, is her strong sense, shared by others of our group, that the community of which she is part is one that, ever since its eighteenth-century emergence, has been caught up in a protracted struggle for survival. 'We've never had it easy hereabouts,' someone comments, referring me to an embittered passage in a 1933 history of the church in whose premises we have met.

'The history of the Scot in the [Cape Fear River] country,' this passage reads, 'is one of . . . defeats and disappointments. The Scotch movement to the American colonies commenced with the migration of a limited number, who were filled with the ambition to create a new life in a new country, where wealth and freedom seemed at the command of the hopeful migrants. But before many Scotch had come this way, the unfortunate experience at Culloden changed the whole tone of the project, and later colonists were . . . compelled to leave their homes . . . More than that, their hands were tied by their oath of allegiance to the British Crown and when the time came [in 1776] to take sides in the Cape Fear uprising, the Scotch were loyal. For their loyalty they were [made] victims . . . and not until another generation had appeared . . . was the feeling between the Whigs [or pro-revolutionaries] and Tories [or loyalists] one of harmony. [Then] the smoke of the Civil War began to show. This time the Scotch elected to stand with the rest of their people, and they loyally followed the Bonnie Blue Flag [the Confederacy's battle banner]. Again disaster . . . attended them. Sherman ravaged the upper Cape Fear country . . . Reconstruction [the period of Northern-dominated rule following the Confederate surrender] . . . added another drastic chapter to the list of terrors. Finally came the war [of 1917–

18] with Germany, and the Scot stood by the Red, White and Blue [the Stars and Stripes] . . . Not only were men and means requisitioned this time, but homes and farms and land and property were taken . . . Two hundred square miles of territory were swallowed . . . on which to establish Fort Bragg . . . Twenty-five miles from east to west, and not a human habitation except the military headquarters.'[64]

Much of this line of argument can readily be demolished. Among the thousands of people from the Highlands and Islands who reached North Carolina in the eighteenth century, there were no more than a handful who had been active Jacobites. If they or other settlers came here under any degree of compulsion, such compulsion had more to do with the estate management practices of their chiefs or landlords than it had to do with policies devised by anti-Jacobite politicians. And when Cape Fear River country settlers of Highlands and Islands background were persuaded to embrace loyalism in the months prior to the Battle of Moore's Creek Bridge, little was made by anyone involved of any oaths those settlers may have taken.

Ultimately, however, none of this matters. What is important is the enduring conviction – a conviction much in evidence during my exchanges with Cary McLeod, Katharine McLeod and others at Bethesda Church – that North Carolina families of Highlands and Islands extraction in those parts have consistently had a raw deal, whether as defeated Jacobites, defeated loyalists or defeated Confederates. And what still rankles most with those folk, even though it happened nearly a century ago, is the loss of so many hard-won farms to the Fort Bragg Military Reservation – where Alex McLeod and I had searched, some days before, for the burial places of Alex's great-great-great-grandparents.

'They went through an awful lot to get here,' Katharine McLeod says of her pioneer ancestors. 'They went through still more in this country. But they hung on. They got hold of land. They cleared it, cultivated it, raised crops on it. All of that made them value their farms. They cherished every inch of those farms, every field, every tree. These things were precious to them.' Heads nod in agreement. 'But none of that stopped the US government taking our farms away,' a voice interjects. 'Maybe not,' another voice counters, 'but we're still here, aren't we? And we're still who we always were. We've got our Highland Games. We've got our clan societies. We've got our Scottish heritage.'

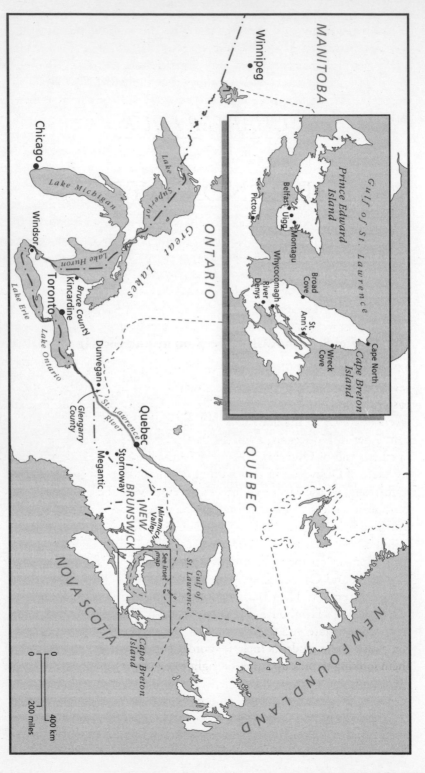

Map 3: Eastern Canada

CHAPTER FOUR

THE LAND OF TREES

Ontario and Scotland: Glengarry County and Glenelg

My journey by road from Ottawa to Dunvegan takes a couple of hours. It is October, and in the wooded country beyond the Canadian capital's eastern suburbs the sideways light from the setting sun is adding extra layers of colour to the deep reds and yellows of an Ontario fall. By the time I get to Dunvegan, a small cluster of white-painted homes at the northern end of Ontario's Glengarry County, it is almost dark. 'You'll see more of Dunvegan in the morning,' I am told by my guide, Barbara Armstrong, whose MacLeod forebears were among the county's earliest European settlers. 'This evening, all you have to do is eat supper.' It is provided by Glengarry farmer Ian MacLeod, whose home we reach five minutes later. Getting out of Barbara's car in the lee of Ian's barn, I stand for a moment on the frost-stiffened grass and watch flight after flight of southbound Canada geese pass overhead – each bird backlit by the sunset's afterglow. Then Barbara cuts her car's engine and, from inside Ian MacLeod's farmhouse, I hear the sound of fiddle music. 'Farming's in so poor a state you need a sideline,' Ian explains. 'Mine's teaching the violin.' Ian's students include more than forty young people – all of them looking to pick up tunes brought to Glengarry by people from the Highlands and Islands.

An early group of those emigrants got here in 1794 after an exceptionally protracted journey. Their leaders were Alexander MacLeod and his father, Kenneth, formerly a tacksman on Norman MacLeod of

Dunvegan's Glenelg estate. Before he left Scotland, Alexander, the 1794 expedition's principal promoter, served with the British army and, though only in his twenties when he set out for Canada, he had reached the rank of captain. Alexander MacLeod, then, was at the start of a promising career. If able to look forward confidently to inheriting his father's position, this young man would not have entertained thoughts of emigrating. By the 1790s, however, Glenelg was a place where neither tacksmen nor their sons could take anything for granted. Rents were again going up steeply. Worse, there was evidence that Glenelg might soon join the long list of Highlands and Islands districts being given over to sheep.

In Glenelg, Kenneth MacLeod tenanted two large tacks or farms. The first, Moyle, was situated at the head of Gleann Mòr, a long and then thickly populated valley. Kenneth's second tack, Caolas Mòr, bordered on Loch Hourn, a saltwater inlet marking the boundary between MacLeod of Dunvegan's Glenelg possessions and the still more extensive lands of Knoydart – owned in the 1790s, as for ages previously, by the MacDonells of Glengarry.

Kenneth MacLeod's principal residence was his Gleann Mòr farm. Hence his Gaelic designation, *Fear na Maoile*, Man of Moyle. No one now living in Glenelg knows anything of this man. But on the evening of my arrival in Glengarry County I hear a lot about Fear na Maoile from one of his Canadian descendants, Flora MacLeod Johnston. Flora is ninety-four. When young, she knew elderly men and women who, when young themselves, were told stories of Kenneth MacLeod by people who had met him. One such story reached Flora Johnston from her great-aunt, Jessie MacLeod.

'Aunt Jessie,' Flora says, 'used to speak of meeting with a woman who'd seen Fear na Maoile. When this woman was a little girl, she was left at home one day by her parents, who were going to a wedding. Upset at being abandoned, as she thought, by her folks, the little girl ran after them. Her mother, it seems, was all for sending her back to the family's cabin, but her father picked up his daughter, set her on his shoulders and took her with him to the wedding. One of the wedding guests was Fear na Maoile, Kenneth MacLeod. And when the little girl who'd ridden to the wedding on her father's shoulders became an old lady she told my Aunt Jessie, then a child, what she remembered of Kenneth. Perhaps there was more, but two things stuck in my aunt's mind. One was the fact that Fear na Maoile wore his hair long. The other was the manner in which everyone treated him – with the greatest of respect.'

In 1794, the place where this tacksman emigrant from Scotland set up home was frontier territory. Now Glengarry County, where farmers like Ian MacLeod are outnumbered by people commuting into Ottawa or equally nearby Montreal, is tamer in appearance than the terrain surrounding Kenneth MacLeod's former tack. There are no commuters in Moyle's vicinity. Take the single-track road into Glenelg from Bealach Ràtagain, and you come, after a mile or two, to a junction where a second such road, less frequented than the first, heads into a tangle of hills, the highest of them rising to around 3,000 feet. Like its neighbours, this hill is covered up to the 1,000-foot contour by plantation forestry of a sort established widely in the West Highlands during the twentieth century. Firs and spruces consequently hem in the spot where Kenneth MacLeod lived.

Towards the end of his time at Moyle, Kenneth must have heard of the uprising launched in July 1792 by some of the many Highlanders who felt themselves under threat as a result of what a contemporary commentator called 'the late and extraordinary rise in the price of sheep'. This price increase was caused by growing demand for wool – more and more of which was needed to clothe the soaring populations of England's cities. In response to the wool boom, sheep farming, previously confined to the southern half of Scotland, spread into the Highlands and Islands. This gave financially hard-pressed lairds a welcome chance to add instantly to their incomes. 'The demand for the raw material of wool by the English manufacturers,' a leading estate manager observed, 'enabled the Highland proprietor to let his lands for quadruple the amount they ever before produced to him.' Sheep duly began to replace the cattle on which the agricultural economy of the Highlands and Islands previously depended.[1]

This development was disastrous from the standpoint of tacksmen like the MacLeods of Moyle, and more disastrous from the standpoint of this group's subtenants. Few tacksmen possessed the capital, skills or inclination to engage in sheep production, and the incoming sheep farmers who now began to take the tacksmen's place mostly wanted to get rid of subtenantries of the traditional type – 'a single unmarried shepherd and a couple of sheepdogs,' as was pointed out, '[being] inhabitants sufficient for the most extensive sheep-walk'.[2]

This accounts for the unrest engendered across the Highlands and Islands by sheep farming's northward expansion – unrest which exploded into open rebellion when, in 1792, people in Easter Ross banded together with the aim of expelling sheep and sheep farmers from their neighbourhood. Especially because it followed hard on the heels of the violence unleashed in France by that country's revolution, this Easter Ross outbreak met with a stern response from the authorities. Troops were rushed north and, much to the relief of Ross-shire's sheriff, who had feared that 'laws and government' were about to be 'set at defiance', Easter Ross's anti-sheep protests were rapidly crushed.[3]

Easter Ross, which borders the Cromarty Firth, was a long ride from Glenelg. But events there are likely to have been followed closely by Kenneth MacLeod of Moyle and his son, Captain Alexander. As it happened, Ross-shire's staunchly pro-establishment sheriff, Donald MacLeod of Geanies, a descendant of the MacLeods who had once been in charge of Assynt, was the Moyle family's fellow clansman. Despite this, it may be that Alexander and Kenneth felt some sympathy for Sheriff Donald's antagonists. During the 1780s, after all, Moyle's MacLeods were well placed to observe sheep farming's advance across nearby Knoydart, and what they witnessed had been anything but comforting.

When, in 1785 or thereby, Alexander MacDonell of Glengarry put large parts of his Knoydart estate under sheep, the main beneficiary was a Dumfries-shire farmer called Thomas Gillespie. At the Glengarry laird's invitation, Gillespie took the tenancy of 'a tract of land' reckoned in 1803 to be 'upwards of twenty miles' across. From this expanse, by one means or another, dozens of families were removed in the 1780s and subsequently. Thus there was initiated a depopulating process so far reaching as to have ensured that nobody in today's Knoydart can trace his or her ancestry from folk who lived there in the eighteenth century. In Ontario's Glengarry County, in contrast, Knoydart ancestries are common. This is because the county was the most popular destination of people set adrift by Thomas Gillespie.[4]

The beginnings of emigration from Knoydart to Glengarry County are bound up with America's Revolutionary War – particularly with the war's impact on a group of MacDonell tacksmen. They were drawn from the original Glengarry, east of Knoydart, as well as from Knoydart itself, and they emigrated in the early 1770s to the Mohawk Valley in what is now upstate New York. Like their counterparts in North Carolina, those tacksmen opposed American independence, becoming guerrilla fighters on the British side in the conflict which began in 1775. Because they fought Britain's American enemies, the Mohawk Valley's MacDonells had little choice, when the Revolutionary War ended in Britain's defeat, but to get out of what had become the United States and accept an offer of a piece of territory in Ontario, then the still British colony of Upper Canada. Naming their new home after their old one, the people who settled this territory called it Glengarry. Further loyalist refugees soon made their way there and, as had happened in the Cape Fear River country, the community thus established went on to attract other emigrants who came from the same Scottish localities as its founders. Inevitably, many of those emigrants were casualties, or people who feared they might become casualties, of the upheavals associated with the introduction of sheep farming.

In a pamphlet touching on the manner in which sheep farming's expansion contributed to emigration from the north of Scotland, a writer of the time commented: 'This plan of improvement has put the whole Highlands into commotion. They who are deprived of [their] possessions . . . feel a reluctance in settling anywhere else, conceive a disgust at their country, and therefore prefer leaving it.' That was what occurred in Knoydart. At about the time of Thomas Gillespie's arrival there, many Knoydart people decided to join the Knoydart folk already resident in Glengarry County.[5]

Among those emigrants was Angus MacDonald of Munial. His Knoydart tack was separated from Kenneth MacLeod's Caolas Mòr farm only by the narrow waters of Loch Hourn. It is probable, therefore, that Angus of Munial was known to Kenneth of Moyle and his son, Captain Alexander. But the Moyle family's sources of information about Glengarry County would not have been limited to such continuing contact as they may have had with their former neighbour. Captain Alexander's wife was a MacDonell who had relatives in Upper Canada, and thanks to earlier MacLeod–MacDonell marriages, Glengarry County's other settlers included cousins or second cousins of Captain Alexander's father. At this time, when writing an account of his parish and its circumstances, Glenelg's Church of Scotland minister mentioned 'flattering accounts' of North America which Glenelg people had received from 'friends' who had already emigrated. It is by no means impossible that the recipients of such letters – all of them doubtless full of Glengarry County's praises – included Moyle's tacksman and his army-officer son.[6]

By 1793, Glenelg's minister continued, much of Knoydart had been occupied by sheep farmers, and Glenelg, where a farm on MacLeod of Dunvegan's estate had been let to a sheep-farming tenant, was going the same way. 'Emigration is thought to be owing in a great measure to the introduction of sheep,' the minister added, 'and if the rage for this mode of farming goes on . . . it is to be apprehended emigration will still increase.' Those words were written in Glenelg's Church of Scotland manse within months of the MacLeods of Moyle leaving Glenelg for Glengarry County on a ship which, as well as conveying the Moyle family to Canada, carried another 120 emigrants.[7]

Captain Alexander MacLeod, 'having determined on emigrating', as he wrote later, travelled 'twice from Glenelg to Greenock' in the spring of 1793 with the aim of chartering a vessel. Once he found a suitable craft, the captain instructed the vessel's skipper to proceed to Glenelg – which the skipper reached on 12 June. For the next three days, while his chartered ship lay at anchor in the vicinity of the slipway used today by the ferry connecting Glenelg with Skye, Alexander supervised the embarkation of his passengers. On 15 June, with everyone safely aboard, he ordered the ship's master to set sail. Neither Alexander MacLeod nor his travelling companions would see Glenelg again – the finality of Captain Alexander's break with Scotland being underlined by the fact that all his close relatives chose to go with him to Canada. Aboard the captain's chartered vessel, then, were three generations of the Moyle family: Alexander himself, his wife and their three small children; Alexander's tacksman father, Kenneth; Alexander's sisters, Mary and Christine; and lastly Alexander's cousin, Norman MacLeod, accompanied by his teenage son.[8]

Since it was summer and since Alexander MacLeod had taken care to hire a seaworthy ship, this 1793 voyage from Glenelg to North America should have been straightforward. That was not how it turned out. About 'half way across the Atlantic,' Alexander recalled, his vessel 'encountered a most tremendous storm which caused her to spring a very dangerous leak'. Their best hope of survival, Captain Alexander and his passengers were informed by the ship's master, lay in an immediate return to Scotland. Several weeks out of Glenelg, therefore, Alexander MacLeod found himself back in Greenock where he 'remained for more than a fortnight . . . until . . . some other vessel could be got ready'. Nor was this the end of Alexander's troubles. His new ship 'had not been out more than four days when a heavy squall of wind carried away her upper masts and sails'. Again there was no alternative but to backtrack – with the result that Captain Alexander's third attempt on the Atlantic did not begin until 1 November.[9]

This meant it was well into winter when the Glenelg emigrants arrived in the Gulf of St Lawrence, where they encountered, in Alexander MacLeod's words, 'a severe snowstorm and excessively cold weather'. With 'a foot of ice on their [ship's] decks', according to Glengarry County tradition, and with access to Upper Canada barred by the freezing over of the St Lawrence River, Captain Alexander and his party had no option but to seek shelter in the nearest harbour – at Charlottetown, Prince Edward Island. There the Glenelg people, some of whom must have wondered if they would have done better to remain in Scotland, spent several months waiting for navigation to resume on the St Lawrence. At last, in May 1794 and on yet another chartered ship, Alexander MacLeod was able to recommence his journey: sailing up the St Lawrence, by way of Quebec, to Glengarry; reaching his destination a full year after his departure from Glenelg.[10]

Somewhere between Glenelg and Glengarry County, Captain Alexander's wife died. In time, however, the captain remarried, and by 1837, when he set down what he remembered of his voyage from Scotland, Captain Alexander, as he put it, had 'been blessed by providence . . . with a family of eleven sons . . . and three daughters'. Equal progress had been made by other members of the captain's emigrant party. 'Having obtained a grant each of 200 acres of land,' he reported, 'they all settled down on their respective lots [or farms] and are now a thriving and numerous body.'[11]

On the evening I arrive in Glengarry County, Flora MacLeod Johnston gives me a photocopied extract from a June 1794 issue of the *Montreal Gazette*. This notes the arrival in Quebec of the schooner *Charlot*, ten days out from Prince Edward Island and carrying 'Mr [Alexander] McCloud [sic] and family, with 115 or 120 men, women and children'. From Quebec, Flora says, her emigrant forebears sailed on to Montreal, where, for the last leg of their St Lawrence voyage, they transferred to several small boats. Not far beyond Montreal, Flora points out, are the Lachine Rapids. Here the Glenelg emigrants would have had to disembark and carry their boats and belongings overland. This last obstacle surmounted, there followed a final passage upstream to Lancaster, where a riverside jetty gave access, as a similar jetty still does, to Glengarry County.

When in Montreal, Captain Alexander's party would have had contact with the British colonial authorities who dealt with land-grant matters. But the land the new arrivals had been allocated was well to the north of Glengarry's St Lawrence River frontage, and the 120-strong emigrant contingent from Glenelg must have had guidance from earlier settlers as to how to get there. A trek of twenty miles or more now followed. At its end, the tired – but surely jubilant – settlers sat down on the ground to eat a meal. 'Their table,' Flora McLeod Johnston says of those settlers, who included her great-great-great-grandfather and two of her great-great-grandparents, 'was a flat stone which is still to be seen, and while gathered around this stone, Captain Alexander and his people were joined by a band of Indians who were invited to sit down beside them and share their food.'

My accommodation in Glengarry County is provided by Dougal and Helen MacLeod. Both are of Highland extraction – Dougal's ancestors having come to Canada from Glenelg in 1794, Helen's having left Lochaber in 1802. Dougal is a dairy farmer and, long before I come down to breakfast at 7 a.m., he is attending to his cattle. 'We thought you'd like to have someone show you round,' Helen says, serving one of the generous meals that punctuate my Clan MacLeod travels. 'Your guide will be Madeleine McCrimmon.'

Before eight, Madeleine and I embark on a tour of places with emigrant associations. By way of MacLeod Road, we reach Glenelg Road, now a paved highway but originally a trail connecting the homesteads established by Captain Alexander's party and by people who followed them. 'My folks left Glenelg in 1816,' Madeleine tells me as we approach Dunvegan, where, though the tourist season is over, the Glengarry Pioneer Museum has been opened for my benefit.

Housed in a set of log buildings of the sort Madeleine's ancestors constructed on getting to Upper Canada, Dunvegan's museum features tools, agricultural implements and other objects of the sort any settler community required to get itself established. Some items, such as hand-operated mills used for grinding small amounts of grain, are modelled on Scottish precursors. Others are distinctively Canadian. Among the latter is a horse-drawn sleigh of a type that was once the standard means of winter transport in this part of North America. 'The sleighbells fitted to Glengarry sleighs were made locally and gave out a really distinctive sound,' Madeleine remarks. 'When Glengarry farmers drove their sleighs into Montreal, Montrealers would hear this sound in the distance and they'd know the Glengarry men were coming to trade with them.'

Not far from Dunvegan, at Kirkhill, I am taken to see Captain Alexander's tombstone in the graveyard of St Columba's Presbyterian Church. Next, Madeleine McCrimmon and I head for the spot where, in 1965, members of Glengarry's Clan MacLeod Society erected their own monument to Captain Alexander MacLeod and his fellow emigrants. As we inspect this neatly maintained memorial, which stands at the end of the dirt track giving access to Captain Alexander's former farm, a yellow school bus slows and stops beside us. A fourteen-year-old girl steps out and, joining Madeleine and me, introduces herself. Her name, she says, is Kaitlin MacLeod, and she is Captain Alexander's great-great-great-great-granddaughter.

Minutes later, I am in the farmhouse kitchen belonging to Kaitlin's father, George MacLeod. On one of George's walls hangs a portrait of Captain Alexander's son, Norman Roy or *Tormod Ruadh*, George's great-great-grandfather. In George's basement, as he shows me, is a heavy iron cauldron which, tradition insists, was brought here from Captain Alexander's original home in faraway Moyle. Outside in the yard, as George also shows me, is the flat-topped granite boulder where, as I heard the previous evening from Flora Johnston, Captain Alexander and his companions laid out the meal they ate to celebrate their arrival in their new homeland.

That night, my Glengarry hosts, Helen and Dougal MacLeod, invite the people I have met to join us for supper. 'What most interested you about what you've seen and heard?' Helen asks. The fact that someone like Kaitlin MacLeod is resident today on a farm first occupied by her great-great-great-great-grandfather, I reply. There is surprise at this. Surely that sort of thing is common where I come from, Helen remarks. But it is not. In much of the Highlands and Islands, dislocation of the sort which caused Captain Alexander MacLeod to come to Canada was so extensive as to make it unusual to find families living on land their forebears cultivated in the eighteenth century.

Of course, Glengarry County too has experienced social change. Because of movement into this part of Ontario from the neighbouring province of Quebec, today's Glengarry is more of an ethnic mix than it used to be. But for a hundred or more years after the commencement of white settlement, this locality consisted, in effect, of Highlands and Islands communities transplanted to North America – a point made repeatedly by contemporary observers. 'Go not to Glengarry if you be not a Highlandman,' prospective emigrants to Upper Canada were warned by one early-nineteenth-century writer. 'Glengarry,' another commentator noted in 1824, 'is . . . inhabited chiefly by Scotch Highlanders who, though they have been many years in Canada, not only speak the Gaelic language but retain much of their original character and customs.' A quarter of a century later, Canadian census takers echoed this point. Of the 17,596 people living in Glengarry County in 1852, they reported, more than three-quarters had either been born in the Highlands and Islands or were of Highlands and Islands descent. One Glengarrian in six was a MacDonell or a MacDonald. Over 400 were MacLeods.[12]

Some of those MacLeods belonged to families who came to Upper Canada with Captain Alexander MacLeod in 1794. Others were products of later emigrations. To begin with, those consisted mostly of folk with Glenelg connections. In 1816 and 1832, however, parties of emigrants reached Glengarry County from the Bracadale area of Skye. Among the second of these groups was a widower, Calum MacLeod, who brought with him five sons and a daughter. In Calum's possession when he arrived in Canada were an axe and a crosscut saw. Those were tools which neither Calum MacLeod nor anyone else would have been in the habit of using in treeless Bracadale. But axes and saws, as Calum must have known when he quit Skye, were basic to the task of creating a farm from a Glengarry land grant – which, when awarded, was likely to consist of virgin forest.[13]

In the Highlands and Islands, especially in the Hebrides, extensive woodland ceased to exist in the Middle Ages or earlier. As was noted by an early visitor to Glengarry County, emigrants from those places were consequently 'unacquainted with the methods by which a practised woodsman can find his way through the trackless forest'. Even the shortest journey could, and often did, end in catastrophe. 'In new settlements,' according to a clergyman who knew Glengarry County well, 'nothing is more common than for persons to lose themselves in the woods . . . When a person is lost, he becomes quite bewildered and stupefied. East from west, and north from south, can no longer be distinguished, and anxiety takes possession of the mind, hurrying one forward, probably in the wrong direction.'[14]

Present-day Glengarry is well wooded. But its tree cover consists now of sadly shrunken descendants of the enormous pines and oaks discovered here by the 1794 pioneers and their successors. Those trees took several generations to remove. Well into the nineteenth century, Glengarry's fields were 'dotted with huge stumps', and many of its farms were little more than clearances in the wilderness. 'There is forest everywhere,' a Glengarry man commented in Victorian times. 'It lines up close and thick along the road, and here and there quite overshadows it. It crowds in upon the little farms and shuts them off from one another and from the world outside, and peers in through the little windows of the log houses looking so small and so lonely.'[15]

'An emigrant set down in such a scene,' it was acknowledged in the early nineteenth century, 'feels almost the helplessness of a child.' Not only was his new environment alien and frightening but his knowledge of how to master this environment was also hopelessly second-hand and incomplete. Calum MacLeod may have purchased an axe and saw before setting out for Upper Canada from Skye. But he would have had no notion of how to bring down a 150-foot high tree; of how to direct its fall; of how to avoid the crippling, even fatal, injuries to which many of Glengarry's aspiring woodsmen fell victim in the course of their first season.[16]

What one Glengarrian called his community's 'fight with the forest', then, was less a single battle than a war. This war was won, however. 'I do not think it is possible,' members of a committee of the British House of Commons were told by a Canadian in 1841, 'that any colony . . . can furnish such numerous instances of competence, affluence and independence . . . as are to be met with in Upper Canada.' Referring in particular to the Highlands and Islands families who had settled Glengarry County, another of the committee's informants said: 'Many of them have excellent farms . . . are possessed of considerable wealth, and live in comfort . . . on their own property.' That last phrase is crucial. The most important thing about their new country, as far as Glengarry's settlers were concerned, was the fact that their hard-won homesteads were theirs and theirs alone. '*Fhuair sinn bailtean dhuinn fhìn,*' runs a song which one of those settlers, Anna Gillis, composed in honour of *Canada Ard*, Upper Canada: 'We got farms of our own [here] with proprietary rights . . . and landlords will no more oppress us.'[17]

India and Egypt

In 1772, at the prompting of Colonel John MacLeod of Talisker, the eighteen-year-old Norman MacLeod moved into Dunvegan Castle, where he was intent, again at the colonel's instigation, on becoming a locally resident chief of the sort Clan MacLeod had not known for the best part of a century. Soon, however, Norman grew disenchanted with the role John of Talisker wanted him to fulfil. 'I remained at home with my . . . clan till the end of 1774,' he wrote later. 'But I confess that I consider this the most gloomy period of my life. Educated in a liberal manner, fired with ambition, fond of society, I found myself in confinement in a remote corner of the world – without any hope of extinguishing the debts of my family or of ever emerging from poverty and obscurity.'[18]

Concluding that no amount of penny pinching on his part would make any difference to borrowings amounting to nearly twenty times the annual rental of his Glenelg, Skye and Harris estates, Chief Norman decided he would do better, both by himself and his clan, to leave Skye and take paid employment. In 1775, Norman accordingly applied for, and obtained, a captaincy in a regiment raised by his cousin, Simon Fraser of Lovat, for service in North America – where Britain, that spring, was being drawn into fighting which soon escalated into the Revolutionary War.

Norman MacLeod's involvement in this war was quickly over. The convoy which his regiment joined when ordered to America in May 1776 was dispersed by an Atlantic storm. Left without an escort, Norman's troopship was seized by an American privateer, and he was taken prisoner. His captivity lasted until 1778, when he was freed in the course of a prisoner exchange. Barred by the terms of this exchange from further service in America, the MacLeod chief was posted to India.

Norman of Dunvegan was by no means the first MacLeod to step ashore in India. Nor was he the last. During the eighteenth and nineteenth centuries, Britain's Indian empire, as Sir Walter Scott remarked in 1821, became something of a 'corn chest for Scotland' – a place where landed families endeavoured to replenish fortunes diminished or destroyed by overspending of the sort that had made Chief Norman's position so precarious. Some Indian-based Scots, such as the founders of the Calcutta trading house known as MacLeod and Company, went into commerce. Others became imperial administrators and civil servants. A third group were, like Chief Norman, soldiers.[19]

One such was Captain William MacLeod who served alongside his chief in Madras in the 1780s and who could trace his descent from Chief Norman's remote predecessor, Ruaraidh Mòr. Captain William's son, grandson and great-grandson were to follow him into Britain's Indian army. The last of these was Lieutenant-General Sir Donald Kenneth MacLeod. His military career began on India's North West Frontier and culminated during the Second World War when General Sir Donald was one of the men in charge of defending British India from its Japanese invaders. Donald Kenneth

MacLeod thus witnessed the beginning of the end of the empire his great-grandfather had helped bring into existence – for, despite the collapse of Japan in 1945, the British presence in India did not survive the 1940s.[20]

In retirement, Donald Kenneth MacLeod went to live in Skye. Lots of the MacLeod military men the Highlands and Islands produced between the eighteenth century and the twentieth did not have this opportunity. Thousands of them are buried in North America, the West Indies, continental Europe, North Africa, the Middle East and southern Asia. In many instances, nothing is known of those soldiers – not even their names. Occasionally, however, individual MacLeods are mentioned in circumstances so unusual as to make one long to know more of what became of them. In this category is John MacLeod who, because of his leadership role in an army mutiny which took place in Edinburgh in 1779, was sentenced 'to receive one thousand lashes on his bare back'. Equally intriguing is the case of an early-nineteenth-century infantryman called Donald MacLeod. He came from Lewis, or just possibly Skye, and he was taken prisoner by Turkish troops during a failed British expedition to Egypt in 1807. Some years later, when encountered by William Yates, an English visitor to Cairo, this Gaelic-speaking Hebridean had become an Arabic-speaking Muslim who went by the name of Osman.[21]

'By reason of his intimate acquaintance with the people [of Egypt], their country and their language,' Yates wrote of Osman, 'he was enabled to render himself useful to all European travellers.' As a result, Yates went on, Osman had accumulated 'considerable' wealth and 'raised [himself] to a society far above that which [his] rank and education entitled him to expect'. The former soldier's conversion to Islam, though it might have had its origins in an attempt to escape the virtual slavery awaiting captured Christians, was thought by William Yates to be sincere. 'He evidently continued where he was by choice,' Yates commented of Osman, 'so I cannot suppose that he had many ties or connections in his own country or that absence from his native land materially disturbed his thoughts . . . He was a tall, fine man of about fifty years of age, with rather a stern aspect, fair, clear complexion and powerful limbs . . . In spite of the disguise occasioned by [his wearing] the long, loose, flowing robes of the East, it required but little penetration to discern the steady, firm and resolute look, and undaunted, determined demeanour of the Scottish Highlander . . . I have often asked Osman to tell me a little about himself; but I remarked that he always endeavoured to change the subject. I did not press it. Possibly the recital of his tale would have occasioned the recollection of many who were dear to him . . . and knew not even that he lived.'[22]

Scotland: Skye

In India, Norman MacLeod of Dunvegan was a success. He helped expand British power in the south of the country, and in the course of campaigns waged against Mysore's native rulers reached the rank of major-general. By the mid-1780s, in consequence, Clan MacLeod's chief was earning the then astronomical sum of £6,000 annually. In addition to his salary, he had been granted a share of the cash yielded by the sale of booty taken during the Mysore fighting. This share amounted, the general's son and successor claimed, to 'about £100,000' – equivalent to more than £6 million today. On his return to Dunvegan from India in 1789, therefore, Norman MacLeod should have been able to make good the damage done to his family's finances by his predecessors in the MacLeod chieftainship. He did not do so, however. A large part of General Norman's fortune, again according to his son, was gambled away before he left India. The rest, and more besides, was spent by the general in the course of the political career on which he embarked as soon as he got back to Scotland.[23]

In 1790, Norman MacLeod became MP for Inverness-shire. He began by adhering to the policies of the government of the day. This government was headed by William Pitt, whose leading ally in Scotland, Henry Dundas, had been instrumental in securing the Dunvegan laird's election. Backbench members of parliament in eighteenth-century Britain were unpaid. But his record in India, Inverness-shire's new MP thought, entitled him to a salaried post of some kind. When no such post was offered, Norman MacLeod fell out with the ruling ministry. 'After having shown every wish to be of use to the government,' he informed Henry Dundas in May 1791, 'and having been so injuriously treated . . . you cannot be surprised if my attachment ceases.' 'From that day until his last hour,' General Norman's son recalled, 'he continued to be one of the most determined opposers of Mr Pitt's administration.' During 1792, in consequence, Norman joined an Edinburgh-based organisation which William Pitt considered a threat to the stability of the state.[24]

This organisation, the Friends of the People, had been launched that summer with the aim of getting the United Kingdom to embrace democratic reform of the type underway in revolutionary France. As a member of the Friends of the People, then, Clan MacLeod's chief was aligning himself with forces set on destroying constitutional arrangements which kept political processes under aristocratic control – by ensuring, for example, that Inverness-shire's electorate consisted of no more than twenty members of the county's landed gentry. Most people of his own class, it followed, now thought Norman MacLeod beyond the pale. Lewis's owner, Francis MacKenzie of Seaforth, described him in 1793 as 'universally disliked'. The

MacLeod chief's pro-reform stance, MacKenzie continued, was founded solely on his desire to be 'revenged' on William Pitt 'for refusing him [the position] his overweening vanity thought his due'. As for the pro-reform philosophy Norman elaborated in a series of speeches and pamphlets, it consisted, Lewis's laird maintained, of 'scraps and saws of political knowledge picked up in alehouses and fermented in debauchery'.[25]

Norman MacLeod may have been inclined, as MacKenzie alleged, to drink too much. And had he been given the government job he craved, he is unlikely to have aligned himself with the Friends of the People. But Norman, for all that, appears to have embraced the cause of reform with genuine passion and to have argued the reform case with skill. Reflecting some years previously on his 'excellent' education, the MacLeod chief had remarked, 'I acquired [in youth] a taste for reading and a desire of general knowledge which has never left me.' Something of this is evident in Norman's writings on the need for democratic change. Also evident in those writings is their author's growing sense of solidarity with the shoemakers, carpenters, shopkeepers and other ordinary folk in whose company he found himself at gatherings of the Friends of the People. 'I particularly rejoice that my countrymen of every rank are well informed,' General MacLeod commented. 'It has been my proud boast . . . that I could scarcely meet with a farmer or tradesman in Scotland with whom I could not enjoy a rational, instructive and well-supported conversation. Such a people are marked by the finger of God to possess, sooner or later, the fullest share of liberty.'[26]

His purse, sword and influence were at their service, Norman MacLeod told the Friends of the People. Neither monarchs nor parliaments should possess unrestricted authority, he declared: 'Sovereignty is derived from the people . . . All the powers lodged in the King, Lords and Commons . . . proceed from the people and ought to be exercised only for their good.'[27]

Such sentiments were commonplace in republican France. They were equally commonplace in the newly independent United States, whose first president, George Washington, Norman MacLeod is said to have met – and talked with – when Washington was a rebel commander and Norman was a prisoner in America. Conservative Britons like Henry Dundas and William Pitt, however, thought the MacLeod chief's opinions dangerously extreme. Government agents were instructed to open Norman's mail and to report to ministers on its contents. Consideration was also given to charging Inverness-shire's MP with sedition. This was not done. But in an attempt to discredit both Norman MacLeod and the Friends of the People, Henry Dundas or one of his acolytes put into circulation a story to the effect that the MacLeod chief, when with the army in India, had embezzled public funds. And when a general election fell due in 1796, Dundas took care to ensure, first, that Norman was deprived of his parliamentary seat and, second, that his attempt to find an alternative seat in England came to nothing.

In 1798, when Irish rebels launched a French-backed uprising intended to bring about Ireland's independence, Norman was mentioned in France as a possible member of the republican government which French politicians believed would seize power in Scotland if, as the same politicians hoped, the Irish crisis precipitated a wider disintegration of the United Kingdom. Had Clan MacLeod's chief actually assumed a prominent role in a Scottish republic, much of what occurred subsequently on his Highlands and Islands estates might not have happened. As it was, the Irish rebellion failed and a republican Scotland never got on to history's agenda. Instead, a deeply demoralised Norman MacLeod was left to wrestle with a financial crisis which, by the later 1790s, was becoming every bit as desperate as the one he had inherited from his long-dead grandfather.

The £15,000 which Norman squandered on his doomed attempt to become an English MP was just one of numerous outlays the MacLeod chief sanctioned in the course of his political involvements. Inevitably, those outlays had a negative impact on the viability of his estates – this impact being all the more disappointing from the standpoint of Chief Norman's land managers because it followed hard on the heels of the drastic, but reasonably successful, steps they had taken with a view to getting the Dunvegan books back into some sort of balance.

In the mid-1770s, when Norman MacLeod left Skye to join the army, his debts, if expressed in present-day terms, were in excess of £2 million, and interest payments on those debts accounted for more than two-thirds of his estate's annual rental. By living for the next fifteen years on his military salary, by authorising the sale of Harris in 1779 and by permitting further sales – of Skeabost, Lynedale, Edinbane, Coisletter and Trumpan in Skye – during 1781, Norman helped greatly to improve the overall position. With his return from India, however, matters began to deteriorate once more. Like his grandfather, Clan MacLeod's chief was duly obliged to raise his tacksmen's rents. Also like his grandfather, Norman found himself confronting something akin to a rent strike on his tacksmen's part.[28]

Back in 1777, a year or so after Norman MacLeod of Dunvegan had fallen into American hands, his tacksmen in Harris, Skye and Glenelg volunteered to increase their annual rent payments by 7.5 per cent. They did so, Norman's tacksmen observed in the course of a circular agreed among them, 'to show [their] attachment to the [chief's] family' and in the hope of contributing to the 'preservation' of the MacLeod estate. 'A more touching proof of his clan's devotion could hardly be conceived,' one of Norman MacLeod's descendants commented of this gesture. But the tacksmen who made it – men who had previously been pressing hard for rent reductions – were not motivated solely by a sentimental regard for their young chieftain. Hard-headed calculation played its part. Many MacLeod tacksmen had themselves lent substantial sums to Norman's grandfather, Old Norman. Now those same tacksmen were intent on staving off a bankruptcy which, by depriving them of any chance of getting their money back, would have ruined them every bit as comprehensively as it would have ruined Old Norman's heir. The helping hand they extended to Young Norman MacLeod, then, was no disinterested act of generosity. The relative stability resulting from the 1777 agreement went a long way to facilitating the land sales which made it possible for Young Norman's business advisers to settle with the chief's tacksmen creditors.[29]

It is significant in this context that when, in the 1790s, General Norman MacLeod MP, as Young Norman had become, began to experience renewed financial difficulty, his tacksmen, far from rushing to their chief's aid, were unanimously unhelpful. From Glenelg, in the early part of 1791, the general's factor reported an 'almost total want of success in collecting the rents'. 'I did not meet with one of the tacksmen who did not profess inability [to meet his obligations],' the factor went on. Since Glenelg's total rental was about to go up by more than 130 per cent, this is not surprising. Nor is it surprising that, faced by rent increases of this magnitude, many of Chief Norman's Glenelg tenants decided to join the Canada-bound emigration led by Captain Alexander MacLeod. So complete was the Glenelg exodus precipitated by Captain Alexander's departure for Glengarry County, in fact, that one of the MacLeod chief's agents professed himself unable to establish who exactly was entitled to occupy land in that locality. Because 'a great number' of 'the original possessors' had left for Canada the year before, this man noted in 1794, 'few or none' of Glenelg's tenants held formal leases. Some tenants could produce 'lines' or letters authorising them to take over particular landholdings. But this was exceptional – 'as the lands were given to any who would take them when the original people . . . emigrated'.[30]

In the later 1790s, with General Norman's financial position continuing to deteriorate, a new round of land sales began. A planned sale of Glenelg was put on hold in the expectation – fulfilled ten years later – that the 'prevalent sheep-farming rage' would eventually produce 'a considerable . . . augmentation' in its price. However, the Waternish peninsula and the neighbouring islands of Isay and Mingay were sold in 1796. These were peripheral parts of Chief Norman's Skye estate. But in 1799, when Orbost, Skinidin, Colbost and part of Glendale were disposed of, the break-up of the general's Skye properties started to affect localities within sight of Dunvegan Castle.[31]

In 1801, General Norman MacLeod died and was succeeded by his teenage son, John Norman. The new chief's inheritance promised little. It certainly held out no prospect of Clan MacLeod's underpinning social structure surviving in anything like its traditional shape. Perhaps the most striking evidence of the clan's accelerating disintegration is to be found in the disappearance of tacksman families of the sort once central to the Skye and Glenelg scene. As John Norman's chieftainship commenced, those MacLeod tacksmen who had not already taken up a career in the military or emigrated to North America were, with just a handful of exceptions, contemplating an early departure.

The exceptions consisted of the few individuals who, by turning their tacks into sheep farms, managed to secure agricultural incomes big enough to enable them to meet the rent demands responsible for driving away so many of their counterparts. Prominent among this new breed of sheep farming tacksmen were the MacLeods of Arnisdale in Glenelg and the MacAskills of Rubh' an Dunain in Skye. Writing of Donald of Arnisdale, whom he visited in 1803, James Hogg, himself a sheep farmer turned novelist and poet, commented: 'His conversation was much confined to that which suited me best, namely sheep farming.' In addition to tenanting the Glenelg tack on which he had followed his father, Hogg noted of Donald MacLeod that he was 'possessed of two large farms in Glenshiel [four or five miles east of Glenelg] . . . which he had lately taken at the yearly rent of £600'. By moving into sheep farming, then, Arnisdale's tacksman had become seriously prosperous. His Rubh' an Dunain contemporary, Kenneth MacAskill, by following the same course, made himself even wealthier.[32]

Rubh' an Dunain, situated at the south-western tip of the Cuillin, four or five miles beyond Glen Brittle, is nowadays uninhabited and can be reached only on foot or by boat. But when Kenneth MacAskill was growing up here towards the close of the eighteenth century, Rubh' an Dunain – its name signifying a fortified promontory – had been home to his MacAskill ancestors for hundreds of years. Kenneth's people, like the MacLeods of Dunvegan, were reputedly of Norse origin and the two families appear to have been linked from the time of their arrival in Skye. Today, that association is reflected in the fact that people called MacAskill are said, in the jargon employed by authorities on these matters, to belong to a sept, or branch, of Clan MacLeod – MacAskills or McCaskills consequently providing a substantial proportion of Clan MacLeod Society membership in the United States and elsewhere. Historically, however, relationships between the Rubh' an Dunain MacAskills and their Dunvegan counterparts were more complicated than is suggested by the notion of the former having been a subset of the latter. In the Middle Ages, Rubh' an Dunain's MacAskill occupants might have been semi-autonomous allies of the MacLeods rather than their subordinates. During the seventeenth and eighteenth centuries, however, the MacAskills lost any independence they possessed and became tacksmen of Clan MacLeod's Dunvegan-based chiefs. As such, they might be expected to have done as most tacksmen did and remove themselves from the Hebrides. Instead, at the start of the nineteenth century and in the person of Kenneth MacAskill, the first Skyeman to become a sheep farmer on any scale, the Rubh' an Dunain family mounted a successful comeback.

In the period just after 1800, by taking over land vacated by other tacksmen, Kenneth MacAskill made himself master of a large slice of the territory still belonging to the MacLeods of Dunvegan. On the enormous acreage thus brought under his control, Kenneth pastured huge numbers of sheep – and did so very profitably. For the most part, this was to the advantage of Kenneth MacAskill's landlord, John Norman MacLeod of Dunvegan, to whom Kenneth paid thousands of pounds annually in rent. But if money flowed from Kenneth MacAskill to the MacLeod chief, power flowed in the opposite direction. The more he became reliant financially on Kenneth MacAskill, the more John Norman was obliged to allow his principal tenant to take land-management decisions of a kind usually reserved to lairds – including decisions as to what was to be done with the hundreds of families who had lived for generations in localities Kenneth was anxious to turn over to his flocks. In the end, many such families were removed from their homes at the instigation of Kenneth MacAskill or his successors. Might John Norman MacLeod have prevented dispossessions and evictions of this type? Arguably, yes, but he did not. John Norman, after all, had a vested interest in the success of Kenneth MacAskill's sheep-farming ventures. Besides, in the early-nineteenth-century Highlands and Islands, it was taken for granted that the generality of folk could be uprooted if their social superiors so decreed.

The consequences of such thinking are illustrated by developments on the Skye estate belonging to the now ennobled MacDonalds of Sleat. There the second Lord MacDonald had 'no objection', it was announced in 1802, 'to try[ing] one or two sheep farms on a proper scale'. Since most MacDonald tacksmen of the old sort had left Skye and since incoming sheep farmers were satisfied with nothing less than vacant possession of several thousand acres, Lord MacDonald's projected sheep farms could not be created without ejecting the people residing on them. The population movements which followed, however, were not intended to result in the affected families leaving Skye – where, as Lord MacDonald's advisers were well aware, those families could be directed into an activity even more lucrative than sheep rearing. This activity was kelp making. Kelp is a type of seaweed.

Around 1800, however, the same term was applied to a crude industrial alkali manufactured from it – this alkali then being much in demand by southern manufacturers specialising in the production of materials like soap and glass.[33]

Making kelp was difficult. First, the growing seaweed had to be cut from semi-submerged rocks, brought ashore and dried. Next, the dried weed had to be incinerated in purpose-built kilns. Finally, the resulting kelp, an ash-like substance, had to be shipped to buyers in ports like Glasgow and Liverpool. Kelpers, as kelp makers were known, consequently worked long hours in dreadful conditions. Describing those conditions, one commentator asked readers to imagine 'a man, and one or more of his children, engaged from morning to night in cutting, drying and otherwise preparing the seaweeds, at a distance of many miles from his home . . . for hours together wet to his knees and elbows . . . living upon oatmeal and water . . . sleeping on the damp floor of a wretched hut'. Nobody, it is clear from this, was likely to take up kelp making voluntarily. That is why the landlords who controlled the kelp industry began to manipulate tenurial arrangements on their estates in ways that left many of their tenants with no choice but to become kelpers. Hence the emergence of crofting.[34]

Until the end of the eighteenth century, most land in the Highlands and Islands was nominally occupied by tacksmen. Much of this land, however, was in the actual occupancy of people who were those tacksmen's subtenants. This large group managed their landholdings collectively – plots being allocated and reallocated among them in accordance with decisions taken on a communal basis. Obviously, those arrangements could not survive the departure of the tacksmen who left for North America between the 1770s and the 1790s. To begin with, admittedly, a tacksman's emigration meant only that his former subtenants found themselves in a more direct relationship with the owner of the land they lived on. Families who had previously paid rent to tacksmen, in other words, were now required to pay rent directly to lairds. This was a significant departure from the way things had been done in clanship's heyday, but it did not greatly alter the day-to-day lives of the folk affected by it. What changed those folk's lives fundamentally and for ever was the landowning class's subsequent decision to do away with communalism of the older variety and make each landholder the individual occupier of a single piece of land known as a croft. Some crofts were created by dividing established settlements into a series of separately tenanted plots. Others took shape on previously uncultivated moorland. But irrespective of their origins, all crofts were small in size – typically extending, especially in the Hebrides, to no more than three, four or five acres. This was because the landlords who oversaw the formation of crofting villages or townships wanted to stop crofting tenants becoming full-time agriculturalists. A crofter, both in principle and in practice, was not, and could not be, a farmer. He was a man who, though tenanting a patch of arable land, had to find a source of non-agricultural income if he was to pay his rent and buy the foodstuffs needed to supplement the output of his minuscule holding. And how might crofters most readily obtain the cash they required? By becoming kelpers.

During the nineteenth century's opening years, the price of kelp reached £20 a ton – equivalent to several hundred pounds today. Of this £20, moreover, just £1 had to be set aside to meet transport costs and just two went to the kelping workforce. The remaining £17 was pure profit. And if that were not gain enough, much of a kelping landlord's wage bill eventually returned to him in the form of rent – because his kelpers, thanks to the spread of crofting, were usually his tenants as well. It is easy to understand, therefore, why possession of a Hebridean estate seemed at this time to be a passport to riches. But it is also easy to understand why the generality of islanders were angered by what was happening to them – their mood reflected in the 'spirit of discontent and irritation' which one contemporary observer detected throughout the Hebrides and, for that matter, the north of Scotland more generally.[35]

This observer was the Earl of Selkirk, a south of Scotland nobleman. 'The progress of the rise of rents and the frequent removal of the ancient possessors of the soil,' Selkirk wrote, 'have nearly annihilated in the people [of the Highlands and Islands] all that enthusiastic attachment to their chiefs which was formerly prevalent, and have substituted feelings of disgust.' What clansfolk-turned-crofters found especially hard to bear, Selkirk went on, was the fact that their chiefs no longer behaved as warm-hearted patriarchs but as coolly calculating businessmen. 'It is not the mere burthen of an additional rent that seems hard to bear; the cordiality . . . which they [as clansfolk] formerly experienced from their superiors are now no more. They have not yet learned to brook [this] neglect; they are not yet accustomed to the habits of a commercial society, to the coldness which must be expected by those whose intercourse with their superiors is confined to the daily exchange of labour for its stipulated reward. They remember not only the very opposite behaviour of their former chiefs; they recollect also the services their ancestors performed for [those chiefs].' Each chief-cum-landlord naturally took the view that his ancestors, by virtue of their having possessed the requisite charters and title deeds, had been outright owners of their clan's territory. People being turned off the land, Lord Selkirk commented, did not agree. 'They well know of how little avail was a piece of parchment and a lump of wax under the old system of the Highlands; they reproach their landlord with ingratitude, and remind him that, but for [the military service rendered by] their fathers, he would now have no property. The permanent possession which they [previously] retained of their paternal farms, they consider only as their just right, from the share their predecessors had borne in the general defence, and [they] can see no difference between the title of their chief and their own.'[36]

Towards the end of the nineteenth century, thinking of this sort underpinned riots and rent strikes which culminated in crofting communities gaining security of tenure. At the century's commencement, however, the means of protest available to crofters, or those who feared they might be forced to become crofters, were different. Just as tacksmen had earlier emigrated, or threatened to emigrate, when asked to pay higher rents, so crofters and prospective crofters now did the same. When offered newly created crofts, Lord MacDonald's estate managers commented in 1801, people responded by saying they would 'much rather try their chance in other countries'. By other countries, aspiring emigrants principally meant the United States – a nation whose citizens, almost miraculously as it appeared from a Highlands and Islands perspective, 'were not troubled with landlords'. Everywhere, it was noted in 1802, 'preparations for emigration' were being put in train. Everywhere families were 'turning their thoughts to America' and beginning to 'correspond . . . with their friends in North Carolina who emigrated thirty years since'.[37]

On the face of things, residents of John Norman MacLeod's Skye estate had less cause to emigrate at this point than Lord MacDonald's tenants. Since John Norman was only fourteen in 1802, he had not yet taken control of his affairs. And because the young laird's trustees or guardians lacked the authority to make far-reaching changes, there was no immediate prospect of the MacLeod chief's people being subjected to upheavals of the kind occurring on Lord MacDonald's property. Already, however, the sheep-farming ambitions of Kenneth MacAskill of Rubh' an Dunain were apparent to everyone in his vicinity. Partly because of well-founded fears as to where those ambitions might lead, many families living on John Norman MacLeod's Skye estate chose to take advantage of the opportunity presented by the arrival in Loch Bracadale of an emigrant ship bound for Wilmington, North Carolina. When this ship, the *Duke of Kent*, sailed for America in August 1802, her 394 'full [or adult] passengers' included 130 of Lord MacDonald's tenants. They also included 264 people from 'MacLeod's country'.[38]

Edward Fraser, then enquiring into the causes of the growing exodus from the Highlands and Islands, wrote an account of this emigrant party's departure. As Loch Bracadale was not a registered harbour, Fraser remarked, there were no customs officers on hand to inspect the *Duke of Kent*, which, in addition to adult emigrants, carried over 200 children. Conditions on the vessel, Edward Fraser insisted, were appalling: 'The accommodations of the ship *Duke of Kent* . . . were so very bad that neither the passengers . . . nor . . . the gentlemen whom I conversed with and who had been on board . . . expect[ed] that they [the ship's passengers] could . . . arrive in life or health.'[39]

Among the Skye folk who left for Wilmington on the *Duke of Kent* was a young woman called Effie McLeod. Effie settled eventually in one of the North Carolina locations I visited in the company of her direct descendant, Alex McLeod. On that occasion, Alex told me what is remembered of his great-great-great-grandmother's Atlantic voyage. Inevitably, MacLeod family tradition has become attenuated with the passage of time. But it confirms that Edward Fraser was right to be concerned about the safety of the people aboard the *Duke of Kent* when, hoisting sail, she slipped out of Loch Bracadale and, rounding Idrigill Point, headed for the open ocean.

Although Effie McLeod was accompanied by her one-year-old son, John, Effie's husband, Murdoch, did not make the Atlantic crossing in her company. 'He was nicknamed "Sailor",' Alex says of his great-great-great-grandfather, 'and maybe, like a lot of other Skyemen, he was serving at the time with the Royal Navy. I just don't know. But what seems to have happened is that Effie's parents, whose surname was MacInnes, decided to leave Skye on the *Duke of Kent*. Murdoch, I guess, was somehow in touch with Effie and was willing to let her and John go too – on the basis, presumably, that he'd follow them to North Carolina as soon as he could.' Alex pauses. 'The one thing that's absolutely clear about all this,' he goes on, 'is that Effie and John were fortunate to survive what came next.'

Like the ship on which Captain Alexander MacLeod and his fellow emigrants from Glenelg had left nine years before, the *Duke of Kent* ran into bad weather. 'I have heard my folks . . . all refer to the long and dangerous voyage,' a North Carolinian wrote much later of what he had learned from people who sailed from Skye on the *Duke of Kent*. 'They were out at sea several weeks longer than usual, having encountered a terrible storm, and they were given up for lost.'[40]

The Atlantic crossing from Loch Bracadale to Wilmington took the *Duke of Kent* three months – months made all the more traumatic for Effie McLeod by the fact that, somewhere in mid-Atlantic, she gave birth to her second son. Named Kent after the vessel taking his mother and brother to America, the baby died and was buried at sea. Such tragedies were frequent. This one is unusual in having had present-day consequences. In 1994, Sue McLeod Christensen, who lives in Greeneville, South Carolina, with her husband Erik, a forensic pathologist, had her second son. Sue is

Effie McLeod's great-great-great-great-granddaughter. Her father, Robert McLeod, is Alex McLeod's brother and, as a result of Alex's research, Robert is well aware of his family history. 'Years ago,' Sue says, 'my dad was talking about Effie coming over to America on the *Duke of Kent*. Dad mentioned that he thought it would be neat if, one day, I named a son after Effie's son, Kent. Well, Erik and I named our firstborn Erik for his father, but Kent seemed right for our second son. We think it's a great name, and Kent himself enjoys knowing why we named him as we did.'

Scotland and Prince Edward Island

Emigration from the Highlands and Islands had ceased with the outbreak of the American Revolutionary War. It resumed in the 1780s and 1790s when, in addition to the people who left Glenelg for Glengarry County, several hundred folk went to other parts of North America from MacLeod lands in Skye. During the mid-1790s, as a result of Britain going to war with revolutionary France, emigration stopped again. In 1801, however, the Peace of Amiens was agreed between the British and French governments – the latter now in the hands of Napoleon Bonaparte. Free movement of shipping was thus restored, and in the Highlands and Islands the consequences were dramatic. 'The emigrations from the Highlands which had been of little account during the continuance of hostilities,' it was said, 'recommenced upon the return of the peace with a spirit more determined and more widely diffused than on any former occasion.' The *Duke of Kent*, then, was one of many emigrant ships which sailed from the Highlands and Islands for North America in 1802. Even more vessels were expected to leave the following year.[41]

As many as 20,000 people were making plans to emigrate, northern Scotland's landlords reported in March 1803. The 'complete depopulation' of entire districts might result, they warned. Because this would have deprived them of the labourers needed to make their kelp, estate owners at once set about trying to convince politicians that emigration ought to be curtailed.[42]

The man on the receiving end of the ensuing anti-emigration campaign was Charles Hope, one of the British government's senior representatives in Scotland. Partly because the administration to which he belonged was in sympathy with what was then called the landed interest, and partly because pro-landlord lobbyists took care to stress that population outflows from the Highlands and Islands might undermine military recruitment, Hope was readily persuaded to intervene in the emigration business. He did so on ostensibly humanitarian grounds – getting parliament to pass, in the summer of 1803, a Passenger Vessels Act which obliged the operators of emigrant ships to limit passenger numbers. His 1803 legislation, Charles Hope wrote, was 'professedly calculated merely to regulate . . . ships carrying passengers to America'. But it was also 'intended,' he admitted privately, 'to prevent the effects of that . . . rage for emigrating to America, which had [lately] been raised among the people [of the Highlands and Islands]'. This was achieved by ensuring that the Passenger Vessels Act pushed the costs of Atlantic passages to levels beyond the reach of many aspiring emigrants.[43]

One of Charles Hope's aims in 1803 was to obstruct the activities of men he described as 'agents of Lord Selkirk'. They were Alexander MacDonald, a retired soldier, and Angus MacAulay, a doctor who was also one of Lord MacDonald's former factors. Both had the job of finding families willing to join a colonising venture which Thomas Douglas, Earl of Selkirk, was trying to get off the ground in North America.

Having begun life as the previous Earl of Selkirk's fifth son, Thomas Douglas did not expect to inherit either his father's title or the Galloway estate which went with it. But because his older brothers died young and childless, Thomas, while still in his twenties, became the possessor in 1799 of an earldom and a substantial income. He was thus in a position to do as he liked, and what the new Lord Selkirk had set his heart on, it became apparent, was accomplishing something constructive on behalf of the increasingly hard-pressed population of the Highlands and Islands.

Thomas Douglas's interest in the north of Scotland dated from the 1780s when, as a student at Edinburgh University, he became friends with the young Walter Scott and came to share Scott's passion – a passion given full rein in novels like *Waverley* – for clanship. In 1792, Douglas toured the Highlands and Islands, where he discovered that the clan-based social order he had expected to find was no more than a fading memory. As mentioned in relation to events in Glenelg, 1792 was marked by an anti-sheep-farming uprising in Easter Ross – an uprising which the future Earl of Selkirk appears to have witnessed. Given the manner in which his romantic illusions must have been shattered by this sudden exposure to late-eighteenth-century realities, it would have been understandable if the young nobleman had left the Highlands and Islands, never to return. But this was not Thomas Douglas's way. True, he turned his back on chiefs or lairds who were evicting their tenantries to make way for sheep. At the same time, however, he embarked on a wide-ranging inquiry into what was happening in the Highlands and Islands – going so far as to learn Gaelic so that he could better understand the feelings and aspirations of the many folk then losing their land to sheep farmers.

Where, Selkirk asked, were those people to go? They could migrate to

Martha MacLeod in her North Carolina home. This home was built by Martha's emigrant ancestor who left Skye for what were then Britain's American colonies in the 1770s.
(*Raleigh News & Observer*)

Roger McLeod in Tragowel, Victoria, Australia. Roger's great-grandfather, who grew up in the Sutherland community of Tongue, came to Australia in 1856 and settled in Tragowel twenty years later. (Ken Jenkins)

Jim McLeod, who lives on Whidbey Island in America's Washington State, visiting the site of the Raasay township of Eyre which his great-great-grandparents left in 1830. (Cailean Maclean)

Canadian teenager Kaitlin MacLeod at the memorial commemorating the arrival in Ontario's Glengarry County of emigrants from Glenelg. Those emigrants got here in 1794. They were led by Alexander MacLeod. He was Kaitlin's great-great-great-great-grandfather and she lives on the farm (in the background) which he settled.
(Deborah Kerr)

Penny McLeod DeGraff (second from right) at Scotland's National Mod in Stornoway, Lewis, where she and her friends, from Seattle on America's Pacific coast, took first prize in a Gaelic singing competition. Penny's great-great-grandmother left Lewis for Canada in 1863.
(*Press and Journal*)

An emigrant shepherd's dog is commemorated by this statue (its plaque in Gaelic) beside Lake Tekapo in New Zealand's South Island. Shepherds from Scotland, many MacLeods among them, played a key role in opening up New Zealand's mountain country to sheep farming.
(Karen Mullaly)

The author (left) interviews brothers Norval (centre) and Harvey McLeod
in Ontario's Bruce County. Norval and Harvey's ancestors left Sutherland
for Cape Breton Island in the early nineteenth century. The family moved
to this part of Canada in the 1850s.
(*Kincardine Independent*)

Texan rancher Don Mack McLeod (right) and his son Michael with some
of the longhorn cattle Michael rears on his ranch. This MacLeod family's
emigrant ancestors left Skye for North America in the 1770s.
(Wayne Willoughby)

Prince Edward Island farmer Martin MacLeod. Martin's forebears, who
were evicted from the Raasay township of North Fearns, emigrated to
P.E.I. in the 1830s.
(Cailean Maclean)

Gesto in Skye, with the Cuillin in the background. The MacLeod ancestor of Poland's Machlejd family left Gesto for Germany in the 1620s. Two centuries later, Gesto was home to James MacLeod, who went on to head Canada's North West Mounted Police and to win the enduring respect of Indian chiefs like the Sioux leader Sitting Bull.
(Cailean Maclean)

Rachael Jackson, who lives in nearby Orbost, at Bharcasaig Bay, Skye, with Loch Bracadale in the background. Rachael grew up in Sydney, Australia, but her great-great-grandfather was an emigrant from Skye and she can trace her MacLeod ancestry back to the thirteenth century.
(Cailean Maclean)

Lowland Scotland's urban centres where, with factories going up on all sides, they would readily obtain work. But such work, Selkirk wrote, held no appeal for the population of the Highlands and Islands: 'The manners of a town, the practice of sedentary labour . . . present to the Highlander a most irksome contrast to his former life . . . A manufactory can have no attraction [to him] except in a case of necessity. It can never be his choice.' What Highlanders and Hebrideans really wanted, Selkirk went on, was an opportunity to make their living, as they had always done, from agriculture: 'Accustomed to possess land, to derive from it all the comforts they can enjoy, they naturally consider it as indispensable, and can form no idea of happiness without such a possession.' It was for this reason, Selkirk observed, that people from the Highlands and Islands were drawn to North America. There, land was in inexhaustible supply; there, land was not subject to 'temporary, precarious and dependent' tenancies of the Highlands and Islands sort; there, farms were owned by the families living on them.[44]

Concluding that emigration from the Highlands and Islands was both unstoppable and in emigrants' best interests, the Earl of Selkirk devoted himself to facilitating it. He also sought to change the emigrant outflow's direction. Although at odds with Highlands and Islands landowners, Selkirk was a British patriot, and it troubled him that emigrants of the sort who left Skye on the *Duke of Kent* were settling in the United States. People quitting the Highlands and Islands, Selkirk reckoned, ought to be going to Britain's remaining colonies where their wealth-creating capacities and their fighting skills would be at the United Kingdom's disposal – not that of a potentially hostile power like the USA. Hence the Earl of Selkirk's decision to buy a tract of territory in British North America – this territory to be populated by settlers from the Highlands and Islands. Initially, Selkirk looked to Upper Canada for the land he needed, but by 1802 he had turned his attention to Prince Edward Island.

Today, Prince Edward Island, in the Gulf of St Lawrence, is Canada's smallest province. At the start of the nineteenth century, it was a colony in its own right. Seized by Britain from France in the mid-eighteenth century, P.E.I. had been parcelled out among a number of purchasers who were expected to establish a population on the island. For the most part, this had not happened. A few emigrants from the Highlands and Islands reached P.E.I. in the 1770s. In the 1780s, they were joined by loyalist refugees – probably including the three MacLeod families recorded by late-eighteenth-century census takers – fleeing north from the United States. But in 1802, when the Earl of Selkirk acquired a big slice of Prince Edward Island from its original owners, P.E.I.'s total population was still below 5,000.[45]

Although Selkirk's intervention boosted this figure by nearly 20 per cent in the course of 1803, it looked for a time as if the earl's P.E.I. colony might founder for lack of colonists. Emigrants from the Highlands and Islands – because, one commentator said, of 'the *clannishness* so peculiar to them' – had long been inclined to settle alongside one another. There was thus a tendency, once a settlement had been founded, for this settlement to be reinforced by what Selkirk called 'repeated emigrations' from the locality which provided its original settlers. By the 1790s, this had begun to be true of Glengarry County – which was attracting successive waves of emigrants from Glenelg and adjacent districts. But so tiny were the initial Highlands and Islands groupings on P.E.I. that the Earl of Selkirk, when first trying to interest further families in joining them, found that the island's name scarcely registered. This was particularly true of Skye which, Selkirk commented, 'had so decided a connection with North Carolina that no emigrants from it had ever gone to any other quarter'. But for the Passenger Vessels Act, this might have continued to be the position. However, on its becoming known in the Highlands and Islands during the early months of 1803 that the price of an Atlantic passage was about to double or treble, intending emigrants panicked. Now the imperative was simply to get away before the Passenger Vessels Act made departure impossible. During the spring and early summer, in consequence, the Earl of Selkirk was able to fill three ships, the *Oughter*, the *Dykes* and the *Polly*, with a total of 800 people. About three-quarters of those folk came from Skye. A lot of them were MacLeods.[46]

Aboard the *Polly* when Selkirk's little flotilla sailed for P.E.I. was *Calum Bàn MacMhannain*, Malcolm Buchanan, a maker of poems and songs. '*Tha na daoine as a' falbh*,' Calum Bàn commented in the course of a composition reflecting on his emigration: 'The people are leaving . . . What would it profit me to remain? I'll go to sea; I'll follow others in search of a new place to dwell. We'll get . . . land [there] which can be bought outright.'[47]

Prince Edward Island: Belfast, Montague and Uigg

The islands I am used to seeing from the ocean are the Hebrides. Most of them are mountainous. Prince Edward Island is not. On the cloudy and breezy day I catch sight of it from the deck of a ferry, therefore, P.E.I. seems singularly featureless – its outline little more than a smudgy line separating a grey sky from a greyer sea. From closer quarters, however, P.E.I. looks more attractive. Its gently undulating terrain, its tidily ploughed fields and its red soils give the place a little of the character of Lowland Scotland's farming districts – Kincardineshire's Howe of the Mearns, for instance. Like the Mearns, P.E.I. is well cultivated, and P.E.I's agriculturalists, like their

Kincardineshire counterparts, are proud of their productivity – as I learn from Martin MacLeod, the island farmer who heads P.E.I.'s Clan MacLeod Society and who meets me at the ferry terminal.

At once, Martin takes me to the spot, near the present-day township of Belfast, where the Earl of Selkirk's emigrant party – which included some of Martin MacLeod's ancestors – stepped ashore in August 1803. Selkirk, who had accompanied them, spent the next month or two helping the new arrivals get established. To begin with, chaos reigned. Everywhere he looked, Selkirk wrote, there were 'confused heaps of baggage'; and, lacking any alternative, families were obliged to 'lodge . . . themselves in temporary wigwams'. But morale, the earl contended, was high. 'They looked to nothing less than a restoration of the happy days of clanship,' he observed of the folk he had brought to P.E.I. This is a telling phrase – for Selkirk, as he busied himself with allocating land and supervising the start of ground clearance, seems to have cast himself in the role of clan chief. 'I [was] talking my best Gaelic,' he recalled of the time he spent with his 1803 emigrants, 'which seemed to have won their hearts.'[48]

At over six feet, Lord Selkirk was tall by nineteenth-century standards. He was also young, slim and red haired. The earl, then, conformed to Highlands and Islands expectations of how a leader of his people ought to look. When he came among them speaking their own language and offering to set them up as farmers on Prince Edward Island, the families with whom Lord Selkirk dealt may well have felt for him a little of the mingled respect and affection their forebears felt for men like Ruaraidh Mòr, Iain Breac and other hero figures of that sort. Something of this is encapsulated by Belfast's monument to Lord Selkirk. On one side is one of Malcolm Buchanan's Gaelic verses. On the other is this sentence: 'In memory of Thomas Douglas, the fifth Earl of Selkirk, philanthropist and coloniser, who, believing that the hardships of the Scottish Highland peasantry could be alleviated only by emigration, came to Canada in 1803 and established a large settlement in this area.'

By way of Belfast's Memorial Church, where I am shown another of the numerous North American cemeteries occupied by people of Hebridean extraction, Martin MacLeod drives me to the small town of Montague. Here I meet with Harold MacLeod, Montague's former mayor and an authority on Prince Edward Island genealogy. 'My great-great-grandfather came over with Lord Selkirk,' Harold tells me. His emigrant ancestor, Harold continues, belonged to the Skye township of Kilmaluag. This township, which Harold has visited more than once, is in the Trotternish area – ten miles north of the village of Uig. In 1803, as for centuries previously, Trotternish was owned by the MacDonalds of Sleat, not the MacLeods of Dunvegan. Both in the nineteenth century and earlier, however, plenty of MacLeods lived on MacDonald land. Harold's great-great-grandfather, Donald MacLeod, was in this category. He first heard of Prince Edward Island, it may be, from Angus MacAulay, whose portrait hangs in Belfast Memorial Church and who, when hired by the Earl of Selkirk to recruit settlers for P.E.I., turned first to Trotternish, a district with which his family had a connection.

"S e seo Eilean an àigh anns a bheil sinn an dràsd", Malcolm Buchanan wrote of P.E.I.: 'This is the isle of contentment where we are now.' Harold MacLeod's forebears, who set up home in Orwell Cove, were of the same opinion. 'They got along pretty good here,' Harold MacLeod says. 'I've heard it said of a later emigrant, a man who arrived in 1829 and who afterwards married one of my great-grandmother's sisters, that he was amazed to discover how well the 1803 settlers had done.'[49]

By way of underlining this point, Harold directs me to a long out-of-print publication in which a Prince Edward Islander of Hebridean descent describes how his family, though starting off in 'shelters built of logs', had graduated to a house 'suitable for a table whereon the proper complement of wine glasses might be displayed . . . for the refreshment of important persons'. Not every P.E.I. resident was quite so upwardly mobile. But by the 1830s, practically all Lord Selkirk's 1803 emigrants, or their children, were occupying 'excellent' farms and raising 'heavy crops'. 'These people,' one of their contemporaries commented, 'have arrived at more comfort and happiness than they ever experienced before.'[50]

Their success notwithstanding, this commentator went on, emigrants from the Highlands and Islands were prone to thinking longingly of the places they had left years earlier. 'There are but few indeed that I have met with who do not, in a greater or lesser degree, feel a lingering wish to see their native country . . . Nothing appears to destroy [their] warm affection for the land where they first drew breath.'[51]

During my time with him, Harold MacLeod says something which reinforces this observation. 'My grandmother,' Harold remarks, 'told me that when she was a little girl she saw old people crying because they'd heard mention of the Cuillin. Of course, my grandmother, who was born here in P.E.I., had never seen the Cuillin and scarcely knew what mountains were. But some of the elderly folk around her were first-generation emigrants who, though they'd made out well since leaving Skye, were saddened to think they'd never again set eyes on the Old Country and its hills.'

We talk of Skye and of Harold's impressions of it. 'I felt like I'd been there before,' Harold says of his first visit to Kilmaluag. 'Isn't that strange? Sometimes I think the memory of the places that were so precious to our people has somehow been implanted in our genes.' I wait, and Harold goes on: 'Back in the 1920s, my father corresponded with people in Skye. He was in touch with an old man in Hungladder, not far from Kilmaluag, who'd been born in the 1840s and who could make connections between our family and families still living there. This made it possible for me, when I went to Skye, to meet with relatives. Nearly 200 years had passed since my great-great-grandfather left Kilmaluag. But there I was, standing where he'd stood and talking with people who, though I'd never set eyes on them before, seemed as familiar to me as my cousins in Orwell Cove. Those Skye people looked the same, talked the same, even walked the same as men and women I grew up with.'

Skye, in Gaelic, is *An t-Eilean Sgiathanach*, the Isle of Skye. Its Gaelic-speaking inhabitants, however, have always known Skye simply as 'an t-eilean', the island. P.E.I. people similarly call P.E.I. 'the island' – as if there is no other. Whether this usage is traceable to emigrants from Skye, I do not know. But it is evident from my evening in Montague that 'the island', meaning P.E.I., has long since taken the place of '*an t-eilean*', meaning Skye, in the affections of families once rooted in the one and now rooted, just as firmly, in the other. Harold MacLeod, being particularly conscious of his people's Hebridean origins, talks movingly of Skye and of what Skye means to him. But like Martin MacLeod and the other P.E.I. folk who join us in Montague, Harold becomes visibly more animated when the conversation moves on to the doings of P.E.I. personalities.

'There was this MacLeod from the island whose sister took a job in Boston,' Martin says, 'and he figured on going there to see her. Seventy, eighty years back it would have been when he made his trip, I reckon. That was a time when, here on the island, you were considered civilised if you had an outhouse – meaning the little shed, somewhere in the yard, that was as close as most folk got to having a bathroom. Now, even in the 1920s, Boston had progressed beyond outhouses. But what wasn't yet to be found even in Boston was air conditioning. So it being high summer when this MacLeod from P.E.I. headed off there, he had to take dinner at tables in the street. He found this kind of odd. So when he got back to the island and they asked him what he thought of Bostonians, he said, "Oh, they're the queerest folk in all the world. They go outside to eat their food, then they go inside to shit."'

'*Ach ma theid gu bràth*,' runs the song Malcom Buchanan made in honour of P.E.I. '*A null thairis air sàil, Thoir mo shoraidh gu càirdean eòlach.*' Skye people should 'flee the [high] rents' levied by their landlords, Buchanan urged, and 'come out as soon as opportune' to Prince Edward Island. Although not necessarily at his prompting, plenty of people did as Malcolm Buchanan advised. Among them, in the summer of 1829, were families whose arrival rated coverage in a P.E.I. newspaper. 'They left their native place about six weeks ago,' the paper reported of this latest influx. 'With prudent foresight characteristic of their race, they came provided with twelve months provisions and an ample stock of warm clothing. They have all relatives already settled in the island, chiefly about Belfast, and . . . it is, we understand, their intention to settle in that thriving settlement.'[52]

The leader of this 1829 emigration was Samuel MacLeod. Before his departure from Skye, Samuel was a schoolteacher in Uig. There, in the course of the 1820s, he became involved with the Baptist Church – a denomination of which the Presbyterian Church of Scotland, operator of schools like Samuel's, disapproved. Uig's Baptist-inclined schoolmaster, Skye's ecclesiastical authorities decided, would have to relinquish his post. It was as a result of church elders making this clear to him, it appears, that Samuel MacLeod made up his mind to emigrate to Prince Edward Island – taking with him his parents and the two dozen further families from the Uig area who had followed their schoolmaster into the Baptist Church.

The settlement founded by Samuel MacLeod and his adherents is today called Uigg. I am shown around it by one of Samuel's great-grandsons, another Harold MacLeod, formerly of Uigg's Dunvegan Farm, now retired. With him Harold has brought a map dating from 1829 and showing land grants made that year in this part of P.E.I. Samuel MacLeod's name features on Harold's map. So do the names of James MacDonald, Murdoch MacLeod, James MacLeod, Angus MacDonald, Donald Ross, Roderick MacLeod, John MacLeod, Alexander Martin, Norman MacLeod, William MacPhee and John Matheson – all of whom accompanied Uig's former schoolteacher to North America. 'They sailed on a ship named the *Mary Kennedy*,' Harold remarks of this emigrant party, 'and judging by the quantity of supplies they brought with them, an awful lot of thought and effort went into planning their departure.'

In his Uigg home, Harold tells me a story about his great-grandfather. 'When the church elders called on Samuel in his schoolroom and told him to quit teaching,' Harold says, 'he turned his back on them and walked right out of the door. But before he left, he picked up his chair – it was a symbol of his authority, I guess – and slung this chair over his shoulder. "Unlike a king," Samuel's supposed to have said, "I can take my throne with me!"' Harold gets up. 'I've something to show you,' he remarks, ushering me into another room where a piece of furniture, clearly of nineteenth-century origin, occupies one corner. Harold nods in this corner's direction. 'That's the chair Samuel MacLeod carried out of Uig School and then brought with him on the *Mary Kennedy* to P.E.I.,' he says.

Nova Scotia: Pictou

Two or three hours into my last night on Prince Edward Island, the wind rises and is soon blowing with all the noisy energy of a Hebridean gale. By afternoon, when I take the ferry from P.E.I. to Pictou, Nova Scotia, the storm has passed. But the sea is still running high and, for the duration of my ferry trip, the mainland coastline is concealed by rain squalls. On a day like this, it is hard to understand what it was about Nova Scotia that caused European countries to fight for control of it. But fight they did, the early-seventeenth-century kingdom of Scotland among them.

Attempts by King James VI and his Edinburgh-based government to establish a settlement in Nova Scotia or New Scotland failed every bit as comprehensively as the same administration's simultaneous attempts to promote a Lowland colony in Lewis. The start of an enduring Scottish connection with Pictou had to wait, therefore, until the district was seized by Britain in the course of the eighteenth-century wars which terminated French rule in North America. Like P.E.I., the Pictou area was sold in the 1760s to faraway entrepreneurs who hoped to profit from its colonisation. Pictou's new owners were mostly resident in already established, and at this point still British, colonies several hundred miles to the south. Prominent among them was a Scots-born cleric, John Witherspoon, president of the College of New Jersey at Princeton and the principal initiator of a scheme which turned on Witherspoon, in collaboration with partners in Scotland, arranging to have as many people as possible shipped from the Highlands and Islands to Pictou.

The liberal-minded John Witherspoon, soon to play a leading part in the American Revolution, thought it good politics as well as good business to help Scots escape their lairds. His Pictou-bound recruits, many of them from the former MacLeod territory of Assynt, became all the keener to get out of Scotland, Witherspoon noted, when 'they found their landlords anxious that they should stay'. However, the Princeton president's commitment to fostering emigration did not extend to having proper checks made on the seaworthiness of the Dutch-built vessel, the *Hector*, his Scottish associates chartered in the summer of 1773 to take intending emigrants to Nova Scotia. The *Hector*, the ship's passengers claimed, was so old and decrepit that 'they could with their hands pick wood out of her sides'. Nor had much been done to ensure the vessel's provisioning. Salt meat went bad before it could be eaten; stores of biscuit and oatmeal were infested with mould; fresh water supplies were inadequate. Inevitably, illness soon broke out. Eighteen children died at sea, and the first act of the *Hector* settlers, when they finally reached Pictou, was to bring ashore for burial the corpses of two of their number – the first an Assynt woman called Christina MacLeod, the second a young son of Alexander MacLeod, also from Assynt – who had died just as Nova Scotia came in sight.[53]

Today a recreated version of the *Hector* is moored alongside Pictou's waterfront. My guide to the ship is Gordon MacLeod, a local businessman who has been involved with the *Hector* project since its inception. The ship, Gordon says, remains 'a work in progress' – its rigging, for instance, still having to be completed. But to walk the *Hector*'s deck and to clamber down into the vessel's hold – where, on the original *Hector*, emigrants were confined for weeks on end – is to get as close as you can now get to experiencing the shipboard conditions of two centuries ago. Much the most terrifying aspect of those conditions derives from the fact that ships like the *Hector* were astonishingly small. Standing in the *Hector*'s bow and looking across Pictou Harbour to the open sea, I remember the answer I got to a question I put to a Nova Scotian fisherman during a previous trip. 'You know what the ocean can be like,' I said to this man. 'How would you feel about sailing the Atlantic in a ship not much bigger than your fishing boat?' He would not even think about it, he replied.

Before leaving Scotland, the *Hector* emigrants, who included at least seventeen individuals called MacLeod, had been told they would get first-rate farmland in Pictou. On disembarking and seeing nothing but unbroken forest, they sat down, it was said afterwards, and wept. Nor was the Pictou settlement's subsequent progress anything like as rapid as that of its counterparts elsewhere. An emigrant who got here at the start of the nineteenth century discovered 'nothing . . . that could with any propriety be called a town. There was one blacksmith's shop, one tavern and two or three small grocery shops. There was no church, no courthouse, no jail.' But despite those alleged inadequacies, Pictou and the hinterland it served shortly afterwards became one of the localities favoured by people quitting the Highlands and Islands for North America. By the close of the 1840s, thousands of Gaelic-speaking emigrants had passed through Pictou en route for the settlements those same emigrants created in this period across much of eastern Nova Scotia.[54]

One early arrival was Donald MacLeod who, with his wife, Ann, and their four children, left Kilmorack, on the eastern side of the mainland Highlands, in the spring of 1801. Among Nova Scotia's attractions to this MacLeod family, and to plenty of others, was the fact that, because it was closer to Scotland than alternative destinations such as Glengarry County or North Carolina, the cost of getting there was theoretically more affordable. But it did not always work out like that – as Angus MacLeod, an 1802 emigrant, was to discover.[55]

Angus, a Sutherland man caught up in Britain's war with revolutionary

France, had spent eight years in the British army. While with the military, he sent home to his wife as big a share as he could manage of his army pay. By scrimping and saving, Angus's wife, in turn, managed to accumulate exactly £50 – and when Angus was discharged from the forces, following the Peace of Amiens in 1801, the couple resolved to spend part of this sum (over £2,500 at today's values) on Atlantic passages for themselves and their two children. Assured by an emigration agent that he and his family could travel from Scotland to Pictou for £30, Angus no doubt intended to spend the remaining £20 on farm equipment. At their port of departure, however, the four MacLeods (like many more emigrants then and later) were informed that, unless their ship's skipper received practically all the cash they were carrying, the vessel would sail without them. When Angus MacLeod disembarked at Pictou to begin life as a Nova Scotia homesteader, therefore, he had only eight pence in his pocket.[56]

Many such tales must have found their way back to Scotland. None of them prevented people trying to get to North America. During 1803, the year which saw the arrival of Lord Selkirk's three vessels off Prince Edward Island, a further three emigrant ships arrived in Pictou from Lewis. With the discharge of their passengers, the now rapidly growing town began to be dominated by people of Highlands and Islands extraction. Frederick Cozzens, an American visitor of 1859, called those people 'a canting, covenanting, oat-eating, money-gripping tribe of Scotch Presbyterians'. A more charitable view was taken by Norman MacLeod, a Scottish churchman whose ancestors were tacksmen at Suardul near Dunvegan. 'Such a true Highland congregation I never saw,' Rev. Norman wrote of the crowd that gathered to hear him preach at Pictou in 1845, 'and when they all joined in singing the Gaelic psalm how affecting was it!'[57]

Gordon MacLeod shows me Pictou's surroundings from a viewpoint on Fitzpatrick Mountain, south of the town. Spread out below is Pictou Harbour, a mile-wide inlet where, during the first half of the nineteenth century, emigrant ships from Scotland dropped anchor most summers. The harbour is shaped like a hand from which the thumb and smallest finger have been removed – each remaining finger being the estuary of one of the watercourses, East River, Middle River and West River, which flow into the sea here. 'You can see how settlement spread out from Pictou by way of those rivers,' Gordon says. 'The earliest settlers got farms with harbour frontages. People who came later had to move further inland.'

Gordon's own emigrant ancestor, Robert MacLeod, reached Pictou in 1817. Robert was a blacksmith by profession, and Gordon still possesses many of the tools he brought from Scotland – where Robert operated a blacksmith's shop, or smiddy, in the village of Auchencairn. 'There's uncertainty as to how Robert came to be in Auchencairn,' Gordon comments. 'There's also a bit of a mystery as to his surname. In Scotland, Robert seems to have called himself Louden. Over here, he called himself MacLeod – a name other members of his family appear to have had all along.'

Auchencairn is in Kirkcudbrightshire. This is the part of Scotland that was home to Thomas Douglas, Earl of Selkirk, but it is not a locality where in 1817 one would have expected to find people of Highlands and Islands background. It is possible, I suggest to Gordon, that Robert MacLeod, blacksmithing in a district where folk of Highlands and Islands descent were seen as more than a little bit alien, might have tried to conceal his origins by adopting a Lowland name like Louden. But this, I acknowledge, is guesswork on my part.

Somehow, copies of a few of Robert MacLeod's outgoing letters have survived. In one of them, Robert tells a friend back in Kirkcudbrightshire that life in North America has its drawbacks. 'Winter here is very long and often very severe,' he observes. Sometimes there is a 'skersity' of cash, and always there is much to be done. 'The land . . . takes a great deal of work to clear it,' Robert remarks when describing the effort that has gone into removing trees from his farm. But that farm, 100 acres in extent, was Robert's own, and it was this which most impressed the Scottish recipient of the emigrant blacksmith's letter. 'I congratulate you on your advancement to a landowner,' his Kirkudbrightshire friend writes to Robert MacLeod, 'and wish you . . . success. You might have swung your great hammer long in Auchencairn before you had become laird of a hundred acres.'[58]

On a farm called MacLeod Meadows, I meet with George MacLeod, whose great-great-grandfather, John MacLeod, came to Pictou from Durness, on Sutherland's north coast, in 1806. John, who sailed from the Caithness port of Thurso, was accompanied by his second wife, Ann, and their six children. The presence of those children, especially the males among them, was important. Because John, born in 1748, was approaching sixty when he came to Nova Scotia, he was too old to qualify for a land grant. However, his grown-up sons counted as settlers in their own right. Not far from Pictou, in the vicinity of Hardwood Hill, one of those sons, Hugh, George MacLeod's great-grandfather, obtained a 200-acre tract of bush and forest. Hugh's 200 acres, George informs me, are still part of MacLeod Meadows Farm, now operated by Alex MacLeod, George's son and Hugh's great-great-grandson.

At their invitation, I stay overnight at MacLeod Meadows with George and his wife, Zena. In the course of an evening dominated by talk of MacLeods past and present, George shows me documentation dealing with his great-grandfather's land grant. In accordance with the regulations governing such matters in colonial times, Hugh MacLeod, prior to his getting title to his farm, had to 'erect a dwelling, clear and work at least three acres of [forest-covered] land, and . . . drain at least three acres of sunken or swampy land'. This was accomplished, and on the morning of my second day in George MacLeod's company – after a breakfast featuring an emblematically Scottish-Canadian dish in the form of porridge doused in maple syrup – I am taken to inspect the long-run results of Hugh's labours.

Because he has bought additional land, George MacLeod's farm is more extensive than his great-grandfather's – so extensive that, to enable me to see as much as possible in the time available, George, who is in his eighties, decides our trip should be made by car. We stop at a barn which went up, George remarks, in 1921 – 'when I was three,' he adds. 'We have around 200 head of cattle on the place,' George says as we head back to his vehicle and set off down the first of a succession of puddled dirtroads. The fields to which those dirtroads give access are the creation of George's ancestors, and George's pride in what they accomplished is evident. So is his appreciation of what he and his family owe to the fact that, nearly 200 years ago, George's great-great-grandfather made up his mind to quit Durness. 'We got something here we'd never have got in Scotland,' George says. 'We got land of our own. That was the making of us. Of course, it's sometimes been a hard pull for us on this farm. Right now, it's a hard pull for my son. I'm hoping, though, that he'll stick with it. Farming can be tough, but this is as good a place as any to hang your hat.'

Scotland: The Highlands and Islands

In 1809, Clan MacLeod's chief, John Norman MacLeod, came of age, married and, as if to conform with what had become a standard pattern, started spending more money than his estates generated. In 1810, in an attempt to bring his income into line with his expenditure, John Norman took three steps which led to further emigration. First, he sold Glenelg to a London businessman for £98,500 (more than £4 million today). Second, he ordered a rent increase so dramatic as to make all previous increases seem insignificant. Third, he began creating crofts with a view to cashing in more effectively on his share of Skye's kelp resources.

When Glenelg was disposed of, Chief John Norman's leading tenant there was Norman MacLeod, whose family had held the tack of Eileanriach, just south of the modern village of Glenelg, for more than a hundred years. Norman greeted news of Glenelg's sale to a stranger by urging all his subtenants to leave for North America and by announcing that he intended to accompany them. In the event, Norman MacLeod changed his mind about emigrating. But most of the Eileanriach tacksman's subtenants quit

Glenelg anyway, and many of their remaining neighbours did likewise in the years following.[59]

If Glenelg's change of ownership was disruptive of former arrangements, so was John Norman's decision to do what Lord MacDonald had done a decade previously – introduce crofting. At the MacLeod chief's instigation, more than a hundred crofts were laid out during 1810 and 1811 in Merkadale, Carbost, Fernilea, Harlosh, Vatten, Roag and Kilmuir, as well as in the parts of Glendale still in John Norman's ownership. By design, each of those places was adjacent to a kelp-rich sea loch: Loch Harport in the case of Fernilea, Carbost and Merkadale; Loch Bracadale in the case of Roag, Vatten and Harlosh; Loch Pooltiel in the case of Glendale; Loch Dunvegan in the case of Kilmuir, now a southern extension of Dunvegan village. Like their counterparts on Lord MacDonald's estate, then, John Norman MacLeod's crofters were also to be kelpers. By way of driving this point home, John Norman's estate managers fixed the rents of his new crofts at extremely high levels – well over £10 annually on average. This was about fifty times more in real terms than the occupants of comparable holdings pay in twenty-first-century Skye, and the MacLeod chief's crofting tenants, it followed, could find the cash he required from them only if they made enormous quantities of kelp. Unsurprisingly, emigration was widely thought preferable to taking a croft on those terms. If they were to get to North America in 1810 or 1811, however, Skye people of modest means – and most of John Norman MacLeod's prospective crofters were in this category – had to find some way of circumventing the provisions of the Passenger Vessels Act. To John Norman's fury, aspiring emigrants among his tenants were helped to do just that by none other than the Dunvegan laird's leading tacksman, Kenneth MacAskill of Rubh' an Dunain.[60]

Since he rented the better part of 30,000 acres from John Norman MacLeod, the Rubh' an Dunain tacksman was hard hit by rent increases which, when they took effect in 1811, raised the overall rental of John Norman's Skye estate, the only one now left to him, by more than 300 per cent. In protest, Kenneth MacAskill adopted the well-tried tacksman tactic of threatening to take himself off to North Carolina. He did so with reluctance and with no intention of depopulating John Norman's property, MacAskill informed the MacLeod chief in August 1810: 'Be assured that I shall never act against the interest of your family by raising any emigrating spirit but, as quietly as I can, remove myself with a few good workmen.' This implied that the Rubh' an Dunain tacksman was going to quit Skye for good – thereby forcing Chief John Norman to find a new farming tenant. But by the following spring Kenneth MacAskill's stance had changed. While agreeing to meet Chief John Norman's rent demands, and thereby securing new leases to his farms, he made clear that he was still intent on leaving – if only temporarily – for America. Now, however, he was not going to go alone. Not only had MacAskill 'resolved . . . to emigrate', John Norman learned in March 1811, 'he had engaged a ship', and in breach of his earlier promise was inviting as many 'small tenants' as possible to go with him. Once the Rubh' an Dunain tacksman had 'announced his intention of heading an emigration', moreover, 'the common people flocked to his standard' – among them men the MacLeod chief had expected to become crofters.[61]

John Norman responded to this development with a mix of blandishments and threats. In the first category is a circular issued by the Dunvegan laird's factor, Charles Robertson: 'MacLeod desires me to inform the tenantry that their interest will ever be his; [and] that in order to ascertain their situation . . . he has determined to spend most of his time upon his estate.' In the second category is a further communication in which Robertson reminds people planning to accompany Kenneth MacAskill to North Carolina that, if they go, they will be in breach of legally binding agreements: 'He [John Norman] desires me communicate . . . his fixed and determined resolution to use every means . . . for forcing those who may prove refractory to implement their agreements [to take crofts]. He has it in his power to prevent the emigration of those who [agreed to take] lands from him and that power he will positively exercise.'[62]

Those intimidatory noises made little impression on the generality of John Norman MacLeod's tenants, and on Kenneth MacAskill they made no impression at all. The Rubh' an Dunain tacksman, Charles Robertson informed his employer in May, had deliberately wrecked the coming summer's kelp harvest by stripping seaweed from the shores adjoining his sheep farms. He 'has not left an ounce [of kelp],' the factor commented of MacAskill – who, Robertson added, was meanwhile deploying 'every argument and calculation to induce people to emigrate'.[63]

By the beginning of August, Kenneth MacAskill's chartered ship, an American-owned vessel called the *Catherine and Edward*, was at anchor in Loch Bracadale and John Norman MacLeod, then resident at Dunvegan Castle, was trying to stop anyone reaching her. First, John Norman sought and received confirmation from the customs authorities in Fort William that, in accordance with regulations deriving from the Passenger Vessels Act, 'no passengers [could] be taken on board any ship unless at a port or place where a customs house is established'. Next, John Norman turned for aid to Donald MacLeod of Talisker, nephew of the now dead Colonel John. Since the law barred emigrants from embarking on the *Catherine and Edward*, John Norman argued, it was the Talisker tacksman's duty, in his capacity as a commander of the local militia, to prevent prospective emigrants from boarding the American ship – by force if necessary. But Donald MacLeod, who was himself to quit Scotland for Tasmania in 1820, had no intention of coming to the MacLeod chief's aid. He said as much to John MacDonnell, a customs man who had been sent to Skye at John Norman MacLeod's request. When MacDonnell told Donald MacLeod that his part-time troops might have to take control of the *Catherine and Edward* if her American skipper put to sea with a ship full of emigrants, the Talisker tacksman disagreed. 'The Local Militia Act,' he said, 'would not admit of [armed men] embark[ing] in boats to assist . . . in seizing the vessel.'[64]

'You are directed by your superiors,' John MacDonnell had been ordered before reaching Skye, 'to seize [the *Catherine and Edward*] should the law be broken . . . and, should she escape with her emigrants illegally, you are the person to whom blame will attach.' But with MacLeod of Talisker refusing to provide the armed force that might have enabled him to take over the *Catherine and Edward*, there was little MacDonnell could do to give effect to his instructions. Everywhere he went on John Norman MacLeod's estate, the luckless customs man reported, he met with abuse. 'That is him who is sent here to distress the oppressed,' MacDonnell heard folk say as he 'passed through their . . . farms'. And despite his doing his best 'to watch the motions of the vessel and the emigrants', he could get no worthwhile information about either. Nor 'could [he] procure for love or money lodgings or meat'. He 'really believe[d],' John MacDonnell concluded, that Skye's people had 'leagued together' to make it impossible for him 'to discover their intentions'.[65]

At the end of August, those intentions became all too apparent when the *Catherine and Edward* up-anchored and sailed away to the south. The ship was bound for Tobermory in Mull, John MacDonnell learned, and it was followed out of Loch Bracadale by several 'large open boats' filled with the emigrants whose departure John Norman MacLeod had been so anxious to stop. Because Tobermory, unlike Loch Bracadale, was a registered port, MacDonnell informed John Norman, the Dunvegan laird's former tenants would be able to emigrate freely from there. And 'as the wind was at north' on the day those same tenants left Skye, their passage from Loch Bracadale to Tobermory would have taken no more than a few hours.

Their transatlantic journey took longer. But before the North American fall had properly set in, families who would otherwise have had to settle for one of John Norman MacLeod's crofts were stepping ashore, as so many Skye folk had done before them, at Wilmington, North Carolina. Some of them gravitated to the Cape Fear River country. Others went to South

Carolina. There, it was reported, the *Catherine and Edward* emigrants were helped to find farms by Kenneth MacAskill who, though holding on to his tenancy of Rubh' an Dunain, had accompanied the *Catherine and Edward* people to the United States – where the Rubh' an Dunain tacksman, perhaps wisely in view of his having so antagonised Dunvegan's laird, remained for several years.[66]

'I should not think he was a man of very marked ability,' one of his grandsons commented of John Norman MacLeod. His deficiencies, however, did not prevent John Norman spending cash he did not have: on lavish improvements to Dunvegan Castle; on extensive tree-planting programmes in the castle grounds; on the re-acquisition of land which his father had sold; on renting fine homes in the south; on vain efforts to purchase a baronetcy; on a successful campaign to become MP for Sudbury in Suffolk; on unsuccessful attempts to follow in his father's footsteps as MP for Inverness-shire. The outcome was that, when John Norman's died in 1833, his debts – despite his having sold Glenelg and despite his having trebled the rents charged on his Skye properties – were nine times larger than his annual income.[67]

At the time of the *Catherine and Edward* episode, John Norman MacLeod, like most landlords in the Highlands and Islands, opposed emigration. Long before his death, again like most landlords in the Highlands and Islands, he became supportive of it. This was mainly because the discovery of new sources of alkali caused the market for Hebridean kelp to collapse in the course of the ten years after 1815. As well as slashing landowners' incomes, this development deprived crofting families of their *raison d'être*. As long as crofters were also kelpers, they were worth retaining. Hence the Passenger Vessels Act of 1803, and hence John Norman MacLeod's efforts to prevent the sailing of the *Catherine and Edward*. On kelp ceasing to be of value, however, crofters were rendered surplus to proprietorial requirements. As early as 1819, one of the Earl of Selkirk's informants was clear as to how Highlands and Islands landlords were reacting to this new situation. 'They are now as eager to get rid of the people as they were formerly to retain them,' Selkirk's contact wrote.[68]

A further expansion of sheep farming followed. So did a further round of evictions. At this time, those evictions began to be known as 'clearances'. All the territories associated historically with Clan MacLeod were affected by them. On the Skye estate still in MacLeod ownership in the 1820s and 1830s, clearances were most widespread in Bracadale and Minginish, the area extending from just south of Dunvegan to the Cuillin.

In 1883, when a royal commission came to Skye to enquire into crofting grievances, old men recited for the commission's benefit the names of dozens of Minginish and Bracadale localities depopulated fifty or sixty years before: Crossal, Drynoch, Satran, Ardtreck, Carbostbeg, Craicinish, Brae Eynort, Heilla, Fiscavaig, Tuasdale, Sumardale, Craig Bhreac, Fearann-nan-Cailleach, Amar, Glen Bracadale, Meadale, Invermeadale and many more. 'There is not a [human] creature in any of these townships now unless [a] shepherd,' the commission of 1883 was told by one witness. This was true. Bracadale and Minginish mostly consisted in the 1880s, as they had done for half a century, of just six sheep farms: Glen Brittle, Talisker, Drynoch with Sumardale and Gesto, Ebost with Ullinish, Ose and Totarder.[69]

Responding to allegations about the extent of clearance in Bracadale and Minginish, MacLeod lairds and their spokesmen stressed that only a tiny part of those areas had ever been in the tenancy of crofters. However, this was not quite the end of the matter – as John Tolmie MacKenzie, factor at Dunvegan towards the end of the nineteenth century, acknowledged. 'On each [tack],' MacKenzie said of the pre-clearance position, 'there was a colony of cottars or squatters who [were] employed . . . to cultivate the land . . . These cottars got a patch of potato ground where they could [also] grow corn . . . That is the rule that was adopted on all the [tacks] on MacLeod's estate.' In the course of his comments, John Tolmie MacKenzie implied – by way of blunting talk of clearance – that the folk he called cottars or squatters were so poverty stricken as to have benefited from their enforced removal. This opinion was challenged by others. 'They were in comfortable circumstances,' one crofting witness to the royal commission of 1883 remarked of pre-clearance cottars. 'They had cattle and sheep and horses. They had a great stretch of hill pasture.' There is no scarcity of early-nineteenth-century testimony to the same effect. When writing about the 'very great' number of subtenants to be found on the typical Hebridean tack, James MacDonald, the author of an 1811 account of island agriculture, noted that such subtenants, John Tolmie MacKenzie's cottars in another guise, often owned 'property in cattle, horses or some other things'.[70]

Although they went on over a long period, clearances in Minginish and Bracadale were at their most intense in the mid-1820s, when John Norman MacLeod undertook to ensure that his sheep farming tenants, whose leases he was then renewing, would have vacant possession of their farms. In April 1825, and again in April 1826, John Norman obtained from Portree's sheriff a series of so-called decrees of removing. These empowered him to dispossess family after family. Sixty years later, the consequent evictions were recalled by a man who, 'when about fifteen years of age', accompanied the sheriff officer given the task of serving eviction orders on dozens of households. 'My duties were to help in filling up each notice to quit and [to] witness each [notice] being served upon the tenant,' this man wrote. 'I cannot now remember the number but it must have been considerable when it took us fully three weeks to serve them all. I can well recall that . . . it was a wholesale affair.'[71]

Also present in Skye at this time was Joseph Mitchell, the civil engineer who supervised the construction of a road which, because it ran from Sligachan to Dunvegan, traversed the southern part of the MacLeod estate. The countryside bordering on his new highway was 'comparatively fertile', Mitchell remarked. He continued: 'A year or two before, it had been cleared of tenantry to the number of 1,500 souls . . . The ruined cottages and green spots of the once cultivated crofts were to be seen scattered on the hillsides . . . But all was then a solitude, and nothing was heard by the passing traveller but the bleating of sheep.'[72]

Today, nearly 200 years after the bulk of its original inhabitants were expelled, the remnants of their field systems can still be seen in Minginish. Those remnants are readily glimpsed from the road which has taken the place of its nineteenth-century predecessor. Should you have the chance to drive northwards on this road, look to your left as, some six or seven miles beyond Sligachan, you approach Drynoch. Especially if it is late in the day and a westering sun is sinking towards the Atlantic, you will see the shadows cast by hundreds of the low ridges on which the people who lived here grew their crops of oats and potatoes. There continues to be debate as to what caused the Highland Clearances and as to who exactly was responsible for them. What there can be no argument about is their occurrence. In Skye, as in much of the rest of the Highlands and Islands, the record of clearance and eviction, as members of the royal commission of 1883 observed, 'is written in indelible characters on the surface of the soil'.[73]

Commenting in 1840 on the fact that Bracadale's population was falling, the parish's minister wrote, 'This decrease is solely to be attributed to the system of farming which has for some time been adopted, viz., throwing a number of farms into one large tack for sheep grazing, and dispossessing and setting adrift the small tenants.' As well as being far less densely populated than tacks of the old sort, then, sheep farms were bigger. This was because tacksmen of the traditional type – the MacLeods of Gesto, Drynoch, Talisker and the like – had to provide, at their own expense, the homes they occupied as well as any barns or other outbuildings they might require. The leases insisted on by sheep farmers, in contrast, made the provision of farmhouses, sheep sheds and other 'fixed equipment' the responsibility of a farm's owner, not its tenant. From a laird's point of view, it follows, there was merit in having a single sheep farmer take over a whole set of former tacks. This kept down costs and maximised revenues.[74]

On John Norman MacLeod's Dunvegan estate, the main beneficiaries of clearance were the MacAskills of Rubh' an Dunain and a family by the name of MacLean who took over Talisker when, nine years after refusing to be drawn into the affair of the *Catherine and Edward*, Donald MacLeod left for Tasmania. As already emphasised, Kenneth MacAskill's landholdings had grown enormously even before he went off temporarily to America on the *Catherine and Edward* – whose emigrant passengers he may have assisted because it was in his interest to sabotage John Norman MacLeod's plan to have crofters established in places Kenneth thought more suitable for sheep. That last point is purely speculative. But if their 1811 quarrel did indeed stem, even in part, from their opposing views on crofting, there was good reason for John Norman of Dunvegan and Kenneth of Ruabh' an Dunain to be reconciled on the latter's return (delayed until 1820 or thereby) from America. Crofts and crofters were now everywhere out of favour – with Merkadale, one of the MacLeod chief's first crofting townships, itself being cleared within twenty years of its creation. Because they enabled him to acquire further acres, such clearances were to Kenneth MacAskill's advantage. They were equally to the advantage of his Talisker contemporary, Lachlan MacLean. It is not surprising, therefore, that both men were accused of having initiated clearances on their own account. This is perfectly believable. While such clearances could not have gone ahead on any scale without the approval of John Norman MacLeod, neither Lachlan of Talisker, also implicated in mass evictions on the island of Rum, nor Kenneth of Rubh' an Dunain would have scrupled to take the lead in ridding their sheep farms of subtenants of the type described by Kenneth's son, Donald, as 'really an encumbrance'.[75]

In expressing such opinions, Donald MacAskill was articulating the standard convictions of sheep farmers and landlords throughout the early-nineteenth-century Highlands and Islands. His views would certainly have been endorsed by William MacLeod, who was at this point the owner of Orbost – one of the several properties sold by General Norman MacLeod of Dunvegan in the 1790s. Like Donald MacAskill, William of Orbost was descended from a long line of Clan MacLeod tacksmen. Also like Donald, William was committed to sheep farming. In his time, therefore, Orbost was comprehensively emptied of people. First one township was cleared or partly cleared, then a second, then a third – with the result, as the royal commission of 1883 heard from a crofting witness, that the same person might find himself or herself made homeless over and over again. 'My father,' this crofter said, 'was born at Ramasaig and is about 75 years of age. He was evicted from there to Idrigill, from Idrigill to Forse, and from Forse back to Idrigill where he was [for] only one year. Then he was removed or evicted [once more] . . . He was removed from [those] places for no other reason than to make way for sheep.'[76]

By the mid-nineteenth century, then, Ramasaig, Idrigill and Forse, along with several more Orbost communities, had ceased to exist. Today Forse's fields have been afforested. But other Orbost townships, despite their having been uninhabited for at least 150 years, are comparatively well preserved – and by no means inaccessible. Take the coastal path which leads south from Orbost House, once the residence of the man responsible for Orbost's clearance, in the direction of the coastal pinnacles known as MacLeod's Maidens, and you will find yourself overlooking a clustered group of ruined cottages – their roofs long gone but their stone walls still standing. Those walls are all that remain of Idrigill.

Orbost became, in effect, a single sheep farm. Glenelg, being more extensive, was able to accommodate four or five. 'In . . . Glenelg,' the district's parish minister noted towards the end of the eighteenth century, 'there are two valleys, through each of which a river runs. The inhabitants reside in separate villages on each side of the rivers, their arable land extending along the banks.' One of those valleys is Gleann Mòr, once home to Kenneth MacLeod, who left for Glengarry County in 1793. Strung out along the glen's lower reaches, in Kenneth's time, were eleven or twelve of the villages or townships mentioned by Glenelg's minister. In the course of Gleann Mòr's clearance, which took place shortly after John Norman MacLeod's disposal of his Glenelg estate, all those townships were swept away and Gleann Mòr was converted into just two sheep farms. One, Beolary, carried 4,500 sheep; the other, Scallasaig, carried 3,100. Those sheep, together with about half a dozen shepherds, took the place of people whose families had lived hereabouts for generations.[77]

What happened in Glenelg happened also in Assynt, where the MacKenzie lairds who took over from the MacLeods of Assynt in the 1670s had themselves given way, by the beginning of the nineteenth century, to the most notorious of all evicting landlords, the first Duke of Sutherland. Clearances in Assynt began in 1812 when much of the district was made over to just five sheep farmers. In the 1880s, it was claimed that 'over fifty' Assynt townships were 'made desolate' as a result of those developments. This, at first reading, may seem a wild exaggeration – but modern research, by no means exhaustive, has identified around thirty Assynt settlements which, though populated prior to 1810, were unoccupied by 1825.[78]

In Lewis, too, there were clearances. There were still more in Harris which, when sold by General Norman of Dunvegan in 1779, was bought by Captain Alexander MacLeod, whose father had been tacksman of Bernera and whose older brother, Norman, had masterminded the ill-starred attempt to sell a boatload of Skye and Harris people into servitude in America. When that episode occurred in 1739, Alexander was far away from the Hebrides. In 1734, at the age of eighteen, he had joined the East India Company, then becoming dominant – commercially, politically and militarily – in British-ruled India. By the 1760s, Alexander was in charge of one of the many company ships trading between London and Bombay. Anyone in that sort of position was at liberty to undertake a good deal of freelance commerce. Not surprisingly, therefore, Alexander MacLeod was said to have 'acquired a considerable fortune', and when he took over what had previously been his clan chief's Harris estate – an estate which included Captain Alexander's native Bernera – it was with the intention of investing heavily in its development.[79]

At Rodel, in the south-eastern corner of Harris, Captain Alexander built a fine home, today's Rodel Hotel, and a harbour. His overriding objective was to provide Harris with a well-financed fishing industry, and had MacLeod of Harris, as Captain Alexander styled himself, succeeded in this aim, the island's subsequent history might have been different. In 1790, however, Captain Alexander died. Tragically, the captain's son and heir, Alexander Hume MacLeod, was an absentee spendthrift very much in the mould of his distant kinsman and contemporary John Norman MacLeod of Dunvegan. Captain Alexander's fishery projects were abandoned, and Harris was given over to kelping. Predictably, the kelp price collapse of the 1820s resulted in the bankruptcy of Harris's last MacLeod owner, Alexander Norman MacLeod, another absentee and Captain Alexander's grandson. By 1834, the island was once more on the market. This time it was bought by the Earl of Dunmore, a Lowland laird.

Dunmore ordered several Harris clearances – one of which provoked so much resistance that it had to be carried out under the protection of a military detachment sent from Glasgow. The earl, however, was not solely responsible for Harris's innumerable evictions. His clearances were simply a continuation of those which took place under the jurisdiction of his MacLeod predecessor, Alexander Norman, whose factor, Donald Stewart, began the process of depopulating Harris's entire Atlantic coastline.

This west side of Harris is an exceptionally attractive place. It is best appreciated by travelling, from south to north, through Scarista, Horgabost and Seilebost, to Tarbert – and then heading, in a more westerly direction now, for Amhuinnsuidhe and Husinish. At practically every point along this route, sea, beaches and mountains combine in patterns that stay for ever in the mind. What is most memorable, especially if the day is fine, are the colours which the ocean takes on where it washes across the white sand that is to be seen everywhere here. This sand, cast up by the Atlantic over thousands of years, consists of the pulverised remnants of seashells. Being rich in lime, the same sand has combined with Harris's otherwise acidic, peaty soil to form huge swathes of the flower-rich meadowland known in Gaelic as *machair*. Machair is even more prevalent on offshore islands like Bernera, Pabbay, Ensay and Taransay than on the Harris mainland, and in all those places it supported settlements which, it was noted as far back as the sixteenth century, were 'verie fertile and fruitful for corn'.[80]

But if, as a seventeenth-century writer commented, 'the west side' of Harris was 'for the most part arable', the island's 'east side' was 'naked without earth'. There, in a locality called the Bays, the landscape is as bleak, barren, rocky and inhospitable as the western machairs are welcoming and productive. This makes all the more unforgivable what was done to the people of Harris by Alexander Norman MacLeod, Donald Stewart and the Earl of Dunmore. By means of clearance on a massive scale, those men organised an almost total transfer of Harris's population, or the part of it left after wholesale departures for North America, from the Atlantic machairs to the Bays.[81]

Most of the sheep farms created in the course of this process, which resulted in the destruction of dozens of settlements and the emptying of whole islands like Pabbay, were first tenanted either by Donald Stewart, who doubled as a sheep farmer, or by Alexander MacRae, a cousin of Stewart's wife. MacRae and Stewart consequently became two of the wealthiest individuals in the Hebrides. As for the families removed to make way for their sheep, they consisted of people categorised – now that kelping had gone – as 'redundant' both by landlords and policy makers. Southern radicals denounced this term. 'Have we not a redundancy of legislators,' one of them asked, '[a redundancy] of clergy . . . of nobility . . . of landed aristocracy?' But such assaults on official thinking had no effect. Gradually it became accepted wisdom in Edinburgh and London that, instead of impeding emigration from places like Harris or Skye, as island lairds had once demanded, British governments should be actively promoting it, as the same lairds were now urging. 'It must be admitted,' a senior administrator commented in 1837, 'that few cases could arise to which the remedy of emigration on a great scale would appear more appropriate than to this . . . of the Hebrides.'[82]

Neither Hebrideans nor mainland Highlanders were hostile to the notion that they might improve their prospects by going overseas. Ever since the start of movement to North Carolina, taking ship for North America had been seen by the generality of people in the Highlands and Islands as a sensible way of responding to each landlord-induced change in their circumstances. In the 1770s, people went to North America – this *dùthaich an duine bhochd*, or poor man's country, as they called it – rather than pay high rents. Around 1800, people emigrated in preference to becoming crofters and kelpers. In the 1820s and 1830s, people wanted to get away in order to avoid the risk of their falling victim to some new clearance. 'The greater number of them are willing to emigrate,' it was observed of Glenelg's remaining residents in 1838, 'and this is not to be wondered at, since by sallying forth upon the world in any direction, they might . . . better their circumstances. To make [those circumstances] worse is all but impossible.'[83]

Why, then, did everyone not leave? Mainly because the price of an Atlantic passage was beyond their reach. Although the provisions of the Passenger Vessels Act were watered down as landlords and politicians alike began to jettison the anti-emigration attitudes of earlier times, the cost of emigration remained high. Alexander Buchanan, a colonial official with a lot of experience of settling people in Canada, thought 'that £60 would be a satisfactory outlay for the removal of a family consisting of a man, his wife and three children from the United Kingdom to British North America, providing them with necessary implements, a log house and fifteen months provisions'. In the Highlands and Islands of the 1820s and 1830s, however, few families were in a position to raise anything like £60 (perhaps £3,000 today). That was why many of them began bombarding the Colonial Department in London with petitions requesting the cash they needed to finance their emigration.[84]

One such document, dating from 1826, was signed by twenty-nine men from Bracadale. 'These persons who, with their families, amount to 229 persons are desirous of obtaining a free passage to Canada,' a civil servant noted of the Bracadale petitioners. 'They and their fathers occupied small farms in the . . . parish [of Bracadale] but their landlord [John Norman MacLeod] having consolidated these farms, let them to two persons [almost certainly Kenneth MacAskill and Lachlan MacLean] for sheep walks, and the petitioners are to quit their houses at Whitsunday 1826.'[85]

Although some emigrants did get help from government in the period between 1815 and 1819, this aid had been withdrawn by 1826, and the Bracadale people were thus left to fend for themselves. But that is not to say they never made it to North America. Prospective emigrants from the West Highlands and Islands were so desperate to be off, an Inverness newspaper reported in 1831, that they were selling their 'whole property' in order to afford transatlantic fares: 'Black cattle . . . small horses . . . the roofs of their huts, their boats, in short everything they have must be converted into money . . . before the necessary sum for defraying the freight can be realised.'[86]

Nor was it necessary, despite Alexander Buchanan's warnings to the contrary, for an emigrant family to spend £60 on their emigration. That may have been the ideal amount to have before quitting Scotland, but by the 1820s dirt-cheap passages could be got in the holds of ships which, on eastward voyages, carried Canadian timber to ports like Glasgow and Liverpool. Rather than sail for North America in ballast, the owners of such vessels, described in the next chapter, were prepared to fill them with emigrants paying just three, four or five pounds per head. Although most such ships, when outward bound from Britain, were making ultimately for Quebec, skippers, in order to minimise the expense of feeding and otherwise caring for emigrants, liked to discharge their human cargoes as close as possible to their first North American landfall. It was for this reason that most of the many thousands of people who emigrated from the Highlands and Islands during the 1820s and 1830s came ashore in localities bordering the Gulf of St Lawrence. There, according to a Gaelic song of the time, emigrants were deposited as casually as 'stones dumped out of nets'. The places where people were thus put ashore included P.E.I. and the Pictou area of mainland Nova Scotia. They also included Cape Breton Island.[87]

At the start of the nineteenth century, Cape Breton Island, treated as a separate colony from 1784 until 1820 when it was added to Nova Scotia, was home to fewer than 3,000 people. By the mid-century, however, the island's population had reached 55,000. Much of this increase was due to emigration from the Highlands and Islands – with some 30,000 people of Highlands and Islands origin arriving in Cape Breton between 1802, when the influx from Scotland began, and the early 1840s, when the island ran out of land for settlement. With them, those 30,000 men, women and children brought a Gaelic-based culture which has shaped the character of this part of Canada ever since.[88]

Cape Breton Island: Broad Cove, Cape North, Wreck Cove and Whycocomagh

On a morning of bright skies and sea-reflected sunlight, Gordon MacLeod from Pictou drives me on to Cape Breton Island by way of the Canso Causeway which now links Cape Breton with the Nova Scotia mainland. On his car's tapedeck, Gordon is playing those songs of drawn-out partings and all-too-brief homecomings which are as redolent of Cape Breton Island as they are of Skye, Lewis or Harris – Cape Breton, like the Hebrides, having seldom been sufficiently buoyant economically to make it possible for more than a small proportion of its people to remain in the places where they were raised. Gordon's tape features the Rankin Family, one of several Cape Breton bands whose output draws on the island's Scottish heritage. As we cross the Canso Causeway, the Rankins are evoking the Cape Breton locality their Highland forebears first settled – a locality where, as this

Rankin Family song laments, spruce trees have reclaimed the abandoned hayfields which nineteenth-century pioneers so painstakingly carved out of virgin forest.[89]

In the writings of Alistair MacLeod, Cape Breton Island inspires a similarly bittersweet affection on the part of exiles who, though they live elsewhere, continue to think of Cape Breton as home. 'It is an evening during the summer that I am ten years old,' one of Alistair's characters recalls, 'and I am on a train with my parents as it rushes towards the end of eastern Nova Scotia. "You'll be able to see it any minute now, Alex," says my father excitedly, "look out of the window, any minute now." He is standing in the aisle by this time with his left hand against the overhead baggage rack while leaning over me and over my mother who is in the seat by the window . . . "There it is," shouts my father triumphantly. "Look, Alex, there's Cape Breton!" He takes his left hand down from the baggage rack and points across us to the blueness that is the Strait of Canso, with the gulls hanging almost stationary above the tiny fishing boats and the dark green of the spruce and fir mountains rising out of the water and trailing white wisps of mist about them like discarded ribbons hanging about a newly opened package.'[90]

Alistair MacLeod's great-great-great-grandfather came, as mentioned earlier, from the island of Eigg. His name was Donald MacLeod, and his father may have moved to Eigg from nearby Skye in the aftermath of the last Jacobite rebellion – which ended six years before Donald's birth. Pioneer Donald, as this eighteenth-century Hebridean is called by his present-day descendants, was one of dozens of Eigg people who sailed for North America between 1788 and 1791. On the other side of the Atlantic, or so a local clergyman commented cynically, those emigrants expected to 'find perfect equality, liberty without control, no lords, no masters . . . as well as land rent free for ever'. The extent to which Pioneer Donald – who lived, before his departure, in the Eigg township of Cleadale – nurtured such hopes is not known. It is clear, however, that Donald, who settled initially at Parrsboro on the Nova Scotia mainland west of Pictou, became increasingly disenchanted with his new surroundings – perhaps, it has been surmised, because he and his family, like practically everyone else from Eigg, were Catholics and, as such, did not feel comfortable in what was a mostly Protestant neighbourhood. Seventeen years after their arrival, at all events, Donald MacLeod and his wife, Jessie, quit Parrsboro. Accompanied by their six children and driving a horse and six cattle ahead of them, the couple made the 200-mile trek to the Strait of Canso, crossed to Cape Breton, where Catholicism was comparatively common, and walked on, along the island's western shore, until they came to Broad Cove – where Gordon and I are now headed.[91]

'One of the differences between the Cape Breton Highlanders and their cousins in the rest of Canada,' Alistair MacLeod has observed, 'was that they alone came to a land that was hauntingly familiar . . . Here again were beautiful if forbidding mountains, sparkling, rushing streams and narrow glens slashing through the hills. Here also the lashing snow and the stinging sleet and the sudden, unexpected, bone-chilling rains and the almost unbelievable winds.'[92]

Driving through Cape Breton Island in Gordon MacLeod's company, I can empathise with those remarks. Cape Breton, from my standpoint, seems a peculiarly homelike place. This, however, owes less to its landscape than it does to the enduring impact made on the island by Pioneer Donald and his numerous counterparts. This impact is everywhere apparent: in placenames like Skye River, New Harris, Skye Glen, Dunvegan, Portree, Mull River, Kiltarlity, McLeod Brook; in a tourism industry relying heavily, like its Highlands and Islands equivalent, on the appeal of tartan; in the survival, even if more and more tenuously, of Gaelic; in internationally acclaimed fiddle music of Scottish derivation; in a longstanding literary tradition, of which Alistair MacLeod is but the latest exponent, founded on the experiences of Cape Breton communities created by refugees from Scotland's clearances.

Reaching Broad Cove, Gordon and I stop at MacLeod Inn, a guest house named for its proprietor, Alistair MacLeod. Like his writer namesake, Alistair traces his descent from Pioneer Donald. 'I'm the sixth generation of my family to live around here,' Alistair says as he introduces other people of MacLeod ancestry he has invited to join us, 'or maybe it's the seventh. I never can remember.' Much genealogical discussion ensues. Shirley Miller from Margaree talks of MacLeod forebears who belonged originally to Raasay. Archie MacLeod from Judique explains how he has traced his family back to Harris – specifically to Donald MacLeod, who was a soldier in one of the Highland regiments which saw service in the American Revolutionary War. 'Donald left Scotland in 1776,' Archie says. 'At one point he was in the Carolinas, at another in the West Indies. Then, when the war ended, he was allocated land in Nova Scotia.' Donald MacLeod received a farm in Guysborough, Archie goes on. Guysborough is on the mainland side of the Strait of Canso, but for whatever reason, Donald did not stay there. Like his namesake, Pioneer Donald, he moved to Cape Breton Island – eventually settling with his wife, Susan, the widow of a New England loyalist, in Mabou, not far from Broad Cove.

This ex-soldier was one of the first people from Harris to come to Cape Breton. When Harris's machair townships began to be cleared in the 1820s, hundreds of others followed. In Cape North, reached by way of coastal scenery as impressive as any in Canada, I meet with some of those people's descendants. Among them are Kathleen MacLeod, my Cape North hostess, and Allister MacLeod, a retired accountant, who lives some miles distant in Ingonish but who has come up to Cape North at Kathleen's invitation. Allister's mother as well as his father was of MacLeod parentage. Before they came to Cape Breton in the 1830s, Allister says, his paternal forebears lived in Assynt – probably in the townships of Clashnessie and Achmelvich. His mother's emigrant ancestors, Allister goes on, were a father and son from Harris, Malcolm and Norman MacLeod.

Malcolm and Norman were casualties of the clearance of Sgarasta Mhòr and Sgarasta Bheag – well-established communities located on an especially attractive tract of machair in Harris's south-western corner. Both Sgarasta Mhòr and Sgarasta Bheag, Big and Little Scarista, were emptied of people in the spring of 1828. As was standard practice in much of the Highlands and Islands at that time, the locality's newly vacated homes, of which there were certainly thirty and possibly as many as fifty, were burned to forestall any possibility of their being reoccupied. Among the houses destroyed in this way was the one occupied by Malcolm MacLeod, his wife, Catherine, their grown-up son, Norman, Norman's wife, also Catherine, and their children. That summer, on a ship called the *City of Edinburgh*, this entire family sailed for Cape Breton Island, settling in Wreck Cove, just south of Ingonish.[93]

Until comparatively recently, Allister MacLeod observes, the Cape Breton descendants of people turned out of the Highlands and Islands were not inclined to dwell on what caused their families to be in Canada. 'They didn't speak much about Scotland,' Allister says of his parents and grandparents. 'It was as if they'd put the country out of their minds – as if they didn't have a good feeling about it. They concentrated on where they were going, not on where they'd been, and they achieved a lot. All my MacLeod ancestors, whether from Harris or Sutherland, did well here. The first generation may have struggled. The second and third generations became merchants, fish buyers and property owners who valued education and who, by sending their sons and daughters to college, helped them into good careers.'

Today, any reticence there may previously have been about Cape Breton Island's Scottish connections has given way to a widespread desire to know more about them. Several of the folk I meet in Cape Breton have travelled to Scotland to visit the localities their forebears left the best part of 200 years ago. One Cape Bretoner who has made this sort of pilgrimage is Anna Mae MacLeod, whose great-grandparents emigrated to Cape Breton from Harris in 1843. Anna Mae is ninety. She and her late husband, Malcolm Angus MacLeod, visited Harris in 1972 – spending two or three weeks there.

Malcolm Angus, in his time one of Cape Breton's leading Gaelic singers, was another descendant of the MacLeod family who left Sgarasta Mhòr for Wreck Cove in 1828. Today, Malcolm Angus's widow, Anna Mae, shares a home in this same Cape Breton community with her brother-in-law, Alex Smith. At his door, Alex, a retired fisherman of Lewis extraction, greets me in Gaelic. In the nineteenth century, there were thousands of homes in North America – not just here in Cape Breton but in the Carolinas, Mississippi, P.E.I., Ontario and lots of other places – where this would have happened automatically. Now only a handful of such homes remain, and when it is assumed in one of them, as it is assumed by Alex Smith, that I, because of my background and interests, must be a Gaelic speaker, I experience in full measure the guilt that goes with having lost your language and, still more, with not having tried hard enough to regain it. 'You speak Gaelic,' I say stupidly, and in English, to Alex. 'It was the first thing that was put in my mouth,' he replies.

Later, Alex and Anna Mae talk about Gaelic and about the efforts presently being made in Cape Breton to sustain it. Anna Mae is strongly supportive of those efforts, but she thinks that Gaelic in Cape Breton is too far gone to be revived. 'When I was a girl,' Anna Mae McLeod recalls, 'everyone in this neighbourhood spoke Gaelic. Now there are only seven or eight Gaelic speakers left. We just gave up on it – and it's too bad we did. Gaelic is beautiful, and though you can try to tell in English the stories our people told for so long in Gaelic, those stories never seem the same in this other language. Something has gone out of them.'

When she visited Harris, Anna Mae continues, she thought it good to hear teenagers and small children speaking Gaelic – something she had not experienced in Cape Breton since her youth. 'It was lovely,' Anna Mae says of her Hebridean excursion. 'Everyone we met was so kind, so friendly. I was sorry that we had to leave. I'm telling you the truth when I say that, after our time over there, I felt real lonesome back here in Wreck Cove. It was in Harris I wanted to be.'

I get up to inspect the view from the window of the room where we are seated. Earlier, when I travelled from Cape North to Wreck Cove by way of Cape Smokey, the day had been overcast and the highway was awash with the remnants of overnight downpours. Now, as breaking clouds are hustled across the sky by a southerly breeze, the ocean in front of me is a moving patchwork of shade and sun. I compliment Anna Mae McLeod and Alex Smith on their home's spectacular outlook. 'There's always something to see,' Anna Mae responds. 'Even on the most bitter winter's night I can sit for a long time by that window watching the moon reflected in the pack ice.'

My travels around Cape Breton started on the island's west coast – a coast bordering the Gulf of St Lawrence. From Wreck Cove, however, I am looking eastward – over the Atlantic. Out there, it occurs to me, are the Harris machair lands where I have often gazed at this same sea from the opposite direction. I share with Anna Mae MacLeod my thought that her Hebridean ancestors exchanged one edge of the Atlantic for the other. 'Yes,' she says. 'And I sometimes wish a hop, a step and a jump could take me over all that water to the places they came from – places I feel I belong to.'

Well into the twentieth century, communities like the one in which Anna Mae MacLeod lives were extremely isolated. Highways did not reach Wreck Cove and Cape North until the 1920s and 1930s. Previously, all communication with those and other so-called outports was by sea. Even the remotest outport, to be sure, acquired a self-sufficiency of sorts – one founded as much on fishing and hunting as on agriculture. But this was no basis for rapid economic growth of the kind that had occurred earlier in, for example, the Cape Fear River country.

In the 1770s, as noted previously, the Hebridean author of *Informations Concerning the Province of North Carolina* portrayed that colony as the next best thing to heaven on earth. No one made any such attempt in the case of Cape Breton Island. Recalling his first sighting of its shores, a sighting made in 1817 from a ship bound for Upper Canada, one emigrant wrote: 'At daybreak . . . we discovered the island of Cape Breton, distant only five or six miles . . . It was very cold . . . The coast, for several miles from the shore, was lined with field ice . . . which extended both north and south as far as the eye could see. The island appeared to be mountainous, rocky and barren, and was partially covered in snow.'[94]

The most telling feature of this account is that it deals with Cape Breton as the island appeared on 22 May – by which date spring, indeed summer, would long since have come to North Carolina or even, for that matter, Glengarry County. Cape Breton, especially inland Cape Breton, was and is a place of late frosts, short growing seasons and what one of the island's early-nineteenth-century administrators called 'terrific winters'. '*Mi 'n seo 's mi 'm fang fo chìs, An tìr an t-sneachda 's nam feur seachte,*' an emigrant from Lochaber lamented in a song about his coming here: 'I am bound, brought low, in the land of snows and sere grasses.'[95]

Those sentiments, admittedly, came under fire from another songmaker. '*'S i 'n tìr a dh' fhàg thu 'n tìr gun chàirdeas,*' the complainer was told, '*Tìr gun bhàidh ri tuath*': 'The land you left is a land without kindness, a land without respect for tenants.' Instead of regretting his departure from Scotland, the Lochaber man should pity the many 'poor people' back in the Highlands and Islands who, being unable to get away to Cape Breton – a 'land of promise', this second song calls it – had no alternative but to endure their 'harsh treatment'.[96]

Others made similar points. 'Even [a] log hut in the depths of the [Cape Breton] forest,' one nineteenth-century commentator remarked, 'is a palace compared with some of the turf cabins of Sutherland or the Hebrides.' And the nineteenth-century occupant of one such hut, an emigrant from Lewis, was in no doubt as to the gains he had secured by quitting the Hebrides for ever: 'I go out and in [my house] at my pleasure. No soul living forces me to a turn against my will, no laird, no factor, having no rent, nor any toilsome work but I [choose] to do myself.'[97]

Getting oneself established in Cape Breton Island was a gruelling business all the same. In Sadie MacLeod's home in Whycocomagh, I meet with Sadie's friend Libby MacLean, who is of Lewis descent and who has brought some genealogical notes composed by her father, Angus Finlay MacLeod, in 1927. Writing of his forebears, who had emigrated to Cape Breton a hundred or so years before, Angus Finlay observed: 'They settled on Lewis Mountain along with . . . Lewis neighbours who came over on the same ship, naming the place after their native [island]. It was a hard proposition to make a home and rear a family in the forest, especially so for one unacquainted with trees or the handling of an axe.'

Things were made all the harder as a result of many emigrants to Cape Breton arriving with almost nothing in the way of financial or other resources. 'In the course of the present year,' Cape Breton's colonial authorities recorded in 1828, 'upwards of 2,100 persons have come into the district from the western part of Scotland, many of whom, on their landing, were quite destitute of food and also of the means of procuring it,' Some of those folk, it appears, were taken in by family members who had arrived before them. But 'great numbers' were said to be 'without friends' and were accordingly 'begging from door to door for a morsel of food'.[98]

In 1829, island officials complained that Cape Breton was being turned into 'a refuge for the poor'. In 1830, they wrote of 'a dreadful inundation' of half-starved Hebrideans and of people 'lying about our beaches to be consumed by want and sickness'. Understandably, the men compiling those reports were of the opinion that immigration into Cape Breton Island from the Highlands and Islands should be drastically curtailed. But nothing, certainly nothing the Cape Breton authorities said or did, could stem the human tide then flowing out of Scotland.[99]

Because Cape Breton's comparatively fertile 'frontlands', the name given to coastal localities, had been settled by earlier emigrants, later arrivals had no alternative but to move on to rocky, scrub-covered and wretchedly poor holdings in the island's 'backlands'. A visitor to one backlands settlement found its occupants confronting difficulties 'that no one except those who experienced them [could] understand'. In weather described as 'very stormy with snow and frost', men who were unable to 'use an axe or adze properly', and who were often 'without proper tools' of any kind, were trying to construct homes from newly felled trees. As a result of everyone in the settlement having to get by with 'little food' and 'scant clothing', men, women and children alike were 'weak with want', 'dispirited', 'fainting with cold'.[100]

'It goes without saying,' another observer noted of families struggling to establish themselves on Cape Breton's backlands farms, 'that their furniture was of the rudest description. Their chairs were blocks of wood. A slab [or plank] with sticks in the four corners to serve as legs formed their table. Their food was served up in wooden dishes or on wooden plates and eaten with wooden spoons, except when, discarding such interventions, they adopted the more direct method of gathering round the pot of potatoes on the floor.'[101]

'I have baptised the child of a parent lying on a pallet of straw with five children in a state of nudity,' a Cape Breton backlands clergyman commented in 1833. 'I have baptised where neither father, mother, nor children could venture out in their tattered rags. I have seen dwellings where six or eight of a family lived for five weeks on the milk of a cow, without any other food. I have endeavoured to afford the consolation of religion at a dying bed in a habitation where no food existed but what was supplied by neighbours who could ill spare it.'[102]

There were many parts of North America where emigrants from the Highlands and Islands, despite the hardships such emigrants faced initially, managed to better themselves in a remarkably short time. Cape Breton Island was not like that. 'Unparalleled distress now exists among the new settlers in the backlands near Baddeck and Middle River,' a Nova Scotia newspaper reported in March 1834. 'It is positively confirmed that in one settlement about forty families consisting of 170 persons . . . are for the most part reduced to one meal per day, and this consisting wholly of potatoes of miserable quality.' Some years later, when even their potato crops failed, many of Cape Breton Island's settlers would abandon their backlands homesteads and become emigrants all over again – sailing this time from Cape Breton to the far side of the world.[103]

CHAPTER FIVE

THE COUNTRY BACK
OF THE SUN

**New Zealand, Scotland, Cape Breton Island and Victoria: Waipu,
Assynt, St Ann's and Melbourne**

It is October, and New Zealand's North Island should be getting
reacquainted with summer. On our way to Waipu from Auckland,
however, Don Hammond and I have driven through rainstorms so
intense as to have left the highway awash with water. Now the weather
has eased a little, but the breeze blowing into Waipu from the Pacific
is unseasonably cool. Few people are about as Don and I approach the
monument Don, a retired aircraft engineer, has brought me here to see.
This monument consists of a stone pillar topped by a sculpted lion of
the sort Scottish kings long ago adopted as their heraldic emblem. At
the pillar's base is an inscription commemorating 'the arrival in New
Zealand' of a 'noble band of empire builders' from 'the Highlands of
Scotland'. Those people were Waipu's founders. They came between
1853 and 1860 on six ships. One of those ships, the *Gertrude*, brought
Don Hammond's great-great-grandfather, Kenneth McLeod, to this
country. Kenneth, Don says, was born in Scotland, but neither he nor
his fellow passengers sailed directly to New Zealand from the British
Isles. Waipu's founding families got here by way of North America and
Australia – their odyssey lasting in some instances for nearly forty years
and involving three or more uprootings of a kind most emigrants found

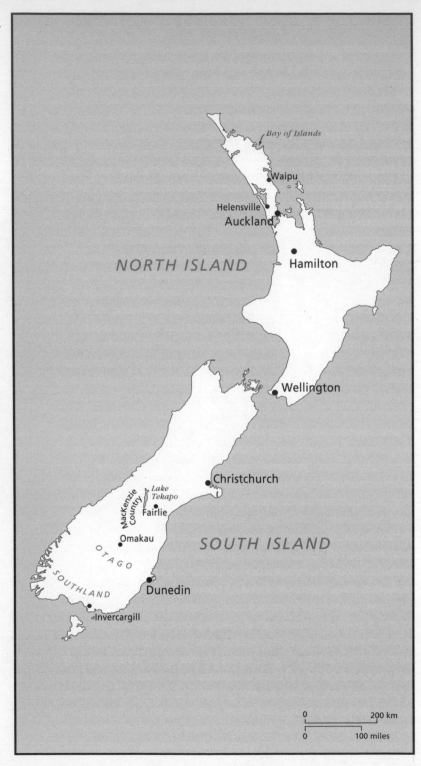

Map 4: New Zealand

hard to undertake just once. There is something reminiscent of the *Book of Exodus* about wanderings of such duration. It is appropriate, therefore, that the people who settled finally at Waipu were led by a man who, even if he did not explicitly model himself on Moses, was every bit as convinced as his biblical predecessor that his journeyings were in accordance with God's will. This man was Norman MacLeod. Waipu's monument celebrates his accomplishments. So do two further memorials. One, standing on land which Norman farmed from the 1820s until the 1850s, overlooks St Ann's Harbour in Cape Breton Island. The other is located at Clachtoll in Assynt.

Clachtoll is a crofting township on Sutherland's Atlantic seaboard – a seaboard consisting of cliff-fringed headlands, rocky creeks and sandy bays. Clachtoll's crofts encircle one such bay. On rising ground at its northern end stands a boulder-like slab of stone dedicated to the memory of Norman MacLeod who was born here in 1780. Overhead, gulls call and circle. Inland, to the east, are low, lumpy hills from which Assynt's grey bedrock juts into the sky. In the opposite direction, if the day is clear, Lewis is visible – at least those bits of it high enough to reach above the horizon.

Like Lewis, Assynt once belonged to Clan MacLeod, also like Lewis, Assynt had been lost to others before Norman's time. While it ended the rule of the district's MacLeod lairds, this change of ownership did not result in immediate expulsions of Assynt's original landholders. Norman's surname was more common than any other in the part of Sutherland where he grew up – with six out of seventeen Clachtoll tenants mentioned in an Assynt rental of 1775 being MacLeods. This continuity of occupation did not last much longer, however. When Norman MacLeod was in his thirties, Sutherland began to be affected by clearances. The ensuing upheavals contributed to Norman's decision to quit Scotland. They also helped ensure he did not leave alone.[1]

Norman MacLeod, according to a religious writer of his day, was 'a clever, irreverent, forward youth' who 'began all of a sudden to join himself to the people of the Lord'. While still a young man, in other words, Norman became a born-again Christian. Soon after, hoping to qualify as a minister, he left for university, in Aberdeen to begin with, then in Edinburgh. At university, however, Norman MacLeod discovered that his fundamentalist faith could not be accommodated into degree courses designed to meet the needs of a state-backed denomination like the then Church of Scotland – a church which Norman, a master of vituperation, lambasted as 'meagre', 'pitiful' and 'degenerate'. Abandoning hopes of a conventional clerical career, but still intent on expounding Christianity as he understood it, the aspiring minister gave up his studies and returned to Assynt, where, though unordained, he began to preach and to gather a following. This following probably grew larger as a result of evictions which took place in the spring of 1812 – when more than 80 Assynt families lost their landholdings and their homes. Although people cast adrift in this way did not automatically align themselves with Norman MacLeod, his teachings probably appealed to folk whose lives had been turned upside down. The same folk, like others in their position, were susceptible to the idea that North America might offer better prospects than Sutherland. When Norman MacLeod announced his intention to organise an emigration to Nova Scotia, there was thus no lack of interest in being part of it.[2]

In 1817, having made arrangements for his wife, Mary, and their three children to join him a year later – as they duly did – Norman sailed from Loch Broom on a ship, the *Frances Anne*, which also carried the bulk of his congregation. The *Frances Anne*'s destination was Pictou. There the Normanites, as the Assynt preacher's adherents were dubbed, established themselves in the vicinity of Middle River. Had they been aiming to found a settlement of the conventional type, their travels would probably have ended here. By 1817, admittedly, land was not so readily to be got in Nova Scotia as it had been formerly. But its flourishing timber trade had made Pictou a boomtown. Labour was in short supply; wages were high; there was every chance of the *Frances Anne* emigrants securing good jobs.

However, his flock's material well-being was not Norman MacLeod's priority. Like the Pilgrim Fathers of 200 years before, he had come to North America to found a community which would conduct itself strictly in conformity with religious teachings, and early-nineteenth-century Pictou, unlike early-seventeenth-century Massachusetts, did not lend itself to such a project. Pictou, Norman declared, was 'a fearful place' – given over to prostitution, 'profanation of the Sabbath' and all sorts of other 'shameless and daring' goings on. Within a year or two of their getting to Middle River, therefore, Norman and the Normanites were making plans to leave.[3]

Their destination was the Ohio country which the United States government had just opened to settlement. Pioneers making for Ohio had a choice of two routes. They could sail up the Mississippi River from New Orleans or they could travel overland from New York. To get to New York or New Orleans from Pictou, the Normanites needed a ship, and being too poor to buy or charter one, they built the necessary vessel themselves. Non-Normanite Pictonians nicknamed this vessel 'the ark' – a designation which its builders, unusual among fundamentalists in having a sense of humour, instantly appropriated. Skippered by Donald MacLeod, one of Norman's fellow emigrants from Assynt, and with Norman himself aboard, the *Ark* sailed from Pictou in the fall of 1819 on a trial cruise which might have ended in disaster had Donald MacLeod, while seeking shelter from a storm, not been able to bring his endangered ship into St Ann's Harbour, an almost enclosed stretch of water on Cape Breton Island's Atlantic coast.

When constructing a fort here in the seventeenth century, a French naval officer described St Ann's Harbour as one of the best anchorages in the world. His opinion had to be revised in the light of repeated winter freeze-ups, but it is easy, on first glimpsing this locality from the Kelly's Mountain section of the Trans-Canada Highway, to appreciate its appeal. The harbour's breaker-free waters are surrounded by timbered hills and by enough flat land to make farming feasible. So, at any rate, thought Norman MacLeod, who now gave up on Ohio. Providence, Norman concluded, had brought him to a spot where he could establish a spiritually cleansed community of the kind he had been unable to sustain in Pictou. Inside a year or two, Norman MacLeod and his followers were staking out farms at the southern end of St Ann's Harbour.

Today, Norman's own former farm is the site of Cape Breton Island's Gaelic College. Since the college promotes activities, such as fiddle playing and dancing, which the puritanical Norman tried to ban, he would not have approved of its being the meeting place chosen by the two dozen MacLeods who got together during my Cape Breton visit to share their family histories with me. Some participants in this St Ann's gathering were of Skye ancestry. Others descended from emigrants who originated in Raasay, Harris, Lewis or Sutherland. But whatever their origins, the MacLeods I met in present day St Ann's sympathised neither with Norman MacLeod's creed nor with the rigorous methods used to enforce it. 'He was next best thing to Adolf Hitler,' one member of the Gaelic College group said of Norman MacLeod. 'Everything I've heard about him makes me think I'd never have got along with him,' someone else remarked.

In New Zealand, where Don Hammond and I talk with another set of MacLeod descendants in Waipu's House of Memories, a community museum, Norman MacLeod is remembered more fondly. Lesley Steenson, a local café owner, mentions that her great-great-grandfather, John Donald MacLeod, born like Norman in Clachtoll, embarked on successive emigrations at the instigation of his preacher namesake. 'He wouldn't have done that unless he felt respect for Norman,' Lesley comments. Ann Reyburn, one of whose emigrant ancestors also came from Clachtoll, makes the same point. 'Norman MacLeod was a born leader,' she says. 'He inspired people. Yes, a lot of bad stuff is told about him, but the good stuff needs to be told as well.' This point of view is endorsed by Norma Venables, one of Norman's great-great-granddaughters, who has driven from nearby Whangarei to join us. Norma directs me to a remark made about Norman

MacLeod by a contemporary. 'His nature and temper were very mysterious,' this man wrote of Norman, 'often . . . clashing with each other. One side was mild . . . while the other was as autocratic and domineering as could be.' Her great-great-grandfather, Norma Venables observes as I read this, must have been a complicated character.[4]

He was certainly an effective pioneer. A colonial official claimed in 1829 that the Normanite community at St Ann's was 'the most sober, industrious and orderly settlement' in Cape Breton Island. Much of the credit for this, the same official went on, belonged to Rev. MacLeod – as Norman had become two years previously when, at the end of a period spent in New York, he was at last ordained a minister.[5]

Soon, however, things were going wrong in the St Ann's Harbour area. The district was not as productive as had been hoped. As a result, its settlers, like many other Cape Bretoners, became reliant on a single crop, potatoes. These could be cultivated by folk whose stock of implements did not extend beyond a spade; they did well in poor soils; and they delivered a greater nutritional yield per acre than cereals. 'It is a well-known fact,' one settler representative noted, 'that the potato is the only article on which a poor man and his family . . . live on [many of] the . . . farms of Cape Breton.' This might have been tolerable if potatoes had not been susceptible to disease. As it was, Cape Breton Island's potato crop was devastated in the summer of 1845, and for several summers thereafter, by blight – the ensuing crisis being all the more acute because it coincided with unusually severe winters. Hunger, even famine, followed. 'Poverty, wretchedness and misery,' it was reported in 1848, 'have spread through the island of Cape Breton.' People were 'running continually from door to door with the ghastly features of death staring [from] their very faces', Norman MacLeod reported. Together with a part of his congregation, he added, he was thinking of quitting this 'desperate and dreary place', as he called Cape Breton, and starting all over again in some more promising part of the world.[6]

Norman intended to settle near Adelaide, South Australia. One of his sons, Donald, had gone there in the 1840s, and the young man's letters home convinced his father that, compared with Cape Breton, Australia was 'a kind . . . of paradise'. Nor was Norman daunted, despite his now being in his seventies, by the prospect of a voyage which, in the event, lasted six months. As he had done when eager to leave Pictou more than thirty years before, Norman persuaded his congregation to build a ship, the *Margaret*. With 140 or so other people, Norman MacLeod sailed out of St Ann's Harbour on this ship in October 1851. Calling first at the Cape Verde Islands, then at Cape Town, the *Margaret* reached Adelaide in April 1852. There Norman learned that his son, like hundreds of other Adelaide residents, had left for

Victoria, where gold had been discovered. The *Margaret* and her passengers duly set sail for Melbourne, Victoria's capital.[7]

Ten or twenty years after the *Margaret*'s arrival, Melbourne, because of its role as service centre to Victoria's Bendigo and Ballarat goldfields, became extremely prosperous. When Roger McLeod, a Melbourne resident introduced earlier, shows me round, I am astonished by the sheer lavishness of buildings dating from what was literally Melbourne's golden age: office and apartment blocks so architecturally ornate as to testify, more than a hundred years later, to the runaway affluence of their original occupants: a bank with an entrance hall so pillared and gilded that you wonder, on entering, if you have strayed into a temple raised, as might have been the case, by money worshippers.

But if it is easy to form an impression of Melbourne as it was at the height of Victoria's goldmining era, it is harder to get a sense of how things were at this era's commencement. The gimcrack buildings of that time, all of them clustering around the Yarra River estuary where Melbourne's founding settlers came ashore in 1835, have long gone. All that survives of early Melbourne – the Melbourne which Norman MacLeod encountered – are contemporary descriptions of it. These are unflattering.

'I must say,' an Australian journalist observed of goldrush Melbourne, 'that a worse regulated, worse governed, worse drained, worse lighted, worse watered town of note is not [to be found] on the face of the globe; and that a population more thoroughly disposed, in every grade, to cheating and robbery, open and covert, does not exist; that in no other place does immorality stalk abroad so unblushingly and unchecked; that in no other place does mammon rule so triumphant; that in no other place is public money so wantonly squandered without giving the slightest protection to life or property; that in no other place are the administrative functions of government so inefficiently managed; that, in a word, nowhere in the southern hemisphere does chaos reign so triumphant as in Melbourne.'[8]

This newspaperman may have exaggerated. He was from Sydney, after all, and Melbourne has always brought out the worst in Sydneysiders. But with thousands of gold-crazed immigrants, from countries as disparate as Britain, the United States, China, Germany and Ireland, coming up the Yarra every month, and with many of the city's policemen having decamped for the diggings, early 1850s Melbourne was definitely a mess. Charles Joseph La Trobe, Victoria's governor, admitted as much: 'Not only have . . . labourers . . . shopmen, artisans and mechanics of every description thrown up their employments and . . . run off to the [gold] workings, but responsible farmers, clerks of every grade, and not a few of the superior classes have followed . . . Business is at a standstill, and even schools are closed.' 'This convulsion has unfixed everything,' another observer commented. 'Religion is neglected, education despised . . . Nobody is doing anything great or generous . . . Everybody is engrossed by the simple object of making money.'[9]

Norman MacLeod had not sailed thousands of miles to set up home in so materialistic a locality. Hence his decision to turn his back on Melbourne and to lead his emigrant party across the Tasman Sea to New Zealand. Here Norman had to surmount one last hurdle in the shape of an expectation, on the part of New Zealand's colonial authorities, that he and his followers, like more conventional settlers of the period, would accept offers of farmland in different parts of the country. Others might be happy to scatter in this way, a Normanite representative told a New Zealand official, but he and the rest of his group were determined to stick together: 'In our case, there exists the . . . strong claim of our being a Gaelic community, requiring to be located near each other . . . as some of our aged people can understand no other language but Gaelic.' This argument prevailed. Norman MacLeod and his congregation were accordingly directed to Waipu, where they were granted some 50,000 acres – an area extensive enough to accommodate both the families who had left St Ann's Harbour on the *Margaret* and those who followed them from Cape Breton Island over the next seven years.[10]

Modern Waipu's population is not so solidly Scottish in background as was the population which established itself here in the 1850s. The district's proximity to Auckland, much the largest of New Zealand's cities, has seen to that. But Waipu still contains plenty of people whose ancestors were among this area's Normanite settlers. Those people help organise Waipu's annual Highland Games; they are prominent in the management of Waipu's House of Memories; they ensure that anyone strolling down Waipu's main street is in no doubt as to who was responsible for creating this community. On banners hung from every Waipu lamp-post are lists of placenames. Some evoke Cape Breton: Baddeck, St Ann's, Boularderie, North River. Others are redolent of the Highlands and Islands: Assynt, Ullapool, Lewis, Skye. More than 150 years after Waipu's founding families got to New Zealand, the places they started out from are at no risk of being forgotten.

Scotland and Australia

Most Scots who emigrated to Australia during the 1850s were happier with what they found than were the Normanites. Norman MacLeod and his disciples, admittedly, were not alone in leaving Australia for New Zealand. But movement of this kind was eclipsed by its opposite – lots of people, including some of Waipu's later-nineteenth-century residents, being enticed away from their New Zealand farms by the prospect of earning high wages, or even finding gold, in localities like Victoria. This is all the more striking because of its representing a reversal of earlier attitudes – Australia, when first incorporated into the United Kingdom's sphere of influence, having been thought to have no future other than as a penal colony.

Eighteenth-century Britain, because it possessed one of the world's most ferocious justice systems, produced innumerable convicts. Since it was expensive to house those convicts in purpose-built jails and much cheaper to ship them overseas, the penny-pinching politicians then in charge of the United Kingdom were attracted by the second option. To begin with, most of the people exiled or transported in this fashion were despatched to North America. Hence the arrival there of Richard Markloud, or MacLeod, whose name appears on a list of 115 'felons' sent from London's Newgate Prison to Maryland in March 1739. But when, in 1776, Maryland and most other American colonies declared themselves independent, they ceased to be available as convict receptacles. With British prisons overflowing, an alternative had to be found, and the choice fell on Australia. Soon the first of a long series of prisoner-laden vessels from Britain had anchored off the future site of Sydney, New South Wales. Those vessels brought Australia its earliest MacLeod settlers. Among them was John McCloud, whose sentence of transportation to New South Wales was passed by magistrates at Lancaster, England, in October 1791. Among them too was Mary MacLeod who was 'sent out' to Australia from Skye 'for the singular crime of . . . having set fire to her neighbour's house in an uncontrollable fit of jealousy'.[11]

In time, Mary MacLeod was released. But she could not afford, or maybe did not want, to go back to Skye. Instead, having found a home in the now burgeoning settlement of Sydney, Mary married a German immigrant by the name of Phillip Shoeffer and set up 'in a respectable way of business' – becoming, among other things, a moneylender whose rate of interest was a highly profitable 20 per cent.[12]

Although he must have been of Scottish ancestry, John McCloud, the transported criminal sentenced at Lancaster in 1791, was technically English – having been born in that country in 1765. This made him more typical of Australia's convict settlers than Mary MacLeod from Skye. Because Scottish judges were less attached to transportation than their counterparts in England, only a small minority of the 150,000 men, women and children conveyed to Australia on the orders of British courts between 1788 and 1868 were Scots. But despite Scottish deportees being few in number, and though most Scots shipped to Australia came from the Lowlands, not the Highlands and Islands, Mary MacLeod was not the only Scots-born representative of her clan to be transported. Particularly if they were so impoverished as to be unable to go overseas, victims of the Highland Clearances commonly fetched up in urban Scotland's slums – where it was all too easy to get on the wrong side of the law. One person who may have been in this category was Margaret MacLeod, a prostitute charged in Edinburgh during 1835 with theft and other crimes. Margaret, described at her trial as 'utterly irreclaimable', had earlier served seven years in jail for receiving stolen goods. Now she was sentenced to lifelong servitude in Australia.[13]

A modern historian has compared Britain's penal settlements in Australia to the twentieth-century Soviet Union's Siberian prison camps. The comparison is all the more apt because, like Josef Stalin's Siberia, Australia became a dumping ground for political dissidents as well as criminals. Indeed, had General Norman MacLeod been prosecuted on account of his participation in the revolutionary politics of the 1790s, as government ministers contemplated, Norman would have shared the same fate as Mary MacLeod, the Skye arsonist, and Margaret MacLeod, the Edinburgh prostitute. In the event, General Norman did not join the other leading members of the Friends of the People who were banished to Australia. In 1820, however, the Australian colonies acquired a man whose family's standing in Clan MacLeod's overall hierarchy was second only to that of the family which produced the clan's chiefs. This man was Donald MacLeod of Talisker.[14]

When Colonel John MacLeod died childless in 1798, his tenancy of Talisker passed to Magnus, Colonel John's younger brother, already tacksman of Claigan, three or four miles north of Dunvegan. On Magnus MacLeod dying shortly after, his place was taken by his eldest son, Donald, who had been brought up at Claigan but who, around 1790, went to India as a serving army officer. Returning to Skye in 1800, Donald MacLeod maintained a toehold in the military by taking the rank of major in one of the militia regiments formed at this time to help safeguard the United Kingdom from a possible French invasion. In 1806, Major Donald married Catherine MacLean, whose father owned the island of Coll, south of Skye. Several of the couple's children were born in Talisker House and, judging by a letter she wrote in 1853, Catherine's memories of Skye were good ones. 'I was then *young* Mrs MacLeod of Talisker,' Catherine recalled of the years around 1810, 'and spent many a happy day at Dunvegan Castle.' Catherine's husband, however, had less reason to remember either the castle or its occupants with affection. In 1811, as mentioned already, Major Donald had refused to comply with Chief John Norman MacLeod's request that the major's militia unit help stop some of the chief's kelpers emigrating to the United States. This inaction on Donald MacLeod's part, the surviving evidence suggests, was bound up with wider disagreements between Talisker's tenant and his laird. Donald of Talisker, it can be deduced from those disagreements, was no more enamoured than his uncle, Colonel John, had been with the aggressively commercial manner in which Clan MacLeod's lands were now managed – Major Donald's disenchantment being all the greater, perhaps, because the fact of his being his chief's kinsman did not shelter him from punitive rent rises. With his rent going up steeply, his income static and his family growing, Donald MacLeod of Talisker faced a bleak future – so bleak, in fact, that he described his circumstances as 'distressed' and, in some desperation, began to think about quitting Scotland.[15]

Commenting on the departure from the United Kingdom of families like the Talisker MacLeods, one of Canada's early-nineteenth-century settlers wrote: 'In most instances, emigration is a matter of necessity, not of choice; and this is more especially true of the emigration of persons of . . . any station or position in the world. Few educated persons, accustomed to the refinements and luxuries of European society, ever willingly relinquish those advantages . . . without the pressure of some urgent cause.' This was certainly true of Major Donald MacLeod. It is unlikely that he would have emigrated if a combination of his own financial situation and the demands made of him by his laird had not left him with little alternative.[16]

Instead of making for North America, emigrating tacksmen's customary destination, Donald MacLeod of Talisker broke new ground by opting for what was then called Van Diemen's Land, today's Tasmania. He did so partly because there were links between the Talisker family and Lachlan Macquarie who, in 1809, became governor of Britain's Australian possessions, Van Diemen's Land among them. Macquarie, himself of Hebridean background, was related to Major Donald's wife, Catherine. This connection explains why Catherine and her husband, at Governor Macquarie's invitation, spent three months in Sydney within a year or two of their getting to Australia. It also explains the comparative ease with which Donald MacLeod obtained the 2,000 acres allocated to him in the vicinity of Hobart, Van Diemen's Land's principal settlement. His Hobart land grant was confirmed before Major Donald left Scotland, but, so strapped for cash had he become, the major might never have taken possession of it had he not got a loan from his father-in-law, Alexander MacLean of Coll. This loan enabled the Talisker tacksman to meet his family's passage costs and, in June 1820, Donald MacLeod, his pregnant wife and their children accordingly made their way to the Lowland port of Leith where they boarded the *Skelton* – bound, as a press announcement put it, for 'Hobart Town, Van Diemen's Land'.[17]

Since Major Donald was also accompanied by four of his Talisker employees and since two of those employees, Roderick and Ann MacDonald, were accompanied by their ten children, the major's party accounted for a quarter of the *Skelton*'s 88 passengers. 'Our passage, on the whole, was uncommonly fine,' the ship's captain, James Dixon, reported. 'Nothing particular occurred until the 16th of July when Mrs MacLeod, a passenger, was delivered . . . of a fine boy.' This boy was Catherine MacLeod's fifth child. 'Her recovery,' James Dixon noted of Catherine, 'was speedy and complete; so much so that she said jocularly a ship was as good for ladies in that way as the shore.'[18]

Towards the end of November 1820, after five months at sea, the *Skelton* put into Hobart. 'The arrival of a vessel with so many settlers was an object of some importance in the colony,' Captain Dixon wrote. The captain was correct. The white population of Van Diemen's Land, prior to 1820, consisted mostly of convicts and their guards. Major Donald, because he had committed himself freely to an Australian future, was bound to generate a lot of interest and to attract a good deal of assistance from a colonial administration looking to foster more such emigration. Soon, as a result, Donald, Catherine and their family were on their way to the landholding they had been promised. There the MacLeods built a home. They called it Talisker.

Victoria: Indented Head and the Western District

Tasmania's Talisker, today a ruin, was not inhabited for long. Major Donald MacLeod died in 1838. Shortly before, he and Catherine, along with several of their now grown-up sons and daughters, had moved to the Australian mainland. There, members of the younger generation of the Talisker family, particularly John Norman MacLeod, Catherine and Donald's third son, were soon at the forefront of efforts to establish sheep stations or ranches in Australia's interior. The area on which they concentrated was Victoria's Western District – extending from Port Phillip Bay, where Melbourne stands, to Victoria's border with South Australia. Here as elsewhere outside Sydney's immediate sphere of influence, agricultural activity had been discouraged by colonial officials who feared that, by permitting it, they would lose control of the settlement process. In 1836, however, a number of sheep farmers from Tasmania or Van Diemen's Land, as it was still called, took matters into their own hands and began shipping flocks across the Bass Strait to Port Phillip Bay – putting those flocks ashore, in the first instance, at Indented Head on the bay's western shore. Where the 1836 pioneers led, others followed – among them John Norman MacLeod who had got into the sheep-rearing business in Tasmania and who was soon to be in charge of one of the Western District's most successful farming operations.

'I landed on Indented Head from Van Diemen's Land with sheep in July 1837,' John Norman recalled. 'In September, I went with a party to explore. We went round Lakes Colac and Korangamite; we were the first

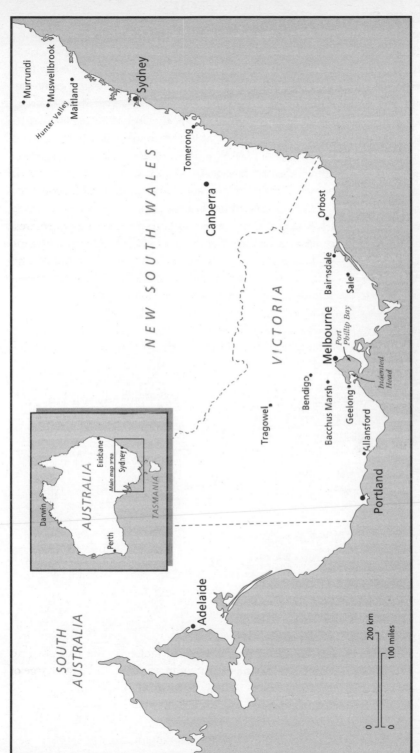

Map 5: South-eastern Australia

[Europeans] who went round the latter . . . As we came along the banks of Lake Korangamite, a great many parties of natives [Aborigines] ran off . . . leaving everything behind them . . . We were stopped by the Pirron Yalloak [River]. At [first] we could not find a ford, so we camped in the centre of a small plain, tethering our horses close around us, and kept a watch all night – there were seven of us. The natives were talking close to us . . . within 100 yards. At daylight two men came to us when we made signs that we would not harm them.'[19]

Victoria's Aborigines clashed frequently with incoming whites – hence John Norman MacLeod's need for the night watch he maintained while pushing into the Lake Corangamite region. Aborigines died in those conflicts. Many more died from diseases introduced by Europeans or as a result of the enforced expulsions which followed white incursions into Aboriginal territory. Given the extent to which Scots-born station owners, shepherds and settlers organised those expulsions, it is ironic that the disaster which overtook Australia's native peoples was a consequence, in part, of the economic forces which also lay behind the Highland Clearances. What happened to the Aboriginal population of Victoria and the rest of Australia in the 1830s and later was more terrible than what was then happening in places like Sutherland, Skye and Harris. But evicted crofters and dispossessed Aborigines had one thing at least in common. Their previous ways of life were ended, whether in Victoria or in the Highlands and Islands, by nineteenth-century Britain's need for wool.

The Highlands and Islands met only a fraction of this need. Australia could meet more – but only if its wool producers gained access to territory from which they had previously been barred. It was with the aim of acquiring such territory that John Norman MacLeod and other sheep farmers from Tasmania moved into Victoria's Western District, where enormous acreages were available for the taking.

With Roger McLeod, I spend two or three days quartering the Western District in search of such traces as it might contain of John Norman and the other members of the Talisker family, including John Norman's widowed mother, Catherine, who followed him here. As John Norman MacLeod did on reaching Victoria, Roger makes Indented Head our starting point. From the sandy promontory where John Norman brought his sheep ashore, the wide waters of Port Phillip Bay stretch away to the north. Out there, projecting above an otherwise unbroken horizon in the way the hills of Lewis do when seen from Assynt, are Melbourne's highrises. Some miles to the south is the Rip – connecting Port Phillip Bay with the open ocean and a place, as its name implies, where crisscrossing currents make navigation hazardous. But Roger and I, though we waste time doing so, have not come to Indented Head to gaze seaward. I want to get a feel for the landscape behind us – the landscape which John Norman MacLeod traversed during his exploratory journey of October 1837.

Then spring was giving way to summer. Now it is May and autumn is well advanced. Even in this southern part of Australia where winters can be chilly, the country's native trees never shed their grey-green foliage. But in Geelong, about twenty miles from Indented Head, yellowing leaves are falling from oaks and elms of the sort which nineteenth-century emigrants from Britain planted in an attempt to give their new homeland something of the appearance of the country they had left. This attempt seems to me to have been vain. There is little that is British, less that is Scottish, about the landscapes which come into view as Roger and I head west.

Thirty or forty years after the arrival here of sheepmen like John Norman MacLeod, much of the Western District of Victoria was redistributed among a different set of farmers who, since they operated on a smaller scale than John Norman and his fellow pioneers, wanted to cultivate the land – instead of using it as pasture. Those later farmers erected buildings, put up fences and built boundary walls of the sort now characteristic of this area. None of these features existed in John Norman MacLeod's time. Striking out from Indented Head, John Norman found himself in open, gently rolling and only lightly wooded terrain. This was, and would remain for several decades, ideal sheep country.

Beyond Geelong, Roger points out the Moorabool River. On its banks, near present-day Meredith, John Norman MacLeod laid claim to the first of his Western District stations – a 25,000-acre tract called Borhoneyghurk. Pausing briefly in Colac, a town which takes its name from one of the lakes mentioned by John Norman in his account of his 1837 explorations, Roger and I press on, and soon I become aware that the midday sun – in the north, I remind myself, not the south – is reflecting dazzlingly from a large body of water to our right. This is Lake Corangamite, where John Norman MacLeod encountered the Aborigines mentioned in his correspondence. I glimpse a bridge. It spans, I realise, the Pirron Yallock River, which John Norman was initially unable to ford and beside which he and his companions took turn to stand guard through the hours of darkness – for fear of their falling victim to an Aboriginal attack.

A day later, Roger and I are in Portland. We drive through the town, and turn into MacLeod Street. At its end, standing on steeply rising ground above Portland Bay and the Southern Ocean, is a house called Maretimo. This large home, enclosing three sides of a central courtyard, was built by John Norman MacLeod when, in the later 1850s, he represented Portland in Victoria's legislative assembly. Castlemaddie, the sheep station which had become John Norman's principal possession by this stage, was close to Portland – and it was here, at Maretimo, the station's owner chose to invest the profits Castlemaddie generated. Those profits were substantial. During Assemblyman MacLeod's lifetime, a lot of his namesakes back in Scotland had every reason to curse sheep. But when you stroll around Maretimo, taking in the quality of the house and its wooded gardens, it is evident that Portland's assemblyman did extraordinarily well out of wool. John Norman, by the 1850s and 1860s, had money to spend. So did his brothers and sisters. This becomes clear when Roger McLeod and I, on our way back to Melbourne, stop at Bacchus Marsh.

Bacchus Marsh was founded, as were many of Victoria's settlements, in the middle years of the nineteenth century, and one of the town's oldest buildings is its Anglican church, Holy Trinity. In this church, overlooking the altar, are two stained-glass windows. Those were commissioned from craftsmen in distant Belgium and shipped to Australia at considerable cost. This cost was met by the children of Catherine MacLeod, the woman Holy Trinity's windows commemorate. For ten years prior to her death in 1863, Catherine lived in Bacchus Marsh. Before that, her home had been in Geelong. This Geelong home, like its Tasmanian predecessor, was called Talisker. That same word from the other side of the world features in the inscriptions on Holy Trinity's windows. Gazing at those windows, illuminated by a bright Australian sun, you get some sense of the Talisker family's determination to ensure that neither time nor distance should be allowed to separate them from the part of Skye where they had been rooted for so long.

New South Wales: Sydney and the Upper Hunter

Today in Australia there are countless people who can trace their roots to Talisker. A lot of those folk owe their Skye connection to Janetta Maria, the youngest daughter of Major Donald and Catherine MacLeod, who was born in Van Diemen's Land in 1824 and who, at the age of eighteen, set up home with her settler husband, Charles Marsh, near Armidale, 250 miles north of Sydney. By 1990, according to an Australian genealogist, this couple's descendants numbered at least 1,500. Peter Macleod, president of the Clan MacLeod Society of New South Wales, takes me to meet one of them. His name is Charles Cooke, and he farms at Long Hill in the valley of New South Wales's Upper Hunter River.[20]

As we drive out of Sydney, where he trades in yacht equipment, Peter Macleod tells me he has traced his ancestry back to the middle part of the eighteenth century. Then, as for the next 150 years, Peter's Macleod forebears lived in or around the Dumbartonshire towns or villages of Helensburgh,

Rhu and Luss – just west of Glasgow. 'There's a tradition to the effect that our people came originally from Skye,' Peter goes on, 'but I can't tie that down. I know they operated a tailoring business, and I've heard it said that my great-grandfather, John Peter Macleod, was swindled out of his share of this business when his father, my great-great-grandfather, died. If that's true, John Peter may have nursed a grudge – something that might explain his tendency to drink too much. I never knew my great-grandfather, but I've been told how, when an old man here in Sydney, he'd sometimes be so full of whisky that he'd wander through the streets, dodging the trams and singing the Will Fyfe song, "I Belong To Glasgow".'

What brought his great-grandfather to Sydney, I ask Peter Macleod. 'He came to join his son, Donald, my grandfather,' Peter replies. This was in the 1920s. Jobs were scarce in Scotland then, and Donald Macleod, a Glasgow shipyard worker who had served with Britain's Royal Flying Corps during the First World War, was convinced that he and his wife, Nellie, could better their prospects by emigrating to Australia. Like his namesake, Major Donald of Talisker, Donald Macleod began by taking up farming in Tasmania. This did not work out. But Donald's later careers as a builder and shopkeeper, first in Melbourne, then in Sydney, were more successful – successful enough to ensure that Ian Macleod, Donald's son and Peter's father, got the start in life that enabled him to qualify as an accountant.

My probing of Peter Macleod's family history occupies the three or four hours it takes to get from Sydney to Muswellbrook, a small town on the Hunter River. 'I'm stopping here,' Peter says, 'to introduce you to Ewen MacLeod. Like my grandfather, Ewen left Scotland in the 1920s. He's elderly now and living in a retirement home. But every March until not so long ago, Ewen staged a MacLeod get-together at his place not far from here. These occasions meant a lot to me and to a lot of other people.'

At ninety-three, Ewen MacLeod walks with the aid of two sticks, but his handshake is strong, his memory clear. 'I grew up on a farm near Aberfoyle in Perthshire,' Ewen tells me. 'My grandfather had a croft in Skye, at Kilmaluag, but my father was one of a big family, so he left the island, settled in Perthshire and got a job as a shepherd. My dad was well set up in Aberfoyle, but he hurt himself in a fall and had to take twelve months off work. This was just two or three years after the First World War, and though my father could have gone back to Skye to recuperate, he headed for Australia instead. He had a brother here, my uncle Malcolm. Before the war, Malcolm had been a seaman, but he'd jumped ship in Melbourne and set up home there. During the war, Malcolm served with the Australian forces, and then, when the fighting was over, he took one of the farms the Australian government gave to ex-servicemen. These were hopeless farms

– far too small. But Malcolm's letters home said nothing of that. According to him, life here could hardly have been rosier, and Dad took Malcolm at his word. My father and my eldest brother emigrated first. My mother took me and my other two brothers out later. We left in 1925. I remember sailing out of London's Tilbury Docks, passing through the Suez Canal, that sort of thing. To a boy like me, it was all a great adventure.'

In Australia, Ewen MacLeod worked first as an agricultural machinery salesman. Later he bought Karingal Farm which became the setting for the Clan MacLeod reunions Peter Macleod recalls with so much warmth. To get to Karingal, which Peter is anxious to show me, we drive out of Muswellbrook in the direction of McCullys Gap.* The forests which fringed our route when we were closer to Sydney have given way now to almost treeless country which, were it not for roadside notices warning of kangaroos, might be in one of the more arid parts of the American West. A recent drought has begun to break and the grass is greening slightly, but creeks remain bone dry. 'People hereabouts are praying hard for more rain,' Peter observes.

At Karingal, Peter points to an enclosed veranda extending all the way along one side of Ewen MacLeod's former farmhouse. 'That's where we'd sit down to dinner when attending Ewen's gatherings,' Peter recalls. 'Some years there would be thirty of us, maybe more. Ewen himself would preside. He'd sit at the head of the table, calling out toasts and ordering anyone who'd been to Scotland to give an account of their trip. Sometimes we'd march out of the house and up that hill over there. Back in 1986, Ewen went to Skye to attend a clan parliament and look up his relatives. While in Skye, though he was well into his seventies, Ewen climbed one of MacLeod's Tables. From then on, he gave the name of MacLeod's Table to the hill he led us up here at Karingal. Once, with a piper playing fit to burst, we unfurled our clan society banner at the summit. I know it sounds crazy, but at moments like that it's really great to belong to Clan MacLeod.'

From Karingal, on a narrow road which follows the course of the mostly waterless Pages River, Peter MacLeod and I head for Charles Cooke's farm at Long Hill. Charles, who greets us at his doorway, is wearing a kilt – not in my honour, he assures me, but because he is just back from a practice stint with his local pipe band. Inside, Charles shows me a prized photograph of Skye's Talisker House which he has visited more than once. Later, over a dinner featuring more beef than I normally eat in six months, I try, and fail, to get this Upper Hunter farmer's Talisker-derived ancestry straightened out – but I do pick up on the fact that there is yet another of Australia's many Taliskers nearby. 'I'll take you there tomorrow,' Charles promises.

---

*Australia and New Zealand have abolished the use of apostrophes in placenames.

The sun is struggling through a morning mist when, next day, Peter Macleod and I board Charles Cooke's car and set out on a tour of this corner of New South Wales. We drive through Gundy – its one building of consequence the Linga Longa Inn. We stop in Aberdeen. We stop in Scone. We stop again in Murrundi, where Charles, who is known to everyone, exchanges greetings with people watching sheepdogs being put through their paces in the town's park. Next we visit a farm, adjacent to a Pages River tributary called Scotts Creek, which Charles's grandparents bought in the early part of the twentieth century and which Charles's grandfather named Talisker. The farm is Talisker no longer. Its name has been changed and its paddocks have been given over to horses – the bloodstock industry being a big thing in today's Upper Hunter Valley. Charles, a cattleman through and through, disapproves of racehorses taking over from the Aberdeen-Angus herds he thinks more appropriate to his home area. Maybe he disapproves too of the way a house he knew in boyhood has all too obviously been neglected. At all events, we do not hang about. Swatting mosquitoes and assailed by grating shrieks from cockatoos, I walk quickly through the remnants of Talisker's orchard. Then we are on the road again.

By afternoon, having said our goodbyes to Charles Cooke, Peter Macleod and I, travelling seaward now, have exchanged the Upper Hunter for the Hunter Valley proper. Today the valley is a mix of vineyards, olive groves and open-cast coalmines. But once it was home to the first big contingent of people to reach Australia from the Highlands and Islands. This group, numbering nearly 300, left Uig in Skye on 7 August 1837. Their ship, the *Midlothian*, reached Sydney four months later. The *Midlothian* emigrants, whose passage costs were met by the British government, had been brought to New South Wales with the aim of their becoming shepherds and the like – a plan which foundered when the *Midlothian* people refused to be dispersed across widely separated sheep stations. Like the families led to New Zealand by Norman MacLeod, the *Midlothian*'s passengers insisted on settling in a single locality where, they explained, 'they might have the ordinances of religion in their own Gaelic, for, failing this, they must live in absolute heathenism as most of them know no English'.[21]

Australia's colonial administrators eventually acceded to those demands – permitting most of the *Midlothian* emigrants to establish themselves around Maitland on the Hunter River's lower reaches. Present-day Maitland, though I do not have time to inspect it, is thus of interest to me – all the more so because of my having an appointment in Sydney, hours after my Hunter Valley trip, with Neil McLeod, a retired accountant whose great-great-grandparents, Donald and Ann MacLeod, together with their seven children, left Skye on the *Midlothian*.

Donald MacLeod, though categorised as a 'farm servant' in documents relating to his emigration, did not lack a distinguished ancestry – thanks to his descent from a further Donald MacLeod who lived at Galtrigil on the western shore of Loch Dunvegan. This earlier Donald, who appears to have been something of an entrepreneur, possessed his own trading vessel. Hence his intimate knowledge of Hebridean waters – and hence his being engaged in 1746 as pilot and guide to Prince Charles Edward Stuart who, during the months following the Battle of Culloden, was ferried by sympathisers from one Hebridean island to the next.

When I meet with Neil McLeod in Sydney, then, I am also meeting with the great-great-great-great-great-grandson of a man who played a vital part in ensuring that Charles Edward Stuart eluded capture and execution. Neil makes little of this. He suggests, however, that his emigrant ancestor, Donald MacLeod, because of this Donald's connection with the ship-owning Donald of Galtrigil, was of more elevated background than most early-nineteenth-century farm labourers. That may be why, Neil goes on, his great-great-grandfather could write – his literacy being proved, Neil points out, by the existence of a letter Donald MacLeod mailed from the Hunter Valley to Scotland in February 1838. Because an edited version of this letter found its way into the columns of the *Inverness Courier*, its contents have been preserved, and they include the information that, within days of getting to Maitland, Donald MacLeod had been 'engaged . . . to a gentleman for fifty pounds a year'. This was Thomas Hardy, proprietor of an extensive landholding on the Paterson River, 30 miles from Maitland. In addition to his wages, Donald wrote, he and his family were in receipt of 'as much as we want of beef, mutton, pork, flour, tea and sugar, tobacco, etc.' Although his voyage from Scotland had been blighted by the death of his two youngest sons, Donald MacLeod went on, he was in no doubt as to the attractions of New South Wales. 'I think this is the best place in the world,' Donald observed. It was certainly a place which enabled him to prosper. By 1850, Donald MacLeod, after just thirteen years in Australia, had saved enough money to buy a property of his own, a 105-acre farm on the Manning River, about fifty miles beyond the Paterson. By way of paying tribute to his origins, Donald, like lots of other MacLeod emigrants all around the world, named his farm Dunvegan.[22]

Victoria: Bairnsdale and Orbost

In the Hunter Valley, I glimpse a sideroad leading to Luskintyre. This is a Harris placename, and it was transferred to New South Wales in the 1820s when a newly arrived emigrant, Alexander MacLeod, acquired land beside the Hunter River. Like John Norman MacLeod, who helped open up Victoria's Western District, Alexander was a tacksman's son and, again like John Norman, Alexander became wealthy. By 1828, Luskintyre's proprietor owned 1,130 cattle and one of the earliest Hunter Valley vineyards. Doing equally well on the Hunter's opposite bank was a quite different Alexander MacLeod. His speciality was sheep. This is not surprising – for, as indicated by his naming his property Ratagan, this Alexander was a son of Donald MacLeod of Arnisdale, the Glenelg tacksman-turned-sheep-producer whose landholdings included the original Ratagan and who made such a positive impression on James Hogg.[23]

There are many Highlands and Islands placenames in New South Wales. There are more in the part of Victoria known as Gippsland – as I discover when, moving on there, I take a southbound and overnight bus out of Sydney. Eight hours into my journey, at three in the morning, the bus comes to a juddering halt and, half emerging from a comfortless sleep, I gaze into the darkness – wondering where on earth I am. What I see does nothing to lessen my disorientation. On the far side of the street is an illuminated shop front with a neon sign above its window. 'Orbost Dairy,' the sign reads.

An hour later, I am in Bairnsdale – which began as Bernisdale and which was named, as was Orbost, by a man with family ties to the Skye originals of those places. At Bairnsdale, though it is barely four a.m., I am met by Frank and Beatty Blennerhassett, whose home is at nearby Bengworden. Beatty's grandfather, one more of this book's dozens of Alexander MacLeods, was a tailor who came to Gippsland in the 1890s from Easter Ross. Frank's forebears were English in origin, but they lived for centuries in Ireland – emigrating from there in 1874. Like Charles Cooke, Frank is a farmer. Unlike Charles, Frank rears sheep, not cattle, and next morning, after an hour or two in bed, I accompany Frank and his son, Stephen, to their farm's shearing shed – having wanted, ever since getting to this country, to see Australian sheep shearing at first hand.

The wool one gets from blackface or cheviot sheep, the breeds which became universal in the Highlands and Islands during the nineteenth century, is very coarse. Today, as a result, it is practically valueless – synthetic fibres having taken its place. This does not mean that sheep farming has ceased in the north of Scotland. Today, however, such farming is geared to the production of lambs for the meat trade – wool being removed from Highlands and Islands sheep mainly because, for animal welfare reasons, it can hardly be left where it is.

At Bengworden, in contrast, wool remains a cash crop. It does so because wool from merino flocks of the Bengworden sort is exceptionally fine – so fine as to attain values of a kind Scottish sheep producers can only dream about. Hence my interest in watching Australian shearing – necessarily a more sophisticated operation than its Highlands and Islands counterpart. As animal after animal passes swiftly through their hands, Stephen and Frank Blennerhasset sort the resulting wool with great care – segments of differing quality going into one or other of a whole set of waiting sacks. 'Bengworden wool always fetches a good price,' Frank says proudly. The readily apparent quality of his sheep, together with the painstaking way they are sheared, make it easy to see why.

Later, Frank and Beatty take me to Orbost. Our road into the town is obstructed temporarily by men loading calves on to a truck. We pull up to wait until the last calf is safely aboard. Then I catch sight of the inscription on the truck's open door: 'L.D. Macalister, Strathaird Farm, Orbost'. Recalling what I have read of Gippsland's history, I walk across and introduce myself to the man in charge. 'Are you Mr Macalister?' I ask, thinking he may be a Strathaird employee, not the farm's owner. 'Yes,' the man replies with excusable wariness. 'I'm Lachie Macalister.'

'So you must be connected,' I continue, 'with Lachlan Macalister from Strathaird in Skye.' Obviously thinking he has fallen in with a madman, Lachie Macalister nods his head. 'That's why my farm's called Strathaird,' he says. Having had no idea, until this moment, that I would find in today's Orbost so direct a link with the town's beginnings, I shake Lachie's hand a second time. 'I'm really pleased to meet you,' I tell him.

More than 200 years ago, the family to which Lachie Macalister belongs moved from Argyll to Skye where they took ownership of the island's Strathaird estate – previously part of the lands of Clan MacKinnon, and as such sandwiched between the territories of the Dunvegan MacLeods, to the north, and those of the MacDonalds of Sleat, to the south and to the east. Lachlan Macalister, the pioneer settler from whom the present-day occupant of Orbost's Strathaird Farm is descended, was a son of the Skye Strathaird's first Macalister laird. He came to Australia as a serving army officer in 1817, and on his discharge from the military, obtained a number of land grants in the Monaro, an area occupying the south-eastern corner of New South Wales. In the early part of 1838, Lachlan Macalister's Monaro station was sought out by a newly arrived emigrant from Skye. His name was Archibald MacMillan. He wanted a job, and Macalister gave him one.

Archibald MacMillan, still in his twenties in 1838, was a lot younger than his Monaro employer. The two, however, had much in common, Archibald's father, Ewen, whose roots were in Lochaber, having migrated to Skye much as the Macalisters had done, though some years later. In Skye, Ewen MacMillan married Marion MacLeod, a local woman of – as the contemporary phrase had it – good family. At about the same time, and conceivably on the recommendation of his MacLeod inlaws, Ewen acquired the tenancy of one of the many tacks or farms belonging to John Norman MacLeod of Dunvegan. This farm was located in Glen Brittle, and Ewen MacMillan's occupation of it must have brought him into contact with the Macalisters of Strathaird, whose estate was close by.

If Archibald MacMillan and Lachlan Macalister exchanged memories of Skye, the chances are they spoke, perhaps with some longing, about the wet weather which has always been characteristic of the Hebrides. Rain, or rather its absence, was certainly a leading topic of conversation in the Monaro throughout the later 1830s – the region then being badly affected, as much of Australia often is, by drought.

With their pastures drying up and their animals dying, Monaro farmers were interested in rumours that, on the other side of the mountains constituting the Monaro's southern boundary, there were comparatively well-watered grazings to be had. It was with the aim of checking out those stories that, during 1839, Archibald MacMillan undertook the first of several journeys which gave him a claim to have been the man who made it possible for whites to establish themselves in Gippsland – the name the authorities attached to the locality, subsequently incorporated into Victoria, which Archibald was instrumental in opening up for settlement.

Today, Archibald MacMillan's reputation is disputed. His admirers point to his achievements as an explorer – and to the fact that, by one of his Gippsland acquaintances, Archibald was described as 'a fine, hearty, affable gentleman, full of Scotch humour'. MacMillan's detractors contrast his warm feelings for his fellow whites with the contempt he demonstrated for those other people who had been living in Gippsland for tens of thousands of years before his arrival. Archibald MacMillan's dislike of Aborigines is evident in his contention that Gippsland was 'too good to be occupied by savages'; it is equally evident in MacMillan's insistence that, when he helped kill the 'savages' in question, he was simply 'an instrument in the hands of the Almighty'. Attitudes of this sort, of course, were common in nineteenth-century Australia, and there is little point in singling out Archibald MacMillan for censure. In a book which makes much of the suffering caused by the Highland Clearances, however, it should not go unnoticed that this Skye-born Scotsman treated Gippsland's original inhabitants with a brutality beside which the activities of Scotland's evicting landlords pale into insignificance.[24]

Archibald MacMillan, who operated initially on Lachlan Macalister's behalf but afterwards acted on his own account, was not the only Scottish beneficiary of Gippsland's forcible expropriation. Around him in the years when Gippsland was being taken over by whites, Archibald gathered a group of fellow station owners whose background, in many instances, was identical to his own. 'They are almost all Highlanders here,' a visitor to Gippsland commented in 1844, 'and one hears a lot of Gaelic.'[25]

Among Gippsland's Gaelic speakers was Archibald MacLeod. The fifth and youngest son of Norman MacLeod of Bernisdale in Skye, Archibald was related to Archibald MacMillan, the explorer of Gippsland, through the latter's MacLeod mother. By way of his own wife Colina, a Campbell from Argyll, Archibald MacLeod was also connected with Lachlan Macquarie. When, in 1821, Colina and Archibald emigrated from Scotland to Van Diemen's Land, it is likely that – like the MacLeods of Talisker – they did so with Governor Macquarie's encouragement.[26]

From Van Diemen's Land, Archibald, Colina and their family, eventually numbering fourteen children, soon sailed for the Australian mainland. Helped by the fact that his elder brother, Donald, was an aide to Thomas Brisbane, Macquarie's successor, Archibald obtained a government post at Bathurst, New South Wales. This was one of the first farming settlements to take shape in the Australian interior, and Archibald MacLeod, as Bathurst's agricultural superintendent, had the task of keeping the authorities in Sydney, on the other side of the Blue Mountains, in touch with progress in the area.

In 1829, Archibald was asked to take on much the same job in Norfolk Island. About a thousand miles north-east of Sydney in the Pacific Ocean, this was the place to which Governor Brisbane shipped the most recalcitrant of Australia's convict settlers. Norfolk Island's consequent role as a centre of 'the extremest punishment' was facilitated by its gruesome climate. That climate, however, struck down the innocent along with the guilty. One of Archibald and Colina's daughters died on Norfolk Island; so did one of their sons. It must have been with some relief, therefore, that the couple and their surviving children returned to New South Wales in 1835 – to begin farming in the Monaro.[27]

Within two or three years of his setting up home there, however, Archibald MacLeod was beset by fresh troubles. First Colina died; then her widower, like everyone else in the Monaro, had to endure a seemingly endless succession of dry seasons. It is hardly surprising, therefore, that on news reaching him of Archibald MacMillan's discovery of less drought-prone localities to the south, Archibald MacLeod abandoned his New South Wales farm and followed in his kinsman's wake.

By the mid-1840s, then, Archibald and his now mostly grown-up children were in Gippsland. There, this MacLeod family contrived to get as many as four or five separate landholdings into their possession. Most of those landholdings were given the names of places with which Archibald's relatives back in Scotland had some association. One Gippsland station, managed by Archibald MacLeod's son Norman, became Bairnsdale or Bernisdale – in tribute to the Skye tack Archibald's father had occupied. Another, managed by Archibald's son John, became Orbost – the original Orbost, at this point, being in the ownership of John's uncle and Archibald's brother, William MacLeod.[28]

How much contact there was between William of Orbost and his emigrant brother, Archibald, is unclear. But both men, coincidentally or not, pursued similar land-management strategies – Archibald MacLeod expanding his flocks and herds at the expense of Gippsland's Aborigines and William, as noted earlier, doing much the same at the expense of the Orbost townships he cleared to make way for sheep.

The people thus lost to Skye were not replaced. In Gippsland, however, incoming whites were soon present in larger numbers than Aborigines had ever been. During the 1860s and 1870s, in consequence, Bairnsdale and Orbost began to develop into towns. Orbost, on the Snowy River, owed its initial success to a flourishing timber industry – based on the extensive forests still to be seen in the Snowy's vicinity. Bairnsdale became an agricultural service centre – and for a time aspired, as Orbost did also, to grow into a city. This did not happen and, though both towns have experienced a good deal of building and rebuilding, their expansion has been insufficient to obliterate all traces of their history. At Orbost, for example, some remnants of an early MacLeod home can still be seen within a few hundred yards of Lachie Macalister's Strathaird Farm. Not far away is McLeod Street. Here a little museum displays a watercolour of the Skye locality to which Victoria's Orbost owes its name.

Back in Bairnsdale, Beatty Blennerhassett organises for my benefit a get-together which turns into a clan gathering. Missing from Beatty's guest list, however, are descendants of Gippsland's first MacLeod settlers, Archibald and his family. This is because their connection with Bairnsdale proved transient – mid-nineteenth-century Gippsland having been too thickly wooded and too distant from good harbours to support a livestock-based economy of the kind then developing at the other, western, end of Victoria. Much of Archibald's land was eventually mortgaged to Sydney financiers and none of his sons or daughters, as a result, made permanent homes in either Bairnsdale or Orbost. Given this circumstance, I tell Beatty Blennerhassett, it is not surprising that the enquiries she has been making on my behalf have failed to turn up anyone connected with Archibald MacLeod. Beatty shakes her head. 'Someone's got to know where to find Archibald's people,' she says.

Next day, still determined to track down Archibald MacLeod's descendants, Beatty escorts me to the Bairnsdale library and archive run by the East Gippsland Family History Society. There one of the society's members provides me with a telephone number in Seaspray, a settlement on Victoria's Bass Strait coast, about sixty miles from Bairnsdale. This number belongs to Bill Macleod, Archibald's great-great-grandson, who agrees to meet me the following morning in Sale – another coastal town where, Bill informs me, his great-great-grandfather is buried.

With Bill Macleod, I visit Sale's cemetery. Together we stand in front of the tombstone Bill has brought me here to see. 'In memory of Archibald MacLeod,' its inscription reads, 'who died at Bairnsdale on 15th November 1861, aged 76 years: an old colonist . . . and one of the early Gippsland settlers.' Norman MacLeod of Bernisdale, Archibald's father and Bill Macleod's great-great-great-grandfather, was a grandson of Roderick MacLeod of Ullinish, whose father, Donald MacLeod of Greshornish, was the fifth son of Clan MacLeod's most acclaimed chief, Ruaraidh Mòr. Since Ruaraidh Mòr's own ancestry can be traced back to Clan MacLeod's medieval beginnings, Bill Macleod possesses a genealogy extending through eight centuries. Bill, a crane operator who works on offshore oil production platforms in the Bass Strait, is dismissive of this fact.[29]

Scotland: Skye, Glenelg and Lewis

In 1835, John Norman MacLeod of Dunvegan died. His son, Norman, inherited both the MacLeod chieftainship and John Norman's Skye estate. The new chief was a young man of twenty-three. As his grandfather, General Norman, had done in similar circumstances more than eighty years before, he began by signalling his intention to live permanently in Dunvegan Castle – where about £8,500 (nearly £500,000 at today's prices) was promptly spent on extensive renovations. Those works were arguably ill advised. Like every MacLeod chief since the time of Ruaraidh Mòr, over 200 years before, Norman took charge of a property weighed down by debt – his rebuilding programme merely adding to the interest payments he had to make each year if he was to keep his creditors at arm's length.[30]

By this point, most Highlands and Islands landlords were absentees, and Norman MacLeod's refusal to adopt this role won him support. In a letter sent in 1838 to Norman's sister Emily, Martin MacLeod of Drynoch commented: 'It is . . . most gratifying to all MacLeod's well-wishers that he has come to reside in the castle . . . He will have the means of becoming well acquainted with the management of his own affairs, which will be advantageous to himself and to the people under him.' This friendly overture notwithstanding, Martin MacLeod's good opinion of his chief and laird did not last. Soon Martin was complaining, as tacksmen had complained for generations, that his chief was never done hounding him for cash. 'He [Chief Norman] clipped me in every way that he could in the narrowest manner,' Martin MacLeod remarked in 1845 when on the point of leaving Skye for North America. But if Martin of Drynoch's departure, which deprived him of Skye's last MacLeod tacksman, came as a blow to Norman MacLeod of Dunvegan, it did nothing to weaken his resolve to be on good terms with the generality of his tenantry. While resident at Dunvegan, Chief Norman remarked, he was 'in very intimate and friendly communication' with the people inhabiting his property. Although Norman's policies did not always meet with their approval, those people, for their part, had reason to think well of him. When, in 1846, Skye's population was plunged into famine, Norman MacLeod at once took on the job of feeding hundreds of families – comprehensively wrecking his already shaky finances in the process.[31]

Had Dunvegan's laird been able to act on one of his impulses, a lot of the folk he helped in 1846 would have been by then in Canada – where, five years previously, Chief Norman tried to buy a 5,000-acre tract of territory with a view to settling on it some of the people left landless as a result of earlier evictions. 'I propose to send out forty families or thereabouts this time next year,' Norman told one of his agents in March 1841. Further families would follow at his expense twelve months later, Norman went on. Each such family, he instructed, was to be provided with a small farm on which 'a cottage' was to be erected. He hoped by those means, the MacLeod chief explained, to 'ease this country of a burden it cannot bear'.[32]

In 1841 and 1842, with a view to making a reality of this plan, lists of prospective emigrants were drawn up. The individuals named on those lists were evidently incapable of funding their own emigration, and they seem to have been eking out an existence on the margins of the sheep farms which had taken shape in localities like Minginish and Bracadale over the preceding thirty years. People of this sort would probably have welcomed an opportunity to start afresh in Canada, but they were not enamoured of the different expedient to which Norman MacLeod resorted on his Canadian venture foundering for lack of the necessary cash. This expedient involved the transfer of families from Bracadale and Minginish to Glendale – where the newcomers were provided with crofts and told that the males among them, in order to supplement the produce of those crofts, should become fishermen.

When challenged about this episode, Chief Norman tried to distinguish between 'eviction' and 'removal from one place to another'. Migration to Glendale from Bracadale, he said, was an example of the latter, not the former. But no linguistic nicety could conceal what happened on the ground.

Glendale became 'overcrowded', one of its crofters said later, because of 'the evicting of most of the tenants of Bracadale' and the resettlement of those tenants in Glendale. This, to be fair, was to conflate a whole series of events. The bulk of Bracadale's many evictions were the responsibility of Norman's father, not Norman. His population-transfer policy, in conception at any rate, was a genuine attempt to assist families who had already lost their landholdings and had not, in the interim, been able to emigrate. Chief Norman's problem was that the families he was trying to help did not want crofts in Glendale. As they afterwards made clear, they wanted the restoration to them of the land from which they had been ejected. This was not on Chief Norman's agenda. Instead, as pointed out by Rev. Roderick MacLeod, parish minister in nearby Snizort, Norman was set on 'enlarging' the sheep farms his father had created.[33]

Although farm enlargement seems to have been accomplished without further evictions, it added to the difficulties facing crofters by depriving them of still more land. Hence Rev. Roderick MacLeod's conviction that poverty was endemic on the Dunvegan estate because sheep farmers 'possess the soil upon which the poor people at one time lived in comparative comfort'. This was particularly true of Minginish and Bracadale. But even in Duirinish, the parish which includes Dunvegan and an area where clearances had been less extensive than in more southerly parts of Norman MacLeod's property, more than 60 per cent of the land which had formerly been cultivated was in the hands of sheep farmers. This could not help but be 'productive of poverty,' Duirinish's minister, Rev. Angus Martin, said in 1844. Despite so much emigration having occurred, Skye's total population, as Martin pointed out, was continuing to rise. More and more people, therefore, were having to be accommodated on less and less land – with the inevitable result, Angus Martin went on, that many families had been left 'without . . . any place . . . on which to settle'. Although those families were in an especially unenviable plight, folk who had crofts, in Angus Martin's opinion, were little better off than folk who did not. 'The crofts are too high rented,' the Duirinish minister contended, 'and they are too small to maintain a family.' Donald MacLeod, Duirinish's medical practitioner, agreed. 'The crofts are so small,' he commented, 'that the people cannot live upon them; the great fault is putting too many people together; they cannot pay their rent out of the land . . . If the people had more land . . . they would be better off.'[34]

Donald MacLeod's call for crofters to have bigger crofts took insufficient account of the fact that crofts were not meant to provide their occupants with an adequate supply of food. Crofts consisted of just four or five acres of indifferent soil because, as stressed already, the men responsible for their creation wanted to leave crofters with no alternative but to turn to non-agricultural employment. This was clearly understood by Sir John McNeill, who became principal administrator of Scotland's poor laws in the mid-1840s and who had to cope, therefore, with the calamity which shortly afterwards engulfed the Highlands and Islands. 'It is a misapprehension,' McNeill wrote of crofters, 'to regard them as a class of small farmers who get . . . their living . . . from the produce of their crofts. They [live] . . . chiefly by the wages of labour.'[35]

Initially, the necessary wages were earned by crofters in their role as kelpers. 'When the manufacture of kelp was brisk,' Chief Norman MacLeod's factor recalled in 1837, 'there was not a small tenant [meaning crofter] on the estate who, after paying his rent, had not an abundant supply of meal for his family.' When the kelp trade collapsed, however, crofters were left with no cash surplus. They could scarcely pay their rents or buy the food they needed – let alone invest in improvements to their ramshackle homes. Most of the people residing on Norman MacLeod's Dunvegan estate, it followed, were undernourished, ill clothed and, above all, badly housed. 'The houses of the crofters,' a mid-nineteenth-century academic observed when investigating conditions in the Hebrides, 'are in the highest degree wretched and miserable'. The average crofter's home, according to the same commentator, contained just one apartment – its floor consisting of earth, its walls of undressed stones and rubble, its roof of 'very permeable' thatch. The crofter's cattle occupied one end of his single room, the crofter and his family lived in the other – 'the whole inhabitants', whether human or animal, entering and exiting by the same door. 'The fire, which is composed of peat, or turf, is in the centre of the floor . . . The smoke escapes by an aperture in the roof . . . and by the door and window, which last is seldom glazed but is shut with straw or heather . . . There can be no question that such a residence . . . has much in it of a tendency to degrade and brutalize the inhabitants.'[36]

In homes of this standard type, furnishings were minimal. Few of the patients attended by Donald MacLeod, Duirinish's medical man, possessed a bed – 'nothing,' Dr Donald said, 'but a wisp of straw upon the ground and a little covering'. Another glimpse into the lives of folk enduring almost unimaginable hardship is provided by notes taken in 1844 by members of a royal commission then visiting Skye to look into the operation of the poor laws. Among the individuals interviewed by commission representatives was Murdoch MacLeod, a crofter at Colbost, not far from Dunvegan: 'Has one half of a croft. Four children. No stock of any kind . . . One bedstead with straw and very poor bedding . . . A little bit of something like an old horserug . . . One coarse earthenware dish, one half of a plate. No furniture to be mentioned. Two of the children nearly naked.'[37]

Readers of this book, were they to make an inventory of their possessions, would have to catalogue thousands of separate items. That is because absolute poverty of the kind experienced by Murdoch MacLeod and his family – their household goods consisting, remember, of a bed, a few scraps of bedding, a worn-out rug, one dish and half a plate – is confined today to countries like Ethiopia. In mid-nineteenth-century Skye, however, Murdoch's plight was not exceptional. Many island families, it was reported, were 'in a state of the most lamentable want'; they were 'destitute'; they 'presented . . . pictures of severe, unmitigated . . . misery'. As their resources dwindled, moreover, Skye folk, like their counterparts in Cape Breton Island, were becoming dangerously reliant on potatoes, the one crop that could be grown in quantity on even an acre or two of poor soil. In Bracadale, where whole families ate little else, potatoes were reckoned to account for more than 90 per cent of each person's nutritional intake. Elsewhere on the Dunvegan estate, dependence on them was hardly less complete. '*Thàinig fortan an àigh ort,*' a MacLeod poet remarked in the course of lines dedicated to this most humble of edible tubers: 'The grace of fortune is on you.' Such praise was misplaced. While potatoes were capable of sustaining people who had no alternative source of food, they were also vulnerable to insect infestation and, still more disastrously, to fungal infections. Cape Bretoners discovered as much in 1845. Skye's population learned the same hard lesson in 1846 and in the years that followed. The cause of catastrophe was the same in both cases: a virulent strain of potato blight to which potatoes of that time had no resistance.[38]

In the summer of 1846, blight's onset was rapid. In August, the *Inverness Courier* sent one of its reporters to Kintail, Lochalsh and Skye. 'In all that extensive district,' the paper commented, 'he had scarcely seen one field which was not affected.' Many crofting townships, the *Courier*'s man noted, were 'enveloped in . . . decay'. 'The blight had taken effect over miles of country,' another observer commented. Everywhere, as potatoes rotted, 'a foetid and offensive smell . . . poisoned the air.'[39]

The Dunvegan estate was among the hardest hit localities. Of the 7,000 or so people living on his property, Norman MacLeod calculated, some 6,000 were 'dependent upon the potato'. Now this irreplaceable crop's ruin, as Norman put it, was complete. In consequence, many hundreds, maybe thousands, of his tenants faced starvation.[40]

In Ireland, where reliance on potatoes was even more total than in Skye, more than a million people were then dying of hunger while their landlords did little to help them. In the Highlands and Islands too, there were plenty of lairds whose reluctance to come to their tenants' aid infuriated the government officials sent north to assess the scale of the crisis. But for

Norman MacLeod, the same officials had nothing but praise. Norman, one of them wrote, was 'an excellent man and a pattern landlord' whose 'untiring exertions' on behalf of the people living on his estate were responsible for keeping those people alive.[41]

Norman MacLeod's actions during the terrible winter of 1846–7, when Skye and the rest of the Highlands and Islands teetered on the brink of a disaster of Irish proportions, testify to the importance he attached to his being his clan's chief. Although Norman was considered by contemporaries to be 'very indulgent' to his crofting tenants, because he was reluctant to evict them for offences such as non-payment of rent, he had not previously departed from the hard-edged land-management strategies developed by his predecessors. Those strategies were predicated on a ceaseless quest for cash flow. In pursuit of this objective, successive MacLeod chiefs had raised rents, sold tens of thousands of acres, introduced new modes of farming, cleared whole communities and, by behaving in this fashion, so alienated their former tacksmen in particular that practically all of them had emigrated. During the winter of 1846–7, however, it seemed briefly as if none of this had happened. During that winter, Dunvegan Castle was occupied by a man who ceased, even if temporarily, to be a revenue-driven landlord and who became instead a patriarchal figure modelled, maybe subconsciously, maybe not, on Ruaraidh Mòr, Iain Breac and other MacLeod chieftains of that sort.[42]

'The famine years,' Chief Norman said afterwards, 'found me at Dunvegan. Every morning . . . hundreds of people awaited my appearance at the castle door. I had at the time large supplies of meal for my workpeople, but these were soon exhausted, and I went to Aberdeen for more.' Why, Norman MacLeod was asked, had he undertaken the feeding of so many families at so great a cost to him personally? 'I only did what every other man similarly circumstanced would have done,' he replied. 'They were my people. It was my duty to assist them.'[43]

'This is a winter of starvation,' it was reported from Bracadale in December 1846. Elsewhere in Skye, things were no better. A 'heavy fall of snow' had added to 'the suffering of the people'. Fields and roadsides had been picked clear of nettles and other semi-edible herbs. No shellfish were left on island beaches. Illness, in the shape of 'dysentry and even scurvy', was widespread – a sure sign that death rates were about to increase exponentially.[44]

That month a printed poster was circulated on Chief Norman's instructions. Headed 'MacLeod's Address to His People' and signed 'your faithful friend, MacLeod', this poster, soon on display all over the Dunvegan estate, was intended to forestall panic. The predicament in which his tenants found themselves, Dunvegan's laird acknowledged, was 'alarming' and 'disheartening'. But they should not give way to despair: 'You are all aware that . . . no exertions on my part have been, or will be, spared to alleviate your distress . . . I intend to remain among you during this time of trial . . . [and] to take care that the country is supplied with a sufficiency of good and wholesome food . . . We will unite together to drive famine from our doors.'[45]

'Not a potato remains,' Norman MacLeod noted on 2 January 1847, but more than 600 men, he went on, had been put to work on drainage schemes and other wage-generating projects – all of them supervised by one of Dunvegan Castle's longstanding staff members, John Campbell, who also had the job of organising regular disbursements of food. 'On Tuesdays and Fridays,' Chief Norman wrote of Campbell's responsibilities, 'he is followed down to the [castle] store by hundreds of poor people who receive stones [measures equivalent to 14 pounds in weight] and half-stones [of oatmeal] according to the number of their families.'[46]

Although John Campbell was nominally in charge on those occasions, Norman MacLeod was often in the background. 'Nothing can be more admirable,' a civil servant commented, 'than the quiet, kind and judicious way in which MacLeod goes about among his people. He seems to know the individual history of every one of them, and they have a mutual confidence in each other which it would be a blessed thing to see more generally in the Highlands [and Islands].' This and the numerous other tributes paid to him must have been of some comfort to Chief Norman during the dark days of early 1847. But the strains inherent in his position were exacting a heavy toll nevertheless. Dunvegan's laird, another official wrote of Norman MacLeod's one-man famine relief programme, had 'taken up the praiseworthy task of finding subsistence for his people with more ardour and benevolence than careful calculation'. Norman's own difficulties, as a result, were multiplying rapidly.[47]

Before the famine, Chief Norman's rental income had been in the region of £6,000 annually. However, interest payments and other unavoidable outlays left him with less than £1,200 clear. Towards the close of 1846, a hike in interest rates bit deeply into this margin. During February and March 1847, the famine's impact eroded it completely. On the one hand, Norman MacLeod had been deprived of almost all his croft rents – his crofting tenants, as he recognised, having 'literally no money'. On the other hand, he was spending huge sums on oatmeal and other supplies. 'The country is now in an awful state,' Norman wrote in February. 'A fearful snowstorm has prevented the men from working, and the entire population . . . is . . . thrown upon my meal store. They come in hundreds. Food cannot be refused, and I can see no possible way in which they can ever hope to pay for what they get . . . [In] three weeks I have not received five pounds.' His income, Chief Norman reckoned, was now 'several hundreds less than nothing', and he was starting – unsurprisingly – to be downhearted. 'I am getting very low,' Dunvegan's laird confessed. 'I have not been very well the last few days, fairly knocked up, mind and body.'[48]

Norman MacLeod's total expenditure on famine relief during the winter of 1846–7 has been estimated at £9,000 – equivalent to £500,000 today. By the following winter, he was bankrupt. Dunvegan Castle was let to a stranger. The wider Dunvegan estate was put in trust, and a large part of it, including the whole of Glendale, was sold. With his wife and family, Chief Norman, at the age of thirty-seven, left for London. There he took 'a very junior post' in the British government's Home Office. It would be fifteen years before Norman MacLeod set foot in Skye again.[49]

Because the Highlands and Islands potato harvest was blighted year after year, the famine which began in 1846 continued into the 1850s. For much of this period, Norman MacLeod's people, as he called his tenantry, were dependent on aid from the government and from charitable organisations. Fortunately, the response to appeals on behalf of hungry crofters and their families was so overwhelming that substantial funds were soon at the disposal of the voluntary agency which channelled those funds into the Highlands and Islands. This agency was the Central Relief Board. Headquartered in the Lowlands, the board was very much a creature of its time and place. Board staff in localities like Skye operated in accordance with a plethora of rules and regulations designed to ensure that recipients of their assistance laboured long and hard for each ounce of meal doled out to them – the Glasgow and Edinburgh professionals who shaped Central Board policy being convinced that no one, however badly situated, should get anything for nothing. The outcome, according to one critic of the board's operations, was that 'a charitable fund' had been turned into 'a screw for oppressing the poor'. Norman MacLeod did not employ such language, but there were moments before he quit Dunvegan for London when he was infuriated by the Central Board's insistence that men who could not turn out to work on its road-building and other projects should be refused help. In a letter sent in March 1848 to the Central Relief Board's senior representative in Skye, Norman commented: 'There will be found many cases that ought to be made exceptions, in my opinion, to your rules . . . John MacLeod, Feorlig [near Dunvegan], a poor man with family, is able to work and very willing. But he is almost blind; so nearly so that he is quite unable to my knowledge, [and] I have long known him, to break stones, and this is the only labour John MacRae [the Central Board's Dunvegan-based official] considers himself authorised to give.'[50]

When Chief Norman left Skye, responsibility for making representations of this type passed to his sister, Emily, who moved from Dunvegan Castle to a nearby house called Kilchoan Cottage. One of the last members of her family to speak Gaelic fluently, Emily was as close to the generality of Skye people as it was possible for someone of her background to be. But neither Emily MacLeod nor any other individual was capable of alleviating human suffering on the scale experienced in the Hebrides during the later 1840s. 'It is impossible for me to describe the misery of this quarter,' one of Emily's correspondents observed of his home district. Among other contemporary testimony of this sort is a description of Skye people lining up for a handout of oatmeal: 'At the appointed time and place, these poor creatures troop down in hundreds, wretched and thin, starved and wan. Some have clothing, some almost none, and some are a mass of rags. Old and young, feeble and infirm, they take their station and wait their turn. Not a murmur, not a clamour, not a word. But they wept . . . as they detailed their . . . miseries.'[51]

Throughout the Highlands and Islands, landlords responded to scenes like these by calling for a renewed exodus to North America. Among pro-emigration lairds were some whose pockets, unlike Norman MacLeod's, were deep enough to finance the population outflow they wished to bring about. Firmly in this category were the owners of Glenelg, Lewis and Assynt – James Baillie, Sir James Matheson and the second Duke of Sutherland. Between 1847 and 1855, those three individuals shipped more than 3,500 people overseas.

Of this total, 344 came from Glenelg. Its inhabitants had once had thousands of acres at their disposal. But by the 1840s, as a result of repeated clearances, Glenelg's remaining residents, about 900 people in all, were crammed into just one or two crofting townships by the seashore. In Glenelg, a journalist wrote angrily, the spread of sheep farming had led to 'fertile land lying waste at one end of a glen and people starving at the other'. Only a handful of the locality's families, it was reported, had access to more than five acres. Most were trying to subsist on the output of one acre or less, and many had no land at all – their plight in stark contrast to the comparative comfort in which emigrants from Glenelg were living, by this point, in Ontario's Glengarry County. Glenelg's remnant population, the parish's minister commented, were well aware of North America's attractions, 'and many would emigrate if they had the means'. In 1849, those means were made available by Glenelg's latest owner, James Baillie, a well-to-do businessman. Subject only to the condition that prospective emigrants 'pull[ed] down their own houses before they set out', a stipulation intended to prevent reoccupation of abandoned homes, Baillie met the cost of shipping dozens of families to Canada.[52]

In Canada, the Glenelg emigrants were joined by 2,337 people from Lewis. Its owner, when the famine commenced, was Sir James Matheson. In 1844, he had bought the island from the last representative of the MacKenzies of Seaforth – who had themselves seized it from the MacLeods of Lewis more than 200 years before. Perhaps the best thumbnail sketch of Lewis's new proprietor, a Sutherland-born tycoon whose wealth derived from his career in India and China, is to be found in *Sybil*, a novel written by Benjamin Disraeli, one of Victorian Britain's leading politicians. There, Matheson features as McDruggy, 'a Scotchman richer than Croesus . . . fresh from Canton with a million of opium in his pocket'. Although the real-life Sir James, a founder of the Hong Kong combine, Jardine Matheson, insisted that he had trafficked in tea, not narcotics, Disraeli was right to portray him as an early beneficiary of the drug business. The basis of Matheson's fortune, then, was ethically suspect, and his opinions of the Chinese with whom he dealt were condescending at best. But nothing of this detracted from Sir James's high status in British society. Nor did his behaviour in Lewis where he was widely disliked. 'Sir James Matheson,' a lawyer of the time observed, 'was . . . most hospitable and sometimes profusely benevolent . . . [But] there was another side to the picture. The policy of [his] estate was a tortuous, subtle, aggressive one in pursuit of territorial aggrandisement and despotic power, so absolute as to be almost universally complained of.'[53]

Both Sir James Matheson and his Glenelg counterpart, James Baillie, were typical of the new men who came to prominence in the Highlands and Islands during the middle years of the nineteenth century. With chieftainly families of the old sort going under or being forced to dispose of large tracts of territory, the way was open for monied individuals to acquire enormous properties at what were, by Lowland or English standards, knock-down prices. Matheson, in particular, began by being convinced he could get a worthwhile return on his investment – pouring a great deal of cash into initiatives intended to regenerate Lewis's moribund economy. Those plans, however, were derailed by the potato failure. In 1846 and subsequently, Lewis's laird, to give credit where credit is due, spent heavily on famine relief measures. But by 1850, with no end to famine in sight, he had had enough. John Munro MacKenzie, Sir James's factor, was duly ordered to begin organising a programme of enforced emigration.

The people he selected for deportation, MacKenzie observed, were drawn from one of 'two classes': the first consisting of everyone who was 'two years [or more] in arrears of rent', the second comprising the inhabitants, whether in arrears or not, of localities which could be 'converted into grazings'. The departure of 1,554 emigrants from Lewis in 1851 was consequently accompanied, as were further emigrations in 1852 and 1855, by widespread clearances. No fewer than 1,180 separate eviction orders were issued by Stornoway's Sheriff Court in a three-year period. Several of Lewis's crofting townships were emptied totally. Others experienced extensive depopulation.[54]

Emigration of the sort financed by James Baillie and Sir James Matheson was not a charitable gesture on its sponsors' part. Being shrewd business operatives, the two lairds were well aware that money laid out in this fashion was by no means money lost. On the income side of his estate accounts, Sir James Matheson's venture into the emigration business brought an immediate return in the form of rents from the sheep farmers who were the ultimate beneficiaries of his clearances. On the expenditure side of the same accounts, there was an equally pleasing gain in the shape of a reduction in the poor rates which the authorities had begun levying on property owners in areas, of which Lewis was certainly one, where social deprivation was both widespread and growing.

Ontario: Bruce County

In mid-May 1851, the first of several hundred families sent that year to Canada from Lewis left Loch Roag, on the island's west coast, aboard a steamer bound for the Clyde – transferring there to a sailing ship of the kind which, in the 1850s, still dominated ocean travel. The Lewis people's journey began badly – the 'heavy swell' their vessel met with on leaving Loch Roag causing 'seasickness among the women and children'. But this was as nothing to the miseries of an Atlantic crossing lasting, in the precise recollection of one 1851 emigrant, 'nine weeks and four days'. So severe were the gales encountered in the course of this two-month voyage that former fishermen among the Lewis emigrants had to turn out at times to help their ship's crew take in sail. In those conditions, loss of life was inevitable. 'They suffered great hardships,' the granddaughter of one emigrant couple recalled. 'My grandmother's first baby died [aboard ship] and was buried at sea.' Her grandparents, the same woman added, were greatly distressed by their having to dispose of their child's body in this way: 'They pleaded [with the ship's captain] to [be allowed to] keep [the baby's corpse] until they got to land to bury him, but the captain [on health grounds] refused. Next day they sighted land.'[55]

On docking in Quebec City, the Lewis emigrants divided, some heading south, others west. The former group settled in a part of Quebec Province which borders with New England. There, in the vicinity of Lac Mégantic, they established a number of communities. The names given to those communities, Galson, Tolsta, Ness Hill, Dell and Balallan, commemorate their founders' Lewis origins every bit as evocatively as a more formal memorial which tells how hundreds of 'Gaelic-speaking people . . . came from the Hebridean Isles of Scotland to pioneer this . . . area'. Unveiled in the autumn of 1999 at a ceremony presided over by a local historian, Duncan McLeod, this memorial strikes a somewhat elegiac note. Perhaps that is appropriate – for such was the pulling power of the nearby United States that, in the 150 years since the victims of Sir James Matheson's clearances came here, their descendants have mostly become American. The same is true of many of the descendants of those other 1851 emigrants who pushed on up the St Lawrence to the Great Lakes region. However, the settlements which this second Lewis group created in Ontario's Bruce County were to retain a Hebridean flavour a little longer than their Quebec counterparts. Indeed, or so it seemed to me when I travelled to Bruce County with Clan MacLeod Society activist Allan MacLeod, something of this flavour lingers there still.[56]

Allan, a retired teacher, lives in Mississauga, a suburb of Toronto, but his roots, Allan tells me, are further east – his emigrant great-great-grandmother, Christina MacLeod, having settled at Big Brook in the River Denys area of Cape Breton Island in 1832. 'My great-great-grandmother was a widow,' Allan says. 'She came, I think, from Skye, and she brought at least two sons, Malcolm and Alex.' Alex was Allan MacLeod's great-grandfather. Alex's son, Duncan, was Allan's grandfather, and Duncan's son, Neil Angus, was Allan's father. 'My father left Cape Breton for the Nova Scotia mainland as a young man,' Allan says. 'That's why I wasn't raised on the family homestead at Big Brook.' When Allan was a boy, however, this Big Brook homestead remained in the occupation of his grandparents, and he was a regular visitor there. 'At that time, people in rural Cape Breton were living much as they'd always done,' Allan remembers. 'Water had to be carried inside from a well. The house was lit only by kerosene lamps. Conversation was mostly in Gaelic, and evenings were given over to telling stories – ghost stories as I recall. Story telling was our ancestors' equivalent of television, I guess.'

As Allan talks, the Ontario countryside is unfolding outside his car's windows. We drive through Brampton, Orangeville, Arthur, Harriston and Mildmay. It is late March, and winter is drawing reluctantly to an end. From a grey sky, rain is falling intermittently on to waterlogged fields where deep snowdrifts linger in every hollow. Then, as we enter Bruce County and approach Kincardine, the weather changes. A breeze picks up, the sky clears and I catch my first glimpse of Lake Huron – extending to the western horizon and looking as limitless as the Atlantic when viewed from Lewis townships of the sort that Bruce County's early settlers left in 1851. There is one marked contrast between Lake Huron and the seas around the Hebrides, however. What I take initially to be waves breaking on an offshore sandbar turn out, on closer inspection, to be something else entirely – upended iceflows glinting in the sun. As is evident from the chilliness of the wind blowing off its surface into Kincardine's main street, Lake Huron, after several weeks of sub-zero temperatures, is frozen clear across.

In a Kincardine restaurant, Allan and I meet with Angus Macleod, a composer whose CD, *The Silent Ones*, a mix of music and speech in both Gaelic and English, is Angus's tribute to his emigrant forebears. From this CD, I have learned a bit about Angus's Lewis antecedents. Now I learn more. 'My principal emigrant ancestor was my great-great-grandfather, Murdo Macleod, who came here with his family,' Angus says. 'He left from Mid-Borve, but his people belonged originally to Galson, a little to the north. Not all of this was known to me when I was growing up, but I've always been aware of Lewis looming large in my background. My grandfather, Billy Macleod, and his six sisters, my great-aunts, talked with each other in Gaelic, and when any of them got together, they spoke about Lewis – which they'd never seen but which they thought of as home.'

Although Angus was not raised here, he came to Bruce County to live in 1998, giving up his previous job as an arts administrator in the university city of Guelph and recording *The Silent Ones* in a studio facility located on a farm once occupied by his great-grandfather and namesake, Angus Macleod. Not many of Bruce County's present-day farms belong to descendants of the county's original homesteaders, Angus remarks. However, he has made arrangements for us to visit one farm in this category. It is home to Allister and Pearl MacKay, Angus goes on, and to get there, he adds, we need to head out of Kincardine by way of Ripley, a small community which took shape in the later nineteenth century at the centre of Huron Township – the Bruce County locality where families from Lewis mostly settled.

The first of those families got here in September 1852. During most of the preceding winter, Bruce County's Lewis settlers had lived in towns like Hamilton, west of Toronto, where the men among them were employed as labourers on railway-construction projects. Work of this type, however, was seen as no more than a stopgap. Like most of the Highlanders and Hebrideans who had preceded them to Canada, the Lewis emigrants of 1851 wanted land to farm.

Because mid-nineteenth-century Ontario was experiencing an immigration-fuelled population boom, with total numbers up from 486,000 in 1842 to 952,000 ten years later, there was intense pressure on the colonial authorities to make additional territory available for settlement. Hence the appearance in Canadian newspapers in July 1852 of notices advertising the disposal of land in the future Huron Township – 'the price to be ten shillings [about £25 in today's terms] per acre, payable in ten annual instalments, with interest'. Here was the opportunity for which the Lewis people had been waiting. Having registered their interest in acquiring land in Bruce County, they made their way to Goderich – a lakeside town forty miles south of Kincardine. Eventually, 109 emigrant families from Lewis, nineteen of them headed by a MacLeod, assembled there. Most had been evicted on Sir James Matheson's orders in the spring of 1851. Some, however, had made the Atlantic crossing more recently; and a few had moved west from Cape Breton Island, where conditions at this point were little better than those prevailing in the famine-stricken Hebrides.[57]

The Canadian government later categorised much of the land in Huron Township as 'first class'. When I reach his farm, Allister MacKay, whose grandmother was a Lewis-born MacLeod, is happy to go along with that description. 'We have good land here,' Allister tells me in the kitchen of his solidly constructed farmhouse – a farmhouse which, back in the 1870s, took the place of the log cabin that had preceded it. Moving on to Allister's porch, we look out across flat fields where, come summer, beef cattle will be pastured. 'When my grandmother came here with her parents in 1852,' Allister MacKay points out, 'this farm didn't look like it looks now. Everything was under trees or brush. But when they began to get the brush cleared, my folks found themselves the owners of a place that was a whole lot better than the one they'd had in Scotland.'[58]

Inside again, I ask Allister and his wife, Pearl, if they have been to Lewis. Yes, they say. 'We made a trip over there in 1978,' Allister explains. Prior to their going, Allister adds, he had been in touch with a distant relative in Lewis and, with the help of this relative, now dead, he and Pearl were able to locate the foundations of the home which Allister's people were 'kicked out of', as he puts it, in 1851. 'It was truly wonderful to be there and to see exactly where my folk's house stood,' Allister comments, 'but what I couldn't figure out was how the poor souls who lived in that house ever earned an income. They must have been fishermen, I guess. They sure couldn't have been farmers. Everywhere you looked, there was only rock and peat. It was pitiful.'

But if Bruce County was an improvement on Lewis, it was not, to start with, much of an improvement. 'The first work he had to do in Canada,' a local schoolmaster noted of one of the district's Lewis-born pioneers, 'was dig his wife's grave.' While such tragedies were common everywhere on the North American frontier, they appear to have been more frequent in Bruce County than in other places – perhaps because the county's settlers, having endured years of malnutrition before their emigration, were more than usually inclined to suffer from poor health and, even when not so afflicted, tended always to be short of money, furnishings, tools and other essentials. 'Very few of the [Lewis people's] original cabins had any floor except the bare ground,' according to the schoolmaster already quoted, 'with only a bundle of straw and some rugs in a corner for a bed.'[59]

Further tales of hard times are to be heard when, on the evening of my arrival in Bruce County, I meet in Kincardine with a succession of people of Highlands and Islands extraction. Because Angus Macleod has publicised my visit in local newspapers and on local radio, I am presented with more than thirty interviewees – to each of whom, unavoidably, I give too little time. Ann Pladsen talks about her great-great-grandparents, Angus and Jessie MacLeod, who, though they appear to have followed Rev. Norman MacLeod from Assynt to St Ann's, declined to accompany him to Australia and New Zealand – opting instead for Bruce County. Also of Assynt descent are brothers Norval and Harvey McLeod, whose forebears, like Ann Pladsen's, got here by way of Cape Breton. All the others I talk with, however, trace their families to Lewis: Heather Ibbotson, whose widowed great-great-great-grandmother, Christina MacLeod, reached Huron Township with her four sons in 1852; Dianne Simpson, whose Lewis ancestor, William MacLeod, arrived that same year; Diane MacLeod, whose great-great-grandfather, John MacLeod, evicted from Galson in the course of one of Lewis's last clearances, settled in Bruce County during 1863.

Two of my Bruce County informants, Mary Phillips and Peggy Chappelle, show me documents containing detailed accounts of emigrant journeys. The narrative in Mary Phillips's possession dates from 1936. It was written by Mary's great-grandmother, whose given name was Alexina, with a view to preserving, for the benefit of Alexina's son, Mary's grandfather, what Alexina could recall of her Scots-born parents, Norman and Sarah MacLeod. This emigrant couple, according to their daughter, were married on 26 July 1850. The marriage took place on the Isle of Mull and, that same day, along with Sarah's mother and several of her brothers and sisters, the newly-weds left Mull for Glasgow, where they boarded the *John Kerr*, a Montreal-bound emigrant ship. 'The *John Kerr* was slow,' Alexina wrote. 'I've heard my father say that boats they could first see far behind them in the morning would be just as far ahead of them at night.' Unsurprisingly, then, Norman and Sarah MacLeod spent eight weeks at sea. But it was in Canada, not on the Atlantic, that their troubles began. No sooner had Norman got to Montreal, Alexina recorded, than he was 'taken down with a fever'. Left behind by the other members of her family, who felt they had no alternative but to press on to Ontario, Sarah found lodgings in Montreal and, moving her ailing husband into those lodgings, took on the protracted job of nursing him back to health. This, for any young woman anywhere, would have been a worrying time. For Sarah MacLeod, two months married, fresh off an emigrant ship and coping with the complexities of life in a city where most people spoke only French, the months that followed must have been a hell on earth. Fortunately, Norman recovered. After the couple had paid for their accommodation, however, they had only a pound or two with which 'to face the winter'. Work which Norman got on a farm on Montreal's outskirts tided them over, and in the summer of 1851, by which point their first child had been born, Sarah and Norman MacLeod were able to travel to Toronto. The next summer, they settled in Bruce County. 'Here,' their daughter commented, 'they met with all the hardships of pioneer life . . . But [they] lived to see . . . good buildings take the place of [their] log shanty, and schools and churches built in the neighbourhood.'

Among this neighbourhood's residents were the Lewis-born forebears of Peggy Chappelle, my other source of a first-hand account of Bruce County's beginnings. This account was written in the 1960s by Peggy's mother, Christina Picot, who lived to be ninety-six and whose MacLeod grandmother, one of Bruce County's 1852 settlers, had told Christina a great deal about her family's early years in Canada. 'My grandmother . . . was gentle and kind,' Christina remembered, 'and must have been very beautiful when she was young. A young man in Lewis [composed] a Gaelic lovesong about her.' Her grandmother, Christina continued, was also well able to look after herself – as underlined by an incident on one of the forest trails which, before the construction of proper roads, connected Huron Township's farms with Ripley and Kincardine. On being accosted on this trail by 'a tramp,' Christina wrote, 'Grandmother took a pistol out of her pocket, and told him to start running, and he did.'

Like many Hebrideans, Christina Picot commented, Bruce County's settlers were 'deeply religious'. 'Their first thought was getting a place to worship God . . . The seats [of their church] were logs and stumps, and there they gathered every Sunday . . . They walked for miles [to attend Sunday service] and those who came a long distance were taken to the homes around [the church] for dinner . . . My mother [who grew up in late-nineteenth-century Bruce County] told me she never heard anything lovelier than the singing of the psalms in Gaelic echoing through the bush.'

Scotland: Skye

By the 1850s, Skye's social collapse was complete. Among its victims was one of the Glendale relatives of John McLeod, the North Carolina farmer whose fine home was described earlier. John's Glendale kinsman was Donald MacLeod, who described his plight in a letter preserved among Emily

MacLeod's papers at Dunvegan Castle. He was 'one of the poorest class,' Donald told Emily, possessing no livestock and having nothing to sow or plant on his croft. He would be obliged, Donald went on, if Emily – known for her 'kindness [in] helping the poor' – could spare him some clothes with which to 'cufer [his] naked childrin'.[60]

Donald MacLeod's English may have been uncertain. His Gaelic was not. In his own language, Donald MacLeod was *Dòmhnull nan Òran*, Donald of the Songs, a published poet and a man who, previous to this point, had managed to make his own way in the world. 'I have a faint recollection of his appearance,' one of Donald MacLeod's younger contemporaries wrote when recalling how the poet had conducted himself in better days. 'He always dressed scrupulously, and wore a tall hat. He was well known all over Skye, not only for his poetry, but also for his . . . conversation. He was a beautiful wit and an eloquent Gaelic speaker, and had a wonderful command of . . . that language.' In a previous era, such a man would have been summoned to Dunvegan Castle to entertain Clan MacLeod's chieftain. Now the Chief of MacLeod was a bankrupt in faraway London, and Dòmhnull nan Òran was reduced to begging children's clothes from Norman of Dunvegan's sister.[61]

'It would be difficult, perhaps impossible, to convey to you an idea of the wretchedness and misery I have witnessed,' a civil servant reported to his superiors at the end of a visit he made to Skye in 1852. 'It must be seen to be understood. Any description that can be given must fall short of the sad reality. It is not too much to say that many of the swine in England are better fed and better housed than are the poor of this island.' At Struan, south of Dunvegan, 'a pauper village of evicted tenants' had come into existence. There '137 souls' were living, and trying to grow crops, on 'about six acres of land'. Nearby, at Coillore, another sixty-two victims of clearance and dispossession were endeavouring to make out on five acres. 'Within the last fortnight,' one of Emily MacLeod's informants told her in February 1852, 'I have had to travel over most of the parishes of Bracadale and Duirinish. I am sorry to say that . . . I have witnessed much distress from want of food. In one wretched locality I found four families, numbering above thirty individuals, who were in a state of actual starvation. They had not an ounce of meal or a single potato amongst them. How they have subsisted since . . . God only knows.'[62]

Skye's sheriff, Thomas Fraser, blamed this state of affairs on what a newspaper of the period called the island's 'sheepocracy'. 'Of the 16,000 arable acres in Skye,' Fraser pointed out in the course of an exchange of letters with Norman MacLeod of Dunvegan, '6,000 are held by 30 [sheep farming] tenants.' Since this left 10,000 arable acres to be shared among the far larger number of people occupying Skye crofts, it meant that the area of crop-bearing land available to the average sheep farmer was fifty times greater than the area available to the average crofter. 'I cannot but think that much of the misery of the population of Skye may be attributed to this cause,' Sheriff Fraser wrote.[63]

Had the sheriff included pasture as well as arable land in his calculations, the disparities he highlighted would have seemed still more glaring – most of Skye's hill grazings having been incorporated, by the 1840s and 1850s, into sheep farms. Even as they stood, however, Thomas Fraser's figures were persuasive. Responding to them, Norman MacLeod did not deny that the growing dominance of sheep-farming interests had left crofters at a disadvantage. But no conceivable redistribution of land, Chief Norman insisted, would solve Skye's problems. There simply was not enough territory to provide for everyone. Hence Norman MacLeod's growing conviction that a large proportion of the island's population, put at around 24,000 by the 1841 census, should be helped to emigrate. 'It is no personal interest of my own, for I have none now, that leads me to urge . . . people's emigration,' Chief Norman commented. 'I think their transfer to a richer soil and a better climate . . . would effect an amelioration of their physical and moral condition.'[64]

Eventually, Thomas Fraser, while not abandoning his belief that Skye could be 'made capable of supporting a much larger population', was 'reluctantly driven' to much the same conclusion as Clan MacLeod's chief. By the close of 1850, the charitable funds raised for famine relief had been spent. But Skye, as the sheriff observed, was still suffering 'widespread, and to all appearance, permanent misery and destitution'. That December in Portree, Fraser convened a meeting of 'local men of influence' to consider 'the present distressed state of [Skye] and what remedy should be adopted for bettering the condition of [its] inhabitants'. The meeting led to the formation of a committee with the remit of persuading as many Skye people as possible to emigrate. In the early part of 1851, the committee, which Thomas Fraser chaired, circulated a 'friendly address' to heads of family throughout the island. Any Skyeman who could not 'reasonably expect to procure sufficient food and clothing for himself and his family', this circular stated, had a 'duty to . . . remove to a country where . . . [he could] procure . . . the means of rising to a comfortable and respectable independence'. As their 'address' made clear, the country Thomas Fraser and his colleagues had in mind was Australia – to which a British government agency, the Colonial Land and Emigration Commission, was then offering assisted passages.[65]

Because even assisted passages were out of reach of the people Sheriff Fraser wanted to help, he launched an appeal for the cash needed to make large-scale emigration possible. Taken up by prominent individuals in the

Scottish Lowlands and England, this appeal culminated in the emergence of a new organisation, the Highland and Island Emigration Society. Its leading office bearers were Sir John McNeill and Sir Charles Trevelyan. Both were senior civil servants: the Edinburgh-based Sir John being in charge, as already mentioned, of Scotland's poor relief arrangements; the London-based Sir Charles holding a key post at the Treasury. Although nominally independent of government, the Highland and Island Emigration Society was thus in touch with ministerial thinking on Highlands and Islands matters. As had been the case since the kelp industry's demise, such thinking tended to the view that Highlands and Islands problems mostly stemmed from the region being overpopulated. In 1851, Lord John Russell's administration accordingly passed an Emigration Advances Act which enabled landlords to borrow from Sir Charles Trevelyan's department the cash they needed to finance the departure of their tenants. This Act's provisions, when taken in conjunction with the emergence of the Highland and Island Emigration Society, allowed Trevelyan, who was notoriously unwilling to spend public money on feeding famine victims, to urge the alternative course 'of adopting a *final* measure of relief for the Western Highlands and Islands by transferring the surplus of [their] population to Australia'.[66]

In advancing this proposition, Charles Trevelyan was assisted by the gold rush which began in Victoria in 1851 – and which caused Rev. Norman MacLeod to move on from Melbourne to New Zealand. The prospect of easy pickings on the goldfields had deprived Australian sheep stations of shepherds and other key workers. The resulting labour shortage could be made good by emigrants from the Highlands and Islands, Sir Charles maintained. Nor would such emigrants simply catch the gold bug in their turn, he insisted. Their 'comparative simplicity and [their] ignorance of the English language,' Trevelyan explained, meant that people from the Highlands and Islands were unlikely to strike out on their own account. Equally helpful in this connection, Sir Charles added, was the fact that he and his Emigration Society colleagues planned to send 'entire families' to Australia. The adult male members of those families, because of their having to provide for wives and children, were bound to be less footloose, or so Trevelyan contended, than the young, single men from whom sheep station owners had formerly been in the habit of recruiting their workforces.[67]

Those arguments appealed to business interests with a stake in the success of Australian agriculture. Among early donors to the Highland and Island Emigration Society were the British agents of Australian sheep producers. Woollen manufacturers, fearing that gold-induced labour shortages in Australia might deprive them of raw materials, were not far behind. Other funds followed, and the Highland and Island Emigration Society was consequently able, by the spring of 1852, to commence operations. First, however, the society had to find people prepared to accept its offers of aid. This proved difficult. The 'long-continued distress' experienced in places like Skye, Sir Charles Trevelyan was informed by Sheriff Thomas Fraser, had engendered so much 'apathy and indifference to the future' as to make the notion of a fresh start unattractive to islanders – all the more so, it emerged, if the fresh start on offer entailed emigrating to Australia.[68]

Because of the distances involved, a voyage to Australia was a much more expensive undertaking than a voyage to North America. Other than serving soldiers or criminals, therefore, the only people from the Highlands and Islands who travelled to Australia during the first third of the nineteenth century were drawn from the minority who, like Donald MacLeod of Talisker, could access the necessary cash. This changed in 1837 when the British government began offering free or subsidised passages to its Australian possessions. This initial experiment in assisted emigration to the southern hemisphere did not last long. Prior to its abandonment, however, several hundred people left Skye for New South Wales. Among them were the *Midlothian* emigrants mentioned earlier. In principle, their positive experiences in the Hunter Valley should have helped the Highland and Island Emigration Society make the case for Australia as an emigrant destination. But what happened to the *Midlothian* people was untypical. Many of the Skye folk who went to Australia in the 1830s appear to have had a difficult time, and some of them made their disenchantment known to friends at home. 'The [emigrants] that wrote back [from New South Wales] did not at all give a favourable account of the place,' Emily MacLeod was told in 1848 by Norman Ferguson who lived in Roag near Dunvegan. If he and his neighbours had their way, Ferguson went on, they would emigrate only to North America – where many of their 'relations and acquaintances' had settled years before and where, by all accounts, emigrants generally did well.[69]

But North America, from a Highland and Island Emigration Society standpoint, was not an option. The society's stated aim was to take people to Australia. Its funds had been raised on this basis, and its office bearers, in order to make those funds stretch as far as possible, were committed to taking advantage of the aid available to Australia-bound emigrants from the Colonial Land and Emigration Commission. Applicants for Emigration Society assistance, Skye's Sheriff Fraser was instructed by Sir Charles Trevelyan, were to have it made plain to them that such assistance was predicated on their going to Australia – and if only for lack of any alternative, the idea of exchanging Skye for New South Wales or Victoria gradually began to gain ground. In July 1852, therefore, the Highland and Island Emigration

Society was able to send 300 or so Skye people to Greenock, where they boarded a ship, the *Georgiana*, bound for Melbourne. 'The spirit which they manifested was in all respects admirable,' Sir Charles Trevelyan wrote of the *Georgiana*'s passengers. Maybe. But prior to those passengers leaving Skye they had been, as Sheriff Fraser observed, 'in a state bordering on starvation'. This was especially true of Dugald MacLeod, who set out for Victoria with his wife, Mary, and their four children. 'Appears to have suffered deeply from want of food,' a Portree-based Colonial Land and Emigration Commission official recorded of Dugald. 'Was ejected from his croft eighteen months ago, and has lived since in a gravelpit by the roadside near Bernisdale'. This was no preparation for a gruelling voyage to the far side of the world.[70]

The Atlantic Ocean

When overseas emigration from the Highlands and Islands began in the eighteenth century, the ships on which emigrants sailed were often of high quality. 'She was a very pretty vessel,' it was noted of one such ship, the *Nestor*, which left Portree for Britain's American colonies in September 1773. Even at this point, admittedly, emigrant ships were not invariably in the *Nestor*'s class – the Pictou-bound *Hector*, another 1773 departure, being little better than a hulk. But the *Hector* was untypical. In the 1770s and for some time after, most America-bound emigrants from the Highlands and Islands made the Atlantic crossing in reasonable comfort. They did so because the standard emigrant ship of the period was chartered by a tacksman of the type then leaving Skye for North Carolina. Since the *Nestor*'s charterer was almost certainly one of her passengers, he would have taken a close personal interest in her crewing, her fitments, her provisioning. Hence the ship's 'commodious and even elegant' cabin – to say nothing of her 'little library, finely bound'.[71]

Every emigrant ship was vulnerable to Atlantic storms, of course. When Janet Schaw, whose impressions of North Carolina were quoted earlier, sailed there from Scotland in 1774, she had a half-share of a well-appointed 'stateroom'. But her voyage was a nightmare all the same. Day after day, with their cabin's windows shuttered to protect them from the shattering impact of breaking waves, Janet and her travelling companion sat in candlelit semi-darkness listening to the 'fury' of the ocean, 'the rattling of the sails', 'the sound of sailors pulling with united strength at the ropes'. 'The sea was now running mountain high,' Janet Schaw's account of her journey continues. 'The waves . . . came aboard like a deluge and, rushing from side to side of the vessel, generally made their way into . . . the stateroom which was often so full of water as almost to reach us in our beds.'[72]

Nearly a week into this mid-Atlantic storm, conditions worsened suddenly: 'Just after the midnight watch was set, it began to blow in such a manner as made all that had gone before seem only a summer breeze. All hands were now called – not only the crew but every man who could assist in this dreadful emergency. Everybody was on deck but my young friend and myself, who sat up in bed, patiently waiting for that fate we sincerely believed unavoidable . . . It is impossible to describe the horror of our situation . . . The waves poured into [our] stateroom . . . The candle was instantly extinguished . . . The vessel which was one moment mounted to the clouds and whirled on the pointed wave [then] descended with such violence as made her tremble for half a minute with the shock . . . Nine hogsheads of water which were lashed to the deck . . . broke from their moorings and, falling backwards and forwards over our heads, at last went overboard with a dreadful noise. Our hen coops with all our poultry [the ship's source of fresh eggs] soon followed, as did the cabhouse or kitchen, and with it all our cooking utensils . . . We heard our sails fluttering into rags. The helm was no longer able to command the vessel tho' four men were lashed to it . . . At last we heard the fore mainmast split from top to bottom.'

Dawn found Janet Schaw's vessel, the *Jamaica Packet*, half-wrecked – 'masts, sails and rigging of all kinds lying on the deck, the ship itself an inactive hulk'. But the wind had dropped at last and Janet, as she at once thanked God, had survived. Weeks later, she was sailing up the comparatively tranquil waters of the Cape Fear River.

When, in 1845, Martin MacLeod of Drynoch emigrated to Canada with his family, their experience of the Atlantic was the opposite of Janet Schaw's. 'The weather was very fine,' Martin's daughter Margaret remembered. 'We had a most pleasant passage from Greenock to Montreal,' Martin himself wrote. 'A lighted candle could have been carried on the deck until we saw land . . . The master was particularly civil and we were as comfortable as we could desire.'[73]

In comparison with most of the thousands of emigrants who quit the Highlands and Islands in the first half of the nineteenth century, Martin MacLeod, though suffering money troubles of the sort that had been afflicting Skye tacksmen for ages, was reasonably well placed financially. Like Janet Schaw, he and his party could afford a cabin or stateroom. Of itself, as Janet's misfortunes proved, this offered no immunity from the effects of ocean gales. But crossing the Atlantic in a passenger ship's cabin was nevertheless very different from making the same voyage in a cargo ship's hold – the only accommodation affordable by the majority of early-nineteenth-century emigrants from the Highlands and Islands to North America.

When not serving as emigrant ships, the vessels on which most Highlands and Islands families crossed the Atlantic were engaged in transporting lumber from Canada to Britain. This trade began to develop during the Napoleonic Wars – which made it impossible to bring timber into the United Kingdom from continental Europe. By the 1820s and 1830s, despite European sources being once more available, the expansion of the country's economy had been such as to make Britain, where shipyards still worked entirely in wood, reliant on Canadian timber. This had implications for those people from the Highlands and Islands who were already in Canada, as well as for those other people who wanted to get there.

In Nova Scotia, Prince Edward Island and Glengarry County's Ottawa Valley hinterland, men of Highlands and Islands extraction were prominent among the lumberjacks who were literally at the cutting edge of the Canadian lumber industry. 'A list of the names of the great lumber families of Canada,' a historian of this industry comments, 'would almost sound like a roll-call of the Scottish clans.' The lumber families thus described may have been headed by men whose fathers, especially if they came from the Hebrides, had scarcely clapped eyes on an axe before leaving Scotland. But the axemanship skills those same men acquired while removing trees from their farms equipped them with the means of earning more dollars than any farm, however productive, could generate. 'From noon until night,' according to one account of early-nineteenth-century P.E.I., 'you hear of nothing but lumber . . . The farmers are all turned timber merchants; every boy that can hold an axe is sent to the woods.' In Glengarry, which had the advantage of easy access to some of the highest yielding forests in Canada, things were much the same. 'There isn't an old family in the county,' it was said by one Glengarrian, 'that hasn't had men in the bush someplace.'[74]

Each winter, throughout the nineteenth century and into the twentieth, Canadian lumberjacks of Hebridean and Highland descent felled millions of the soaring pines, spruces and oaks which constituted the Atlantic timber trade's raw material. Working in temperatures far below zero, and living in isolated 'shanties' which were as dirty as they were overcrowded, the same lumberjacks next dragged tree trunk after tree trunk across frozen and snow-covered ground to the banks of the nearest stream. Then, after the springtime snowmelt flooded every watercourse, they floated those tree trunks, in the form of ungainly rafts, to Quebec, Pictou or one of the other harbours from which Canadian lumber was shipped to British ports like Liverpool and Greenock.

As noted with reference to Sweyne McLeod, the Mississippi lumberman who featured in this book's opening paragraphs, moving timber from North America's inland forests to the sea was dangerous, as well as back-breaking, work. Perhaps because of this, lumberjacks lived hard. 'Great quantities of spurious whisky [meaning illegally distilled rotgut] are drunk,' according to a contemporary description of shanty life, 'and many battles are fought.' 'They asked only a good belt of pine and an open river,' it was said of Glengarry's lumbermen by an admirer. 'Their moral character, with few exceptions, is dishonest and worthless,' commented one of the same lumbermen's detractors. 'I believe there are few people in the world on whose promises less faith can be placed . . . The epithet "lumberer" is considered synonymous with . . . spendthrift habits and [with] villainous and vagabond principles.'[75]

If lumberjacks attracted condemnation, the vessels to which they delivered their rafts of freshly felled timber attracted more. 'Of all ships,' remarks the timber trade historian already quoted, 'the worst and the craziest were those that "came down", as the phrase went, to carrying wood.' This was because of the nature of a lumber ship's cargo. Silk, tea and other goods of that kind were of high unit value and could be ruined by contact with seawater. They were consigned, therefore, to the best available vessels. Lumber, in contrast, was of low value in relation to its bulk – and it did not matter, since it had just spent weeks afloat in Canadian rivers, if such lumber got wet. When a ship was fit for nothing else, then, it remained fit for the timber trade; and because no worthwhile skipper or seaman wanted anything to do with these 'sailors' coffins', as they were called, lumber ships were frequently captained and crewed by drunkards, derelicts and ex convicts who could find no better jobs.[76]

When sailing from Britain to Canada, ships of this sort found it difficult to get conventional cargoes – since exporters of the manufactured goods making up the bulk of westward-bound trade had no wish to entrust such goods to vessels known to be among the worst afloat. In those circumstances, it seemed little short of providential to the owners of timber-carrying ships that people from places like the Highlands and Islands were so desperate to get to North America as to be prepared to cross the Atlantic in the holds of their usually leaking, and invariably decrepit, vessels. Semi-destitute emigrants, paying no more than three, four or five pounds apiece, might not have been a profitable trade in their own right. But they were a valuable adjunct to the lumber-shipping business – all the more so since, like timber, they did not need to be kept dry.

Once an inward-bound lumber ship had discharged its cargo in a British port, therefore, a temporary deck was installed in its hold. On this deck there were erected two tiers of bunks made from 'rapidly nailed together . . . planks'. Because partitions would have wasted valuable space, those bunks occupied a single compartment, extending all the way from bow to stern and measuring perhaps one hundred feet in length by twenty-five feet in breadth, with an average headroom of five feet or less. Visiting a vessel which took on emigrants at the Skye port of Uig, Joseph Mitchell, the civil engineer mentioned earlier, described its accommodation as 'very rough'. Such space as remained between the ship's 'two rows of berths,' Mitchell went on, 'was piled with boxes, bags, chests, etc. Into this den – for it could not be called anything else – were huddled some 200 or 300 men, women and children.'[77]

If any of those people read the advice British civil servants churned out for the benefit of prospective emigrants, they might have come across this passage: 'The following supply will be sufficient for a family of five persons for a voyage to North America, viz. 48 stones [or 672 pounds] of potatoes if in season; 2½ hundredweights [or 280 pounds] of oatmeal or flour; half a hundredweight [or 56 pounds] of biscuits; 20 pounds of butter in a keg; one gallon of molasses; 20 pounds of bacon; 50 pounds of [salted] fish in a small keg; one gallon of spirits; and a little vinegar.' Such advice was well meant, but during the 1820s, 1830s and 1840s, scarcely any of the emigrants embarking on ships of the kind inspected by Joseph Mitchell could afford more than a tiny fraction of those provisions. The typical emigrant's last penny was invested in his or her passage. For food and water, most emigrants were reliant on their ships' skippers, and they, needless to say, kept daily rations to a minimum. The less emigrants were given to eat, after all, the bigger was the profit to be made from carrying them.[78]

William Bell, a Church of Scotland minister, sailed for Canada on an emigrant ship in 1817. Being a clergyman, he probably fared better than most of his ship's passengers, but not, it seems, a lot better. The water he was given to drink, Bell wrote, was filthy: 'But its dirty appearance was not its worst quality. It had such a rancid smell that to be in the same neighbourhood was enough to turn one's stomach.' Such food as was on offer was equally off-putting: 'The bread, by the captain himself, was admitted to be more than a year old, and the [salt] beef much older; indeed, I have never seen anything like the latter presented to human beings.'[79]

Although no stoves were permitted below decks on emigrant ships, for fear of fire, cooking facilities were to be had in what Janet Schaw, back in the 1770s, referred to as a 'cabhouse' or caboose. This was a galley on deck. But when the weather was bad, as it often was in the Atlantic, any such galley was inaccessible – because, when waves began to break across an emigrant ship's decks, its hatches were battened down and its passengers incarcerated in the vessel's hold. 'The ship rolled so much,' William Bell recalled of stormy days and nights he spent confined to his bunk, 'that we were often dashed from one side of our beds to the other with great violence. She [the ship] sometimes lay so long on one side that I feared she would never rise more. Those who had young children found it difficult to avoid crushing them . . . Our [berths] cracked frightfully; and everything moveable was dashed from its place.'[80]

Because winds in the Atlantic blow generally from west to east, a sailing ship heading for Britain from North America could often make the ocean crossing in three weeks. A westward-bound vessel, however, often took more than two months to travel the same distance – most of this time spent tacking to and fro in the face of stubbornly prevailing westerlies. On emigrant ships, especially on those where it was necessary to keep passengers below decks for long periods, the consequences of a long passage were so bad as almost to defy description. A vile mix of seawater, urine, excrement, vomit and rotten food accumulated steadily in the hold until, as members of a British parliamentary committee were informed, 'the between-decks were like a loathesome dungeon'.[81]

Given their recognised unseaworthiness, it is not surprising that many emigrant ships were wrecked. Equally predictable, in view of the conditions they had to endure, was the susceptibility of early-nineteenth-century emigrants to disease. Babies and children in particular died of nothing more complicated than persistent seasickness, coupled with the dehydration to which it gave rise. Children and adults alike died of influenza, measles, smallpox, cholera and typhus – the latter spread by the lice with which all emigrant ships were infested. Most deaths went unreported. Occasionally, however, some record of them has survived. Thus of the 200 emigrants who sailed from Lewis for Canada on the ill-named *Harmony* in 1827, thirteen died in mid-Atlantic, twenty-two died after they had been put ashore in some uninhabited corner of Cape Breton Island and a further five perished after their ship docked. Twenty years later, it was calculated that one in six, perhaps one in five, of all transatlantic emigrants died at sea. The voyage of the *Circassian*, which carried people from the Skye and Lochalsh area to Canada in 1847, was typical in this regard. Of her 300 passengers, seventy never as much as glimpsed North America.[82]

Those facts need to be kept in mind by readers of this book. Much of it focuses on the more positive aspects of the emigrant experience: on families and individuals from the Highlands and Islands who grasped the opportunities available to them in their new countries; on the present-day New Zealanders, Australians, Canadians, Americans and others who are rightly proud of what their emigrant ancestors achieved. As preceding paragraphs have stressed, however, the story of emigration from the Highlands and Islands, and especially from the early-nineteenth-century Highlands and Islands, has its darker side as well. For every ten emigrants who made it to their intended destinations during the 1820s, 1830s, 1840s and 1850s, there were at times as many as two or three whose journeys ended with their deaths.

The Southern Ocean

Sailing to Australia from Scotland took longer than sailing to North America – passages averaging sixteen weeks and extending to twenty-four on occasion. Adding to any such journey's discomforts and dangers were the marked contrasts in weather experienced on voyages to the southern hemisphere. Emigrants were buffeted, to begin with, by the gales they commonly encountered in the Irish Sea and the Bay of Biscay. Then came the cloying, windless heat of the tropics – when, between Africa and Brazil, ships might be becalmed for days on end. But even harder to bear than tropical temperatures in excess of 100 degrees Fahrenheit was bitter cold of the sort met with when, on clearing the Cape of Good Hope, emigrant ships, in order to shorten sailing times, swung towards Antarctica. During this most hazardous stage of any Australia-bound vessel's trip, its passengers were exposed to the sleet-laden storms and blizzards plaguing the sub-Antarctic latitudes which nineteenth-century sailors christened the Roaring Forties. Down there in the Southern Ocean, lots of emigrants lost their lives.

Their deaths appear to have been of little consequence to the owners and masters of the ships which carried them. When, in 1852, Captain James 'Bully' Forbes, the aptly nicknamed skipper of the *Marco Polo*, crammed on all possible sail, plunged exceptionally deep into the Roaring Forties and offered his crew a choice of two destinations, 'Hell or Melbourne', he completed the Britain–Australia run in an astonishing sixty-eight days. Newspapers of the time made much of this. They made little or nothing, however, of the fact that, of the 701 passengers on the *Marco Polo*, a lot of them people from Skye, fifty-three died. Most of the *Marco Polo* casualties, it appears, were children. Hence the contents of a letter received, in the early part of 1853, by Alexander, or Sandy, MacKinnon, a Roag crofter. Posted in Melbourne, on 8 November 1852, this letter was written by John MacKinnon, Alexander's brother and a *Marco Polo* emigrant. 'Sandy,' John wrote, 'throwing out my two boys into the deep sea, it will never go out of my heart. The youngest died with the measles . . . The other died six days after him.'[83]

Despite the greater distances involved, death rates among mid-nineteenth-century emigrants from Scotland to Australia were, generally speaking, lower than among emigrants to the United States and Canada. Passengers for Australia normally qualified for assistance from governmental or quasi-governmental organisations, the Highland and Island Emigration Society among them. This made for comparatively strict supervision of onboard accommodation and provisioning. It also meant, in the case of people in receipt of Highland and Island Emigration Society aid, that poorer emigrants were provided with supplies of clothing, food and toiletries. But many such emigrants had endured years of poverty and hunger before their departure. Even if only a minority of them were as badly situated as Dugald MacLeod, the Skyeman whose home in advance of his leaving for Victoria was a gravelpit, few had escaped extreme privation of one kind or another. Among the passengers who died on Australia-bound vessels, it followed, a high proportion were of Highlands and Islands origin. Thus of the 754 people packed into the *Bourneuf*, which sailed under Highland and Island Emigration Society auspices, eighty-four died at sea. Another ninety-six died on the *Ticonderoga*, forty-one on the *Priscilla* and some three dozen on the *Ontario*. Still more catastrophic was the fate of the *Hercules*. This was a naval ship put at the Highland and Island Emigration Society's disposal by the British Admiralty, and it set out for Australia from the Argyll port of Campbeltown on 26 December 1852.[84]

The 742 emigrants on the *Hercules* came largely from Skye and Harris. They had been taken to Campbeltown by steamer and, according to a press report of the time, they boarded the *Hercules* in good spirits: 'The young women came first – some looking cheerfully round, some sad and some in tears; but all took pains to adjust their shawls and handkerchiefs, their tresses and their caps, as they made their appearance before strangers. The married women and the children followed: the latter skipping and dancing on the broad deck, overjoyed at their escape from the confinement of the steamboat; the former so completely absorbed by the care of their children . . . that they did not seem to be conscious of where they were . . . The men looked dark and stern, like men about to confront danger, and not likely to shrink from the encounter, but [they] relaxed into a smile at the first kind word.'[85]

There would be few smiles from the *Hercules*' passengers in the months that followed. Less than 24 hours out of Campbeltown, a subsequent commission of enquiry heard, they and their ship came close to falling victim to 'a storm of the most violent description'. For five days, the *Hercules* rode out the gale in the Firth of Clyde – eventually putting in to Rothesay where, it was reported, the vessel's sails were found to be in shreds, her rigging badly damaged and her passengers prostrate with seasickness. This was bad enough; but still more ominous was the appearance among the *Hercules* emigrants of 'fever [meaning typhus] . . . smallpox and measles'. When, a fortnight later, the *Hercules* set out once more, disease took hold in earnest. By mid-January, after encountering another 'perfect hurricane' in the Irish Sea, the *Hercules* was at anchor off Cork, in the south of Ireland, with thirty-four cases of smallpox among her passengers and with typhus also spreading. Because the authorities in Cork refused to allow anyone from the infection-ridden *Hercules* to come ashore, the emigrant families on the ship were left to cope as best they could with what now turned into a runaway epidemic. Eventually, 237 people fell victim to smallpox, typhus or both. Of this total, fifty-six died.[86]

The survivors of the *Hercules* disaster sailed from Cork on 14 April 1853 and arrived in Adelaide, South Australia, on 26 July. Another eight emigrants died during those three and a half months. One of them was a woman called Ann MacLeod. During her shipboard funeral service, held off West Africa, 'no less than eight sharks,' it was said, 'followed close to the ship, watching every movement until her body was thrown overboard, when they immediately disappeared [with] her remains'.[87]

Victoria: Point Henry and Melbourne

Point Henry, on the western shore of Port Phillip Bay, Victoria, is not much visited by tourists. The place is dominated by an aluminium works and, to get there, you have to drive past a long series of scenically dreary saltpans. Nor is the seaward view from Point Henry, a flat and exposed promontory, much more enticing. But beside a car park where mine is the only vehicle, I discover a historical marker which confirms what I have read in advance of coming here. Off Point Henry, according to its inscription, hundreds of emigrant ships from Britain once dropped anchor. Among those ships in the early 1850s were several vessels chartered by the Highland and Island Emigration Society.

Melbourne, Victoria's capital, was the emigration society's favoured destination, receiving well over two-thirds of its several thousand emigrants. The city, however, could not be reached by ocean-going craft. From Point Henry, therefore, shallow-draft steamboats conveyed emigrants across Port Phillip Bay and up the Yarra River to docks and wharfs which, to mid-nineteenth-century arrivals from the Highlands and Islands, must have seemed anything but welcoming.

Because of its goldrush, Victoria was then experiencing, in words used at the time, 'a vast and hitherto unprecedented influx of population'. In 1851, there had been 77,000 people living in the colony; in 1854, the total stood at 237,000; by 1857, that figure had doubled. In those circumstances, emigrants were vulnerable to all sorts of disasters. Liable to be robbed, cheated and swindled at every turn, few of them could afford decent lodgings. Some slept in a tented town which the colonial authorities erected on boggy ground beside the Yarra. Others, incapable of meeting the weekly charge of five shillings for a tent, were to be found 'sleeping under wood heaps' or simply squatting in Melbourne's roadways. This was not so bad between October and March. But from April and May onwards, when warmth gave way to chill, Melbourne could be miserable. 'Those who have not witnessed a Victorian winter,' one city resident commented in May 1853, 'have little conception of the depth of water, and the filth, found in the streets of Melbourne.' Everywhere, 'desolate creatures' were eking out a precarious existence in crude shelters made from barrels, planks and pieces of scrap. Down by the Yarra, meanwhile, people were continuing to pour into a place that had neither homes nor sustenance to offer them: 'The daily exhibitions of distress endured by the hapless stranger . . . are truly heart rending; females, young children, invalids, all hurry from the newly arrived ship . . . to what is called the Queen's Wharf; ankle-deep in Port Phillip mud; no friend to greet them, no friendly hand to point the way, or cheering voice to offer comfort to the perplexed.'[88]

This lack of a friendly hand must have been all the more difficult to cope with when, as happened regularly, emigrants from the Highlands and Islands encountered abuse of the kind which comfortably situated men and women often direct at refugees and itinerants thought to pose a threat to the settled order of things. Anyone reaching Victoria from Skye, Harris, Lewis and other famine-ravaged parts of Scotland was almost automatically described as 'indolent' or 'dirty' – many such comments carrying the stamp of official approval. 'I am put to great difficulty with these people,' one immigration officer noted of the Gaelic speakers with whom he dealt, 'because I am unable to communicate with them except by signs . . . I do not understand one word of Gaelic, and they do not understand one word of English.' Having next complained about 'the uncleanliness of their habits', the same man went on to categorise the Highland and Island Emigration Society's clients as 'intractable'. People from the Highlands and Islands, he wrote, were 'as near an approach to barbarians as any [emigrants] I have ever met with'.[89]

Bigotry of this sort would have mattered less if people reaching Victoria from the Highlands and Islands had been able to establish tightly knit communities of the sort resulting from earlier emigrations. In localities such as the Cape Fear River country, Glengarry County, Pictou and Prince Edward Island, successive groups of Gaelic-speaking emigrants from Scotland managed to recreate in new settings something of their former way of life. Absolutely basic to this achievement, however, was the ready availability in all those places of cheap, even free, farmland that could be taken over in blocks big enough to permit numerous families from the same Highlands and Islands localities to settle side by side. No such farmland was on offer in mid-nineteenth-century Victoria. Here, by the 1850s, landholdings typically consisted of huge sheep stations of the kind developed by Archibald MacLeod in Gippsland and by John Norman MacLeod in Victoria's Western District. Those stations were incompatible with homesteading of the North American variety. In Victoria, it followed, people of Highlands and Islands background had no alternative but to accept roles that bore little resemblance to those that might have come their way had they had the chance to go to Canada. There they could have become self-employed agriculturalists. In Victoria, for better or worse, most Highlanders and Hebrideans instead became labourers and servants. Sometimes they were driven into dependence on charity.

In March 1853, a Mrs MacLeod, who appears to have been abandoned by her husband, was rescued from Melbourne's streets by the city's Ladies Benevolent Society. Some weeks later, a Highland and Island Society was formed in Victoria with the aim of raising funds for distribution to Gaelic-speaking Scots in need of similar assistance. Among the individuals proffering this sort of aid was Catherine MacLeod, formerly of Talisker but then living, as already mentioned, in Geelong, not far from Point Henry. Possibly at their mother's prompting, Catherine's landholding sons gave jobs to hard-pressed emigrants from Skye. Other sheep station operators of Highlands and Islands extraction did likewise, among them Gippsland's Archibald MacMillan. 'For his Highland countrymen newly arrived in Victoria,' it was reported of MacMillan, 'he made special arrangements with the licensee of [Melbourne's] Port Phillip Club Hotel . . . to entertain them until they obtained employment in the country.'[90]

'The Scotch stick together like bricks,' one Australian observed caustically of this tendency for folk from the Highlands and Islands to help one another. But the beneficiaries of such help, especially men hired as shepherds and the like, were grateful for it. 'I feel obliged to everyone that ever advised me to come to this colony,' one of them wrote. Lots of others made comments to the same effect.[91]

In a letter mailed to his sister in Bracadale in November 1852, Donald MacAskill tells how he and his four sons are employed on a Victoria sheep station where they expect to earn £200 annually between them. He has 'left starvation behind,' Donald informs his sister. 'I can give as much [food] to my dogs now as I was giving to my family at home [in Skye],' he adds. Then, maybe thinking this sounds too good to be true and being aware of the widespread suspicion back in the Hebrides that the Highland and Island Emigration Society pressurised emigrants into putting a gloss on their experiences, Donald switches to a language his sister will know no emigration society representative understands. '*Tha mi beò, slàn, làn thoilichte ann am fàsach Astrailia,*' Donald MacAskill writes in Gaelic: 'I am alive, well and happy in the wilds of Australia.'[92]

Even John MacKinnon, the man whose two small sons died on Bully Forbes's *Marco Polo*, is pleased with what he finds in Victoria. 'I heard at home good accounts of Australia,' John tells his brother towards the close of 1852, 'but I never believed [these accounts] until I saw [the country] with my own eyes . . . I am only six weeks and two days at work, and I have in my possession this night, after clearing all my debts, twenty pounds sterling, and that may tell you what kind of place this is. How long I would be in Skye before I would gather as much.'[93]

Occasionally, in letters reaching Skye from Victoria, a disenchanted note is struck. Margaret MacLeod, working as a washerwoman in Melbourne, considers the city 'a very wicked place' where people, 'especially women', are 'given greatly to drink'. John MacKinnon, however, is more complimentary – and more typical. 'Now I have to tell you that I live here [in] as little fear as I would in Roag,' John informs his brother, Sandy. 'They will be speaking at home that [in Australia] a person would be in danger of his life, day and night, but it is not true. I saw some of the natives [Aborigines] going bare-naked, but they will hurt no person.'[94]

Another Skyeman, John MacDiarmid, is equally enthusiastic. 'I have to tell you that this country is the best country in the world,' he informs a friend at home. 'I hope I will be a gentleman before ten years time.' MacDiarmid's ambition is unlikely to have been fulfilled, however. 'Not many of the families shipped here from Scotland in the 1850s made instant successes of themselves,' I am told by Jim McLeod, whose great-great-grandparents, Alexander and Mary McLeod, got to Australia on the *Araminta*, a Highland and Island Emigration Society vessel which reached Point Henry in October 1852.[95]

Jim, a retired school principal, lives in Sale, Victoria, where he serves as a lay preacher in Australia's Uniting Church. His great-great-grandfather, he says, was known in Gaelic as *Alasdair Ruadh*, Red-Headed Sandy, and prior to his quitting Scotland this Alasdair Ruadh was the tenant of a three-and-a-half-acre croft at Culnacnoc in the Staffin area of Skye. 'I couldn't find the slightest trace of my great-great-grandfather's home when I went to Culnacnoc to look for it,' Jim goes on. 'I suppose that's because there wasn't much to his place to begin with. But that's not to say my great-great-grandparents found things easier here. Yes, Red Sandy got a job as a shepherd in the Ballarat area – and, yes, this job brought him more money than he'd ever earned in Skye. But it wasn't until well into the twentieth century, by which point Sandy's grandson had his own tailoring business in Melbourne, that you could say our family was doing well.'

Shepherds like Jim McLeod's great-great-grandfather were each in charge of a mob, or flock, of about a thousand sheep. During the hours of daylight, with the help of two or three dogs, a shepherd moved his mob from one piece of pasture to the next. Then, when evening approached, he drove the animals back to the shack that served as his base. There the shepherd's assistant, known as a hut keeper, took over – keeping watch through the hours of darkness for dingoes and other predators. All such shepherding was hazardous because of the ever-present risk of death or serious injury from snakebites, Aboriginal attacks or simple accidents. But what got to most shepherds in the end was the loneliness that was their occupation's defining characteristic. Englishmen, it was claimed, just could not cope single-handedly with the Australian bush. Men from the Highlands and Islands, on the other hand, being 'inured to solitude and wide tracts of open land', were said to be 'quite at home' in the wilderness.[96]

This rings a little false. Emigrants from the Highlands and Islands, despite Sir Charles Trevelyan's assurances to the contrary, were every bit as prone as other groups to prefer the life of a goldminer to that of a shepherd or stationhand. 'The last cargo of Highlanders landed at Port Phillip Bay spoke no English,' according to a report that reached London in 1852. 'They were closely questioned in the Bay as to their knowledge of the [Ballarat and Bendigo] diggings. They professed to know nothing. They enquired "whether she [the diggings] was a man or a beast". Nothing could be more satisfactory [to Victoria's sheep station owners] and already the [sheepmen's] agents saw these fine families tending sheep at the old [pre-goldrush] wages. But no sooner was the small Gaelic army, some three hundred, fairly landed than they gave three cheers for the diggings and marched off.'[97]

Many other people of Highlands and Islands origin did likewise. 'The German camps are strong in music,' a contemporary commentator noted of the multinational population which sprang into existence around goldrush Bendigo, 'but they lapse into silence when stirring martial strains are commenced on the bagpipes by enthusiastic Scottish Highlanders who are very numerous in Bendigo, every gully indeed having its pipes and pipers.'[98]

Bendigo, where the last working goldmine closed in 1954, is today a comfortable-looking city. Bendigo in the early 1850s was something else entirely. Then, thousands of miners, or diggers, worked claims just a few square yards in area – each digger burrowing deep into the ground in search of the metal that could bring him instant wealth. For miles around, every tree had been felled. When it was hot and dry, dust swirled chokingly in the wind. When it rained, the diggings turned into a swamp.

Few miners struck it rich. All of them, however, gloried in the personal liberty, the egalitarianism and the anarchic disrespect for authority which flourished on the goldfields – and which, to some degree, have been characteristic of Australian society ever since. 'There's no masters here to oppress a poor devil,' runs one digger ballad. 'Out in Australia we're all on a level.'[99]

Beliefs of this sort struck a chord with miners from the Highlands and Islands. Bendigo's Gaelic-speaking diggers expressed themselves well pleased with Australia's freedom from 'tyranny and oppression', 'lairds and factors'. Similar sentiments surface in *An Teachdaire Gaidhealach*, a Gaelic newspaper which began to circulate through the goldfields in 1853. *An Teachdaire*, The Teacher, naturally compared Australia with Scotland. It did so to Scotland's disadvantage. In the Highlands and Islands, the paper observed, 'the poor man who rents [a] croft, which has descended to him from his father's father, must, when [this croft] is required for the accommodation of sheep, turn out family and all'. No such crime, *An Teachdaire* went on, could occur in Australia, a country which was founded, the paper insisted, on fraternity and equality: 'Here a man is respected as a man, and Jack is as good as his master.'[100]

People who imbibed such thinking were dismissive of the notion that they were indebted to the Highland and Island Emigration Society. Emigrants in receipt of emigration society assistance were contractually bound, on their establishing themselves in Australia, to reimburse a proportion of the society's costs. But a Melbourne immigration officer who questioned many such emigrants found 'not one' who 'appeared to be in any degree aware that he had [agreed] to pay anything at all'. The Highland and Island Emigration Society could not do much about this. No emigration society debt collector was likely to be well received by Bendigo's goldminers – or, for that matter, by Victoria's widely scattered shepherds and hut keepers. As a result, six-sevenths of the total amount due to the society from its emigrant clients remained unpaid.[101]

John and Isabella McLeod, who emigrated from Raasay to Australia in 1854 with Highland and Island Emigration Society help, owed the society £30. This debt was never settled. John and Isabella's great-great-great-grandson, Graeme McLeod, when I meet with him in Allansford, Victoria, is unapologetic about that. Most of the people who left Raasay in 1854 were evicted, Graeme points out. Their departure, he goes on, was greatly to the advantage of their landlord. 'Raasay is a beautiful island,' Graeme says. Why, he asks, should folk expelled from it have felt obliged to meet the cost of their expulsion?

Scotland: Raasay

In 2001, according to that year's United Kingdom census, Raasay's population was 194. During the early part of the nineteenth century, however, this small island was home to well over a thousand people. Between the 1820s and the 1850s, most of them left – usually on emigrant ships. Today, as a result, many countries contain people who claim Raasay ancestry. In my experience, they do so with a striking intensity of feeling. Why this should be so, I am not sure. Perhaps Raasay is easier to identify with than larger islands containing lots of separate communities. Or perhaps there simply persists among people of Raasay descent a sense of the island's undeniable distinctiveness. All islands are thought special by their inhabitants, of course. But Raasay is arguably more special than most. By Hebridean standards, it is, and looks, productive. Unlike Lewis, Harris and other treeless islands of that sort, Raasay is also heavily wooded, and views from the island – to the Cuillin on one side and to the mainland hills above Applecross on the other – are without parallel in Scotland.

Raasay became a MacLeod possession during the Middle Ages. Its ruling family, who claimed to have held the island 'since time immemorial', were descended from the MacLeods of Lewis. Raasay's MacLeod chiefs, then, owed no allegiance to the MacLeods of Dunvegan. This was made clear in 1745 when the then MacLeod of Raasay declared for Prince Charles Edward Stuart and Jacobitism – thus putting himself at odds with Dunvegan's anti-Jacobite laird. Although its chief's adherence to Charles Edward led to Raasay being ransacked by government troops in the months following the Battle of Culloden, the MacLeods of Raasay emerged from the 1745–6 rebellion with their lands intact. As far as Raasay's other residents were concerned, this proved a mixed blessing. Like their counterparts elsewhere, Raasay's chiefs now started to spend money at an unsustainable rate. They equipped themselves, for example, with a lavishly constructed and still surviving mansion, Raasay House. This home's cost was far in excess of what the MacLeods of Raasay could afford. Their debts, in consequence, began to grow spectacularly. They grew further when, in 1823, John MacLeod, who turned out to be the island's last MacLeod laird, inherited Raasay from his father.[102]

John MacLeod, an army officer by profession, was a notorious gambler who, by the time his gambling career ended, owed his creditors some £61,000 – in excess of £3 million at present-day values. In the hope of reducing this figure, Raasay's laird put part of his estate under sheep. Murdoch MacLeod, the great-great-grandfather of Martin MacLeod, my guide to Prince Edward Island, was one of the victims of those clearances – which led to a good deal of emigration from Raasay to P.E.I. 'My people left from a place called

North Fearns,' Martin told me. 'Recently, I read somewhere that they and their neighbours came here to Canada of their own free will. That made me angry. My great-great-grandfather didn't want to leave Raasay. He was evicted.'

John MacLeod's clearances, however, were as nothing to those unleashed as a result of John's failure to lay hands on a fortune he had hoped would come his way. This fortune belonged to the Raasay laird's father-in-law, General Sir Donald MacLeod. The general came from Skye, and his involvement with the military began when he served alongside Norman MacLeod of Dunvegan in India during the 1780s. Like Norman of Dunvegan, General Donald made a lot of money in India. Unlike Norman, Donald managed to hang on to his wealth. For some years, then, John MacLeod of Raasay was able to stave off bankruptcy by cultivating the impression that, on his father-in-law's death, he would be in a position to discharge his debts. When General Sir Donald finally died in 1843, however, Raasay's laird got not a penny. His creditors duly pounced. John MacLeod was sequestrated and Raasay sold. Unfortunately for its former owner, the selling price failed to meet all his obligations. In an attempt to avoid further legal proceedings, John MacLeod of Raasay duly fled Britain – sailing for Australia and settling on a sheep station near Nalang in Victoria.

Raasay's purchaser was George Rainy, a Lowland businessman who had made a fortune from the West Indies sugar trade. Rainy, very much in the manner of Lewis's James Matheson, was anxious to take on the persona of a landed gentleman. Like Matheson, he came to his tenants' aid when, in 1846, their potatoes failed. Also like Matheson, Raasay's new laird tired of this endeavour. By the early 1850s, then, George Rainy was committed to a drastic reduction in his island's population. He achieved this by means of especially far-reaching clearances.

A Raasay crofter called Donald MacLeod told a government commission of enquiry that he remembered George Rainy 'clearing fourteen townships'. 'I have seen [Rainy's agents] knocking [down] the houses over [people's] heads when they were evicting them,' Ronald MacLennan, another crofter, said. 'In one day I have seen no less than 300 evicted and leaving the island . . . I have seen them going to the churchyard in their grief at being separated from their homes, and taking . . . as mementoes . . . handfuls of the soil and grass that covered the graves of their kindred.'[103]

One morning in 1982, I visited the cemetery where Raasay's departing emigrants came for the mementoes mentioned by Ronald MacLennan. My visit was made in the company of the late Sorley MacLean, *Somhairle MacGill-Eain*, born in Raasay in 1911 and, without question, the most eminent Gaelic poet of modern times. In 1982, Sorley was living in retirement at

Braes, the part of Skye closest to Raasay and the place where, in 1882, there began the crofting revolt which brought the Highland Clearances to an end. A hundred years on from this revolt, I was helping to make a television documentary to mark its centenary, and by way of preface to our account of the events of 1882, my producer and I were trying to convey something of the emotions still surrounding evictions of the sort George Rainy organised. Hence our having asked Sorley MacLean to join us. Partly we wanted a television audience to hear Sorley talk, as only he could, about Raasay's past. But mostly we wanted to film, on his home ground, the man responsible for the most forceful condemnation of the clearances that has ever been, or ever will be, written.

This condemnation is Sorley MacLean's *Hallaig*, a poem which, as the Nobel laureate Seamus Heaney has commented, 'is at once historical and hallucinatory'. Heaney, an Irishman as conscious of Ireland's history as Sorley was of Scotland's, goes on: 'Hallaig is an actual place, a ghost clachan north of Beinn na Lice on the poet's native island. The poem begins with an image of screening and blotting out, the familiar sad sight of a boarded-up window, so common in Ireland and Scotland and so suggestive of emigration, eviction, famine, clearance . . . But miraculously, by the third line, the screen is removed and the sorrowful recognitions transposed into a paradisal key. Suddenly, unbewilderingly, the woods have become women. The poem is set at twilight, in the Celtic twilight, in effect, at that time of day when the land of the living and the land of the dead become pervious to each other, when the deserted present becomes populous with past lives, when the modern conifers make way for the native birch and rowan, and when the birch and rowan, in their turn, metamorphose into a procession of girls walking together out of the nineteenth-century hills.'[104]

Here, in Sorley's translation from his original Gaelic, are some of *Hallaig*'s fourteen verses:

> I will wait for the birch wood
> until it comes up the cairn,
> until the whole ridge from Beinn na Lice
> will be under its shade.
> If it does not, I will go down to Hallaig,
> to the Sabbath of the dead . . .
> They are still in Hallaig,
> MacLeans and MacLeods . . .
> The men lying on the green
> at the end of every house that was,
> the girls a wood of birches,
> straight their backs, bent their heads.

> Between the Leac and Fearns
> the road is under mild moss,
> and the girls in silent bands
> go to Clachan as in the beginning,
> and return from Clachan
> from Suisnish and the land of the living:
> each one young and light-stepping,
> without the heartbreak of the tale.[105]

Reflecting on those lines, another twentieth-century Gaelic poet, Iain Crichton Smith, observed: 'Sometimes in certain texts . . . we sense that the poet has reached levels of intuition that go beyond the intelligence and the reasoning mind, that he has made contact with his theme in a very direct way. I have myself sensed this often in Shakespeare and in some Greek poetry. We find it . . . very finely in *Hallaig*. In this poem, it is as if MacLean felt . . . quite clearly the desolation, the sadness, the terrible emptiness of the Highlands, its ghosts and presences, in an absolute intuitional music.'[106]

Crichton Smith was right. But when you have spent time, as I have done and as I suspect Sorley MacLean did also, sitting among the ruins of townships long ago swept clean of their inhabitants, you begin to grasp that there is more to *Hallaig* than its evocations of emptiness and desolation. Such evocations are present in *Hallaig*, certainly. But something else is present also: a reaching out to how the Highlands and Islands would be had what happened here in the nineteenth century not taken place. In *Hallaig*, Sorley MacLean imagines this Raasay township as it might have existed without, in Sorley's phrase, the heartbreak of the tale – as it might be, in other words, if there had been no clearances, no evictions, no dispossessions, no enforced emigrations. In such a Hallaig, there would be MacLeods and MacLeans to greet you; there would be young, light-stepping women; there would be men seated each summer's evening on turf benches of a sort which, in actuality, have crumbled into the earth beside Hallaig's disintegrated homes.

Scotland and Victoria: Hallaig and Allansford

On a March afternoon when the wind is from the west and Raasay is beginning to be spring-like, I walk to Hallaig in the company of Cailean Maclean, Sorley's nephew and the source of several of this book's photographs. Our starting point is North Fearns, the township to which Prince Edward Island's Martin MacLeod traces his roots. At North Fearns, the modern road gives way to a footpath which Cailean and I follow northward. On our right is the Inner Sound, separating Raasay from Applecross. On our left are the slopes of Beinn na Lice – covered by birch trees of the slim, delicate sort which, in Sorley's great poem, turn into straight-backed girls. In Hallaig, two or three miles beyond North Fearns, we find neither girls nor anyone else – just some sheep, the inheritors of this and every other depopulated township, nibbling the beginnings of the new season's grass. While Cailean takes some pictures, I inspect the ruins of Hallaig's houses. Where walls still stand, I notice, they are strong and well made. By the standards of their time and place, the people who lived here, or so their buildings suggest, were not lacking in resources.

Hallaig was cleared in 1854. A diary kept that year in Raasay House details some of the principal events in the life of the island: 'May 4th, The [first] cuckoo [of the summer] was heard'; 'May 22nd, The Coolins capped with snow last night'; 'June 6th, The *Chevalier* steamer put into the bay and took aboard 129 Raasay people, emigrants to Australia.' The *Chevalier* conveyed those 129 men, women and children to Birkenhead near Liverpool. There they boarded a sailing ship, the *Edward Johnstone*, from which, on 4 September, they disembarked in Portland – the town where John Norman MacLeod, Major Donald MacLeod of Talisker's third son, would shortly construct his grand house with its fine views of the Southern Ocean.[107]

In 1854, Portland Harbour had not yet been equipped with deepwater wharfs. Accordingly, the *Edward Johnstone* lay out to sea while her passengers were ferried ashore in rowboats. Awaiting the rowboats' arrival were local representatives of the Highland and Island Emigration Society. Although Sir Charles Trevelyan, the society's principal spokesman, disavowed all such intention, the assisted passages it made available to Hallaig's former residents had helped George Rainy clear the township. But this did not prevent the emigration society's Australian agents demanding the payments they believed due to them. From Donald MacLeod, John MacLeod, Widow Ann MacLeod and a further John MacLeod, the heads of four Hallaig families, Sir Charles Trevelyan's representatives requested £179 in total. This was then a large amount. Little if any of it was ever forthcoming.[108]

On our return from Hallaig to North Fearns, since we have an hour to spare before catching the ferry for Skye, Cailean Maclean and I drive up the narrow road giving access to Raasay's west coast. We skirt Churchton Bay, where the *Chevalier* moored on 6 June 1854. We pass Raasay House. We pass Oscaig, where Cailean's grandparents once lived and where his father and his Uncle Sorley were brought up. We stop at Balachuirn. There, with the sun dipping towards the Cuillin, we turn around, and heading south now, make for the waiting boat.

Six weeks later, at the close of a day spent traversing Victoria's Western District, I reach Allansford, a small town a little to the east of the larger

Warrnambool. Here I am put up by Graeme and Barbara McLeod. Theirs is the latest in a long series of MacLeod homes in which I have been made welcome while researching this book, but it is the only such home I enter to the sound of a Gaelic song. The song is one of several on a videotape which Graeme is playing for my benefit. It is being sung, I realise as Graeme ushers me inside, at a Skye ceilidh where, as I watch, the singer gives way to the ceilidh's *fear an taighe* or presenter. He is Cailean Maclean, the man with whom, back there on the other side of the world, I visited Hallaig, North Fearns, Oscaig and Balachuirn. It is with the last of those townships, I learn, that Graeme is connected by way of his great-great-great-grandparents, John and Isabella McLeod. 'They were part of the Raasay group who came here on the *Edward Johnstone* in 1854,' Graeme says of Isabella and John. 'Before that, they lived in Balachuirn, where John was a crofter.'

Barbara and Graeme are teachers who have quit the profession. Graeme now grows tomatoes commercially. Barbara's various involvements in her local community have included work on a number of historical projects. Drawing on research skills acquired in the course of those projects, Barbara McLeod has accumulated a lot of information about the *Edward Johnstone* emigrants.

John and Isabella, her husband's McLeod ancestors, were in their fifties when they left Scotland, Barbara tells me. In their home at Balachuirn, where John was tenant of a three-acre croft, the couple had raised six children, Murdoch, Margaret, John, Christina, Angus and Donald, all of whom came to Australia with their parents. Donald, the youngest, was still a teenager at that point. His siblings were already adults – Margaret, Donald's eldest sister, being old enough to have married two years before the family's emigration. Margaret's husband was another McLeod, John by name, who came from Arnish, one of Raasay's more northerly townships, where his father was a stonemason. When John and Margaret left Raasay, they were accompanied by their first child, a further John McLeod, then just over one year old. Days after their departure from Raasay, while John, Margaret and their little boy waited to board the *Edward Johnstone* at Birkenhead, Margaret's second son, Alexander, was born. Did this experience, which could not have been other than traumatic, have a damaging effect on Margaret McLeod's health? Possibly. At all events, in 1860, when barely thirty, Margaret died. 'She's buried in Warrnambool,' Barbara McLeod says of Margaret. 'Her fifth and last child, Donald, born in 1859, was Graeme's great-grandfather.'

'It was tough for these people,' Barbara says of the *Edward Johnstone*'s passengers. 'A lot of them were old by nineteenth-century standards. John and Isabella were certainly in that category, and back in Scotland, they'd not had things easy. They'd brought up a big family. They'd been through a famine, the clearances, all of that. Now they had to make a fresh start in a new country which, despite what they might have been told before leaving Raasay, had little to offer them. In Balachuirn, John and Isabella had their croft. Here, where they couldn't get land of their own, they had to take jobs on a sheep station. On top of everything else, I suspect that Isabella would have had no alternative but to care for five small grandchildren when Margaret, her daughter, died.'

Because many of his forebears set up home in the Allansford area, Graeme McLeod grew up surrounded by uncles, aunts, cousins and other relatives. Few members of his family talked much about their background, however, and Graeme when younger was under the impression that his emigrant ancestors came from Skye, not Raasay. This mistake was cleared up when Graeme first visited Scotland. That was in the 1980s and, since then, Graeme has been back several times – staying for six weeks, on one occasion, with friends he has made in Balachuirn. 'It's difficult for me to explain my feelings for Raasay,' Graeme says. 'When I'm in Balachuirn, I go for long walks – to Arnish sometimes, other times to Hallaig. Those places are full of meaning for me – so much that, when I leave Raasay, I'm in tears. Once I laughed when I heard Aborigines talk about the spiritual relationships they say they have with particular localities. I don't laugh any more. Being in Raasay has made me realise how Aborigines connect with the land. I'm not sure if my bond with Raasay is the same as an Aborigine's bond with his piece of Australia. But I certainly appreciate his feelings in a way I didn't before I went to Balachuirn.'

CHAPTER SIX

ALMOST ALL GONE NOW

Saskatchewan and Alberta: Calgary, Fort McLeod and the Cypress Hills

On a dead-straight, empty highway about forty miles out of Shaunavon, Saskatchewan, I stop my car, get out and walk to the crest of one of the gently sloping ridges which ensure that anyone driving across this segment of the prairies is presented with a succession of almost limitless panoramas. An unyielding wind from the west is pushing bank after bank of low, but broken, cloud across the sky – with the result that the landscape in front of me is a shifting mix of shade and sunlight. Out there, I know, Saskatchewan stops and Montana begins. From where I am standing, however, I can detect no difference between the two.

On maps, because it is also the Canadian–US frontier, the Montana–Saskatchewan border is instantly apparent. On the ground it is less obvious. But borders, even if hard to detect, can matter greatly. This one certainly mattered when, on 15 October 1877, General Alfred H. Terry of the United States army stepped across it. By so doing, the general, accompanied by several aides and escorted by a cavalry detachment, entered the North West Territories of the Dominion of Canada, a country which, though it had recently acquired its own government, remained part of the British Empire. Waiting to greet Terry, and to make clear he had no jurisdiction here, were the empire's local representatives, men responsible for enforcing instructions emanating from Queen Victoria's

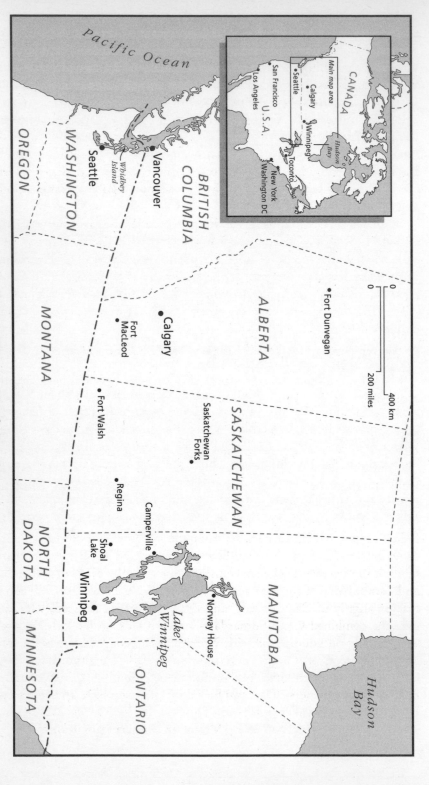

Map 6: Western North America

ministers in distant Ottawa or more distant London. Because those ministers and their monarch set great store by show and glitter, Alfred H. Terry, his own dark blue uniform darkened further by the effects of much hard riding, found himself confronting, as a New York journalist accompanying Terry's party put it, 'a small but brilliant retinue'. This retinue consisted of troopers belonging to Canada's North West Mounted Police – 'their red uniforms,' the same American reporter went on, 'contrast[ing] beautifully with the monotonous dun colour of the plains around them.' Detaching himself from his companions, one scarlet-coated officer approached General Terry. He was, this officer said, the North West Mounted Police's commissioner, and his name was James MacLeod.[1]

MacLeod of the Mounties, as prairie people called the man who welcomed Alfred H. Terry to Canada, spent his early years in Gesto. Situated on a little bay near the mouth of Loch Harport, this is the Skye locality where, in the early seventeenth century, the founder of Poland's Machlejd family lived before he left for Central Europe. Gesto is an attractive spot and the MacLeods, according to James's sister, Margaret, were happy there. Her childhood home, Margaret wrote, was 'the sweetest place under the sun. [Our] house stood close to the sea, a stone wall in front enclosing a garden . . . To the west, [was] the broad Atlantic.'[2]

Margaret and James's father was Martin MacLeod of Drynoch. Martin's roots, as his designation indicates, were in Gesto's vicinity, Drynoch being no more than four or five miles from the spot his daughter remembered so fondly. In the early eighteenth century, however, the MacLeods of Drynoch, in the person of Norman MacLeod, Martin's great-grandfather, had transferred their main base of operations to Glenelg where Norman, while hanging on to Drynoch, took over the tack of Eileanriach. There the Drynoch family stayed until 1811 when, as noted earlier, John Norman MacLeod of Dunvegan sold Glenelg. At that point, Martin of Drynoch's father, despite having toyed with the notion of going to North America, came back to Skye where, in addition to continuing as Drynoch's tenant, he took the tenancy of the previously distinct landholdings of Sumardale and Gesto. None of this was accomplished amicably. The Drynoch family reacted angrily to Glenelg's sale, and though Martin MacLeod, who took over the combined Gesto-Sumardale-Drynoch tack on his father's death, was initially on good terms with Norman MacLeod of Dunvegan, John Norman's successor, the two men soon quarrelled. With the aim, Martin said, of placing his children 'in a position where they, by their own efforts, may obtain independence', he and his family duly quit Skye and emigrated, as already mentioned, to Ontario. This was in 1845 when Martin's son James, the future MacLeod of the Mounties, was just eight years old.[3]

In Ontario, where Martin MacLeod settled in the neighbourhood of Toronto, his disagreements with Norman of Dunvegan, despite their now having to be conducted at long range, intensified further. For reasons which are obscure, but which probably had to do with legal and other complications surrounding the terms on which Martin relinquished his tenancy, the MacLeod chief retained in his possession some £2,000, then a large sum, which Gesto's former tacksman expected to come to him. On the disputed cash evaporating in the course of Norman of Dunvegan's bankruptcy, Martin of Drynoch was left embittered. By failing to separate his ex-tenant's funds from his own, Chief Norman had committed, Martin thought, an 'utterly dishonourable act'.[4]

Martin MacLeod wanted his son, James, to embark on a legal career. James, however, had other ideas. Against his father's wishes, he joined a Canadian militia regiment, served with distinction in the course of frontier troubles on the prairies, and having thus acquired an appetite for action and adventure, was well positioned, on the North West Mounted Police being formed in 1873, to assume a leading role in the organisation.

The mounted police owed their existence to Canada's first prime minister, Sir John Macdonald. Like James MacLeod, Macdonald had come to North America from Scotland as a boy. Also like James, Sir John was both a Canadian nationalist and a British imperialist. When, in 1867, several of Britain's previously distinct North American colonies constituted themselves into a single federation, Macdonald, the new country's foremost politician, committed himself to an agenda of westward expansion. Canada, he proclaimed, should aspire to be a transcontinental nation – stretching, as the United States did by the 1860s, from the Atlantic to the Pacific. This bold vision was eventually made a reality. Before that happened, however, two related objectives had to be secured by Sir John Macdonald and his allies: first, already-existing British settlements in the vicinity of Vancouver had to be cajoled, as they soon were, into joining the Canadian federation; second, steps had to be taken to ensure that the then unsettled prairie region between the Great Lakes and the Rockies was secured for Canada and the empire. It was with the latter aim in view that the North West Mounted Police were formed. Their role was to keep present-day Saskatchewan and Alberta out of American clutches – while simultaneously pressuring the Indian peoples living in this vast area to accept Queen Victoria as their sovereign. Given those aims, *The Times* of London explained to its readers, it made sense to equip the mounted police with scarlet uniforms of the kind long associated with the British military – 'in order that no misconception may exist in the minds of either Yankee ruffians or Indian warriors as to the nationality of the force'.[5]

The ruffians mentioned by *The Times* were American traders who had moved out of Montana into the Alberta and Saskatchewan prairies. There, from fortified posts with well-chosen names like Fort Whoop-Up, they sold rotgut liquor to the prairie region's Indian tribes. This, from a Canadian and British perspective, was a worrying development – partly because of the disorder which whiskey peddling of the Whoop-Up type always brought in its wake, and still more because Fort Whoop-Up's operators had hoisted the United States flag in territory nominally under the British Empire's jurisdiction. Within months of the North West Mounted Police's formation, therefore, a detachment of the force's troopers, including James MacLeod, at this stage the mounted police's assistant commissioner, were ordered to put an end to whiskey trading on the prairies.

Ironically, given the nature of his mission, the assistant commissioner was himself a hard drinker – as demonstrated by a story deriving from a trip he made, in his dual capacity of mounted policeman and Canadian militia colonel, to one of the US army's frontier posts. There his American hosts, looking to have fun at their visitor's expense, drank with him in relays – convinced that, sooner or later, he was bound to succumb. According to an eyewitness, however, James MacLeod saw off a succession of drinking partners: 'As the evening wore on and the bottle circulated freely, man after man disappeared, either under the table or into an armchair . . . and when Colonel MacLeod assisted the one solitary survivor up the stairs to his bed, the man stopped short . . . and said, "By God, Colonel, where do you put it?"'[6]

His own fondness for alcohol notwithstanding, James MacLeod dealt easily with Fort Whoop-Up. The fort, at the junction of the St Mary and Oldman rivers near present-day Lethbridge, Alberta, had been largely abandoned prior to James's arrival, and was taken without bloodshed. Moving on west from Whoop-Up, the Mounted Police's assistant commissioner now established two new posts. The first, on the Oldman, was christened Fort McLeod by James's subordinates. The second, further north on the Bow River, was named by James MacLeod himself. He called this post Fort Calgary – by way of tribute to his sister, Alexandra, whose home was in the original Calgary on the Isle of Mull. Today's Albertan Calgary, its nucleus the settlement which sprang up around James MacLeod's fort, is Canada's third largest city. Appropriately, it contains a Clan MacLeod Society. Among this society's founders, I am told by Alma MacLeod, a current member, was the late Mary Dover, a prominent Calgary citizen and Colonel James MacLeod's granddaughter.

Alma and one of her Clan MacLeod Society colleagues, Randy MacLeod, take charge of my Alberta travels. We begin at the spot where Fort Calgary took shape in the 1870s, its site now overshadowed by the glittering highrises which dominate modern Calgary's downtown. Next, driving out of the city on a street called MacLeod Trail, we make for Fort McLeod. It is June, but the weather has been chilly and the Rocky Mountains, a constant presence on our right as we head south, are coated in snow.

Fort McLeod, nowadays a small town serving the cattle ranchers whose herds are to be seen everywhere in this corner of Alberta, boasts one significant tourist attraction – a reconstructed version of the fort which, for a time, was home to James MacLeod and a 150-strong detachment of the North West Mounted Police. Here Randy, Alma and I meet with Jasper Buckskin, whose grandfather was one of the mounted police's Indian scouts.

Jasper's people, the Bloods, are one of the tribes constituting the Blackfoot nation, an Indian confederacy which dominated this region before whites got here. Blackfoot independence ended when James MacLeod, who took overall charge of the mounted police in 1876, persuaded Blackfoot and other chiefs to accept treaties he presented to them on behalf of his political superiors in Ottawa. By putting their names to those treaties, the Blackfoot and neighbouring First Nations, as Canada's Indian groupings are called, also assented to large-scale immigration into their former territories. James MacLeod thus opened the way for white settlement in Alberta – which is why his Indian treaties are often portrayed as his career's crowning glory. From Jasper Buckskin's standpoint, however, the mounted police commissioner's agreements with the Blackfoot look like unequal, if not quite forcibly imposed, pacts. Jasper, then, is no uncritical admirer of James MacLeod. But in his dealings with Alberta's First Nations, Jasper Buckskin concedes, MacLeod of the Mounties was not without redeeming features, one of them being the high esteem in which he held Indians.

'All the Indians I have so far met appear to be a very intelligent lot of men,' James MacLeod wrote shortly after his arrival on the prairies. The same lack of racial prejudice is evident in the mounted police commissioner having become the close friend and drinking companion of a Mountie scout called Jerry Potts, whose father was Scottish by birth but whose mother was Blackfoot. His comparative freedom from bigotry, of course, did not stop James MacLeod subjecting the Blackfoot to white rule. But it does seem to have gained him a reputation among his First Nation contacts as a man who could be trusted, as not all whites could, to stick by any deal he made. 'I doubt if anyone ever had such influence with them,' one of the mounted police commissioner's colleagues commented of James MacLeod's relationships with the Blackfoot. 'He kept his place, never accepted a present, never gave one, and was respected by [Indians] all the more for it.' Those qualities were much in evidence when, in 1877, James MacLeod became embroiled in the diplomatic crisis which, that fall, led to the US army's General Alfred H. Terry becoming the mounted police commissioner's guest.[7]

This crisis had its origin in troubles precipitated by the advance of miners, ranchers and settlers into territories which afterwards became the American states of North Dakota and Montana. In response to those incursions, a number of Sioux and Cheyenne bands, under the joint leadership of Chiefs Sitting Bull and Crazy Horse, went to war with the intruders. An immediate result was the Battle of the Little Bighorn, when an American force under the command of General George A. Custer was wiped out. This was in June 1876. Months of fighting followed, and Crazy Horse and Sitting Bull were forced on the defensive. In time, the former surrendered to the United States military, while the latter, with several thousand followers, sought safety across the border in Canada where the Sioux set up camp in the Wood Mountain area of southern Saskatchewan.

By crossing the 'medicine line', as Indians of that time called the American–Canadian frontier, Sitting Bull and his people put themselves out of reach of their US army pursuers. They also presented Mounted Police Commissioner James MacLeod with a problem which, in a dispatch to Ottawa, the commissioner described as 'very grave'. If Sitting Bull launched an attack on the American army from his Wood Mountain camp, James MacLeod pointed out, this might trigger an American invasion of the Canadian prairies. Hence the speed with which the commissioner went to meet Chief Sitting Bull, by whom he was well received. Invoking Queen Victoria, known to Indians as 'the Grandmother', the police commissioner informed Sitting Bull and other Sioux chiefs that, as long as they kept the Grandmother's peace, their safety would be guaranteed. 'There was a wall raised up behind them [on the border],' James MacLeod informed his Sioux audience, 'that their enemies dare not cross.' However, the police commissioner went on, he wanted Sitting Bull and his subordinate chiefs to accompany him to a meeting at which the US authorities, in the person of General Terry, would make proposals to them. Reluctantly, the commissioner's Sioux listeners agreed to do as he requested. The upshot was a conference, held on 17 October 1877 and attended by, among others, James MacLeod, Alfred H. Terry and Chief Sitting Bull.[8]

This conference took place in the mess hall at Fort Walsh, a North West Mounted Police post in the Cypress Hills, a little to the east of the provincial border separating modern Saskatchewan from Alberta. Abandoned by the Mounties after a fire in the 1880s, but rebuilt sixty years later, Fort Walsh, a cluster of wooden buildings surrounded by a log stockade, is too isolated to attract many visitors. When I visit, on a summer afternoon of sun and thundershowers, mine is practically the only vehicle parked at the end of an approach road so quiet as to have deer grazing on its verges. Birdsong and the rattle of swiftly running water in a nearby creek are the only sounds to be heard in a valley which, on the day Chief Sitting Bull came here, must have echoed to the din of conversation and the clattering of horses.

Sitting Bull's behaviour, on his entering Fort Walsh's mess hall, was significant. Walking up to James MacLeod, the Sioux chief took his hand and shook it warmly. General Terry he ignored – and when the latter attempted to assure Sitting Bull that the chief and his people, if they returned to United States territory, would be permitted to live quietly on reservations set aside for that purpose, Sitting Bull cut the American short. 'You come here to tell us lies,' he said. 'Go back . . . [and] take your lies with you. The country we came from belonged to us; you took it from us; we will live here.' With this, the Sioux delegation left the Fort Walsh conference – and though James MacLeod, at Alfred H. Terry's request, promptly sought a private word with Sitting Bull, there was no changing the Sioux chief's mind. 'We like you and the [mounted] police very much,' Sitting Bull told James MacLeod, 'and it is only for this reason we came to see [General Terry and his colleagues] and to hear what they had to say.' But there was no way, Sitting Bull insisted, he could be persuaded to take his people back to the American side of the medicine line. For the foreseeable future, it was clear, the Sioux were to remain Commissioner MacLeod's responsibility.[9]

Sitting Bull's intransigence owed something to his Wood Mountain camp having gained, just prior to the abortive Fort Walsh gathering, a further Indian contingent led by Chief White Bird of the Nez Perce. White Bird's people, like Sitting Bull's, had been battling with the United States military – most recently in Montana's Bear Paw Mountains where the Nez Perce, at the end of a fighting retreat which began hundreds of miles to the west, were encircled by a hugely superior American force. Although this Bear Paw episode ended in the death or surrender of most of the Nez Perce caught up in it, White Bird and about a hundred others had managed to get away under cover of darkness – subsequently making their way, much as Sitting Bull and the Sioux had done, into Canada. 'Many of them were wounded,' one of James MacLeod's officers reported of White Bird's party. 'Some were shot badly through the body, legs and arms.' From a Sioux perspective, the same officer went on, the suffering inflicted on the Nez Perce by the US army served to confirm that Sitting Bull was right to have as little as possible to do with Alfred H. Terry. 'You see these men, women and children, wounded and bleeding,' one Sioux spokesman said of White Bird and his party. 'We cannot talk with [soldiers] who have [those people's] blood on their hands. They [the Americans] have stained the grass of the Grandmother with it.'[10]

In Sitting Bull's camp, Chief White Bird was joined by a young man who was the chief's close relative and who afterwards compiled, on the basis of what he heard from White Bird at Wood Mountain, a belligerently pro-Indian account of the origins, course and outcome of the Nez Perce War. Although this man's mother was Nez Perce, his father was a Scots-born fur trader – which is how it came about that Chief White Bird had a kinsman called Duncan McDonald.[11]

On the face of things, Duncan McDonald and James MacLeod inhabited separate universes – James being the Canadian government's principal agent on the prairies, while Duncan, part Nez Perce by birth and wholly Nez Perce by inclination, was one of the people categorised in the nineteenth century as 'half-breeds'. Duncan McDonald's background, then, made him unacceptable to many whites. This, however, would not have prevented James MacLeod from speaking with him – the police commissioner's good friend Jerry Potts, after all, being another half-breed of identical provenance. It is tempting, therefore, to speculate that, somewhere in the vicinity of Wood Mountain, Saskatchewan, Duncan McDonald and James MacLeod might have met and talked – for if they did they would have discovered that their family histories overlapped. The overlap derives from James's grandfather, Donald MacLeod, having been tacksman of Eileanriach in Glenelg towards the close of the eighteenth century – when Donald is bound to have had contact with one of his neighbours, Angus MacDonald of Munial, whose own tack on Knoydart's north coast was not far from Donald MacLeod's Eileanriach home. Angus MacDonald, as mentioned earlier, was among early Knoydart emigrants to Glengarry County, Ontario. With him to Canada, the Munial tacksman took his son Finan, who, during the 1790s, joined a fur-trading combine on whose behalf, in the opening years of the nineteenth century, he helped explore and map the territory which James MacLeod was afterwards ordered to pacify. Other members of this McDonald family came west in Finan's footsteps. One of them was the father of Duncan McDonald, Chief White Bird's mixed-blood kinsman. Thus there arises the mildly tantalising possibility that Sitting Bull's Wood Mountain encampment might have been visited simultaneously by two men – one a white of high social standing, the other a so-called half-breed – whose divergent circumstances arose out of emigrant journeys which, despite their contrasting outcomes, started in much the same place and involved much the same sorts of people.

Alberta and Manitoba: Athabasca and Winnipeg

The fur-trading concern which recruited Finan McDonald, Angus of Munial's son, was the North West Company. Based in Montreal, this most aggressive of corporations, which took shape around 1780, was created by men from the Highlands and Islands. Among the more renowned Nor'Westers, as the company's ruling partners called themselves, was Alexander MacKenzie, originally from Lewis and the first white to make an overland crossing of North America. One of MacKenzie's older contemporaries was Normand MacLeod, a Skyeman who, when he got to North America around 1760, was a British army officer. On quitting the military, Normand, whose name has always been spelled thus, settled in the Mohawk Valley area of colonial New York where he began dabbling in the fur trade. During America's Revolutionary War, the pro-British Normand abandoned New York for Canada. There he began trading in opposition to the infant North West Company. Soon, however, Normand merged his interests with it – thereby ensuring that several other MacLeods acquired key roles in the company's management structure.[12]

An early member of this group was Alexander MacLeod, a further Skyeman and Normand's nephew. Alexander's principal sphere of operations was the then newly opened up Athabasca region in the far north of present-day Alberta. It was from Athabasca, first penetrated by whites in the 1780s, that Alexander MacKenzie made his pioneering trip to the Pacific in 1793 – MacKenzie's westward route taking him up the Peace River on which, a few years later, the North West Company established a post called Fort Dunvegan. This post, soon the leading fur trade centre in the Peace River country, was named by Archibald Norman MacLeod – almost certainly from Skye, probably another of Normand MacLeod's relatives, and by all accounts a flamboyant character given to 'flounc[ing] around . . . in a . . . military uniform of his own design, complete with sword and cocked hat'.[13]

In 1806, when Fort Dunvegan was still under construction, the post was run by one more of the North West Company's MacLeods, Alexander Roderick. Like Archibald Norman, Alexander Roderick MacLeod spent several winters in the Athabasca country. Since orders from faraway Montreal reached him just once a year, Alexander Roderick was in sole charge of Nor'Wester operations across a huge tract of territory populated only by itinerant Indian bands. His role, however, was one which Alexander Roderick MacLeod, despite his isolation, appears to have relished. In this, he was typical of his numerous North West Company counterparts. According to one early-twentieth-century historian, men from the Highlands and Islands made more effective fur traders than anyone else: 'Self-dependent, inured to spartan conditions, accustomed to scattered communities, their character was suited to their new surroundings, and the clan system, whatever may have been its faults, certainly produced men who knew how to rule in their own small circle.'[14]

Those men's commercial ambitions were unlimited. Thanks to their adoption of Indian technologies such as snowshoes and birchbark canoes, they were able to range across the North American continent in pursuit of the beaver pelts that were the fur trade's staple. Demand for beaver, the source of the felt then used for making hats, was fuelled by forces similar to those which generated demand for wool – and just as the expansion of sheep farming created all sorts of social dislocation, whether in Scotland or Australia, so the fur trade helped bring about the destruction of Canada's tribal societies.

North West Company traders did not trap beavers. They paid Indians for pelts. Partly, payment took the shape of comparatively innocuous goods like knives and axes. Notoriously, it also took the form of whiskey – and, because Indian peoples had never previously encountered alcohol, whiskey's arrival could result in whole tribes falling victim to catastrophic addictions of the kind associated more recently with heroin or crack cocaine.

In their dealings with Indian suppliers, fur traders relied heavily on the native women they took as partners. In fur-trade jargon, those women were 'country wives' and, inevitably, they became the mothers of mixed-blood children. When, as almost all of them did eventually, a fur trader left a locality like the Peace River area and headed back east, his colleagues expected him to abandon his country wife and children. This did not always happen, however. It certainly did not happen in the case of Alexander Roderick MacLeod who, following the North West Company's 1821 merger with the Hudson's Bay Company, became one of the Bay Company's chief traders. In his will, Chief Trader MacLeod stressed that he considered his Indian partner to be his 'legitimate wife' and went on to underline his 'serious determination' that, after his death, his mixed-blood children should be treated as his heirs. In the event, a legal judgement on the validity or otherwise of Alexander Roderick's wishes was sought from two English lawyers who concluded that the former chief trader, who died in 1840, was indeed his Indian partner's husband – even though their wedding, a mostly Indian ceremonial, involved neither church nor state. 'This marriage,' the lawyers commented, 'took place . . . where there were no established clergymen, and was solemnised in accordance with the customs of the country.'[15]

Sadly, this judgement failed to secure the well-being of Alexander Roderick's mixed-blood children. When, in 1836, Sarah MacLeod, one of those children, married a Hudson's Bay Company employee, John Ballenden, she seemed assured of a good future. Sarah's husband, after all, was one of the Bay Company's rising stars and, by 1848, he had taken charge of company operations in the Canadian West. But neither Sarah nor John Ballenden anticipated the difficulties that came their way when they made their home in Manitoba's Red River Settlement, the future Winnipeg. Red River, by the 1840s, was attracting growing numbers of white women. As also happened in Britain's Asian and African colonies, their arrival changed attitudes to white–native liaisons. Sexual, particularly marital, relationships between white men and Indian women were now declared taboo in the Red River area – while the mixed-blood offspring of such relationships were subject to abuse. Despite, or perhaps because of, the fact that her husband was one of the most prominent members of the Red River community, Sarah Ballenden's life was made miserable. On grounds that were flimsy at best, spurious at worst, she was said to have committed adultery – something to be expected, it was added, from a half-breed. John Ballenden stood by his wife. But Sarah, even with his backing, found it impossible to cope. Ostracised, persecuted, gossiped about endlessly, her health broke down. Soon Sarah MacLeod Ballenden was dead.[16]

In modern Canada, people of mixed blood continue to struggle for parity of esteem. I hear a little of what this struggle involves when, in today's Winnipeg, I meet with Mary Richard. Her surname, before her marriage, was McLeod and she is among the ten per cent of Winnipeg residents who are classified officially as 'Aboriginal'. This term, Mary explains, comprises two formerly distinct categories – one consisting of First Nations like the Blackfoot, the other made up of mixed-blood people like herself. Especially in Manitoba, where such people have been common since the era of the fur trade, they possess their own identity. Mary Richard, then, as well as being Aboriginal is Métis – a name first adopted by Manitoba's mixed-blood population some 200 years ago. At that time, the Manitoba Métis were a force to be reckoned with – their effectively autonomous society underpinned by their role as suppliers of dried buffalo meat, or pemmican, to the fur traders who passed through Red River on their way to Athabasca and points west. By the nineteenth century's close, however, the Métis, together with Canada's First Nations, had been excluded from the Canadian mainstream – and both groups, as a result, were increasingly beset by all sorts of troubles. Those troubles, though their nature has altered in the interim, have not gone away. While waiting for my appointment with Mary Richard in Winnipeg's Thunderbird House, described in its introductory literature as 'a home for Aboriginal spirituality and culture', I leaf through the current issue of *Indian News*. It includes an interview with Canada's prime minister, Paul Martin. His government, Mr Martin tells the paper, 'faces no greater challenge than those that confront Aboriginal Canada. Simply put, we must break the cycle of poverty, indignity and injustice in which so many Aboriginal Canadians live.'

Mary Richard, a community activist, shares this objective. We speak about how it might be achieved. We speak about the difficulties which have always faced anyone, whether in present-day Manitoba or in the post-clearance Highlands and Islands, who tries to give new purpose to people whose former ways of life have been destroyed. Most of all, because this is what has brought me to Thunderbird House, we talk about Mary Richard's background. 'Somewhere,' Mary says, 'I have a family tree.' On its being produced, its contents highlight a key difference between Métis MacLeods and the MacLeods who became Anglophone, or English-speaking, Canadians. The latter, even when separated from Scotland by several generations, favoured first names that were variations on a familiar Norman-Alexander-Roderick theme. Mary Richard's McLeod forebears, in contrast, preferred Baptiste, Michel, François and the like. I ask Mary if this means that her family spoke French. 'No,' she says, 'they didn't, not exactly.'

Mary Richard grew up in Camperville, about 200 miles north of Winnipeg and a place which, during Mary's childhood, was inhabited by just a few hundred people. Camperville, despite its tiny population, was home to several languages. 'In our household alone,' Mary Richard recalls, 'we spoke four. Papa spoke English and Ojibway. Mama spoke Cree, English and Michif.' Michif, which Mary also speaks, is an important aspect of Métis uniqueness. Its basis is Québécois French, the lingua franca of the Montreal-based fur trade. But mixed into Michif, and accounting for much of its vocabulary, are words drawn from Indian languages, notably Saulteaux and Cree. So the Michel, Baptiste and François McLeods in her family tree, I put it to Mary Richard, would have spoken Michif. 'Probably,' Mary says. 'But some of them spoke Bungay.' This, Mary tells me, was another linguistic offshoot of the fur trade. Now extinct, Bungay, like Michif, was part-French, part-Indian in origin. Unlike Michif, however, Bungay included a sprinkling of Gaelic.

Even the earliest McLeod listed on Mary Richard's family tree was born in Manitoba. But when I spend an hour or two with Albert McLeod, another of Winnipeg's Métis residents, I am in the company of someone who can name the Lewis township which one of his Scots-born ancestors left to join the mid-nineteenth-century Hudson's Bay Company. Albert is a policy analyst in the Aboriginal Health Department of Manitoba's provincial government. 'I'm a Métis person,' he says as he introduces himself. 'What this means, in my case, is that I'm a product of two nations, the Scots and the Cree. Because of the fur trade, those nations intermingled, and I'm one of the results.'

Albert McLeod shares with me an anecdote drawn from his family history: 'Way back in the early days of the fur trade, one of the Hudson's

Bay Company's traders was leaving this country for the last time – sailing out of Hudson Bay for Europe on one of the company's ships. The trader was abandoning his Cree wife. But their children, the trader had decided, were to go away with him. The abandoned wife, though desperately distressed, couldn't stop her older sons and daughters being taken. But she managed to get hold of the youngest child, a baby boy, and clutching him to her, she ran away into the bush. Of course, the trader searched for his wife and his baby. But he couldn't find them, and soon he had to board his ship. When the ship sailed, the Cree woman watched from her hiding place as it carried all except one of her children to Europe. You can imagine her feelings. But you can also imagine the comfort she got from having been able to hang on to her baby.'

Albert McLeod pauses. 'My grandmother told me that story,' he says. 'It meant a lot to her. The little boy whose mother hid him in the bush, you see, was my grandmother's grandfather. He was brought up to be Cree. But starting in his time, and I guess he was born in the early nineteenth century, there's been European blood in our family.'

Albert directs me to a sheaf of photocopied documents spread across his floor. The earliest of those documents, dated 1875, is headed thus: 'Treaty 5 between Her Majesty the Queen [Victoria] and the Saulteaux and Swampy Cree Tribes of Indians at Beren's River and Norway House.' In 1908, as another of Albert's documents makes clear, this treaty was amended by an 'adhesion' or addition dealing with territories then occupied by 'the Split Lake and Nelson House bands of Indians'. This adhesion had two signatories, one an Indian, the other a Hudson's Bay Company man. The first of those, Chief Peter Moose, assented to the 1908 agreement by placing 'his x mark' alongside 'his name in Cree characters'. Albert points to this name. 'Peter Moose was my mother's great-uncle,' he tells me. Next Albert points to the name of the chief's co-signatory, a Bay Company post manager called Henry McLeod. 'He was my father's grandfather,' Albert says.

Henry McLeod was Scottish, Albert explains, but his wife, Christina Morrison, Albert's great-grandmother, was part-Cree, having had an Indian mother and a Scots-born father – the latter being Hector Morrison, Albert McLeod's great-great-grandfather. Hector came from Sandwick in Lewis. He joined the Hudson's Bay Company in 1832.

'My father's father,' Albert says, 'was William McLeod. He made a living as a Bay Company fisherman. He supplied the fish fed to the company's dog teams in winter.' William's wife was a further McLeod, whose given name was Sarah Jane. Like William, she was part-Cree, part-Scottish – her father, Donald McLeod, having been another of the Bay Company's Scottish recruits.

For much of the twentieth century, the mixed-blood or Métis family founded by Albert McLeod's Cree and Scottish forebears lived, as some of its members still do, in the northern part of Manitoba – either in the vicinity of The Pas, on the Saskatchewan River, or around Norway House, a Bay Company base located near the point where Nelson River exits Lake Winnipeg. Up there on the edge of the Arctic, Albert McLeod believes, his people could have evolved a stable and successful society. 'We were Cree and we were Scottish,' Albert says. 'We were comfortable with that. We had our own way of living. We had a vision of how our future might be. But we could only have found our way to that future if we'd been left alone – and we weren't left alone. New values began to be imposed on us from back east; we ran up against racism; we were made to feel worthless. A lot of what we'd had just fell apart.'

There is silence for a moment. 'Let me tell you about one of my uncles,' Albert says. 'His name was Norman, Norman McLeod. That's a real Scots name, I guess, and Norman, with his reddish hair and blue eyes, looked real Scottish as well. But his language was Cree, and so was his life. This life was all fishing, all boats, all trapping – a Cree life, as I say. Anyway, Norman began to be ill. He knew he was ill, very ill, but he wasn't the sort of man who'd ever consult a western or westernised doctor – a doctor who wasn't part of his world. So as winter began, Norman left home to set out his trap line as usual. Then Christmas came. Norman should have been back for Christmas, and he wasn't. They went looking for him, and they found him in his cabin in the bush. He was dead. He'd been dead for some time.'

New South Wales: Tomerong

The Métis McLeods I met in Winnipeg take pride in an ancestry that is Scottish as well as Cree. In Tomerong, New South Wales, when I talk with Bobby McLeod, an Australian Aborigine, it is apparent that Bobby is equally anxious to embrace those elements of his family history which derive from Scotland. 'When I was young,' Bobby says, 'I ran up against a lot of racism, a lot of prejudice. When you meet with that, it makes you angry – and I got angry about everything European. I blamed whites for the way we were robbed of our land, for all the bad times we've had. But now I've moved on. Now, as well as being angry about what happened, I want to know why it happened. So I was glad to get the chance, back in 1997, to go to Scotland. When there, I went to Skye and visited Dunvegan Castle. It was important for me to do that. I wanted to know more about the MacLeods – the MacLeods I got my name from. I needed to understand who they were, why they left Scotland, what brought them here.'

In notes attached to one of his published poems, Bobby McLeod is introduced with those words: 'Bobby's belonging is to the Monaro peoples through his father and to the Tomakin, Wandandian and Yuin groupings through his mother. Defining Bobby is a difficult task as he . . . is a multifaceted individual . . . He is regarded by many as an Aboriginal leader, while also singer, songwriter, poet, activist, teacher of Aboriginal lore and culture, director and founder of . . . the Doonooch Dance Company.'[17]

Bobby McLeod's links with the Monaro's Aboriginals account for his surname. It was in the Monaro, as mentioned earlier, that Archibald MacLeod settled before he moved into mid-nineteenth-century Gippsland. It is to Archibald's son John, the man in charge of Gippsland's Orbost Station, that Bobby traces the McLeod component of his background.

There are parallels here with what happened in Canada. Just as white fur traders became the sexual partners of North American Indians, so white sheep rearers in Australia became the sexual partners of Aborigines. When looking after Orbost Station during the 1840s and 1850s, John MacLeod is known to have had around him so-called blacks with names like Billy and Jack MacLeod. According to one interpretation of this fact, those blacks, some of them boys and young men who had come south from the Monaro, were pure-blood Aborigines to whom John MacLeod simply attached his surname. An alternative explanation allows for the possibility that some at least of the black, or not quite black, MacLeods employed at Orbost were, in fact, mixed-blood children resulting from the station manager's relationships with Aboriginal women.[18]

Such relationships, some coercive, others less so, developed against a backdrop of generalised hostility between Aborigines and Australia's white colonisers. Gippsland's Aborigines were naturally resentful of the way in which MacLeod-owned livestock encroached on to hunting-and-gathering territories that had formerly been their exclusive preserve. More than once, in consequence, Orbost Station's flocks and herds were decimated by Aboriginal raiders. At those times, as is evident from a letter describing his reaction to the killing of a number of cattle, John MacLeod was virtually at war with his Aborigine neighbours: 'I rode down unarmed [to inspect the dead animals] as I had a young horse [easily startled by gunshots]. About two miles from [my] hut, I saw a native dog and, having no gun, took [my foot] out of the stirrup . . . to kill him [the dog] with the [stirrup] iron. [At this,] my horse took fright and pitched me . . . on the ground. Instantly the scrub . . . seemed alive with blacks. I am sure the whole tribe was there; [their] yells made my flesh creep. I was in a deuce of a fright, but I [normally] had a brace of pistols in my belt, and this was known to the blacks. So I took out a round brass tinder box and, holding it like a pistol, made the best of my way home. Although they [the Aborigines] followed me in the scrub, I never saw one. I think the fright was mutual.'[19]

Although this confrontation ended innocuously, others were bloodier. The outcome was predictable. In Gippsland as elsewhere in Australia, Aboriginal ways of life that had developed over tens of thousands of years began to disintegrate. It has not been easy for Aborigines to repair the ensuing damage. This is evident from what Bobby McLeod has to say about himself.

Bobby McLeod grew up in a Sydney suburb to which his family had been moved compulsorily from their original home in the New South Wales countryside. In Sydney, Bobby went to a predominantly white school. 'I was always told I wasn't good enough,' he recalls. 'Kids in the playground thought I was dirty and they wouldn't even hold my hand, just my little finger.'

Like many Aborigines, Bobby McLeod took refuge in alcohol. 'By the time I'd turned thirty-six, I'd been drunk every day for seven years,' he says. Gradually, however, he began to turn his life around. As he did so, he became politically active, participating in battles for Aborigine rights, travelling overseas during the 1970s and 1980s to meet with representatives of other, also disadvantaged, indigenous peoples. On a visit to Canada, where Bobby saw something at first hand of how the country's First Nations were looking to rediscover their ancestral belief systems, it became clear to this Australian Aborigine that he too might find inspiration, even salvation, in the past. Hence his decision in 1990 to set up the healing and cultural centre which has given rise to the Doonooch dance group.

Doonooch is an Aboriginal concept having to do with what Aborigines call dreaming, a mystical means of being in touch with the earth and with one's ancestors. When introduced in those terms, the philosophy to which Bobby McLeod's Doonooch Dancers give expression might sound distant from day-to-day realities. In fact, his dance group provides Bobby with a practical means of helping young people of Aboriginal background gain the sense of purpose he himself lacked when he was their age. Far from engaging in flight from the modern world, then, the Doonooch Dancers, who starred in the opening ceremony of Sydney's Olympic Games in 2000, are a striking demonstration of the extent to which Aboriginal Australia is capable of devising constructive alternatives to drink, drug addiction and all the other manifestations of breakdown which have scarred Aboriginal society for so long.

Bobby McLeod and the Doonooch Dancers have travelled to several European countries. Hence Bobby's trip to Scotland and his consequent discovery that, before they left for Australia, many people from the Highlands and Islands were on the receiving end of oppressive policies similar to those they later imposed on Aborigines. Bobby McLeod would like to explore how this could have occurred. 'There should be more contact between Scots and Aborigines,' he says. 'We ought to take more interest in each other.'

South Carolina: Mayesville

Although they suffered at the hands of emigrants from countries like Scotland, Australia's Aborigines and Canada's First Nations mostly retained, in theory at any rate, their personal freedom. By definition, this was not true of the African-American slaves belonging to Scottish settlers in North Carolina's Cape Fear River country. 'Young healthy negroes are bought [in North Carolina] for between £25 and £40,' prospective settlers were informed in the early 1770s. 'Five of these will clear and labour a plantation the first year.' From the start of Highlands and Islands settlement in the vicinity of the Cape Fear River, then, black slaves were basic to the area's economy. Among the surviving papers of MacLeod and other settler families in North Carolina, it follows, are documents concerning the buying and selling of human beings. Also still in existence are the remnants of huts in which MacLeod-owned slaves were accommodated.[20]

Because imported slaves originated in different parts of Africa, they could communicate with each other only by adopting the language of their owners. This meant that Cape Fear River country slaves commonly spoke Gaelic. Other African-Americans, on managing to escape from the United States into Canada, where slavery was outlawed from a relatively early period, became Gaelic speaking as a result of their setting up home among emigrant communities of the kind established in Cape Breton Island. Hence the otherwise mystifying appearance in Rudyard Kipling's 1897 novel, *Captains Courageous*, of a 'jet-black' ship's cook who 'comes from the innards of Cape Breton' and whose language of choice – a 'huffy-chuffy . . . home-made Scotch' – turns out to be Gaelic.[21]

The linguistic curiosities to which it gave rise do not detract from the fact that the enslavement of millions of black people has to be ranked, as a United States president remarked when visiting Africa in 2003, among the most heinous of all history's crimes. To their credit, some individuals of Highlands and Islands background were of much the same opinion more than 200 years ago. John MacLeod, a naval surgeon who served at one point on a slave ship, was in this category. So was Alexander MacLeod, a New York clergyman who arrived in the United States from Scotland in 1792. Alexander's father, Neil MacLeod, the son of a Skye tacksman, was parish minister of Kilfinichen in Mull. In 1773, Neil was described by Samuel Johnson as 'the clearest-headed man that he [Johnson] had met in the Western Islands'. A similar clear-headedness is discernible in the anti-slavery sermons preached in early-nineteenth-century New York by Neil's son, Alexander. The Bible, Alexander MacLeod pointed out, stated that anyone who 'stealeth a man and selleth him . . . shall surely be put to death'. This text caused Alexander to conclude: 'The practice of buying, holding or selling our unoffending fellow creatures as slaves is immoral.' All the world's inhabitants, black Africans every bit as much as white Europeans, were 'different members of the same great family,' Alexander MacLeod went on. 'Can you be sincere friends to liberty,' he asked his fellow Americans, 'and tolerate this dreadful traffic?'[22]

The question thus posed was settled finally in the course of America's Civil War. MacLeods lined up with both sides in that conflict – men from northern states joining the Union army, men from southern localities like the Cape Fear River country serving in big numbers with Confederate forces. Often, when visiting North Carolina cemeteries, I have come across the graves of MacLeods who died in Confederate uniforms. Sometimes, beside those men's tombstones, I have seen freshly planted Confederate flags. Present-day African-Americans see those flags as suggestive of a continuing reluctance in some quarters to accept that slavery was wrong. But if Confederate flags are placed on the graves of Confederate dead for white supremacist reasons, they are placed there for other, more complex, reasons as well. MacLeods who left the Cape Fear River country to fight for the Confederacy may have done so, in part, to defend slaveholding. At bottom, however, they considered themselves to be fighting on behalf of communities that they and their emigrant ancestors had created – communities where much that was Scottish in origin survived into the nineteenth century. I do not go along with a recently fashionable, but overblown, thesis to the effect that the American Civil War saw a Celtic South pitted against an Anglo-Saxon North. But I do accept that, in the Cape Fear River country anyway, pro-Confederate feeling was, to some extent, the political expression of a deep-seated desire to safeguard a local identity rooted ultimately in the Highlands and Islands of Scotland. Because I want to keep alive in today's Highlands and Islands a heritage similar to the heritage defended by people living in the mid-nineteenth-century Cape Fear River country, those people's commitment to sustaining their area's distinctiveness is one component of Confederate ideology which, a little to my alarm, I can readily connect with.

Whatever one thinks of Confederate motivations, the fact remains that the Confederate cause was lost. In 1865, the Cape Fear River country was overrun, as described already, by a Union army and the region's slaves were freed. After their liberation, a few African-Americans adopted surnames of their own devising. Others settled for the surnames of their former owners – which is why there are plenty of African-Americans called MacLeod. Not all those folk have an ancestral connection with the Highlands and Islands, but some do. Slaveholders, and still more the unmarried sons of slaveholders, frequently made mistresses of, or raped, female slaves. It is for this reason, as a white descendant of slaveholders has commented, that 'the progeny of slaves' and 'the progeny of slave owners' are for ever linked: 'We have been in each other's lives. We have been in each other's dreams. We have been in each other's beds.' African-American MacLeods, it follows, include people of Highlands and Islands descent.[23]

Whether a nineteenth-century African-American called Sam McLeod was in this category, I do not know. Sam was born into slavery in the Mayesville area of South Carolina, a locality settled by families moving down from the Cape Fear River country. Two such families, McLeod and Wilson by name, acquired substantial landholdings near Mayesville. On their properties, the McLeods and Wilsons kept slaves – Sam growing up on a McLeod-owned plantation, and Sam's future wife, Patsy, being raised on a Wilson place. Because those plantations were not far apart, it was easy for Patsy and Sam to meet and to get to know one another. But having done so, they wanted to marry, and this was more difficult. Married slaves, particularly those attached to different plantations, risked being sold separately. Even if this did not happen, a slave couple's children could be seized and sold with no more ceremony than might surround the marketing of calves or lambs.

Prior to 1865, several of Sam and Patsy McLeod's children were taken in this way. Patsy and Sam could not prevent that. But somehow they managed to keep track of each child, and when liberation came, they gathered their family together again. At the same time, Sam McLeod, now a free man, left the plantation where he had lived and took over a 35-acre farm on which he and his eldest son built a log cabin. In this cabin in 1875, Sam and Patsy's fifteenth child, Mary, was born. From the same cabin, when a little girl, Mary McLeod walked five miles each morning into Mayesville to attend a mission school. This school, by enabling her to acquire the beginnings of an education, made it possible for Mary to embark on a career which ended in her becoming one of the most influential African-American women of her generation.

With the help of a scholarship, Mary McLeod went on from Mayesville to Scotia Seminary, North Carolina, and then to the Moody Bible Institute in Chicago where she was, on her arrival, the institute's only African-American student. Mary's ambition was to be a missionary in Africa. But she soon learned that missionaries, even missionaries to Africa, had to be white – and so Mary McLeod, at the end of her Chicago studies, returned to South Carolina where she became a teacher, and where in 1898 she married Albertus Bethune. For several years, Mary McLeod Bethune moved from one teaching job to another. Then, in 1904, she founded in Dayton, Florida, her own school for African-American girls.

Mary McLeod Bethune believed that, by educating her fellow African-Americans, she would restore to them the self-esteem which slavery had taken away. 'If our people are to fight their way up out of bondage,' Mary commented, 'we must arm them with the sword and the shield and the buckler of pride.' Predictably, those sentiments attracted hostility from white supremacists of the sort who, well into the twentieth century, were able to operate across America's then segregationist South. As a result, Mary McLeod Bethune tangled occasionally with the Ku Klux Klan, a racist and semi-secret society which had been founded by whites who wanted their organisation to embody the heroic qualities which Sir Walter Scott's novels had taught the South to associate with clans of the Scottish variety. Although the Ku Klux Klan contained more thugs than warriors, it was more than capable of intimidating, even lynching, anyone who got in its way. This makes it all the more remarkable that Mary McLeod Bethune, even when confronted by mobs of Klansmen, refused to abandon her work. She pressed ahead with her educational programmes. She became prominent in African-American politics nationally. She accepted, from President Franklin D. Roosevelt, a senior post in the US federal government. 'Hold your heads up high!' Mary McLeod Bethune once told an African-American audience. 'Look every man straight in the eye . . . Look at me. I am black, I am beautiful.'[24]

South Africa: Gauteng and the Western Cape

Mary McLeod Bethune was convinced, because of what she had heard from her maternal grandmother, that some of her African forebears were people of power. If so, they would have occupied positions similar to those held by the ancestors of Nelson Mandela, who emerged from prison to become South Africa's first democratically elected president. Mandela's family was one of high standing in his country's pre-colonial society. This society was dominated by kin-based groupings organised in much the same way as Scottish clans. Unsurprisingly, then, Nelson Mandela outlines his lineage in language of the kind used by many of the people featured in this book – Mandela setting great store, as the typical member of a Clan MacLeod Society does also, by his ability to root himself in the place where his family originated.

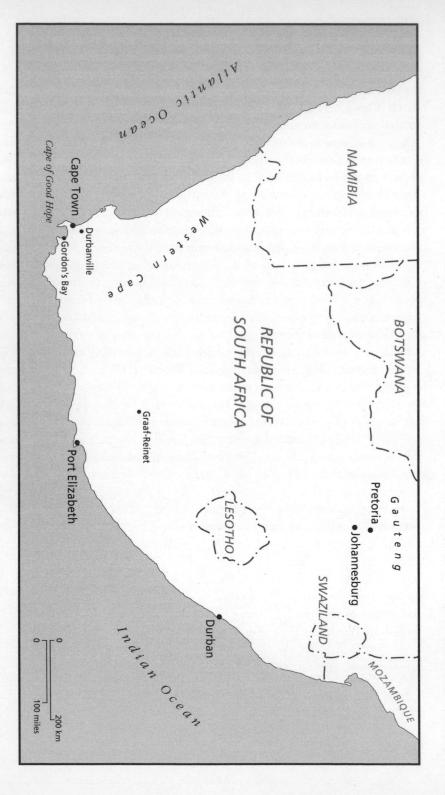

Map 7: South Africa

This place was South Africa's Transkei region which Nelson Mandela describes as 'a beautiful country of rolling hills, fertile valleys and a thousand rivers'. The Transkei, Mandela writes, 'is home to the Thembu people, who are part of the Xhosa nation, of which I am a member'. Mandela continues: 'Each Xhosa belongs to a clan that traces its descent back to a specific forefather. I am a member of the Madiba clan, named after a Thembu chief [an African equivalent of Leod] who ruled . . . in the eighteenth century.' Going into greater detail, Nelson Mandela outlines the structure of Thembu society as it was at the time of Ngubengcuka, a chief who died in 1832. The Thembu then consisted of three houses or sub-groups, one of them the Ixhiba. Mandela comments: 'The eldest son of the Ixhiba House was Simakade, whose younger brother was Mandela, my grandfather.'[25]

I come across those words in the middle of a Gauteng night which has brought rain and thunder of such intensity that sleeping is impossible. Gauteng, formerly the Transvaal, is South Africa's heartland. It includes both the country's capital, Pretoria, and its foremost business centre, Johannesburg. Centurion, the suburb where I am spending a couple of days with Andrew and Alida McLeod, is located between the two.

When Andrew's emigrant grandfather, John McLeod, died in the 1930s, a piece of paper was found among his belongings. On this piece of paper, John had summarised what he knew of his background. 'Sometime about the year 1820,' he wrote, 'Donald McLeod . . . came down from the north of Scotland to work on the Great North Road between Perth and Queensferry. Old Donald settled around Dunfermline in Fifeshire [where he] married Rachel Creighton and had five of a family, four boys and a girl.' Old Donald was Andrew McLeod's great-great-grandfather – and the road he helped construct was the main highway into the Highlands from Edinburgh. Because he was described by his grandson as coming from 'the north of Scotland', not from an island like Lewis or Skye, Donald McLeod may have moved south from Sutherland, then the scene of extensive clearances. At all events, once established in Dunfermline, Fife's principal town, Donald remained there. So did John, Donald's third son and Andrew McLeod's great-grandfather. In 1895, however, one of John's own sons, also John and the source of this family history, left Scotland for South Africa. Here he settled in Bloemfontein, soon marrying Martha van der Walt. Martha, as her name suggests, was an Afrikaner. So is Andrew McLeod, Martha's grandson and my Gauteng host.

South Africa's Afrikaners constitute a majority of the country's white population, and during the twentieth century they were a major source of support for apartheid – the racist belief, entrenched in South Africa's constitution before the adoption of democracy in 1994, that only whites should exercise control of government. Afrikaner history begins with the mid-seventeenth-century seizure of the Cape of Good Hope and its immediate hinterland by the Dutch East India Company – which saw in Africa's southern tip a convenient staging post on the sea route linking the company's Amsterdam headquarters with its Far Eastern empire. The Dutch, German and other settlers attracted to South Africa in the period of Dutch East India Company dominance, which lasted until the end of the eighteenth century, evolved into today's Afrikaner community. This community possesses its own language, Afrikaans; it possesses also a strong sense of its separateness from South Africa's other, mostly English-speaking, whites. 'I'm an Afrikaans speaker who doesn't have an Afrikaner name,' Andrew McLeod says as members of his family gather for the *braai* or barbecue which Andrew has organised on my behalf. 'That doesn't make me any less an Afrikaner, but it does make me aware that, as well as being an Afrikaner, I'm also Scottish.'

It is late April, and in Gauteng the autumn evenings are beginning to be chilly. Grateful for the heat from Andrew's outdoor fireplace, I cup my hands around my mug of *rooibos*, a so-called bush tea which is rapidly replacing coffee in my affections. Not for the first time in the course of my travels among Clan MacLeod, I reflect while listening to the conversations going on around me, I am among people whose language I cannot understand. This remains the case when, next day, Andrew and Alida, anxious to provide some insights into the way South Africa is changing, take me to Mamelode to meet with Peggy Letsoala, who speaks Twsana, Sotho and Afrikaans, but not a lot of English.

Mamelode is one of Pretoria's black townships – its rows of jerry-built homes and shacks dating from the apartheid era when, in theory, black South Africans were not entitled to live permanently in cities. Peggy Letsoala is one of Mamelode's residents. She and Alida McLeod have known each other for nearly twenty years – Peggy being a cleaner in Pretoria's Transvaal Museum where Alida has worked since the mid-1980s. But this is the first time Alida, Andrew and Peggy have socialised together – Alida having asked Peggy if she would be willing to show me a little of the South Africa that can be accessed only by going to communities other than predominantly white suburbs like Centurion. Peggy Letsoala was happy to oblige a foreigner from Scotland – and so I find myself in her front room, eating cakes from her best china and trying to discover how post-apartheid South Africa looks from Mamelode's perspective. Much has been accomplished, Peggy Letsoala says, but much still remains to be done.

As we drive out of Mamelode, Andrew McLeod talks about his family's past and about the way this past intersects with the wider history of South

Africa. 'My father,' Andrew says, 'was an adamant Afrikaner. He was a civil servant, a steadfast member of the Dutch Reformed Church, equally loyal to the National Party, the political movement which enforced apartheid. My boyhood, then, was an Afrikaner boyhood lived in what our people thought would always be an Afrikaner country. Now we're no longer in charge, and everything that makes us what we are, including our language, seems to be under threat.'

For much of his life, Andrew McLeod was an agricultural scientist and college teacher. Then he suffered a stroke which has left him partly disabled. Rather than sit around, Andrew explains, he returned to university to study history. Today he is completing a thesis on the Anglo-Boer War. This conflict, starting in 1899, ended in disaster for South Africa's Boers or Afrikaners, as they would now be called. Above all else, Boer South Africa wanted to establish its independence from Britain – which, a century before, had ejected the Dutch East India Company from its Cape of Good Hope possessions. But Boer autonomy was not won in 1899 or in the course of the fighting which followed. Instead, the Afrikaner republics of Transvaal and the Orange Free State were conquered by British forces. As things turned out, this was not the end of Afrikaner nationalism. By the 1940s, it was the dominant political force in South Africa, which, with the gradual demise of Britain's empire, had become a self-governing, though still white-ruled, country. But today, with South Africa firmly in the hands of its majority black population, Afrikaner dominance is no more – leaving people like Andrew McLeod to wonder, and worry about, what comes next.

Outside Pretoria, Andrew introduces me to his friend, Piet Basson, an Afrikaner farmer. Several of Piet's neighbours have been killed by the criminal gangs which sometimes raid isolated homesteads like the one Piet occupies. Despite this, he is determined to hang on. 'We belong here,' Piet tells me. 'We've been here for hundreds of years. But we know that, though once it was easy to be an Afrikaner, it will be hard for us in future.'

Some Afrikaners are attempting to resolve this dilemma by abandoning Afrikaans for English. One of them is Arno McLeod. We meet when, having flown south from Johannesburg, I spend some time in the vicinity of Cape Town. 'My Scots-born McLeod ancestor arrived here 200 years ago,' Arno tells me. 'I've been told he was a guard on a ship taking prisoners to Australia. The ship put in at Cape Town, and my ancestor must have taken a liking to South Africa – because he came ashore and never left.' Having good reason to get out of British-controlled Cape Town, Arno's ship-jumping forebear moved east – settling, finally, 300 miles from the cape, in the Graaff-Reinet district. Two centuries and six or seven generations later, the family this McLeod founded by marrying into Graaff-Reinet's Boer or Afrikaner population is still there. Arno McLeod, a chemical engineer, is among its younger members. 'At home and in school,' Arno says, 'I spoke Afrikaans. That was the way things were. But Afrikaans no longer has the standing it had in the apartheid period. Today you have to be able to conduct yourself in English. I speak English all the time – at work, with my wife, to our three kids.'

Arno McLeod's strategy for survival in the new South Africa involves a conscious cultivation of the Scottish dimension of his heritage – something which, though not ignored entirely by his parents and grandparents, meant less to them than their Afrikaner connections. One of Arno's companies, I learn, traded under the name Dunvegan. 'I'd like to visit Scotland,' Arno comments. 'I'd like to wear a kilt. I'd like to know more about my McLeod background.' Detecting a potential recruit, my guide to the Cape Town area, Alistair MacLeod, responds to this by handing Arno a leaflet about South Africa's Clan MacLeod Society – a society which, thanks to Alastair's determination to introduce me to a big cross-section of its membership, I am getting to know well.

Although I travel many miles in the company of Alistair MacLeod and his wife, Hazel, I manage to take in only the southernmost corner of the Western Cape, the South African province which includes Cape Town and its suburbs. But I have seen enough of the province's beaches, mountains and wineries, I assure Hazel and Alistair, to be minded to come back. At this point, we are seated high above Gordon's Bay, an Indian Ocean resort about fifty miles out of Cape Town, and Alistair is telling me how his grandfather, George MacLeod, emigrated from Delny in Easter Ross to Somerset West – a locality clearly visible from our viewpoint – where he got a job as a gamekeeper. This was around 1900, and a century after George MacLeod's arrival here, Alistair, who lives in nearby Durbanville, is back where his grandfather started. In between times, however, there have been further migrations, emigrations and re-emigrations – Alistair, who was born in Kimberley, between Cape Town and Johannesburg, having spent quite a bit of his life in Northern Rhodesia, now Zambia, where he organised mineral surveys.

The Western Cape's MacLeods arrived in ones and twos at different times, for different reasons. Betty Salmon, born in England and a MacLeod before her marriage, met her late husband, Richard, when he was serving with South Africa's armed forces during the Second World War. Sheila Douglas's MacLeod connection derives from her McLeod grandfather – 'a big man with a strong Scottish accent,' Sheila remembers – who emigrated to South Africa from the Easter Ross town of Tain in 1883. Peter MacLeod, who runs a guest house called Dunvegan Lodge at Clovelly, between Cape

Town and Simonstown, is a member of a family which has been here for more than 150 years. Guy McLeod and Sally Newill descend from William MacLeod, who was one of early-nineteenth-century Cape Town's port captains or harbourmasters. The same man's other descendants include Chris MacLeod, an estate agent or realtor in Constantia, one of Cape Town's most attractive suburbs. In his Constantia home, Chris shows me a family tree which describes William MacLeod, who got here in 1822, as the son of a younger brother of Colonel John MacLeod of Talisker. If this is correct, then William MacLeod reached Cape Town just as his cousin, Major Donald MacLeod, was getting established in Tasmania.

Some of today's South Africans are following in Major Donald's footsteps – Australia being one of the destinations favoured by whites who have chosen to leave the country. Precipitated by uncertainties stemming from the advent of democracy, this outflow includes members of the MacLeod families I meet in the Western Cape and in Gauteng. That makes for one key difference between South African MacLeods and their counterparts elsewhere. In most countries mentioned in this book – the USA or Canada, for instance – emigration, as far as people of Scottish extraction are concerned, is usually in the past. In South Africa, it is a present-day reality. 'Sometimes I think we're witnessing the start of a second Great Trek,' Andrew McLeod's farmer friend, Piet Basson, tells me. The original trek – a consequence of the nineteenth-century Boer population's determination to shake off British domination – took thousands of families into frontier regions which later evolved into autonomous Boer republics. The Great Trek's modern equivalent is more diffuse but involves greater distances. Andrew McLeod's son, Ponty, lives and works in New Jersey. Alistair MacLeod's daughter, Carole, has spent the last four years in London. As it happens, Carole is holidaying in Cape Town when I visit. 'Will she ever come back permanently?' I ask. Carole MacLeod shakes her head. 'No,' she says, 'I don't think so.'

Scotland: Strathnaver and Skye

Emigrants from the Highlands and Islands often denigrated the previous populations of the areas where they settled. In nineteenth-century Scotland, however, people from the Highlands and Islands were themselves on the receiving end of a good deal of racially inspired abuse – it being taken for granted at this time that Anglo-Saxons, a category thought to include Scottish Lowlanders as well as English people, were innately superior to Celts. 'The people of Skye are an indolent, ignorant and dirty race' whose troubles were 'the consequence of their own vices,' the *Scotsman* reported in 1846. 'Ethnologically,' another Lowland newspaper commented, 'the Celtic race is an inferior one and, attempt to disguise it as we may, there is . . . no getting rid of the great cosmical fact that it is destined to give way . . . before the higher capabilities of the Anglo-Saxon.' There could be no argument, it was thought, with an anthropologist's finding that skulls from Celtic regions like Ireland or the Highlands and Islands were characterised by 'a low type of cranial formation' approximating that of 'the negro races'. Anglo-Saxon skulls, in contrast, were considered 'fully equal in point of development' to those of the ancient Greeks – who were well known to have been at 'the summit of . . . intelligence and beauty'.[26]

Convictions of this sort surface regularly in the correspondence of Patrick Sellar, the lawyer and sheep farmer who organised hundreds of evictions on behalf of the Duke and Duchess of Sutherland, owners of almost all the large county from which the couple derived their titles. According to Sellar, Sutherland's 'aborigines', as he called the county's inhabitants, were on a par with North America's native population. Like American Indians, he went on, Sutherland folk lived 'in turf cabins in common with the brutes'. It followed, in Patrick Sellar's opinion, that Sutherland's population was bound to gain from the destruction of its traditional way of life. 'It surely was a most benevolent action,' he wrote of the people he dispossessed, 'to put these barbarous hordes into a position where they could better associate together, educate their children and advance in civilisation.'[27]

During the opening weeks of 1814, in weather so bitterly cold that some of his assistants were said to have contracted frostbite, Patrick Sellar served eviction notices on families then occupying Strathnaver – a lengthy valley which opens on to Sutherland's north coast near the village of Bettyhill. Four or five months later, the clearance of Strathnaver, afterwards tenanted by Sellar in his sheep-farming capacity, got underway. One Strathnaver resident wrote this account of what followed: 'I was an eyewitness of the scene . . . Strong parties, furnished with faggots and other combustibles, rushed on [Strathnaver's] dwellings . . . and immediately commenced setting fire to them, proceeding in their work with the greatest rapidity till about three hundred houses were in flames. The consternation and confusion were extreme. Little or no time was given for removal of persons or property . . . The cries of the women and children [and] the roaring of the affrighted cattle hunted . . . by the yelping dogs of [Patrick Sellar's] shepherds amid the smoke and fire . . . presented a scene that completely baffles description: it required to be seen to be believed.'[28]

The author of that passage is commemorated by a little monument which, when driving down Strathnaver's single-track road in the direction of Bettyhill, you reach a mile or two south of Syre. 'In memory of Donald MacLeod, stonemason, who witnessed the destruction of Rossal in 1814,' this monument's inscription reads. Nearby is the swiftly flowing River Naver. On the river's other bank is a conifer plantation. This plantation encircles the remnants of Rossal's homes. Before their destruction in 1814, those homes housed about a hundred people – one of them the Strathnaver stonemason whose writings played a big part in bringing the Highland Clearances to the attention of people who might not otherwise have heard of them.

Donald MacLeod's accounts of events in Strathnaver first surfaced in Scottish newspapers. Those accounts reached a wider audience courtesy of the American anti-slavery campaigner, Harriet Beecher Stowe, whose best-selling novel, *Uncle Tom's Cabin*, helped popularise calls for slavery's abolition. Invited to tour Britain by one of the country's abolitionist groups, Stowe arrived from the United States in April 1853, and was fêted everywhere she went. Stowe was especially pleased to be entertained to lunch by the second Duke and Duchess of Sutherland – at whose London home, she wrote, guests were 'received . . . by two stately Highlanders in full costume'. Had the visiting American stopped there, all might have been well. But in *Sunny Memories*, a book about her travels, Harriet Beecher Stowe took issue with critics of her London host and hostess's part in the Highland Clearances. Stories of evictions and burnings in Sutherland were 'ridiculous' and 'absurd', Stowe insisted. What had actually happened in places like Strathnaver, she went on, was 'an almost sublime instance of the benevolent employment of superior wealth and power in shortening the struggles of advancing civilization, and elevating, in a few years, a whole community to a point of education and material prosperity which, unassisted, they might never have obtained'.[29]

Donald MacLeod, living by this point in Edinburgh, was no apologist for slavery, which he thought 'damnable'. But neither was he prepared to permit Harriet Beecher Stowe's pro-clearance views to go unchallenged. In a publication pointedly entitled *Gloomy Memories*, MacLeod, writing more in sorrow than in anger, told Stowe: 'For the sake of aristocratic adulation . . . you have exposed yourself to be publicly chastised by an old . . . broken-down stonemason.' Despite Harriet Beecher Stowe's assertions to the contrary, Donald MacLeod continued, virtually nothing done in the Highlands and Islands by the area's proprietors had been done for altruistic reasons: 'The motive of the landlords was self-interest; and in the Highlands it has been pursued with a recklessness and remorselessness to which the proverbial tyranny and selfishness of that class elsewhere furnishes no parallel. Law and justice, religion and humanity, have been either totally disregarded or, what was still worse, converted into instruments of oppression.'[30]

Donald MacLeod's arguments were taken up by Karl Marx, soon to be

Communism's leading theoretician, but then the London correspondent of the *New York Daily Tribune*. 'The history of the wealth of the Sutherland family,' Marx commented in an article addressed to his United States readership, 'is the history of the ruin and expropriation of the Scotch-Gaelic population from its native soil.' In Sutherland, as elsewhere in the Highlands and Islands, Karl Marx believed, clan lands 'belonged [in the past] to the clan'. This had continued to be case, Marx asserted, until 'the forcible transformation of *clan property* into the *private property* . . . of the chief' had opened the way for clearances of the Strathnaver sort. Among the principal beneficiaries of such clearances, Marx wrote, were the Duke and Duchess of Sutherland who, notwithstanding the delight they took in parading their anti-slavery credentials, had subjected their tenants to treatment which did not differ greatly, Karl Marx contended, from that endured by African-Americans.[31]

Like many of the people set adrift by the Highland Clearances, Donald MacLeod went in the end to Canada. There he settled in Woodstock, Ontario, where he opened a bookshop and where he died – 'in comparative poverty,' it was reported – around 1860. Back in Scotland, meanwhile, other voices were beginning to be raised in opposition to clearing landlords. One such voice belonged to a Skye clergyman, Rev. Roderick MacLeod, whose background could not have differed more sharply from that of the Strathnaver stonemason turned Woodstock bookseller. Roderick's father was a younger son of one of Raasay's MacLeod chiefs and when, in 1823, Roderick became parish minister of Bracadale, soon to be the scene of extensive evictions, it was not anticipated that he would identify with those evictions' victims.[32]

In the early nineteenth century, Church of Scotland clergymen were appointed by landlords, not by their congregations. Partly for this reason, and partly because of their usually belonging to the same social class as the lairds to whom they owed their jobs, few such clergymen took issue with the land-management policies being put into effect around them. At the height of Patrick Sellar's clearances in Sutherland, according to Donald MacLeod, the county's Church of Scotland ministers told their congregations 'that all their sufferings came from God and were a just punishment for their sins'. Roderick MacLeod, when gifted his Bracadale pulpit by the parish's landlord, John Norman MacLeod of Dunvegan, was doubtless expected to take a similar line. However, he failed to do so, having meanwhile embraced a version of Christianity which owed little to the less-than-impassioned convictions he had held previously. This new faith was an emotionally charged and intensely evangelical Presbyterianism of much the same sort as another MacLeod clergyman, Rev. Norman, afterwards of Waipu, was then preaching in Cape Breton Island.[33]

Like his fellow clansman in Cape Breton, Roderick MacLeod was accused of subjecting his congregation to a clerical dictatorship. Bracadale's communion roll was reduced to less than ten on the grounds that only 'God-fearing' and 'consistent' Christians were entitled to receive so sacred a sacrament. Baptism was similarly withheld from children whose parents were considered by Rev. Roderick to be 'deficient in religious knowledge'. Among the several infants who consequently died unbaptised was one of the sons of Martin MacLeod of Drynoch, father of the North West Mounted Police's future commissioner and, before he left for Ontario, a member of the Bracadale congregation. In Canada years later, Martin's daughter, Margaret, recalled the circumstances surrounding her little brother's death: 'The dear baby was seized with croup after being taken to [Roderick MacLeod's] manse for baptism, which was refused. A heavy rain came on, he [the baby] took cold and, after a few hours' illness, died.' In reaction to this tragedy, Martin of Drynoch quit the Church of Scotland. Rev. Roderick was not perturbed. His enemies among the gentry – of whom he made a lot – were outweighed, numerically anyway, by allies drawn from the other end of Skye's social spectrum.[34]

Among those allies was Donald Munro, one of many lay preachers then setting up in opposition to Church of Scotland ministers of the traditional, pro-laird variety. Their critics portrayed men like Munro as dangerous agitators who tended to 'intermix their spiritual instructions [with] . . . reflections on . . . the conduct of . . . landlords whom they compare to the taskmasters of Egypt'. But when another clergyman, offended by the Bracadale minister's friendship with Donald Munro, put it to him that he should disown a man who expounded doctrines of this kind, Rev. Roderick was in no way abashed. 'I expect to spend eternity in Donald Munro's society,' he said. Soon Roderick MacLeod, instead of condemning the anti-landlord views of his lay associates, had made those views his own. 'Mr MacLeod . . . considers that the earth ought to be cleared of sheep and not of men,' it was reported of Bracadale's minister. 'He affirms that the island [of Skye] is capable of maintaining every soul upon it, but under different rule.'[35]

When, in 1843, its evangelical faction left the Church of Scotland to set up a new denomination, the Free Church, Roderick MacLeod was at the forefront of this ecclesiastical revolution. Because several island landlords, thinking the Free Church seditious, refused to sell sites for church buildings to Rev. Roderick and his colleagues, their services had to be held for a time out of doors. On one especially icy winter's morning, Roderick MacLeod was said to have 'preached . . . with the hailstones dancing on his forehead, the people wiping away the snow before they could sit down'. But such was Rev. Roderick's pulling power that, even in the worst weather, he was guaranteed huge congregations. Among the minister's favourite venues was the natural amphitheatre surrounding Fairy Bridge on the Dunvegan–Portree road. Here in 1843 and after, thousands came to listen to *Maighstir Ruaraidh*, as Rev. Roderick was called in Gaelic. About forty years later, Fairy Bridge's role as an open-air church was recalled by Skye supporters of the Highland Land League, who made it one of their meeting places. Thus it came about that, throughout the 1880s, the hills above Fairy Bridge resounded to Land League denunciations of Skye's landowning families, the MacLeods of Dunvegan included.[36]

A good deal of the crofting unrest which gave rise to the Highland Land League can be traced to Glendale. In 1852, when Clan MacLeod's bankrupted Chief Norman was in London, the trustees appointed to administer his Dunvegan estate sold Glendale to Sir John MacPherson MacLeod. Although he had family links with the Hebrides, Sir John, much of whose life was spent in India, visited his Skye property only once. Otherwise, he entrusted Glendale's management to his factor, Donald MacDonald. As the agents of absentee proprietors often did, MacDonald appears to have used his position to advance his own interests. Soon he was tenanting no fewer than five Glendale sheep farms and when, in 1882, a further Glendale farm, Waterstein, went out of lease, Donald MacDonald made clear that he intended to become its tenant too. This might not have mattered had the thirty-plus crofters living in two Glendale townships, Upper and Lower Milovaig, not banded together – in a then unprecedented move – to make their own bid for Waterstein's lease. On hearing that Glendale's factor was himself to have Waterstein, the Milovaig men were furious. Since Sir John MacPherson MacLeod had just died, the Milovaig crofters demanded and got a meeting with the lawyers who were settling his affairs. Urged at this meeting to be patient, the Milovaig people responded by stating that they were about to take matters into their own hands: 'We told them that our forefathers had died in . . . patience, and that we ourselves had been waiting in patience until now, and that we could not wait any longer.'[37]

By the end of May 1882, cattle belonging to Glendale's crofters had been moved on to Waterstein's pastures. This was in breach of the law. But the court order which the estate's administrators obtained, and which instructed the offending crofters to remove their animals from Waterstein, was ignored. The farm remained in crofting occupation, and when, in November, one of the Glendale estate management's employees tried to remove crofters' livestock from it, he was attacked.

Shortly before Christmas, warrants were issued for the arrest of more than twenty men implicated in the November assault. On 16 January 1883, with the aim of enforcing those warrants, an attempt was made to station a police sergeant and three constables in Glendale. Alerted to the approach of this police detachment by sentries they had posted on the hills overlooking the road into the glen from nearby Dunvegan, a crowd mustered to await the policemen's arrival. The unfortunate constables and sergeant, together with an inspector who was accompanying them, were knocked down and manhandled as a prelude to their being herded back the way they had come. Four days later, by way of demonstrating their mastery of the situation, a column of Glendale crofters – armed, it was said, with clubs, scythes, graips and other makeshift weapons – marched on Dunvegan itself. This time there was no confrontation with the forces of law and order. On hearing of the Glendale column's approach, the several policemen then in Dunvegan took to their heels and fled, by way of Fairy Bridge, to Portree.

Those dramatic events led to government intervention. The possibility of sending troops to Glendale was considered but, for the moment, rejected. Instead an official emissary was despatched on a naval gunboat to negotiate with the Glendale rebels. During the ensuing discussions, a token five crofters agreed to stand trial in Edinburgh, where they were jailed. But this concession was matched by ground given on the other side – government ministers announcing the appointment of a royal commission whose remit was to enquire into crofting grievances and to report on how they might be remedied. In May, the commission, chaired by Francis Napier, a Scottish peer, began taking evidence in Skye.

Having heard a lot of testimony to the effect that crofting communities had suffered greatly at the hands of landlords, Lord Napier outlined ways in which the tenurial position of crofters might be strengthened. But because politicians declined to give immediate effect to his recommendations, disturbances of the Glendale type proliferated. More sheep farms were seized. Crofters everywhere suspended rent payments. Skye policemen, normally unarmed in accordance with British practice, were authorised to carry guns. Eventually, the military were deployed. Crofters were not intimidated, however. Organising politically under the banner of the Highland Land League, they succeeded in giving their campaign a national dimension. In the United Kingdom general election of 1885 – the first, coincidentally, in which crofters were entitled to vote – most Highlands and Islands constituencies, previously represented in parliament by landowners, sent Land League MPs to Westminster.

The Highland Land League's platform consisted of three demands: first, that crofters be freed from the threat of eviction; second, that croft rents be reduced; third, that the land lost to crofters during the clearances be restored to them. By way of justifying those positions, Land League members quoted the Bible – with which, thanks to men like Maighstir Ruaraidh, they were well acquainted. In an exchange of correspondence with Norman MacLeod of Dunvegan, now back in Skye, John MacPherson, a Glendale crofter who became a leading Land Leaguer, cited a series of scriptural texts which amounted, MacPherson insisted, to 'letters of agreement from God pronouncing our claim and right in the land'. 'God commanded the land [of Israel] to be divided among the Israelites,' John MacPherson went on, and the Highlands and Islands should be treated similarly. Not only would this be in accordance with biblical precedent; it would remedy the injustice done when clan chiefs took ownership of clan lands which had formerly belonged, or so the Highland Land League maintained, to clanspeople as a whole.[38]

When they urged parliament to grant them immunity from eviction, then, crofters did not think they were requesting something new. The United Kingdom legislature, the Land League said, was simply being asked to recognise that everyone living in the Highlands and Islands had once been entitled, and should be entitled again, to undisturbed occupancy of their landholdings. Although fiercely disputed by Scotland's lairds, this argument was accepted by the man who most mattered in the United Kingdom of the 1880s, Britain's prime minister, William Gladstone. While property rights deserved respect, Gladstone told his cabinet colleagues, no such respect could be extended to landed property founded – as the prime minister believed was the case in the Highlands and Islands – on the appropriation by clan chiefs of land to which they had no exclusive claim. It was because the generality of clansfolk had been deprived of their stake in the land, William Gladstone commented in 1885, that he proposed to legislate in the crofting interest: 'It is . . . this historical fact that constitutes the crofters' title to demand the interference of parliament. It is not because they are poor, or because there are too many of them, or because they want more land to support their families, but because . . . they . . . had rights of which they have been surreptitiously deprived to the injury of the community.'[39]

In 1886, Gladstone's government accordingly passed a Crofters Act. The Act did little to add to the total acreage at the crofting population's disposal – that would come later. But it met the Highland Land League's other key demands. A judicial tribunal, the Crofters Commission, was established to set the level of croft rents. At the same time, every crofter was granted security of tenure. This security, moreover, was of an unusually all-encompassing type – crofters, as well as being freed from the threat of eviction, now having an absolute right to hand on croft tenancies to their heirs. By this means, the Crofters Act guaranteed the continuation of crofting. It also brought about a marked improvement in housing conditions – as crofters, in the knowledge that they would be able to hang on to their homes, began to invest in the slate-roofed and white-painted cottages which, for much of the twentieth century, were characteristic of crofting localities.

But if crofters hailed the Act of 1886 as a Scottish equivalent of the American legislation that terminated slavery, landlords were unanimous in their condemnation of what parliament had done. The Crofters Act had 'deprived [him] of the power of letting his own lands,' Norman MacLeod informed William Gladstone, and this opinion was confirmed, as far as Norman and his family were concerned, when the Crofters Commission first reduced their crofting rental by almost a quarter, then cancelled more than half of the Dunvegan tenantry's outstanding arrears. This 'wiping out' of rent arrears was 'despotic', a 'confiscation' and an 'iniquity,' according to Reginald MacLeod, one of Norman's sons and himself a future laird. All in all, the Crofters Act had been 'a disaster,' Reginald observed; and if, as the Highland Land League wanted, sheep farms were broken up and returned to crofters, this would be state-endorsed robbery.[40]

What Norman MacLeod of Dunvegan found hardest to accept as the Land League crisis of the 1880s swirled around him was the dismissal by crofters of the efforts he had made, forty years before, to feed the very families now intent on demonising him. 'You say in the years 1847 and 1848 you kept alive the whole people on your property,' John MacPherson observed in one of his letters to Chief Norman. 'I cannot say anything about other people, but I shall challenge you if ever my father got one shilling's worth [of meal] from you without payment.'[41]

Was John MacPherson right? Almost certainly not. But such stories of the famine years as had reached MacPherson and his generation were concerned less with Norman MacLeod's generosity than with a deeply etched sense of grievance deriving from the behaviour of relief agencies which insisted that starving people did several hours of hard labour in return for every pound of oatmeal given to them. One thing was remembered about Norman MacLeod's period as Glendale's laird, however. 'You placed Bracadale people in Glendale,' MacPherson told Chief Norman on one occasion. On another, he recalled that every croft in Glendale townships like Upper and Lower Milovaig had been halved to accommodate the Bracadale families Norman MacLeod sent there. The solution to Glendale's overcrowding, John MacPherson and the Land League insisted, lay in reversing this process. In Bracadale and Minginish, Land Leaguers pointed out, Chief Norman was content to have a tiny number of sheep farmers occupying areas which were extensive enough, or so the Napier Commission heard repeatedly, to meet the needs of hundreds of people. 'Is there not plenty of land waste in the Isle of Skye?' one of the commission's crofter witnesses declared. 'Is not the property of MacLeod waste altogether?'[42]

Emily MacLeod, Chief Norman's sister, was the one member of her family to express sympathy for views of this sort. 'I have always thought that the people should have more hill pasture, and that it should not have been taken away as it was about sixty years ago,' Emily commented in 1885. The Land League notion that clansfolk had somehow shared possession of land with clan chiefs 'had no foundation in fact,' Emily believed. 'But the chiefs,' she thought, 'had no right to turn off the people as was done in . . . the early part of this century. There were till then no large sheep farms and the people were allowed to pasture their cattle on the outlying hills . . . When sheep farmers came and offered large sums for these pastures, the poor people were sent to the seashore and to inferior lands. Many were forced to emigrate, and one cannot wonder at their descendants feeling the hardship bitterly.' As Emily was well aware, her own father had introduced many of the changes she condemned. '[He] was a very poor man,' Emily wrote by way of explaining her father's conduct, '[and] one can scarcely wonder at selfish human nature welcoming the large sheep farmer with his punctually paid rent. But it was a cruel alteration.'[43]

Nova Scotia and South Carolina: New Glasgow, Bethune, Antioch and Florence

One of the best-known land reformers in the Highlands and Islands of the 1880s was an Inverness-based author and journalist, Alexander MacKenzie. MacKenzie's books include the first comprehensive account of the origins and development of Clan MacLeod. This account is, for the most part, celebratory. Hence the disillusioned note struck by Alexander MacKenzie when, elsewhere in his writings, he turns from the deeds of long-dead chiefs to the doings of their more recent successors: 'There is nothing in history so absolutely *mean* as the eviction of Highlanders by chiefs solely indebted for every inch of land they ever held to the strong arms and trusty blades of the progenitors of those whom the . . . chiefs of the nineteenth century have so ruthlessly evicted and despoiled.'[44]

But though he denounced the Highland Clearances, Alexander MacKenzie was in no doubt that emigrants from the Highlands and Islands gained as a result of their emigration. In 1879, MacKenzie did what I have also done while compiling this book. He visited several of the North American districts where people from the Highlands and Islands settled. Nowhere in the course of his travels, Alexander MacKenzie was honest enough to admit, did he meet folk who would have preferred to be in Scotland: 'I have taken considerable pains to find out the feeling here, regarding the mother country, among those who came out themselves, as well as among their descendants, and I cannot recall a single instance in which any of those who have settled down here, on their own lands, would wish to go back and live in the Highlands.' Many of the younger men and women he met, MacKenzie noted, 'expressed a desire to *see* the country of their ancestors, but the idea of going back to remain in it [had] never crossed their minds'.[45]

This was because the emigrant population was much better off than the population of the Highlands and Islands, Alexander MacKenzie concluded. After attending a Gaelic service in the New Glasgow area of Nova Scotia, he wrote: 'Imagine nearly 200 carriages, four-wheeled, scattered all about the church. It was such a sight as I never saw, and never could have seen, in the Highlands; yet here there is hardly a family which does not drive to church, and market, in a nice light wagon.'[46]

Nova Scotia, Alexander MacKenzie went on, was not the wealthiest Canadian province – 'though to me,' he added, '[its farms appear] a paradise . . . in comparison with the wretched patches on which the crofter has to eke out an existence'. But whether in Nova Scotia or elsewhere in North America, it is apparent from the tenor of his reports that MacKenzie was amazed by how well people of Highlands and Islands extraction were doing: 'From what I could learn at home of the position of my countrymen who had crossed the Atlantic . . . I was led to believe that they occupied a much better position in the New World than those who remained [in Scotland]. I could never, however, believe that the difference was so great as it really is.'[47]

Their comparative affluence did not mean that people of emigrant descent were content to remain in the districts their forebears settled. By the later nineteenth century, those districts were producing their own migratory outflows. This onward movement had various causes. In part a response to opportunities on offer in North America's growing cities, it was also a consequence of the United States and Canada constantly opening up new areas of settlement – beyond the Appalachians, around the Great Lakes, across the prairies, on the far side of the Rocky Mountains. In those places, the children, grandchildren and great-grandchildren of men and women who had emigrated to North America from the Highlands and Islands became pioneers in their turn.

In North Carolina's Cape Fear River country, the commencement of outward migration can be traced to the years around 1800. At this period, people whose emigrant parents had left the Highlands and Islands during the 1770s moved in growing numbers into South Carolina – where they were joined, over the next ten or twenty years, by folk who came directly from Scotland. Today, as a result, South Carolina contains many members of America's Clan MacLeod Society. One of them, Purdy McLeod, a retired military man who lives in Columbia, takes me to see the area, in the vicinity of Bishopville and Bethune, where the Highlands and Islands presence in South Carolina had its starting point.

My day with Purdy begins with a visit to Bethune's Scotch Cemetery. The morning is hot, and as Purdy McLeod and I crunch across the cemetery's sun-dried grass, I experience, as always in emigrant graveyards, the disorienting impact of seeing familiar-looking names in wholly unfamiliar surroundings. I pause in front of the tombstone commemorating Kenneth McCaskill, who died in 1878. 'He lived a long and useful life,' his tombstone's inscription states of Kenneth. Much of that life was spent in South Carolina, but it began elsewhere. Kenneth McCaskill, his tombstone informs me, 'was born, in March 1800, in the Isle of Skye, Scotland, in the shire of Minginish'. Minginish, a locality rather than a shire, is mentioned on several of the tombstones I inspect in Bethune's Scotch Cemetery. In this graveyard, I suspect, I am in the company of people taken to America in 1811 by the Rubh' an Dunain tacksman, also Kenneth MacAskill, whose emigrant party was recruited mainly in the Minginish area.

But if Minginish looms large in the Scotch Cemetery, its people do not have the place completely to themselves. One headstone, for example, commemorates John McLeod, who was born in Glenelg and who died in Bethune in 1830. Beside John's grave is that of his wife Mary, 'the mother of ten children'. Propped against Mary McLeod's tombstone is a bouquet of fresh-cut flowers. 'Someone still cares,' Purdy says.

Soon we are driving through Bethune, where Purdy was raised. Fifteen miles to the south is Bishopville. Here Purdy points out McLeod's Pharmacy – 'established 1803', its shopfront sign proclaims. Eight miles beyond Bishopville, we come to Antioch Baptist Church where Purdy's great-grandfather, Alexander McLeod, is buried. 'Alexander was born in this country in 1815,' Purdy tells me. 'His father, my great-great-grandfather, another Alexander McLeod, was then in his twenties and had been born in Scotland – but where exactly I don't know.'

By way of McCaskill Road, Purdy next makes for the spot his folk farmed in the nineteenth century – its location indicated by a stretch of water still known as McLeod Mill Pond. Purdy mentions a cousin, Jesse McLeod, we might have called on had time permitted. But the morning is getting late, and we have a lunch date in Florence, an hour or so west of Antioch. Here we are scheduled to meet with Florie McLeod Ervin and her brother Jim, grandchildren of Dr Frank Hilton McLeod, who came south from North Carolina in the 1890s to establish a hospital now known as the McLeod Medical Center. Doctor Frank's father was Samuel McLeod who, in circumstances already described, shot and killed a Union army trooper on his mother's North Carolina farm in March 1865. Since the then teenage Sam was himself the grandson of Skye people who had settled in the Cape Fear River area more than sixty years before, Florie and Jim, my Florence hosts, are separated from Skye by two whole centuries. This is also true of their McLeod cousins, Dorothy Rhodes and Helen Bradham, who have driven north from Charleston to join us. But though Skye is far in those folk's past, a little of its influence survives among them. Florie McLeod Ervin's fine home is wholly of its setting in America's South. So is the food we are served, and so are the accents round the table. At one point, however, I look up and catch sight of Dorothy Rhodes deep in conversation with the person beside her. There are people whose facial features are of a type – though I should be hard pressed to demonstrate this scientifically – seen only in the Hebrides. Dorothy seems to me to have those features.

Texas: Galveston, Houston and Edna

On a spring-like January evening in Galveston, Texas, I am dining in the city's Artillery Club. This is the oldest such institution west of the Mississippi River and its mission, a club brochure informs me, 'is to provide . . . an environment that remembers, maintains and promotes the great heritage of Texas and its distinguished citizens'. Among the earliest of those citizens was one of the Artillery Club's first captains, as club presidents are called. His name was Hugh McLeod and his father, who came from Skye, arrived in New York not long after America's Revolutionary War. In the 1830s, when US-born settlers in Texas made their successful bid for independence from Mexico, which had previously controlled this part of North America, Hugh McLeod, an American army officer, resigned his commission, volunteered for service with the newly proclaimed Republic of Texas and helped secure the republic's victory. Some years later, when Texas joined the United States, Hugh McLeod, who had gone on to fight Indians on Texas's western frontier, was a well-set-up lawyer in Galveston – then as now a flourishing port connecting Texas, by way of the Gulf of Mexico, with the wider world.[48]

My Artillery Club host, Douglas McLeod, is also a Galveston lawyer. Douglas has no connection with his Indian-fighting predecessor, but he has something in common with other Texans of Scottish extraction I meet. All those Texans are descended from people who, like Hugh McLeod back in the 1830s, reached Texas from elsewhere in North America. Douglas McLeod's father came here from neighbouring Mississippi. Bill McLeod, a prominent figure in Clan MacLeod USA, knows that his great-grandfather, who ran barges on the Mississippi River, was raised in Prince Edward Island.

Rev. Jim McLeod, who lives in Cat Spring, and Gloria McLeod, a Houston resident, owe their surnames to John McLeod, an 1802 emigrant from Skye to the Cape Fear River country, where, because his farm was near a creek of that name, John became known as 'Buffalo'. 'Buffalo McLeod,' Rev. Jim explains, 'was my great-great-great-grandfather. Gloria's late husband, Harry, was Buffalo's great-great-grandson.'

Also with us in the Galveston Artillery Club are Don Mack McLeod and his wife Kathrine. Don Mack, a tall, strongly built and proudly conservative cattleman, is as close to an archetypal Texan as it is possible to get. He is also deeply rooted in this most American of American states. In the course of our Artillery Club evening, somebody mentions Jim Bowie – one of several Scots-descended frontiersmen who died at the Battle of the Alamo during the Texan War of Independence. 'He was my grandmother's great-uncle,' Don Mack comments. And what of his MacLeod background, I ask Don Mack. Where did his MacLeod ancestors come from? 'Skye,' he replies. 'Way back, or so I've been told, they were of the same family as the MacLeods of Dunvegan.'

Initially, I am inclined to put this down to the Texan habit of never allowing the facts, genealogical or otherwise, to get in the way of anything that might add to your standing. But I am wrong to be sceptical. Don Mack's great-great-great-grandfather, John MacLeod, who emigrated from Scotland to North Carolina around 1770, came of a long line of Skye tacksmen, the MacLeods of Glendale, whose ancestry can be traced to a fifteenth-century MacLeod chief. While all MacLeods of their rank were of necessity warriors, the Glendale family, being steadfast Jacobites, saw more action than most – successive generations fighting, on the Stuart side, at the Battles of Worcester (1651), the Boyne (1690), Sheriffmuir (1715) and Culloden (1746). Each of those battles ended in Stuart defeat – and the MacLeods of Glendale, militarily at any rate, were to experience similar setbacks in North America. Don Mack's emigrant forebear, John MacLeod, who appears to have operated a slaving ship out of Wilmington, North Carolina, died at sea in 1775. His family, however, opted for the loyalist – and thus losing – side in the Revolutionary War that broke out the same year. This may explain why Don Mack's great-great-grandfather, Daniel, subsequently moved from North to South Carolina – and why Daniel's older brother John, the Long Johnny McLeod mentioned in this book's opening sequence, embarked on the more ambitious migration which took him to Greene County, Mississippi.[49]

'I guess I was kinda rowdy in my day,' Don Mack McLeod says as, on the morning following our dinner date in Galveston, he takes me to a cattle auction in Edna, a small town fifty miles out of Houston. Hearing this, it is tempting to conclude that Don Mack's great-grandfather, William Alexander McLeod, must have been an earlier version of his great-grandson. According to a family history in Don Mack's possession, William Alexander, who was born and raised in Marlboro County, South Carolina, left that quarter just after the Civil War, in which he had served with the Confederate army, and took a berth on a ship bound for Texas. With him when he sailed into Galveston, William Alexander had $2,800 (then a big sum) which, or so Don Mack's history states, 'he wished to invest'. What happened next is unclear. But 'instead of investing his money' in Galveston, Don Mack's family history goes on, William Alexander 'spent it on strong drink for the pleasure of himself and his friends'. Don Mack McLeod, I gather, does not entirely disapprove.

Despite, or maybe because of, his having got through so much cash in Galveston, William Alexander McLeod was taken with Texas. Going home to South Carolina, he sold his farm and came back here – settling this time in the Alto area, north of Galveston, with his wife and their several children. Among those children was Don Mack's grandfather. He had been born during the Civil War – at a point when his father, William Alexander, was home on leave. On the morning following the birth, it seems, Don Mack's great-grandmother asked her husband how the baby should be named. 'Call him after my commander,' William Alexander said. This commander was Albert Sidney Johnston, a Confederate general who, like the Galveston Artillery Club captain, Hugh McLeod, had taken part in the Texan independence struggle. To Don Mack's satisfaction, then, the first of his McLeod ancestors to spend the greater part of his life in Texas bore the name of a military man who was both a Texan and a Confederate hero.

At the Edna auction, Don Mack, a familiar figure anywhere that cattle are bought or sold, is greeted warmly by everyone we meet. Perched on a wooden bench high above the sale ring, I listen uncomprehendingly to the auctioneer's rhythmic chant and try to make sense of what is going on. As each batch of animals enters the ring, Don Mack provides a low-voiced commentary on their provenance. Dutifully, I take notes. But having glimpsed one or two of the discreet hand movements employed by buyers looking to make a bid, I worry all the time that, were I absent-mindedly to scratch my nose or my ear with my pen, I might find myself the owner of half a dozen Holsteins.

At Edna, Don Mack McLeod and I are joined by Don Mack's son, Michael, whose nearby ranch we visit when the Edna sale is done. 'This is not some fancy lawyer's ranch house,' Michael says as he shows me into his kitchen. 'This is a working rancher's ranch house.' On every wall there are beautifully mounted hunting trophies – guns and taxidermy being two of

Michael McLeod's enthusiasms. Another of Michael's passions – and much the most important – is his herd of longhorn cattle. 'Michael,' Don Mack remarks proudly, 'is one of our leading longhorn breeders.'

To be around longhorns is to be around Texan history. In the nineteenth century, those long-legged, lanky animals – half-wild descendants of the cattle Mexico's Spanish conquerors brought from Europe – were what got Texan livestock rearing off the ground. In more recent times the longhorn went out of fashion – giving way to heavier, beefier breeds. Now, however, it is being restored to prominence by men like Michael McLeod. 'You'd maybe like to look at some longhorns,' Michael says. This is less of a question than a statement. 'Sure,' I respond nonchalantly.

On Michael McLeod's ranch, just twenty or thirty miles from the Gulf of Mexico, I am on the southern rim of the same huge flatlands I encountered in faraway Saskatchewan. Today a cold-edged breeze is blowing from that direction. But the visibility is good, and as we approach the spot where some of Michael's longhorns are grazing, they can be picked out easily. Soon I am standing among a bunch of the most fearsome-looking cattle I have ever encountered – their dark, strong, swept out horns measuring, in some instances, more than six feet from tip to tip. A week or so later, when I am in California, word reaches me that Don Mack McLeod – who probably had me pigeon-holed as one more weak-kneed European of lamentably liberal inclinations – was greatly impressed by my courage. Don Mack, my friend, no bravery was involved – just a mix of ignorance and stupidity.

Illinois and New Zealand: Naperville, Auckland and Helensville

The onward migration which took Don Mack McLeod's ancestors from the Carolinas to Texas had parallels elsewhere. In Pictou, Nova Scotia, I meet with Gertrude McLeod Hilton, whose family tree, rooted in the Scotland of 200 years ago, has sprouted branches which extend into practically every corner of Canada and the United States. 'Whenever McLeods had ten cents to their name, they bought a ticket to go somewhere,' Gertrude says. Among the family histories which bear this out is that of Bill MacLeod, who lives in Naperville, Illinois, and who is president of Clan MacLeod USA, the American component of the Associated Clan MacLeod Societies.

William MacLeod, Bill's great-great-grandfather, emigrated from Skye in the 1840s. His destination was Prince Edward Island. But William – because, Bill has heard, he thought P.E.I. too flat – quickly left the island and headed instead for Cape Breton. There William and his wife Margaret, who came from Raasay, obtained land in the River Denys area, south of Whycocomagh, where they raised seven children, one of whom was John

MacLeod, Bill's great-grandfather. He became a fisherman whose trade took him as far afield as Massachusetts. There, when fishing out of the Cape Cod port of Provincetown in the mid-1860s, John MacLeod met and married Sarah McDermid. From Provincetown, John took his wife back to River Denys, where, in time, the two had eight children. When they grew up, no fewer than six of those children, including John William, Bill's grandfather, quit River Denys for Boston.

This sort of thing was common in Cape Breton in the years around 1900. Unable to compete with the cheaply produced food pouring out of Canada's newly opened-up prairies, farming communities of the River Denys type could not retain their young people. To begin with, many of those young people found work in the coalmines which developed during the later nineteenth century in the vicinity of Cape Breton towns like Sydney and Inverness. Eventually, however, mining proved no more secure than farming. That is why the Cape Bretoners who populate Alistair MacLeod's fiction seem always to be grappling with the implications of leaving home. 'I have decided that almost any place must be better than this one with its worn-out mines and smoke-black houses,' comments one of Alistair's characters. A further character greets news of her son's departure from Cape Breton with those words: 'It is just as well. There is nothing for one to do here anyway. There was never anything for one to do here.'[50]

Boston, the biggest city within striking distance of Cape Breton, was an obvious destination for Cape Bretoners in search of betterment. Men from Cape Breton got jobs in the city's shipyards and factories. Women were in demand as domestic servants. From a Cape Breton perspective, then, Boston was endlessly enticing – though when actually encountered, the city, like other urban centres, could all too readily seem unwelcoming to folk from rural backgrounds. Mae MacLeod, who went to Boston from Cape Breton in the early twentieth century, recalled: 'Some nights you would cry yourself to sleep . . . People had it hard when they left [home] . . . [But] we had to be brave . . . You couldn't afford to [go] back.'[51]

John William MacLeod, Bill MacLeod's River Denys grandfather, married in Boston in 1907. Soon he was the father of two boys, the eldest of whom, John Archie, became Bill's father. Within four years of his marriage, however, John William had divorced and had arranged for John Archie and his other son to be taken north to Cape Breton, where they were raised by one of their uncles on the MacLeod family farm at River Denys. This farm was eventually inherited by Bill MacLeod and his brother, John. Following the discovery of marble deposits in its vicinity, John and Bill sold their landholding to a quarrying company which, at Bill's suggestion, has put up a monument to River Denys's pioneer families. Speaking at the monument's unveiling in the summer of 2003, Bill MacLeod said of those families: 'They emigrated from Scotland under very difficult conditions, then persevered and survived in this new land. Over time their sons and daughters moved throughout Canada and the United States.'[52]

Not all such movement was confined to North America. Some people ranged further afield. One of them was John McLeod. His parents were early-nineteenth-century emigrants from Sutherland to Nova Scotia where John, born in 1825, was raised on his father's Pictou farm. When still in his teens, John left Nova Scotia for the neighbouring province of New Brunswick. There he joined his older brother Isaac, who had quit Pictou some years previously and who, when John put in an appearance, was farming in the vicinity of Newcastle on New Brunswick's Miramichi River. Although John may have come to New Brunswick, as Isaac had done, with the intention of acquiring a farm, he scented more promising prospects in the Miramichi area's then booming timber trade. As a lumberman, John McLeod excelled and, by 1846, was doing well enough to marry. His wife, the twenty-one-year-old John's junior by five years, was Helen Alexander. Soon the couple had two sons and seemed intent on spending their lives together. During 1848, however, word reached New Brunswick that gold had been found in California. Leaving his wife and children, John McLeod quit the Miramichi country and made the transcontinental trip to California's goldfields. There, no doubt, John expected to make his fortune. Instead he lost everything in one of the floods which devastated goldrush California as a result of unsuccessful attempts to divert mountain watercourses in the vicinity of Sacramento. This was in January 1850. For a long time thereafter, no news of John reached either Helen, his wife, or Isaac, his brother, both of them still in New Brunswick. 'As far as Helen and Isaac were concerned,' I am told by John McLeod's great-great-grandson, 'my great-great-grandfather must have seemed as good as dead.'

But John McLeod had not died. As is indicated by the fact that his great-great-grandson, also John McLeod, lives in Auckland, New Zealand, the original John McLeod, having narrowly escaped drowning in California, reacted by taking himself off to the other side of the Pacific. 'Perhaps he was too proud to return penniless,' the present-day John McLeod says of his forebear. 'Perhaps he'd simply got to like the mining life. At all events, my great-great-grandfather, instead of going home, went looking for gold in Australia.'

Having fared no better in Australia than he had done in California, John McLeod next sailed for New Zealand, where gold had been discovered on North Island's Coromandel Peninsula. Again John failed to strike it rich, but in nearby Auckland he made the acquaintance of one of the entrepreneurs then trying to develop North Island's timber resources. At last, John McLeod, whose period in the Miramichi country had made him an expert lumberjack and sawmiller, was presented with an opportunity to acquire the wealth he had been seeking since quitting New Brunswick. The Auckland area, when John McLeod got there, was studded with stands of kauri, a valuable hardwood that grew to a huge size. Unlike most of his New Zealand contemporaries, John knew how to bring down even the most gigantic kauri, how to handle the resulting logs, how to transform those logs into boards and other semi-finished products prior to shipping them to eager buyers in Australia. Soon 'Long John the Yank', as this tall and North American-accented timberman was dubbed in Auckland, had serious money at his disposal. Hence Long John's decision to get in touch once more with his wife, his children, his brother and the rest of his relatives in New Brunswick.

Among those relatives was John's niece, Elizabeth, then a little girl living on the Miramichi Valley homestead belonging to Isaac McLeod, her father. 'It was a beautiful farm,' Elizabeth McLeod wrote later of her New Brunswick birthplace, 'streams running right through and beautiful meadows.' At this farm, towards the close of the 1850s, there turned up a letter addressed to Isaac McLeod and mailed in New Zealand by the brother from whom Isaac had not expected to hear again. Enclosed with John's letter to Isaac was a sum of money. This was intended for Helen, John's wife. He had not written directly to Helen, John explained to Isaac, because he feared she might – presuming him dead – have remarried. If Helen had done so, John went on, he had no wish to re-enter her life. 'Father wrote back [to his brother],' runs Elizabeth McLeod's account of what happened next, 'and said that [Helen had not married again and that] she was a credit to herself and to everyone.' Thus reassured, John McLeod left Auckland for New Brunswick.[53]

Travelling by way of India, Egypt and Britain, John McLeod reached the Miramichi country during the early part of 1861. The district, he learned, had hit a bad patch. New Brunswick's timber reserves were depleted; its agriculture was depressed; Isaac McLeod, in consequence, was in some difficulty. To John, the way out of this difficulty was obvious. Isaac and his family, together with John and *his* family, should emigrate at once to New Zealand. So it was agreed. By selling Isaac's farm and by drawing on cash which John had brought back from Auckland, the McLeod brothers bought a small schooner, *The Seagull*. Sailing first to Pictou, where they bade farewell to family members still in Nova Scotia, John, Isaac, their wives and their children set off across the Atlantic at the beginning of October 1861. Their intention was to make for Auckland by way of the Cape of Good

Hope and Australia. In principle, this was straightforward. In practice, the voyage turned into a series of disasters.

'Some time after we left Nova Scotia,' the then thirteen-year-old Elizabeth McLeod recalled of her months on *The Seagull*, 'we noticed a crack in the foremast. In a terrific storm the foremast went.' Shelter was sought in the Brazilian port of Pernambuco where repairs were effected. More trouble followed, however. Somewhere in the Southern Ocean, one of Isaac's sons died. Although Helen, John's wife, shortly after gave birth to a daughter, such celebration as occurred was cut short when, off Tasmania, *The Seagull* encountered a further ferocious gale. Again the vessel was dismasted. 'For over six weeks we drifted about and did not know where we were,' Elizabeth McLeod remembered. But for a chance encounter with another ship that towed the stricken schooner into Portland, Victoria, neither *The Seagull* nor her passengers would have survived. As it was, a further set of repairs sufficed to take the battered craft safely to Auckland.

Having unloaded the sawmilling equipment they had brought from New Brunswick, John and Isaac McLeod installed themselves and their families on land they purchased north-west of Auckland on North Island's Tasman Sea coast. Its original Maori inhabitants called this spot Te Awaroa. John McLeod renamed it Helensville, in honour of his long-neglected wife. For much of the second half of the nineteenth century, Helensville prospered on the back of its trade in kauri logs. Today there are few kauris hereabouts. But on the rainy Sunday morning when I drive out of Auckland to visit Helensville, where a sizeable congregation is emerging from a Presbyterian church dedicated to Scotland's St Andrew, it proves easy to find signs of continuing local involvement in the timber business. It proves equally easy to track down present-day descendants of Helensville's McLeod founders – those descendants, I learn, now totalling at least 1,500.

Barbara McLeod, my source of this information and one of Isaac McLeod's great-great-granddaughters, is proud of what her ancestor accomplished. 'My great-great-grandfather was born in Scotland,' Barbara says. 'He emigrated to Nova Scotia when a child. He provided himself with a first-rate farm in New Brunswick. Then, when a man of his age would nowadays be thinking of retirement, he came to New Zealand and, in partnership with his brother, created Helensville. So yes, I've a lot of time for Isaac. I've a lot of time, too, for John. Most of all, perhaps, I value the way they collaborated with – rather than tried to do down – the Maoris they employed in their sawmills. My great-great-grandfather, when he went into New Zealand politics towards the close of his career, spoke up repeatedly on behalf of Maori causes. Maoris reciprocated by honouring Isaac and other McLeods.'

This point is reinforced by an 1866 newspaper cutting in the possession of John McLeod, the original John McLeod's great-great-grandson. The cutting reads: 'A monster feast in honour of Mr John McLeod of Helensville was given a few days since by over three hundred natives . . . The feast was conducted with all ceremony and was intended to show the esteem and good feeling entertained by the natives for Mr McLeod. The native fashion of giving a dinner as a mark of respect to an individual differs from our own mode in this particular: that whereas the givers of a dinner with us sit down and consume the good things provided, native hosts hand over *kai-kai* [food] to a guest to use as he may think fit. The provisions gathered together on this occasion consisted of some 50 tons of potatoes, a large quantity of pumpkins, kumara [sweet potatoes], corn, pigs and sundry other produce.'

New Zealand: Christchurch, Martins Bay, Dunedin and the MacKenzie Country

The financial pressures which propelled people out of late-nineteenth-century New Brunswick were identical to those making for a continuing outflow from the Highlands and Islands. Gradually, however, the nature of this Scottish exodus was beginning to change. Formerly, emigrants had tended to travel in family groups, often in the company of friends and neighbours. Now, emigrants were more commonly single men, single women or recently married couples who, following their departure, were unlikely to be seen again by parents, brothers and sisters left at home. In some ways, then, emigration of this new sort was more disruptive of relationships than emigration of the older variety. In extreme cases, it could lead to members of the same family being spread across as many as three or four continents.

In Christchurch, New Zealand, I am introduced to Jessie McLeod Gourdie and her cousins, Betty Moss and Janet McLeod Lawrie. Although all three descend from the same emigrant ancestor, Murdoch McLeod, who arrived in New Zealand from Raasay in 1865, they belong, they tell me, to a family with branches in several countries. 'Murdoch was our great-grandfather,' Jessie explains. 'His parents, our great-great-grandparents, were Malcolm and Peggy McLeod, whose home, before they were evicted in the 1850s, was in the Raasay township of Manish.' Peggy and Malcolm, Jessie goes on, had eight sons. 'Two of those sons died as children,' Jessie says. 'Of the six who survived, just one, Donald, remained in Raasay. The other five emigrated. One went to Australia; one went to Prince Edward Island; the other three, including our great-grandfather, came here to New Zealand.'[54]

My Christchurch host is Ian MacLeod, whose emigrant forebear, like Jessie McLeod Gourdie's, got to New Zealand in the 1860s. Ian's roots are in the Assynt township of Balchladich where, he informs me, his great-

great-grandfather, John MacLeod, organised one of the few attempts made
to resist the clearances ordered by successive Dukes of Sutherland. This
episode occurred in 1843, when, at the instigation of the duke who afterwards
entertained Harriet Beecher Stowe in London, further removals were taking
place in an area which had already been extensively depopulated. 'He set
His Grace [the duke] and the [duke's] managers at utter defiance,' a Scottish
newspaper reported of John MacLeod, 'in violent and threatening letters
which he addressed to them.' Predictably, the main effect of those letters
was to make John MacLeod's eviction all the more certain. When the Duke
of Sutherland's representatives came to Balchladich to eject him from his
croft, however, they found their intended victim at the head of a small band
of men and women who, with the help of sticks and stones, managed to
drive off the evicting party. When the same party returned to Balchladich
some days later with the backing of no fewer than thirty policemen, John
MacLeod wanted to take them on, too. 'But his little army,' as one of the
few historians to take note of those events has commented, 'drifted away
in despair until he was left alone with his son and two other young men.
They were arrested and carried in manacles to Dornoch Gaol, eighty miles
away.'[55]

Several hundred miles north of Christchurch, in their home at Martins
Bay near Auckland, I meet with Joan Tattersfield and her daughter, Nitia
Wilkinson. Outside a semi-tropical downpour is sending rivers of rainwater
cascading from roofs and verandas. Inside Nitia – a seventh-generation New
Zealander, she says proudly – is recounting her family history. This history
starts with the birth, in Portskerra on Sutherland's north coast in 1801, of
John MacLeod who, by the time of his marriage to Christian Bremner in
1821, was a shoemaker in the Caithness fishing port of Wick. Nothing is
known of what caused John MacLeod to move to Wick, about forty miles
from Portskerra. Nor is anything known of what motivated John, Christian
and their three teenage children to leave Wick, and Scotland, for ever in the
summer of 1838. All that can be said with certainty is that Christian, John,
their daughter and their two sons were among the earliest Scots to take up
residence in New Zealand: John, Nitia's great-great-great-great-grandfather,
getting here, after a five-month stopover in New South Wales, on 12 June
1839; his wife and children following some months later.

John MacLeod and his family settled in hilly, well-wooded country
fronting the Bay of Islands, a North Island locality well known to early-
nineteenth-century whites because its coves and inlets provided whaling
crews with sheltered anchorages. Within months of his arrival, according
to documentation preserved in New Zealand's national archives, John had
'built a house' at Waikare on the Bay of Islands' northern shore. Nearby is

Waitangi. Here in February 1840, at a gathering involving John MacLeod, whose signature appears on one of the resulting documents, Maori chiefs put their names to the still-controversial treaty which had the effect of transferring New Zealand's sovereignty from those same chiefs to Britain's monarchy. The Waitangi agreement led to much of New Zealand being made available to settlers at bargain-basement prices. The treaty, however, came too late to ease John MacLeod's purchase of the land he wanted to farm. To become owner of this land, John had to strike his own deal with local Maoris. The resulting bargain – by no means entirely one sided – brought those Maoris a supply of guns, gunpowder, blankets, axes and iron cooking pots.[56]

Although other emigrants from Scotland came to North Island during the 1840s, the focus of Scottish involvement in New Zealand shifted, by the end of that decade, to South Island – specifically to the region known as Otago and, even more specifically, to this region's principal port of access, the then newly created settlement of Dunedin. Dunedin's name is an anglicised version of *Dùn Èideann*, meaning Edinburgh in Gaelic. The present-day city is dominated architecturally by Presbyterian churches; its street names are those of Scotland's capital; its shops sell tartan souvenirs; it even possesses a whisky distillery. Nothing of this is accidental. Dunedin was established in 1848 by emigrant Scots, and the society they created here was modelled on that of Scotland. Dunedin's founders, however, wished to do more than replicate what they had left behind. Because many of them were staunch members of the recently formed Free Church, they wanted their community to be organised – in a way Scotland itself, with its diversity of denominations, could not be – in accordance with Free Church doctrine. Many of Dunedin's early residents, therefore, were people with impeccably Presbyterian pedigrees – among them Neil and Esther McLeod, a brother and sister who arrived in Dunedin from Scotland in 1860.

Esther's great-grandson, John Gertson, tells me that Esther and Neil's father was John McLeod, the owner and operator of a fish-curing business in Wick. Although expanding rapidly on the back of a booming herring fishery, nineteenth-century Wick was a small town. It is likely, therefore, that John McLeod, the Wick fish curer, knew of John MacLeod, the Wick shoemaker who, as a result of his setting up home at Waikare in 1839, must have brought New Zealand to the attention of people back in Caithness. But when, following their father's death, Esther and Neil McLeod decided to quit Scotland, their choice of destination probably owed less to Wick's Bay of Islands connection than it did to the fact that two of Neil and Esther's uncles were Free Church ministers. Given the extent to which Otago was then under Free Church influence, this must have helped Neil obtain the teaching post he took up on getting to New Zealand, where Esther, until her marriage, acted as her brother's housekeeper.

Historically, MacLeod is a Sutherland name, not a Caithness one. It is probable, then, that many of mid-nineteenth-century Caithness's MacLeod residents were refugees from nearby Sutherland's clearances. Because those clearances resulted in a massive expansion of sheep farming, they created a demand for shepherds. Initially, most such shepherds were imported from elsewhere in Scotland. But by the 1840s and 1850s, in Sutherland as in the Highlands and Islands more generally, young men of crofting background were acquiring sheep management skills of a high order. This made them obvious candidates for recruitment by New Zealand's pioneer sheep farmers, who were soon looking to the Highlands and Islands for the men they needed to operate their sheep runs. During the nineteenth century's third quarter, as a result, Gaelic-speaking shepherds poured into New Zealand. Among them was James McLeod, who arrived in 1865 – and whose story I am told by his great-grandson, Donald Warrington, a physicist on the staff of the University of Otago in Dunedin.

James McLeod grew up in the Sutherland settlement of Elphin, where his father's tombstone is still to be seen. 'Sacred to the memory of Murdo McLeod,' this tombstone reads, 'esteemed for Christian simplicity, self-denial and faithfully discharging his duties.' As those words hint, Murdo McLeod was another of the already mentioned lay preachers who were responsible for the success of the Free Church in crofting areas. Murdo was blind. Even in old age, however, his disability did not stop him trudging from township to township on evangelising journeys which made this elderly Elphin preacher, according to obituary material in the possession of his Dunedin great-great-grandson, one of the best-known people in mid-nineteenth-century Sutherland.

When, in 1872, Murdo McLeod died in Elphin, his son James was shepherding on a sheep station in the vicinity of Fairlie, about 150 miles north of Dunedin. James's brother Donald, another emigrant shepherd, was employed in the same vicinity – and such was their mastery of their trade that Donald and James McLeod, both of whom went on to acquire flocks of their own, were reckoned to be 'the best judges of sheep in [New Zealand]'.[57]

With Graeme McLeod, my guide to South Island, I visit Fairlie on an October morning when the district's trees are coming into leaf and its fields and hillsides – still given over to sheep rearing – are awash with lambs. As we leave Fairlie and head for Burkes Pass, Graeme, a teacher by profession, tells me about his own emigrant forebears. They left for New Zealand from Caithness, where Graeme's great-great-grandfather, John McLeod, was tenant of a small farm in Clyth, a coastal community south of Wick. As was common in nineteenth-century Caithness, John McLeod's tenancy depended on his satisfying his landlord that he was improving his farm by bringing adjacent moorland into cultivation. Because he had no alternative, John complied with this condition. As one of his New Zealand granddaughters recalled, however, the bigger John McLeod's cultivable acreage became, the more rent he was obliged to pay: 'Grandfather would . . . make arable land from heather and whin [gorse] at his own expense, and the laird would clap on a couple of pounds for every acre reclaimed, until the land wouldn't support [his] family and they had to leave their homeland.'[58]

'Six of my great-great-grandfather's twelve children emigrated from Scotland,' Graeme McLeod says. 'Four went to Australia. Two, George and Robert, came here in 1874. The New Zealand railway system was being constructed at that time, and Robert, my great-grandfather, got a job as a platelayer.' In 1876, Graeme goes on, Robert McLeod married Jane McLaren, also of Scottish origin. The couple loom large in a family history compiled by their grandson, Gordon McLeod, Graeme's father. There, Robert is described as 'a tall, spare man of few words [who] was thrifty, energetic, thorough'. Jane, for her part, is remembered as 'a solid, sturdy woman who made butter, baked . . . scones and bannocks, and produced an excellent wine from apples, gooseberries or blackcurrants'.

At the end of the nineteenth century, the road through Burkes Pass, which Graeme and I have now reached, was used by stagecoaches operated by a man called Calum McLeod. Calum, whose origins I cannot pin down, held the contract to carry mail from Fairlie, by way of Burkes Pass, to Tekapo, a settlement at the southern tip of a mountain lake of the same name. For the most part, Calum McLeod's Fairlie–Tekapo excursions were uneventful, but sometimes he met with blizzards. 'The [thirteen-mile] journey from Fairlie to Burkes Pass occupied six hours,' Calum wrote of a trip he made one wintry July morning. 'The snow from the summit of Burkes Pass to Bullocky Creek averaged four feet [in depth].'[59]

Spring is well advanced when Graeme McLeod and I take the modern road for Tekapo, and there is no snow in our immediate vicinity. But the upper reaches of the mountains we are approaching – mountains more than twice as high as Scotland's – are blanketed in deep drifts which sparkle in the sun. The region we are entering, Graeme explains, is the MacKenzie Country. It owes its name to James MacKenzie, another Scots-born shepherd. He settled here in the 1850s and afterwards acquired almost mythical status as a result of his quarrels with the district's wealthy runholders – folk whose sheep MacKenzie first looked after and later stole. Most of those runholders or station owners were English, and according to a MacKenzie Country historian, the area was not to their taste: 'The primeval forces of nature here hold sway and the struggle against winters, winds . . . and, above all, loneliness was too much for these English folk. By the [eighteen] eighties, almost all the Englishmen had left, leaving the contest to Highland shepherds. Crofter heredity and environment had conditioned these shepherds . . . to loneliness and to fighting it out . . . So this stern upland basin became a Highland stronghold . . . [and] the names of MacKenzie Country pioneers read like a gathering of the clans: the Hays and the MacPhersons; Burnetts and MacRaes; Grants and MacKenzies; Frasers and MacGregors; Sinclairs and MacKinnons; Cowans and MacLeods.'[60]

In Omakau, two or three hours' drive south of Tekapo, I call on Don MacLeod, whose father, back in the 1920s, became first manager then part owner of a MacKenzie Country station called Birchwood. 'My dad's name was William,' Don says. 'He belonged originally to Achiltibuie, where my grandfather, also William MacLeod, was a crofter and stonemason.' His father, Don goes on, had four brothers and three sisters: 'One brother was drowned when serving in the British Royal Navy during the First World War. Another brother and a sister stayed on in Scotland. The rest of the family emigrated. The two girls who left went to Canada. So did one of the boys. The other two lads, Dad and his brother Roderick, chose New Zealand.'

'Do you know Achiltibuie?' Don asks. Yes, I reply, wondering which of this Wester Ross township's crofts, strung out along the Atlantic coast not far from Ullapool, was home to Don MacLeod's father. 'I've never been there,' Don says. 'During the Second World War, I was with the New Zealand army in Italy, and at one point I was selected for an officer-training course in England. When I reach England, I thought, I'll get some leave, I'll go up to Scotland and I'll make straight for Achiltibuie. But just before I was due to get away from Italy, I was wounded – badly wounded – in the fighting at Monte Cassino. They shipped me home, and I spent three years in a Christchurch hospital. So I never did get to England. That doesn't bother me. But I would have liked to see Achiltibuie. I'd have liked that very much.'

Because his father died while Don MacLeod was recuperating from his wounds and because Don's family then lost its stake in Birchwood, Don has not lived there since he left to go to war. His boyhood affection for the place remains undimmed, however. This would not have surprised a further McLeod, David by name, who came from England in the 1920s to take charge of another of New Zealand's high country sheep stations. 'I believe that association with a particular piece of land is a fundamental need for human beings,' David McLeod observed. 'Nowhere perhaps in the modern world is this longing so well fulfilled as in the high country of New Zealand. Nowhere can a man be so nearly monarch of all he surveys as there.'[61]

Birchwood, as described by Don MacLeod, conforms exactly to this notion of a MacKenzie Country sheep station being, in effect, an independent kingdom. 'We were totally self-sufficient,' Don says. 'We had to be. Collecting our mail meant a sixteen-mile ride to the nearest pick-up point, a sixteen-mile ride back. Visits to grocery stores just weren't an option. We made our own bread, we made our own butter, we milked our own cows, we butchered our own sheep.'

At just under 150,000 acres, Birchwood – even by MacKenzie Country standards – was a larger-than-average station. 'We had about 12,000 sheep and 800 breeding cattle,' Don MacLeod recalls. 'Dad ran the place with the help of four or five shepherds who were with us permanently. But when mustering times came round and the sheep had to be brought in for shearing and the like, we'd take on another two dozen or more musterers – young, single blokes who were regularly on the move from one station to the next.'

Drawing on his memories of New Zealand sheep runs of the Birchwood type, one musterer wrote: 'I do not think anyone knows what it is like to be thoroughly and really cold to the bones till he has slept out for a moonlight night on the ground with [just] one red blanket over him and a sharp, keen frost gradually changing the red of the blanket to a crisp, glittering white. Though we were dead tired, we could sleep but little.'[62]

'She could be pretty tough going,' Don MacLeod comments of his own mustering experiences. 'There were winters when the snow was so deep you could walk across a fence and never know it was there. I remember spending one night in the mountains in a rickety old hut where the boards had shrunk so much there were gaps between them. The wind came whistling through those gaps, and when a blizzard got going in the early hours, so did the snow. In the morning, my blanket had line after line of snow across it – each line corresponding exactly to one of the cracks in the wall.'

Did you ever go hungry, I ask. 'No, no,' Don replies. 'Nobody ever went hungry up there in the high country. When we went out mustering in the mountains, we'd take a string of pack horses to carry our grub. And we'd have a cook with us. If he was a good cook, and a lot of them were, he'd bake scones in a camp oven, even turn out a roast some nights. Most times, then, we had pretty good tucker. We had oatmeal porridge every morning, I remember, and as much tea as you could handle. We never did have strong drink with us in the mountains. But we had plenty of tea. And cheese, always cheese. That was at my dad's insistence. I never saw such a joker for cheese. He'd eat the stuff when it was so high there were all sorts of things crawling out of it.'

I get up and walk across the room to where two framed photographs are hanging on the wall. Each is a panoramic shot. One shows a narrowing valley enclosed by snow-capped peaks; the other, clearly taken from the same spot, shows the same valley widening gradually as it slopes away downhill. Rising stiffly from his chair, Don joins me. 'These are views you get from Birchwood,' he says of his paired photographs. 'Come here,' Don MacLeod adds, turning to a window which looks northwards out of Omakau. 'See that faraway range of mountains,' Don says, pointing. 'See that pass a little to the right. If you were to take a horse, cross that pass and ride just a bit beyond it, you'd be looking into Birchwood. Believe me, in all the world there's no better sight.'

New Zealand: Otago, Invercargill and Southland

When I leave the MacKenzie Country, pass through Omakau and head for Invercargill, I am traversing the part of Otago which, in the early 1860s, was the site of New Zealand's most significant goldrush. As had already happened to Melbourne, Dunedin was transformed by its becoming a stepping-off point for a goldfield. As their infant city was overwhelmed by an incoming tide of miners, moneymen, prostitutes and hucksters of every kind, the settlement's Free Church founders were close to despair. 'Gold, gold, gold is the universal subject of conversation,' one of them commented. 'The fever is running at such a height that, if it continues, there will scarcely be a man left in town.'[63]

Among the men who abandoned homes and jobs in the hope of picking up a fortune was George McLeod, originally from Tongue in Sutherland. Because the beginnings of Otago's goldrush coincided with the onset of winter, neither George McLeod nor his fellow miners had things easy. 'Tent life was miserable,' one prospector recalled. 'About the beginning of July a heavy fall of snow took place which lay until the second week of August. The cold was intense. Boots and clothes were frozen like boards in the night-time, and had to be taken under the blankets and thawed before being put on in the morning.'[64]

Persevering, George McLeod discovered gold. Most miners would have continued digging. George, however, was of a more calculating disposition. Was the gold he had found a pointer to a large deposit? Or might it be all there was to find in this particular location? Taking the more pessimistic view and declining, in consequence, to push his luck further, George McLeod, having registered his claim, sold it for the then hefty sum of £900. 'George was now a rich man,' I am told by Judith Moore, one of the miner's descendants. 'First, he got in touch with his family back in Sutherland and arranged for his father, his mother, his four sisters and his three brothers to join him in New Zealand. Next, he bought a couple of parcels of land and set himself up as a farmer.'

Stan Gilmore, Judith's cousin and George McLeod's great-great-grandson, shows me a collection of faded newspaper cuttings containing references to his great-great-grandfather. George, it appears from these, was a piper of some local renown. A big, burly man, he was also a heavyweight athlete. At Invercargill's first Highland Games, held in January 1863, George McLeod, in addition to taking a prize for his piping, won a number of stone-throwing contests. 'It was said of George that he could ford a stream with a 200-pound sack of wheat under each arm,' Stan remarks.

George McLeod's farms were in the vicinity of Hedgehope and Mabel Bush, neighbouring settlements some twenty miles out of Invercargill in the part of New Zealand known today as Southland. With Graeme McLeod, who lives in Invercargill, I drive through Southland on an October evening of a sort which makes it obvious why one of its Scots settlers said of this area's grassy hills that they were 'grand for sheep'. Spring being well advanced, the Southland landscape has taken on the bright green colouration which is a New Zealand speciality. Travelling through this landscape, consisting of neatly fenced fields and paddocks, it is difficult to imagine that, until the nineteenth century was well advanced, neither fences nor fields existed here. What, I want to know, did Southland look like prior to the arrival of men like George McLeod? Next morning, Graeme takes me to meet someone who can answer my question.

This is Ned McLeod, who farms near Centre Bush, west of Invercargill. Although mountains can be seen on the horizon, the land around Centre Bush is flat, and on the day of my visit it is being raked by a southerly wind which feels as if it has blown straight off Antarctica. Ned owns some 3,000 sheep, and like the numerous shepherds who came from Scotland to New Zealand in the past, he is an expert dog handler. Gesturing in the direction of Winton, a nearby town, Ned comments as we look across his farm from his front door: 'I haven't missed the annual sheepdog trials at Winton in nearly fifty years.'

Ned's grandfather, another Edward or Ned McLeod, emigrated to New Zealand from Caithness more than a century ago. Inside Ned's farmhouse, while Mateen, Ned's wife, serves scones and cheese of exactly the sort I have eaten in the homes of crofting families all over the Highlands and Islands, I ask Ned about his grandfather's background. He shrugs his shoulders. 'I could tell you a lot more about my dogs' pedigrees than I can tell you about my own,' he says. What is clear is that the original Ned McLeod's father, the present-day Ned's great-grandfather, was a tailor back in Scotland. What is also clear is that the tailor's emigrant son, Ned's grandfather, settled near Gore, north-east of Invercargill, where he raised sheep on land which, before being reseeded with imported grass of the type now dominant in Southland, had to be stripped of its natural vegetation. This vegetation consisted mainly of the coarse and wiry native grasses that New Zealanders call tussock. Ned, whose father eventually took over his grandfather's farm, is old enough to have helped root out tussock. Much the same sort of effort, Ned McLeod explains, was required to turn his own farm, which he acquired in 1956, into a worthwhile enterprise. 'Here the problem was peat,' Ned says. 'I had to drain the place before I could put sheep on her.'

Sheep and their management are Ned McLeod's great passions. His ewes, rams and lambs have won trophy after trophy at Southland's agricultural shows, and nothing angers him more than the extent to which dairy cattle are replacing sheep on Southland farms. 'Plenty of dairy farmers have looked around here,' Ned says. 'My place would be ideal for dairying, they tell me. But I tell them to keep their hands off it. There'll be no cattle on this farm as long as I'm in charge of it.'

Scotland, Canada, New Zealand, Australia and the United States

In 1883, when giving evidence to Lord Napier's royal commission, John MacLeod, a sixty-two-year-old widower whose home was in the Harris township of Ardhasaig, described how, one by one, his children had emigrated: 'The end of it was that my [whole] family . . . scattered into all parts of the earth . . . Some of them are dead in a foreign land . . . Others I know not where they are . . . I am alone.' The likely consequences of his having to cope unaided with encroaching old age were not spelt out by John MacLeod. They did not have to be. In the 1880s, when state pensions for the elderly were still far in the future, everyone knew exactly what lay in wait for men or women who had been deserted, in effect, by their children: poverty and an early death.[65]

Among the people questioned in the course of his enquiries, Napier noted, were some who thought emigration a panacea for all the ills of the Highlands and Islands. But this opinion, Lord Napier went on, was held only by spokesmen for northern Scotland's 'upper and middle classes'. Crofters, in contrast, viewed the prospect of further outflows from the Highlands and Islands with 'aversion' and 'repugnance'. There were good reasons for this, Napier acknowledged. Among them was the fact that what Napier called the 'residuary', or non-emigrating, part of the population of the Highlands and Islands had 'received little benefit' from emigration in the past. Landlords might have implied, and might even have promised, that land relinquished by departing emigrants would be used to enlarge crofts occupied by departing crofters' neighbours. However, this had seldom happened – cleared townships having almost always been turned into sheep farms. Hence the Highland Land League's insistence that there should be no renewed government backing for emigration from the Highlands and Islands until all the land taken from crofters during the Highland Clearances had been restored to them. 'I feel called upon to warn [you] against any such proceedings,' one of the Land League's Skye representatives informed a pro-emigration politician, 'so long as we have thousands of acres . . . which, if properly and economically used, would [provide for] victims of . . . oppression and eviction.'[66]

With one exception, then, no public money was spent in the 1880s on emigration initiatives of the sort common earlier. The exception, involving the resettlement of a hundred or so crofting families on the Canadian prairies, arose out of difficulties in Lewis and Harris. Those were islands where people struggled at the best of times, and where 1887's poor harvest threatened to turn the ensuing winter into a rerun of the famine of forty years before. Civil servants sent from Edinburgh to Lewis in January 1888 reckoned that 'actual starvation' might soon occur. 'On all sides,' they reported, 'we observed evidence of the deepest poverty and dejection.' In one Balallan croft house, occupied by Murdo MacLeod and his family, the visiting officials found 'no meal' and 'no money'. Because he already owed large sums to local merchants, Murdo could get no credit. He and his wife, their food resources consisting of a couple of barrels of potatoes, possessed just two blankets – their children sleeping under 'bags and sails'. In those circumstances, it is not surprising that when, in the spring of 1888, the British government advertised in Lewis and Harris for families willing to make a fresh start in Canada, there was no shortage of eager volunteers.[67]

Their initial enthusiasm notwithstanding, many of those aspiring pioneers were bitterly to regret their decision to emigrate. Because they did not sail for North America until mid-May 1888, summer was so far advanced by the time they got to their new homeland that they were too late to plant a crop. Cash advances which should have been used to buy essential equipment were spent instead on emergency supplies, and when seeds were got into the ground during the spring of 1889 they quickly succumbed to drought. Eventually, the larger of the two 'crofter colonies' thus created on the prairies, at Killarney in the south-western corner of Manitoba, failed completely. Its twin settlement, near Saltcoats in what were then the North West Territories, fared only slightly better.[68]

Despite the Saltcoats and Killarney fiasco, and despite the Highland Land League's insistence that land reform at home would obviate the need for further population outflows, the twenty or thirty years prior to the outbreak of the First World War in 1914 produced a steady stream of emigrants from the Highlands and Islands. Clearances had ceased with the passing of the Crofters Act. But Highlands and Islands living standards, though starting to rise, remained far below those prevailing in the overseas countries and colonies which, throughout this period, made strenuous efforts to recruit settlers from the northern half of Scotland. Everywhere, it seemed, new farms were being brought into existence, and everywhere families were needed to fill them.

On a hill outside the New Zealand town of Palmerston, there is a monument to John Mackenzie, who arrived in this part of Otago from Easter Ross in 1860. MacKenzie, who became one of New Zealand's leading politicians, was committed to breaking up the colony's huge sheep runs in order to prevent New Zealand acquiring a landed aristocracy like Scotland's. In 1892, when Minister of Lands in the New Zealand government, John MacKenzie was asked to explain his thinking to the House of Representatives in Wellington. Addressing the house's speaker, he said: 'The Minister for Lands, sir, got his ideas as a boy when [in the Scottish Highlands] he saw the poor people evicted from their houses in the most cruel manner . . . Is it any wonder that I should have opinions . . . in connection with the land question in this country?'[69]

John MacKenzie had plenty of counterparts in Australia where, from the 1860s onwards, the colonial authorities were under pressure to 'unlock the lands' by giving the generality of settlers access to the enormous acreages accumulated by wealthy station owners like the MacLeods of Talisker. In response, the Victoria and New South Wales legislatures passed a series of Selection Acts which entitled families, such as the Tragowel McLeods mentioned in this book's opening chapter, to choose, or select, blocks of land in areas formerly closed to them.

The promoters of Australia's Selection Acts were inspired by the prairie settlement policies pursued by governments in the United States and Canada. At the centre of those policies was the American Homestead Act of 1862. This measure, soon copied by Canadian administrations, permitted any US citizen to claim 160 acres of previously unsettled land. In return for a nominal upfront payment of $1.25 an acre, homesteads formed in this way instantly became the private property of their occupants – who, even if they were unable to afford the acreage payment, were granted full ownership rights at the end of their first five years. Ten years prior to the Homestead Act, there had been 1.5 million farms in the United States. Fifty years after the Act became law, there were more than four times as many – most of them located on recently opened-up land west of the Mississippi

River. It was on such land that Angus McCaskill, the Scots-born narrator of a novel set in nineteenth-century Montana, settled alongside his friend, Rob Barclay. 'On the Declaration of Applicant there in front of me,' Angus remarks of the moment he takes possession of his homestead, 'my land's numbers were registered as *SW ¼ Sec. 31, Tp. 28N, Rge. 8W*, on Rob's they were *NE ¼ Sec. 32, Tp. 28N, Rge. 8W*, and with our grins at each other we agreed that ink had never said anything better.'[70]

In Montana, towards the close of the nineteenth century and in the opening years of the twentieth, there were pioneer farmers, cowboys and shepherds who spoke much better Gaelic than English. To the north of Montana's border with Canada's prairie provinces, there were many more settlers of Highlands and Islands extraction. Some of those people were the Canadian children or grandchildren of earlier emigrants. But also present in growing numbers were folk who had come directly from places like Skye, Harris, Lewis and Sutherland. As compared with their predecessors of fifty or a hundred years before, those emigrants travelled quickly and in comfort. First, they crossed the ocean on steamships; next, courtesy of the Canadian Pacific Railway (CPR), they were conveyed westward on the trains which, by the later 1880s, linked Atlantic ports like Halifax with the numerous railroad halts then springing up across Manitoba, Saskatchewan and Alberta.

Because Canada's government wanted, for reasons mentioned already, to have the prairies populated as densely as possible, potential settlers were targeted by Canadian government agents. The agent responsible for emigrant recruitment in the Highlands and Islands was Hugh McKerracher, a Gaelic-speaking Ontarian whose parents had originated in Perthshire. McKerracher travelled regularly through the Highlands and Islands on a horse-drawn wagon 'emblazoned', as a Scottish journalist put it in 1907, with 'the inspiring and much-favoured name [of] Canada'. Having accompanied McKerracher to the Lewis township of Carloway, the same journalist filed an account of the evening lecture, illustrated by magic lantern slides, which the agent gave one evening in the township's primary school: 'Before eight o'clock, the accommodation of the school . . . was taxed to its utmost capacity, extra seats having had to be arranged . . . Mr McKerracher spoke first in Gaelic and afterwards in English. He undoubtedly had a good subject in Canada, and . . . he dealt with it in all its aspects, forcefully and eloquently, describing [the country] as . . . of vast extent and inexhaustible resources.'[71]

A Lewis clergyman and poet, John MacLeod from Arnol, was in no doubt as to the impact of such performances. Having been exposed to a succession of cleverly posed slides featuring 'cows up to their ears in grass' and 'a lovely girl leaning on a gate', lots of Lewis's young men, or so one of Rev. MacLeod's poems comments, came home and announced their intention to be off as soon as possible to Canada. Those who acted on this intention, and many did, embarked on journeys liable to end with their stepping off crowded trains into the architecturally splendid railway station which, by way of demonstrating its corporate faith in a glittering prairie future, the CPR built in the middle of Winnipeg.[72]

Manitoba and Saskatchewan: Winnipeg and Saskatchewan Forks

Winnipeg's best years began in February 1881, when it was decided that the Canadian Pacific Railway, the means by which Canada's politicians consolidated their grip on the prairies, should pass through Winnipeg on its way to distant Vancouver. Today, the boom thus unleashed – a boom which lasted until the First World War cut off the flow of prairie-bound emigrants from Europe – has receded into history. Winnipeg's CPR station is now the city's Aboriginal Centre, and little is left of the shed-like buildings where immigration officials once processed hundreds of thousands of arrivals from Scotland, England, Ireland, Sweden, Germany, Iceland, Estonia, Latvia, Poland, Russia and the Ukraine. As for the Red River Settlement, the pioneering outpost that was Winnipeg's early-nineteenth-century precursor, virtually all trace of it disappeared under the CPR's tracks and under the sprawling city which developed around them. Among today's Winnipeggers, however, are people whose family links with this area date from Red River Settlement times. One is Roy McLeod, a security guard whose great-great-grandfather, John McLeod, got here from Lewis nearly 200 years ago. John came with a party of settlers recruited by Thomas Douglas, Earl of Selkirk, whose earlier involvement with Prince Edward Island had given way to a conviction that Manitoba ought to be colonised by emigrants from the Highlands and Islands.

Selkirk's Manitoba venture began with his acquiring from the Hudson's Bay Company an enormous tract of territory bisected by the Red River, which flows into Lake Winnipeg from the south. Since Red River was then hundreds of miles west of the frontier of white settlement on the Great Lakes, and since the canoe routes from the lakes to Red River were firmly in the hand of the Bay Company's great rivals, the Montreal-based Nor'Westers, Selkirk's prospective colonists had to access Manitoba from York Factory, located on the western shore of Hudson Bay.

The Earl of Selkirk's first party of Manitoba-bound settlers arrived at York Factory on 24 September 1811 – at the end of what John McLeod, who had accompanied them from Scotland, called 'a very tedious passage' of sixty-one days. 'The season was now so far advanced,' John McLeod wrote, 'that we could not proceed to the interior [because Manitoba's rivers were already freezing] and consequently remained at the seacoast all winter.' This was no small inconvenience. Forced to endure Hudson Bay's sub-Arctic weather for month after month, and with little in the way of fresh food available to them, about three-quarters of the hundred-strong emigrant group went down with scurvy and other illnesses. As a result, it was well into the summer of 1812 before Manitoba's aspiring colonists arrived at their ultimate destination – the forks, or junction, of the Red and Assiniboine rivers. Here, where riverside walkways and souvenir stores now attract tourists, John McLeod helped establish the tiny community which, over the next thirty years, grew into the Red River Settlement.[73]

The settlement, which remained small in size until the coming of the CPR, was nearly strangled at birth by the North West Company – whose principals were opposed to what they regarded, with some justice, as a Bay Company plot to obstruct their westward expansion. It was for this reason that John McLeod, although a Bay Company employee rather than one of Lord Selkirk's intending settlers, found himself spending a lot of time at the Red and Assiniboine forks – where he supervised the construction of log-built fortifications designed to fend off the assaults made on the Red River Settlement by the Nor'Westers and their Métis allies. 'On June 25th, 1815,' John McLeod reported of one of those assaults, 'a sudden attack was made by an armed band . . . They numbered about seventy or eighty, well armed and on horseback . . . I assumed command . . . [and], mustering with inferior numbers and only a few guns, we took a stand . . . For many days after, we were under siege, living under constant peril, but unconquerable [behind] our bullet-proof log walls.'

In 1818, John McLeod married Charlotte Pruden, the mixed-blood daughter of another Hudson's Bay Company trader. 'My great-grandfather, a second John McLeod, was one of John and Charlotte's children,' Roy McLeod tells me. 'He was a very big man, just under seven feet tall, and he became a fur trader like his father.' Not all John McLeod Senior's children remained in the West, however. Malcolm, John's oldest boy, was sent to Scotland, where he was educated in Edinburgh's High School. Afterwards, Malcolm McLeod studied law in Montreal and went on to become one of Quebec's judges. In the 1870s, drawing on what he had learned of western geography from his father, one of the first traders to establish a Hudson's Bay Company presence on North America's Pacific coast, Malcolm published a series of newspaper articles and pamphlets making the case for a Canadian transcontinental railway – the railway which, during the 1880s, took shape as the CPR.

In Winnipeg, I stay with Bob and Connie McLeod. Bob's great-grandparents, Donald and Margaret McLeod, were married in the Assynt township of Clashnessie in 1848. That same year, the couple emigrated – settling initially and briefly in Pictou, Bob thinks, before moving to Bruce County, Ontario, where Bob's grandfather, Thomas McLeod, the sixth of Donald and Margaret's eleven children, was born in 1861. Like a lot of other Bruce County people, Thomas, while still a teenager, headed west – getting to Manitoba well in advance of the CPR and, as a result, having to come by way of the United States. 'Thomas went by train to Minneapolis and then travelled overland to Fargo, North Dakota,' Bob says. 'From Fargo, in those days, a Red River steamboat took you on to Winnipeg.'

Thomas McLeod's destination was the then newly opened-up community of Shoal Lake, about 250 miles west of Winnipeg, where he got a job as a farmhand with a family who had also moved there from Bruce County. Four or five years later, at about the time the CPR reached Shoal Lake, Thomas McLeod, now twenty-one, began farming himself – taking on the ownership of a quarter section, or 160 acres, of previously uncultivated land which, like other prairie pioneers, he aimed to turn into crop-yielding fields. Sod busting, the term applied to this process, was not easy. Even the heaviest of nineteenth-century ploughs, all of them still drawn by horses or oxen, could make little impression on prairie turf laid down over thousands of years. 'Much of the work had to be done by hand,' Bob McLeod comments. 'For my grandfather, and for thousands like him, it must have been a real tough life.' This is confirmed when, heading out of Winnipeg, I take the Trans-Canada Highway to Saskatchewan.

My previous visits to the Saskatchewan prairies were made in late summer, when weeks of baking heat had left the landscape drained of colour, or in the depths of winter, when bitter winds blew across uninterrupted expanses of snow. This time, it is June. It has been wet, and everywhere the new-grown grass is green. In a steady rain that would do credit to the Hebrides, I drive out of Prince Albert to visit a farm situated in the neck of land lying just west of the forks of the North and South Saskatchewan Rivers, once the leading fur trade routes to Athabasca and the Rockies. As I approach the forks, the paved highway gives way to a dirt road, and my rented car makes heavy going of four-inch-deep mud. Spotting a couple of men fixing agricultural machinery in a roadside shed, I stop and ask if this is the way to the MacLeod place. My overseas accent and my much-too-lightweight vehicle line me up for what follows. 'Boy, are you lost,' says one of the two. 'The MacLeod place is a good forty miles from here.' But after a moment, my informant relents, grins and points into the still-falling rain. 'Next turn-off but one on the right,' he tells me. Half an hour later, I am lunching lavishly on pickerel, a lake fish that is a prairie delicacy, and Donald MacLeod, who first came to this Saskatchewan Forks farm as a three year old in 1935, is telling me a little of his family's experience of prairie homesteading.

This experience began with the arrival in Saskatchewan of Donald's father, John MacLeod, who had been born in the Lewis township of Portvoller in 1898 and who, before he reached his teens, was orphaned. 'My dad's father died when he was five or six,' Donald MacLeod says. 'His mother died when he was twelve. Two years later, he came to Canada. He had three uncles here, Malcolm, Andrew and Alex MacKenzie, brothers of Dad's mother. They'd left Lewis for Saskatchewan four or five years before, and I guess it made sense for my father to join them. He lived with his uncle Malcolm, who was homesteading alongside his two brothers in a place called Chipperfield in southern Saskatchewan.'

When Malcolm MacKenzie took possession of his homestead, Donald MacLeod goes on, it consisted of nothing but prairie – and because trees were non existent in his area, there was no question of Malcolm building a log cabin of the kind which North America's earlier settlers constructed. 'Malcolm and another fellow dug a hole in the ground and, to begin with, they lived in that,' Donald says.

In 1917, at the height of the First World War, John MacLeod, only four years in Canada at this point, was back in Europe with the Canadian army. At the war's end, after spending a couple of months with his grandparents in Portvoller, John returned to Saskatchewan, where, in the interim, one of his uncles, Alex MacKenzie, had died. Taking on Alex's homestead, John now became a prairie farmer on his own account. 'Dad wasn't working with the best of soils,' Donald MacLeod remarks. 'Back in Portvoller, his uncles had been fishermen. Their crofts, to them, would just have been sidelines. When selecting homesteads, then, the MacKenzies had no eye for what was good and what was bad – and the places they picked were so full of stones they were real hard to break in.' This makes it all the more impressive that, throughout the 1920s, John MacLeod did well. The wheat, oats and flax he grew sold profitably. In partnership with one of his uncles, John invested in a threshing machine. He bought one of the first motorcars, a Model T Ford, seen in his district. In 1925, he married Elizabeth Plaxton, an elementary school teacher.

Then came the decade that prairie people still call the Dirty Thirties. As the North American economy collapsed in the wake of 1929's Wall Street crash, so did agricultural prices. At the same time, there was drought, record-breakingly cold winters, searingly hot summers and even swarms of crop-eating grasshoppers so dense, on occasion, that it was barely possible to keep your feet in the streets of Saskatchewan's towns. 'In retrospect,' Donald MacLeod comments, 'it's easy to see that much of the prairie around

Chipperfield should never have been ploughed. Things were fine as long as it kept raining. But when the dry years came, the soil just blew away.'

All across Saskatchewan at this time, the summer sky was darkened by semi-perpetual dust storms. The province's roads, together with the CPR's transcontinental tracks, were blocked by wind-blown earth which drifted across them like snow. In cities like Saskatoon and Regina, thousands of jobless men stood in line for welfare handouts. Out on the prairie, meanwhile, homestead after homestead was abandoned. 'In the end,' Donald MacLeod says, 'my mother and father just walked away from their place. It was worth nothing and, even if it had been worth something, there was no one to buy it. So, in the spring of 1935, they loaded everything worth taking into the Model T, which they'd turned into a small truck, left Chipperfield for ever and came up here.'

Donald is talking now about the Saskatchewan Forks farm on which he still lives. It belonged originally to his mother's parents – who, in effect, took in their daughter, their son-in-law and their grandchildren. Being further north, and comparatively well wooded, the Saskatchewan Forks area was less drought stricken than localities like Chipperfield. But prairie life when Donald MacLeod was growing up continued to be hard. A freezer then consisted of blocks of ice cut from the South Saskatchewan in winter. The principal source of water was the barrel which held the rain that fell on the MacLeod home's roof. Mains electricity did not arrive until 1952. A telephone was unavailable until 1971. Food, especially in the early days, mostly took the form of fish which John MacLeod – 'much the best fisherman I ever saw,' his son says – caught in one or other of the nearby rivers.

Has he visited Lewis, I ask Donald MacLeod. 'Yes,' he says. 'Back in the 1950s, I left for Alberta and got a job in the oil industry. From Alberta, I went to work in Turkey, and in 1960, when on my way home, I stopped off in Scotland and went up to Lewis. When I got to Portvoller, I saw a man at work by the roadside. He was shearing sheep, and I stopped to speak with him. He turned out to be my dad's first cousin.'

Scotland: Skye, Raasay and Harris

At Totara, on New Zealand's Pacific coast north of Dunedin, a roadside monument commemorates the dispatch from here, in February 1882, of the first cargo of frozen lamb and mutton sent successfully from the southern hemisphere to the United Kingdom. This event signalled the end of the sheep-farming economy which took shape in the Highlands and Islands during the early nineteenth century. Since the 1870s, northern Scotland's sheep farmers had been contending with downward pressure on wool prices

A nineteenth-century Skye crofter working his croft with
a *cas-chrom* or foot-operated plough.
(Aberdeen University Library)

A SKYE COTTAGE.

A mid-nineteenth-century Skye cottage. Better-off Skye people
lived in homes like these. Less fortunate families had to make
do with makeshift shacks.
(*Illustrated London News*)

This North Carolina home was built in the 1830s by John McLeod, who
emigrated from Skye with his mother in 1802. The contrast between
John's farmhouse and its Skye equivalents is striking.
(Collection of Alexander C. McLeod)

John McLeod's son, Alexander, a farmer like his father,
built this home in the 1880s.
(Collection of Alexander C. McLeod)

Alexander's son, Robert Lee McLeod, a lumber merchant, built this fine
home in the North Carolina town of Maxton around 1910. In the space of
three generations, as shown by the succession of homes pictured here, this
McLeod family proved that the American Dream – a conviction that
prosperity could readily be won in the US – sometimes came true.
(Collection of Alexander C. McLeod)

Rev. Norman MacLeod, raised in the Sutherland township of Clachtoll, led an emigrant party from Sutherland to Pictou, Nova Scotia, in 1817. From Pictou, in the 1820s, Norman and his congregation moved to St Ann's, Cape Breton Island. From there, in the 1850s, the minister and his followers emigrated again – sailing first for Australia and settling eventually at Waipu in New Zealand. (Waipu Heritage Centre)

Representatives of three of the families, all of them originating in the Scottish Highlands, who accompanied Norman MacLeod from Cape Breton Island to Waipu.
(Waipu Heritage Centre)

A naval ship, the *Hercules*, leaving Scotland for Australia in December 1852. The *Hercules* carried 742 emigrants, mainly from Skye and Harris. More than 60 of those people were to die of smallpox and typhus before the *Hercules* reached Adelaide.
(*Illustrated London News*)

DIGGERS OF HIGH DEGREE.

Gold-diggers at Bendigo, Victoria, in the 1850s. 'Scottish Highlanders are very numerous in Bendigo,' an Australian commented, 'every gully having its pipes and pipers.'
(National Library of Australia)

A sod house on the Canadian prairies. In the years around 1900,
homesteaders from Scotland commonly lived in such homes while
breaking in the land.
(Glenbow Archives)

More prairie scenes, including (top) a snowed-in train.
(Glenbow Archives)

Dunvegan Castle, ancestral home of Skye's MacLeod chiefs, as it appeared in the nineteenth century. (Aberdeen University Library)

MacLeod clan members attend a homecoming, or family gathering, at Old Bethesda Presbyterian Church, North Carolina, in 1940. A spirit of clanship had survived what was then a 150-year separation from Scotland. However, tartan is not much in evidence. The Scottish diaspora's fondness for kilts is a more recent phenomenon.

– this pressure stemming from Australian and New Zealand competition. Now that frozen meat was also becoming available at prices well below those required to sustain large-scale sheep production in places like Skye and Sutherland, sheep farmer after sheep farmer began to get out of the Highlands and Islands. For the region's landowners, this was a catastrophic development. Within months of the Totara shipment arriving in London, Norman MacLeod of Dunvegan found himself unable to obtain tenants for several of the formerly lucrative sheep farms established on his estate some sixty years before.[74]

As far as crofters were concerned, it was a cause of celebration that their emigrant kin on the far side of the world – by flooding the British market with cheap wool and cheaper mutton – were weakening the financial position of Norman MacLeod and his fellow landlords. With sheep farming in retreat, the notion that crofters might again occupy territory from which their forebears had been ejected – a notion previously thought far fetched – began to be taken seriously by senior politicians, and before the nineteenth century ended had become government policy. Shortly thereafter, a state agency bought the first of many tracts of land that the nation acquired in the course of the next thirty years in order to create new crofts in localities cleared in the past. The two areas purchased initially were Glendale in Skye and a part of Strathnaver in Sutherland.

The Glendale and Strathnaver experiments led in 1911 to the formation of a further organisation, the Board of Agriculture for Scotland, which had the task of embarking on a wider resettlement programme. This programme, however, was delayed by lack of funds and by the legal obstacles placed in its way by landlords. Inevitably, this caused frustration among families hoping to gain the crofts politicians had promised. This frustration came to a head in the aftermath of the First World War. During Britain's four-year conflict with Germany, recruitment to the country's armed forces had been boosted in the Highlands and Islands by repeated assertions to the effect that at the war's end, 'the people of the Highlands,' as one government minister put it, 'must be placed in possession of the soil'. When this did not happen in the months following the Allied–German armistice of November 1918, young men – mostly newly back from military service on the killing grounds of the Western Front – took the law into their own hands. All over the Highlands and Islands, plans were made to have sheep farms occupied illegally. Many of the ensuing land raids, as seizures of this type were called, took place in areas once controlled by Clan MacLeod.[75]

During 1920 and 1921, for example, land raiders moved into the deserted Raasay townships from which, seventy years before, hundreds of people had been shipped to Australia. Those raiders came from Rona. This little island, just north of Raasay, had been made a dumping ground for Raasay families who could not, or would not, go overseas. According to the Scottish Land Court, a rent-fixing tribunal which had replaced the earlier Crofters Commission, conditions in Rona were 'miserable in the extreme'. Rona's land, the court reported in 1920, was of 'the poorest quality' and its homes were of 'the most primitive description'. 'It is difficult to know,' the Land Court went on, 'how anyone can carry on under such conditions, and still more [difficult] to understand how a living can be obtained.'[76]

Rona's inhabitants endorsed this judgment. 'The circumstances under which we live here,' they informed the Board of Agriculture by letter in February 1920, '[are] most deplorable, the place being hardly fit for goats, let alone human beings, while the good land [at] the south end of Raasay from which we could have a decent living and for which the best of our manhood has bled and died in Flanders [on the Western Front] is as a sporting ground.' Four of this letter's nine signatories were MacLeods. Like everyone else on Rona, they wanted to reoccupy the Raasay townships from which their ancestors had been evicted. Following sheep farming's collapse, several of those former townships, as the Rona people pointed out to the Board of Agriculture, had been rented to a shooting tenant. Rona's residents, as they made clear, were determined to bring this situation to an end: 'Most of us have fought [in] the war . . . and we are . . . determined to fight, and [to] shed our last drop of blood if necessary, for our liberties at home.'[77]

The threatened raids duly occurred, and the raiders, of whom the most prominent was a man named Donald MacLeod, were imprisoned as a result. Their cause triumphed all the same. In 1922, the Board of Agriculture bought Raasay, most of which has been in public ownership ever since. One or two of the island's cleared townships, including Hallaig, were left empty. The others, however, were resettled, some by the now released raiders.

Elsewhere in the Highlands and Islands, there were analogous developments. In Glenelg, families moved back into the previously depopulated Gleann Mòr. In Harris, large numbers of crofters were installed in new townships on the machair lands which had been emptied by the island's landlords during the 1820s and 1830s. In Skye, where there was growing pressure for something similar to be done, the Board of Agriculture began to target sheep farms on the Dunvegan estate.

Dunvegan's laird at this point was Norman Magnus MacLeod, a retired soldier and diplomat who had succeeded his father, Norman, on the latter's death in 1895. Like most landlords, Norman Magnus took a dim view of the Board of Agriculture's operations. 'To propose settling crofters within a few hundred yards of [Dunvegan] Castle is extremely harsh,' one of his agents complained when the board announced its intention to establish crofts on former farmland at Claigan. The Board of Agriculture, however, had little option but to press ahead with its plans. Like Raasay, Skye was not short of militant ex-soldiers prepared to seize the land they wanted. 'Unless this farm is promised to us immediately,' the Board of Agriculture was informed by men demanding crofts at Claigan, 'we shall take possession of it.' Other demobilised soldiers made identical threats. 'We have fought on sea and land in defence of the Empire,' declared the nine signatories to a letter giving notice of a raid on one of Norman Magnus MacLeod's sheep farms. 'The same spirit is alive in us today and we are determined to fight for our rights to this land without delay.'[78]

Not much fighting was necessary, mainly because of Norman Magnus falling victim to the latest of the financial crises which, from as far back as the eighteenth century, had blighted the lives of successive MacLeod chieftains. The previous such crisis had culminated in the mid-nineteenth-century bankruptcy of Norman Magnus's father. This bankruptcy had ushered in a period of careful management at Dunvegan Castle. By the 1920s, however, matters were deteriorating once more – because cuts in croft rents had combined with the downturn in sheep farming to bring about a marked reduction in the income available to Dunvegan's laird from his estate. In response, Norman Magnus MacLeod borrowed heavily. By 1920, his debts were in the order of £40,000 (equivalent to about £1 million today) and, like earlier chiefs, he was left with no alternative, if his finances were to be stabilised, but to sell a large slice of his property.

Because prospective private buyers of Hebridean estates had been scared away by crofting unrest and by sheep farming's continuing difficulties, there was only one possible source of the cash Dunvegan's laird needed. This was the Board of Agriculture with whose representatives Norman Magnus MacLeod was in discussion before the end of 1919. Soon it had become clear that the board was willing to buy the greater part of Bracadale and Minginish – some 60,000 acres in total – for a price which, after protracted haggling, was fixed at £56,809.

The southernmost of Norman Magnus's farms, Glen Brittle, was excluded from the sale. This meant that Dunvegan's laird retained ownership of much of the Cuillin. During most of the several centuries since Clan MacLeod had acquired those peaks, they were thought to have no great value. In the course of the Victorian period, however, growing fascination with wild landscapes – whether in the Scottish Highlands and Islands, the Alps or the Rockies – had given the Cuillin worldwide renown. Norman Magnus MacLeod, in consequence, was almost as anxious to keep the Cuillin as he was to hang on to Dunvegan Castle. His deal with the Board of Agriculture, despite its depriving Norman Magnus of the bulk of his previous acreage, allowed him to do so. This, together with its enabling him to escape from indebtedness, was what made the Board of Agriculture's offer so attractive from Norman Magnus MacLeod's standpoint. As his younger brother, Roderick, commented: 'If we sold, the debt could all be paid and the castle and the Coolins, the two jewels of the estate, would be safe.'[79]

The Board of Agriculture's acquisition in 1920 of most of Minginish and Bracadale made this government agency the owner of sheep farms which, a couple of centuries before, had been the tacks occupied by families like the MacLeods of Talisker, Drynoch and Gesto. Those families were long gone by 1920, mostly to North America and Australia. Now the sheep farmers who had succeeded them were also to give way – this time to crofters. Over the next three or four years, as a result, about 150 families were settled by the Board of Agriculture in localities from which hundreds of other such families had been evicted during the 1820s. Some of the new settlers – most notably those allocated land on the north shore of Loch Harport and in Glen Drynoch – acquired holdings extending to several hundred acres apiece. The majority, however, had to be content with more typically sized crofts. About half of those went to people from Skye. The remainder went to folk from Lewis and Harris.

Forty-three Harris families and twenty more from Lewis moved on to what had been Talisker Farm in the spring of 1923. Talisker House, from which Major Donald MacLeod of Talisker had left for Tasmania in 1820, was sold by the Board of Agriculture to a man by the name of James Cameron. The arable land fronting Talisker Bay also went to Cameron. But this left space in North Talisker, the part of the former farm bordering Loch Harport, for three new settlements, Fernilea, Portnalong and Fiscavaig, in which the Lewis and Harris people were accommodated.

Among those people was a thirteen-year-old boy, Calum MacLeod, from Portvoller in Lewis. Calum came to Fernilea with an older brother and when the two were getting themselves established on the former Talisker Farm, the challenges they faced were not very different from those confronting one of their cousins, John MacLeod, also originally from Portvoller and then homesteading, as already described, in Saskatchewan. 'The Fernilea settlers ran into a lot of difficulty in the later 1920s,' I am told by Calum MacLeod's son, John Norman, head of studies at Sabhal Mòr Ostaig, Skye's Gaelic College. 'My father left for Glasgow where he got a job on the railways. From Glasgow, he went for three or four years to the Falkland Islands – to work on a sheep farm there.'

Despite their problems, the communities of Fiscavaig, Portnalong and Fernilea survived, and when, not long before the outbreak of the Second World War, they were visited by Neil Gunn, a well-known novelist, the townships appear to have been doing well. 'The[ir] houses,' Gunn wrote of Fernilea, Portnalong and Fiscavaig, 'are all built to the same pattern: stone gables, corrugated iron sides with front-door porch, and roof of grey artificial slate. With rare exceptions they are freshly painted or whitewashed, look very well and fit into the landscape.' All around, Gunn went on, 'potatoes and corn were springing up in small but healthy patches; milch cows were everywhere'.[80]

Initiatives of the North Talisker type had generated a good deal of political controversy, Neil Gunn observed: 'But however one may argue or discuss the merits of the [Talisker] settlement, there can be no doubt of the happy contrast in which it stands to the same land under the dominion of the old lairds or chiefs. Less than a century ago, Portnalong was cleared of its inhabitants [who were] . . . transported . . . to America . . . As we wandered in the hilly lands about Portnalong, we came on new houses everywhere . . . and their bright faces seemed like the mind of a folk who throve for untold centuries, and would thrive for centuries more, if the greed and egoism of the landed and plutocratic designers of our worldly affairs gave them half a chance.'

CHAPTER SEVEN

AWAY FOR A WHILE

Cape Breton Island: St Ann's

In the early summer of 1947, Flora MacLeod, Dunvegan's latest laird, got a letter from Canada. It was written by Angus MacKenzie, founder of Cape Breton Island's Gaelic College. The college, at St Ann's, hosted an annual Gaelic mod, or festival, and MacKenzie's letter invited Flora, in her capacity as Clan MacLeod's chief, to open the mod scheduled for that August. What followed is summarised in jottings Flora MacLeod made at the end of the day she flew into Sydney, Cape Breton Island's capital: 'Arrived Sydney Airport. Pipes, press, photographers, crowds; representatives of provincial government, mayor, Gaelic College . . . Reception and refreshments; speeches; drive to Isle Royal Hotel, Sydney, accompanied by Canadian Mounted Police in red uniforms.'[1]

Flora took charge at Dunvegan when Reginald MacLeod, her father, died in 1935 – six years after inheriting the Dunvegan estate and the Clan MacLeod chieftainship from Norman Magnus, his elder brother and Flora's uncle. Until her uncle's death and her father's subsequent move to Skye, Flora lived mostly in London. There, in 1901, she married Hubert Walter, whose family owned *The Times*. The marriage was not a success. The couple lived increasingly apart, and when Hubert died in 1933 his widow, as she noted, 'felt [this] a liberation'. Changing her name back to MacLeod, Flora joined her father at Dunvegan. There she entered local politics and – believing that something had to be done to provide places like Skye with new sources of employment and income

– went on to take a prominent role in a government-backed committee set up to devise a development strategy for the Highlands and Islands.[2]

One of the industries which Flora MacLeod thought might help turn around the Highlands and Islands economy was tourism. It was partly to promote its growth that she agreed to go to Canada in 1947. However, the warmth of the welcome she got in Cape Breton, especially from the island's MacLeods, convinced her that she should have more contact with her clansfolk, as she called them, wherever they might be. Despite being sixty-nine when she opened the St Ann's mod, Dame Flora MacLeod, as she became in 1953, duly embarked on a series of tours which took her to practically every part of Canada, the United States, Australia and New Zealand. One outcome of those tours was a worldwide mushrooming of Clan MacLeod Societies.

Not everyone enthused about this development. Hugh MacLennan, a leading literary figure and a Cape Bretoner by birth, thought it pathetic that so many of his fellow Scottish-Canadians clung, as he saw it, to clanship. The evictions which propelled Scots out of Scotland were nothing less than crimes, MacLennan believed. 'If [those] crimes . . . were not denounced as were the crimes committed against the Irish,' he wrote, 'it was because the Highlanders took so long to be weaned from the family concept of society in which they were reared . . . The clan system of the Old Country had so stupefied the race with loyalty that, even after their chiefs had sold them out, most of the people pretended it wasn't so.'[3]

Hugh MacLennan was scathing about festivals of the type which Flora MacLeod opened in Cape Breton. 'Today there's a Gaelic College at St Ann's,' MacLennan observed in 1964. 'Every summer there is a Highland Mod . . . and chiefs are invited from the other side, most of them arriving with Oxford accents and not a word of Gaelic. Now there is a trade in tartans, and you occasionally see, as you never did thirty years ago, Cape Breton boys and girls wearing kilts. An older generation would have known, I think, that the romance about the kilt as a distinctive uniform of the clan was largely a Victorian invention . . . I record it as a plain fact that the kilt was never worn in Cape Breton before the tourists came.'[4]

Hugh MacLennan's opinions are echoed by a present-day novelist, D.R. MacDonald, also a Cape Bretoner, who brings one of his youthful characters to the Gaelic College at St Ann's on a Sunday afternoon when a 'gathering of the clans' is getting underway. In the college grounds, the young man talks with 'an old guy, a local by his accent, still in his church necktie, his dark coat slung over his arm, his silver hair carefully parted and slicked down'. The older man indicates a kilt-wearing passer-by. 'My dad got Gaelic from his mother's milk,' he says, 'but you wouldn't get him in a rig like that.' Referring to the people attending 'this Gathering of the Clans thing', the older man continues: 'They're mostly from away, you know . . . It's them that got those booths set up out there with the names of clans on them. You find your clan and they have brochures and bits of paraphernalia. I'm a MacLachlan myself. "These Are Your People," the sign says on the MacLachlan booth. No, they're not, I says to myself. Never set eyes on them. My people were in church with me this morning.'[5]

'When the natural water dries up,' Hugh MacLennan remarked, 'it is human for people to try to drink at the mirage.' By implication, then, North America's *real* Scottish heritage died with the passing of Gaelic – the language's demise taking out of circulation the songs, poems and traditions to which it alone gave access. On this reading, clan societies and other continuing manifestations of North American Scottishness are necessarily synthetic, maybe even spurious. Much the same point has been made by North American academics.[6]

Writing as Dame Flora MacLeod's international travels were commencing, Charles W. Dunn, Professor of Celtic at Harvard, commented: 'The degree to which people [in the United States and Canada] have remained truly Highland may be measured by their retention of the Gaelic language. Only by retaining their language can the people preserve their oral traditions and their music; when they lose the language, they lose with it much that marks them off from the other people settled in the New World.' A younger American academic, Michael Newton, in a book to which Charles Dunn contributed a foreword, goes further. From his perspective, celebrations of the Highlands and Islands contribution to the United States are pointless unless they are informed, as such celebrations seldom are, by the Gaelic component of the emigrant experience. 'If Americans with Scottish Highlanders in their ancestry choose to identify with this [Gaelic] heritage,' Newton wrote in 2001, 'there is surely much to enjoy . . . If they choose instead to sublimate their passion into the trappings of nineteenth-century Highlandism – clan tartans, militarism, pseudo-Jacobite songs in English, and so on – they will lose the chance to delve into the substance of their ancestors' culture.'[7]

By Highlandism, also known as tartanry, Michael Newton means the conviction that pro-Scottish feeling can only be expressed by embracing a highly romanticised version of the Highlands and Islands past. This conviction is traceable to the novels of Walter Scott; it was boosted by Queen Victoria's infatuation with the fairytale palace built for her at Balmoral; and it has been roundly castigated in modern Scotland as a hopelessly reactionary diversion from efforts to equip Scots with a forward-looking vision of what they and their country ought to be about. Hence the unease which many Scottish commentators experience when dealing with overseas clan societies of the type Flora MacLeod did so much to promote. Because those societies appear to have embraced a variant of Scottishness which many of us in Scotland consider outmoded and artificial, it is easy for Scots to conclude that neither clan society members nor the Scottish diaspora as a whole deserve to be treated seriously. As indicated at the outset, this book rejects that approach. It takes the diaspora's interest in Scotland at face value, and it deals with overseas Scots as they are, not as I or anyone else would like them to be.

My approach, then, owes less to Michael Newton than to Celeste Ray, whose book, *Highland Heritage*, is an illuminating study of clan societies and other manifestations of Scottishness in the American South. Ray is an anthropologist who comes originally from North Carolina and who went to Edinburgh in 1990 to study the archaeology of Europe's Iron Age. While in Scotland, this visiting academic became used to overhearing condescending comments about heritage tourists from the United States. However, it was not until she went home that it occurred to her that she might accidentally have come across a research topic with greater potential than the Iron Age. 'When I returned from Edinburgh to North Carolina,' Celeste Ray explains, 'I began attending Scottish-related events. I went to the dances and the Highland Games simply because I was missing Scotland and the Scots, and I was surprised to meet people there who had never been to Scotland yet "missed" it too. They spoke often and with empathy of the nostalgia and homesickness felt by their Scottish immigrant ancestors. I was struck by their strong transnational identification and sense of place nine or more generations removed from the immigration experience. I began to wonder if my Scottish friends were perhaps too quick to assume insincerity in Americans' search for heritage . . . My research interests turned from Celtic hill forts to the North Carolinian settlement sites of . . . Scottish immigrants – only to shift again when descendants of those immigrants introduced me to their genealogical and community lore and had little trouble convincing me that their persisting ethnic identity was . . . far more intriguing than house foundations of any period.'[8]

From a Scottish standpoint, perhaps the single most mystifying feature of the 'persisting ethnic identity' which Celeste Ray goes on to analyse is the extent to which, since the mid-twentieth century, it has treated clan chiefs as celebrities. Rowland T. Berthoff, an American historian who, like Celeste Ray, spent time in Edinburgh, was dismissive of this. 'The rising tide of American clan fervour has . . . refloated some long-stranded vessels in Scotland,' Berthoff wrote in 1982. 'A number of Scottish country gentlemen and London businessmen, some of them otherwise rather obscure, who happen to hold the nominal headship of long since scattered Highland clans and Lowland families, have been restored to unquestioning adulation on the circuit of American . . . clan banquets.' Understandably, cynicism of the Berthoff variety does not play well in diaspora circles. Older members of Clan MacLeod Societies, when sharing with me their memories of Flora MacLeod, are universally admiring of her and say over and over again that she provided them with links to Scotland they would not otherwise have possessed. When discussing the impact of Flora's trip to St Ann's with Allister MacLeod from Ingonish, I ask if it ever seemed odd to him or to Cape Bretoners more generally that the Canadian descendants of people thrown out of their homes by Scotland's nineteenth-century landlords should make so much fuss of one of those landlords' twentieth-century successors? Allister is well equipped to answer this question, one of his relatives having hosted Flora MacLeod in 1947, and he thinks before replying. 'What we knew of the Highland Clearances we knew from books,' Allister says. 'Our ancestors might have experienced eviction [as Allister's, in fact, did] but nothing of this had come down to us. There was no discussion of it. When Dame Flora came to Cape Breton Island and was treated like royalty, that was simply because, to people like us, she was the head of our family and a very lovely lady.'[9]

Today, the Associated Clan MacLeod Societies recognise two chiefs. One, John MacLeod, Dame Flora's grandson and successor lives in Dunvegan Castle. The other, Donald MacLeod, lives in Tasmania. Donald, an electrical engineer by profession, is the great-great-grandson of Raasay's last MacLeod laird who, as mentioned earlier, emigrated to Australia in 1846. In 1988, the Scottish authorities which deal with those matters recognised Donald's late father as chief of the MacLeods of Lewis – the Sìol Thorcuil of medieval times and the grouping to which Raasay's MacLeod lairds belonged. Donald MacLeod has inherited his father's position, while his younger brother John, a marketing manager with a Tasmanian agricultural supplies company, is formally MacLeod of Raasay. Both men, when I meet with them, decline to make much of their titles. However, both are active participants in clan society affairs, Donald appearing from time to time at clan gatherings alongside his Dunvegan, or Sìol Thormoid, counterpart.

At such gatherings, much use is made of a word Allister MacLeod from Ingonish employs when talking of Dame Flora. This word is *family*, and it was used repeatedly by Flora MacLeod herself. Whatever Clan MacLeod may have been, she maintained, it had become a worldwide family whose members, irrespective of their nationality, were to remember that Dunvegan Castle, where they would always be welcome, was their home as well as hers. This is a powerful message – one that speaks strongly to people looking, as many are, for ways of restoring some communality or rootedness to a society characterised increasingly by its tendency to isolate and make anonymous its component human beings.

Benedict Anderson, an influential theorist of nationalism, famously defined the nation as 'an imagined political community'. 'It is *imagined*,' Anderson went on, 'because the members of even the smallest nation will never know most of their fellow members, meet them or even hear of them, yet in the minds of each lives the image of their communion.' Clans, as nowadays conceived by clan society members, are also imagined communities. But they are smaller and more intimate than nations; and unlike nations, as Flora MacLeod stressed, they are not geographically confined.[10]

An American, as Benedict Anderson pointed out, believes his American-ness links him with millions of other Americans. If the same person is a member of Clan MacLeod USA, he also considers himself to have clanship ties with lots of non-American MacLeods. It follows that the Associated Clan MacLeod Societies, though they can be seen as a rejection of globalisation's tendency to make everyone and everywhere the same, are also a manifestation of globalisation's capacity to facilitate the emergence of new forms of human association. The MacLeod clan parliaments which Dame Flora inaugurated at Dunvegan in 1956, and which have been held regularly ever since, could not happen if it were not now possible to get easily to Scotland from other countries. Nor would ACMS's future be so assured in the absence of the worldwide web, where Clan MacLeod, a localised tribe transformed into a transnational collective, increasingly transacts its business.

Clan MacLeod Magazine, a twice-yearly publication which helps ACMS members keep in touch, rarely contains anything controversial. In 1976, however, the magazine carried a letter from Gregory MacLeod, a Cape Bretoner, who wanted to hear less from men 'concerned about the correct length of their kilts' and more from people interested in 'traditional cultural and community values'. Internet-based clanship has helped grant this wish. While tartanry of the type to which Gregory MacLeod took exception is to be found in large measure on Clan MacLeod websites, it is beginning to be overshadowed there by MacLeod genealogy. Like the expansion of clan societies, the current growth of interest in family history may be bound up psychologically with people's need for greater interconnectedness than modern lifestyles generally permit. In relation to the Highlands and Islands diaspora, however, the particular significance of its genealogical obsessions lies in the way those obsessions connect clanship as now practised internationally with clanship as it existed in the north of Scotland several hundred years ago.[11]

'*Cuimhnich air na daoine bhon tànaig thu*,' advises a Gaelic proverb: 'Remember the men from whom you descend.' Doing this was essential in the pre-Culloden Highlands and Islands, where, as emphasised earlier, a person's rank and status depended on that person's lineage. But even when clanship of the Highlands and Islands variety fell apart and people's social position no longer depended on who their forebears were, an astonishingly detailed knowledge of those forebears persisted, not least among emigrant populations. 'Without the aid of any documents,' Charles Dunn observed, 'many a third and fourth generation descendant in Nova Scotia who visited Scotland during the First or the Second World War was able to trace out his remotest relations. It is not uncommon in Cape Breton to find those who can name their father, grandfather and great-grandfather, all of whom were perhaps born on this [Canadian] side of the Atlantic, and their great-great-, great-great-great-, and great-great-great-great-grandfathers, who were born in Scotland.' This book could not have been written but for the willingness of Clan MacLeod society members to share information of this sort with me. Listening to them as they spoke of men and women who lived and died in the eighteenth and nineteenth centuries, it was tempting to sense the survival into modern times of a cast of mind which Anne Grant, an early and perceptive analyst of Highlands and Islands society, described thus in 1811: 'No Highlander ever once thought of himself as an individual . . . He considered himself . . . with reference to those who had gone before, and those who were to come after him.'[12]

Victoria, Ontario, Scotland, England, California, Washington State and British Columbia

In Bendigo, Victoria, Harold MacLeod unrolls the family tree on which he has worked for more than twenty years. It is sixteen feet long and the raw material on which it is based, Harold tells me, occupies thirty-four box files. In Guelph, Ontario, Irene MacCrimmon, whose late husband's ancestors were hereditary pipers to the MacLeods of Dunvegan, shows me the hundreds of genealogies she has collected from Canadian MacLeods. Everywhere in the world of clan societies one finds the same consuming interest in roots, beginnings, origins. This is most in evidence abroad, but it is true nearer home as well.

The world's first Clan MacLeod Societies were formed in Glasgow and Edinburgh in or about 1890. The Glasgow society did not last long, but its Edinburgh counterpart has survived. Stella Henderson, a member for more than half a century, shows me a scrapbook which gives an insight into how the society functioned during the 1930s. Then its president was Sir John Lorne MacLeod, also Edinburgh's provost or mayor, and the society, as it had been since its inception, was conducted on a very formal basis.

This is no longer the case. Today's Clan Macleod Society of Scotland has no direct line to Edinburgh's business and political elite, nor does it stage balls and other grand occasions as once it did. Members meet in a church hall and, like their counterparts elsewhere, they come from a wide cross section of social backgrounds. Also like clan society members universally, they know – or are trying to establish – precisely how their families came to be where they now are. John Davidson Kelly's MacLeod connection derives, by way of his mother, from the MacLeods of Suardal, Skye tacksmen whose other descendants have included George MacLeod, churchman, Christian Socialist, pacifist and founder of the Iona Community. Brian MacLeod descends from a long line of MacLeod soldiers whose ultimate origins he is still trying to trace. Donald MacLeod is looking for a Highlands and Islands starting point for a family whose nineteenth-century forebears were farm labourers or millers in Fife. Mary King outlines a MacLeod ancestry which begins in Sutherland and which, I realise, includes Murdo MacLeod, the Elphin lay preacher I heard about from his Dunedin great-great-grandson, Donald Warrington. 'Murdo had two sons who emigrated to New Zealand,' Mary says, 'but what became of them I've no idea.' I can help remedy that, I tell her.

Analogous linkages emerge when I meet with members of the Clan MacLeod Society of England. Ewan MacLeod's family tree, like that of John Davidson Kelly in Scotland, begins with the Suardal MacLeods, whose remote progenitors were armourers to the MacLeods of Dunvegan. Iain Breac MacLeod descends from Skye and Harris tacksmen whose children or grandchildren included Donald MacLeod, one of the British officers killed at the Battle of Moore's Creek Bridge, and Alexander MacLeod, the early-nineteenth-century New York clergyman who was prominent in anti-slavery circles. One of Rev. Alexander's cousins was John MacLeod, born in Skye in 1784. Having first served as a doctor with the East India Company, this man became surgeon-general of Madras. Iain Breac is his great-great-grandson.[13]

Some members of England's Clan MacLeod Society belong to families whose founders came directly south from Scotland. John MacLeod is in this category – his ancestors, who went on to become brewers in London, having moved to Tyneside in the eighteenth century. James Donald McCrimmon's story contains more twists and turns. It begins with his great-great-grandfather's emigration from Skye to Canada in 1844. 'My father was the 1844 emigrant's great-grandson,' James continues. 'He was an ice-hockey star known as Silver McCrimmon, and in 1915 he moved from Canada to the United States. There my father took out US citizenship, but after he died in 1934 my mother, who was English, came home and took me with her. So

I'm an Englishman who owes his Scottish name to an American father who was born a Canadian.'

Bunty McLeod joined England's Clan MacLeod Society with her late husband, David McLeod, who was the grandson, Bunty says, of an Australian emigrant to Latin America. In the early nineteenth century, she explains, her husband's great-great-grandfather, Roderick McLeod, left Skye for Angus on the Scottish mainland. In time, Roderick's grandson, Alan McLeod, emigrated from Scotland to Australia. There, Alan became an active trade unionist. In 1893, when William Lane, another labour activist, quit Australia for Paraguay with the intention of founding a colony where everyone would 'labour on the common ground for the common good', Alan McLeod joined him. Like most such projects, Lane's venture did not turn out as planned. However, it lasted long enough for David McLeod, Alan's grandson and Bunty McLeod's late husband, to have spent his early years in a Paraguayan log cabin.[14]

David McLeod came to England from South America. Norman MacLeod, with whom I spend a morning in San Francisco, emigrated to California from England in 1965. Norman is a lawyer. He is also the great-grandson of *Dòmhnull nan Òran*, Donald of the Songs, whose begging letter to Emily MacLeod of Dunvegan was quoted in the course of my account of nineteenth-century Skye's famine years. Donald's son Neil, Norman's grandfather, was another Gaelic poet and songmaker who quit the Glendale area, where he grew up, for Edinburgh. There Neil MacLeod became a sales representative in a tea firm run by a cousin, and there he composed verses which are still known in the Gaelic-speaking Highlands and Islands. One of Neil MacLeod's productions, dating from the 1880s and entitled *Na Croitearan Sgiathanach*, the Skye Crofters, is a celebration of the attack launched on the island's lairds by the Highland Land League. In this composition, Neil MacLeod looks forward to the destruction of 'the arrogant landlords' whose former clansfolk had been 'tossed off the land'. When the crofting cause triumphs as it surely will, Neil writes, '*Thèid crìoch air gach fòirneart*': 'All oppression will crumble.'[15]

Neil MacLeod's son, another Neil and my Californian informant's father, was a doctor in Yorkshire. Shortly after the Second World War, he was murdered by a soldier to whom he had given a lift in his car – with the result that Norman, the murder victim's son, grew up with little knowledge of his Scottish ancestry. 'In 1979,' Norman MacLeod tells me in the San Francisco coffee shop where we have breakfast, 'I went to Skye to see if I could find any trace of the house where my grandfather was born. In Glendale, I was directed to the home of a local man, then in his nineties, who knew my grandfather. Meeting with this man – something I found very moving –

gave me one of the few glimpses I've had into the Gaelic-speaking world my family left behind. My life has been so different from the lives lived by my forebears.'

Moving on from San Francisco to Seattle, I meet with Steve Thomas, whose MacLeod great-grandfather emigrated to Portland, Oregon, from the Wester Ross township of Laide in the 1880s. This makes Steve's family history comparatively straightforward – most of the people I encounter in the Seattle area being products of more complicated, and often generations-long, migratory journeys. Margaret van Nus's McLeod ancestors emigrated from Skye to Ontario in the 1830s. Thomas McLeod Bremerton's Scottish forebears began farming in New Brunswick's Miramichi Valley in the early nineteenth century. Cy Cook's great-grandfather, Robert McLeod, came from Glasgow to New York in the mid-nineteenth century. Then he emigrated twice more, first to South Africa and next to Australia, before returning to the US, where, after settling briefly in Vermont, he made three further moves – to Missouri, Colorado and Kansas.

The Clan MacLeod Society get-together which is organised for my benefit in Vancouver demonstrates that British Columbia too was often the end point of continent-spanning migrations. Neil McLeod's emigrant ancestors came to Cape Breton, probably from the island of Pabbay near Harris, in the 1830s. Ian MacLeod's Lewis forebears also settled in Cape Breton – in the vicinity, as it happens, of St Ann's. Ann Bryant and Bob MacLeod descend from Raasay people who emigrated to Prince Edward Island. Ray MacLeod knows that his family were in Nova Scotia or New Brunswick as far back as the eighteenth century – having moved there, he suspects, from the United States at the close of the Revolutionary War.

Elizabeth Louise Rivera, her husband José and their four small children are late for my date with Vancouver's Clan MacLeod Society because Vancouver is a hundred miles from their home in Chilliwack. José is himself an emigrant – having left Guatemala for the United States with his parents when he was six and having subsequently moved from the US into Canada. Elizabeth is a seventh-generation Canadian, whose surname before her marriage was McLeod. Her emigrant great-great-great-grandparents, she tells me, were Alexander and Christina McLeod, who arrived in Ontario from the Harris township of Kyles Stockinish in 1863. Elizabeth Rivera has put a lot of effort into establishing those facts – questioning her older relatives back in Ontario, spending many hours on the Internet, even contacting people in Scotland. What is it, I ask, that motivates a busy twenty-six-year-old woman with a big family to take such an interest in her ancestry? 'I want to be able to teach our children about their background,' Elizabeth says. 'It would be good if José was able to speak with them in Spanish. It would be good if I could talk with them in Gaelic. Gaelic was my family's language. Your language makes you who you are, and it's upsetting to me that we were robbed of it.' Acting on those convictions, Elizabeth Rivera has contacted Sabhal Mòr Ostaig, Skye's Gaelic College, to explore her chances of embarking on a distance-learning course in Gaelic. She is also committed to visiting Harris. 'One of my most important goals is to see where Alexander and Christina lived before they came to Canada,' Elizabeth comments.

As stressed previously, this wish to set foot in the place that was home to one's emigrant forebears is characteristic of the Highlands and Islands diaspora. When Elizabeth Louise Rivera speaks of Kyles Stockinish, I am reminded of Don MacLeod telling me in Omakau, New Zealand, of his lifelong regret that his war wound took away his one opportunity to get to Achiltibuie; reminded too of Graeme McLeod talking passionately of the trips he made from his home in Allansford, Victoria, to Raasay; reminded, above all, of the similar pilgrimage described in Alastair MacLeod's novel, *No Great Mischief.* 'You are from here,' Alastair's fictional creation, Catriona MacDonald, is informed when she travels to the West Highland locality which her great-great-great-grandparents left in the eighteenth century. 'No,' Catriona says, 'I'm from Canada.' 'That may be,' she is told. 'But you are really from here. You have just been away for a while.'[16]

'From way back,' Alastair MacLeod said when we met in Ontario, 'Scots outside Scotland wanted to visit the Old Country. But there was no chance of significant numbers of them doing so until the First World War came along. The fighting in France took hundreds of thousands of young men from Canada and other countries to Europe. For the first time, people whose family origins were in the Highlands and Islands were able to return.'

One of them was William Angus McLeod, a Texan chaplain who crossed the Atlantic on a troopship in the summer of 1918. William Angus, whose great-grandfather emigrated from Skye to the Cape Fear River country, did not take kindly to the ocean. He was seasick; he slept badly; he feared, with justification, that his ship might fall victim to German submarines. On 4 September, however, William Angus McLeod's morale improved for reasons he set out that evening in a letter to his wife, Mattie: 'This has been to me a truly wonderful day . . . To begin with, I slept soundly last night, owing to the presence of our increased escort, a number of British destroyers. But quite early I was awake and soon I heard a soldier's voice call out, "Come on boys, here's land!" . . . And what was more, this first foreign land I ever laid eyes on was none other than Bonny Scotland. I was almost overcome by my emotions and wondered long if it were not, after all, a dream. But there it was; great old hills . . . planted here and there with farms. In fancy I saw, more than a century ago, the old sailboat with prow headed in the opposite direction from the way we were going – towards the west. And on board, leaning far over the sides with tears streaming down weather-beaten cheeks, my own forefathers, straining to see as long as they could a bit of their homeland. After a century or more, a son of theirs greets these same old hills . . . It was a sight I shall never forget, but shall retain the recollection of as a treasure above all price. *I have seen Scotland!'*[17]

In February 1919, the war now over, William Angus McLeod travelled to Skye. 'I found a good many Canadians, Australians and New Zealanders . . . on much the same mission,' he reported. Those young men were acting on their own initiative, but later the urge to make such trips was encouraged by Flora MacLeod. In 1937, to mark King George VI's coronation, Flora invited her clansfolk, wherever they might be, to visit Dunvegan Castle. A number of overseas MacLeods took up this offer, among them Jerzy Machlejd who was to die at Katyn.

In 1939, the Second World War began. During the war, Flora MacLeod made it known that any British Commonwealth or American serviceman called MacLeod would be welcome at Dunvegan Castle when on leave – there being no way such a serviceman, if stationed in the United Kingdom, could go home. 'My trip to Skye and my visit to the castle,' a Canadian soldier recorded at the time, 'was, without a doubt, the grandest experience of my life . . . I wrote mother a twelve-page letter telling her of my trip.' While at Dunvegan, a New Zealander commented, he felt he was with his 'own people' – 'even though in a different country and thousands of miles from home'.[18]

Just before the Second World War, about half of the Clan MacLeod Society of Scotland's 500 or so members lived overseas. This was an early indication of diaspora interest in clanship. So were developments like the launch in 1936 of a Clan MacLeod Society in Glengarry County, Ontario. When Dame Flora MacLeod set out to foster the emergence of more such groupings, then, she had something to build on. She also had assistance from ex-servicemen to whom she had offered hospitality between 1939 and 1945. One of them was Norman Macleod, a Canadian. 'My father spent three of his wartime furloughs at Dunvegan,' I am told in Toronto by Norman's son Colin.

Norman Macleod helped establish a network of clan societies across Canada. His son's commitment to those societies has been unwavering for over fifty years. Now this same commitment is evident in Colin's daughter Karen, a schoolteacher. She is president of her local Clan MacLeod Society and in collaboration with another young woman, Emma Halford MacLeod from Scotland, she edits *Clan MacLeod Magazine*. When a student, Karen Macleod spent a year at Edinburgh University, where she studied Scottish history and managed to vote – 'on the winning side,' she says – in the 1997 referendum which led to Scots regaining self-government. 'Who you are and where you come from are things that matter greatly,' Karen Macleod insists.

This philosophy is shared by Jim McLeod, a college teacher I talk with in his home on Whidbey Island, north of Seattle. Jim was raised in Spokane, near Washington State's boundary with the Idaho panhandle which separates Washington State from Montana. 'My dad was orphaned when he was a child,' Jim McLeod says, 'so I had no contact with grandparents and no real sense of where our family started out from. I'd heard we were descended from a Norman McLeod who emigrated from Portree to Prince Edward Island in the early nineteenth century, but that was all I'd heard.'

In 1969, Jim McLeod visited Skye. On a wet and stormy day and on a single-track road, he crashed his rented car and, waiting for it to be repaired, booked into a bed-and-breakfast establishment in Portree. Among his fellow guests were a McLeod couple from Australia who, chancing to meet Dame Flora while visiting Dunvegan Castle, mentioned Jim's mishap. That evening, Jim McLeod was contacted by Flora and invited to move to the castle – which he did. Quizzed by his hostess about his background, Jim provided the few facts he knew, while deciding, there and then, to find out more.

The obvious place to start was Prince Edward Island, where Jim McLeod next headed. In P.E.I., he was put in touch with relatives he had not known of. With their help, a family history began to be pieced together. Soon Jim learned that Alexander McLeod, the grandfather he had never met, moved from the P.E.I. community of High Bank to Montana in 1906. Alexander's father, it transpired, was a High Bank farmer named Donald McLeod – Donald's father being Norman McLeod, or *Tormod Bàn* as he was called in Gaelic, who came to Prince Edward Island from Scotland in 1830. Tormod Bàn, as Jim McLeod had been informed, did indeed sail from Portree. But before that he lived in the Raasay township of Eyre with his wife, Margaret, a granddaughter of one of the island's eighteenth-century tacksmen, Malcolm MacLeod of Brae. 'I've been to Eyre several times,' Jim says. 'I don't know which of its piles of stones was my great-great-grandparents' home. What I do know is that Raasay is important to me. It's part of my identity.'

What Raasay means to Jim McLeod, Lewis means to Penny McLeod DeGraff, who lives in Seattle. Penny combines a commitment to Clan MacLeod with an equal commitment to Gaelic. Both enthusiasms stem from Penny DeGraff's discovery of her Hebridean roots – a discovery resulting from enquiries made by Peggy's late aunt, Jean McLeod, who lived in California. 'My aunt was aware that our McLeod ancestors had emigrated from Lewis to Canada in 1863,' Penny says. 'She tried for years to establish where exactly our people came from. In 1989, she succeeded.'

This was when Jean McLeod sent a letter to a Lewisman who, she had been told, might be one of her kinsfolk. 'Dear Jean,' this man wrote in response, 'what a surprise to hear from a long-lost relative. It is amazing and somehow sad that we can go through life and not know of each other's existence . . . We [meaning both the writer and his Californian correspondent] are descendants of Murdo Macleod and Mary Murray, who spent most of their married life at Glen House [*Taigh a' Ghlinne*], some three miles from the village of Barvas . . . For generations their descendants were known as People of the Glen [*Muinntir a' Ghlinne*], and indeed, Jean, you have every right to identify yourself as one of them. It is a title you can bear with pride because you come from fine people.'

The Murdo and Mary mentioned in this 1989 letter were Penny McLeod DeGraff's great-great-grandparents. Their home was an inn or hostelry on the Barvas–Stornoway road. The building has long since disappeared, but its remnants can still be seen. Murdo lived here until his death – Mary, his widow, moving to nearby Barvas before emigrating to Bruce County, Ontario, with two of her six children, Donald and Neil.

Neil McLeod was Penny DeGraff's great-grandfather. In Bruce County, Neil, still a teenager when he got there, married Jessie Smith, whose parents, also emigrants from Lewis, had moved to Bruce County from Cape Breton. In 1878, taking with them their four-year-old son, John, and Neil's now elderly mother, Mary, Neil and Jessie left Bruce County for Winnipeg. Their aim was to farm in Manitoba, but the land then available there was not to Neil's liking. In 1882, therefore, the family moved south to the US, and homesteaded near Milton on the North Dakota prairie. This was where Mary McLeod, once of Glen House, Barvas, spent her last years; this was where John McLeod, Mary's grandson and Penny DeGraff's grandfather, was brought up; this, in turn, was where John married and raised ten children of his own. One of those children was Penny's father, Neil McLeod; another was her Aunt Jean. 'My dad had no great interest in his ancestry,' Penny De Graff says. 'Aunt Jean was fascinated by it. When she finally managed to get in touch with our Lewis relatives, she was eighty-nine and too old to travel. But she lived for another eight years and, before her death, I was able to sing Aunt Jean a Gaelic song I'd learned in Lewis. That meant a great deal to her.'

Penny and her husband, Dale DeGraff, made the first of several journeys to Lewis in 1990. There they were warmly received by several of Penny's third cousins – with whom Penny has since kept in close contact. 'Until I went to Lewis, I scarcely knew Gaelic existed,' Penny McLeod DeGraff tells me. 'Whenever I heard it spoken, I knew I had to speak it too.' Now she does – not fluently, Penny insists, but competently enough to make herself understood by Gaelic speakers and to be able to understand most of what they say to her. Today Penny DeGraff listens to BBC Scotland's Gaelic broadcasts on the worldwide web; she helps organise *Fèis Shiàtail*, Seattle's regular Gaelic festival; and she sings with the Gaelic musical groups she and some like-minded friends have established. With one of those groups, Penny travelled in 2001 to Scotland's National Mod, held that year in Stornoway. There this American McLeod and her Seattle colleagues came first in a mod competition – one requiring a traditional rendition of the so-called waulking songs which Lewis women sang when making tweed. While in Stornoway, Penny McLeod DeGraff, as she had done before, went to stand on the spot once occupied by her great-great-grandparents' home. 'It's so good just to be there,' she says.

Scotland: Lewis and Skye

On 21 April 1923, 260 people, more than fifty of them named MacLeod, left Stornoway for the St Lawrence on a liner called the *Metagama*. This was one of the biggest groups to quit Lewis since the sailing of the *Friendship* for Philadelphia in 1774. Newspapers accordingly carried grainy, black-and-white photographs of the departing emigrants. Those photographs inspired a Lewis-born poet, Iain Crichton Smith, to write:

> Your faces cheerful though impoverished,
> you stand at the rail, tall-collared and flat-capped . . .
> What are you leaving now? –
> The calm routine of winding chimney smoke,
> the settled village with its small sparse fields,
> the ceilidhs and the narratives. Deceived
> by chiefs and lairds, by golden promises,
> you set off, smiling towards a new world,
> Canada with its Douglas firs and snow,
> the miles of desolate emptiness.[19]

'Why do I weep,' Crichton Smith asks as he inspects a *Metagama* photograph, 'to see these faces, thin and obsolete?' There is anger in this question. Partly that anger was fuelled by what Smith heard of the generalised experience of Hebridean emigrants to 1920s Canada – people caught up often in the horrors of the Dirty Thirties. What gave Crichton Smith's poem its cutting edge, however, was the fact of his knowing a 1920s emigrant who was also his uncle: 'My uncle worked building railways, and sometimes did not work at all, and slept in dosshouses where shoes had to be nailed to the floor lest they be stolen during the night. His underwear, like that of his friends, was at last in rags. Many of them died of drink, others starved. He was lucky, eventually reaching Vancouver where he became a fire officer . . . Latterly he would fly to Lewis, even at 80 years of age, and every week read the *Stornoway Gazette* which he had sent to him from home. When I saw him, and later . . . when in Australia I heard of Highland exiles who had drifted into hopelessness and alcohol, I was angered by the waste, the dreadful waste, of our island humanity . . . It is not right that a whole culture should have been treated in this way.'[20]

Most of the people I meet during my travels among Clan MacLeod have no regrets about their own, or more usually their forebears', emigration. Yes, they wish to retain or recover something of their Scottish heritage. But they are generally doing well; they are comfortable with, indeed proud of, being Americans, Canadians, Australians, South Africans, New Zealanders. Those folk, then, find it hard to think about emigration other than positively. The same is true of the nations which emigrants from Scotland joined. From the perspective of countries like Australia or the US, the arrival of thousands of men, women and children from the Highlands and Islands constituted a huge gain in human capital. But from a Scottish standpoint, the opposite is true. To us, the people who left represent a great loss. This is why emigration's dark side, as Iain Crichton Smith recognised, is not simply a matter of Lewismen yielding to booze and despair in the icebound streets of prairie cities. What will forever make emigration problematic, as far as Scots remaining in Scotland are concerned, is its unremittingly negative impact on the communities our hundreds of thousands of emigrants left behind.

Recalling the day the *Metagama* pulled away from Lewis to the sound of a vast crowd of well-wishers singing the Hundredth Psalm in Gaelic, Sheila MacLeod, a Lewis woman, wrote: 'Some consequences were immediate: the sense of loss felt by those returning from their farewells in the town [of Stornoway] to the village homes bereft of a son or brother. Other results were slower to make themselves felt: the marriages that would not take place, the children that would not now be reared in Lewis, the homes that would not be built, the land that would not be tilled. For of [those] who sailed that day, all but 20 were young men, young men on the threshold of maturity. Their average age was 22.'[21]

To think about our Highlands and Islands exodus in the places where it began is always to reflect on the possibilities this exodus denied to communities where, if anything, the rate of emigration accelerated as the twentieth century got underway. In many parts of the Highlands and Islands, between 1931 and 1951, the population fell by between 20 and 25 per cent. 'A decrease of population, however small, is usually a matter for concern,' the authors of a 1955 study commented. But when the loss amounted to 'a quarter or a fifth in the short space of 20 years', it could legitimately be reckoned 'grave indeed'. The township of Clashnessie in Assynt served as an example of what was going on more generally. 'In 1910,' it was reported in 1952, 'there were 138 people in Clashnessie; now there are only 20. The youngest "boy" is 28 and the youngest "girl" will not see 45 again.'[22]

For much of the twentieth century, then, there was every reason to be pessimistic about the Highlands and Islands. Presently, however, there is cause for optimism, not least in the success story that is Skye. By the 1960s, Skye's population, which reached 24,000 in the early 1840s, had fallen to just above 6,000, and the downward trend seemed set to continue. Hearteningly, the opposite has happened. Skye, at the start of the twenty-first century, has thousands of new residents and contains hundreds of new homes. The island's total population is up by more than 40 per cent on its low point. At Sabhal Mòr Ostaig, soon to be a component part of the emerging University of the Highlands and Islands, students occupy an architecturally spectacular campus and take degree courses taught in Gaelic. A diversifying and growing economy, which includes a number of high-tech businesses, is sustaining a wide range of previously missing facilities. Among those is the Three Chimneys restaurant, at Colbost near Dunvegan, which in 2002 an international panel of food writers placed twenty-eighth on a list of the top fifty restaurants in the world.

By no means everywhere is doing as well as Skye. Lewis and Harris, for instance, continue to lose population. Nevertheless, the Highlands and Islands as a whole have experienced 20 per cent population growth since the 1960s. During this period, the part of northern Scotland administered by Highland Council, an area comprising much of the mainland as well as inshore islands like Skye, has gained no fewer than 50,000 people. For ages, this same area, like the north of Scotland overall, was characterised by a complete absence of job opportunity and by the high unemployment rates which underpinned the longstanding Highlands and Islands belief that prosperity could be got only elsewhere. More recently, in contrast, Highlands and Islands unemployment rates have stood at 3 per cent or less – with many employers reliant on workers recruited in countries like Poland, Latvia and Croatia. Today, for the first time in several centuries, more people are coming to the Highlands and Islands than are going away.

There is reason to expect inward migration of this sort to continue. Across the modern world, new communications technologies are enabling the emergence of a more dispersed pattern of economic activity than the one familiar to us since the industrial revolution of the eighteenth and nineteenth centuries. Age-old barriers of distance and remoteness – barriers which the Highlands and Islands once found insurmountable – are starting to break down. Internationally, leading companies are increasingly located in places where their owners and workforces can simultaneously earn a good living and have access to natural environments of the highest quality. Hence the attraction of North American regions like Colorado or British Columbia. Hence our growing conviction in Scotland that, where those North American localities have led, the Highlands and Islands, one of Europe's most attractive areas, can aspire to follow.

But if much has changed and is changing in the Highlands and Islands, some things remain the same. At Dunvegan Castle, John MacLeod confronts problems of a type familiar to his ancestors. He does so without the financial cushion available to his grandmother and predecessor, Dame Flora. Her father, a successful businessman, left his daughter well provided for. Even Flora, however, found it hard to invest adequately in the repair and maintenance of Dunvegan Castle. When John MacLeod took charge of his inheritance, it was consequently apparent to him that some means had to be found of generating the cash which, sooner or later, would have to be poured into Dunvegan Castle if it were not to go the way of most such buildings and become uninhabitable. This was why Dunvegan Castle was turned into a tourist attraction. But though visitor numbers at Dunvegan peaked at over 140,000 annually, and though lots of tourism-related jobs were created, sums of the kind required if the castle was to be renovated properly remained as unobtainable as ever. In the spring of 2000, therefore, John MacLeod did what many of his forebears had done when they wanted to raise capital. He put land up for sale, placing the Cuillin on the market at an asking price of £10 million.

Ten or twenty years before, the planned disposal of the Cuillin might have proceeded without challenge. But in 1999, Scotland, although remaining in the United Kingdom, had acquired for the first time since 1707 its own parliament and government. This government was committed to land reform. In those circumstances, neither politicians nor the wider public, whether in Skye or beyond, were supportive of the idea that Scotland's most iconic mountain range should simply be sold to the highest bidder. A great deal of controversy was generated, no offers were received for the Cuillin and, in the summer of 2003, a different approach was duly adopted. The Cuillin, it was announced, would be gifted to the Scottish people and ownership of Dunvegan Castle would be transferred from John MacLeod to an appropriate trust – on the understanding that public agencies, in advance of the Cuillin deal going ahead, would help finance the castle trust and thus allow it to keep the castle functioning. Predictably, none of this proved easy. In the summer of 2004, architectural consultants reported that the bill for putting Dunvegan Castle and its associated tourism enterprise on a sound footing would be in the region of £20 million. Finance on that scale, it was obvious, would be impossible to obtain from public sources. There, as of this writing, the matter rests.*

Although the Cuillin's fate is undecided, other territories associated with Clan MacLeod continue to change hands – but in the direction now of the people living on them. This process began in 1904 when Glendale was bought by the British government and made over to the locality's inhabitants. In the Glendale case, both existing crofts and the new smallholdings created on former sheep farms were sold to their occupiers. But when, about twenty years later, Stornoway parish was acquired by its residents, a new model emerged – the parish, extending to 70,000 acres, becoming the collective property of the people whose homes were within its boundaries. The elected body set up to administer the community-owned estate which thus took shape was named the Stornoway Trust. It still survives. For much of the twentieth century, however, it seemed likely to remain a curious exception to the Highlands and Islands norm – most people taking it for granted that the overwhelming bulk of the region's land resource would for ever remain in the ownership of a tiny number of mostly absentee lairds.

This expectation was shattered in June 1992, when the Swedish property company which owned the North Assynt estate advertised the property for sale, and when local crofters, in a then unprecedented move, decided to make a joint bid for it. 'My grandfather was cleared, you've got to do this,' Assynt's crofters were informed by one of the many people – from elsewhere in Scotland and from further afield – who contributed a total of £130,000 to their fighting fund. With this fund's help, North Assynt, long part of Clan MacLeod's heartland, was formally acquired by a crofting trust in February 1993. As a result, community control began to seem feasible in other places. Assisted by the new Scottish government's commitment to land reform, and by grants and loans from public sources, whole islands like Eigg and Gigha, together with a series of large estates elsewhere in the Hebrides and on the Highland mainland, took the community ownership route. In the area once dominated by Clan MacLeod, Stornoway parish and North Assynt, the twin pioneers of community ownership, were joined by Lewis's 1,700-acre Bhaltos estate as well as by the 55,000-acre North Harris estate, one of Scotland's biggest rural properties. As of this writing,

---

* Here, I should declare an interest. From 1998 until 2004, I chaired Highlands and Islands Enterprise, one of the organisations involved in those developments.

moreover, further community ownership bids have just succeeded, or are under consideration, in several parts of Lewis, on an additional estate in Assynt and on the Orbost estate in Skye.[23]

The case for community ownership does not rest on emotion. It is founded on the fact that self-confidence is boosted and all sorts of enterprise unleashed when formerly dependent populations take charge of their own destinies. In the present context, however, one piece of sentiment may be allowed. As mentioned more than once already, people in the Highlands and Islands were traditionally of the view that, during clanship's heyday, land belonged to the generality of clansfolk, not just to clan chiefs. Community ownership can be interpreted as a restoration of this position. It might be appropriate, therefore, if overseas clan societies, when looking for symbols with which to identify in Scotland, did not confine themselves to castles. While a medieval stronghold can certainly be seen as an embodiment of what clanship stood for, so can clan lands now in the ownership of people to whom those lands are home.

New Zealand and Scotland: Auckland, Dunvegan and Orbost

The thousands of people who have settled recently in the Highlands and Islands do not include many returning members of the area's overseas diaspora. This is unsurprising. As underlined at the outset, Canadians, Americans, Australians and others of Highlands and Islands extraction may look to their Highlands and Islands origins for some sense of who they are; they may be anxious, as this book has stressed, to visit the Highlands and Islands; but they have no desire, for the most part, to come and live here. 'When I beheld that old land my heart was thrilled,' William Angus McLeod wrote at the end of his 1919 trip to Skye. 'I love every vale and hilltop in Skye. I love her landscapes and prize her dauntless people. They are my people and for real worth I will match them with any other people on God's green earth. But I breathed a silent prayer of thanksgiving . . . for a benign providence that sent our race over the seas, so making it possible for us to be Americans.'[24]

In Auckland, I spend an evening with John and Cathy Macleod. Both are members of the city's Clan MacLeod Society and both come originally from Lewis, John having grown up in Back, Cathy in Point. She emigrated here with her parents in 1958, Cathy says, and she has loved the place ever since. Not long after her arrival, Cathy goes on, she went back to Britain to train as a teacher and there, in London, she met and married John, who had come south to work as a joiner and shopfitter. In 1964, at Cathy's prompting, the couple left London for New Zealand. They have been in Lewis only

AWAY FOR A WHILE

twice since then, John tells me, their second trip preceding my meeting with them by just two or three months. 'One of my Lewis nephews came to see us off on the ferry,' John says of this trip's conclusion. 'I'd made clear to him that I'm getting old and that I'll take no more flights to Scotland. As we were saying our goodbyes on the pier, my nephew, speaking about the long journey ahead of Cathy and myself, suggested we'd spend much of this journey thinking about Lewis. "You're bound to feel homesick," he said. "No," I told him, "I won't be homesick. Yes, I'll feel sad when I reflect that, if you and the rest of the family don't come out to Auckland, I'll never see any of you again. But homesick? No, not homesick. How can I be homesick when I'm leaving Lewis to go home?"'

But such thinking is not universal. At their home on the outskirts of Dunvegan, I call on Donald and Rosemary MacLeod. Donald is a rarity in present-day Skye. He is the only person on the island, as far as I can establish, who can claim to be the current head of one of Clan MacLeod's once numerous tacksmen families – families whose close kinship with their chiefs failed to prevent their departure in the face of soaring rents. But Donald MacLeod, although his ancestors were tacksmen in Glenelg in the eighteenth century and in Glendale the century before, is nevertheless the son, the grandson and the great-grandson of men who were born in Australia. 'My great-great-grandfather emigrated in 1835,' Donald explains. 'Much later my father came to Britain. He lived in Edinburgh, and I grew up there. As a boy, however, I spent a lot of time in Skye and got to really like the island. So when I retired from the diplomatic service, Rosemary and I moved to Dunvegan. To me especially, this seemed a natural thing to do. I feel that I belong here.'

Leaving Dunvegan, I take one of Skye's unimproved roads to Orbost. In 1921, about ninety years after the place was cleared, several young men who lived in nearby Roag, and who had just come home from wartime service with the military, notified the authorities that they intended 'to take forcible seizure' of Orbost with a view to re-establishing crofts on the property. This did not happen. But in 1997, when the 6,000-acre Orbost estate was put up for sale by its then owners, it was bought by Highlands and Islands Enterprise, a government-funded development agency.* HIE's objectives were similar to those of the prospective raiders of more than seventy years before. Looking to give a further boost to Skye's economy, HIE wanted to create new opportunities in a locality that had remained largely depopulated since its early-nineteenth-century laird removed Orbost's original inhabitants.

---

* Again, a declaration of interest. When HIE acquired Orbost, I was chairman of Skye and Lochalsh Enterprise, the HIE subsidiary which initiated and handled the purchase.

HIE's plans were not endorsed universally in Skye – which meant that the immediate outcome of the agency's purchase was a great deal of argument and dispute. Now things are quieter. Community ownership of Orbost is on the cards. Houses have been built, croft-type smallholdings laid out and several businesses established. Today, as a result, there are more people resident at Orbost than there have been for a long time.[25]

One of them, Rachael Jackson, is an Australian who, though she makes nothing of this, possesses one of the most prestigious ancestries I have come across in all my travels. Unravelling this ancestry's complexities is difficult, but a good starting point is Rachael's great-great-great-great-grandfather, John MacLeod. Although a tacksman at Rigg in the Trotternish area of Skye and thus a tenant of the MacDonalds of Sleat, John was descended from one of the MacLeods of Raasay. In the early 1770s, like many other tacksmen, John MacLeod of Rigg emigrated to the Cape Fear River country. There he became a loyalist soldier and took part in the Battle of Moore's Creek Bridge, where he was captured by pro-independence forces. After this, John MacLeod returned to Skye, married and raised a family – including Archibald, John's second son and Rachael Jackson's great-great-great-grandfather. Archibald MacLeod trained in medicine and became a doctor. His wife, Rachael's great-great-great-grandmother, was Flora MacLeod, a daughter of Donald MacLeod of Arnisdale, Glenelg's pioneer sheep farmer. Since her Arnisdale forebears were descended from one of the MacLeods of Dunvegan, and since her huband's *sloinneadh* or lineage began with the Lewis chiefs who were the MacLeods of Raasay's forebears, Flora MacLeod's son, Donald Archibald, had ancestral links with both of Clan MacLeod's leading families. So, it follows, does Donald Archibald's great-great-granddaughter, Rachael Jackson. 'Donald Archibald MacLeod was trained as a civil engineer,' Rachael comments. 'In 1865, he and his wife emigrated to New Zealand. Afterwards our family moved to New South Wales. That's where I'm from. I went to school and university in Sydney.'[26]

In 1994, partly at the suggestion of her Sydney grandmother, Peggy Staas, a Clan MacLeod enthusiast and a granddaughter of Donald Archibald MacLeod, Rachael Staas, as she then was, attended a Young MacLeod Week organised in conjunction with that year's clan parliament at Dunvegan. 'I'd always been interested in my MacLeod ancestors,' Rachael says, 'and I just loved being in Skye. In 1995, I came back for a month. Then, in 1997, I took a year out, headed here again and got a job in the Dunvegan Castle restaurant. That's when I met Keith Jackson, who became my husband. He was a shepherd on the Dunvegan estate, and he'd come to Skye from England with his parents when he was eleven. We were married in 1998, and soon I was pregnant. Both Keith and I wanted to make our home in Skye, but we couldn't find anywhere to live. HIE had just bought Orbost, and we applied for a place here. At that point, however, we were turned down – so we had to go off to Perthshire where Keith got a shepherd's post that came with a house. We spent three years in Perthshire, but it wasn't at all like Skye. I never felt at home there the way I do here. Keith wasn't happy either, and we were thinking about leaving Scotland when we saw that HIE were advertising a new round of places at Orbost. This time we were lucky.'

Rachael Jackson is now thirty. She has two children, and she and Keith, who has become the Orbost estate's shepherd, are jointly launching a number of commercial ventures. 'I can't tell you exactly why it's so important to me to be in Skye,' Rachael says, 'but I know it has to do with my family's roots being here. I've studied genetics, and sometimes I think there must be MacLeod genes in my body, and in our children's bodies, that were here in Skye hundreds of years ago and are now in Skye once more. To me, that's a good thought.'

Rachael Jackson is a member of the trust which has been formed with the aim of taking Orbost into community ownership. 'One of the things I'd like our trust to do,' Rachael says, 'is to lease or give a little piece of land to the Clan MacLeod Society of Scotland. The trust's intention is to commemorate the MacLeods who have emigrated from places like this by building some sort of memorial wall. I hope we might get people from many different countries to send stones from the places where their families settled. Those stones would become part of our wall and, in this way, we'd create here at Orbost something symbolic of Skye's links with the rest of the world.'

From Keith and Rachael Jackson's home, I walk down the track that leads to Bharcasaig Bay, passing the ruins of houses left empty when their occupants were evicted. Christmas is five days away, and the weather is wintry. In the night, a hard frost gave way to squalls of rain and sleet moving in from the Atlantic. Now deep snow covers the Cuillin, and beyond Bharcasaig Bay's narrow entrance Loch Bracadale's wide waters are grey and wind raked beneath a stormy-looking sky.

Out there in August 1802, a half-broken-down emigrant ship, the *Duke of Kent*, embarked on a near-disastrous voyage to Wilmington, North Carolina. Among the passengers who must have crowded on to the *Duke of Kent*'s decks to get their last glimpse of Skye was a woman who had lived, until this point, not far from Orbost. Her name was Effie McLeod, and it was in her great-great-great-grandson's home in Nashville, Tennessee, that I agreed to write this book. What Alex McLeod and the rest of the MacLeod diaspora will make of its contents, I do not know. But whatever Alex and my other informants think of what I have produced, they can be assured of this: my admiration for their emigrant ancestors is unstinting; so is my gratitude to all the MacLeods who have shared their stories with me. From them I learned, among many other things, that it is possible for our emigrant people's descendants, even when separated from Scotland by thousands of miles and by hundreds of years, to feel real and deep affection for places like the one where I am standing this December afternoon. Long may all the world's MacLeods remember where they came from.

ACKNOWLEDGEMENTS

By Alexander C. McLeod

When visiting the Isle of Skye in 1773, Samuel Johnson commented: 'Books are faithful repositories, which may be a while neglected or forgotten; but when they are opened again, will again impart their instruction: memory, once interrupted, is not to be recalled. Written learning is a fixed luminary, which, after the cloud that had hidden it has past away, is again bright in its proper station. Tradition is but a meteor, which, if once it falls, cannot be rekindled.'

Acting on this truth, Clan MacLeod has long been committed to creating a permanently available source of information about the clan. We aimed to publish a trilogy dealing with our evolution and development. The first volume would tell the story of the clan in Scotland; the second would record what is known about Clan MacLeod genealogy and family history; the third would deal with the emigration of MacLeods from Scotland to other parts of the world.

This has been a long-term project. The first instalment of our trilogy, *The MacLeods: The History of a Clan*, by the late Dr Isabel F. Grant, was published in 1959, reprinted in 1981 and is now available on CD-ROM. Our trilogy's second instalment, *The MacLeods: The Genealogy of a Clan*, by the late Rev. Donald MacKinnon and Mr Alick Morrison, was published in five separate sections between 1968 and 1976. The first of these sections was revised by Alick Morrison and republished as *The Chiefs of Clan MacLeod* in 1986. Further sections, after further revision in one instance, were most recently reprinted in 1999. What remained to be tackled was our trilogy's third instalment, to which we gave the working title of *The MacLeods: The Migration of a Clan*. It was with a view to getting this job done that we commissioned James Hunter to research and write this book. Along the way, our original title has changed. Our aims, however, have not.

With the appearance of *Scottish Exodus: Travels Among a Worldwide Clan*, we have completed a task we first embarked on half a century ago. This book shows how Clan MacLeod became an international family. It celebrates the bravery and determination of people who emigrated from Scotland to other countries. It has a lot to say about those people's present-day descendants. Among them, as Jim Hunter's book demonstrates, there is often a longing both to return to the land whence their ancestors came and to know more about those ancestors – who they were, how they lived, why they left Scotland. This book will help members of Clan MacLeod – and families of Highlands and Islands origin more generally – to make connections with their history and with each other. We are, as this book's contents demonstrate, united by shared experiences as well as by our common links with the places where Clan MacLeod began.

But does the concept of Clan MacLeod have any meaning in a world now so different from the one in which our clan took shape? I believe it does. To me, our clan is a microcosm of the United Nations – embodying all that organisation's hopes and exhibiting many of its problems. Like the United Nations, Clan MacLeod is today a reflection of the family of man – all this family's colours and all of its religious and political differences being overshadowed ultimately by an awareness of common kinship. In Clan MacLeod as it now exists, we have preserved something of the spirit which made clanship such a powerful force in the Scottish Highlands and Islands during the Middle Ages and subsequently. But we have adapted this spirit in the light of today's democratic ideals. We are a worldwide fellowship joined together by our history, our shared culture, our unity and our hope that our Scottish heritage will endure into the future.

As Jim Hunter told me repeatedly in the course of the four years during which he worked on *Scottish Exodus*, the book could not have been written but for Clan MacLeod's commitment to it. Hundreds of clan members – in places as far apart as Poland and New Zealand – spent time with Jim, told him their family stories, put him up in their homes, drove him around their countries and shared with him the results of their often painstaking enquiries into their people's past. Others helped in different ways. Here in the United States, James R. McLeod and W. Reynolds McLeod, both of them college professors and both of them able historians in their own right, reviewed Jim Hunter's drafts and made many helpful suggestions as to content and approach. In the United Kingdom, meanwhile, the project had from the outset the constant support of Chief John MacLeod of MacLeod and Malcolm L. A. MacLeod of Raasay – each of them central to the work of the Associated Clan MacLeod Societies.

No exercise of this kind – involving as it did long hours in archives and libraries as well as extensive travel internationally – could have been undertaken without the availability of the necessary funding. Hence the significance of the lists of Sponsors and Subscribers which follow. But for their generous backing, this book would not exist.

MEMORIALS
John Holmes Macleod
Dame Flora MacLeod of MacLeod
Joan Wolrige Gordon and Alice MacNab of MacNab
Robert Wolrige Gordon and Patrick Wolrige Gordon
Murdoch McLeod and Effie McInnis McLeod
John McLeod and Flora Johnson McLeod
Alexander McLeod and Margaret Warner McLeod
Robert Lee McLeod and Margaret Elizabeth McIver McLeod
Mattie Andie McLeod Rice and Edward Laurence McLeod, Sr
Walter Guy McLeod and Vida Canaday McLeod
Malcolm Lee McLeod and Julia Mixon McLeod
Ruth McLeod Allen and Inez Canaday Macfarlane
James Carlisle McLeod and Floramay Holliday McLeod
Agnes McLeod Stephens

SPONSORS
Helen Cornelia McLeod Bradham
John MacLeod of MacLeod
Mr Roderick Kingman Macleod
Florence McLeod Ervin and James Carlisle McLeod, Jr
Alexander Canaday McLeod and Dorothy Woods McLeod
Laura Margaret McLeod
Robert Franklin McLeod and Jean Messervy McLeod
Dorothy McLeod Rhodes
Jack McLeod Stephens and Sue A. Stephens

SUBSCRIBERS
Australia
Clan MacLeod Society of Australia
Mrs R.E. Cropper

Ian and Ruth MacLeod
Peter Robert Macleod and Wendy Patricia Macleod
Torquil Roderick Macleod of the Lewes and Mary Macleod
W.A. McLeod

Canada
Clan MacLeod Foundation of Canada; Hugh Ross MacCrimmon
Clan MacLeod Societies of Canada
Robert G. and Barbara MacLeod Armstrong
Clan MacLeod Society of Greater Vancouver (Canada)
Jean MacLeod McKenna and John Edward McKenna
Colin Macleod and Beth Macleod
Donald R. and Eleanor I. MacLeod
John D. MacLeod and Helen C. MacLeod Grant
Ian Charles MacLeod and Ardis Elaine MacLeod
Mary McQueen MacLeod and Mae I. MacLeod Blackmore
Ian A. McCrimmon; Mary Lou McCrimmon
Jean Telfer Ottosen and Pauline Crooker Fevens
Norman MacLeod Rogers; Ian MacFee Rogers
Edmund Stewart Telfer and Corey Stuart Telfer
George and Ruth Toller

England
Alistair Angus MacLeod and Jill Alexandra MacLeod
Andrew P. MacLeod
David MacLeod
Iain Breac Cameron MacLeod and Elizabeth Mavis MacLeod
Moira B.S. MacLeod
Peter McLeod
Caroline A.R. Macleod and Malcolm L.A. Macleod OBE
Dr Leonard McLeod and Dr Andrew McLeod
Susanna L. Smithson and Christina McLeod Morley
The Clan MacLeod Society of England
Sheila Alice Wilson

France
Association Française du Clan MacLeod

Germany
Clan MacLeod Society of Germany

New Zealand

Clan MacLeod Society of New Zealand
Don Hammond and Janet Pullan
Graeme and Barbara MacLeod
Maxwell Ian Muldrew
Ian F. MacLeod

Poland

Michal Machlejd and Joanna Machlejd
Wanda Machlejd Szymonowicz

Scotland

Clan MacLeod Heritage Trust
Edward William Henderson and Stella McLeod Henderson
Sir Hamish MacLeod KBE
Brian McLeod
Alick and Jenny Morrison
Nancy MacLeod Nicol
The Clan MacLeod Society of Scotland

South Africa

Clan MacLeod Society of South Africa
Alistair and Hazel MacLeod

United States of America

Patricia and Michael Barger
Anne McLeod Bleggi
Coralane and Harry Boyes
John McLeod Bradham
Sue McLeod Christensen
Clan MacLeod Society USA, Inc.
Dunvegan Foundation of Clan MacLeod Society USA, Inc.
Mr Albert J. Lewis
Anthony and Dorothy Macleod
Emma I. Link
Col Bill and Betty Macleod
Kimberly Margaret MacLeod Hamelin and Benjamin Robin
	MacLeod Hamelin
Mabelle Luman
Angus and Mary MacLeod
Andrew Giles Calhoun and Josephine MacLeod

Colin Bruce MacLeod and Karen Susan Quanbeck MacLeod
Colin C. MacLeod, Jr and Ann Kivlighan MacLeod
Donald B. MacLeod
Donald B. MacLeod and Janet S. MacLeod
Dr John and Katherine MacLeod
Mr and Mrs Louis H. MacLeod
Kimberly Avery MacLeod and David Albert MacLeod
Dr Norman W. MacLeod
Robert E. MacLeod, Jr, and Kathleen Armstrong MacLeod
Richard Patrick MacLeod and Richard Alexander MacLeod
Roderick J. MacLeod and Karen L. MacLeod
Sayre and Eugenie MacLeod
Mr and Mrs Thomas W. MacLeod
Virginia Louise MacLeod
William C. and Irene P. MacLeod
N. Douglas MacLeod, Jr, and Nancy F. MacLeod
Raymond and Nora McCabe
Daniel Mead McClure
Alexander Woods McLeod
C. Anderson and Jean McLeod
Don Mack and Kathrine McLeod
Gustavus Arius McLeod and Mary Alice Von Lockmuller McLeod
Harry M. and Deborah McLeod
Harry Myles McLeod and Mildred Gloria McLeod
James R. McLeod and J. Brock McLeod
James S. McLeod and Doris A. McLeod
Katharine McLeod
Lamar and Juanita McLeod
Mary Darden McLeod and Michael Joseph Dotson
Milton K. and Barbara McLeod
Col Purdy B. and Odell McLeod
Rev. Purdy Belvin McLeod, Sr, and Gertrude Horres McLeod
Mr and Mrs Richard H. McLeod
Robert G. McLeod
Robert Lee McLeod, Jr and Ann McNeer McLeod
Ross and Lois McLeod
W.R. and V.B. McLeod
Judge William Lasater McLeod, Jr
Col William R. and Ceebee McLeod
William Swinton McLeod and Alice McLeod
Dale McLeod Messervy

The Rev. Canon Peter M. Norman and Janet W. Norman
Frances Pearson
Donna Compton Testini and Deanna Marie Testini Mirabile
Julia Elizabeth Bradham Pelzer
Dorothy Seward McLeod Poli
Margaret Claire Bradham Thornton
John Randolph Bradham Thornton
Alexandra Lee McLeod Thornton
Elliott McLeod Lawson Thornton
Elisha Poinsett Richardson Thornton
John MacLeod Tutterow, Esq. and Lisa MacRae Tutterow
Virginia Macleod Westbrook

NOTES AND REFERENCES

CDM – Clan Donald Muniments
CM – Celtic Magazine
CMM – Clan MacLeod Magazine
DCM – Dunvegan Castle Muniments
NAS – National Archives of Scotland
NLS – National Library of Scotland
NS – Northern Scotland
PRO – Public Record Office
SHR – Scottish Historical Review
SS – Scottish Studies
TGSI – Transactions of the Gaelic Society of Inverness

Without adding unacceptably to its size, it is impossible to equip a book like this with sources for every statement it contains. Sources have been provided, however, for every quotation and for genealogical or other details which readers might wish to follow up.

Chapter One

1 F.L. Riley (ed.), 'A Trip Through the Piney Woods', *Publications of the Mississippi Historical Society*, IX, 1906, 521, 530.
2 This and ensuing quotations from A. MacLeod, *No Great Mischief*, New York, 2000, 1, 4–6, 10, 89–90, 160–1.
3 A. MacLeod, 'Introduction', in R. Rankin (ed.), *Mabou Pioneers II*, Mabou, 1977.

4 F. Grinton, *Pastures Old and New: A Record of Our Pioneers*, Kerang, 1970, 23.

5 B. & N. Wilson, *Settling the Plains: A History of Tragowel*, Snowdon, 1978, 7.

6 *Genesis* 12: 1.

7 *Exodus* 3: 6–8.

8 Scotus Americanus, *Informations Concerning the Province of North Carolina Addressed to Emigrants from the Highlands and Western Isles of Scotland*, in W.K. Boyd, *Some Eighteenth-Century Tracts Concerning North Carolina*, Raleigh, 1927, 434.

9 E.J. Cowan, *For Freedom Alone: The Declaration of Arbroath*, East Linton, 2003, 143–6. See also W. Ferguson, *The Identity of the Scottish Nation: An Historic Quest*, Edinburgh, 1998.

Chapter Two

1 H. Palsson and P. Edwards (eds), *Eyrbyggja Saga*, London, 1989, 25.

2 M. Magnusson and H. Palsson (eds), *Laxdaela Saga*, London, 1969, 49; H. Palsson and P. Edwards (eds), *Landnámabók: The Book of Settlements*, Winnipeg, 1992, 23.

3 M. Magnusson and H. Palsson (eds), *The Vinland Sagas: The Norse Discovery of America*, London, 1965, 75.

4 Magnusson and Palsson, *Laxdaela Saga*, 51–2.

5 Palsson and Edwards, *Landnámabók*, 55.

6 D. Ó Cróinín, *Early Medieval Ireland*, London, 1995, 234–5.

7 T.O. Clancy (ed.), *The Triumph Tree: Scotland's Earliest Poetry*, Edinburgh, 1998, 216; E. Monsen and A.H. Smith (eds), *Heimskringla: The Lives of the Norse Kings*, New York, 1990, 592–3.

8 Palsson and Edwards, *Landnámabók*, 97.

9 R. Shepherd, *Iain Macleod*, London, 1994, 2.

10 J.C. Watson (ed.), *Gaelic Songs of Mary MacLeod*, Edinburgh, 1982, 48–9.

11 The most recent, most authoritative and most persuasive account of MacLeod origins is W.D.H. Sellar, 'The Ancestry of the MacLeods Reconsidered', *TGSI*, LX, 1998. Earlier views can be found in: R.C. MacLeod, *The MacLeods of Dunvegan: From the Time of Leod to the End of the Seventeenth Century*, Edinburgh, 1927; I.F. Grant, *The MacLeods: The History of a Clan*, London, 1959; W. Matheson, 'The Ancestry of the MacLeods', *TGSI*, LI, 1977; A. Morrison, *The Chiefs of Clan MacLeod*, Edinburgh, 1987; A. Morrison, 'The Kingdom of Man and the Isles', *TGSI*, LVIII, 1995.

12 J. Abernethy, 'The Genetics of Clan MacLeod', *CMM*, XIII, 2004, 760–3.

13 J. MacInnes, 'West Highland Sea Power in the Middle Ages', *TGSI*, XLVIII, 1972, 527.

14 Clancy, *Triumph Tree*, 302–3.

15 D. Rixon, *The West Highland Galley*, Edinburgh, 1998, 190.

16 R.W. Munro (ed.), *Monro's Western Isles of Scotland and Genealogies of the Clans*, Edinburgh, 1961, 161.

17 Watson, *Songs of Mary MacLeod*, 32–5.

18 J. Lydon, 'The Scottish Soldier in Medieval Ireland', in G.G. Simpson (ed.), *The Scottish Soldier Abroad*, Edinburgh, 1992, 12.

19 J. MacDonald (ed.), 'An Elegy for Ruaidhri Mor', *Scottish Gaelic Studies*, VIII, 1958, 40–9.

20 T. Riis, *Should Auld Acquaintance Be Forgot: Scottish–Danish Relations, 1450–1707*, 2 vols, Odense, 1988, II, 123–4.

21 J. Ferguson (ed.), *Papers Illustrating the History of the Scots Brigade in the Services of the United Netherlands*, 3 vols, Edinburgh, 1899–1901, I, 571–2, II, 394, III, 22; 'Admiral Norman MacLeod', *CMM*, 1, 1935, 25–6; R.C. MacLeod, *The MacLeods: A Short Sketch of their Clan History*, Edinburgh, 1906, 96–100.

22 T. Coulson, *Mata Hari: Courtesan and Spy*, London, 1930, 29. Also, J. Keay, *Spy Who Never Was: The Life and Loves of Mata Hari*, London, 1987.

23 W.F. Leith (ed.), *The Scots Men-at-Arms and Lifeguards in France*, 2 vols, Edinburgh, 1882, I, 19.

24 Adv 20.1.2: 'Letter and memoire concerning the Macklot family in France', 1754. Also, MacLeod, *MacLeods of Dunvegan*, 59. The fullest account of Maclot origins is in: *Clan MacLeod Society of France Bulletin*, 9, 1983. See also E. Bonner, 'French Naturalization of the Scots in the Fifteenth and Sixteenth Centuries', *Historical Journal*, XL, 1997; L. McLeod, 'The MacLeods of Vendôme', *CMM*, IX, 104–7.

25 N. Davies, *Heart of Europe: A Short History of Poland*, Oxford, 1984, 78; N. Ascherson, *The Struggles for Poland*, London, 1988, 127. Also, N. Davies, *Rising '44: The Battle for Warsaw*, London, 2003.

26 W. Machlejd, 'Experiences in the Polish Home Army', *CMM*, I, 1946, 369. For the original of this article, see DCM (5/172): 'Article by Wanda Machleid'.

27 My principal sources of information about Machlejd descent are Moira MacLeod of Whitley Bay, England, and Michele L. Winter of Montville, New Jersey, who has drawn on a book authored by Stanislaw Loza and published in Warsaw in 1932. This book's title translates as: *Polish Families of Foreign Origin Settled in Warsaw and its Surroundings*.

28 T.C. Smout, N.C. Landsman and T.M. Devine, 'Scottish Emigration in the Seventeenth and Eighteenth Centuries', in N. Canny (ed.), *Europeans on the Move: Studies in European Migration*, Oxford, 1994, 80; A. Bieganska, 'A Note on the Scots in Poland', in T.C. Smout (ed.), *Scotland and Europe, 1200–1850*, Edinburgh, 1986, 158; W. Borowy, *Scots in Old Poland*, Edinburgh, 1941, 6. Also, T.M. Devine, *Scotland's Empire*, London, 2003, 10–11.

29 Machlejd, 'Experiences', 367, 369.

30 *Ibid.*, 369.

31 *Ibid.*, 370–1.

32 *Ibid.*, 371. This paragraph also draws on information supplied by Moira MacLeod.

33 For Stuart MacLeod's Skye ancestry, see D. MacKinnon and A. Morrison, *The MacLeods: The Genealogy of a Clan: Section Three*, Clan MacLeod Society, n.d., 63–6, 81–3.

Chapter Three

1 C. Boyer (ed.), *Ship Passenger Lists: National and New England, 1600–1825*, Newhall, 1977, 154–61; D. Dobson (ed.), *Directory of Scots Banished to the American Plantations, 1650–1775*, Baltimore, 1984, 143.

2 B. Lawson, *The MacLeods of Lewis and Harris*, Northton, 2002, 1.

3 Acreages from: R.C. MacLeod (ed.), *The Book of Dunvegan*, 2 vols, Aberdeen, 1938–9, II, 69.

4 C. Ó Baoill and M. Bateman (eds), *Gàir nan Clàrsach*: *The Harps' Cry: An Anthology of Seventeenth-Century Gaelic Poetry*, Edinburgh, 1994, 198–9, 205.

5 MacLeod, *Book of Dunvegan*, I, 186–9.

6 PRO State Papers (SP63/402): Montgomery and Bailie to Ward, 10 November 1739.

7 PRO State Papers (SP63/402): MacLeod to McGown, 19 June 1739; SP63/402: Montgomery and Bailie to Ward, 10 November 1739.

8 PRO State Papers (SP63/402): Examination of W. Murdoch and A. McLeod, 7, 12 November 1739.

9 PRO State Papers (SP63/402): Examination of J. Johnston, 7 November 1739.

10 PRO State Papers (SP63/402): Montgomery and Bailie to Ward, 10 November 1739.

11 PRO State Papers (SP63/102): Montgomery and Bailie to Ward, 10 November 1739; Examination of D. Crawford, 7 November 1739; R.H. Duff (ed.), *Culloden Papers*, London, 1815, 154; PRO State Papers

(SP63/102): Examination of D. MacKay, 8 November 1739; D. Warrand (ed.), *More Culloden Papers*, 5 vols, Inverness, 1923–30, III, 141; CDM (MEP333): L. St Lawrence to A. Cunningham, 26 November 1739.

12 Duff, *Culloden Papers*, 204.

13 S. MacLean, *Ris a' Bhruthaich: Criticism and Prose Writings*, Stornoway, 1985, 51.

14 DCM (4/295): MacLeod of Talisker to W. Fraser, 2 April 1772; *Book of Dunvegan*, II, 145.

15 DCM (1/382/1): 'Copy of correspondence betwixt A.B. and Mr Fraser', 28 January 1772; J. Walker, *An Economical History of the Hebrides and Highlands of Scotland*, 2 vols, London, 1812, I, 51–2; S. Johnson, *A Journey to the Western Islands of Scotland*, London, 1984, 74; T. Pennant, *A Tour in Scotland and a Voyage to the Hebrides*, Edinburgh, 1998, 342.

16 DCM (2/264): 'Essay on the Late Emigrations by a Highlander', 1774.

17 Pennant, *Tour in Scotland*, 309–10.

18 Dobson, *Scots Banished to the American Plantations*, 143.

19 Johnson, *Journey to the Western Islands*, 75; DCM (1/466/24): Description of Harris, 29 February 1772; *A Candid Enquiry into the Causes of the Late and Intended Migrations from Scotland*, Glasgow, 1771, 56.

20 P. Griffin, *The People with No Name: Ireland's Ulster Scots, America's Scots Irish, and the Creation of a British Atlantic World*, Princeton, 2001, 73, 96.

21 Scottish Americanus, *Informations*, 436–7, 441, 447.

22 *Ibid., Informations*, 450.

23 *Ibid., Informations*, 429–30.

24 *Ibid., Informations*, 434–5.

25 W. Matheson (ed.), *The Songs of John MacCodrum*, Edinburgh, 1938, 199–203.

26 M. MacDonell (ed.), *The Emigrant Experience: Songs of Highland Emigrants in North America*, Toronto, 1982, 36–7.

27 DCM (4/113): A. MacLeod to N. MacLeod, 8 February 1771; H. Paton (ed.), *The Lyon in Mourning*, 3 vols, Edinburgh, 1895–6, III, 259.

28 DCM (4/221): A. MacDonald to N. MacLeod, 26 June 1771; DCM (4/113): A. MacLeod to N. MacLeod, 8 February 1771; DCM (4/306/1): Letter from D. MacLeod, 18 March 1771; NLS Lee Papers (MS 3431): 'Observations upon Harris', 1772; DCM (4/306/3): A. Morrison to N. MacLeod, 18 March 1771; B.P. Robinson, *A History of Moore County, North Carolina, 1747–1847*, Southern Pines, 1956, 32–4.

29 M.I. Adam, 'The Highland Emigration of 1770', *SHR*, XVI, 1919, 283; *Scots Magazine*, September 1772, 515–16.

30 M. Martin, *A Description of the Western Islands of Scotland*, Edinburgh, 1994, 248; Johnson, *Journey to the Western Islands*, 101.

31 DCM (4/392/1): J. MacKenzie to N. MacLeod, 11 August, 1773; A. MacKenzie, *History of the MacLeods*, Inverness, 1889, 151.

32 DCM (4/294): J. MacLeod to W. Fraser, 3 April 1769.

33 DCM (4/304/1): A. MacLeod to N. MacLeod, 21 April 1772; DCM (4/304/2): A. MacLeod to W. Fraser, 28 April 1772; J. Boswell, *The Journal of a Tour to the Hebrides*, London, 1984, 300.

34 DCM (4/312): N. MacLeod to W. Fraser, 27 April 1772.

35 NLS Delvine Papers (MS 1306): F. MacDonald to J. MacKenzie, 12 August 1772; Delvine Papers (MS 1306): A. MacDonald to J. MacKenzie, 2 March 1773.

36 NLS Delvine Papers (MS 1306): A. MacDonald to J. MacKenzie, 2 March 1773; DCM (4/319): A. MacLeod, Circular, 13 April 1772.

37 Pennant, *Tour in Scotland*, 289.

38 Boswell, *Journal of a Tour*, 313; DCM 4/228: J. MacLeod to Lady MacLeod, 9 October 1772.

39 DCM (4/394): J. MacLeod to N. MacLeod, 23 November 1772.

40 DCM (4/394): J. MacLeod to N. MacLeod, 23 November 1772; DCM (4/228): J. MacLeod to Lady MacLeod, 9 October 1772.

41 DCM (4/396): J. MacLeod to N. MacLeod, 22 February 1773.

42 Boswell, *Journal of a Tour*, 286.

43 MacKenzie, *The MacLeods*, 152. This passage is drawn from an autobiographical sketch written by Norman MacLeod in 1785. The original is preserved at Dunvegan: DCM (5/45/1–4).

44 R.H.M. MacLeod, 'The Clans Retain Little Now of their Original Character', *CMM*, VIII, 1979, 92; MacKenzie, *The MacLeods*, 152; DCM (4/397): J. MacLeod to N. MacLeod, 30 April 1773.

45 A.W. Parker, *Scottish Highlanders in Colonial Georgia: The Recruitment, Emigration and Settlement at Darien*, Athens, 1997, 112, 122–3.

46 R.J. Adam (ed.), *Home's Survey of Assynt*, Edinburgh, 1960, xxiv; A.R. Newsome (ed.), *Records of Emigrants from England and Scotland to North Carolina*, Raleigh, 1962, 23–4.

47 B. Bailyn, *Voyagers to the West: Emigration from Britain to America on the Eve of the Revolution*, London, 1986, 40; *Scots Magazine*, October 1773, 557.

48 Bailyn, *Voyagers to the West*, 309.

49 PRO State Papers (SP 54/48): Gillanders to Davidson, 22 April 1774; State Papers (SP 54/48): Memorial of the Earl of Seaforth, n.d.

50 PRO State Papers (SP 54/48): Gillanders to Davidson, 22 April 1774; State Papers (SP 54/48): Memorial of the Earl of Seaforth, n.d.

51 Bailyn, *Voyagers to the West*, 312.

52 D. Dobson (ed.), *Directory of Scottish Settlers in North America, 1625–1825*, 6 vols, Baltimore, 1984–6, I, 169–71; D. Whyte (ed.), *A Dictionary of Scottish Emigrants to the USA*, Baltimore, 1972, 321.

53 *Candid Enquiry*, 50.

54 W.R. Brock, *Scotus Americanus: A Survey of the Sources for Links between Scotland and America in the Eighteenth Century*, Edinburgh, 1982, 82. Also, C. MacIver, 'Parish of Glenelg', in D.J. Withrington and I.R. Grant (eds), *The Statistical Account of Scotland*, 20 vols, Wakefield, 1981, XVII, 74; R. MacLeod, 'Parish of Bracadale', Withrington and Grant, *Statistical Account*, XX, 155; W. Bethune, 'Parish of Duirinish', Withrington and Grant, *Statistical Account*, XX, 161; R.H. MacLeod, *Flora MacDonald: The Jacobite Heroine in Scotland and North America*, London, 1995, 127.

55 NLS Delvine Papers (MS 1306): A. MacDonald to J. MacKenzie, 30 November 1772; A. MacDonald to J. MacKenzie, 2 March 1773.

56 E.W. Andrews (ed.), *Journal of a Lady of Quality: Being the Narrative of a Journey from Scotland to the West Indies, North Carolina and Portugal in the Years 1774 to 1776*, New Haven, 1939, 141, 145, 158.

57 D. Meyer, *The Highland Scots of North Carolina*, Chapel Hill, 1961, 112, 116; A. Morrison, *The MacLeods: The Genealogy of a Clan: Section Four*, Clan MacLeod Society, n.d., 91.

58 Robinson, *History of Moore County*, 36.

59 B. Lawson, *The Teampull on the Isle of Pabbay: A Harris Church in its Historical Setting*, Northton, 1994, 17–18; MacKinnon and Morrison, *MacLeods: Section Three*, 214–15.

60 L.S. Butler and A.D. Watson (eds), *The North Carolina Experience: An Interpretative and Documentary History*, Chapel Hill, 1984, 143; B.G. Moss, *Muster of the Loyalists in the Battle of Moore's Creek Bridge*, Blackburgh, 1992, 45–52; MacKinnon and Morrison, *MacLeods: Section Three*, 214–25.

61 I.C.C. Graham, *Colonists from Scotland: Emigration to North America, 1707–1783*, New York, 1956, 178–9.

62 Robinson, *History of Moore County*, 71.

63 Bailyn, *Voyagers to the West*, 504.

64 B.H. Butler, *Old Bethesda: At the Head of Rockfish*, Southern Pines, 1933, 274–6.

Chapter Four

1 G. Dempster, *A Discourse Containing a Summary of the Proceedings of the Society for Extending the Fisheries*, London, 1789, 6; J. Loch, *An Account of the Improvements on the Estates of the Marquess of Stafford*, London, 1820, xvii.

2 Dempster, *Discourse*, 6.

3 E. Richards, *A History of the Highland Clearances: Agrarian Transformation and the Evictions*, London, 1982, 258.

4 W.F. Laughlan (ed.), *James Hogg's Highland Tours*, Hawick, 1981, 69.

5 A. Irvine, *An Enquiry into the Causes and Effects of Emigration from the Highlands*, Edinburgh, 1802, 36.

6 C. MacIver, 'Parish of Glenelg', in Withrington and Grant, *Statistical Account*, XVII, 76; M. MacLean, *The People of Glengarry: Highlanders in Transition, 1745–1820*, Toronto, 1991, 123–4.

7 MacIver, 'Parish of Glenelg', 76.

8 A. McLeod, Land Grant Petition, 31 December 1837, in Clan MacLeod Society of Glengarry, *The MacLeods of Glengarry: The Genealogy of a Clan*, Dunvegan, 1971, 58; MacLean, *People of Glengarry*, 123. Also, information from Flora MacLeod Johnston.

9 McLeod, Land Grant Petition, 58–9.

10 McLeod, Land Grant Petition, 59; Clan MacLeod Society of Glengarry, *MacLeods of Glengarry*, 112.

11 McLeod, Land Grant Petition, 59; MacKinnon and Morrison, *MacLeods: Section Three*, 159–85.

12 J. MacTaggart, *Three Years in Canada*, 2 vols, London, 1829, I, 193; W. Bell, *Hints to Emigrants*, Edinburgh, 1824, 53; MacLean, *People of Glengarry*, 215.

13 'MacLeods in Canada', *CMM*, I, 1937, 81; Clan MacLeod Society of Glengarry, *MacLeods of Glengarry*, 291.

14 T. Douglas, *Observations on the Present State of the Highlands of Scotland*, Edinburgh, 1806, 185; Bell, *Hints to Emigrants*, 135–6.

15 R. Connor, *The Man from Glengarry*, Toronto, 1993, 36, 39.

16 Douglas, *Observations*, 185.

17 R. Connor, *Glengarry School Days*, Toronto, 1990, 26; *Report from the Select Committee Appointed to Enquire into the Condition of the Population of the Highlands and Islands of Scotland and into the Practicability of Affording the People Relief by Means of Emigration*, London, 1841, 135, 163; MacDonell, *Emigrant Experience*, 136–7.

18 MacKenzie, *The MacLeods*, 165.

19 A.M. Cain (ed.), *The Cornchest for Scotland: Scots in India*, Edinburgh, 1986, 7; A.D. Gibb, *Scottish Empire*, London, 1937, 252.

20 B. Mitford, 'The MacLeods of Ullinish', *CMM*, I, 1942, 279–80. Also, 'Congratulations', *CMM*, I, 1942, 245; 'Obituaries', *CMM*, III, 1959, 235.

21 J. Prebble, *Mutiny: Highland Regiments in Revolt*, London, 1977, 208.

22 W.H. Yates, *The Modern History and Condition of Egypt*, 2 vols, London, 1843, I, 285–9. Osman is the basis of a novel which includes a detailed historical appendix: H. Hopkins, *The 1001 Nights of Drummer Donald MacLeod*, Edinburgh, 2000.

23 DCM (5/47): Account of His Own Life by J.N. MacLeod, 1802. Norman MacLeod's military career is summarised in three articles by J.R. McLeod: 'Tipu and the General: Skye Folk Tradition and History', *CMM*, XII, 1997; 'The General and the Bibi of Canmore: Romantic Folk Tale or History?', *CMM*, XII, 1998; 'The General and the Seaforth Doom', *CMM*, XIII, 2001. See also Grant, *The MacLeods*, 513–18.

24 DCM (4/762/18): N. MacLeod to H. Dundas, 7 May 1791; DCM (5/47): Account of His Own Life by J.N. MacLeod, 1802.

25 R.G. Thorne (ed.), *The House of Commons, 1790–1820*, 5 vols, London, 1986, IV, 507.

26 MacKenzie, *The MacLeods*, 156; N. MacLeod, *Two Letters to the Chairman of the Association for Parliamentary Reform in Scotland*, Edinburgh, 1793, 3.

27 MacLeod, *Two Letters*, 6; H.W. Meikle, *Scotland and the French Revolution*, Edinburgh, 1912, 96.

28 MacLeod, *Book of Dunvegan*, II, 98, 136–8.

29 DCM (2/112/1): Obligation of the Tenants of Glenelg, 19 September 1777; MacLeod, *Book of Dunvegan*, II, 137.

30 DCM (4/765): N. MacLeod to W. MacDonald, 23 February 1791; Grant, *The MacLeods*, 542; NAS Fraser McIntosh Papers (GD128/43/2): W. MacDonald to N. MacLeod, 16 December 1794.

31 NLS (Adv. 35.6.18): 'State of Emigration from the Highlands of Scotland', 1802, 11.

32 Laughlan, *Hogg's Highland Tours*, 56. Also, D. MacKinnon, *The MacLeods of Arnisdale*, Dingwall, 1929, 17–18.

33 J. Hunter, *The Making of the Crofting Community*, Edinburgh, 1976, 19.

34 W. MacGillivray, 'Report on the Outer Hebrides', *Transactions of the Highland and Agricultural Society*, II, 1831, 301.

35 Douglas, *Observations*, 123,

36 Douglas, *Observations*, 124–5.

37 Hunter, *Making of the Crofting Community*, 20; J.M. Bumsted, *The People's Clearance, 1770–1815: Highland Emigration to British North*

America, Edinburgh, 1982, 112; NLS (MS 9646): 'On Emigration from the Scottish Highlands and Isles by Edward Fraser', 55.

38 NLS (MS 9646): 'Fraser on Emigration', 23.

39 NLS (MS 9646): 'Fraser on Emigration', 25, 278.

40 J.A. McLeod to W.A. McLeod, 15 March 1907: correspondence in the possession of James A. McLeod, Cat Spring, Texas.

41 R. MacLeod, 'Parish of Bracadale', 155; Douglas, *Observations*, 4.

42 I. Adams and M. Somerville, *Cargoes of Hope and Despair: Scottish Emigration to North America*, Edinburgh, 1993, 170.

43 Hunter, *Making of the Crofting Community*, 25; J. Stewart, *An Account of Prince Edward Island in the Gulph of St Lawrence*, London, 1806, xi.

44 Douglas, *Observations*, 50–2.

45 H.S. MacLeod, *The MacLeods of Prince Edward Island*, Montague, 1987, v.

46 Howison, John, *Sketches of Upper Canada*, Edinburgh, 182, 1173; Douglas, *Observations*, 183.

47 J.B. MacLeod, 'A Rona Family in Canada', *CMM*, I, 1940, 176; MacDonell, *Emigrant Experience*, 108–9.

48 Selkirk, *Observations*, 198, 200; P.C.T. White (ed.), *Lord Selkirk's Diary, 1803–04: A Journey of His Travels*, Toronto, 1958, 17.

49 MacDonell, *Emigrant Experience*, 112–13.

50 A. MacPhail, *The Master's Wife*, Montreal, 1939, 1; J. MacGregor, *Historical and Descriptive Sketches of the Maritime Colonies*, London, 1828, 13.

51 MacGregor, *Sketches of the Maritime Colonies*, 71.

52 MacDonell, *Emigrant Experience*, 110–13; L.H. Campey, *A Very Fine Class of Immigrants: Prince Edward Island's Scottish Pioneers, 1770–1850*, Toronto, 2001, 84.

53 Cowan, *For Freedom Alone*, 128; G.G. Patterson, *A History of the County of Pictou*, Montreal, 1877, 80, 456.

54 D. Campbell and R.A. MacLean, *Beyond the Atlantic Roar: A Study of the Nova Scotia Scots*, Toronto, 1975, 45.

55 D. Dobson (ed.), *Directory of Scottish Settlers in North America*, 6 vols, Baltimore, 1984–6, I, 170.

56 G. MacLaren, *The Pictou Book: Stories of Our Past*, New Glasgow, 1954, 101–2.

57 D. MacArthur, 'Some Emigrant Ships from the West Highlands', *TGSI*, LV, 1987, 341; I. MacKay, 'Tartanism Triumphant: The Construction of Scottishness in Nova Scotia, 1933–54', *Acadiensis*, XXI, 1992, 10; D. MacLeod, *Memoir of Norman MacLeod*, London, 1882, 158.

58 W.A. MacLeod, *MacLeod Family History: The Story of the MacLeod Family from Galloway, Scotland, from 1770 to 2001*, Langley, 2001, 5, 7, 26.

59 MacKinnon and Morrison, *Section Three*, 145.

60 MacLeod, *Book of Dunvegan*, II, 118; DCM (2/709/1): Memo by MacLeod, 1 March 1893.

61 DCM (2/208/1): Documentation relating to the tack of Rhuandunan, 15 August 1810; DCM (4/860): Robertson to MacLeod, 9 March 1811; DCM (4/862): Robertson to MacLeod, 8 April 1811.

62 DCM (4/862): Robertson to MacEwen, 5 April 1811.

63 DCM (4/863): Robertson to MacLeod, 11 May 1811.

64 DCM (4/883): Falconer to MacLeod, 5 August 1811; DCM (4/884): MacLeod to Talisker, 14 August 1811; DCM (4/885): MacDonnell to MacLeod, 26 August 1811.

65 DCM (4/887): MacDonnell to MacLeod, 1 September 1811.

66 DCM (4/1808/1): E. MacLeod to R. MacLeod, 10 February 1887.

67 DCM (5/45/4): Canon R. C. MacLeod's addition to Norman MacLeod's Memorial of his Father, n.d.

68 Bumsted, *People's Clearance*, 218.

69 *Report of the Commissioners of Inquiry into the Conditions of the Crofters and Cottars in the Highlands and Islands of Scotland*, 5 vols, London, 1884, I, 15–16; II, 331, 337–8, 341, 343; *Report of the Royal Commission, Highlands and Islands*, 2 vols, London, 1895, I, 45–6.

70 *Highlands and Islands Commission*, I, 49; *Conditions of Crofters and Cottars*, II, 214; J. MacDonald, *General View of the Agriculture of the Hebrides*, Edinburgh, 1811, 79–80.

71 NAS Portree Sheriff Court Records (SC 32): Roll Book, 7 April 1825, 3 April 1826; L. Reid, *The Soay of Our Forefathers*, Isle of Skye, 1995, 31.

72 J. Mitchell, *Reminiscences of My Life in the Highlands*, 2 vols, Newton Abbott, 1971, II, 110.

73 *Conditions of Crofters and Cottars*, I, 2.

74 J.R. Glass, 'Parish of Bracadale', *New Statistical Account of Scotland*, 15 vols, Edinburgh, 1845, XIV, 296.

75 DCM (644/7/2): List of tenants on Rhuedunan, n.d.

76 *Conditions of Crofters and Cottars*, II, 201–2.

77 MacIver, 'Parish of Glenelg', 73. Also, *Conditions of Crofters and Cottars*, IV, 2055; T.M. Murchison, 'Glenelg, Inverness-shire: Notes for a Parish History', *TGSI*, XL, 1957, 317.

78 *Conditions of Crofters and Cottars*, IV, 1734. Also, M. Bangor-Jones, *The Assynt Clearances*, Dundee, 1998.

79 NLS Delvine Papers (MS 1310): A. MacDonald to Delvine, 30 July 1771. Also, B. Lawson, *Harris Families and How to Trace Them*, Northton, 1990.

80 Munro, *Monro's Western Isles*, 86.

81 Martin, *Western Islands*, 110.

82 *Report from the Select Committee Appointed to Enquire into the Expediency of Encouraging Emigration from the United Kingdom*, London, 1826, 3; H.I. Cowan, *British Emigration to British North America: The First Hundred Years*, Toronto, 1961, 93; *Report from the Agent General for Emigration on the Applicability of Emigration to Relieve Distress in the Highlands*, London, 1841, 1.

83 A. Fullarton and C.R. Baird, *Remarks on the Evils at Present Affecting the Highlands and Islands of Scotland*, Glasgow, 1838, 44; S.M. Kidd, 'Caraidh nan Gaidheal and Friend of Emigration: Gaelic Emigration Literature of the 1840s', *SHR*, LXXXI, 2002, 66.

84 A.C. Buchanan, *Emigration Practically Considered*, London, 1828, 19.

85 *Select Committee on the Expediency of Encouraging Emigration*, 356.

86 Campey, *Fine Class of Immigrants*, 82.

87 J. Shaw, 'Brief Beginnings: Nova Scotian and Old World Bards Compared', *Scottish Gaelic Studies*, XVII, 1996, 345.

88 R. Morgan, *Early Cape Breton: From Founding to Famine*, Wreck Cove, 2000, 136. For a detailed survey of settlement in Cape Breton, see: S. Hornsby, *Nineteenth-Century Cape Breton: A Historical Geography*, Toronto, 1992.

89 'Gillis Mountain', *The Rankin Family Collection*, EMI Music Canada.

90 A. MacLeod, *Island: The Collected Stories*, Toronto, 2000, 79–80.

91 Documentation in the possession of Allister MacLeod, Broad Cove. Also, C. Dressler, *Eigg: The Story of an Island*, Edinburgh, 1998, 58; J.L. MacDougall, *History of Inverness County*, Belleville, 1972, 352–5.

92 A. MacLeod, 'Introduction', in Rankin (ed.), *Mabou Pioneers*, ix.

93 For details of this Scarista clearance and of the people affected by it, see Lawson, *Teampull at Northton*, 30–2.

94 Bell, *Hints to Emigrants*, 31.

95 P. Cumming, H. MacLeod and L. Strachan, *The Story of Framboise*, Framboise, 1984, 17; MacDonell, *Emigrant Experience*, 84–5.

96 MacDonell, *Emigrant Experience*, 88–93.

97 Campbell and MacLean, *Beyond the Atlantic Roar*, 23; Hornsby, *Nineteenth-Century Cape Breton*, 75.

98 D.C. Harvey, 'Scottish Immigration to Cape Breton', in D. MacGillivray and B. Tennyson (eds), *Cape Breton Historical Essays*, Sydney, 1980, 37.

99 Hornsby, *Nineteenth-Century Cape Breton*, 47; Harvey, 'Scottish Immigration', 47.

100 H. MacPhee, 'The Trail of the Emigrants', *TGSI*, XLVI, 1969, 192.

101 G.G. Patterson, *A History of Victoria County*, Sydney, 1978, 82.

102 R. Mathieson, *Survival of the Unfittest: The Highland Clearances and the End of Isolation*, Edinburgh, 2000, 111.
103 Harvey, 'Scottish Immigration', 38.

Chapter Five

1 Adam, *Survey of Assynt*, 12–13.
2 J. Kennedy, *The Days of the Fathers in Ross-shire*, Inverness, 1979, 153; N. Robinson, *Lion of Scotland: Norman McLeod*, London, 1974, 49; E. Richards, *Patrick Sellar and the Highland Clearances*, Edinburgh, 1999, 87.
3 F. MacPherson, *Watchman Against the World: The Remarkable Journey of Norman McLeod*, Wreck Cove, 1993, 41; M. Molloy, *Those Who Speak to the Heart: The Nova Scotian Scots at Waipu*, Palmerston North, 1991, 31.
4 N.R. McKenzie, *The Gael Fares Forth: The Romantic Story of Waipu and Sister Settlements*, Christchurch, 1935, 210.
5 Molloy, *Those Who Speak*, 32.
6 Morgan, *Early Cape Breton*, 138, 141; D.C. Harvey (ed.), *Bulletin of the Public Archives of Nova Scotia: Letters of the Rev. Norman McLeod, 1835–51*, Halifax, 1939, 21–2; Morgan, *Early Cape Breton*, 149.
7 Morgan, *Early Cape Breton*, 149.
8 G. Serle, *The Golden Age: A History of the Colony of Victoria, 1851–1861*, Melbourne, 1963, 67.
9 Serle, *Golden Age*, 22; D. Goodman, *Gold Seeking: Victoria and California in the 1850s*, St Leonards, 1994, 37.
10 G. MacDonald, *The Highlanders of Waipu: Or Echoes of 1745*, Dunedin, 1928, 112, 117.
11 B.D. McLeod, *Everyone Has a Granny Called MacLeod*, Clan MacLeod Society of New South Wales, 1994, 70; C. Boyer (ed.), *Ship Passenger Lists: The South, 1538–1825*, Newhall, 1979, 17; J.D. Lang, *Reminiscences of My Life and Times*, Melbourne, 1972, 129; E. Richards, 'Scottish Australia', in E. Richards (ed.), *That Land of Exiles: Scots in Australia*, Edinburgh, 1988, 22.
12 Lang, *Reminiscences*, 129.
13 L.L. Robson, *The Convict Settlers of Australia*, Melbourne, 1976, 82.
14 For comparisons between Stalin's gulag and Britain's penal colonies, see R. Hughes, *The Fatal Shore: A History of the Transportation of Convicts to Australia*, London, 1987.
15 DCM (4/1574): C. MacLeod to E. MacLeod, 30 July 1853; D.S. MacMillan, *Scotland and Australia, 1788–1850: Emigration, Commerce and Investment*, Oxford, 1967, 81.

16 S. Moodie, *Roughing It in the Bush*, London, 1987, xv.

17 J. Dixon, *Narrative of a Voyage to New South Wales and Van Diemen's Land*, Edinburgh, 1822, 13–14.

18 Dixon, *Narrative of a Voyage*, 14, 24–5, 139–42.

19 T.F. Bride (ed.), *Letters from Victorian Pioneers*, Melbourne, 1898, 147–9.

20 For a full genealogy of the Talisker family, see: B.D. McLeod, *Genealogy of the Family of MacLeod of Talisker in Australia*, Neutral Bay, 1990.

21 Family history by N. Beard in possession of Neil McLeod, 11.

22 *Ibid.*, 11.

23 MacLeod, *Granny Called MacLeod*, 24–30; MacKinnon, *MacLeods of Arnisdale*, 26.

24 G. Dunderdale, *The Book of the Bush*, London, 1898, 200; R. MacKay, *Recollections of Early Gippsland Goldfields*, Traralgon, 1916, 28; E. Richards, 'Highland Emigrants to South Australia in the 1850s', *NS*, V, 1982, 2.

25 D. Watson, *Caledonia Australis: Scottish Highlanders on the Frontier of Australia*, Sydney, 1984, 133.

26 For details of Archibald's background, see P. MacLeod, *From Bernisdale to Bairnsdale: The Story of Archibald and Colina MacLeod and their Descendants in Australia*, Nar Nar Goon North, 1994. This detailed account has been followed in preference to other published genealogies from which it differs in some particulars.

27 Hughes, *Fatal Shore*, 456–67.

28 MacLeod, *Bernisdale to Bairnsdale*, 39.

29 Bill Macleod's line of descent can be traced in D. MacKinnon and A Morrison (eds), *The MacLeods: The Genealogy of a Clan: Section Two*, Associated Clan MacLeod Societies, n.d.

30 W.D. Simpson, 'A Chronicle History of Dunvegan Castle', *TGSI*, XXXVII, 1937, 390.

31 DCM (4/1573/3): M. MacLeod to E. MacLeod, 17 October 1838; M. Crauford-Lewis, *Macleod of the Mounties*, Ottawa, 1999, 17; *Conditions of Crofters and Cottars*, I, Appendix A, 24.

32 DCM (4/1354/2): MacLeod to Craigie, 6 March 1841.

33 *Condition of Crofters and Cottars*, I, Appendix A, 25; *Report from the Select Committee on Emigration*, 1841, 73; *Condition of Crofters and Cottars*, II, 362–3.

34 DCM (2/659/26): R. MacLeod to N. MacLeod, 9 May 1839; T.M. Devine, *The Great Highland Potato Famine*, Manchester, 1988, 23; *Report from the Commissioners Appointed for Inquiring into the Administration and Practical Operation of the Poor Laws in Scotland*, 8 vols, 1844, III, 393–4.

35 *Report to the Board of Supervision by Sir John McNeill on the Western Highlands and Islands*, 1851, x.

36 NAS Highland Destitution (HD7/9): Graham to Maule, 20 April 1837; Fullarton and Baird, *Remarks*, 14–15.

37 *Report of Poor Law Commissioners*, III, 391, 394.

38 J. Barron (ed.), *The Northern Highlands in the Nineteenth Century*, 3 vols, Inverness, 1907–13, II, 98–9, 196–7; Devine, *Highland Famine*, 16; A. Nicolson, *History of Skye*, Isle of Skye, 1994, 210.

39 Barron, *Northern Highlands*, III, 109; Mitchell, *Reminiscences*, I, 222.

40 *Correspondence Relating to the Measures Adopted for the Relief of Distress in Ireland and Scotland*, London, 1847, 64.

41 NAS Highland Destitution (HD6/2): Eliott to Coffin, 27 April 1847.

42 NAS Highland Destitution (HD7/9): Graham to Maule, 20 April 1837.

43 *Condition of Crofters and Cottars*, I, Appendix A, 28; *Highlands and Islands Commission*, I, 130.

44 *Measures for the Relief of Distress*, 255–6; N. MacLeod (ed.), *Extracts from Letters to the Rev. Dr Norman MacLeod Regarding the Famine in the Highlands and Islands*, Glasgow, 1847, 8.

45 DCM (2/659/23/5): MacLeod's Address, 26 December 1846.

46 *Measures for the Relief of Distress*, 279; DCM (2/659/23/7): MacLeod to his mother, 26 January 1847.

47 DCM (4/1431): Forbes to Perceval, 24 April 1847; NAS Highland Destitution (HD6/2): Haliday to Coffin, 4 March 1847.

48 DCM (2/659/23/7): MacLeod to his mother, 26 January 1847; *Measures for the Relief of Distress*, 353; DCM (2/659/23/10–12): N. MacLeod to E. MacLeod, 10, 27 February 1847.

49 MacLeod, *Book of Dunvegan*, I, xi; MacKenzie, *The MacLeods*, 184.

50 T. Mulock, *The Western Highlands and Islands of Scotland Socially Considered*, Edinburgh, 1850, 91; NAS Highland Destitution (HD10/27): MacLeod to Fishbourne, 21 March 1848.

51 DCM (2/659/2): A. Allan to E. MacLeod, 5 May 1849; Lady McCaskill, *Twelve Days in Skye*, London, 1852, 16, 35.

52 R. Somers, *Letters from the Highlands on the Famine of 1847*, Inverness, 1977, 92; Devine, *Highland Famine*, 323; *Report of Poor Law Commissioners*, III, 438; *McNeill Report*, xxvi.

53 Devine, *Highland Famine*, 212; R. Blake, *Jardine Matheson: Traders of the Far East*, London, 1999, 39; N. Nicolson, *Lord of the Isles*, Stornoway, 2000, 43; B. Disraeli, *Sybil*, London, 1957, 62.

54 J.S. Grant (ed.), *Diary 1851: John Munro MacKenzie, Chamberlain of the Lews*, Stornoway, 1994, 20; Devine, *Highland Famine*, 217, 329.

55 Grant, *Diary*, 74; N. Robertson, *The History of the County of Bruce*, Toronto, 1906, 419–20. Also, letter in the possession of Peggy Chappelle, Ripley, Ontario, referred to below.

56 L. MacLeod, *Lingwick: Last of the Quebec-Hebridean Crofters*, Brampton, 2002, 19.

57 Robertson, *History of Bruce*, 535.

58 *Ibid.* 415.

59 A. McCharles, *Bemocked of Destiny*, Toronto, 1908, 28–9.

60 DCM (4/1504): D. MacLeod to E. MacLeod, April 1854.

61 R.C. MacDiarmid, 'Donald MacLeod the Skye Bard: His Life and Songs', *Transactions of the Gaelic Society of Glasgow*, I, 1887, 23.

62 W.B. Clarke (ed.), *Emigration from the Highlands and Islands of Scotland*, Bicheno, 2002, 35; J. McNeill, 'Emigration from the Isle of Skye', *Illustrated London News*, 15 January 1853; McCaskill, *Twelve Days in Skye*, 18; Devine, *Highland Famine*, 253; DCM (2/659/7/6): Ferguson to MacLeod, 23 February 1852.

63 R.A.C. Balfour, 'The Highland and Island Emigration Society, 1852–58', *TGSI*, LVII, 1986, 433; DCM (2/659/10): Fraser to MacLeod, 18 February 1847.

64 Balfour, 'Emigration Society', 434.

65 Devine, *Highland Famine*, 246; Balfour, 'Emigration Society', 434; Clarke, *Emigration from the Highlands and Islands*, 3.

66 NAS Highland Destitution (HD4/1): Trevelyan to Fraser, 3 April 1852.

67 NAS Highland Destitution (HD4/1–3): Trevelyan to Nicholson, 7 June 1852; Trevelyan to Murdoch, 15 March 1853.

68 Clarke, *Emigration from the Highlands and Islands*, 1.

69 DCM (2/659/8/1–2): Ferguson to MacLeod, 4 April and 2 June 1848.

70 Clarke, *Emigration from the Highlands and Islands*, 60–1; DCM (2/656/7): Chant to Trevelyan, 8 August 1852; NAS Highland Destitution (HD4/2): Trevelyan to editor of *Daily News*, 20 July 1852; M.D. Prentis, *The Scots in Australia: A Study of New South Wales, Victoria and Queensland, 1788–1900*, Sydney, 1983, 70.

71 Boswell, *Journal of a Tour*, 262.

72 Andrews, *Journal of a Lady of Quality*, 43–54.

73 Crauford-Lewis, *MacLeod of the Mounties*, 26; T. Coleman, *Passage to America: A History of Emigrants from Great Britain and Ireland*, London, 1972, 108.

74 A.R.M. Lower, *Great Britain's Woodyard: British America and the Timber Trade, 1763–1867*, Montreal, 1973, 187; J.M. Bumsted, *The Peoples of Canada: A Pre-Confederation History*, Toronto, 1992, 191–2; R. MacGillivray and E. Ross, *A History of Glengarry*, Belleville, 1979, 445.

75 J. MacGregor, *Historical and Descriptive Sketches of the Maritime Colonies*, London, 1828, 167; Connor, *Man from Glengarry*, 17; J. MacTaggart, *Three Years in Canada*, 2 vols, London, 1829, I, 242.

76 Lower, *Great Britain's Woodyard*, 235.

77 H. Melville, *Redburn: His First Voyage*, London, 1976, 320; Mitchell, *Reminiscences*, II, 111–12.

78 A.C. Buchanan, *Emigration Practically Considered*, London, 1828, 87.

79 W. Bell, *Hints to Emigrants*, Edinburgh, 1824, 12, 26.

80 Bell, *Hints to Emigrants*, 6, 11.

81 E.C. Guillet, *The Great Migration: The Atlantic Crossing by Sailing Ship since 1770*, London, 1937, 72.

82 Lower, *Great Britain's Woodyard*, 243; C.W. Dunn, *Highland Settler: A Portrait of the Scottish Gael in Nova Scotia*, Toronto, 1953, 20; Devine, *Highland Famine*, 61; Coleman, *Passage to America*, 151.

83 Serle, *Golden Age*, 58; D. Charlwood, *The Long Farewell: The Perilous Voyages of Settlers Under Sail in the Great Migrations to Australia*, Warrandyte, 1998, 29; DCM (4/1579/1): J. MacKinnon to A. MacKinnon, 8 November 1852.

84 Balfour, 'Emigration Society', 462; Charlwood, *Long Farewell*, 98, 163.

85 Charlwood, *Long Farewell*, 79.

86 *Report of the Select Committee on Emigrant Ships*, London, 2 vols, 1854, I, 35–6; Balfour, 'Emigration Society', 457–62.

87 Balfour, 'Emigration Society', 463.

88 R. Broome, *The Victorians: Arriving*, Melbourne, 1984, 75; D. Baines, *Emigration from Europe, 1815–1930*, London, 1991, 225; E. Richards, 'St Kilda and Australia: Emigrants at Peril, 1852–53', *SHR*, LXXI, 1992, 145–50.

89 Charlwood, *Long Farewell*, 80, 93; E. Richards, 'The Highland Scots of South Australia', *Journal of the Historical Society of South Australia*, IV, 1978, 56–8.

90 R. MacKay, *Recollections of Early Gippsland Goldfields*, Traralgon, 1916, 28.

91 Prentis, *Scots in Australia*, 103; DCM (4/1578): A. MacKenzie to N. Farquharson, 5 December 1852.

92 Balfour, 'Emigration Society', 470–1.

93 DCM (4/1579/1): J. MacKinnon to A. MacKinnon, 8 November 1852.

94 DCM (4/1580): M. MacLeod to her brother and sister, December 1852; DCM (4/1579/1): J. MacKinnon to A. MacKinnon, 8 November 1752.

95 DCM (2/661/2): J. MacDiarmid to a friend in Skye, 5 September 1852.

96 T. Dingle, *The Victorians: Settling*, Melbourne, 1984, 32.

97 Serle, *Golden Age*, 54.

98 E. Richards, 'Australia and the Scottish Connection, 1788–1914', in R.A. Cage (ed.), *The Scots Abroad: Labour, Capital and Enterprise*, London, 1985, 136.

99 Goodman, *Gold Seeking*, xv.

100 Richards, 'Australia and the Scottish Connection', 136; E. Richards, *A History of the Highland Clearances: Emigration, Protest, Reasons*, London, 1985, 272.

101 Charlwood, *Long Farewell*, 80.

102 N. MacLeod, *Raasay: The Island and Its People*, Edinburgh, 2002, 12.

103 *Conditions of Crofters and Cottars*, II, 449; *Highlands and Islands Commission*, I, 13.

104 S. Heaney, 'The Trance and the Translation', *The Guardian*, 30 November 2002.

105 S. MacLean, *O Choille gu Bearradh: From Wood to Ridge: Collected Poems in Gaelic and English*, Manchester, 1990, 227–9.

106 I.C. Smith, *Towards the Human: Selected Essays*, Edinburgh, 1986, 130–1.

107 R.B. Molloy (ed.), *The Record Books of Raasay House, 1851–1869*, Isle of Raasay, 1974.

108 I am indebted to Barbara McLeod, Allansford, for her permission to use the results of her researches into the *Edward Johnstone* emigrants.

Chapter Six

1 R. Atkin, *Maintain the Right: The Early History of the North West Mounted Police*, London, 1973, 120–1.

2 Crauford-Lewis, *MacLeod of the Mounties*, 21–2.

3 S. MacLaren, *Braehead: Three Founding Families in Nineteenth-Century Canada*, Toronto, 1986, 53. For background on the Drynoch family, see: MacKinnon and Morrison, *MacLeods: Section Three*, 128–57.

4 MacLaren, *Braehead*, 62.

5 Atkin, *Maintain the Right*, 40.

6 Atkin, *Maintain the Right*, 106.

7 MacLaren, *Braehead*, 163. Also, material in the historical exhibition at Fort McLeod.

8 Atkin, *Maintain the Right*, 119; R.M. Utley, *The Lance and the Shield: The Life and Times of Sitting Bull*, London, 1998, 194.

9 Utley, *Lance and Shield*, 196–7; J. Wallace, *A Double Duty: The Decisive First Decade of the North West Mounted Police*, Winnipeg, 1997, 193.

10 Utley, *Lance and Shield*, 193–4.

11 For Duncan McDonald's account of the Nez Perce War, see D. McDonald,

'Through Nez Perce Eyes', in, L. Laughy (ed.), *In Pursuit of the Nez Perces*, Wrangell, 1993. For the MacDonald family story, see J. Hunter, *Glencoe and the Indians*, Edinburgh, 1996. This book is published in the US as *Scottish Highlanders, Indian Peoples: Thirty Generations of a Montana Family*, Helena, 1997.

12 The best account of Normand MacLeod's career is in *Dictionary of Canadian Biography*, 14 vols, Toronto, 1966–8, IV, 505–6. Several other MacLeod fur traders feature in the same source.

13 P.C. Newman, *Caesars of the Wilderness: The Story of the Hudson's Bay Company*, London, 1987, 127–8. For an account of fur trade activity in the Peace River country, see J.N. Wallace, *The Wintering Partners on Peace River*, Ottawa, 1929.

14 Wallace, *Wintering Partners*, 30.

15 S. van Kirk, *Many Tender Ties: Women in Fur Trade Society*, Winnipeg, 1983, 117.

16 For Sarah MacLeod Bellenden's story, see Kirk, *Many Tender Ties*, 211–19.

17 B. MacLeod, *Baby Gudjagah*, Nowra, 2002, 17.

18 For background on the Aboriginal presence at Orbost, see L. Wilkinson, 'Aboriginal Historical Places Along the Snowy River', *Gippsland Heritage Journal*, XXIII, 1999. Also, P. Pepper, *The Kurnai of Gippsland*, Melbourne, 1985.

19 MacLeod, *Bernisdale to Bairnsdale*, 83.

20 Boyd, *Eighteenth-Century Tracts*, 445.

21 R. Kipling, *Captains Courageous: A Story of the Grand Banks*, London, 1897, 42.

22 MacKinnon and Morrison, *MacLeods: Section Three*, 316–17; Boswell, *Journal of a Tour*, 368; A. MacLeod, *Negro Slavery Unjustifiable: A Sermon*, New York, 1802, 5, 7, 10, 41. Also, J. McLeod, *A Voyage to Africa with Some Account of the Manners and Customs of the Dahomian People*, London, 1820.

23 E. Ball, *Slaves in the Family*, London, 1999, 14.

24 J.A. Hanson, *Mary McLeod Bethune and Black Women's Political Activism*, Columbia, 2003, 80. Additional material from the many websites devoted to Mary McLeod Bethune.

25 N. Mandela, *Long Walk to Freedom*, London, 1995, 3–5.

26 J. Bruce, *Letters on the Present Condition of the Highlands and Islands*, Edinburgh, 1847, 50; K. Fenyó, *Contempt, Sympathy and Romance: Lowland Perceptions of the Highlands and the Clearances during the Famine Years, 1845–1855*, East Linton, 2000, 61, 85; Watson, *Caledonia Australis*, 54–5.

27 R.J. Adam, *Papers on Sutherland Estate Management*, 2 vols [I], E156, Edinburgh 175–6.

28 D. MacLeod, *Gloomy Memories: The Highland Clearances of Strathnaver*, Bettyhill, 1996, 49.

29 H.B. Stowe, *Sunny Memories of Foreign Lands*, 2 vols, London, 1854, I, 301–2, 313.

30 C.D. Rice, *The Scots Abolitionists*, Baton Rouge, 1981, 182; MacLeod, *Gloomy Memories*, 21.

31 K. Marx, 'The Duchess of Sutherland and Slavery', in K. Marx and F. Engels, *Articles on Britain*, Moscow, 1971, 143–6; K. Marx, *Capital: A Critique of Political Economy*, 3 vols, London, 1976, I, 891.

32 'D.M.', 'Donald MacLeod: Author of Gloomy Memories', *CM*, X, 1885, 556. For Rev. Roderick MacLeod, see R. MacLeod, 'The Bishop of Skye: The Life and Work of Rev. Roderick MacLeod', *TGSI*, LIII, 1983.

33 D. Ansdell, *The People of the Great Faith: The Highland Church, 1690–1900*, Stornoway, 1998, 138.

34 Ansdell, *People of Great Faith*, 116–20; Crauford-Lewis, *MacLeod of the Mounties*, 21.

35 Hunter, *Crofting Community*, 96; M. MacKay, *Brief Memorials of the Life, Character and Ministry of the Rev. Roderick MacLeod*, Edinburgh, 1869, 9; McCaskill, *Twelve Days in Skye*, 22.

36 MacLeod, 'Bishop of Skye', 189.

37 Hunter, *Crofting Community*, 138–9.

38 DCM (4/1382): J. MacPherson to N. MacLeod, 11 November 1884.

39 E. Cameron, *Land for the People: The British Government and the Scottish Highlands, 1880–1925*, East Linton, 1996, 33.

40 DCM (4/1374/5): N. MacLeod to W. Gladstone, 17 November 1890; Cameron, *Land for the People*, 43; R. MacLeod, 'The Crofter Commission', *Blackwood's Magazine*, CXLVI, 1889, 518–23.

41 DCM (4/1382): J. MacPherson to N. MacLeod, 11 November 1884.

42 DCM (4/1382): J. MacPherson to N. MacLeod, 11 November 1884; *Condition of Crofters and Cottars*, II, 187.

43 DCM (2/698): Emily MacLeod's View of the Condition of the People, 1885.

44 A. MacKenzie, *History of the Highland Clearances*, Inverness, 1986, viii–ix.

45 A. MacKenzie, 'The Editor in Canada', *CM*, V, 1880, 21.

46 *Ibid.*, 72.

47 *Ibid.*, 20.

48 For an account of Hugh McLeod's career, see P.N. Spellman, *Forgotten*

Texan Leader: Hugh McLeod and the Texan Santa Fe Expedition, College Hill, 1999.

49 For the MacLeods of Glendale, see, MacKinnon and Morrison, *MacLeods: Section Three*, 14–22, 62–79. Additional information from Don Mack McLeod and Weeden Nichols, Kansas, a great-great-great-grandson of Long Johnny McLeod.

50 MacLeod, *Island*, 33, 42.

51 Cumming, *Framboise*, 102.

52 Newspaper cuttings, from August 2003, in the possession of Bill MacLeod.

53 Memoir by Mrs Elizabeth Oxley, 1849–1934: typescript in possession of John McLeod, Auckland.

54 For further details of this family, see, J. Smyth, *One Hundred Years: A Family History of Murdoch McLeod and His Descendants*, Auckland, 1965. Donald, the family member who remained in Raasay, was the forebear of the late Calum MacLeod, a Raasay crofter who, in the 1980s, became famous for building a road single-handedly to his croft.

55 J. Prebble, *The Highland Clearances*, London, 1969, 169.

56 G. Kelly, *The Descendants of John and Christian McLeod of Waikare*, Titirangi, 1998, 12–13.

57 Obituary information in possession of Donald Warrington, Dunedin.

58 Family correspondence in possession of Gordon McLeod, Ashburton. Gordon is Graeme's father.

59 W. Vance, *High Endeavour: The Story of the MacKenzie Country*, Wellington, 1980, 95.

60 Vance, *High Endeavour*, 3–4.

61 D. McLeod, *Down From the Tussock Ranges*, Christchurch, 1980, 13.

62 Vance, *High Endeavour*, 51.

63 V. Pyke, *History of the Early Gold Discoveries in Otago*, Dunedin, 1887, 28.

64 Pyke, *Gold Discoveries*, 64.

65 *Condition of Crofters and Cottars*, III, 1171.

66 *Condition of Crofters and Cottars*, I, 101–3; SRO (AF51/134): M. MacInnes to Lothian, 6 February 1889.

67 *Report on the Condition of the Cottar Population of the Lews*, London, 1888, 5–7, 18–19.

68 For a detailed account of the Killarney and Saltcoats settlements, see W. Norton, *Help Us to a Better Land: Crofter Colonies in the Prairie West*, Regina, 1994.

69 T. Brooking, *Lands for the People: The Highland Clearances and the Colonisation of New Zealand*, Dunedin, 1996, 18.

70 I. Doig, *Dancing at the Rascal Fair*, New York, 1987, 90.

71 M. Harper, *Adventurers and Exiles: The Great Scottish Exodus*, London, 2003, 152–3.

72 R. Black (ed.), *An Tuil: Anthology of Twentieth Century Scottish Gaelic Verse*, Edinburgh, 2002, 414–15.

73 This and subsequent quotations draw on extracts from John McLeod's journal in the possession of R. McLeod, Winnipeg. The journal has also appeared in print: H.G. Gunn (ed.), 'Diary of Chief Trader John McLeod', *North Dakota State Historical Society Collections*, II, Bismark, 1908.

74 For an account of the late-nineteenth century crisis in sheep farming, see J. Hunter, 'Sheep and Deer: Highland Sheep Farming, 1850–1900', *NS*, I, 1973.

75 Hunter, *Crofting Community*, 195.

76 *Ibid.*, 203.

77 NAS Crofting Files (AF67/149): M. MacKay and others to Board of Agriculture, 19 February 1920.

78 L. Leneman, *Fit for Heroes: Land Settlement in Scotland after World War I*, Aberdeen, 1989, 140; NAS Crofting Files (AF67/148): A. MacAskill and others to Board of Agriculture, 4 December 1919; NAS Crofting Files (AF67/150): D. Ferguson and others to Board of Agriculture, 1 September 1920.

79 MacLeod, *Book of Dunvegan*, II, 101.

80 N.M. Gunn, *Off in a Boat: A Hebridean Voyage*, Isle of Colonsay, 1998, 92–5.

Chapter Seven

1 DCM: Diary and Papers of Flora MacLeod, uncatalogued.

2 A.W. Gordon, *Dame Flora: The Biography of Dame Flora MacLeod of MacLeod*, London, 1974, 106.

3 H. MacLennan, *Seven Rivers of Canada*, Toronto, 1977, 116; H. MacLennan, 'The Scottish Touch: Cape Breton', in E. Cameron (ed.), *The Other Side of Hugh MacLennan: Selected Essays Old and New*, Toronto, 1978, 216.

4 MacLennan, 'Scottish Touch', 221–2.

5 D.R. MacDonald, *Cape Breton Road*, London, 2001, 240.

6 MacLennan, 'Scottish Touch', 221.

7 C.W. Dunn, *Highland Settler: A Portrait of the Scottish Gael in Nova Scotia*, Toronto, 1953, 138; M. Newton, *We're Indians Sure Enough: The Legacy of the Scottish Highlanders in the United States*, Auburn, 2001, 269.

8 C. Ray, *Highland Heritage: Scottish Americans in the American South*,

Chapel Hill, 2001, xi. For a summary of tartanry's significance, see D. McCrone, *Understanding Scotland: The Sociology of a Stateless Nation*, London, 1992, 174–96.

9 R.T. Berthoff, 'Under the Kilt: Variations on the Scottish American Ground', *Journal of American Ethnic History*, I, 1982, 21.

10 B. Anderson, *Imagined Communities: Reflections on the Origin and Spread of Nationalism*, London, 1998, 6.

11 Letter from G. J. MacLeod, *CMM*, VII, 1975, 129.

12 M. Newton, *A Handbook of the Scottish Gaelic World*, Dublin, 2000, 111; Dunn, *Highland Settler*, 53; A.M. Grant, *Essays on the Superstitions of the Highlanders of Scotland*, 2 vols, London, 1811, 51.

13 Those connections can be traced in MacKinnon and Morrison, *MacLeods: Section Three*, 198–244.

14 Documentation supplied by Bunty McLeod.

15 D.E. Meek, *Tuath is Tighearna: Tenants and Landlords*, Edinburgh, 1995, 104, 224–6.

16 MacLeod, *No Great Mischief*, 160.

17 This and subsequent quotations from correspondence and other material in possession of William Angus's grandson, Rev. Jim McLeod, Cat Spring, Texas.

18 Extracts from letters to Flora MacLeod: *CMM*, I, 1942, 238, 267.

19 I.C. Smith, *Collected Poems*, Manchester, 1992, 314–15.

20 Smith, *Towards the Human*, 49.

21 S. MacLeod, 'The Day the *Metagama* Sailed from Stornoway', *Eilean an Fhraoich Annual*, 1973, 25.

22 Hunter, *Claim of Crofting*, 58.

23 J. MacAskill, *We Have Won the Land: The Story of the Purchase by the Assynt Crofters Trust of the North Lochinver Estate*, Stornoway, 1999, 68.

24 Material in possession of Rev. Jim McLeod.

25 NAS Crofting Files (AF67/147): D.G. MacSween and others to BoAS, 15 January 1921.

26 Rachael's ancestry can be traced in MacKinnon and Morrison, *MacLeods: Section Three*, 101–13; Morrison, *MacLeods: Section Four*, 91–7.

BIBLIOGRAPHY

CDM – Clan Donald Muniments
CM – Celtic Magazine
CMM – Clan MacLeod Magazine
DCM – Dunvegan Castle Muniments
NAS – National Archives of Scotland
NLS – National Library of Scotland
NS – Northern Scotland
PRO – Public Record Office
SHR – Scottish Historical Review
SS – Scottish Studies
TGSI – Transactions of the Gaelic Society of Inverness

1. Unpublished manuscripts

Dunvegan Castle, Isle of Skye
Dunvegan Castle Muniments: DCM.

Clan Donald Centre, Isle of Skye

Clan Donald Muniments.

National Archives of Scotland, Edinburgh

Seaforth Papers: GD46.
Fraser McIntosh Papers: GD128.
Material Relating to Highland Destitution: HD.
Papers Relating to Highland Destitution: AD58/81.
Records of the Highland and Island Emigration Society: HD4/1–5.
Portree Sheriff Court Records: SC32.
AF51: Scottish Office Emigration Files: AF51.
Scottish Office Crofting Files: AF67.
Scottish Office Estate Management Files: AF83.
Exchequer Land Settlement Files: E824.

National Library of Scotland, Edinburgh

Observations on the North of Scotland, 1796: MS1034.
MacKenzie of Delvine Papers: MS1102–310.
Observations or remarks upon the barony called Harries, 1772: MS3431.
Liston Papers: MS5696–7.
On Emigration from the Scottish Highlands and Isles: MS9646.
Letter and memoire concerning the Macklot family in France, 1754: Adv. 20.1.2.
State of Emigration from the Highlands of Scotland, 1802: Adv. 35.6.18.

Public Record Office, London

State Papers: Kidnapping of people in Skye and Harris, 1739: SP 63/402/129–43.
State Papers: Emigration from Lewis, 1774: SP 54/45/697–706.

Inverness Public Library

Joseph Maidment's Collection of Material Relating to Inverness-shire.

2. Other unpublished material

Basu, Paul, *Highland Homecomings: Genealogy and Heritage Tourism in the Scottish Highlands and Islands: A Report for Moray, Badenoch and Strathspey Enterprise*, Elgin, 2000.
Cultural Projects Unlimited, *Report to the Associated Clan MacLeod Societies*

on the Feasibility of Creating a Clan MacLeod Centre, Crawfordjohn, 2000.

Maclean, Cailean, Orbost Surveys: A Report for Skye and Lochalsh Enterprise, Isle of Skye, 2000.

3. Published contemporary material

A Candid Enquiry into the Causes of the Late and Intended Migrations from Scotland, Glasgow, 1771.

Adam, R.J. (ed.), Home's Survey of Assynt, Edinburgh, 1960.

—, Papers on Sutherland Estate Management, 2 vols, Edinburgh, 1972.

Adams, Ian H. (ed.), Papers on Peter May, Land Surveyor, 1749–93, Edinburgh, 1972.

Alison, William P., Observations on the Famine of 1846–47 in the Highlands of Scotland and in Ireland, Edinburgh, 1847.

—, Letter to Sir John McNeill on Highland Destitution, Edinburgh, 1851.

Amicus, Eight Letters on the Subject of the Earl of Selkirk's Pamphlet on Highland Emigration, Edinburgh, 1806.

Anderson, James, An Account of the Present State of the Hebrides and Western Coasts of Scotland, Edinburgh, 1785.

Andrews, Evangeline W. (ed.), Journal of a Lady of Quality: Being the Narrative of a Journey from Scotland to the West Indies, North Carolina and Portugal in the Years 1774 to 1776, New Haven, 1939.

Antiplagarius, 'On Emigration and the Means of Preventing It', Farmer's Magazine, IV, 1803.

Barron, James (ed.), The Northern Highlands in the Nineteenth Century, 3 vols, Inverness, 1907–13.

Bell, William, Hints to Emigrants, Edinburgh, 1824.

Bethune, William, 'Parish of Duirinish', in Withrington, D.J. and Grant, I.R. (eds), The Statistical Account of Scotland, 20 vols [XX], Wakefield, 1981.

Billis, R.V. and Kenyon, A.S., Pastoral Pioneers of Port Phillip, Melbourne, 1974.

Booklidge, J.W., County of Bruce Directory, Montreal, 1867.

Boswell, James, The Journal of a Tour to the Hebrides, London, 1984.

Botfield, Beriah, Journal of a Tour through the Highlands of Scotland, Norton Hall, 1830.

Boyd, William K. (ed.), Some Eighteenth-Century Tracts Concerning North Carolina, Raleigh, 1927.

Boyer, Carl (ed.), Ship Passenger Lists: National and New England, 1600–1825, Newhall, 1977.

— (ed.), *Ship Passenger Lists: New York and New Jersey, 1600–1825*, Newhall, 1978.

— (ed.), *Ship Passenger Lists: The South, 1538–1825*, Newhall, 1979.

— (ed.), *Ship Passenger Lists: Pennysylvania and Delaware, 1641–1825*, Newhall, 1980.

Bride, Thomas F. (ed.), *Letters from Victorian Pioneers*, Melbourne, 1898.

Brown, Robert, *Strictures on the Earl of Selkirk's Observations on the Present State of the Highlands*, Edinburgh, 1806.

Bruce, James, *Letters on the Present Condition of the Highlands and Islands*, Edinburgh, 1847.

Buchanan, Alexander C., *Emigration Practically Considered*, London, 1828.

Buchanan, John L., *Travels in the Western Hebrides from 1782 to 1790*, Isle of Skye, 1997.

Bumsted, J.M. (ed.), *The Collected Writings of Lord Selkirk, 1799–1809*, Winnipeg, 1984.

— (ed.), *The Collected Writings of Lord Selkirk, 1810–1820*, Winnipeg, 1988.

Cameron, Alexander (ed.), *Reliquiae Celticae*, Inverness, 1894.

Cameron, Viola R. (ed.), *Emigrants from Scotland to America, 1774–1775*, Baltimore, 1976.

Campbell, John L. (ed.), *Songs Remembered in Exile: Traditional Gaelic Songs from Nova Scotia*, Aberdeen, 1990.

Campbell, Ruby (ed.), *Correspondence and Documents pertaining to the Bethune, Keahey, McLeod . . . and other Highlander families of North Carolina*, Harnett, 1987.

Clancy, Thomas Owen (ed.), *The Triumph Tree: Scotland's Earliest Poetry, AD 550–1350*, Edinburgh, 1998.

Clarke, W.B. (ed.), *Emigration from the Highlands and Islands of Scotland*, Bicheno, 2002.

Creighton, Helen and MacLeod, Calum (eds), *Gaelic Songs in Nova Scotia*, Ottawa, 1964.

De Crèvecoeur, Hector St John, *Letters from an American Farmer*, London, 1981.

Cunningham, Peter, *Two Years in New South Wales*, Sydney, 1966.

'D.M.', 'Donald MacLeod: Author of Gloomy Memories', *Celtic Magazine*, X, 1885.

Dempster, George, *A Discourse Containing a Summary of the Proceedings of the Society for Extending the Fisheries and Some Thoughts on the Present Emigrations from the Highlands*, London, 1789.

Dickens, Charles, *American Notes*, London, 1985.

Dixon, James, *Narrative of a Voyage to New South Wales and Van Dieman's Land*, Edinburgh, 1822.

Dobson, David (ed.), *Directory of Scots Banished to the American Plantations, 1650–1775*, Baltimore, 1984.

— (ed.), *Directory of Scottish Settlers in North America, 1625–1825*, 6 vols, Baltimore, 1984–6.

— (ed.), *Directory of Scots in the Carolinas*, Baltimore, 1986.

— (ed.), *Emigrants and Adventurers from Argyll and the Northern Highlands*, 2 vols, St Andrews, 1993–2000.

— (ed.), *Scottish Soldiers in Colonial America*, 2 vols, St Andrews, 1995–97.

— (ed.), *Ships from Scotland to America, 1628–1828*, Baltimore, 1998.

— (ed.), *Scots in Poland, Russia and the Baltic States, 1550–1850*, Baltimore, 2000.

Douglas, Thomas, *Observations on the Present State of the Highlands of Scotland*, Edinburgh, 1806.

Duff, R.H. (ed.), *Culloden Papers*, London, 1815.

Dunderdale, George, *The Book of the Bush*, London, 1898.

Dunn, Douglas (ed.), *The Faber Book of Twentieth-Century Scottish Poetry*, London, 1992.

Ferguson, James (ed.), *Papers Illustrating the History of the Scots Brigade in the Services of the United Netherlands*, 3 vols, Edinburgh, 1899–1901.

Foote, William H., *Sketches of North Carolina: Historical and Biographical*, New York, 1846.

Fox, Denton and Palsson, Hermann (eds), *Grettir's Saga*, Toronto, 1974.

Fraser, A., 'The Gael in Canada', *TGSI*, XXIII, 1899.

Fullarton, Allan and Baird, Charles R., *Remarks on the Evils at Present Affecting the Highlands and Islands of Scotland*, Glasgow, 1838.

Fyfe, J.G. (ed.), *Memoirs of the Life and Gallant Exploits of Sergeant Donald MacLeod*, London, 1933.

Gilpin, William, *Observations, Relative Chiefly to Picturesque Beauty, made in the year 1776, Particularly the Highlands of Scotland*, 2 vols, London, 1789.

Girvin, John, *An Address to the Landholders, Factors and Tenantry in the Highlands of Scotland for Preventing Emigration*, Edinburgh, 1803.

Grant, Anne M., *Essays on the Superstitions of the Highlanders of Scotland*, 2 vols, London, 1811.

Grant, James S. (ed.), *Diary 1851: John Munro MacKenzie, Chamberlain of the Lews*, Stornoway, 1994.

Gunn, Neil M., *Off in a Boat: A Hebridean Voyage*, Isle of Colonsay, 1998.

Hall, James, *Travels in Scotland by an Unusual Route*, 2 vols, London, 1807.

Hancock, W. Neilson, *What are the Causes of the Distressed State of the Highlands of Scotland?*, Belfast, 1852.

Harvey, Daniel C. (ed.), *Bulletin of the Public Archives of Nova Scotia: Letters of the Rev. Norman McLeod, 1835–51*, Halifax, 1939.

— (ed.), *Journeys to the Island of St John or Prince Edward Island, 1775–1832*, Toronto, 1955.

Hassam, Andrew (ed.), *No Privacy for Writing: Shipboard Diaries, 1852–79*, Melbourne, 1995.

Headrick, James, *Report on the Island of Lewis*, London, 1800.

Heron, Robert, *Observations made in a Journey through the Western Counties of Scotland*, 2 vols, Perth, 1799.

Highlander, *The Present Conduct of the Chieftains and Proprietors of Land in the Highlands of Scotland*, Glasgow, 1773.

Hogg, James, *A Tour in the Highlands in 1803*, Edinburgh, 1986.

Homer, P.B., *Observations on a Short Tour to the Western Highlands of Scotland*, London, 1804.

Howison, John, *Sketches of Upper Canada*, Edinburgh, 1821.

Hughes, Edward (ed.), 'The Scottish Reform Movement and Charles Grey, 1792–94: Some Fresh Correspondence', *SHR*, XXXV, 1956.

Hunter, James (ed.), *For the People's Cause: From the Writings of John Murdoch*, Edinburgh, 1986.

Inverness Society for the Education of the Poor, *Moral Statistics of the Highlands and Islands of Scotland*, Inverness, 1826.

Irvine, Alexander, *An Enquiry into the Causes and Effects of Emigration from the Highlands*, Edinburgh, 1802.

Johnson, Samuel, *A Journey to the Western Islands of Scotland*, London, 1984.

Johnston, J.G., *The Truth: Consisting of Letters Just Received from Emigrants to the Australian Colonies*, Edinburgh, 1839.

Kennedy, David, *Pioneer Days at Guelph and the County of Bruce*, Toronto, 1903.

Kennedy, John, *The Days of the Fathers in Ross-shire*, Inverness, 1979.

Knox, J., *A Tour through the Highlands of Scotland and the Hebride Isles*, London, 1787.

Lang, Andrew (ed.), *The Highlands of Scotland in 1750*, Edinburgh, 1898.

Lang, John D., *Reminiscences of My Life and Times*, Melbourne, 1972.

Laughlan, W.F. (ed.), *James Hogg's Highland Tours*, Hawick, 1981.

Leith, William F. (ed.), *The Scots Men-at-Arms and Lifeguards in France*, 2 vols, Edinburgh, 1882.

Leyden, John, *Journal of a Tour in the Highlands and Western Islands of Scotland in 1800*, Edinburgh, 1903.

Loch, James, *An Account of the Improvements on the Estates of the Marquess of Stafford*, London, 1820.

McCaskill, Lady, *Twelve Days in Skye*, London, 1852.

McCharles, Aeneas, *Bemocked of Destiny*, Toronto, 1908.

MacCulloch, John R., *A Description of the Western Islands of Scotland*, 3 vols, London, 1819.

—, *The Highlands and Western Isles of Scotland*, 4 vols, London, 1824.

MacDonald, Duncan, 'Through Nez Perce Eyes', in Laughy, Linwood (ed.), *In Pursuit of the Nez Perces*, Wrangell, 1993.

MacDonald, James, *General View of the Agriculture of the Hebrides*, Edinburgh, 1811.

MacDonald, John (ed.), 'An Elegy for Ruaidhri Mor', *Scottish Gaelic Studies*, VIII, 1958.

MacDonald, Kenneth, 'A Run through Canada and the States', *CM*, VIII, 1883.

MacDonald, Rowland H., *The Emigration of Highland Crofters Shown to Be Inevitable*, Edinburgh, 1885.

MacDonell, John A., *Sketches Illustrating the Early Settlement and History of Glengarry in Canada*, Montreal, 1893.

MacDonell, Margaret (ed.), *The Emigrant Experience: Songs of Highland Emigrants in North America*, Toronto, 1982.

MacGillivray, W., 'Report on the Outer Hebrides', *Transactions of the Highland and Agricultural Society*, II, 1831.

MacGowan, Douglas (ed.), *The Stonemason: Donald Macleod's Chronicle of Scotland's Highland Clearances*, Westport, 2001.

MacGregor, John, *Historical and Descriptive Sketches of the Maritime Colonies*, London, 1828.

MacIver, Colin, 'Parish of Glenelg', in Withrington, D.J. and Grant, I.R. (eds), *The Statistical Account of Scotland*, 20 vols [XVII], Wakefield, 1981.

MacKay, John, 'Sutherland's Evictions and Burnings', *CM*, IX, 1884.

MacKay, M., *Sermon Preached in the Free Church, Snizort, on the Occasion of the Decease of the Rev. Roderick MacLeod*, Edinburgh, 1869.

McKay, Margaret M. (ed.), *The Rev. Dr John Walker's Report on the Hebrides of 1764 and 1771*, Edinburgh, 1980.

MacKay, Richard, *Recollections of Early Gippsland Goldfields*, Traralgon, 1916.

MacKay, William (ed.), *The Letterbook of Bailie John Steuart of Inverness, 1715–1752*, Edinburgh, 1915.

MacKenzie, Alexander, 'The Editor in Canada', *CM*, V, 1880.

—, 'Social Unrest in Skye', *CM*, VII, 1882.

—, 'The Highlanders of New Zealand and Their Distressed Countrymen at Home', *CM*, VIII, 1883.

McLaughlan, Thomas, *The Depopulation System in the Highlands*, Edinburgh, 1849.

MacLennan, Farquhar (ed.), *Duanagan, Duain is Dualchas a Eilean Ratharsair, Fladaidh is Eilean Tighe*, Isle of Raasay, 2001.

MacLeod, Alexander, *Negro Slavery Unjustifiable: A Sermon*, New York, 1802.

MacLeod, Donald, *Gloomy Memories: The Highland Clearances of Strathnaver*, Bettyhill, 1996.

MacLeod, John, 'Parish of Harris', in Withrington, D.J. and Grant, I.R. (eds), *The Statistical Account of Scotland*, 20 vols [XX], Wakefield, 1981.

McLeod, John, *A Voyage to Africa with Some Account of the Manners and Customs of the Dahomian People*, London, 1820.

MacLeod, Malcolm, 'Parish of Snizort', in Withrington, D.J. and Grant, I.R. (eds), *The Statistical Account of Scotland*, 20 vols [XX], Wakefield, 1981.

MacLeod, Norman, *Two Letters to the Chairman of the Association for Parliamentary Reform in Scotland*, Edinburgh, 1793.

—, *Considerations on False and Real Alarms*, London, 1794.

MacLeod, Rev. Norman, *Reminiscences of a Highland Parish*, London, 1833.

— (ed.), *Extracts from Letters to the Rev. Dr MacLeod Regarding the Famine in the Highlands and Islands*, Glasgow, 1847.

MacLeod, Reginald, 'The Crofters: How to Benefit Them', *Blackwood's Magazine*, CXXXIX, 1886.

—, 'The Crofter Commission', *Blackwood's Magazine*, CXLVI, 1889.

MacLeod, Roderick, 'Parish of Bracadale', in Withrington, D.J. and Grant, I.R. (eds), *The Statistical Account of Scotland*, 20 vols [XX], Wakefield, 1981.

MacLeod, Roderick, *Sermon Preached at a Gathering of MacLeods in St Clement's Church*, Lochmaddy, 1971.

MacLeod, Roderick C. (ed.), *The Book of Dunvegan*, 2 vols, Aberdeen, 1938–9.

McNeill, John, 'Emigration from the Isle of Skye', *Illustrated London News*, 15 January, 1853.

MacPhail, J.R.N. (ed.), *Highland Papers*, 4 vols, Edinburgh, 1914–34.

MacRae, Donald, *The Americans at Home: Pen and Ink Sketches of American Men, Manners and Institutions*, Glasgow, 1885.

MacTaggart, John, *Three Years in Canada*, 2 vols, London, 1829.

Magnusson, Magnus and Palsson, Hermann (eds), *Njal's Saga*, London, 1960.

— (eds), *The Vinland Sagas: The Norse Discovery of America*, London, 1965.

— (eds), *Laxdaela Saga*, London, 1969.

Mangan, James J. (ed.), *Robert Whyte's Famine Ship Diary: The Journey of an Irish Coffin Ship*, Dublin, 1994.

Martin, Martin, *A Description of the Western Islands of Scotland*, Edinburgh, 1994.

Marx, Karl, 'The Duchess of Sutherland and Slavery', in Marx, Karl and Engels, Friedrich, *Articles on Britain*, Moscow, 1971.

—, *Capital: A Critique of Political Economy*, 3 vols, London, 1976.

Masson, D., 'The Gael in the Far West', *TGSI*, III, 1873.

Matheson, William (ed.), *The Songs of John MacCodrum*, Edinburgh, 1938.

— (ed.), *The Blind Harper: The Songs of Roderick Morrison and His Music*, Edinburgh, 1970.

Mayhew, Henry, *London Labour and the London Poor*, 4 vols, London, 1861.

Meek, Donald E. (ed.), *Tuath is Tighearna: Tenants and Landlords*, Edinburgh, 1995.

Miller, Hugh, *The Cruise of the Betsey*, Boston, 1858.

Mitchell, Joseph, *Reminiscences of my Life in the Highlands*, 2 vols, Newton Abbott, 1971.

Molloy, Robert B. (ed.), *The Record Books of Raasay House, 1851–1869*, Isle of Raasay, 1974.

Monsen, Erling and Smith, A.H. (eds), *Heimskringla: The Lives of the Norse Kings*, New York, 1990.

Moodie, Susanna, *Roughing It in the Bush*, London, 1987.

Moorsum, W., *Letters from Nova Scotia*, London, 1830.

Morley, J.D.I. (ed.), *An American Venture: Letters Home from James and William McLeod, 1770–1776*, Clan MacLeod Society USA, 1988.

Mulock, Thomas, *The Western Highlands and Islands of Scotland Socially Considered*, Edinburgh, 1850.

Munro, James (ed.), *Acts of the Privy Council of England: Colonial Series, 1766–1783*, 6 vols, London, 1912.

Munro, Jean and Munro, R.W. (eds), *Acts of the Lords of the Isles, 1336–1493*, Edinburgh, 1986.

Munro, R.W. (ed.), *Monro's Western Isles of Scotland and Genealogies of the Clans*, Edinburgh, 1961.

Murray, Charles A., *Travels in North America*, 2 vols, London, 1839.

Newsome, A.R. (ed.), *Records of Emigrants from England and Scotland to North Carolina, 1774–1775*, Raleigh, 1962.

Ó Baoill, Colm and Bateman, Meg (eds), *Gàir nan Clàrsach: The Harps' Cry: An Anthology of Seventeenth-Century Gaelic Poetry*, Edinburgh, 1994.

Palsson, Hermann and Edwards, Paul (eds), *Egil's Saga*, London, 1976.

— (eds), *Orkneyinga Saga: The History of the Earls of Orkney*, London, 1978.

— (eds), *Eyrbyggja Saga*, London, 1989.

— (eds) *Landnámabók: The Book of Settlements*, Winnipeg, 1992.

Paton, Henry, *The Lyon in Mourning*, 3 vols, Edinburgh, 1895–96.

Pennant, Thomas, *A Tour in Scotland and a Voyage to the Hebrides*, Edinburgh, 1998.

Pyke, Vincent, *History of the Early Gold Discoveries in Otago*, Dunedin, 1887.

Remarks on the Earl of Selkirk's Observations on the Present State of the Highlands of Scotland, Edinburgh, 1806.

Report on the Proceedings of the General Assembly of the Church of Scotland in the Case of the Rev. Roderick MacLeod, Edinburgh, 1826.

Riley, Franklin L. (ed.), 'A Trip through the Piney Woods', *Publications of the Mississippi Historical Society*, IX, 1906.

Roberts, Richard A. (ed.), *Calendar of Home Office Papers in the Reign of George III*, 3 vols, London, 1899.

Robson, James, *General View of Agriculture in the County of Argyll and Western Part of Inverness-shire*, London, 1794.

Ross, Donald, *The Scottish Highlanders: Their Present Sufferings and Future Prospects*, Glasgow, 1852.

—, *Real Scottish Grievances*, Glasgow, 1854.

Rural Economist, 'Cursory Reflections on the Means of Preventing Emigration from the Highlands', *Farmer's Magazine*, IV, 1803.

Scots Magazine, Edinburgh, 1739–1804.

Scotus Americanus, *Informations Concerning the Province of North Carolina addressed to Emigrants from the Highlands and Western Isles of Scotland*, in, Boyd, William K. (ed.), *Eighteenth Century Tracts Concerning North Carolina*, Raleigh, 1927.

Scrope, G. Poulett, *Some Notes of a Tour in England, Scotland and Ireland*, London, 1849.

Seton, Bruce G. and Arnot, Jean G. (eds), *The Prisoners of the '45*, 3 vols, Edinburgh, 1928.

Sharpe, Richard (ed.), *Raasay: A Study in Island History: Documents and Sources*, London, 1978.

— (ed.), *Adomnan of Iona: Life of St Columba*, London, 1995.

Sinclair, Catherine, *Scotland and the Scotch*, Edinburgh, 1841.

Smith, Alexander, *A Summer in Skye*, Hawick, 1983.

Smith, Leonard H. and Smith, Norma H. (eds), *Nova Scotia Immigrants to 1867*, 2 vols, Baltimore, 1994.

Somers, Robert, *Letters from the Highlands on the Famine of 1847*, Inverness, 1977.

Steuart, A. Francis (ed.), *Papers Relating to the Scots in Poland, 1576–1793*, Edinburgh, 1915.

Stevenson, Robert L., *The Amateur Emigrant*, London, 1984.

—, *The Silverado Squatters*, London, 1984.

Stewart, David, *Sketches of the Character, Manner and Present State of the Highlanders of Scotland*, 2 vols, Edinburgh, 1822.

Stewart, Iain A.D. (ed.), *From Caledonia to the Pampas: Two Accounts by Early Scots Emigrants to Argentina*, East Linton, 2000.

Stewart, John, *An Account of Prince Edward Island in the Gulph of St Lawrence*, London, 1806.

Stowe, Harriet B., *Sunny Memories of Foreign Lands*, 2 vols, London, 1854.

Tabler, Edward C. (ed.), *Trade and Travel in Early Barotseland: The Diaries of George Westbeech and Norman MacLeod*, London, 1963.

Tepper, Michael (ed.), *Passengers to America: A Consolidation of Ship Passenger Lists*, Baltimore, 1980.

Thompson, Elizabeth (ed.), *The Emigrant's Guide to North America by Robert MacDougall*, Toronto, 1998.

Tregelles, Edwin O., *Hints on the Hebrides*, Newcastle, 1855.

Trevor-Roper, Hugh (ed.), *Lord Macaulay: The History of England*, London, 1986.

Walker, John, *An Economical History of the Hebrides and Highlands of Scotland*, 2 vols, London, 1812.

Wallace, William S. (ed.), *Documents Relating to the North West Company*, Toronto, 1934.

Warrand, Duncan (ed.), *More Culloden Papers*, 5 vols, Inverness, 1923–30.

Watson, J. Carmichael (ed.), *Gaelic Songs of Mary MacLeod*, Edinburgh, 1982.

White, Patrick C.T. (ed.), *Lord Selkirk's Diary, 1803–04: A Journal of his Travels*, Toronto, 1958.

Whyte, Donald (ed.), *A Dictionary of Scottish Emigrants to the USA*, Baltimore, 1972.

— (ed.), *A Dictionary of Scottish Emigrants to Canada before Confederation*, 2 vols, Toronto, 1986–95.

Willard, Margaret W. (ed.), *Letters on the American Revolution*, Port Washington, 1968.

Yates, William H., *The Modern History and Condition of Egypt*, 2 vols, London, 1843.

4. British parliamentary papers

A Survey and Report of the Coasts and Central Highlands of Scotland by Thomas Telford, 1802.

Reports from the Committee to whom the Survey and Report of the Coasts and Central Highlands of Scotland was Referred, 1802.

Reports from the Select Committee Appointed to Enquire into the Expediency of Encouraging Emigration from the United Kingdom, 1826–27.

Report from the Select Committee on Timber Duties, 1835.

Distress in the Highlands: A Letter Addressed to Mr Fox Maule by Mr Robert Graham, 1837.

Report from the Select Committee Appointed to Enquire into the Condition of the Population of the Highlands and Islands of Scotland and into the Practicability of Affording the People Relief by Means of Emigration, 1841.

Report from the Agent General for Emigration on the Applicability of Emigration to Relieve Distress in the Highlands, 1841.

Report from the Commissioners Appointed for Inquiring into the Administration and Practical Operation of the Poor Laws in Scotland, 8 vols, 1844.

Copy of Correspondence Respecting the Emigrant Ships Catherine *and* John and Robert, 1844.

Documents Relative to the Distress and Famine in Scotland in the Year 1783, 1846.

Correspondence Relating to the Measures adopted for the Relief of Distress in Ireland and Scotland, 1847.

Report to the Board of Supervision by Sir John McNeill on the Western Highlands and Islands, 1851.

Papers Relative to Emigration to the North American Colonies, 1852.

Report of the Select Committee on Emigrant Ships, 2 vols, 1854.

Report of the Commissioners of Inquiry into the Conditions of the Crofters and Cottars in the Highlands and Islands of Scotland, 5 vols, 1884.

Memorandum of Arrangements for Starting a Colonisation Scheme for the Crofters and Cottars of the Western Highlands and Islands, 1888.

Report on the Condition of the Cottar Population of the Lews, 1888.

Report of the Royal Commission, Highlands and Islands, 2 vols, 1895.

Annual Reports of the Board of Agriculture for Scotland, 1912–30.

5. Local history, family history and genealogy

Abernethy, Julia, 'The Genetics of Clan MacLeod', *CMM*, XIII, 2004.

Acland, L.G.D., *The Early Canterbury Runs*, Christchurch, 1975.

Adams, John, *Path Among the Years: History of the Shire of Bairnsdale*, Bairnsdale, 1987.

'Admiral Norman MacLeod: Royal Navy of the Netherlands', *CMM*, I, 1935.

American National Biography, 24 vols, New York, 1999.

Anderson, Frank W., *Fort Walsh and the Cypress Hills*, Humboldt, 1999.

Aragon, Lorraine V., *Sandhills Families: Early Reminiscences of the Fort Bragg Area*, Fort Bragg, 2000.

Australian Dictionary of Biography, 15 vols, Melbourne, 1966–2000.

Bangor-Jones, Malcolm, *The Assynt Clearances*, Dundee, 1998.

—, *Historic Assynt*, Lochinver, n.d.

Barron, Evan M., *Prince Charlie's Pilot: A Record of Loyalty and Devotion*, Inverness, 1913.

Bassin, Ethel, *The Old Songs of Skye: Frances Tolmie and her Circle*, London, 1977.

Beith, Alexander, 'Parish of Glenelg', *New Statistical Account of Scotland*, 15 vols, Edinburgh, 1845.

Berry, Gerald L., *The Whoop-Up Trail: Early Days in Alberta*, Lethbridge, 1995.

Bolger, Francis W.P., *Canada's Smallest Province: A History of PEI*, Charlottetown, 1973.

Boss, W., *The Stormont, Dundas and Glengarry Highlanders, 1783–1951*, Ontario, 1952.

Bryan, Tom, *Rich Man, Poor Man, Indian Chief: Fascinating Scots in Canada and America*, Insch, 1997.

Bryson, Jefferson W. and Boyes, Harry E., *The First Forty Years: The History of the Clan MacLeod Society in the United States of America, 1954–94*, Columbia, S. Carolina, 1995.

Buchanan, Joni, *The Lewis Land Struggle: Na Gaisgich*, Stornoway, 1996.

Budge, Eleanor M., *The Budges of Skye*, Inverness, 1975.

Bumsted, J.M. (ed.), *Dictionary of Manitoba Biography*, Winnipeg, 1999.

Butler, Bion H., *Old Bethesda: At the Head of Rockfish*, Southern Pines, 1933.

Byers, Mary and McBurney, Margaret, *Atlantic Hearth: Early Homes and Families of Nova Scotia*, Toronto, 1994.

Caird, James B., 'The Isle of Harris', *Scottish Geographical Magazine*, LXVII, 1951.

Caliri, David J., *Pine and Thistle: Two Hundred Years of Bethesda Presbyterian Church*, Aberdeen, 1989.

Cameron, Alexander, *History and Traditions of the Isle of Skye*, Inverness, 1871.

Cameron, James M., *Pictou County's History*, New Glasgow, 1972.

Campey, Lucille H., *A Very Fine Class of Immigrants: Prince Edward Island's Scottish Pioneers, 1770–1850*, Toronto, 2001.

Cheape, Hugh, 'The MacCrimmon Piping Dynasty and its Origins', *TGSI*, LXII, 2002.

Clan MacLeod Magazine, Edinburgh, 1935–2005.

Clan MacLeod New Zealand, *Annual Newsletter*, 1959–2004.

Clan MacLeod Society of France Bulletin, 1981–2004.

Clan MacLeod Society of Glengarry, *The MacLeods of Glengarry: The Genealogy of a Clan*, Dunvegan, 1971.

Clerk, Archibald, 'Parish of Duirinish', *New Statistical Account of Scotland*, 15 vols, Edinburgh, 1845.

Collins, Robert, *Prairie People: A Celebration of my Homeland*, Toronto, 2003.

Cooper, Derek, *Skye*, London, 1970.

Coulson, Thomas, *Mata Hari: Courtesan and Spy*, London, 1930.

Coupe, Robert L.M., *A MacLeod Family in Easter Ross During the Nineteenth Century*, Vancouver, 1991.

Cox, Kenneth, *Angus McMillan: Pathfinder*, Olinda, 1973.

Crauford-Lewis, Michael, *MacLeod of the Mounties*, Ottawa, 1999.

Cumming, Peter, MacLeod, Heather and Strachan, Linda, *The Story of Framboise*, Framboise, 1984.

Currie, Jo, *Mull: The Island and Its People*, Edinburgh, 2000.

Dempsey, Hugh A., *Charcoal's World: The True Story of a Canadian Indian's Last Stand*, Calgary, 1998.

Dictionary of Canadian Biography, 14 vols, Toronto, 1966–8.

Douglas, Hugh, *Flora MacDonald: The Most Loyal Rebel*, London, 1994.

Douglas, Rosemary and Perry, Margaret, *Eastern Gippsland: A Pictorial Journey*, Bairnsdale, 2002.

Douglas, William, *New Light on the Old Forts of Winnipeg*, Winnipeg, 1956.

Dressler, Camille, *Eigg: The Story of an Island*, Edinburgh, 1998.

Entwistle, Evelyn R., *History of the Gaelic Society of New Zealand*, Dunedin, 1981.

Farrell, Rita H., *Our Mountains and Glens: The History of River Denys, Big Brook and Lime Hill*, Truro, 1993.

Fedosov, Dimitry, *The Caledonian Connection: Scotland–Russia Ties: A Concise Biographical List*, Aberdeen, 1996.

Ferguson, Calum, *Children of the Black House*, Edinburgh, 2003.

Ferguson, Ronald, *George MacLeod: Founder of the Iona Community*, London, 1990.

Fletcher, Meredith and Kenneth, Linda, *East Gippsland Shire Council: Thematic Environmental History*, Monash, 2001.

Fowler, Malcolm, *They Passed This Way: A Personal Narrative of Harnett County History*, Harnett, 1992.

Fraser, Barry, *The Norman MacLeod Heritage Series*, St Anns, 1996.

Galbraith, John K., *The Non-Potable Scotch: A Memoir on the Clansmen in Canada*, London, 1967.

Gallant, Peter, *Scottish Immigrants to PEI*, Charlottetown, 1993.

Gilbert, Mary, *Personalities and Stories of the Early Orbost District*, Orbost, 1972.

Gillies, Donald, *The Life and Work of the Very Rev. Roderick MacLeod*, Portree, 1969.

Glass, John R., 'Parish of Bracadale', *New Statistical Account of Scotland*, 15 vols, Edinburgh, 1845.

Gordon, Anne W., *Dame Flora: The Biography of Dame Flora MacLeod of MacLeod*, London, 1974.

Gordon, R.E., *Dear Louisa: History of a Pioneer Family in Natal*, Durban, 1976.

Grant, I.F., *The MacLeods: The History of a Clan*, London, 1959.

—, *The Clan MacLeod*, Edinburgh, 1966.

Grey, Frank, *History of the McLeods of Helensville*, Otahuhu, 1962.

Grinton, Frederick, *Pastures Old and New: A Record of Our Pioneers*, Kerang, 1970.

Hackler, Rhoda E.A., *The Story of Scots in Hawaii*, Honolulu, 2001.

Hairr, John, *From Mermaid's Point to Raccoon Falls: A Guide to the Upper Cape Fear River*, Erwin, 1996.

Harkness, John G., *Stormont, Dundas and Glengarry: A History*, Ottawa, 1946.

Harrison, Gwen S. (ed.), *Families and Farms of Huron Township*, Ripley, 1985.

Hawkes, John, *The Story of Saskatchewan and its People*, 3 vols, Regina, 1924.

Hedrick, Joan D., *Harriet Beecher Stowe: A Life*, New York, 1994.

Henderson, Alexander, *Henderson's Australian Families: A Genealogical and Biographical Record*, Melbourne, 1941.

Henderson, Ann M., *Kildonan on the Red*, Steinback, 1981.

Hildebrandt, Walter and Hubner, Brian, *The Cypress Hills: The Land and Its People*, Saskatoon, 1994.

Hoar, Myra M. and Hoar, William S., *A Hebridean Heritage*, Vancouver, 1991.

Hornby, Susan, *Celts and Ceilidhs: A History of Scottish Societies on Prince

Edward Island, Charlottetown, 1981.

Hubbert, Mildred Y., *Split Rail Country: A History of Artemesia Township*, Owen Sound, 1987.

Hunter, James, *Skye: The Island*, Edinburgh, 1986.

Inverness Field Club, *Rossal: A Clearance Village in Strathnaver*, Inverness, n.d.

Johnston, Helen E., *McLeods by the Barque Bride: The History of Donald and Janet McLeod and their Descendants*, Auchenflower, 1997.

Johnston, Jim A., *Strathnaver Trail: The Story of North Highland Landscape*, Inverness, 2003.

Kane, Sharyn and Keeton, Richard, *Fiery Dawn: The Civil War Battle at Munroe's Crossroads, North Carolina*, Fort Bragg, 1999.

Keay, Julia, *Spy Who Never Was: The Life and Loves of Mata Hari*, London, 1987.

Kelly, Douglas F., *Carolina Scots: An Historical and Genealogical Study of Over 100 Years of Emigration*, Dillon, 1998.

Kelly, Glenys, *The Descendants of John and Christian McLeod of Waikare*, Titirangi, 1998.

Kennedy, David, *Pioneer Days at Guelph and the County of Bruce*, Toronto, 1973.

Lamb, James B., *Hidden Heritage: Buried Romance at St Ann's*, Wreck Cove, 2000.

Lawson, Bill, *Register of Emigrant Families from the Western Isles of Scotland to the Eastern Townships of Quebec*, Eaton Corner, 1988.

—, *Harris Families and How To Trace Them*, Northton, 1990.

—, *St Clement's Church at Rodel*, Northton, 1991.

—, *Register of Emigrant Families from the Western Isles of Scotland, 1750–1900: Isle of Harris*, Northton, 1992.

—, *The Teampull at Northton and the Church at Scarista*, Northton, 1993.

—, *The Teampull on the Isle of Pabbay: A Harris Church in its Historical Setting*, Northton, 1994.

—, *Register of Emigrant Families from the Western Isles of Scotland to Ontario*, Northton, 1996.

—, *Harris in History and Legend*, Edinburgh, 2002.

—, *The MacLeods of Lewis and Harris*, Northton, 2002.

Leah, Bill, 'Soay: The Island and some of its Folktales', *TGSI*, LVIII, 1994.

Lotz, Jim and Lotz, Pat, *Cape Breton Island*, Newton Abbott, 1974.

Love, John A., *Rum: A Landscape Without Figures*, Edinburgh, 2001.

MacAlister, Florence, *Memoir of the Right Honourable Sir John McNeill*, London, 1910.

MacAskill, John, *We Have Won the Land: The Story of the Purchase by the Assynt Crofters Trust of the North Lochinver Estate*, Stornoway, 1999.

MacCowan, Roderick, *The Men of Skye*, Portree, 1902.

McCrimmon, Madeleine and MacLeod, Donaldson R., *Lochinvar to Skye, 1794–1987: A History of the Roads East and West of McCrimmon*, Glengarry, 1988.

MacCrimmon, Malcolm, *The Family of MacCrimmon: Hereditary Pipers to MacLeod of MacLeod*, Vancouver, 1978.

MacDiarmid, R.C., 'Donald MacLeod the Skye Bard: His Life and Songs', *Transactions of the Gaelic Society of Glasgow*, I, 1887.

MacDonald, Donald, *Lewis: A History of the Island*, Edinburgh, 1978.

MacDonald, Donald, *Cape North and Vicinity Pioneer Families: History and Chronicles*, Cape North, 1996.

MacDonald, Donald J., *Clan Donald*, Loanhead, 1978.

MacDonald, Duncan, *Genealogical Sketches of the Families of MacRae and MacLeod of Glengarry*, Brockville, 1995.

MacDonald, Finlay J., *Crowdie and Cream and Other Stories: Memoirs of a Hebridean Childhood*, London, 1994.

MacDonald, Gordon, *The Highlanders of Waipu: Or Echoes of 1745*, Dunedin, 1928.

MacDonald, Isobel, *A Family in Skye, 1908–16*, Stornoway, 1980.

MacDougall, J.L., *History of Inverness County*, Belleville, 1972.

MacEwan, Grant, *Fifty Mighty Men*, Saskatoon, 1982.

MacFarlane, Norman C., *The Men of the Lews*, Stornoway, 1924.

MacGillivray, Royce and Ross, Ewen, *A History of Glengarry*, Belleville, 1979.

Machlejd, Wanda, 'Experiences in the Polish Home Army', *CMM*, I, 1946.

MacInnes, John, *The Brave Sons of Skye*, Edinburgh, 1889.

MacInnes, John, 'Gleanings from Raasay Tradition', *TGSI*, LVI, 1985.

MacIver, Matthew M., 'A Social and Economic Survey of the Island of Lewis, 1790–1850', *TGSI*, LII, 1982.

MacIvor, John, 'Parish of Harris', *New Statistical Account of Scotland*, 15 vols, Edinburgh, 1845.

MacKay, M., *Brief Memorials of the Life, Character and Ministry of the Rev. Roderick MacLeod*, Edinburgh, 1869.

McKenna, Kenneth J., 'Documents and Letters Relating to the Lochaber Emigrants of 1802', in Fleming, Rae (ed.), *The Lochaber Emigrants to Glengarry*, Toronto, 1994.

McKenna, Ken, *Highland Paths: Tales of Glengarry*, Alexandria, 1998.

MacKenzie, Alexander, 'First Highland Emigration to Nova Scotia: Arrival of the Ship *Hector*', *CM*, VIII, 1883.

—, *History of the MacLeods*, Inverness, 1889.

—, *History of the Highland Clearances*, Inverness, 1986.

MacKenzie, Greta, *Why Patagonia?*, Stornoway, 1996.

McKenzie, N.R., *The Gael Fares Forth: The Romantic Story of Waipu and Sister Settlements*, Christchurch, 1935.

MacKenzie, William, *Old Skye Tales: Traditions, Reflections and Memories*, Isle of Skye, 1995.

MacKenzie, William C., *History of the Outer Hebrides*, Paisley, 1903.

—, *The Book of the Lews*, Paisley, 1919.

MacKinnon, Donald, *The MacLeods of Arnisdale: Compiled from Family and Other Documents*, Dingwall, 1929.

—, *The Clerical Sons of Skye*, Dingwall, 1930.

MacKinnon, Donald and Morrison, Alick, *The MacLeods: The Genealogy of a Clan: Section One*, Clan MacLeod Society, n.d.

—, *The MacLeods: The Genealogy of a Clan: Section Two*, Clan MacLeod Society, n.d.

—, *The MacLeods: The Genealogy of a Clan: Section Three*, Clan MacLeod Society, n.d.

McKissack, Patricia and McKissack, Frederick, *Mary McLeod Bethune*, Hillside, 1991.

McLaren, David J., *David Dale of New Lanark*, Glasgow, 1999.

MacLaren, George, *The Pictou Book: Stories of Our Past*, New Glasgow, 1954.

MacLaren, Sherill, *Braehead: Three Founding Families in Nineteenth-Century Canada*, Toronto, 1986.

MacLean, Alasdair, *A MacDonald for the Prince*, Stornoway, 1982.

MacLean, Charles, *Island on the Edge of the World: The Story of St Kilda*, Edinburgh, 1996.

MacLean, Magnus, 'Skye Bards', in MacLeod, Fred T. (ed.), *Eilean a' Cheo: Isle of Mist*, Edinburgh, 1918.

MacLeod, Alastair, 'Introduction', in Rankin, Reginald (ed.), *Mabou Pioneers II*, Mabou, 1977.

McLeod, Bruce D., *Genealogy of the Family of MacLeod of Talisker in Australia*, Neutral Bay, 1990.

—, *Everyone Has a Granny Called MacLeod*, Clan MacLeod Society of New South Wales, 1994.

MacLeod, C.E. Alexander, *The Clan Mac Mhic Alasdair Ruaidh: The MacLeods of St Kilda*, London, 1968.

McLeod, Claude A., *Our MacLeod Ancestry*, (no place of publication), 1942.

MacLeod, Colina A.C., 'MacLeods in Gippsland', *The Gap*, 1921.

McLeod, David, *Many a Glorious Morning*, Christchurch, 1970.

—, *Down from the Tussock Ranges*, Christchurch, 1980.

MacLeod, Donald, *Memoir of Norman MacLeod*, London, 1882.

MacLeod, Douglas C., *The MacLeod Family of Lynchburg, Virginia: Ancestors and Descendants*, Franklin, 1993.

MacLeod, Frederick T., *Reminiscences of Skye*, Edinburgh, 1900.

—, *The MacCrimmons of Skye: Hereditary Pipers to the MacLeods of Dunvegan*, Edinburgh, 1933.

McLeod, Grover S. and Wright, Ophelia M., *Neal McLeod: His Genealogy*, US, Wedowee, 1961.

MacLeod, Harold B., *The Clan MacLeod of Australasia Pipe Band*, Bendigo, 2003.

MacLeod, Harold S., *The MacLeods of Prince Edward Island*, Montague, 1987.

McLeod, Ian, *McLeods and Malseeds*, Hobart, 2002.

MacLeod, Ian G., *A History of the Church in St Ann's*, St Ann's, 1970.

MacLeod, Isabel C., *Fifty Years of History: Glengarry Clan MacLeod*, Dunvegan, 1986.

MacLeod, J.B., 'A Rona Family in Canada', *CMM*, I, 1940.

MacLeod, J.F.M., 'Notes on Waternish in the Nineteenth Century', *TGSI*, LIX, 1995.

MacLeod, J.N., *Memorials of the Rev. Norman MacLeod*, Edinburgh, 1898.

MacLeod, J.R. Stuart, *An Enquiry into the Origin of the MacLeods*, Melbourne, 1912.

McLeod, James B. (ed.), *Patriarchal Papers*, 11 vols, Lumberton, 1985.

McLeod, James B., 'Early Pioneers from Skye to Prince Edward Island', *CMM*, VIII, 1980.

McLeod, James R. 'Tipu and the General: Skye Folk Tradition and History, *CMM*, XII, 1997.

—, 'The General and the Bibi of Canmore: Romantic Folk Tale or History?', *CMM*, XII, 1998.

—, 'The General and the Seaforth Doom', *CMM*, XIII, 2001.

McLeod, Jean, *The Dunosdale Story*, London, 1995.

McLeod, Jock, *Clan McLeod Helensville*, Helensville, 1995.

MacLeod, Joseph, *Highland Heroes of the Land Reform Movement*, Inverness, 1917.

MacLeod, Leòdhas, *Lingwick: Last of the Quebec-Hebridean Crofters*, Brampton, 2002.

McLeod, Leonard, 'The MacLeods of Vendôme', *CMM*, IX, 1983.

McLeod, Loris M., *From the Hebrides to Here*, Warrnambool, 1991.

MacLeod, Marjorie, MacLeod, Margaret and MacCrimmon, Madeleine, *Canadian Clan MacLeod, 1936–92*, Toronto, 1992.

MacLeod, Mary K., 'The MacLeod House', in MacLeod, Mary K. and St.Clair, James O., *Pride of Place: The Life and Times of Cape Breton Heritage Houses*, Sydney, 1994.

MacLeod, Norma, *Raasay: The Island and its People*, Edinburgh, 2002.

MacLeod, Phyl, *From Bernisdale to Bairnsdale: The Story of Archibald and Colina MacLeod and their Descendants in Australia*, Nar Nar Goon North, 1994.

McLeod, Rod, *The McLeods of Pabbay*, Adelaide, 1992.

MacLeod, Roderick, 'The Bishop of Skye: The Life and Work of Rev. Roderick MacLeod, Minister of Bracadale and Snizort', *TGSI*, LIII, 1983.

MacLeod, Roderick C., *The MacLeods: A Short Sketch of their Clan History*, Edinburgh, 1906.

—, 'A West Highland Estate During Three Centuries', *SHR*, XXII, 1925.

—, *The MacLeods of Dunvegan: From the Time of Leod to the End of the Seventeenth Century*, Edinburgh, 1927.

—, *The MacLeods: Their History and Traditions*, Edinburgh, n.d.

—, *Norman Magnus MacLeod: A Memoir of a Noble Life*, Inverness, 1930.

MacLeod, Ruairidh H. (ed.), *Chief Flora: A Memorial*, Association of Clan MacLeod Societies, 1977.

—, 'The Clans Retain Little Now of their Original Character', *CMM*, VIII, 1979.

—, *Flora MacDonald: The Jacobite Heroine in Scotland and North America*, London, 1995.

MacLeod, Sheila, 'The Day the *Metagama* Sailed from Stornoway', *Eilean an Fhraoich Annual*, 1973.

MacLeod, W. Allan, *McLeod Family History: The Story of the McLeod Family from Galloway, Scotland from 1770 to 2001*, Langley, 2001.

MacLeod, William S., *William McLeod: Progenitor of the Clan in the Bahamas*, Fresno, 1998.

'MacLeods in Canada', *CMM*, I, 1937.

MacMillan, A.J., *To the Hill of Boisdale: A Short History of the Pioneer Families of Boisdale, Cape Breton*, Sydney, 1986.

MacPhail, Andrew, *The Master's Wife*, Montreal, 1939.

MacPhail, Margaret, *Loch Bras d'Or*, Windsor, 1970.

McPhee, John, *The Crofter and the Laird*, New York, 1992.

MacPherson, Flora, *Watchman Against the World: The Remarkable Journey of Norman McLeod*, Wreck Cove, 1993.

MacQueen, Malcolm A., *Skye Pioneers and the Island*, Winnipeg, 1929.

—, *Hebridean Pioneers*, Winnipeg, 1957.

MacSween, Ann, *Skye*, Edinburgh, 1990.

Matheson, William, 'The Ancestry of the MacLeods', *TGSI*, LI, 1977.

—, 'The MacLeods of Lewis', *TGSI*, LI, 1979.

Miket, Roger, *Glenelg, Kintail and Lochalsh: Gateway to the Isle of Skye: An Historical Introduction*, Isle of Skye, 1998.

Miket, Roger and Roberts, David L., *The Medieval Castles of Skye and Lochalsh*, Isle of Skye, 1990.

—, 'The MacLeods of Ullinish', *CMM*, I, 1942.

Morgan, Patrick, *The Settling of Gippsland: A Regional History*, Traralgon, 1997.

Morley, J.D.I. (ed.), *An American Venture: Letters Home from James and William McLeod, 1770–1776*, Clan MacLeod Society USA, 1988.

Morrison, Alick, 'The Contullich Papers', *TGSI*, XLIII, 1962.

—, 'Harris Estate Papers, 1724–54', *TGSI*, XLV, 1967.

—, 'Early Harris Estate Papers, 1679–1703', *TGSI*, LI, 1978.

—, 'The Feu of Berneray and the Sale of Harris', *TGSI*, LI, 1979.

—, 'The Grianan Case, the Kelp Industry and the Clearances in Harris', *TGSI*, LII, 1980.

—, *The Chiefs of Clan MacLeod*, Edinburgh, 1987.

—, *The MacLeods: The Genealogy of a Clan: Section Four*, Edinburgh, n.d.

—, *The MacLeods: The Genealogy of a Clan: Section Five*, Edinburgh, n.d.

Moss, Bobby Gilmour, *Muster of the Loyalists in the Battle of Moore's Creek Bridge*, Blackburgh, 1992.

Munro, R.W., 'Some Hebridean Hosts: The Men Behind the Travellers' Tales', *TGSI*, XLIII, 1962.

Murchison, T.M., 'Glenelg, Inverness-shire: Notes for a Parish History', *TGSI*, XL, 1957.

Nelson, Larry E., *McLeod: A History of the Development of a Medical Center*, Florence, 1988.

Nicholson, John *et al.*, *Middle River: Past and Present History of a Cape Breton Community*, Cape Breton, 1985.

Nicol, Nancy M., *Tell Your Children About the Stones: A Short History of the Clan MacLeod Society*, Edinburgh, 2002.

Nicolson, Alexander, *Handbook to the Isle of Skye*, Glasgow, n.d.

—, *History of Skye*, Isle of Skye, 1994.

Nicolson, John, *I Remember: Memories of Raasay*, Edinburgh, 1989.

Oates, John A., *The Story of Fayetteville and the Upper Cape Fear*, Raleigh, 1972.

Olssen, Erik, *A History of Otago*, Dunedin, 1984.

Osborn, Betty, *The Bacchus Story*, Bacchus Marsh, 1973.

—, *A History of Holy Trinity Church*, Bacchus Marsh, 1997.

Patterson, George G., *A History of the County of Pictou*, Montreal, 1877.

—, *A History of Victoria County*, Sydney, 1978.

Patterson, M.A. and Carswell, A.D., *History of Sandy Grove Presbyterian Church*, Raeford, 1925.

Peterson, Richard and Catrice, Daniel, *A Short History of Bacchus Marsh and District*, Bacchus Marsh, 1995.

Pinney, Robert, *Early Northern Otago Runs*, Auckland, 1981.

Porter, Hal, *Bairnsdale: Portrait of an Australian Country Town*, St Ives, 1977.

Poulter, George C.B., *The MacCrimmon Family*, Camberley, 1936.

Reed, A.H., *The Story of Early Dunedin*, Dunedin, 1956.

Reid, Laurance, *The Soay of our Forefathers*, Isle of Skye, 1995.

Reynolds, Robert J., 'Over the Sea to Scotland's Skye', *National Geographic Magazine*, July 1952.

Robertson, Norman, *The History of the County of Bruce*, Toronto, 1906.

Robinson, Blackwell P., *A History of Moore County, North Carolina, 1747–1847*, Southern Pines, 1956.

Robinson, Neil, *Lion of Scotland: Norman McLeod*, London, 1974.

—, *To the Ends of the Earth: Norman McLeod and the Highlander Migration to Nova Scotia and New Zealand*, Auckland, 1997.

Ross, Malcolm, *Rivers of America: The Cape Fear*, New York, 1965.

Roy-Sole, Monique, 'Keeping the Métis Faith Alive', *Canadian Geographic Magazine*, March 1995.

Salierna, Antonietta, *East Gippsland Past and Present*, Lakes Entrance, 1987.

Schaitberger, Lilian B., *Scots of McIntosh*, Darien, 1986.

Scott, Hew (ed.), *Fasti Ecclesiae Scotticanae*, 8 vols, Edinburgh, 1915–50.

Sellar, W.D.H., 'The Ancestry of the MacLeods Reconsidered', *TGSI*, LX, 1998.

—, *The Highland Clan MacNeacail*, Isle of Skye, 1999.

Sharpe, Richard, *Raasay: A Study in Island History*, London, 1977.

Shepherd, Robert, *Iain Macleod*, London, 1994.

Sherwood, Roland H., *Pictou Pioneers*, Windsor, 1973.

Simpson, W. Douglas, 'A Chronicle History of Dunvegan Castle', *TGSI*, XXXVII, 1937.

—, *Dunvegan Castle, Isle of Skye: Official Guide*, Aberdeen, 1951.

Smyth, Jean, *One Hundred Years: A Family History of Murdoch McLeod and His Descendants*, Auckland, 1965.

Spellman, Paul N., *Forgotten Texan Leader: Hugh McLeod and the Texan Santa Fe Expedition*, College Hill, 1999.

Stanley, Laurie, *The Well-Watered Garden: The Presbyterian Church in Cape Breton*, Sydney, 1983.

Stewart, Walter, *The Early History of Bacchus Marsh Schools*, Bacchus Marsh, 1983.

Sullivan, Buddy, *Early Days on the Georgia Tidewater: The Story of McIntosh County and Sapelo*, Darien, 1992.

Swire, Otta, *Skye: The Island and its Legends*, Edinburgh, 1961.

Vance, William, *High Endeavour: The Story of the MacKenzie Country*, Wellington, 1980.

Vining, Elizabeth G., *Flora MacDonald: Her Life in the Highlands and America*, London, 1967.

Wallace, Stegner, *Wolf Willow: A History, a Story and a Memory of the Last Plains Frontier*, New York, 1990.

Wellman, Manly W., *The County of Moore, 1747–1947: A North Carolina Region's Second Hundred Years*, Southern Pines, 1962.

—, *The Story of Moore County: Two Centuries of a North Carolina Region*, Moore County Historical Association, 1974.

Wells, John, *Gippsland: A People, A Place and Their Past*, Drouin, 1986.

West, Charles S., *History of Helensville and Kaipara*, 1952.

Wheelwright, Julie, *The Fatal Lover: Mata Hari and the Myth of Women in Espionage*, London, 1992.

Wilson, Betty and Wilson, Neil, *Settling the Plains: A History of Tragowel*, Snowdon, 1978.

Yemen, Jane F., *Scrapbooks: 1850–1950*, Ripley, 1983.

6. Imaginative literature

Black, Ronald (ed.), *An Lasair: Anthology of Eighteenth Century Scottish Gaelic Verse*, Edinburgh, 2001.

—, *An Tuil: Anthology of Twentieth Century Scottish Gaelic Verse*, Edinburgh, 2002.

Connor, Ralph, *Glengarry School Days*, Toronto, 1990.

—, *The Man from Glengarry*, Toronto, 1993.

Disraeli, Benjamin, *Sybil: Or the Two Nations*, London, 1957.

Doig, Ivan, *Dancing at the Rascal Fair*, New York, 1987.

Gunn, Neil M., *Butcher's Broom*, London, 1977.

Hopkins, Harry, *The 1001 Nights of Drummer Donald MacLeod*, Edinburgh, 2000.

Johnson, Gerald, *By Reason of Strength*, Laurinburg, 1994.

Kidman, Fiona, *The Book of Secrets*, Auckland, 1987.

Kipling, Rudyard, *Captains Courageous: A Story of the Grand Banks*, London, 1897.

MacDonald, Ann-Marie, *Fall on Your Knees*, New York, 1998.

MacDonald, D.R., *Cape Breton Road*, London, 2001.

MacLean, Rory, *The Oatmeal Ark: From the Western Isles to a Promised Sea*, London, 1998.

MacLean, Sorley, *O Choille gu Bearradh: From Wood to Ridge: Collected Poems in Gaelic and English*, Manchester, 1990.

MacLennan, Hugh, *Each Man's Son*, Boston, 1951.

MacLeod, Alistair, *Island: The Collected Stories*, Toronto, 2000.

MacLeod, Alistair, *No Great Mischief*, New York, 2000.

McLeod, Bobby, *Baby Gudjagah*, Nowra, 2002.

Melville, Herman, *Redburn: His First Voyage*, London, 1976.

Morgan, Patrick (ed.), *Shadow and Shine: An Anthology of Gippsland Literature*, Traralgon, 1988.

Smith, Iain C., *Consider the Lilies*, Oxford, 1977.

Smith, Iain C., *Collected Poems*, Manchester, 1992.

7. General history, comment and analysis

Aberg, Alf, 'Scottish Soldiers in the Swedish Armies in the Sixteenth and Seventeenth Centuries', in Simpson, Grant G. (ed.), *Scotland and Scandinavia*, Edinburgh, 1990.

Adam, Margaret I., 'The Highland Emigration of 1770', *SHR*, XVI, 1919.

—, 'The Causes of the Highland Emigrations of 1783–1803', *SHR*, XVII, 1920.

Adams, Ian and Somerville, Merdyth, *Cargoes of Hope and Despair: Scottish Emigration to North America, 1603–1803*, Edinburgh, 1993.

Adamson, Ian, 'The Ulster–Scottish Connection', in Wood, Ian S., *Scotland and Ulster*, Edinburgh, 1994.

Andersen, Per S., 'Norse Settlement in the Hebrides', in Wood, Ian and Lund, Niels (eds), *People and Places in Northern Europe, 500–1600*, Woodbridge, 1991.

Anderson, Benedict, *Imagined Communities: Reflections on the Origin and Spread of Nationalism*, London, 1991.

Ansdell, Douglas, *The People of the Great Faith: The Highland Church, 1690–1900*, Stornoway, 1998.

Armit, Ian, *The Archaeology of Skye and the Western Isles*, Edinburgh, 1996.

Ascherson, Neal, *The Struggles for Poland*, London, 1988.

Atkin, Ronald, *Maintain the Right: The Early History of the North West Mounted Police*, London, 1973.

Bailyn, Bernard, *Voyagers to the West: Emigration from Britain to America on the Eve of the Revolution*, London, 1986.

—, *The Peopling of British North America: An Introduction*, New York, 1986.

Baines, Dudley, *Emigration from Europe, 1815–1930*, London, 1991.

Balfour, Roderick A.C., 'The Highland and Island Emigration Society, 1852–58', *TGSI*, LVII, 1986.

Ball, Edward, *Slaves in the Family*, London, 1999.

Bangor-Jones, Malcolm, 'From Clanship to Crofting: Landownership, Economy and the Church in the Province of Strathnaver', in Baldwin, John R. (ed.), *The Province of Strathnaver*, Edinburgh, 2000.

Bannerman, John W.M., 'The Lordship of the Isles', in Brown, Jennifer M. (ed.), *Scottish Society in the Fifteenth Century*, London, 1977.

Bardon, Jonathan, *A History of Ulster*, Belfast, 1992.

Barnhill, J.W. and Dukes, Paul, 'North-East Scots in Muscovy in the Seventeenth Century', *NS*, I, 1972.

Barrow, G.W.S., *The Kingdom of the Scots: Government, Church and Society from the Eleventh to the Fourteenth Century*, London, 1973.

Baynes, John, *Soldiers of Scotland*, London, 1988.

Bayly, C.A., *The Birth of the Modern World*, Oxford, 2004.

Belich, James, *Making Peoples: A History of the New Zealanders from Polynesian Settlement to the End of the Nineteenth Century*, Auckland, 2001.

—, *Paradise Reforged: A History of the New Zealanders from the 1880s to the Year 2000*, Auckland, 2001.

Bennett, Margaret, *The Last Stronghold: The Scottish Gaelic Traditions of Newfoundland*, Edinburgh, 1989.

—, *Oatmeal and the Catechism: Scottish Gaelic Settlers in Quebec*, Edinburgh, 1997.

Berg, Jonas and Lagercrantz, Bo, *Scots in Sweden*, Edinburgh, 1962.

Berthoff, Rowland T., *British Immigrants in Industrial America, 1790–1950*, Cambridge, 1953.

—, 'Under the Kilt: Variations on the Scottish-American Ground', *Journal of American Ethnic History*, I, 1982.

—, 'Celtic Mist Over the South', *Journal of Southern History*, LII, 1986.

Berton, Pierre, *The National Dream: The Great Railway, 1871–1881*, Markham, 1989.

—, *The Last Spike: The Great Railway, 1881–1885*, Markham, 1989.

—, *The Promised Land: Settling the West, 1896–1914*, Toronto, 1990.

Best, Henry B.M., 'The Auld Alliance in France', in Reid, Stanford W. (ed.), *The Scottish Tradition in Canada*, Toronto, 1976.

Bewley, Christina, *Muir of Huntershill*, Oxford, 1981.

Bieganska, Anna, 'A Note on the Scots in Poland', in Smout, T.C. (ed.), *Scotland and Europe, 1200–1850*, Edinburgh, 1986.

Bitterman, Rusty, 'Economic Stratification and Agrarian Settlement: Middle River in the Early Nineteenth Century', in Donovan, Kenneth (ed.), *The Island: New Perspectives on Cape Breton History*, Sydney, 1990.

Black, George F., *Scotland's Mark on America*, New York, 1921.

Blainey, Geoffrey, *A Shorter History of Australia*, Sydney, 2000.

Blair, Peter H., 'Olaf the White and the Three Fragments of Irish Annals', in Lapidge, M. and Blair, Peter H. (eds), *Anglo-Saxon Northumbria*, London, 1984.

Blake, Robert, *Jardine Matheson: Traders of the Far East*, London, 1999.

Blethen, H. Tyler and Wood, Curtis W., *From Ulster to Carolina: The Migration of the Scotch-Irish to Southwestern North Carolina*, Raleigh, 1998.

Bodnar, John, *The Transplanted: A History of Immigrants in Urban America*, Bloomington, 1985.

Bogucka, Maria, 'Scots in Gdansk in the Seventeenth Century' in Macinnes, Alan I., Riis, T. and Pedersen, F.G. (eds), *Ships, Guns and Bibles in the North Sea and the Baltic States, 1350–1700*, East Linton, 2000.

Bogue, Allan G., 'An Agricultural Empire' in Milner, Clyde A., O'Connor, Carol A. and Sandweiss, Martha A. (eds), *The Oxford History of the American West*, Oxford, 1994.

Bonner, Elizabeth, 'French Naturalization of the Scots in the Fifteenth and Sixteenth Centuries', *Historical Journal*, XL, 1997.

Borowy, W., *Scots in Old Poland*, Edinburgh, 1941.

Brander, Michael, *The Emigrant Scots*, London, 1982.

Bray, Elizabeth (ed.), *The Discovery of the Hebrides: Voyagers to the Western Isles, 1745–1883*, London, 1986.

Brock, Jeanette M., *The Mobile Scot: A Study of Emigration and Migration, 1861–1911*, Edinburgh, 1999.

Brock, William R., *Scotus Americanus: A Survey of the Sources for Links Between Scotland and America in the Eighteenth Century*, Edinburgh, 1982.

Broderick, George (ed.), *Chronicle of the Kings of Man and the Isles*, Edinburgh, 1979.

Brooking, Tom, 'Tam McCanny and Kitty Clydeside: The Scots in New Zealand', in Cage, R.A. (ed.), *The Scots Abroad: Labour, Capital and Enterprise*, London, 1985.

—, *Lands for the People: The Highland Clearances and the Colonisation of New Zealand: A Biography of John McKenzie*, Dunedin, 1996.

—, 'Sharing Out the Haggis: The Special Scottish Contribution to New

Zealand History', in Brooking, Tom and Coleman, Jennie (eds), *The Heather and the Fern: Scottish Migration and New Zealand Settlement*, Dunedin, 2003.

Broome, Richard, *The Victorians: Arriving*, Melbourne, 1984.

Broun, Dauvit, *The Irish Identity of the Kingdom of the Scots*, Woodbridge, 1999.

Brown, Wallace, *The King's Friends: The Composition and Motives of the American Loyalist Claimants*, Providence, 1965.

Bruce, Duncan A., *The Mark of the Scots*, Secaucus, 1997.

Bryan, Tom, *Twa Tribes: Scots Among the Native Americans*, Edinburgh, 2003.

Bryant, G.J., 'Scots in India in the Eighteenth Century', *SHR*, LXIV, 1985.

Bull, Esme, *Aided Immigration from Britain to South Africa*, Pretoria, 1991.

Bumsted, J.M., 'Sir James Montgomery and Prince Edward Island, 1767–1803', *Acadiensis*, VII, 1978.

—, *The Scots in Canada*, Toronto, 1982.

—, *The People's Clearance, 1770–1815: Highland Emigration to British North America*, Edinburgh, 1982.

—, *Land, Settlement and Politics on Eighteenth-Century Prince Edward Island*, Montreal, 1987.

—, *The Peoples of Canada: A Pre-Confederation History*, Toronto, 1992.

Burton, Anthony, *Thomas Telford*, London, 1999.

Butler, Lindley S. and Watson, Alan D. (eds), *The North Carolina Experience: An Interpretative and Documentary History*, Chapel Hill, 1984.

Byock, Jesse L., *Medieval Iceland: Society, Sagas and Power*, Enfield, 1993.

—, *Viking Age Iceland*, London, 2001.

Cage, R.A., *The Scottish Poor Law, 1745–1845*, Edinburgh, 1981.

Cain, Alex M. (ed.), *The Cornchest for Scotland: Scots in India*, Edinburgh, 1986.

Caird, James B., 'The Creation of Crofts and New Settlement Patterns in the Highlands and Islands', *Scottish Geographical Magazine*, CIII, 1987.

—, 'Early Nineteenth-Century Estate Plans', in MacLeod, Finlay (ed.), *Togail Tir: Marking Time: The Map of the Western Isles*, Stornoway, 1989.

Calder, Angus, *Revolving Culture: Notes from a Scottish Republic*, London, 1994.

—, *Revolutionary Empire: The Rise of the English-Speaking Empires*, London, 1998.

Calder, Jenni, *Bonny Fighters: The Story of the Scottish Soldier, 1600–1914*, Edinburgh, 1987.

—, *Scots in Canada*, Edinburgh, 2003.

Cameron, A.D., *Go Listen to the Crofters: The Napier Commission and Crofting*, Stornoway, 1986.

Cameron, Elspeth (ed.), *The Other Side of Hugh MacLennan: Selected Essays Old and New*, Toronto, 1978.

Cameron, Ewen A., *Land for the People: The British Government and the Scottish Highlands, 1880–1925*, East Linton, 1996.

—, *The Life and Times of Fraser Mackintosh, Crofter MP*, Aberdeen, 2000.

Campbell, D. and MacLean, R.A., *Beyond the Atlantic Roar: A Study of the Nova Scotia Scots*, Toronto, 1975.

Campbell, Marjorie W., *The North West Company*, Vancouver, 1983.

Campbell, Randolph B., *Gone to Texas: A History of the Lone Star State*, New York, 2003.

Campbell, Wilfred, *The Scotsman in Canada: Eastern Canada*, London, 1911.

Campey, Lucille H., *Fast Sailing and Copper-Bottomed: Aberdeen Sailing Ships and the Emigrant Scots they Carried to Canada*, Toronto, 2002.

Cannadine, David, *The Decline and Fall of the British Aristocracy*, London, 1990.

Cannon, Roderick D., *The Highland Bagpipe and its Music*, Edinburgh, 1995.

Cardell, Kerry and Cumming, Cliff, 'Scotland's Three Tongues in Australia: Colonial Hamilton in the 1860s and 1870s', *SS*, XXXI, 1992.

Charlwood, Don, *The Long Farewell: The Perilous Voyages of Settlers Under Sail in the Great Migrations to Australia*, Warrandyte, 1998.

Cheape, Hugh, *Tartan: The Highland Habit*, Edinburgh, 1995.

—, 'A Dance Called America: Migrating Music', *The Voice*, Winter 2003.

Ciechanowski, Jan M., *The Warsaw Rising of 1944*, Cambridge, 1974.

Clark, Andrew H., *Three Centuries and the Island: A Historical Geography of Settlement and Agriculture in PEI*, Toronto, 1959.

Clark, H. Wallace, *The* Lord of the Isles *Voyage: Western Ireland to the Scottish Hebrides in a Sixteen-Oar Galley*, Kildare, 1993.

Clyde, Robert, *From Rebel to Hero: The Image of the Highlander, 1745–1830*, Edinburgh, 1995.

Cohen, Robin, *Global Diasporas: An Introduction*, London, 1997.

Coldham, Peter W., *Emigrants in Chains: A Social History of Forced Emigration to the Americas, 1607–1776*, Baltimore, 1992.

Coleman, Terry, *Passage to America: A History of Emigrants from Great Britain and Ireland*, London, 1972.

Colley, Linda, *Britons: Forging the Nation, 1707–1837*, London, 1992.

—, *Captives: Britain, Empire and the World, 1600–1850*, London, 2002.

Constantine, Stephen, 'Empire Migration and Imperial History', in Constantine, Stephen (ed.), *Emigrants and Empire: British Settlement in the Dominions between the Wars*, Manchester, 1990.

Contamine, Philippe, 'Scottish Soldiers in France in the Eighteenth Century', in Simpson, Grant G. (ed.), *The Scottish Soldier Abroad*, Edinburgh, 1992.

Cookson, J.E., 'The Napoleonic Wars, Military Scotland and Tory Highlandism in the Early Nineteenth Century', *Scottish Historical Review*, LXXVIII, 1999.

Cooper, Derek, *Road to the Isles: Travellers in the Hebrides, 1770–1914*, London, 1979.

Corbin, Carol and Rolls, Judith A., *The Centre of the World at the Edge of a Continent: Cultural Studies of Cape Breton Island*, Sydney, 1996.

Cowan, Edward J., 'Norwegian Sunset, Scottish Dawn: Hakon IV and Alexander III', in Reid, Norman H. (ed.), *Scotland in the Reign of Alexander III*, Edinburgh, 1990.

—, 'The Myth of Scotch Canada', in Harper, Marjory and Vance, Michael E. (eds), *Myth, Migration and the Making of Memory: Scotia and Nova Scotia, 1700–1990*, Edinburgh, 1999.

—, *For Freedom Alone: The Declaration of Arbroath*, East Linton, 2003.

Cowan, Helen I., *British Emigration to British North America: The First Hundred Years*, Toronto, 1961.

Craig, David, *On the Crofters' Trail: In Search of the Clearance Highlanders*, London, 1990.

Crawford, Barbara E., *Scandinavian Scotland*, Leicester, 1987.

Cregeen, Eric R., 'The Tacksmen and their Successors: A Study of Tenurial Reorganisation in Mull, Morvern and Tiree in the Early Eighteenth Century', *SS*, XIII, 1969.

—, 'The Changing Role of the House of Argyll', in Phillipson, N.T. and Mitchison, Rosalind (eds), *Scotland in the Age of Improvement*, Edinburgh, 1970.

Critchett, Jan, *A Distant Field of Murder: Western District Frontiers, 1834–1848*, Melbourne, 1990.

Cróinín, Dáibhí Ó, *Early Medieval Ireland, 400–1200*, London, 1995.

Cumming, Cliff, 'Scottish National Identity in an Australian Colony', *SHR*, LXXII, 1993.

Cunliffe, Barry, *Facing the Ocean: The Atlantic and Its Peoples*, Oxford, 2004.

Cunningham, Tom F., *The Diamond's Ace: Scotland and the Native Americans*, Edinburgh, 2001.

Darling, F. Fraser, *West Highland Survey*, Oxford, 1955.

Davies, Norman, *Heart of Europe: A Short History of Poland*, Oxford, 1984.

—, *Rising '44: The Battle for Warsaw*, London, 2003.

Day, David, *Claiming a Continent: A New History of Australia*, Sydney, 2001.

Day, J.P., *Public Administration in the Highlands and Islands*, London, 1918.

DeMond, Robert O., *The Loyalists in North Carolina During the Revolution*, Hamden, 1964.

Derry, T.K., *A Short History of Scandinavia*, Minneapolis, 1979.

Devine, T.M., 'Temporary Migration and the Scottish Highlands in the Nineteenth Century', *Economic History Review*, XXXII, 1979.

—, 'Highland Migration to Lowland Scotland, 1760–1860', *SHR*, 63, 1983.

—, *The Great Highland Potato Famine*, Manchester, 1988.

—, 'Landlordism and Highland Emigration', in Devine, T.M. (ed.), *Scottish Emigration and Scottish Society*, Edinburgh, 1992.

—, *Clanship to Crofters' War: The Social Transformation of the Scottish Highlands*, Manchester, 1994.

—, 'A Conservative People: Gaeldom in the Age of Improvement', in Devine, T.M. and Young, J.R. (eds), *Eighteenth-Century Scotland: New Perspectives*, East Linton, 1999.

—, *Scotland's Empire*, London, 2003.

Dingle, Tony, *The Victorians: Settling*, Melbourne, 1984.

Ditchburn, David, *Scotland and Europe: The Medieval Kingdom and its Contacts with Christendom*, East Linton, 2000.

Dobson, David, *Scottish Emigration to Colonial America, 1607–1785*, Athens, 1994.

Dodgshon, Robert A., *From Chiefs to Landlords: Social and Economic Change in the Western Highlands and Islands, 1493–1820*, Edinburgh, 1998.

Donaldson, Gordon, *The Scots Overseas*, London, 1966.

Donnachie, Ian L., 'Scottish Criminals and Transportation to Australia, 1786–1852', *Scottish Economic and Social History*, IV, 1984.

—, 'Economy and Society in the Seventeenth Century in the Highlands', in MacLean, Loraine (ed.), *The Seventeenth Century in the Highlands*, Inverness, 1986.

—, 'The Making of Scots on the Make: Scottish Settlement and Enterprise in Australia', in Devine, T.M. (ed.), *Scottish Emigration and Scottish Society*, Edinburgh, 1992.

Dow, F.D., *Cromwellian Scotland, 1651–1660*, Edinburgh, 1979.

Duffy, Sean, 'Irishmen and Islesmen in the Kingdoms of Dublin and Man, 1052–1171', *Eriu*, XLIII, 1992.

Dukes, Paul, 'The First Scottish Soldiers in Russia', in Simpson, Grant G. (ed.), *The Scottish Soldier Abroad*, Edinburgh, 1992.

Duncan, K.J., 'Patterns of Settlement in the East', in Reid, Stanford W. (ed.), *The Scottish Tradition in Canada*, Toronto, 1976.

Dunlop, Jean, *The British Fisheries Society, 1786–1893*, Edinburgh, 1978.

Dunn, Charles W., *Highland Settler: A Portrait of the Scottish Gael in Nova Scotia*, Toronto, 1953.

Dunthorne, Hugh, 'Scots in the Wars of the Low Countries, 1572–1648', in Simpson, Grant G. (ed.), *Scotland and the Low Countries, 1124–1994*, East Linton, 1996.

Ekirch, Roger A., *Bound for America: The Transportation of British Convicts to the Colonies, 1718–1775*, Oxford, 1987.

Emmerson, George S., 'The Gaelic Tradition in Canada', in Reid, Stanford W. (ed.), *The Scottish Tradition in Canada*, Toronto, 1976.

Erickson, Charlotte J., *Invisible Immigrants: The Adaption of English and Scottish Immigrants in Nineteenth-Century America*, London, 1972.

—, 'Who Were the English and Scottish Emigrants to the United States in the Late Nineteenth Century?', in Glass, D.V. and Revelle, R. (eds), *Population and Social Change*, London, 1972.

Fay, C.R., *Adam Smith and the Scotland of his Day*, Cambridge, 1956.

Fellows-Jensen, Gillian, 'Viking Settlement in the Northern and Western Isles: The Placename Evidence', in Fenton, Alexander and Palsson, Hermann (eds), *The Northern and Western Isles in the Viking World: Survival, Continuity and Change*, Edinburgh, 1984.

Fenyó, Krisztina, *Contempt, Sympathy and Romance: Lowland Perceptions of the Highlands and the Clearances during the Famine Years, 1845–1855*, East Linton, 2000.

Ferguson, Niall, *Empire: How Britain Made the Modern World*, London, 2004.

Ferguson, William, *The Identity of the Scottish Nation: An Historic Quest*, Edinburgh, 1998.

Fischer, David H., *Albion's Seed: Four British Folkways in America*, Oxford, 1989.

Fischer, Thomas A., *The Scots in Germany*, Edinburgh, 1902.

—, *The Scots in Eastern and Western Prussia*, Edinburgh, 1903.

—, *The Scots in Sweden*, Edinburgh, 1907.

Fitzpatrick, Rory, *God's Frontiersmen: The Scots-Irish Epic*, London, 1989.

Flinn, Michael W., 'Malthus, Emigration and Potatoes in the Scottish North-West, 1770–1870', in Cullen, L.M. and Smout, T.C. (eds), *Comparative Aspects of Scottish and Irish Economic and Social History, 1600–1900*, Edinburgh, 1974.

—, *Scottish Population History*, Cambridge, 1977.

Fogleman, Aaron, 'Migration to the Thirteen British North American Colonies, 1700–75: New Estimates', *Journal of Interdisciplinary History*, XXII, 1992.

Forrest, Denys, *Tiger of Mysore: The Life and Death of Tipu Sultan*, London, 1970.

Foster, Gilbert, *Language and Poverty: The Persistence of Scottish Gaelic in Eastern Canada*, St John's, 1988.

Friesen, Gerald, *The Canadian Prairies: A History*, Toronto, 1987.

Fry, Michael, *The Dundas Despotism*, Edinburgh, 1992.

—, *The Scottish Empire*, Edinburgh, 2001.

Gardner, P.D., *Gippsland Massacres: The Destruction of the Kurnai Tribes, 1800–1860*, Warragul, 1983.

Gibb, Andrew D., *Scottish Empire*, London, 1937.

Gibbon, John M., *Scots in Canada*, London, 1911.

Gibson, Rob, *Plaids and Bandanas: From Highland Drover to Wild West Cowboy*, Edinburgh, 2003.

Gifford, John, *The Buildings of Scotland: Highlands and Islands*, London, 1992.

Giliomee, Hermann, *The Afrikaners: Biography of a People*, Cape Town, 2003.

Gjerde, Jon, *From Peasants to Farmers: The Migration from Balestrand, Norway, to the Upper Middle West*, Cambridge, 1985.

Goldring, Philip, 'Scottish Recruiting for the Hudson's Bay Company, 1821–80', *Scottish Tradition*, IX, 1979.

—, 'Lewis and the Hudson's Bay Company in the Nineteenth Century', *SS*, XXIV, 1980.

Goodare, Julian, 'The Statutes of Iona in Context', *SHR*, LXXVII, 1998.

Goodman, David, *Gold Seeking: Victoria and California in the 1850s*, St Leonards, 1994.

Gourievidis, Laurence, 'The Strathnaver Clearances in Modern Scottish Fiction', in Baldwin, John R. (ed.), *The Province of Strathnaver*, Edinburgh, 2000.

Graham, Ian C.C., *Colonists from Scotland: Emigration to North America, 1707–1783*, New York, 1956.

Graham-Campbell, James, *The Viking World*, London, 2001.

Grainger, John D., *Cromwell against the Scots: The Last Anglo-Scottish War, 1650–1652*, East Linton, 1997.

Grant, Alexander, 'Scotland's Celtic Fringe in the late Middle Ages: The MacDonald Lords of the Isles and the Kingdom of Scotland', in Davies,

R.R. (ed.), *The British Isles, 1100–1500: Comparisons, Contrasts and Connections*, Edinburgh, 1988.

Grant, I.F., *Highland Folk Ways*, London, 1961.

Grant, I.F. and Cheape, Hugh, *Periods in Highland History*, London, 1987.

Grant, James, *Scottish Soldiers of Fortune*, London, 1890.

Gray, John M., *Lord Selkirk of Red River*, London, 1963.

Gray, Malcolm, *The Highland Economy, 1750–1850*, Edinburgh, 1957.

—, 'The Course of Scottish Emigration, 1750–1914: Enduring Influences and Changing Circumstances', in Devine, T.M. (ed.), *Scottish Emigration and Scottish Society*, Edinburgh, 1992.

Greene, Jack P., *Pursuits of Happiness: The Social Development of Early Modern British Colonies and the Formation of American Culture*, Chapel Hill, 1988.

Griffin, Patrick, *The People with No Name: Ireland's Ulster Scots, America's Scots Irish and the Creation of a British Atlantic World*, Princeton, 2001.

Grimble, Ian, 'Emigration in the Time of Rob Donn, 1714–1778', *SS*, VII, 1963.

—, *Chief of Mackay*, London, 1965.

—, *The World of Rob Donn*, Edinburgh, 1979.

—, *The Trial of Patrick Sellar*, Edinburgh, 1993.

Guillet, Edwin C., *The Great Migration: The Atlantic Crossing by Sailing Ship since 1770*, London, 1937.

Haines, Robin F., *Emigration and the Labouring Poor: Australian Recruitment in Britain and Ireland, 1831–60*, Basingstoke, 1997.

Haldane, A.R.B., *The Drove Roads of Scotland*, Edinburgh, 1971.

Hance, William A., *The Outer Hebrides in Relation to Highland Depopulation*, New York, 1949.

Hanson, Joyce A., *Mary McLeod Bethune and Black Women's Political Activism*, Columbia, 2003.

Harper, Marjory, *Emigration from North-East Scotland*, 2 vols, Aberdeen, 1988.

—, 'Crofter Colonists in Canada: An Experiment in Empire Settlement in the 1920s', *Northern Scotland*, XIV, 1994.

—, *Emigration from Scotland Between the Wars: Opportunity or Exile*, Manchester, 1998.

—, *Adventurers and Exiles: The Great Scottish Exodus*, London, 2003.

Harvey, D.C., 'Scottish Immigration to Cape Breton', in MacGillivray, Don and Tennyson, Brian (eds), *Cape Breton Historical Essays*, Sydney, 1980.

Hassam, Andrew, *Sailing to Australia: Shipboard Diaries by Nineteenth-Century British Emigrants*, Manchester, 1994.

Haws, Charles H., *Scots in the Old Dominion, 1685–1800*, Edinburgh, 1980.

Hayes-McCoy, G.A., *Scots Mercenary Forces in Ireland, 1565–1603*, Dublin, 1937.

Heaney, Seamus, 'Introduction', in Ross, Raymond J. and Hardy, Joy (eds), *Sorley MacLean: Critical Essays*, Edinburgh, 1986.

—, 'The Trance and the Translation', *The Guardian*, 30 November 2002.

Hearn, Terry, 'Scots Miners on the Goldfields', in Brooking, Tom and Coleman, Jennie (eds), *The Heather and the Fern: Scottish Migration and New Zealand Settlement*, Dunedin, 2003.

Henderson, Diana, *Highland Soldier: A Social Study of the Highland Regiments*, Edinburgh, 1989.

Hewitson, Jim, *Tam Blake & Co: The Story of the Scots in America*, Edinburgh, 1993.

—, *Far Off in Sunlit Places: Stories of the Scots in Australia and New Zealand*, Edinburgh, 1998.

Hill, Douglas, *Great Emigrations: The Scots to Canada*, London, 1972.

Hitchins, Fred H., *The Colonial Land and Emigration Commission*, Philadelphia, 1931.

Hook, Andrew, *Scotland and America: A Study of Cultural Relations, 1750–1835*, Glasgow, 1975.

Hornsby, Stephen, *Nineteenth-Century Cape Breton: A Historical Geography*, Toronto, 1992.

Hughes, Robert, *The Fatal Shore: A History of the Transportation of Convicts to Australia, 1787–1868*, London, 1987.

Hunter, James, 'Sheep and Deer: Highland Sheep Farming, 1850–1900', *Northern Scotland*, I, 1973.

—, *The Making of the Crofting Community*, Edinburgh, 1976.

—, *The Claim of Crofting: The Scottish Highlands and Islands, 1930–1990*, Edinburgh, 1991.

—, *A Dance Called America: The Scottish Highlands, the United States and Canada*, Edinburgh, 1994.

—, *On the Other Side of Sorrow: Nature and People in the Scottish Highlands*, Edinburgh, 1995.

—, *Glencoe and the Indians*, Edinburgh, 1996.

—, *Last of the Free: A Millennial History of the Highlands and Islands of Scotland*, Edinburgh, 1999.

Hutchinson, Roger, *The Soapman: Lewis, Harris and Lord Leverhulme*, Edinburgh, 2003.

Insh, George P., *Scottish Colonial Schemes, 1620–1686*, Glasgow, 1922.

Jackson, W. Turrentine, *The Enterprising Scot: Investors in the American West after 1873*, Edinburgh, 1968.

James, Lawrence, *Raj: The Making and Unmaking of British India*, London, 1998.

Jedrey, Charles and Nuttall, Mark, *White Settlers: The Impact of Rural Repopulation in Scotland*, Luxembourg, 1996.

Jesch, Judith, *Women in the Viking Age*, Woodbridge, 1994.

Johnston, Hugh J.M., *British Emigration Policy, 1815–1830: Shovelling Out Paupers*, Oxford, 1972.

Jones, Gwyn, *A History of the Vikings*, Oxford, 1984.

— (ed.), *The Norse Atlantic Saga*, Oxford, 1986.

Kaminska, Elzbieta, *Powstanie Warszawskie: The Warsaw Uprising*, Warsaw, 2004.

Karlsson, Gunnar, *Iceland's 1100 Years: History of a Marginal Society*, London, 2000.

—, *A Brief History of Iceland*, Reykjavik, 2000.

Karras, Alan L., *Sojourners in the Sun: Scottish Migrants in Jamaica and the Chesapeake, 1740–1800*, Ithaca, 1992.

Keay, John, *The Honourable Company: A History of the English East India Company*, London, 1993.

Kennedy, Michael, 'Lochaber No More: A Critical Examination of Highland Emigration Mythology', in Harper, Marjory and Vance, Michael E. (eds), *Myth, Migration and the Making of Memory: Scotia and Nova Scotia, 1700–1990*, Edinburgh, 1999.

Kidd, Sheila M., 'Caraidh nan Gaidheal and Friend of Emigration: Gaelic Emigration Literature of the 1840s', *SHR*, LXXXI, 2002.

Kiddle, Margaret, *Men of Yesterday: A Social History of the Western District of Victoria*, Melbourne, 1961.

Kiernan, Victor, 'Scottish Soldiers in the Conquest of India', in, Simpson, Grant G. (ed.), *The Scottish Soldier Abroad*, Edinburgh, 1992.

Kingston, Simon, 'Trans-Insular Lordship in the Fifteenth Century', in Devine, T.M. and MacMillan, J.F. (eds), *Celebrating Columba: Irish–Scottish Connections, 597–1997*, Edinburgh, 1999.

Kirk, Sylvia van, *Many Tender Ties: Women in Fur Trade Society*, Winnipeg, 1983.

Knightley, Phillip, *Australia: A Biography of a Nation*, London, 2000.

Knowles, Norman, *Inventing the Loyalists: The Ontario Loyalist Tradition and the Creation of Useable Pasts*, Toronto, 1997.

Lacy, Terry G., *Ring of Seasons: Iceland, Its Culture and History*, Reykjavik, 1998.

Landsman, Ned C., *Scotland and its First American Colony, 1683–1765*, Princeton, 1985.

—, 'The provinces and the empire: Scotland, the American colonies and the development of a British provincial identity', in Stone, Lawrence (ed.), *An Imperial State at War: Britain from 1689 to 1815*, London, 1994.

Lawson, Alan, 'The North West Company of Canada: The Highland Connection', in MacLean, Loraine (ed.), *An Inverness Miscellany*, Inverness, 1987.

Lee, Stephen J., *The Thirty Years War*, London, 1991.

Lefler, Hugh T. and Newsome, Albert R., *North Carolina: The History of a Southern State*, Chapel Hill, 1973.

Lefler, Hugh T. and Powell, William S., *Colonial North Carolina: A History*, New York, 1973.

Lehman, William C., *Scottish and Scotch-Irish Contributions to Early American Life and Culture*, Port Washington, 1978.

Leneman, Leah, *Fit for Heroes: Land Settlement in Scotland after World War I*, Aberdeen, 1989.

Lenman, Bruce, *The Jacobite Risings in Britain, 1689–1746*, London, 1980.

—, *Scotland, Integration, Enlightenment and Industrialisation*, London, 1981.

—, *The Jacobite Clans of the Great Glen, 1650–1784*, London, 1984.

—, 'The Highland Aristocracy and North America, 1603–1784', in MacLean, Loraine (ed.), *The Seventeenth Century in the Highlands*, Inverness, 1986.

Lindsay, Isobel, 'Migration and Motivation: A Twentieth-Century Perspective', in Devine, T.M. (ed.), *Scottish Emigration and Scottish Society*, Edinburgh, 1992.

Lindsay, Maurice, *The Castles of Scotland*, London, 1986.

Little, Jack I., *Crofters and Habitants: Settler Society, Economy and Culture in a Quebec Township, 1848–1881*, Montreal, 1991.

—, 'Ethnicity, Family Structures and Seasonal Labor Strategies on Quebec's Appalachian Frontier, 1852–81', *Journal of Family History*, XVII, 1992.

—, 'Popular Voices in Print: The Local Newspaper Correspondents of an Extended Scots-Canadian Community, 1894', *Journal of Canadian Studies*, XXX, 1995.

—, 'The Bard in a Community in Transition and Decline: Oscar Dhu and the Hebridean Scots of the Upper St Francis District, Quebec', *Canadian Papers in Rural History*, X, 1996.

Lloyd, T.O., *The British Empire, 1558–1983*, London, 1984.

Logan, G. Murray, *Scottish Highlanders and the American Revolution*, Halifax, 1976.

Logan, Robert A., 'Highlanders from Skye in North Carolina and Nova Scotia', *Scottish Genealogist*, XII, 1966.

Logue, Kenneth J., *Popular Disturbances in Scotland, 1780–1815*, Edinburgh, 1979.

Love, John A., *Rum: A Landscape Without Figures*, Edinburgh, 2001.

Lower, Arthur R.M., *Great Britain's Woodyard: British America and the Timber Trade, 1763–1867*, Montreal, 1973.

Lydon, James, 'The Scottish Soldier in Medieval Ireland: The Bruce Invasion and the Galloglass', in Simpson, Grant G. (ed.), *The Scottish Soldier Abroad*, Edinburgh, 1992.

Lynch, Michael (ed.), *The Oxford Companion to Scottish History*, Oxford, 2001.

MacArthur, Dugald, 'The Breadalbane, 1844–53, and her work for the Highland Destitution Committee', *TGSI*, LV, 1986.

—, 'Some Emigrant Ships from the West Highlands', *TGSI*, LV, 1987.

McCrae, Alister, *Scots in Burma*, Edinburgh, 1990.

McCrone, David, *Understanding Scotland: The Sociology of a Stateless Nation*, London, 1992.

McCrone, David, Morris, Angela and Kiely, Richard, *Scotland the Brand: The Making of Scottish Heritage*, Edinburgh, 1995.

MacDonagh, Oliver, *A Pattern of Government Growth, 1800–1860: The Passenger Acts and their Enforcement*, London, 1961.

MacDonald, D.F., *Scotland's Shifting Population, 1770–1850*, Glasgow, 1937.

McDonald, Forrest and McDonald, Ellen S., 'The Ethnic Origins of the American People, 1790', *William and Mary Quarterly*, XXXVII, 1980.

MacDonald, Norman, *Canada, 1763–1841: Immigration and Land Settlement*, London, 1939.

—, *Canada: Immigration and Colonisation, 1841–1903*, Aberdeen, 1966.

MacDonald, Norman, 'Putting on the Kilt: The Scottish Stereotype and Ethnic Community Survival in Cape Breton', *Canadian Ethnic Studies*, XX, 1988.

McDonald, R. Andrew, *The Kingdom of the Isles: Scotland's Western Seaboard, 1100–1336*, East Linton, 1997.

—, *Outlaws of Scotland: Challenges to the Canmore Kings*, East Linton, 2003.

MacDonald, Sharon, *Reimagining Culture: Histories, Identities and the Gaelic Renaissance*, Oxford, 1997.

MacDonald, Stuart, 'Crofter Colonisation in Canada, 1886–1892: The Scottish Political Background', *Northern Scotland*, VII, 1986.

MacDougall, Norman, 'Achilles Heel: The Earldom of Ross, the Lordship of the Isles and the Stewart Kings, 1449–1507', in Cowan, E. J. and McDonald, R. Andrew, *Alba: Celtic Scotland in the Middle Ages*, East Linton, 2000.

McFarland, Elaine W., *Ireland and Scotland in the Age of Revolution: Planting the Green Bough*, Edinburgh, 1994.

—, 'Scottish Radicalism in the Later Eighteenth Century', in Devine, T.M. and Young, J.R. (eds), *Eighteenth-Century Scotland: New Perspectives*, East Linton, 1999.

McGeachy, Robert A.A., 'Captain Lauchlin Campbell and Early Argyllshire Emigration to New York', *Northern Scotland*, XIX, 1999.

Macinnes, Allan I., 'Scottish Gaeldom: The First Phase of Clearance', in Devine, T.M. and Mitchison, Rosalind (eds), *People and Society in Scotland, I, 1760–1830*, Edinburgh, 1991.

—, Allan I., *Clanship, Commerce and the House of Stuart, 1603–1788*, East Linton, 1996.

MacInnes, John, 'The Oral Tradition in Scottish Gaelic Poetry', *Scottish Studies*, XII, 1968.

—, 'Gaelic Poetry and Historical Tradition', in MacLean, Loraine (ed.), *The Middle Ages in the Highlands*, Inverness, 1981.

—, 'Clan Sagas and Historical Legends', *TGSI*, LVII, 1990.

MacInnes, Rev. John, 'West Highland Sea Power in the Middle Ages', *TGSI*, XLVIII, 1972.

Macintyre, Stuart, *A Concise History of Australia*, Cambridge, 1999.

MacKay, Donald, *Scotland Farewell: The People of the* Hector, Edinburgh, 1980.

MacKay, Ian, 'Tartanism Triumphants: The Construction of Scottishness in Nova Scotia, 1933–54', *Acadiensis*, XXI, 1992.

—, *The Quest for the Folk: Antimodernism and Cultural Selection in Twentieth-Century Nova Scotia*, Montreal, 1994.

MacKenzie, A.A., 'Cape Breton and the Western Harvest Excursions, 1890–1928', in Donovan, Kenneth (ed.), *Cape Breton at 2000: Historical Essays in Honour of the Island's Bicentennial*, Sydney, 1985.

MacKenzie, John M., 'A Scottish Empire: The Scottish Diaspora and Interactive Identities', in Brooking, Tom and Coleman, Jennie (eds), *The Heather and the Fern: Scottish Migration and New Zealand Settlement*, Dunedin, 2003.

MacKenzie, W.C., *The Highlands and Isles of Scotland: A Historical Survey*, Edinburgh, 1949.

McKerral, Andrew, 'West Highland Mercenaries in Ireland', *SHR*, XXX, 1951.

MacKillop, Andrew, 'Highland Estate Change and Tenant Emigration', in

Devine, T.M. and Young, J.R. (eds), *Eighteenth-Century Scotland: New Perspectives*, East Linton, 1999.

—, *More Fruitful than the Soil: Army, Empire and the Scottish Highlands, 1715–1815*, Edinburgh, 2000.

MacKinnon, John E., 'Sentiment and Community', *Scottish Tradition*, XXII, 1997.

MacLean, Alasdair, 'Jacobites at Heart: An Account of the Independent Companies', in Scott-Moncrieff, Lesley (ed.), *The '45: To Gather an Image Whole*, Edinburgh, 1988.

—, 'Highlanders in the Forty-Five', *TGSI*, LIX, 1996.

MacLean, J.P., *An Historical Account of the Settlements of Scotch Highlanders in America Prior to the Peace of 1983*, Glasgow, 1900.

MacLean, Malcolm and Carrell, Christopher (eds), *As an Fhearann: From the Land*, Stornoway, 1986.

McLean, Marianne, *The People of Glengarry: Highlanders in Transition, 1745–1820*, Toronto, 1991.

MacLean, Sorley, *Ris a' Bhruthaich: Criticism and Prose Writings*, Stornoway, 1985.

MacLennan, Hugh, *Seven Rivers of Canada*, Toronto, 1977.

McLeod, Mona, *Leaving Scotland*, Edinburgh, 1996.

—, *Agents of Change: Scots in Poland, 1800–1918*, East Linton, 2000.

MacLeod, R.C., 'Canadianizing the West: The North-West Mounted Police as Agents of the National Policy', in Francis, R. Douglas and Palmer, Howard (eds), *The Prairie West: Historical Readings*, Edmonton, 1995.

MacLeod, Roderick C., 'The Western Highlands in the Eighteenth Century', *SHR*, XIX, 1922.

—, 'The Norsemen in the Hebrides', *SHR*, XXII, 1925.

—, 'The West Highlanders in Peace and War', *SHR*, XXIV, 1927.

—, *The Island Clans during Six Centuries*, Morganstown, 1984.

McLynn, Frank, *Charles Edward Stuart: A Tragedy in Many Acts*, London, 1988.

MacMillan, David S., 'Sir Charles Trevelyan and the Highland and Island Emigration Society', *Royal Australian Historical Society Journal*, XLIX, 1963.

—, *Scotland and Australia, 1788–1850: Emigration, Commerce and Investment*, Oxford, 1967.

McNaught, Kenneth, *History of Canada*, London, 1988.

MacNeil, Alan, 'Scottish Settlement in Colonial Nova Scotia: A Case Study of St Andrew's Township', *Scottish Tradition*, XIX, 1994.

MacNeill, Seumas and Richardson, Frank, *Piobaireachd and its Interpretation: Classical Music of the Highland Bagpipe*, Edinburgh, 1987.

MacPhail, I.M.M., *The Crofters' War*, Stornoway, 1989.

MacPhee, Hugh, 'The Trail of the Emigrants', *TGSI*, XLVI, 1969.

McWhiney, Grady, *Cracker Culture: Celtic Ways in the Old South*, Tuscaloosa, 1988.

McWhiney, Grady and Jamieson, Perry D., *Attack and Die: Civil War Military Tactics and the Southern Heritage*, Alabama, 1986.

Magnusson, Magnus, *Viking Expansion Westwards*, London, 1973.

—, *Iceland Saga*, London, 1987.

Mandela, Nelson, *Long Walk to Freedom*, London, 1995.

Marsden, John, *Sea-Road of the Saints: Celtic Holy Men in the Hebrides*, Edinburgh, 1995.

—, *The Fury of the Northmen: Saints, Shrines and Sea-Raiders in the Viking Age*, London, 1996.

Marshall, David W.H., *The Sudreys in Early Viking Times*, Glasgow, 1929.

Marshall, P.J. (ed.), *Cambridge Illustrated History of the British Empire*, Cambridge, 1996.

Mason, Philip, *The Men Who Ruled India*, London, 1985.

Mathieson, Robert, *The Survival of the Unfittest: The Highland Clearances and the End of Isolation*, Edinburgh, 2000.

Meek, Donald E., 'The Land Question Answered from the Bible: The Land Issue and the Development of a Highland Theology of Liberation', *Scottish Geographical Magazine*, CIII, 1987.

—, 'Evangelicalism and Emigration: Aspects of the Role of Dissenting Evangelicalism in Highland Emigration to Canada', in MacLennan, Gordon W. (ed.), *Proceedings of the First North American Congress of Celtic Studies*, Ottawa, 1988.

Megaw, Basil R.S., 'Norseman and Native in the Kingdom of the Isles: A Reassessment of the Manx Evidence', *SS*, XX, 1976.

Meikle, Henry W., *Scotland and the French Revolution*, London, 1912.

Meyer, Duane, *The Highland Scots of North Carolina, 1732–1776*, Chapel Hill, 1961.

Middleton, Richard, *Colonial America: A History*, Oxford, 1966.

Mitchell, Elaine A., 'The Scot in the Fur Trade', in Reid, Stanford W. (ed.), *The Scottish Tradition in Canada*, Toronto, 1976.

Mitchison, Rosalind, *The Old Poor Law in Scotland: The Experience of Poverty, 1574–1845*, Edinburgh, 2000.

Molloy, Maureen, *Those Who Speak to the Heart: The Nova Scotian Scots at Waipu*, Palmerston North, 1991.

Morgan, Hiram, *Tyrone's Rebellion: The Outbreak of the Nine Years War in Tudor Ireland*, Woodbridge, 1993.

Morgan, Robert, *Early Cape Breton: From Founding to Famine*, Wreck Cove, 2000.

Morrison, Alick, 'The Kingdom of Man and the Isles, 839–1266', *TGSI*, LVIII, 1995.

Munro, Alasdair and Sim, Duncan, *The Merseyside Scots: A Study of an Expatriate Community*, Birkenhead, 2001.

Munro, Jean, 'The Lordship of the Isles', in MacLean, Loraine (ed.), *The Middle Ages in the Highlands*, Inverness, 1981.

Murdoch, Alexander, *A Scottish document concerning emigration to North Carolina in 1772*, Raleigh, 1990.

Murdoch, Steve, 'More than Just MacKays and Mercenaries: Gaelic Influences in Scandinavia, 1580–1707', *TGSI*, LX, 1997.

—, 'Cape Breton: Canada's Highland Island', *NS*, XVIII, 1998.

Newman, Peter C., *Company of Adventurers: The Story of the Hudson's Bay Company*, London, 1985.

—, *Caesars of the Wilderness: The Story of the Hudson's Bay Company*, London, 1987.

Newton, Michael, *A Handbook of the Scottish Gaelic World*, Dublin, 2000.

—, *We're Indians Sure Enough: The Legacy of the Scottish Highlanders in the United States*, Auburn, 2001.

Newton, Michael and Newton, Judy A., *The Ku Klux Klan: An Encyclopaedia*, New York, 1991.

Nicolson, Nigel, *Lord of the Isles*, Stornoway, 2000.

Norton, Wayne, 'Malcolm McNeill and the Emigrationist Alternative to Highland Land Reform, 1886–1893', *SHR*, LXX, 1991.

—, *Help Us to a Better Land: Crofter Colonies in the Prairie West*, Regina, 1994.

Nugent, Walter, *Crossings: The Great Transatlantic Migrations, 1870–1914*, Bloomington, 1992.

O'Gallagher, Marianna, *Grosse Ile: Gateway to Canada, 1832–1937*, Quebec, 1984.

Ommer, Rosemary E., 'Primitive accumulation and the Scottish *clann* in the Old World and the New', *Journal of Historical Geography*, XII, 1986.

Orr, Willie, *Deer Forests, Landlords and Crofters: The Western Highlands in Victorian and Edwardian Times*, Edinburgh, 1982.

Parker, Anthony W., *Scottish Highlanders in Colonial Georgia: The Recruitment, Emigration and Settlement at Darien, 1735–1748*, Athens, 1997.

Paul, Allen, *Katyn: The Untold Story of Stalin's Polish Massacre*, New York, 1991.

Pearce, Gilbert L., *The Scots of New Zealand*, Auckland, 1976.

Pepper, Phillip, *The Kurnai of Gippsland*, Melbourne, 1985.

Perceval-Maxwell, M., *The Scottish Migration to Ulster in the Reign of James I*, London, 1973.

Pittock, Murray, *The Myth of the Jacobite Clans*, Edinburgh, 1995.

Power, Rosemary, 'Magnus Barelegs' Expeditions to the West', *SHR*, LXV, 1986.

—, 'Scotland in the Norse Sagas', in Simpson, Grant G. (ed.), *Scotland and Scandinavia*, Edinburgh, 1990.

Prebble, John, *The Highland Clearances*, London, 1969.

—, *Mutiny: Highland Regiments in Revolt, 1743–1804*, London, 1977.

—, *The King's Jaunt: George IV in Scotland*, London, 1989.

Prentis, Malcolm D., *The Scots in Australia: A Study of New South Wales, Victoria and Queensland, 1788–1900*, Sydney, 1983.

Price, Lynda, *Introduction of the Social History of Scots in Quebec, 1780–1840*, Ottawa, 1981.

Priestley, Susan, *The Victorians: Making their Mark*, Melbourne, 1984.

Quarles, Chester L., *The Ku Klux Klan and Related American Racialist and Antisemitic Organisations*, Jefferson, 1999.

Rankin, Hugh F., *The Moore's Creek Bridge Campaign*, Conshohocken, 1986.

Ranlet, Philip, *The New York Loyalists*, Knoxville, 1986.

Rattray, W.J., *The Scot in British North America*, 4 vols, Toronto, 1880–84.

Ray, Celeste, *Highland Heritage: Scottish Americans in the American South*, Chapel Hill, 2001.

Redmond, Gerald, *The Sporting Scots of Nineteenth-Century Canada*, Toronto, 1982.

Rethford, Wayne and Sawyers, June S., *The Scots of Chicago: Quiet Immigrants and their New Society*, Dubuque, 1997. [HP3.99.323]

Reynolds, Henry, *The Other Side of the Frontier: Aboriginal Resistance to the European Invasion of Australia*, Ringwood, 1982.

Rice, C. Duncan, *The Scots Abolitionists*, Baton Rouge, 1981.

Richards, Eric, 'The Highland Scots of South Australia', *Journal of the Historical Society of South Australia*, IV, 1978.

—, *A History of the Highland Clearances: Agrarian Transformation and the Evictions*, London, 1982.

—, 'Highland Emigrants to South Australia in the 1850s', *NS*, V, 1982.

—, *A History of the Highland Clearances: Emigration, Protest, Reasons*, London, 1985.

—, 'Varieties of Scottish Emigration in the Nineteenth Century', *Historical Studies*, XXI, 1985.

—, 'Australia and the Scottish Connection, 1788–1914', in Cage, R.A., *The Scots Abroad: Labour, Capital, Enterprise,* London, 1985.

—, 'Scottish Australia', in Richards, Eric (ed.), *That Land of Exiles: Scots in Australia,* Edinburgh, 1988.

—, 'Scotland and the uses of the Atlantic Empire', in Bailyn, Bernard and Morgan, Philip D. (eds), *Strangers within the Realm: Cultural Margins of the British Empire,* Chapel Hill, 1991.

—, 'St Kilda and Australia: Emigrants at Peril, 1852–53', *Scottish Historical Review,* 71, 1992.

—, 'The Decline of St Kilda: Demography, Economy and Emigration', *Scottish Economic and Social History,* XII, 1992.

—, 'How Did Poor People Emigrate from the British Isles to Australia in the Nineteenth Century?', *Journal of British Studies,* 32, 1993.

—, *Patrick Sellar and the Highland Clearances,* Edinburgh, 1999.

—, 'Leaving the Highlands: Colonial Destinations in Canada and Australia', in Harper, Marjory and Vance, Michael E. (eds), *Myth, Migration and the Making of Memory: Scotia and Nova Scotia, 1700–1990,* Edinburgh, 1999.

—, 'The Last of the Clan and Other Highland Emigrants', in Brooking, Tom and Coleman, Jennie (eds), *The Heather and the Fern: Scottish Migration and New Zealand Settlement,* Dunedin, 2003.

—, *Britannia's Children: Emigration from England, Scotland, Wales and Ireland Since 1600,* London, 2004.

Richards, Eric and Clough, Monica, *Cromartie: Highland Life, 1650–1914,* Aberdeen, 1989.

Riis, Thomas, *Should Auld Acquaintance Be Forgot: Scottish–Danish Relations, 1450–1707,* 2 vols, Odense, 1988.

Ritchie, Anna, *Viking Scotland,* London, 1993.

Ritchie, John, *Lachlan Macquarie: A Biography,* Melbourne, 1986.

Rixon, Denis, *The West Highland Galley,* Edinburgh, 1998.

Robertson, I.R., 'Highlanders, Irishmen and the Land Question in Nineteenth-Century Prince Edward Island', in Cullen, L.M. and Smout, T.C. (eds), *Comparative Aspects of Scottish and Irish Economic and Social History,* Edinburgh, 1977.

Robson, L.L., *The Convict Settlers of Australia,* Melbourne, 1976.

Robson, Lloyd, *A Short History of Tasmania,* Melbourne, 1997.

Roesdahl, Else, *The Vikings,* London, 1992.

Ross, Alexander M., 'Loch Laxford to the Zorras: A Sutherland Emigration to Upper Canada', *Scottish Tradition,* XVIII, 1993.

Ross, Peter, *The Scot in America,* New York, 1996.

Sawyer, June S., *The Complete Guide to Celtic Music,* London, 2000.

Sawyer, Peter (ed.), *The Oxford Illustrated History of the Vikings*, Oxford, 1997.

Sellar, W.D.H., 'Hebridean Sea Kings: The Successors of Somerled, 1164–1316', in Cowan, E.J. and McDonald, R. Andrew, *Alba: Celtic Scotland in the Middle Ages*, East Linton, 2000.

Serle, Geoffrey, *The Golden Age: A History of the Colony of Victoria, 1851–1861*, Melbourne, 1963.

Shaw, Frances J., *The Northern and Western Islands of Scotland: Their Economy and Society in the Seventeenth Century*, Edinburgh, 1980.

Shaw, John, 'Brief Beginnings: Nova Scotian and Old World Bards Compared', *Scottish Gaelic Studies*, XVII, 1996.

Shepperson, George, 'Harriet Beecher Stowe and Scotland, 1852–53', *SHR*, XXXII, 1952.

—, *Scotland and Africa*, Edinburgh, 1982.

Shepperson, Wilbur S., *British Emigration to North America: Projects and Opinions in the Early Victorian Period*, Oxford, 1957.

Sher, Richard B. and Smitten, Jeffrey R, *Scotland and America in the Age of Enlightenment*, Edinburgh, 1990.

Sigurdsson, Gisli, *Gaelic Influence in Iceland: Historical and Literary Contacts*, Reykjavik, 2000.

Simpson, Peter, *The Independent Highland Companies, 1603–1760*, Edinburgh, 1996.

Sinclair, Keith, *A History of New Zealand*, Auckland, 2000.

Smailes, Helen, *Scottish Empire: Scots in Pursuit of Hope and Glory*, Edinburgh, 1981.

Smith, Abbott E., *Colonists in Bondage: White Servitude and Convict Labor in America, 1607–1776*, Williamsburg, 1947.

Smith, Iain Crichton, *Towards the Human: Selected Essays*, Edinburgh, 1986.

Smout, T.C., 'Famine and Famine-Relief in Scotland', in Cullen, L.M. and Smout, T.C. (eds), *Comparative Aspects of Scottish and Irish Economic and Social History*, Edinburgh, 1974.

Smout, T.C., Landsman, Ned C. and Devine, T.M., 'Scottish Emigration in the Seventeenth and Eighteenth Centuries', in Canny, Nicholas (ed.), *Europeans on the Move: Studies in European Migration, 1500–1800*, Oxford, 1994.

Smyth, Alfred P., *Scandinavian Kings in the British Isles, 850–880*, Oxford, 1977.

—, *Warlords and Holy Men: Scotland, AD80–1000*, London, 1984.

Steer, K.A. and Bannerman, John W.M., *Late Medieval Monumental Sculpture in the West Highlands*, Edinburgh, 1977.

Steuart, A.F., *Scottish Influences in Russian History*, Glasgow, 1913.

Stevenson, David, *Alasdair MacColla and the Highland Problem in the Seventeenth Century*, Edinburgh, 1980.

Stewart, A.M., *Scots in the Baltic*, Aberdeen, 1977.

Strange, Ian J., *The Falkland Islands*, Newton Abbott, 1983.

Szasz, Ferenc M., *Scots in the North American West, 1790–1917*, Norman, 2000.

Thomson, Derick S., *An Introduction to Gaelic Poetry*, London, 1974.

— (ed.), *The Companion to Gaelic Scotland*, Oxford, 1983.

Thorne, R.G. (ed.), *The House of Commons, 1790–1820*, 5 vols, London, 1986.

Turner, Alan R., 'Scottish Settlement of the West', in Reid, Stanford W. (ed.), *The Scottish Tradition in Canada*, Toronto, 1976.

Turner, C. Frank, *Across the Medicine Line: The Epic Confrontation between Sitting Bull and the North West Mounted Police*, Toronto, 1973.

Tyson, Robert E., 'Landlord Policies and Population Change in North-East Scotland and the Western Isles, 1755–1841', *NS*, XIX, 1999.

Utley, Robert M., *The Lance and the Shield: The Life and Times of Sitting Bull*, London, 1998.

Vance, Michael E., 'The Politics of Emigration: Scotland and Assisted Emigration to Upper Canada', in Devine, T.M. (ed.), *Scottish Emigration and Scottish Society*, Edinburgh, 1992.

—, 'British Columbia's Twentieth-Century Crofter Emigration Schemes: A Note on New Sources', *Scottish Tradition*, XVIII, 1993.

Van Vogt, William E., *Britain to America: Mid-Nineteenth-Century Immigrants to the United States*, Urbana, 1999.

Wahlgren, Erik, *The Vikings and America*, London, 2000.

Wallace, J.N., *The Wintering Partners on Peace River*, Ottawa, 1929.

Wallace, Jim, *A Double Duty: The Decisive First Decade of the North-West Mounted Police*, Winnipeg, 1997.

Wallace, W. Stewart, *The Pedlars from Quebec and Other Papers on the Nor'Westers*, Toronto, 1954.

Waters, Mary, *Ethnic Options: Choosing Identities in America*, Berkeley, 1990.

Watson, Don, *Caledonia Australis: Scottish Highlanders on the Frontier of Australia*, Sydney, 1984.

Welch, James, *Killing Custer: The Battle of the Little Bighorn and the Fate of the Plains Indians*, New York, 1994.

Welsh, Frank, *A History of South Africa*, London, 2000.

Whyte, Ian D., *Migration and Society in Britain, 1550–1830*, London, 2000.

Wigan, Michael, *The Scottish Highland Estate: Preserving an Environment*, Shrewsbury, 1991.

Wightman, Andy, *Who Owns Scotland*, Edinburgh, 1996.

Wilkie, Jim, *Metagama: A Journey from Lewis to the New World*, Edinburgh, 2001.

Wilkinson, Linda, 'Aboriginal Historical Places Along the Snowy River', *Gippsland Heritage Journal*, XXIII, 1999.

Williams, Keith, 'A Way Out of Our Troubles: The Politics of Empire Settlement', in Constantine, Stephen (ed.), *Emigrants and Empire: British Settlement in the Dominions Between the Wars*, Manchester, 1990.

Williamson, Arthur H., 'Scots, Indians and Empire: The Scottish Politics of Civilization, 1519–1609', *Past and Present*, CL, 1996.

Withers, Charles W.J., *Gaelic in Scotland: The Geographical History of a Language*, Edinburgh, 1984.

—, *Gaelic Scotland: The Transformation of a Culture Region*, London, 1988.

—, *Urban Highlanders: Highland–Lowland Migration and Urban Gaelic Culture*, East Linton, 1998.

Wood, John D., 'Transatlantic Land Reform: America and the Crofters' Revolt, 1878–1888', *SHR*, LXIII, 1984.

Wood, Stephen, *The Scottish Soldier*, Manchester, 1987.

—, *The Auld Alliance: Scotland and France, The Military Connection*, Edinburgh, 1989.

Woodcock, George, *A Social History of Canada*, London, 1989.

Woolcock, Helen R., *Rights of Passage: Emigration to Australia in the Nineteenth Century*, London, 1986.

Womack, P., *Improvement and Romance: Constructing the Myth of the Highlands*, London, 1989.

Wright, Esther C., *The Loyalists of New Brunswick*, Fredericton, 1955.

Young, Michael, *The Aboriginal People of the Monaro: A Documentary History*, Sydney, 2000.

Youngson, A.J., *After the Forty-Five: The Economic Impact on the Scottish Highlands*, Edinburgh, 1973.

Index